Digital
Design and
Manufacturing

Digital Design and Manufacturing: CAD/CAM Applications in Architecture and Design

by
Daniel Schodek, Martin Bechthold, Kimo Griggs,
Kenneth Martin Kao, and Marco Steinberg

WILEY

JOHN WILEY & SONS, INC.

Library of Congress Cataloging-in-Publication Data:
Digital design and manufacturing: CAD/CAM technologies in architecture/
by Daniel Schodek . . . [et al.].
    p.   cm.
  Includes bibliographical references and index.
  ISBN 0-471-45636-5 (cloth)
  1. CAD/CAM systems. I. Schodek, Daniel L., 1941-
TS155.6.D55 2004
670'.285—dc22
2004014940
Printed in the United States of America

10 9 8 7 6 5 4 3 2 1

Contents

Preface

This book is for architects and industrial designers interested in knowing more about the ever-growing field of computer-aided design and manufacturing (CAD/CAM), as it is particularly related to these two professions. Use of these technologies has had a liberating effect on the work of many designers in both fields. There is an optimism that design vocabularies can be expanded and that these same designs can be made with a quality and precision previously difficult to achieve. Implicit in these technologies are paradigms for interactions among design, analysis, and production activities that both challenge current approaches and provide positive alternative approaches for the future. Traditional tenets that have long characterized fundamental design attitudes—such as needs for standardization and repetition in the design of components for efficient industrialized production techniques to be brought to bear—are already being challenged by mass customization and other ideas made feasible by new design and production capabilities. In architecture, the structure of role definition and responsibilities within the building and construction industry is also being challenged as modes of professional practice develop. In industrial design, larger roles are envisioned for designers as they harness these techniques.

In architecture, however, an appreciation of what these technologies are actually all about is surprisingly underdeveloped. A few practitioners who have adopted the use of these techniques have achieved wide recognition, but these same techniques have been slow to be adopted in the profession as a whole. One reason is

undoubtedly that CAD/CAM technologies are simply not well understood. Individuals well versed in CAD techniques often find it difficult to understand connections to the world of computer numerically controlled (CNC) machines and related sophisticated manufacturing processes—or even to understand that the kinds of digital design environments that best support downstream manufacturing processes are quite different than those they might be so familiar with and use in everyday practice. Similarly, individuals accustomed to craft-based environments or traditional construction processes often do not fully appreciate the ever-increasing role of computers in the world of fabrication and construction. There is indeed a vast amount of literature available on CAD/CAM technologies that could be helpful, but it is very difficult to access. Most books dealing with the subject are primarily technical books oriented toward mechanical or manufacturing process engineers. This book seeks to provide a one-volume coverage of the field appropriate to the needs and interests of architects. It is also appropriate for use in educational curricula at colleges or universities for more advanced students, or in continuing education courses for practicing architects.

In industrial design, there is little doubt that CAD/CAM techniques have been widely adopted by product design groups and widely used in the production of all kinds of products. Typical consumer products are now invariably made within a CAD/CAM environment. Curiously, however, many industrial designers often pick up their knowledge of these techniques more as part of professional practice rather than during their education. Again, the lack of an accessible treatment of the material is a primary hindrance in introducing this material into an educational program. Part of this book explicitly addresses the needs of the industrial design community.

An underlying premise of the book is also that while application domains differ, the general design aspirations, sensibilities, and specific needs to understand fundamental digital design and production tools are similar for both the architecture and industrial design communities. The general processes for making complex digital surface or solid models of objects in a suitable way that supports following manufacturing processes, extracting information from the models and using it to control CNC machines, and other integral parts of the overall CAD/CAM process are inherently the same. Obviously different for each profession are the types of the products made, their sizes, their product uniqueness and numbers produced, the role of the designer in the design process, and many other factors. Ultimately, the issues involved in using CAD/CAM techniques in making a building, and the specific technologies used, are quite different than those involved producing a line of consumer products. On the other hand, there are areas where the two professions have directly overlapping interests and involvement, as is the case in products produced for primary use in buildings (lighting fixtures, furniture, etc.).

This book provides a relatively succinct, self-contained overview of the world of computer-aided design and manufacturing appropriate to both groups. Well-known existing design and production attitudes based on the use of digital models are first reviewed as a way of understanding how newer developments in automation either build upon or differ significantly from past approaches. Recent initiatives in the use of newer CAD/CAM technologies within this world are then explored. Several case studies are provided that are intended to illustrate not only the potential of these new technologies in design but the many difficulties and problems inherent in their implementation as well. More technically oriented chapters are included for those actually interested in how to implement CAD/CAM technologies in design. Characteristics of modeling environments (e.g., CATIA, SolidWorks, Pro/ENGINEER, Unigraphics) commonly used in CAD/CAM applications are reviewed, including sections on parametric modeling, dimensionally driven design, feature-based design, assembly modeling, and other topics. Larger system structures, data models, and Internet-based applications are also covered. Computer numerical control (CNC) technologies are discussed in detail, as are related application-oriented CAM software. Fundamental manufacturing processes and their CNC counterparts are next surveyed. General production attitudes and strategies are also discussed. In addition, differences between prototyping, low-volume production techniques, and high-volume production techniques are discussed.

This book is the result of a collaboration among several individuals who have different kinds of expertise and backgrounds with respect to CAD/CAM applications in architecture and industrial design. It evolved over a number of years through various studio, coursework, and symposia offered at the Harvard Design School by the authors, as well as their own professional practices.

Daniel Schodek, Martin Bechthold,
Kimo Griggs, Kenneth Martin Kao, and
Marco Steinberg
Harvard Design School
Cambridge, Massachusetts
December 2003

Acknowledgments

We would like to acknowledge the contributions of the many associates, assistants, and current or former employees who worked on this project, including Tom Karlhuber, Andrea Lamberti, Amy Sheehan, Michelle Tarsney, Juan Villafane, Winifred Wang, Nick Maynard, Chris Kucinski, Zach Kramer, and Yong Gib Yun.

Numerous contributors who very generously shared their work with us include: Tim Eliassen and Michael Mulhern of TryPyramid Structures, Inc.; Frances O'Neill and Mike Maguire of Architectural Skylight Co., Inc.; Brian Forster and Neil Noble of Arup Group Ltd; Fred Adickes of C-Tek; Damian Murphy of Dewhurst Macfarlane; David Derocher of East Coast CADCAM; Frank Gehry, Jim Glymph, and Christopher Mercier of Gehry Partners LLP; Michael Taylor at Michael Hopkins & Partners; Albert Kahn Associates; Alberto de Gobbi of Permasteelisa; Renzo Piano and Shunji Ishida of Renzo Piano Building Workshop; Charles Blomberg of Rafael Viñoly Architects; Kappa S.R.O. of Prague; Kevin Rotheroe of Free Form Research Studio; Volkder Ruhl; Condé Nast; Herald Kloft of osd; and Bernhard Franken of franken architekten. Others include Andoni Borjabaz from IDOM; Klaus Linkwitz; Vikas Gore of DP Architects Pte Ltd; Shiro Matsushima; Bill Zahner and Roger Reed of A. Zahner Company; Christine Clemens of Cannon Design; Ann Lawless and John Alexander at The American Precision Museum; John I. Parsons; Brian Matt and Heather Andrus of Altitude, Inc.; Catharina Lübke of Recaro GmbH; Tero Purosto of Puro Oy; Dan Williams of Motorola; Juhani Salovaara of Studio Salovaarat Oy; Vivie Thonet of Gebrüder Thonet GmbH; Minna Staffans of Kvaerner-Masa Yards; Kati Heikkila of Nokia; Scott Underwood of IDEO; Mike Reissig of Colt Firearms; Chris Hunter of the Schenectady Museum; the Wedgwood Museum; Stala Oy, Eastman Kodak Company; GE, John A. Dreyfuss and Gail Dreyfuss Wilson; the ALCOA Company; Pingtel; and Cindy Roth of Ergonomi Technologies Corp.

Each of us also would like to thank our family members for their continued support: Martin Bechthold—Marina Sartori, Fosca and Natalia Bechthold; Kenneth Martin Kao—Deborah, Hannah, and Louise Martin Kao, Charles and Susana Kao, Ken and Chris Martin; Kimo Griggs—Susan Tang and Wesley Yi-Fan Griggs; Daniel Schodek—Kay and Ben Schodek, Ned Schodek and Johanna Maron; Marco Steinberg—Riikka and Carlo Steinberg; Marja, Edward and Sonia Steinberg; Jani Paasonen and Marja Acs; Liisa and Jussi Tenkku.

CHARACTERISTICS AND ORIGINS

The first chapter in Part I consists of a self-contained overview of computer-aided design and manufacturing (CAD/CAM) applications in architecture. It places topics presented in subsequent chapters into a larger perspective. The second chapter briefly traces the origin and evolution of digital design and production techniques.

CHAPTER 1

Characteristics of CAD/CAM Environments

1.1 THE NATURE OF CAD/CAM TECHNOLOGIES

The use of computer-aided design and manufacturing (CAD/CAM) technologies in architecture and design is no longer simply an exciting but still emerging interest area. These technologies are here to stay. They have opened up new design vocabularies that have changed the face of architecture and design (see Figure 1-1 A and B). They are also the leading edge of a chain of innovations in the whole design and production environment that have been ushered in by evolutions in the fields of information technology and highly sophisticated, numerically controlled machines. The focus of this book is on imparting an understanding and sensibility to designers of how to use these new technologies in a creative way. It emphasizes the actual techniques by which products, components, or assemblies are designed and manufactured through the use of computer-aided design and manufacturing processes (see Figure 1-2 A and B).

Figure 1-1 The utilization of CAD/CAM techniques has enabled architects such as Frank Gehry of Frank O. Gehry & Associates to develop new design vocabularies. The "Der Neue Zollhof" in Düsseldorf, Germany, is shown.

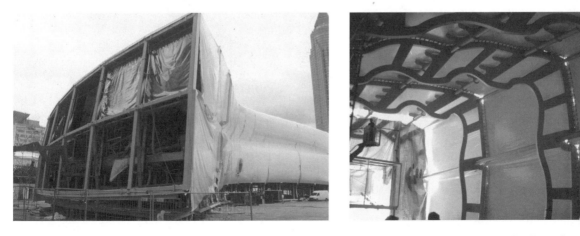

Figure 1-2 The design of the "Dynaform" BMW pavilion by Bernard Franken & Associates in Frankfurt, Germany, utilized new digital design techniques in the development of its form and computer-aided manufacturing techniques in the development of its components.

In the following chapters, the evolution of CAD/CAM technologies will be first discussed as a way of understanding what they are all about. In particular, you will see that computers and numerically controlled machines did not develop independently of one another. Rather, a symbiotic relationship existed. Subsequently, you will see that the continued evolution of CAD/CAM technologies has led to the development of a number of building blocks that can be used to configure different systems for supporting varying design and production activities. These many different building blocks may be put together in a variety of ways to serve different purposes. Fundamentally, the core of a computer-aided design and manufacturing system consists of three major components: a digital interactive design and analysis environment for making digital geometric models of the object to be eventually produced (a CAD system), a computer-aided manufacturing (CAM) software wherein the user specifies how the digital design model is to be actually manufactured and creates a series of digital instructions for controlling specific machines, and one or more computer numerically controlled (CNC) machines and related tools that translate these digital instructions into actual machine operations that make the object.

The interactive design system allows a designer to create sophisticated digital models. These digital environments have advanced surface and solid modeling capabilities. They support parametric design and assembly modeling. Design histories can be recovered and steps modified because of the hierarchical structure of these systems. They are dimensionally driven and feature-based, and they support specific material-oriented design applications, for example, sheet-metal bending. The manufacturing applications package that interfaces between the design and the machine environment may be integral to the whole system or exist as a stand-alone package. The different machines that are ultimately numerically controlled include CNC milling machines, drills, saws, laser cutters, water jets, electric discharge machines, welders, and others. These and other machines can be used to fabricate objects directly or to create negative molds for indirect processes such as casting or injection molding.

More comprehensive CAD/CAM systems may include one or more analysis packages (e.g., structural, thermal, tolerance-buildup) that are normally found in a computer-aided engineering (CAE) system. Some systems are particularly well suited to design evaluation, including ergonomic analyses, cost analyses, and so forth. Special design for manufacturing and assembly procedures are often embedded in related software. A component of a complete CAD/CAM installation that may or may not be present is a capability for reverse engineering (digitally scanning an existing physical model and converting it into a digital model for further manipulation).

Many CAD/CAM environments also include technologies for quickly making evaluation prototypes directly from a computer model (see Figure 1-3). These 3-D printing or free-form fabrication (or rapid prototyping) technologies have caught the imagination of many designers and seemingly characterize the CAD/CAM field to them. Many are based on "additive" manufacturing processes that build up a three-dimensional object slice by slice. While attractive, these technologies may or may not be part of a specific CAD/CAM installation. Likewise, there are many other ways of rapidly creating prototypes for evaluation that may be more appropriate than just additive manufacturing technologies.

In addition to the components noted, a fully automated design and production environment might also include material handling systems, robots for assembling parts, machine vision systems, process management and control systems, material resource planning systems, quality assurance systems, and a whole host of other possible systems and technologies. It must be emphasized, however, that few installations actually contain *all* of these components. In a limited working fabrication environment, for example, an installation might consist simply of some sort of low-level computer-aided drawing package that is coupled directly to a CNC machine of one type or another via a basic software manufacturing applications package that allows the user to directly control the machine (e.g., setting toolpaths, cutting head speeds, tool changes, and so forth).

The great power of CAD/CAM technologies comes into play when the core systems are embedded in a larger networked information system that brings into

Figure 1-3 The product design world has been strongly influenced by the development of sophisticated computer-aided design and manufacturing systems. Functional prototypes for components for the Pingtel telephone designed by Altitude were made using a stereolithography system. (Source: Pingtel®)

play the full spectrum of different participants ultimately involved in the planning, design, supply, production, installation, marketing, distribution, and use of any product. Information exchange needs are, of course, crucial in these relationships. Many different business and management models have been developed that ultimately hinge on how these relationships are structured. It is within this larger context that the power of computer-aided design and manufacturing systems comes into play in many industries, and it is via this context that many design and production industries have revolutionized how they operate.

The remainder of this chapter presents a relatively self-contained overview of CAD/CAM systems. It provides a nontechnical introduction to what CAD/CAM systems are all about and how they are structured. It is still assumed, however, that most readers have a basic familiarity with one or more common computer-aided design environments. Subsequent chapters will deal in more depth with the history, application, and theory of computer-aided design and manufacturing systems.

1.2 DIGITAL DESIGN AND ANALYSIS ENVIRONMENTS

Introduction

The most fundamental of the building blocks of a complete CAD/CAM system is a digitally based *computer-aided design system* that provides the basic interactive design capabilities. A whole host of sophisticated digital environments are available that support an array of different modeling and representation needs. Their power and versatility are evident in the many striking computer-generated images that virtually surround us today. Digital environments have been developed to serve specific industry needs (aerospace, entertainment, architecture) or to target specific roles in the design and production process (conceptual design, visualization or rendering, design development, engineering, etc.). Modes of representation and primary applications vary (e.g., two- or three-dimensional representations based on wireframe, surface, or solid models, and animations) as do related internal database structures. Capabilities among environments vary enormously as well.

Not all of these digital environments, however, are equally useful in supporting connections to subsequent manufacturing and assembly processes. An image that appears strikingly three-dimensional and photorealistic does not mean that the underlying computer model can be used directly within a computer-aided manufacturing environment. Indeed, a fundamental conceptual issue discussed in this book centrally revolves around defining the kind of computational model that can be built to represent a design; the capa-

bilities and limitations of the computational model; and the ease with which it can be used for a variety of design, analysis, and manufacturing purposes. The kind of model used can either pose extreme barriers to the creative designer or can open up new possibilities for defining and making new forms.

Many early- or first-generation CAD systems offered only limited drafting capabilities and were specifically intended to support only visualization or documentation applications (e.g., the preparation of working drawings). Descendants of these kinds of systems, which fundamentally focus on two-dimensional representations of three-dimensional objects, remain in common use in the design professions and are undoubtedly familiar to most designers. They are extremely good for basic drawing and the production and annotation of plans, sections, elevations, and other traditional representational views of designs. As has been observed on countless occasions, however, early versions of these same systems were cumbersome for use in preliminary design stages, nor were connections easy to make with the evolving field of computer-aided manufacturing. Three-dimensional forms could not be quickly developed or explored. Other common problems existed. Even developed designs could remain essentially ambiguous. There was no computationally inherent way of checking, for example, whether or not a drawn floor plan, section, and elevation were actually fully consistent with one another. In using early-generation CAD systems, it was also extremely difficult to model designs that involved highly complex geometrical surfaces that were not easily described as parts of circles or other common geometrical shapes. With time the capabilities of these systems improved dramatically, but their fundamental role as representation and documentation tools largely remained.

Design offices wanting to forge new directions were forced to look into the kinds of geometric modeling approaches first developed and used in other design and production industries (e.g., automotive, aerospace) to obtain more robust software that was more tuned to supporting downstream applications. This software is inherently based on the development and use of three-dimensional models, from which two-dimensional views and other information may be derived. This same type of software also allows the parametric variation of a basic geometric configuration to produce different "instances" of a design for evaluation. Designs can be dimensionally driven, and feature-based approaches are common. Design histories are recoverable and can be manipulated because of the hierarchical structure used in which parent-child relationships are clearly established. Connections to analysis modules (e.g., structural) are normal. Geometry can be exported to be used in connection with CNC machines. All of these capabilities are extremely useful in a design development and subsequent production environment. They are by no means present in all digital modeling packages. By and large, current systems that have these capabilities have typically been developed to support *design development* activities. They are not intuitive "design conceptualization" tools, but rather tools that support the kind of detailed design work that ultimately has to go into any product before moving to subsequent stages aimed toward manufacturing.

The following section reviews basic modeling approaches, establishes some definitions, and generally seeks to understand what is needed in a design-oriented modeling environment that is useful in supporting downstream applications. This review is at a general level only. Part IV of this book looks at modeling environments in greater technical detail.

Fundamental Digital Representations and Modeling Environments

Basic Issues

In most digital design systems, there are common ways for a user to make a basic digital model. A variety of graphical and numerical interfaces allow users to create, edit, and manipulate points, lines, curves, and surfaces. Simple three-dimensional *wireframe* models may be created directly from simple points and lines. In these models, line segments outline the basic edges of a volume. Approaches of this type formed the basis for many pioneering computer-aided design systems. Other approaches are based on the development of *surface models*. In these models, space is enclosed by surfaces that can be created and manipulated in a variety of ways. These models focus on the surface definition and surface qualities of a three-dimensional object. Excellent systems based on surface modeling approaches have been created that are directed specifically toward producing striking visual representations of objects (e.g., an automobile body) complete with exceptional shading and lighting effects. The power of these same modeling environments has also allowed architects to create new design vocabularies, such as those based on free-form shapes.

While much can be done with surface modeling environments, there are a great many instances within the larger world of computer-aided design and manufacturing in which there is a real need for even more elaborate geometric models. Depending on the surface modeler used, the curves and surfaces represented may or may not be fully defined in a numerical sense. A related issue is that surface models are sometimes not without geometrical ambiguity—created surfaces that may visually appear all right on the screen may be in actuality not very exact. Surfaces may not quite touch, for example, or unattached lines may exist. These conditions may be nonproblematic for many visualization purpose, but

cannot normally be tolerated by typical machine environments, which demand that the digital model be totally unambiguous in a geometric sense. How can a machine make something that is not completely defined? Additionally, many important technical analyses require that measures such as the center of gravity or the center of mass of an object cannot be determined. Applications of this type simply cannot be done with wireframe or surface models. More fully defined representations are often needed.

In response to some of the concerns noted, more sophisticated digital modeling systems have been developed for use within the world of computer-aided design and manufacturing that are based on more fully defined three-dimensional representations called *solid models*. These are essentially volumetric models. In these systems, complex curved lines and bounding surfaces that define model configurations are numerically defined in an exacting sense. These numerical definitions also allow a determination to be made of the unique intersections that result when different volumetric objects with complex geometries intersect one another. These same definitions allow the computation of the volume or mass of an object, its center of gravity or mass, and other needed information.

As will be seen, most sophisticated digital environments that support downstream analysis or computer-aided manufacturing applications have both advanced surface modeling capabilities and solid modeling capabilities. In sophisticated digital environments intended to support computer-aided manufacturing applications, the specific steps used in model development can also be recorded and subsequently manipulated. Constraint management and dimensional control capabilities are likewise embedded in the digital systems (see Figure 1-4).

Curves, Surfaces, and Solids

Defining and representing curves and complexly shaped surfaces in a surface or solid modeling system is no easy matter. Many objects having highly complex geometries—the hull of a sailing boat, for example—cannot easily be precisely described by a series of two-dimensional drawings, which often leave much to chance or to the interpretation of the builder. In the boat hull example, one might imagine defining the shape via a series of two-dimensional cross sections and traditional plan and elevation views (a common practice in the history of boat-building). While it is easy to sketch a curve connecting one cross-sectional profile to another, a knowledgeable geometer or builder instantly knows that the surface connecting the profiles can actually assume many different shapes that may resemble one another but that are actually different. In historical boat-building processes, the intended shape was approximated via cross sections that were, in turn, built.

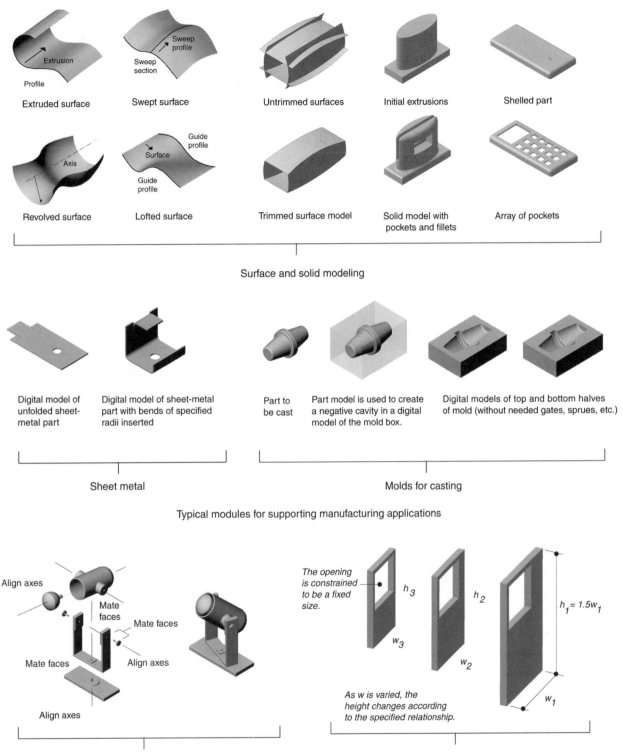

Figure 1-4 Digital modeling environments used in CAD/CAM environments provide many different kinds of modeling and analysis capabilities. Design histories can be recorded and subsequent changes can be propagated throughout a model.

The exact shape of the hull then resulted from the shape the planking assumed as it was bent to conform to the cross sections. The same general arguments can generally be made with respect to how many complex roof shapes were given their final forms, as is the case with Le Corbusier's chapel at Ronchamp. This lack of precise numerical definition of the final surface shape may well pose no problem to the experienced craftsperson skilled in building boat hulls who uses his or her craft knowledge to create the exact shape of the hull. Nor would it be to the skilled craftsperson making a complex roof shape. Attempting to make the same hull or roof shape in an automated machine environment, however, poses a completely different problem. The final shapes would have to be exactly defined a priori. Machines must be told exactly what to do, which in turn means that it is necessary for the designer to exactly specify the complex shape of the hull in a numerically based language that the machine control system can understand. Someone making a small-scale model of the roof of Ronchamp by using a milling machine, for example, would have to define the roof shape in a numerically precise way. Providing the capability to precisely numerically model highly complex curves, and, consequently, for related complex surfaces, has been one of the driving forces behind the development of more sophisticated computer modeling systems.

As discussed in Chapter 10, several different ways have been developed to more precisely model and numerically define various curves and related surfaces. Surface shapes based on these curve definition methods can be created in a variety of different ways, such as via extrusions, sweeps, or lofts. Additionally, surfaces can be intersected, trimmed, and joined in a variety of ways.

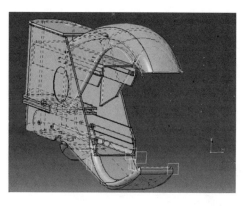

Surface model of a hand held paper stapler

Final rendered image of surface model

Figure 1-6 Common consumer products, such as this handheld paper stapler, often represent difficult digital modeling challenges. (Source: Courtesy of Alex Gil)

These are common processes for making surfaces from curves that are now common in virtually any surface or solid modeling system. (See Figures 1-5 and 1-6.)

Three-dimensional models can subsequently be developed from surfaces to enclose space. A whole host of techniques exist for placing, orienting, and intersecting multiple surfaces to create volumetric shapes. Similarly, many techniques exist for editing resulting surface intersections—for instance, two intersecting surfaces may be "trimmed." Convincing and useful representations of volumetric objects may be obtained. While surface models representing volumetric objects are extremely useful, it does not axiomatically follow that the underlying geometry is always fully developed throughout the whole of the object or actually makes a true volumetric shape. Sometimes adjacent surfaces do not exactly meet, and they leave gaps. These same characteristics may not be overly problematic, however, in early design stages where design elements are indeed often unresolved and ambiguous, or for many render-

Surface model—This surface model was made by first creating cross-sectional profiles, and then lofting a surface over the profiles. Ribs were made by sweeping rib cross sections along the profiles.

Figure 1-5 The model shown is a digital reconstruction of a building in Vienna—the Nationale Nederlandanden, Hungary, Ltd., and ING Bank, Budapest—by Erick van Egeraat. Egeraat was an early user of sophisticated digital modeling environments to produce unusually shaped buildings. (Source: Feng Guo (Harvard Design School))

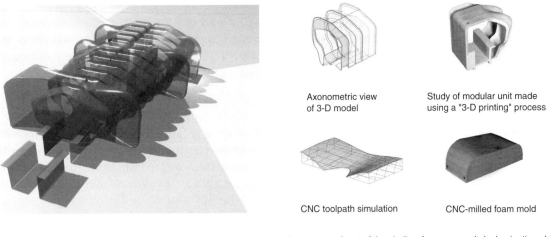

Axonometric view
of 3-D model

Study of modular unit made
using a "3-D printing" process

CNC toolpath simulation

CNC-milled foam mold

Proposal for an urban diner composed of modular thin-shell elements.

A prototype of part of the shell surface was made by laminating glass-reinforced plastic over a CNC-milled mold.

Figure 1-7 Surface models are often used in preliminary design stages when shapes are complex. A "3-D print" was used to study the design, and an evaluation physical mock-up was made based on the surface model via a CNC milling operation. (Source: Courtesy of Alex Gil)

ing applications where visualization issues are of paramount importance. As previously noted, however, these issues become problematic for other applications. Surface models need not have these problems. If carefully constructed, an assembly of surfaces can indeed constitute a true volumetric unit (see Figure 1-7).

Other approaches to making three-dimensional models are possible. Classical methods for defining simple three-dimensional geometric shapes (spheres, etc.) rely on long-known direct mathematical equations, or on their alternative parametric representations (see Chapter 10). Current approaches also utilize what are called *boundary representation approaches* that resemble surface models, but whose data structures typically contain much more information regarding surface topology (e.g., information is kept on all surfaces with respect to adjacencies to other nodes and surfaces, and whether particular sides are on the outside or inside of a volume). These are the "solid models" mentioned previously.

A clear value of these solid modeling approaches is that they provide digital models that are numerically well defined and geometrically unambiguous. Additionally, their data structures allow many properties of a volumetric entity, such as its weight or center of mass, to be calculated. They can also support other analytical activities such as structural analyses based on the use of finite element techniques. These same modelers, however, are normally more cumbersome to use than so-called concept modelers or surface modelers directed toward visualization purposes.

Hierarchical Structures

The process of developing a conceptual design into an end model suitable for supporting fabrication is a truly arduous one. During the design development process, specific features of designs are normally revised many times. In many common modeling systems, the need to revise a model often means literally rebuilding it (depending on the location and extent of the revision). In these systems, the user makes a series of specific moves to create a final model (e.g., drawing a curve, sweeping it, intersecting it with another, etc.). Literally hundreds of such steps can be made in a complex model. No record is made, however, of the steps taken; nor is the specific model construction process recoverable. Specific changes, albeit seemingly simple ones, may require laborious rebuilding of the whole model.

In response to these problems, digital environments with hierarchically based structures have been developed that allow the design history (steps in creating a model) to be recorded and subsequently manipulated. Steps are recorded and listed. They can be assigned specific names that are meaningful to the user (e.g., "outer shell thickness" or "cut hole"). The variable present in any step—for example, the diameter of a circle for a hole—is always identifiable and accessible to the user for change at any point in the design process.

These capabilities are achieved via the establishment of a series of "parent-child" relationships in the way the digital model is conceptualized and built. Models are hierarchically structured with a base model established (a "parent"). Features and other components subsequently added to the model become "children," which inherit characteristics of the parent. If the parent changes, children follow the changes, but not vice versa. These hierarchical relationships can be reordered or a user can intervene at any level.

The general hierarchical nature of parent-child relationships is illustrated in Figure 1-8. The parent can exist without the children, but not vice versa. A change made to a parent high in the hierarchy affects all models subsequently created. In some events, changing the form of some high-level element may make subsequent operations (i.e., the configuration of certain children) impossible because of impossible geometric demands. Chapter 11 discusses this subject in greater detail.

Parametric Variation

During any design process, the configuration, size, and shape of an object is seemingly in a state of constant turmoil—at least in early design stages. There is normally a need to study various proportions of a shape. Even once a basic shape is established, the exact dimensions of specific elements frequently change as a result of structural analyses, detailing considerations, and so forth. Hence, there is a general need to be able to alter quickly certain basic dimensions of a shape being designed. The broad need is to be able to vary the basic parameters of an object to obtain one or more *parametric variations*. A family of parametric variations all stem from the same characteristic shape but slightly vary in dimension or shape from one to another. They are *instances* of the same design. The essential shape and constituent elements of the design are clearly set within certain specified constraints, but the exact dimensions and shapes of individual elements vary from shape to shape. While making these different

instances can be done "by hand" (e.g., building a series of new models for each dimensional variation), parametric modeling systems facilitate this process by allowing certain dimensions to be specified as variables (see Figure 1-9).

What can be parametrically varied in a design? The answer to this question lies with the intent of the designer in building the model. Parametric variation can occur at any level. In a building, the overall shape of the external envelope may be parametrically varied, with certain key parameters governing the way the shape varies. Specific elements, such as façade elements—including windows and doors—could be varied. Bay proportions could be the targets. The list could

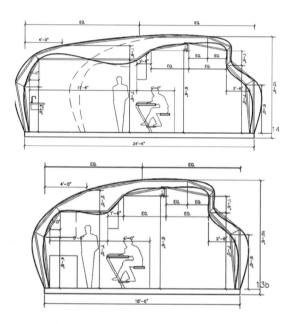

Model of a parametrically variable rib — critical dimensions defining the rib shape can be varied to produce a range of rib shapes (two instances are shown; a design table was used to define the full set of instances).

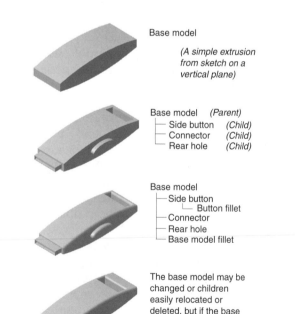

Base model

(A simple extrusion from sketch on a vertical plane)

Base model   *(Parent)*
  ├─ Side button   *(Child)*
  ├─ Connector   *(Child)*
  └─ Rear hole   *(Child)*

Base model
  ├─ Side button
  │ └─ Button fillet
  ├─ Connector
  ├─ Rear hole
  └─ Base model fillet

The base model may be changed or children easily relocated or deleted, but if the base model is deleted all children disappear.

Different instances may be combined in an assembly model to produce a building complex.

This proposal for an urban diner explored using different rib modules to fit different site conditions. The interior shape was driven by internal layout and height requirements.

Figure 1-8 A robust digital model in a CAD/CAM environment is built on parent-child relationships that can be defined within a hierarchically organized tree structure. This structure allows changes to be easily made without the model being completely rebuilt.

Figure 1-9 The design proposal depicted is based on a parametrically variable solid model of a single rib part that has been instantiated in many different forms in an assembly model. (Source: Courtesy of Evan Brinkman)

go on—down to the shapes of handrails or doorknobs. The way a specific parameter is varied, say, a critical dimension, can be at the will of the designer or can be made dependent upon some other factor via explicit rule structures. The width of an entryway could be made proportional to the number of people expected in the space, or the number of lug bolts used in the rim of a car wheel might be proportional to the diameter of the wheel. It is the designer's role to create a parametric model that allows him or her to explore the issues of identified importance.

Constraints, Dimensionally Driven Variations, and Rule Structures

The concept of parametric variation is accomplished by making systems that are constraint-based and dimensionally driven. Specific rule structures, including formulas, are also normally used. Constraints may assume the form of dimensions, angles, or any of several relationships between them. Specific values may be fixed throughout a complex design process where part shapes are being frequently varied. In a simple window example, it might be important for the bottom edge of the rectangle representing the window to always be a certain distance from a horizontal reference line (such might be the case if the rectangle represented a window in some façade designs).

Specific dimensions may also be used as control variables that determine the final geometry of a part. The term *dimensionally driven* is used to describe a digital model in which one or more specific critical dimensions are identified as governing parameters for a whole configuration. A change made by a user in one of these critical dimensions alters its configuration. The dimensional change thus "drives" the design. Critical dimensions in a design may be independently specified, or they may be used to drive the value of another dimension via a specified *formula* or *rule structure*. In the window example, a decision for all windows to have the same proportion regardless of their absolute size, could be implemented by having the width of the window directly dependent on the height of the window via a specified formula (e.g., width = 0.75 × height) wherein the height would be specified as the driving dimension. Inputting a value for the window height automatically causes the width to assume a value of 0.75 times the height. Other more complex relations could be established. The width could be specified in a fashion such as this: width = 0.8 × height − 4 inches.

Capabilities for establishing and managing constraints and making dimensionally driven models, are not found in a typical conceptual modeling system or one used for normal drawing and design representation. These kinds of capabilities, however, are found in the kinds of digital environments commonly used in the CAD/CAM field, for example, Pro/ENGINEER, CATIA, SolidWorks, and Unigraphics.

Feature-Based Design

Additional needed capabilities include what is commonly called *feature-based design*. Features are commonly used geometric manipulations, additions, or insertions that are straightforward in idea but frequently extremely tedious to implement. Constructing a simple fillet where a cylindrical shaft meets a curved surface can be frustratingly difficult and tedious if done directly. If the user then wants to vary the size of the fillet, the model would have to be significantly reconstructed. In response to these needs, *feature-based* design systems have evolved. Common processes such as chamfering corners, making slots or bolt holes, and so on are rendered easier in feature-based design systems. Capabilities exist for rapidly creating these elements and then allowing them to be parametrically varied.

Application Modeling

Good digital environments for CAD/CAM work support explorations between digital modeling and material and manufacturing dictates via a number of specialized modules. The output from a modeling environment that is specially created to support objects made by bending and folding thin sheet products (e.g., sheet metal) is seen in Figure 1-4 earlier in the chapter. Additionally, many special features associated with the reality of thin-sheet bending, such as the need for specified bend radii for different kinds of materials and plate thickness, and the need for "relief cuts" at certain places, are also typically supported by these packages.

Several other applications are also shown in Figure 1-4. In a casting process, for example, a three-dimensional model is first made to be used as a "pattern" to make a cavity in a mold material (such as sand). The cavity is then filled with molten metal. The part is removed from the mold after the piece is solidified. In the digital world, if a part is ultimately to be cast, the objective of the digital design process is to make a digital model for a negative mold for a part, rather than the part itself. The geometry of the original design model would be used to create a reverse-image model within an encompassing block—that is, a negative cavity. The resulting mold model would then be modified to contain all of the necessary sprues, vents, and connecting elements for making a complete mold. Any change in the original part model would be propagated through the derived mold model.

Assemblies

A fundamentally important characteristic of a good design system includes an ability to support the creation of *assemblies* of parts. Most large-scale design works, obviously including works of architecture, can be characterized in production terms as being complex aggregations of parts—each with specific functionalities—that have been configured to be assembled into a larger whole. This is certainly not to say that the whole design process itself necessarily proceeds as a process of designing individual pieces and fitting them together (often referred to as a "bottom-up" process). The process often proceeds in the opposite way—as a constant definition and refinement of a holistic design until the components have been fully detailed (often referred to as "top-down" design). More often than not, however, the design process is iterative in nature and cycles through whole/part relationships many times.

High-end digital design environments used in the CAD/CAM arena have modules devised to aid in the process of assembly modeling. Constituent parts can be first designed and then placed within a new model that reflects the whole assembly, or a large form can be subdivided into constituent elements. Tools exist for moving and positioning specific parts in relation to one another. Special constraining tools, for instance, alignment and mating relationships, exist that help place pieces in proper relationship to one another. Parts in mechanisms can be allowed to move or rotate as anticipated or needed.

Good digital environments also allow for "interference checks" wherein zones where pieces that overlap or conflict with one another are highlighted. This interference check feature is extremely important, since the problem of physical objects inadvertently running into one another, or being inadvertently designed to occupy the same space, has long plagued designers.

Robust assembly modelers always allow changes made in constituent part models to be propagated through the whole assembly. Thus, a change to a constituent part made in the part design file will be reflected in any final assembly model containing the part. Error messages will result if the change is so dramatic that the assembly configuration is no longer valid. Since critical dimensions between parts in an assembly can also be stipulated, the whole assembly model can thus be parametrically varied. Different instances of it can be developed.

Design for Production

It is well known that the process of how something is made frequently dictates or influences many design features of the part to be made. Over the course of time, many principles for how to design artifacts in light of production considerations have been developed. Many of these principles have been formally delineated and codified and embedded in *design-for-manufacturing* or *design-for-assembly* approaches. Design principles embedded in these approaches range from configurational

issues for supporting different fabrication technologies to larger principles having to do with minimizing the number of parts used in a design via consolidation of part functionalities, assembly order, and so forth. These design principles are further explored in Chapter 16.

Analysis Systems

Analysis systems are powerful components of any comprehensive environment supporting both CAE and CAD/CAM applications. For example, just because a beam can be modeled within a digital design environment and even ultimately fabricated via a CNC machine, it does not follow that the size and shape of the beam is adequate for its intended role in a building. While not necessarily a digital modeling problem, a collapsing beam is nonetheless indicative of a severe shortcoming in the design process. To meet analysis needs of this general type that help ensure the design value of the object, robust digital design environments typically include one or more analysis systems that seek to predict certain kinds of performances or evaluate the designed object from specific points of view. Structural analysis packages are common, as are other packages for analyzing the thermal or electromechanical behavior of an element. These and other analysis capabilities are explored in more depth in Chapter 11.

Integrated and Collaborative Models

Many different participants from different disciplines are invariably involved in designing and ultimately constructing buildings or products. The use of shared digital design environments based on 3-D digital design models with their many associated reporting functions does offer the potential for better information flows and interactions among different groups. Chapter 7 explores the more practice-oriented applications of 3-D models.

1.3 THE MANUFACTURING ENVIRONMENT

CNC Machines and Related Manufacturing Processes

Artifacts are ultimately made via the application of one or more manufacturing processes. Many of these processes are quite ancient in origin. Many are based on material removal processes via mechanical or other means. Other techniques are based on deformation processes that involve the bending or shaping of materials. Yet others are based on various casting or molding processes. Many of these processes have time-honored origins and have been used long before the advent of any kind of computer technologies, and only recently have they been adapted to newer control approaches. Other technologies have only been introduced rather recently (e.g., water jets or lasers) and are clearly dependent on computer technologies in their operation and control.

Most of the actual production machines of interest herein are based on *numerical control technology.* Instead of a person directly operating a machine, a set of numerically encoded instructions are prepared and then read and decoded by the machine, causing it to operate in an automatic mode. Today, it is common that the machine instructions are derived from a digital design model via a CAM program (see the section that follows). These numerically encoded instructions in turn cause the servomechanisms and other devices within a CNC machine to execute specific movements, including actions such as cutting in a straight line or along a prespecified curve.

Many types of different CNC machines are currently in use, including drill presses, saws, milling machines, facing and longitudinal lathes, grinders, and other machines that create objects via material removal processes by mechanical means (see Figure 1-10). Machines supporting newer material removal processes, such as abrasive-jet technologies (e.g., water jet machines) are invariably numerically controlled. Machines can be simple or complex. *Machining centers,* for example, are multifunctional, numerically controlled machine tools with capabilities for different types of machining and with automatic tool changing. Chapter 13 looks at CNC technologies and machine types in detail.

Modeling for Specific Manufacturing Processes (CAM Models)

To employ CNC machines, it is normally necessary to extract geometric and other information from the digital design model. This can be a simple or complex step depending on what is actually to be made—the part itself or some type of additional tooling to make the part using a specialized process of some type or another. It must be remembered that what is to be done at this stage may not actually look like the design model (albeit obviously related to it). If a piece is to be cast, then the objective is to make the negative molds, not the part itself. It is thus important to decide on how an object is to be made as soon as possible.

Once the decision is made as to what is actually going to be manufactured, then the digital model is converted via a manufacturing applications package or, as it often described, *computer-aided manufacturing software,* into a set of instructions appropriate for making the object by use of a specific machine technology. Manufacturing applications packages form a key building block in a CAD/CAM system by providing a software link between the computer-aided design model and actual numerically controlled (NC) production equipment. They provide a structured environment for establishing and evaluating how a particular object might actually be made by a specific machine or set of machines. These software packages allow the specification of toolpaths, tool changes, sequences of tooling operations, and so forth. In addition, they prepare "machine language" instructions to govern the actual movements of an NC machine. In these systems, the user has to literally think through what actions he or she wants the machine to accomplish (and in what order). These actions then need to be formally specified. For example, in a simple machining system, here is where a user decides on the specific cutting tool that is to be used for machining (e.g., a ball end mill of a particular diameter), the location of the first cut and the direction that the tool follows (the *toolpath*), the speed of the cut, the depth of the cut (hence, the number of passes the initial tool makes to create a surface), whether or not the tool end doing the initial rough passes is the same as the tool doing the final finishing, and other similar factors. (See Figure 1-11.) Many packages have useful graphic interfaces. Once the user specifies all needed machine actions, these actions are translated by the software into specific code that can ultimately be used to control the NC machine that makes the final parts. A typical part is shown in Figure 1-12.

COMMON TYPES OF CNC MACHINES
Routers
Lathes
Milling Machines
Saws
Drills
Laser Cutters
Water Jets
and Others

COMPUTER with CAD/CAM software

CNC MACHINE

3-axis CNC router

Figure 1-10 There are many different types of computer numerically controlled (CNC) machines. A three-axis CNC router is shown on the right.

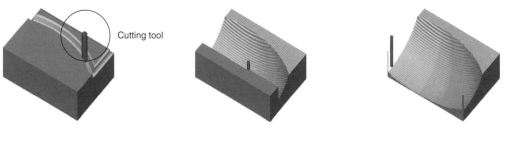

Simulation of block and tool— the tool and cutting are animated and follow the digital model.

The cutting marks indicate the cutting path of the tool that has been specified by the user.

The scalloped surface results from the shape of the tool end and the spacing of the tool passes.

Figure 1-11 These images show a toolpath simulation for a CNC milling machine. The toolpath is first derived from the basic digital model. The simulation is used for verification of the toolpath prior to actual machining.

It must be emphasized that the design of the manufacturing application package is closely tied into the nature of the actual manufacturing process envisioned as well as the material nature of the artifact itself. Creation of a good digital manufacturing application model fundamentally requires that the user be completely familiar with the manufacturing process itself. Typical CAM software is not a replacement for knowledge of the process involved and related constraints that surround it.

Related Technologies
Free-Form Solid Fabrication ("3-D Printing")

The need and value for making initial prototypes for understanding and evaluating proposed designs is well understood by all designers. Chapter 15 explores in more detail the many ways of making prototypes. Of

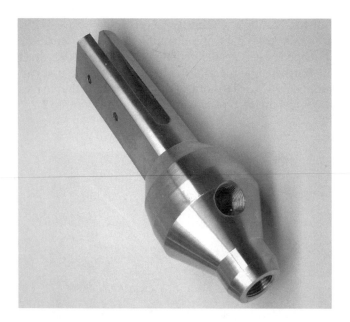

Figure 1-12 This stainless steel connector was made by TriPyramid Structures, Inc. It was turned, machined, and threaded. (Source: © TriPyramid Structures, Inc.)

particular interest at this point is that there are a number of new digitally based tools that greatly assist in prototype production. In particular, there are a whole host of newer technologies—typically called solid free-form fabrication technologies—that rely on "additive" methods of making objects. Basically, these systems build up a model using a sequential "slice by slice" approach. Most build up sequential slices by a material solidification process or a template-cutting process. Common technologies include that of stereolithography, fused deposition modeling, laminated object manufacturing, and others. Originally widely known as "rapid prototyping systems" and still commonly called "3-D printing," the term *solid free-form fabrication* is now used as a better descriptor of the processes involved.

The use of these systems falls into several distinct applications. One set of applications for so-called concept modelers is to be able to quickly generate models that are useful for conceptualizing complex objects that are difficult to visualize. These are especially good for improving communications among participants in the design process. Another set of technologies is directed toward the direct use of solid free-form fabrication models either as direct production parts or in indirect support of production processes via their use as patterns for mold making. Chapter 14 explores these technologies in detail.

Reverse Engineering

Many designers prefer to start design with a physical model. The model is scanned and a related digital model is created and subsequently revised or modified as desired. A design model might come in the form of an actual physical study model executed in clay or some other material, or it might be an actual functional part whose drawings and representations are long lost. In all cases, however, there are no existing digital representations whatsoever. The first part of the reverse engineering process is to digitally capture the geometry of a physical study model or original part via a three-dimensional digitization process. Various digitizing devices are available. Electromechanical means or laser scanning technologies are common. The scanning system records the three-dimensional geometry of an object and records it into a file. This file is then brought over into a geometric modeling system where it is first edited and then used as a basis for creating a new digital model (e.g., curves are fitted through sets of points). This process normally requires extensive editing and intervention (surfaces need to be stitched together, gaps filled, etc.). The model is then used as before. Ultimately, the resulting new digital model would then be used to control the fabrication process within a CNC environment. (See Figure 1-13.)

This general approach is a powerful one in many instances. Certainly it is useful in any kind of building restoration work where the intent is to create a new object that is a replacement for an existing part. As discussed in subsequent chapters, it has also been used by well-known designers such as Frank O. Gehry & Associates in connection with many of the projects coming from this office.

Manufacturing Systems

There are a myriad of different ways in which different manufacturing processes can be organized. The process or processes chosen depends upon many factors, including the size and configuration of the objects, the anticipated volume of production, and many other factors. Assembly-line productions are clearly aimed at high-volume production. Here the intent is to lower unit production costs by as much rationalization of the manufacturing process as possible. These systems produce high volumes, but adapting for changing designs is costly, since major retooling is invariably involved.

As production volume expectations decrease, the use of high-cost but volume-efficient technologies decreases. Specific approaches—such as flexible manufacturing systems—to machine organization and other processes can be adopted that are aimed at low- and medium-volume production ranges. Groups of machines are organized to produce families of varying elements with reduced setup time.

Production Strategies

At a broader level, the term *computer-integrated manufacturing (CIM)* is often used to describe an approach to manufacturing that includes a technological component but further includes many other activities. The approach includes the design and production activities previously discussed, as well as material purchasing, delivery, and inspection, and it further extends into marketing activities, sales, and post-sale support.

There are also techniques for orchestrating and managing the more or less simultaneous participation in the design and fabrication process of many participants. It is well known that the widespread use of communication and networking technology has both allowed and encouraged the many participants in the process to be geographically, and often organizationally and administratively, removed from one another. Concurrent design software facilitates the interactive flow of information among participants while at the same time allowing controls to be exerted. (See Figure 1-14.)

There are also broad strategic approaches that represent manufacturing philosophies and attitudes that reflect different business models, for example, just-in-time and lean manufacturing. Indeed, a whole host of new business models have evolved from adoption of the capabilities offered by comprehensive CAD/CAM

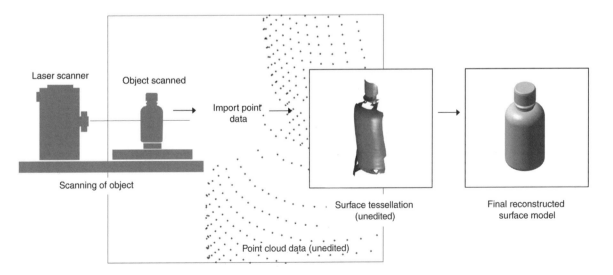

Figure 1-13 Three-dimensional scanning and the "reverse engineering" process. A physical model is scanned, resulting point clouds are edited and aligned, the surface is tessellated and edited, and a new surface model is developed. The new model can then be modified as desired.

Fundamental Processes

Manufacturing Systems

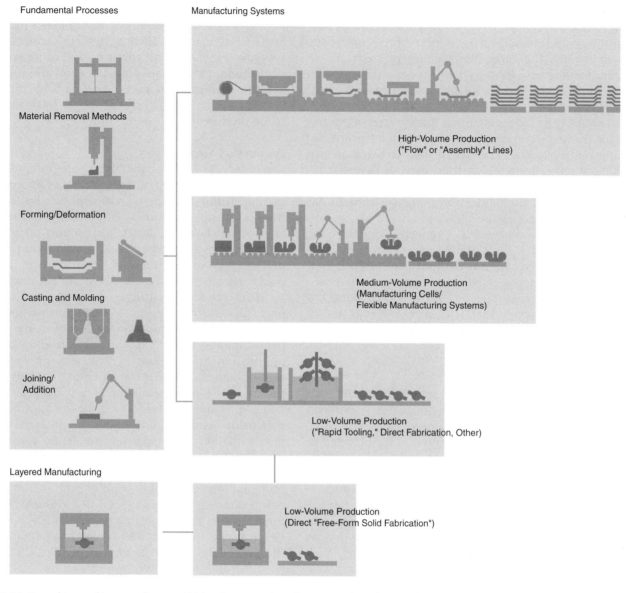

Material Removal Methods

Forming/Deformation

Casting and Molding

Joining/
Addition

High-Volume Production
("Flow" or "Assembly" Lines)

Medium-Volume Production
(Manufacturing Cells/
Flexible Manufacturing Systems)

Low-Volume Production
("Rapid Tooling," Direct Fabrication, Other)

Layered Manufacturing

Low-Volume Production
(Direct "Free-Form Solid Fabrication")

Figure 1-14 General types of low-, medium-, and high-volume manufacturing systems (see Chapter 17).

environments. One of the more interesting models is that of "mass customization." Here the general intent is to use highly efficient production facilities to produce objects custom-specified by a user. Specific strategies, for instance, component swapping, are part of the general approach. Mass customization obviously has great conceptual appeal and has formed the basis for many polemics about the relationship between design and production. They typically entail much more in the way of technology, organization, and comprehensive business strategy than typically meets the eye. Chapter 18 addresses mass customization in greater detail.

CHAPTER 2

An Evolutionary Perspective

2.1 PARALLEL STREAMS

As a way of both defining and understanding the characteristics of computer-aided design and manufacturing systems, as we now know them, we need to look at their origin and development. This is no easy task, however, since these systems have diverse origins. Obviously, they have origins in the very fields encompassed by the terms themselves—"computers" and "manufacturing." More generally, however, they are also a response to changing attitudes toward the interrelationship between design and production activities.

Perhaps the best way to engage the topic is to first look at several parallel streams of development that have strongly contributed to the development of CAD/CAM systems. One stream of development is undoubtedly coupled with the rise of industrialization and the concurrent development of machine technologies intended to support the design and production paradigms associated with the age of industrialization, particularly process specialization. Closely allied to this major stream of development is the rise of automation. In many instances the rise of automation is synonymous with the rise of industrialization, but there are many other contributing influences as well—including the wonderful and curious automata of the nobility of eighteenth-century France. Surely the evolution of computer technology forms another source of development, but again this evolution overlaps and is influenced by developments in both machine technology and automation. Jacquard's famous power looms governed by punch tapes that came into use at the beginning of the nineteenth century form the example par excellence here. The approach used here is to initially describe these three initial streams of development independently and as occurring in a more or less parallel mode. This is not to say that these streams occurred independently of one another, only that it is easier to trace the development of certain key concepts when they are considered separately.

2.2 THE RISE OF INDUSTRIALIZATION AND AUTOMATION

Industrialization: Early Developments

The development of tools has long been acknowledged as one of the defining characteristics of human evolution. They have served to increase human power, improve precision, and generally be the enabling devices that have defined our unique ability to make tools used in turn to make other tools, and thus ultimately create a stunning world of artifacts. The current culmination of our age-old quest to create new and better tools is the development of the CAD/CAM technologies. These technologies as we now know them are inextricably linked with the early rise of material processing techniques and the subsequent rise of industrialization in the eighteenth and nineteenth centuries. Here also is where traditional craft-based approaches to production initially gave way to process-specialization approaches that ultimately redefined whole production environments—which in turn led to changes in basic societal structures. Attitudes toward not only how to make artifacts changed but also how to design them in view of the new capabilities afforded by the new production environments.

The actual origins of underlying material processing and production technologies lie deep in antiquity, of course, as do the origin of tools themselves. The era of most relevance here, however, is the eighteenth century, and the place is England.

In this place and beginning with this period, manufacturing changed from a collection of local cottage industries to more organized and systematic production environments—at least in England and then subsequently in other countries. The change began occurring in an environment still dominated by a craft production model—a model characterized by individual craftsmen making custom-made products for specific individuals. Normally, a craftsman worked on a product from start to finish, using a small set of relatively general tools. Consequences of the emerging industrial revolution, however, would challenge this approach. Pots and other products were made by the

Figure 2-1 The Crystal Palace built in London between 1851 and 1852 remains the fundamental icon of how the rise of industrialized building techniques impacted architecture.

thousands, for example, in the mid-1700s in places such as Iron Gorge at Coalbrookedale, where the cast-iron industry was developing. As described in Chapter 8, Wedgewood ushered in not only new ways of making ceramics but new design attitudes as well that would be familiar to any industrial designer.

The complexity of making many products in high demand led to the development of many technological innovations. Of particular importance with respect to the ultimate development of numerical control technology and automated machines is the work of Joseph-Marie Jacquard (1752–1834) and his predecessors, who ultimately developed a power loom that used punched cards to govern the weaving of complex patterns. Complex woven patterns had long been tediously woven by hand. The emerging textile industry had long sought ways to mechanize the process. Jacquard built upon the work of his predecessors—Basile Bouchon, Jean-Baptiste Falcon, Jacques de Vaucanson, and Edmund Cartwright—in developing a method for using preprepared punched cards to control the operation of looms. An early Jacquard machine was basically a frame containing a number of wire hooks, which were raised or lowered according to the pattern to be woven. A straightforward but nonetheless ingenious mechanism was developed for using perforated paper to raise or lower any pattern of hooks as desired. Designs for complex weaving patterns could thus be made and transferred to perforated cards, and these cards would in turn govern the mechanical weaving operation itself. The Jacquard loom is an example par excellence of an early type of programmable machine (see Figure 2-2). The machine was subsequently introduced into England in 1818 and Scotland in 1824, and rapidly became the mainstay of the great textile industries in these regions.

In other arenas, the rise of mechanized processes proceeded on many fronts. Working in the United States, Eli Whitney is generally credited with the development of an early form of the milling machine—a machine in which a multitoothed rotary cutter removes metal from a workpiece attached to a table. This versatile machine provided the basic enabling technology for making many kinds of products and for parts used in yet other machines, including his well-known cotton gin. Additionally, Whitney's work proved pivotal in accelerating both the development of *standardized processes* for making parts and the associated concept of part *interchangeability*. He was thus instrumental in developing *process specialization* approaches based on the *division of labor,* wherein each worker produced only individual parts, to be later assembled by others. The approach demanded new manufacturing approaches and controls, hence the development of devices such as jigs and other kinds of fixtures to ensure that each part produced was the same as every other part produced. The basic idea of process specialization itself, so obvious today, was novel at the time.

Many machine developments had occurred by the mid-1800s. The Lincoln Miller of 1855, for example, was a milling machine built by Pratt and Whitney (see Figure 2-3). The Browne and Sharpe machine of 1861 was perhaps the first "universal" milling machine (see Figure 2-4). With time, more and more machines were being designed to support more specialized tasks (e.g., machines were made specifically to produce complexly shaped wood moldings). The process wherein new machines were quickly devised to meet new needs was

Figure 2-2 A Jacquard loom with a weaving pattern controlled by perforated cards.

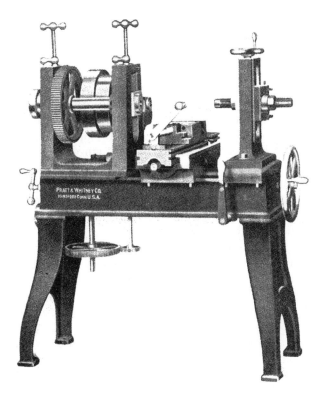

Figure 2-3 The Lincoln milling machine was a very early machine tool that was manually operated. It was capable of great accuracy.

a self-accelerating one made possible by the very existence of earlier machines. Machines were used to build ever more sophisticated machines.

By the mid-1800s, the concepts of process specialization and the associated division of labor became the central means of increasing production. Associated with emerging trends in process specialization were specific design attitudes. The development of designs based on the interchangeability of parts was inherently associated with process specialization. Not only was production increased, but there were also positive benefits in the use and maintenance of products once they were in use, which further encouraged propagation of these production techniques. As workers only needed to be trained for specific processes—often of limited complexity in themselves—overall required worker skill levels were ultimately reduced. Initially, however, these approaches based on new machines were used to increase the productivity and quality of products produced by already skilled workers. The success of these approaches depended to a large degree on the abilities of workers still trained in earlier craft traditions and perfectly capable of providing generalized functions. This same era saw the more widespread organization of the supply industry as specific groups invested in the development of specific machines to make general materials and components used by a great number of final end-product producers.

As the end of the nineteenth century approached, there were distinct changes occurring in how industries made use of labor. Earlier attitudes that used machine developments in conjunction with an already skilled labor force to increase both productivity and quality, as well as the sophistication of products, began giving way. Skill levels declined and labor exploitation began. The simultaneous change in the role of labor, and consequently authorship, proved to have not only long-lasting technical consequences but also political and social ones. In high-volume production areas—such as textiles—the evolution of this approach reached extremes that eventually led to massive labor exploitation and unrest. (See Figure 2-5.) Of specific interest herein, however, is that process specialization approaches did not dominate all production arenas.

Figure 2-4 The Browne and Sharpe screw machine of 1902 represented the full development of the automatic machine.

Figure 2-5 This Ingersoll cross-rail milling machine was developed for high-volume production setups.

Where demand and related production volumes were not high, skilled workers using multipurpose machines still provided the only way to produce needed objects.

Industrialization: Later Developments

The process specialization approach represented a radical change from the earlier craft attitudes toward production. The nineteenth-century paradigm of process specialization as a primary means of increasing productivity involved labor, but it mostly focused on improvements in machine processes. Developments in and around 1900 looked more toward lowering costs through developing efficiencies in the overall process of production. While retaining the primary elements introduced in the nineteenth century, these developments focused on improving production flows. The innovations introduced in the Ford Company are well known. Flows were organized to bring work to men and women at specific stations, where they repetitively performed small, well-defined tasks. The labor component of the flow was studied extensively. F. W. Taylor's famous experiments on labor performance in workshop settings sought to increase production by looking at the performance of both machines and labor, and in particular, their interaction. Henry Ford used these techniques to constantly reduce the price of his Model T automobile. The need for process control (including the role of labor) led to more and more vertical management organization as well. Product standardization was a natural by-product of this way of thinking. The results were rewarding. As automobile prices fell, the size of the available market dramatically increased as the automobile changed from a specialized luxury item to a commodity. The pattern became self-reinforcing. The allied notions of economy of scale, flow processes, labor performing small specialized tasks, and emphasis on cost lowering even at the expense of product sophistication became synonymous with the term *mass production*. Images of "assembly lines" became familiar to most consumers and persuasively affected the design and production thinking of the day in all fields, not just in the automotive arena.

With time, entrenched notions of mass production based on product standardization and economies of scale began to falter, with perhaps the most dramatic evidence being the decline of the American automotive industry in the late 1960s and 1970s. The stability of demand markets, so fundamental to the concept of mass production, began to decline as demographic and general societal changes began sweeping the world and causing market fragmentation. No longer was there an ever-increasing market for limited product types so essential to mass production. Instead, there were increasing demands for different types of products. Competition from abroad soon offered highly differentiated products that appealed to a wide range of consumers. Mass production was no longer as attractive as it once was.

Even while mass production attitudes dominated the manufacturing scene, there always remained an active and important segment within the production sphere that retained its high skill levels and ability to produce specialized products. As before, in areas where demand volume remained low—for high-value unique or specialized products or custom models—reliance continued to be placed on relatively skilled operators using multipurpose machines. Indeed, this segment of the industry remained apart from major trends in other production spheres.

The development of numerically controlled machine equipment in the late 1940s and early 1950s—discussed more in a following section—was at least partly targeted toward this same low-volume, high-value production sector. Among the development goals was how to create a means for low-volume production while minimizing the need for highly skilled operator assistance. The response was both pragmatically driven by desires to reduce costs but also by perceptions of national defense needs. The military-industrial complex that sponsored some of the initial developments in this area saw a dwindling of the vast store of skilled labor built up during World War II and sought ways to mitigate the problem via the development of computer-assisted tools.

The ultimate success of the attempts to improve production via numerically controlled technologies is clear (otherwise this book surely would not be here). These techniques ushered in both technology and process innovations. Many new manufacturing processes, for instance, laser cutting, can exist only because of them. The development of numerical control technology and machine design continued to reach higher states of refinement. One development path was directed toward the development of machines that acted semi-autonomously (and sometimes autonomously), usually called robots. As discussed more in the next section, the successful thrust here was not on the creation of fully autonomous, mobile, and thinking robots that sought to emulate human actions and intelligence, but rather on task-specific industrial robots. Another thrust was directed toward how to arrange constellations of machines to better support "group technologies" and other different kinds of manufacturing strategies. Here you find the world of manufacturing cells, flexible manufacturing systems, and so forth. "Agile manufacturing" and other buzzwords surround the ever-changing portrait of manufacturing sectors as they seek to find new ways to be cost-effective and productive. Many of these approaches were driven by perceived needs to draw away from traditional hard assembly-line approaches oriented toward large-volume production and to find better ways of dealing with needs for low-volume runs of customized products.

These more recent developments will be explored in detail in following sections. At this point it can be noted that together they subsequently became the driving forces behind a reconceptualization and eventual retooling of many industrial segments in America and abroad. They led to major changes in fields such as the aerospace and automotive industries. The new technologies, coupled with new management approaches, provided a way of breaking out of the limitations imposed by older mass production paradigms by allowing the efficient making of highly differentiated goods. Emphasis focused on processes for making differentiated, varied products. Great efficiencies were obtained when single processes could be applied to multiple products. Interestingly, these new processes did not necessarily reduce costs of specific products when volumes were high, and could not necessarily compete with older mass production economies of scale. They did, however, achieve broadly lowered costs over a larger range of product types, which in turn enjoyed a large market in the aggregate. These trends have become canonized in some industries. Words such as "mass customization" were introduced to characterize the trend and to explore how these approaches could be made even more efficient (see Chapters 9 and 18).[1]

Automata

At this point it is useful to again return to a historically earlier time and focus on yet another thread of development. Here we focus briefly on different quests to develop various "automata," or devices that in some way emulated the actions of living animals or people. At first these devices were seemingly mere curiosities designed to delight or amuse, or perhaps be magical. In many direct and indirect ways, however, they significantly contributed to the development of the computer itself. In a more obvious manner, they provided much of the inspiration underlying the development of modern robotics and machine "intelligence." While surely the subject of how automata evolved is ultimately thoroughly interwoven with both the rise of industrialization and with the development of computer technology, there are some threads to the story that seemingly stem from unrelated roots.

The literature of this field is vast. We can identify various attempts to develop automata that can be traced back to ancient Greece and China. Archytas of Tarentum—a friend of Plato—constructed a pigeon controlled by a jet of air or steam. At about the same time in China, evidence of a mechanical orchestra exists. In medieval times, the rapid development of clock technology was accompanied by all manner of figures that moved to celebrate different times. The 1500s saw the development of lifelike figures based on clock technologies and the wonderful orreries.

The 1700s saw a rise of interest in these devices, particularly in France. Many were built for entertainment. Nonetheless, these seeming diversions ultimately played a major role in the development of industrial automation and the computer itself. Nowhere is this impact clearer than in the work of Jacques de Vaucanson. In 1738 he made three automata—a musician that played on the flute, a boy with a tambour, and a duck. The flute player could play 11 melodies and moved the levers of his flute with his hands and seemingly blew with his mouth. The actions of various rotating cams that caused the movements were regulated by heavy weights. Reputedly, the life-size duck quacked and flapped its wings. It even swallowed and, in a manner, digested its food and excreted it through rubber tubing that simulated intestines. These devices, along with many later ones, were enormously complicated and required considerable mechanical skill and ingenuity, as well as necessitating the development of the concept of deliberate movement sequences designed to achieve a specific effect. There is little doubt that this preparation served Vaucanson well in his subsequent role as inspector of silk factories, where he frequently introduced many innovations into the manufacturing apparatus used at the time. Vaucanson was a major contributor to the development of the automated loom, subsequently perfected by Jacquard, and hence to both the development of mechanical automation and to the computer itself via development of the concept of programmable operations.

While the fascination with idle automata designed to only amuse slowed in the nineteenth century, the idea of machines having both the mechanical capacity and intelligence necessary to emulate humans was a recurrent one. The idea of chess-playing automata, for example, was explored many times during this period. The specific image of the automata with humanlike physical appearances that would indeed emulate human capabilities remained persuasive. Writing in the early part of this century, the Czech dramatist Karel Capek played a role in the development of automation and societal attitudes toward it. In a 1917 story, Capek used the word *robot* from the Czech words *robota* (obligatory work) and *robotnik* (an obligated worker). In a 1922 play, *R.U.R.* ("Rossum's Universal Robots"), Capek describes intelligent mechanical machines that were initially created to serve their human makers. In his play, these same machines eventually destroyed humankind's creations and ultimately humankind itself.

Capek not only introduced a word that caught the public's imagination for a class of intelligent machines; his portrayal of robots as substitutes for humans still remains in the popular imagination. While this popularized image of robots was ever-present in the interwar period and afterward, the actual development of what we now think of as true robots was much slower and awaited many further developments in electronics, servomechanisms, and, of course, the modern computer. The development of servomechanisms during the World War II period was critical. The further development of computer-based numerical control technology in the early 1950s (discussed in more detail later) was equally pivotal. Ultimately, the continued development of numerically controlled machines coupled with improved programming and control capabilities naturally led directly to the evolution of a whole series of special-purpose robotic devices.

One of the first true robots was the Unimation 2000. This robot could move an arm and close a gripper. Robots based on these initial technologies were introduced in the 1970s for material handling and spot welding applications. Early robots by Unimation and Cincinnati Milacron (a CNC machine tool builder) were hydraulic-powered and often simple polar coordinate devices. The subsequent development of electric motors with sufficient torque levels was a major breakthrough. These early robots used in industry applications, however, are a far cry from society's vision of an intelligent machine with anthropomorphic features and human capabilities. While later versions became quite sophisticated, they made no pretense to having "human intelligence." They became the workhorses of many industries.

In the 1980s, industrial robots became much more sophisticated and possessed many more degrees of freedom in their movement capabilities. Capabilities were developed for "teaching" a robotic device to perform a sequence of operations by literally guiding the end effector (the final gripper or other end tool) by hand. Robotic devices could thus be taught to mimic experienced spray painters and welders. New developments in sensors and other technologies enabled industrial robots, as well as more traditional machines, to be designed to have remarkable capabilities. Machine vision systems were introduced to allow a machine to interpret images. Automated decision-making capabilities for the machines as based on vision and other sensor systems were increased as well. The development of robotic devices continues today, with the incorporation of more and more capabilities, albeit they have still not quite achieved the capabilities of our two friends in *Star Wars*.

2.3 THE COMPUTATIONAL ENVIRONMENT

Early Developments

The development of the modern computer is surely one of the great achievements of our age and has obviously had an enormous impact on our society and the way it functions. The origins of computers can be arguably traced to very early times. In Greek and Roman times, a calculating device based on the manipulation of stones on a flat surface was used. While other early precedents could be noted as well, more recent developments are central to our argument and will be focused on herein.

The scientific revolution ushered in not only a whole new way of thinking about the world but also an increased demand for improved calculation capabilities. Within specific areas, such as astronomy, these same demands were heightened by broad intellectual quests to further our understanding of the makeup and movement of astronomical objects and were coupled with pragmatic demands to use these understandings in the furtherance of practical needs, such as navigation, that were associated with the great trade and territorial expansions of the day. A direct consequence of developments such as these was a renewed focus on the problem of dealing with vast quantities of digital information and the need to make precise calculations rapidly. The development of logarithms with their associated vast tables of numbers and ways of manipulating these numbers to perform rapid but nonetheless precise calculations, for example, directly addressed these kinds of needs. John Napier is generally considered the primary developer of logarithms (in 1614). He went on to develop a device for performing arithmetic operations that relied upon the manipulation of rods with digits imprinted upon them (they were often called "bones," since they were literally made of bones). In the 1620s, the mathematician William Oughtred brought to bear the powerful computational capabilities of logarithms in the development of one of the world's most remarkable instruments—the slide rule—when he observed that logarithms could be represented in length measures. In the 1642, Blaise Pascal produced a mechanical arithmetic machine that implemented simple algorithmic procedures. Pascal produced some 50 different models of calculating machines. There was considerable outcry at the time from some about his machine, the Pascaline, namely, that it would replace humans and put many tabulators out of work.

During the same general era as the scientific revolution, largely concurrent development in other branches of mathematics provided new ways of conceptualizing and describing not only physical phenomena but of exploring the world in more geometric terms. Developments in the field of mathematics, such as descriptive geometry by Gaspard Monge and others, are certainly influential, since they laid the basis for many of the kinds of manipulations now implicitly part of the geometric modeling systems now in common use in any computer-aided design environment. The development of calculus by individuals such as Gottfried Wilhelm Leibniz further enhanced our understanding of the geometric world by providing specific tools for the precise description of complex curves and surfaces.

Charles Babbage (1792–1871) and others subsequently developed calculating machines capable of many sophisticated operations. He proposed an early form of a large-scale digital calculator: the "Analytical Engine." Although never truly finished, these remarkable mechanically based engines clearly anticipated the modern digital computer. The Analytical Engine was conceived so that it could be programmed to solve many computational problems. It had a punched card reader reminiscent of those in Jacquard machines. It had a form of memory—a number could be entered, stored, and retrieved from any location. Registers could be used to perform a variety of operations, and a special storage unit was developed for machine instructions. A form of machine language similar to that used today was used.

Babbage developed a relationship with Ada Lovelace, daughter of the poet Lord Byron. She became as taken with the machine as with Babbage and soon contributed many programming ideas. She introduced the loop and subroutine. Arguably, she was the world's first computer programmer. She went on to speculate about the capacity of the machine and others like it to perform activities associated with human intelligence. Interestingly, she concluded that the Analytical Engine could not be regarded as capable of thinking as humans understand it but could accomplish many activities that would otherwise demand human thought.

Another significant step occurred around 1854 when the mathematician George Boole developed a logic system based on the use of mathematical symbols. Through symbols and rules, evaluations could be made as to whether statements were logically true or not. This system for dealing with logical problems via algebraic notations ultimately provided an intellectual basis for the development of mathematical logic. Ultimately, this development helped lay the foundation for the truly modern computer, with its roots in both symbolic logic and in logic circuits.

The quest for practical and reliable calculating machines for serving many business and scientific purposes continued throughout the nineteenth century. William Burroughs (1857–1898) repeatedly tried to market a reliable machine until he finally succeeded. In response to a competition for more efficient tabulation methods, Herman Hollerith created an electrically operated machine-readable punch card and card-processing system for use with the 1890 census. From 1894 to 1896, Herman Hollerith formed the Tabulating Machine Company.

The Twentieth Century

Developments became rapid during the interwar period. In 1924 the International Business Machines Corporation (IBM) was formed. Organized by Thomas J. Watson, a former National Cash Register Company executive, the company was formed out of a holding company called Computer-Tabulating-Recording Company that in turn had been formed out of the Tabulating Machine Company by Herman Hollerith.

The interwar period was a time of great innovation in the rapidly developing computer field. In Germany, a civil engineer, Konrad Zuse, developed one of the world's first fully programmable digital computers (to automate what he termed the "awful calculations" required to be done by civil engineers). His final machine, completed in 1940, was programmable. It had a built-in memory of 1,408 bits organized into 64 words and had 1,408 relays to make random memory access possible. He went on to develop a language that presaged C. Curiously, his work was never exploited to any great extent by the Nazi war machine.

Vannevar Bush (1890–1974) and colleagues at M.I.T. developed the "Differential Analyzer"—an analog computer using thermionic valves or tubes that was completed in 1930. It was an electronic version of George Boole's logic system. In an analog device, the amplitude of a continuous signal typically represents the numerical value of data represented. (Later digital devices, by contrast, use an electrical signal that changes from one state to another in separate steps.) Alan Turing provided a theoretical description of a more general-purpose computer. He extended the work of others and ultimately founded modern computational theory. Turing developed the idea of what has come to be known as a Turing machine, which is a theoretical idea of a computer. He developed a famous test for determining whether or not a machine is intelligent, which largely hinges around the ability of a computer to imitate human performance.

Intense development activity continued in other areas during the interwar period. In 1939, a project directed at developing a versatile programmable computer was started at Harvard University under the direction of Howard Hathaway Aiken. The general-purpose computer, the Harvard-IBM Mark I Automatic Sequence Controller, was completed in 1944 by Howard Aiken. The Mark I contained around 760,000 parts and 500 miles of wire. It took around 4 seconds to perform simple multiplication tasks and 11 seconds to perform simple division tasks. Other machines followed. Grace Murray Hopper developed libraries of subroutines for the Mark series and wrote high-level language compilers. Interestingly, she also helped originate the term "debug." The Mark series used many mechanical relays. A problem was caused when a moth died inside one of them. Subsequently, having problems with the computer was commonly referred to as "having bugs" in it. The Mark series attracted a lot of attention, but it was evident that it was computationally slow because of its electromechanical relay technology.

Spurred by a wartime environment and special computing needs in aeronautics and ballistics, J. P. Eckert and J. W. Mauchly of the University of Pennsylvania developed the Electronic Numerical Integrator and Calculator (ENIAC) between 1943 and 1945. Completed in 1946, this remarkable but enormous electronic computer—weighing some 30 tons—used 18,000 electron tubes, but it had no internal storage and had to receive its instructions from external switches and plugs. A primary problem with the ENIAC was the incredible trouble required to change a program, which involved setting 6,000 switches. The notion of the "stored program" was introduced to mitigate these problems. The ideas underlying the stored program containing everything from algorithmic methods to recursive techniques are primarily attributed to the Hungarian-American mathematician John von Neumann, although the contributions of Eckert and Mauchly are evident. The Remington Rand company acquired the ENIAC and subsequently introduced it as the Universal Automatic Computer (UNIVAC I). This machine used magnetic tape for input and output. It was the first commercially available computer. UNIVAC did not prove to be a commercial success, but it did wake up IBM to the need to increase its presence in the market. Its popular 700 and 1400 series were introduced, with the famed 360 series following shortly afterward.

On other fronts developments occurred rapidly. A practical silicon transistor—a device based on semiconductor materials used for voltage and current amplification—was produced in 1954. Microprocessors—integrated circuits that contain the entire central processing unit of a computer on a microchip—were developed in the 1970s.

By now there is almost a bewildering array of computer types and technologies. There also have been changes in how computers are used and societal attitudes toward them. Early systems tended to be large, general-purpose mainframe installations intended for multiple users. They were taken up aggressively by the scientific, engineering, and business communities, but they remained a novelty to most of the population at large. Use remained largely within a domain of self-selected specialists operating within a centralized framework. The subsequent development in the 1970s of minicomputers, workstations, and, eventually, microcomputers, changed the face of computing. The empowerment engendered by the introduction of the microcomputer is known to have altered societal perceptions toward computing by making computing a relatively ubiquitous and decentralized phenomenon that is readily accessible. With this increase of accessibility came an explosion of creative uses of the computer.

2.4 THE DEVELOPMENT OF NUMERICAL CONTROL TECHNOLOGY

The marriage between programmable computers and associated digital design and engineering environments, numerical control technology, and sophisticated numerically controlled production machines for making objects has yet to be culminated. This marriage marks the crystalline point in the evolutionary process that has led to the development of the attitudes, tools, and systems that comprise what we now call computer-aided design and manufacturing.

As already noted, the basic idea underlying numerical control technologies can be traced back to the industrial revolution and the use of punched paper cards, tapes, or other devices to control the operations of machines. The idea was not new. In the evolution to a new plateau, the Servomechanism Laboratory at the Massachusetts Institute of Technology was an early leader in the development of not only the all-important servomechanisms that are crucial to how numerically controlled machines actually operate but in numerical control technology itself. In 1949, John T. Parsons of the Parsons Corporation of Traverse City, Michigan, worked with the Servomechanism Laboratory to propose specifications for the "Cardmatic Milling Machine"—a milling machine intended to be operated by a computer via input by punched cards. In June of 1950, the Servomechanism Laboratory submitted a report outlining the performance and design specifications of a three-axis, numerically controlled milling machine. In February of 1951, Parsons terminated its sponsorship of the project in view of the expected need to spend large amounts of time and money to develop the machine. The U.S. Air Force, perceiving the ultimate value of numerically controlled manufacturing technologies for the aircraft industry, chose to continue the contract.

The major components of the machine ultimately developed included the "Tape Preparation Unit," the "Director," and the "Machine" itself. Tapes were prepared by typing series of numbers that represented the type and order of machine instructions. The Director unit was a custom-designed digital processor that accepted instructions from the paper tape and translated them into analog electrical pulses that drove the machine's servomechanisms. The machine itself was a well-developed Cincinnati Hydro-Tel milling machine. The existing drive and control of the three machine motions was replaced with power servomechanisms developed at the Servomechanism Laboratory. Several sample pieces were executed by the completed machine. One was a launching socket made of aluminum alloy. Programming time took 68 hours, tape preparation time was 58 hours, fixing the workpiece took fully 80 hours, and actual machining time took 3.6 hours. The original project culminated in a major demonstration in 1952 while still under a contract to the U.S. Air Force. A demonstration was given to 242 representatives from 130 government groups and industry organizations. This event was an important milestone in the development of computer numerically controlled machine technology. (See Figure 2-6.)

It is conceptually important to note that this pivotal development married the fruits of several parallel developments briefly described earlier, especially emergent digitally based computer technologies with a truly mature product of the age of industrialization—the milling machine. The latter was by this time a highly developed machine. The rise in sophistication in the design and use of so-called traditional machines engendered by prior industrialization efforts can only be described as truly remarkable. The brilliance of the marriage between mature fabrication technologies and strong but still emerging computer technologies can hardly be overstated.

After this marriage was initially consummated in the 1950s, technologies continued to evolve. Punched-card technologies proved cumbersome and subject to breakdown, and new methods were sought to input instructions. The time-consuming nature of specifying machine movements through direct numerical language led to the development of an English-like programming language, APT (Automatically Programmed Tools), in 1959. Control systems were developed for orchestrating a series of related numerically controlled machines. Still other NC machines were subsequently developed with local memory and to incorporate a local programmable control unit. The independent CNC machine remained quite attractive for many application environments. Their stand-alone capability empowered many previous nonusers, small shops, and organizations seeking to reduce their dependency on large centralized computing administrations and structures, with their associated cumbersomeness and resistance to change. The result was a burgeoning of new applications.

The 1990s saw a literal explosion of improved technologies for both actual machine types and for specifying and controlling machine movements. So-called CAM software evolved that made the whole process of writing numerical control code considerably easier. It became possible to directly extract geometric information from a digital model and use it to ultimately guide the operations of a CNC machine. The direct marketing of these packages to small operators helped accelerate the use of CNC technologies throughout all industries. Many new types of machines were also developed about this time whose operation and use is conceivable only within the context of an advanced computer-based technological environment, for instance, electric discharge machining systems, water jets, laser cutters, free-form fabrication machines, and so forth.

The 1990s also saw the flowering of sophisticated software environments that provided not only exceptional digital design capabilities (e.g., parametric modeling, feature-based design) but other capabilities as well. Analysis programs became linked to digital models. Related design packages that began embedding manufacturing information (e.g., sheet metal or mold-making modules) also became available in a widespread way. These same digital environments also became linked to CAM software that facilitated direct connections to the CNC environment used to produce objects. These large integrated environments—discussed more in Part IV—became the mainstay of the automotive, aerospace, and other industries.

Today, systems have achieved a high degree of sophistication. New machine types and methods of facilitating ever more direct connections to the manufacturing world continue to evolve.

The "Director"

Cincinnati Hydro-Tel machine refitted for CNC operations

Machined aircraft part, NC paper tape, and milling bit

Figure 2-6 The 1952 demonstration by the Servomechanism Laboratory of MIT of its numerically controlled milling machine was a pivotal point in the development of CNC technology.

THE ARCHITECTURAL DESIGN CONTEXT

The chapters in Part II first present a number of application studies of how CAD/CAM processes have been used in different architectural and product design arenas. Some early examples and transitional buildings are included to provide a perspective of how the field has evolved to its present state. Special problems associated with complex geometries are also covered. The final chapter in Part II addresses the impact of CAD/CAM processes on project implementation and discusses impacts on professional practice in general.

CHAPTER 3

Transitions:
Digital Design for Fabrication

Since the 1960s, computer applications began to transform architectural design and engineering practices for fabrication by enhancing the capacity for managing complex geometries, with greater precision, faster execution, and increased automation. Computer-aided design provided a new design development framework for collaboration among architects, engineers, and fabricators. The creation of digital models allowed the design development team and consultants to shape design concurrently. This development preceded the advent of extranet and intranet digital framework for concurrent engineering from remote locations.

CAD initially was employed to translate handmade sketches and models into digital 2-D and 3-D wireframe and surface models. In the design development phase, digital databases facilitated collaboration through computer-aided engineering. It also provided master geometries for consultation with fabricators. In the construction document phase, digital models provided the shape description for translation into the patterns and templates of the building components' subassemblies for prototyping and fabrication.

Computer-aided applications facilitated the exploration of iterative design variations and provided a fuller understanding of the consequences of the materials and methods. Full-scale mock-ups of building components allowed a means to validate and evaluate the attributes of a design as well as to simulate the fabrication process and final production. The increasing application of the computer numerically controlled machine led to more precise digital models and more useful data for fabrication application.

The projects discussed in this chapter illustrate early computer applications for design and their translation for fabrication. The Sydney Opera House by Jørn Utzon exemplifies an early effort to use mainframe computers to model the building's sail-shaped shells and glazing for structural engineering and fabrication to produce templates for its concrete precast shell ribs, glazed precast tile roofs, and glazing panels. The Menil Collection and the Kansai Airport by the Renzo Piano Building Workshop illustrate a design process emphasizing the prototyping and crafting of building components for

the structure, sunshade, and cladding. The Schlumberger Cambridge Headquarters and the SAGA Group Headquarters by Michael Hopkins & Partners illustrate the use of computers for fabric structure for concurrent engineering with Ove Arup & Partners engineers, who were key collaborators in engineering and fabrication for these case studies. The Fish and the Rasin Building by Gehry Partners Associates initiated collaboration with Permasteelisa in using CATIA software for modeling and fabrication of complex surfaces.

3.1 SYDNEY OPERA HOUSE (SYDNEY, AUSTRALIA, 1956–1973)

Utzon's winning competition entry proposed complex curved shell structures, freehand sketched to evoke the forms of billowing sails (see Figure 3-1). This design challenged its architects and engineers at Ove Arup & Partners to find the means to describe the building's forms for structural analysis and a method to translate them into fabrication.[1] Sydney Opera House illustrates a pioneering application of computer-aided design and engineering for manufacture in architecture. Digital modeling facilitated structural analysis as well as detailed layout of building assemblies. Detailed component models of its concrete ribs, precast roof tiles, glass panels, and steel structures were generated to produce full-size patterns for fabrication.

Computer Modeling and Applications

From 1957 until 1974, the engineers from Ove Arup & Partners in collaboration with Utzon and Hall, Todd and Littlemore architects, and University of Melbourne used an I.C.L. 1900 series mainframe computers to model the complex intersection of the sail-like shell structure and the faceted glass walls of the opera house. The engineers also wrote with Fortran software for structural analysis. Ove Arup and Jack Zunz recalled: "It was clear in these early days that to achieve a solution at all, to make it possible to build the structure, extensive use of electronic digital computers was necessary. It

Figure 3-1 Utzon's winning entry for the competition for the Sydney Opera House evokes billowing sails. The final geometry of the shells was the result of collaboration among the architects and engineers. (Source: Photo by Marta Sartori.)

would otherwise have been almost impossible to cope with the sheer quantity of geometric problems, let alone the complexity of the analytical work."[2] Computers were critical to the execution of this project in the surface modeling of the roof shells and glazing.

The computer modeling of the opera house's shell and glazing geometries determined the base geometries and its parts assemblies for the varying shapes of roof tile and glass panel assemblies. As a critic noted, "With computers, the engineers were confident, they could calculate the dimensions of every component part so that the whole structure would fit together perfectly like a giant jigsaw puzzle."[3] The use of computers ex-

tended to the setting out of the project and its dimensional controls during construction on-site.[4] Even with the expediting use of the computers, this project remained an extraordinary undertaking. Its engineering required over 2,000 hours of computer time, as well as 350,000 man-hours to complete the design of the new roof system.[5]

The Search for Shape and Structure

The complexity of Utzon's concept of sketched curved shell surfaces was simplified through a seven-year design development phase. From 1957 until 1963, 12

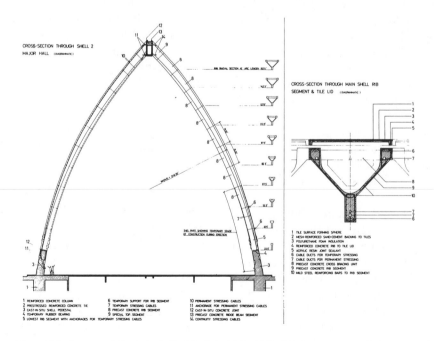

Figure 3-2 Cross sections through Shell 2 of the Major Hall of Sydney Opera House, a main shell rib segment, and tile lid. (Source: © Arup. Reproduced by permission from *The Arup Journal*.)

shell solutions were considered, with each successive form becoming more rationalized and structural elements more repetitive. The initial freeform complexly curved concrete shells proved unrealizable. Other alternate solutions included elliptic paraboloid, single parabolic shell, and double parabolic shell. Circular ribs were then introduced, and ellipsoid geometry tested with elliptical ridges and ribs. A steel space frame was considered as an option. To facilitate the modeling, engineering, and fabrication of the shell structure, the complex curved surfaces were abandoned in favor of basing the shells on the standardized curvature of a sphere. A solution was found defining sail-shaped sections from a 75-meter-diameter sphere with a post-tensioned precast concrete rib structure.[6] (See Figure 3-2.)

The radial ribs' cross section changed from T to Y, from 1.2 to over 2 meters deep at the ridge, and widened from 0.9 to over 3 meters with unique end conditions at the ridge intersection. The shell structure consists of over 2,400 precast concrete structural rib segments, clad with over 4,000 tiled roof panels (see Figure 3-3).

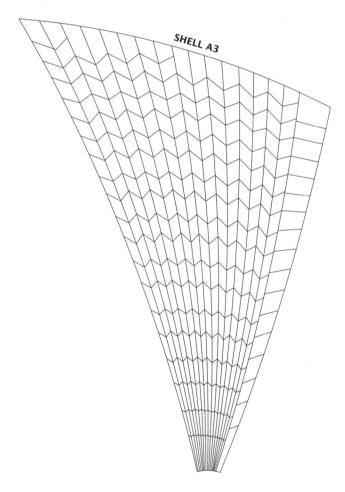

Figure 3-3 Layout of roof panels for part of the Major Hall. (Source: © Arup. Reproduced by permission from *The Arup Journal*.)

Precast Roof Panels

Although the roof geometry was substantially standardized, the large variation of the roof tile configuration again demonstrated the necessity for computer modeling with associated inventory documentation. For the roofs, 996,112 tiles were needed, and 1,055,950 tiles were ordered. These tiles were cast over 25 precast concrete roof lids. Six standard tiles were highly repetitive, while the tiles on the panel edges changed dependent on their location on the chevron-shaped precasts. The panels were limited to 19.5 square meters for ease of handling. Within each chevron panel, the square tiles were identical, with edge tiles custom-cut to fit each edge condition (see Figure 3-4). The design team encoded all tile types, generating a system to document and transmit the variations of tile dimensions to the factory for cutting and their subsequent precasting assembling.

Glazing Geometries

The glass enclosure is a composition derived from a cylinder intersecting an upper cone and a lower cone (see Figure 3-5). These forms and their intersections were described in a series of faceted planes, with intersection points fully described in three axes displacements, with individual panels identified with corner points to ensure full continuity and alignment for a precisely fitted silicon glazing joint (see Figure 3-6).

In addition to the computer-modeled glass geometries, the steel and bronze mullion system and its attachment points to the concrete rib of the shell were also engineered to anticipate wind loads and concrete deflections from creep and post-tensioning of the shell superstructure. To hand-calculate the complexity and

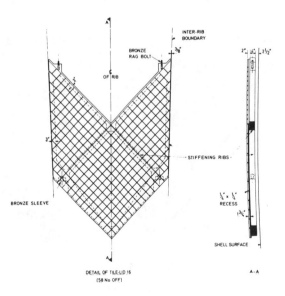

Figure 3-4 Within each chevron panel, the square tiles were identical, with edge tiles custom-cut to fit each edge condition. (Source: © Arup. Reproduced by permission from *The Arup Journal*.)

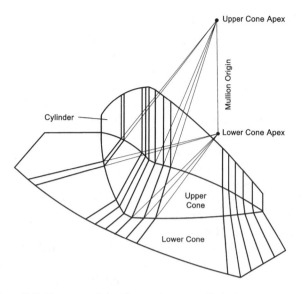

Figure 3-5 Geometry of the glass enclosure: a cylinder intersecting two cones. (Source: © Arup. Reproduced by permission from *The Arup Journal.*)

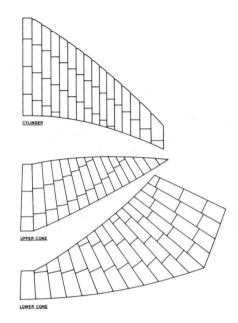

Figure 3-7 Approximately 700 different sizes and shapes of glass panes were needed. (Source: © Arup. Reproduced by permission from *The Arup Journal.*)

details of the intersections would have proved to be cost-prohibitive. Begun in 1967, the computer model allowed the engineers to study the glazing geometry and its structural behavior. By adjusting key displacement points within the glass wall, variations of geometry could be explored via subroutines to calculate the coordinates of all key structural glass surfaces. Of the approximately 2,000 glass panes, approximately 700 different sizes and shapes were needed for the enclosure during its construction between 1970 and 1972.[7] (See Figure 3-7.)

The three-dimensional geometries were translated into individual glazing templates. They were plotted, cut, test-fitted in situ, and cut on site. These glazing

panels' digital file was an early prototype for the subsequent application of the CNC cutting of glass panels (see Figure 3-8).

Geometric Variations

An early example of parametric modeling was evident in the algorithmic relationship established between the shell and glass geometries. It managed multiple changes in the design development of form and structure. The tightly fitted enclosure assembly required a high level of precision and tight tolerances throughout. Thus, a small change resulted in modifications throughout the building. In his book *Sydney Opera House Glass Walls,* a photographic record of the construction, Harry Sowden recalls:

> By the time the programme was complete, there were approximately 60 constants in the A4 glass wall, ranging from the defining parameters of the shell ribs, the position of the mullion origin and cone apices, to the offset dimension of the glass from the structure, the width of the silicone rubber joints and the diameter of the corbel reinforcing bars. . . . During the development of the design, it was not uncommon for a small design change in one area to alter every dimension throughout the whole wall. It was, therefore, necessary to develop the final details concurrently with the geometry so that they could be fitted into the computer programmes.[8]

By setting out geometric constants and variables, the design was adjusted until a satisfactory solution was

Figure 3-6 These forms and their intersections were described in a series of faceted planes, with intersection points fully described in three axes' displacements, with individual panels identified with corner points to ensure full continuity and alignment for a precisely fitted silicon glazing joint. (Source: Photo by Marta Sartori)

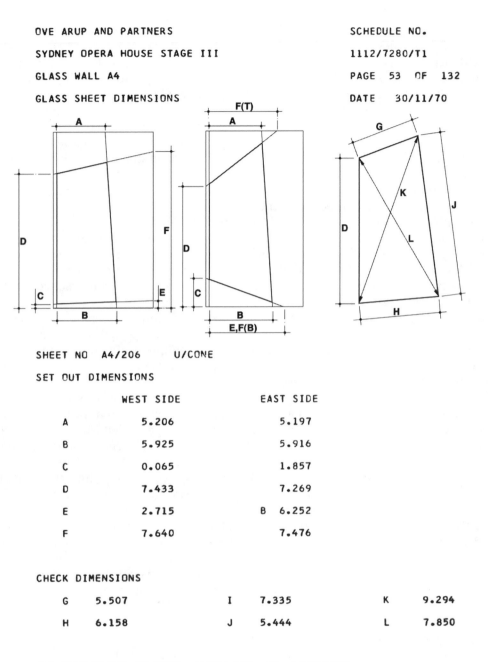

OVE ARUP AND PARTNERS

SYDNEY OPERA HOUSE STAGE III

GLASS WALL A4

GLASS SHEET DIMENSIONS

SCHEDULE NO.

1112/7280/T1

PAGE 53 OF 132

DATE 30/11/70

SHEET NO A4/206   U/CONE

SET OUT DIMENSIONS

	WEST SIDE		EAST SIDE
A	5.206		5.197
B	5.925		5.916
C	0.065		1.857
D	7.433		7.269
E	2.715	B	6.252
F	7.640		7.476

CHECK DIMENSIONS

G	5.507	I	7.335	K	9.294
H	6.158	J	5.444	L	7.850

ALL DIMENSIONS IN FEET. REFER DRG. NO. 1112/7473

Figure 3-8 Glass sheet dimensions. The digital file for the glazing panels was an early prototype for CNC cutting of glass panels. (Source: © Arup. Reproduced by permission from *The Arup Journal*.)

obtained. As the design evolved, the computer produced key dimensions and component templates that were transferred onto working drawings and schedules. The surface modeling of the shell geometries and the glazing were also translated into various dependent structural geometries, offset from the surface to describe the post-tensioned concrete structures and the steel glazing supports. These subassemblies' geometries were controlled by the surface geometry, mathematically determined.

Patterns for Manufacturing

Computer-plotted glass panel templates were produced to generate trapezoid glass-cutting outlines on-site. The templates were test-fitted against the actual building. With on-site tolerance marked from the test fit, each panel was custom-cut to match the concrete shell and steel glass framing. This tedious process ensured a precise fit for the glass, adjusting its modeled dimensions for deviations on-site. Over 30,000 measurements for the glass were supplied to the contractor for the cutting of the glass shapes. There were 67,000 square feet of glass, cut into over 2,000 panes and over 700 different sizes. The three-dimensional coordinates of 2,310 glass fixing points were modeled, and verified in the field. Over 40 bronze glazing extrusions were employed and precut to match the theoretical model.

Dimensional Verifications on Site

The mathematical models of the shells, glazing, and base were used to coordinate with a computerized building survey model. This allowed the survey team to continually monitor the theoretical geometry with the constructed reality on-site. Construction tolerance was entered via survey points throughout the project in a dynamic feedback loop comparing computerized coordinate displacements with site measurements. This became the methodology for all shape verification for the project. Site survey points of key concrete shell dimensions were used to generate an "as-built" shell displacement, to be used for the recalculation of glass panel geometry and panel sizes. The first generation of the glass panel templates was based on idealized dimensions of concrete shells. The second generation of glass templates was based on as-built recalculation adjusted to the constructed dimensional tolerances and concrete creep. These site survey updates allowed for continued adjustments of the design and its engineering from the design phase all the way through fabrication and construction. Through the application of the computers in multiple facets of this project's architectural, engineering, and manufacturing disciplines, innovations in professional practice were achieved.

3.2 THE MENIL COLLECTION (HOUSTON, TEXAS, 1981–1986)

Renzo Piano Building Workshop and Ove Arup & Partners' design, engineering, and prototyping of the Menil Collection's light baffles exemplify a component-based approach to designing building assemblies.[9] This design process offers a model upon which the digital environment can be emulated, as the CAD/CAM programs strive to facilitate dispersed collaboration toward rapid prototyping and concurrent engineering.

RPBW's crafting of the building assemblies, employing a "piece by piece" strategy, illustrates a prototyping process during design development. This approach encourages full-scale mock-up and close collaboration among designers, engineers, and fabricators. The integration of hand-sketched design with computer modeling and engineering analysis is combined with the crafting of a physical model. Each refinement cycle brings about design improvements and reevaluation of the design concept, materials, and methods. Quick feed-

back during concept design is followed by more systematic development via scaled and full-size physical modeling for lighting analysis and component shaping. By improving the prototypical performance of each unit, RPBW could array and regenerate aggregative improvement to the whole. Each component's incremental design variation could be translated digitally. This project's emphasis on handcrafting key components offers a collaboration strategy in an increasingly digital environment.

Light Baffle

The light baffles illustrate an early attempt to hand-model building components in combination with three-dimensional computer analysis. Piano initially sketched a quarter barrel vaulted sun baffle design (see Figure 3-9). With Peter Rice and Tom Barker, this was developed into a sweeping curvilinear wavelike baffle, incorporating refracting and reflecting surfaces, while supporting lighting attachments along its edges, and thickened supports to attach to the cast ductile iron roof trusses above.

These early concept sketches were translated into precise drawings, from which the team of Shunji Ishida from RPBW and Neil Noble and Alistair Gutherie from Ove Arup & Partners hand-built a sun refracting model on a sun angle device. The solar path and resulting lighting effects were simulated and studied first in a cardboard model. Subsequently, a full-size gallery and sun baffle was constructed on the building site to further study the light quality and fine-tune the building elements. An 8-foot-long master model for the sunshade units was fabricated by hand, developed by the designers and engineers for its performance and its fab-

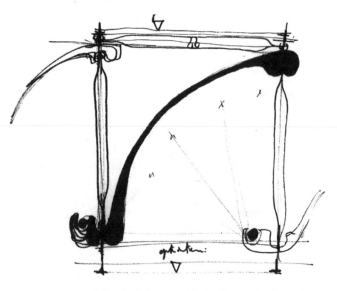

Figure 3-9 An initial sketch of the sun-baffle for the Menil Collection. (Source: Reproduced by permission from Renzo Piano Building Workshop.)

rication. This became the model from which subsequent forms were copied for reinforced laminated ferro-cement sun baffles. The engineers produced digital models of the cast-metal support for finite-element analysis. The team evaluated methods of casting laminated layering of the ferro-cement. They selected the layered ferro-cement, which produced the most precise shape and finish (see Figure 3-10).

Modern Craftsmanship

The prototype phase is an integral part of RPBW's design process, reflecting Piano's design philosophy. Piano felt that "the modern meaning of craftsmanship lies in the production stage preceding the industrial stage: the prototype."[10] This process is distinguished in its "united thinking and doing" process, which integrates the engineering, design, and fabrication disciplines in its exploration of form, performance, materials, and methods.[11] For Piano, it is important to develop an understanding of the craft of architecture before integrating the computer-aided technologies into the development of a building. Although the designs can be created with great facility using CAD, they frequently lack the informed discipline of its integration with engineering, along with their translation into fabrications and constructions.[12] CAD offers unprecedented precision in the modeling of geometry and multidisciplined engineering simulations, yet the screen images alone often lack the necessary reality of a physical model. Piano cautioned that CAD can be superficial and the design insufficiently resolved when it is studied only in its graphic mode. It is preferable to work with a physical model whenever possible. This is especially needed when a design is unresolved. Because the computer-aided manufacturing facilitates the translation of the digital model into three-dimensional proof-of-concept mock-ups, it can be integrated with

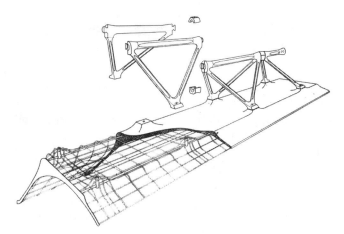

Figure 3-10 Ferro-cement light-baffles. (Source: Reproduced by permission from Renzo Piano Building Workshop.)

this design strategy by expanding upon the traditional handcrafted prototyping method through the integration of computer-aided manufacturing of rapid prototyped mock-ups.

3.3 KANSAI AIRPORT (OSAKA, JAPAN, 1988–1994)

Renzo Piano Building Workshop's Kansai Airport Terminal design demonstrates an increased application of computer-aided design integrated with computer-aided engineering in structural, mechanical, and engineering disciplines. The resulting digital models were used to aid the fabrication for the constituent roof structure, cladding, mechanical scoop, and light-refracting ceiling. Peter Buchanan considers Kansai to be one of the foremost examples in the use of the computer in architecture, citing it as "an essential tool of the modern craftsman."[13]

Integrated Computer-Aided Design and Engineering

The engineers at Ove Arup & Partners worked closely with RPBW to shape key designs for the Kansai enclosure and structure. The building geometry incorporated engineering concepts. The air-conditioning and illumination scoops were generated from Tom Barker's concept sketch in 1988 (see Figure 3-11). He proposed a discharge of airstream from one end of the terminal, traveling 80 meters to achieve macroenvironmental control within the main terminal ceiling.[14] This internal airflow geometry complemented the structural geometry designed by Peter Rice and integrated into the central theme of the building, rationalized via computer models by the architect and engineer.

These digital models allowed for structural airflow analysis, and fire and smoke damage computer analysis. Computational fluid dynamic modeling simulated the airflow for the macro-jets and refined the shaping of the air scoop ceilings. These internal ceiling membranes are airflow channels as well as ceiling light refractors. Nineteen white lustrous Teflon open ducts were fabricated and their shape translated from computer drawing files provided by Ove Arup & Partners and Nikken Sekkei.[15]

Roof Geometry

At Kansai, the roof geometry was rationalized from a freehand concept drawing of a proposed building section, informed by the nature of a macro-jet air supply scoop, and translated into transitional curved segments composed into a tholoid curve along its length. By repeating and offsetting the main steel roof trusses along its length on a section-shifting method, the design allowed for standardization of its main struc-

Figure 3-11 Concept sketch for the roof of the Kansai Airport from 1988. (Source: Reproduced by permission from Renzo Piano Building Workshop.)

tures, while adjusting to its changing angles at the pivot points of its supports from its base to the trusses.[16] (See Figure 3-12.)

Avoiding a repeat of the roof cladding complications at Sydney Opera House and at Bercy, the team at Kansai detailed the roof using 82,000 identical panels of a standardized roof cladding. The roof tiles, dimensioned 1.8×0.6 meters and 1 mm thick, are interlocked perpendicularly and spaced with a reveal longitudinally. This outer roof allows for movement and drainage down on top of the inner roof, constructed of insulated double corrugated steel.[17] The strategy to standardize a roof cladding design, using "loose-fit" panel connections, allowed the roof cladding panel to adapt to varying geometries, thus simplifying the double-curved form of its cladding assembly. This team's rationalization of the roof geometry and its development of a geometrically adaptable roof panel limited the complexity to the curvilinear three-dimensional truss, and the crafting of the fireproof cladding for the steel tubular truss supports.

Curved Steel Trusses

The steel trusses' digital design and engineering provided the database for the steel fabricator to interpret and translate the geometric information into its fabrication. The structural engineers, in consultation with the architect, determined the center axis of the three-dimensional steel geometry and intersections. The curved steel roof trusses are composed of prefabricated sections that are

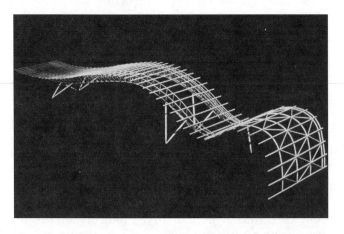

Figure 3-12 Three-dimensional computer model of a bay of the roof showing the structural steel layout. (Source: Reproduced by permission from Renzo Piano Building Workshop.)

clad with standardized roof panels. The steel fabricator further developed the structure in a shop drawing, working from " . . . geometric analysis [that] began with the Building Workshop model and computer work. Based on the structural intersection points drawn by a large computer at Ove Arup & Partners, a steel manufacturer drew up the final data for the geometry."[18] With the demand for steel precision at 0.5 millimeter and overall tolerance of 1 millimeter, robotic welding ensured a high level of accuracy with increased digitally controlled fabrication. Buchanan illustrated the sequenced steps of steel manufacture: "Robotic welding of tubes into required lengths, bending tubes to required radius, positioning upper chords and welding secondary structure, assembly of sections of truss, welding in rotating jigs, test assembly and checking."[19]

GFRC Fire Protection

Glass reinforced cement cladding of the steel truss props. Peter Buchanan recounted the steel structure's highly crafted enclosures:

> After much sketching and modeling, the Building Workshop created CAD drawings from which the Japanese manufacturer made 1:5 scale clay models. After many versions of these had been made, full-size models were made in wood and Styrofoam. These underwent yet further refinement before manufacture.[20]

The GFRC steel cladding, developed from this iterative process of design, allowed the architect, the engineer, and the fabricator to evaluate these components in CAD and actual mock-ups. These full-scale prototypes combined the geometric precision of digital models with the tactile handcrafting of the Workshop's design methodology. In this manner, the digital tools were used to augment and expand the design vocabulary.

3.4 SCHLUMBERGER CAMBRIDGE RESEARCH CENTER (CAMBRIDGE, UNITED KINGDOM, 1982–1992)

The architects at Michael Hopkins & Partners and the engineers at Ove Arup & Partners collaborated and expanded their work beyond geometric modeling and structural analysis, and included the generation of the fabric structure's cutting pattern, and the numerical modeling of the contractor's method for the step-by-step tensioning of each of the membrane's three roof modules, thereby integrating computer-aided design and engineering processes with the manufacturing. The design of a fabric roof results directly from shaping the forces within the fabric itself (see Figure 3-13). It results in an immediate synthesis of architecture and engineering in the nature of materials, demanding a highly integrated and concurrent design and engineering process.

Physical Concept Study Model

The design of the structure at Schlumberger began under Michael Hopkins' direction in a roundtable brainstorming session with key architects and engineers. Rough concept sketches with order-of-magnitude structural configurations were generated and evaluated. The team began to develop guiding design principles and define boundary conditions for the fabric structure. During this stage, the team digitally modelled the design as well as used physical models made of spandex to study various roof shapes for early evaluation (see Figure 3-14). The fabric allowed the team members to elastically stretch and pull various shapes for consideration.

The fabric roofs' geometry were formed by the boundary conditions set by the rectangular buildings surrounding the inner courtyard. The fixed base geometry remained constant during the design phase, while the fabric surface forms were investigated for various shapes and stress configurations through physical and digital modeling.

In this project, the fabric structure was suspended from steel outriggers, covering the space between perimeter steel buildings. The fabric roof's shape is the numerical equivalent of a soap film forming within the same set of "boundaries." It is the choice of boundaries and prestress ratio that determines the surface shape. The base condition was precisely fitted, while the suspended fabric retained a greater dimensional tolerance provided by length adjustment in the aerial hanger cables.

Fablon Software: Concurrent Design and Engineering

Ove Arup & Partners developed the Fablon software for form finding and stress analysis, as well as for detailed shape definition. Using Fablon, the design and engineering team combined physical modeling in the concept phase with computer modeling and engineering to produce a quadrilateral database for the generation of fabric panel shapes for manufacture. The engineers configured the forms of the spandex model into a series of triangulated quadrilateral geometry. (See Figure 3-14.)

The Fablon model allowed the engineers to analyze the whole membrane system's response to a variety of wind and snow conditions. Parametrically the engineers evaluated the position and flexibility of fabric suspension points and generated theoretical fabric shapes, considering pre-stressing, erection, and site adjustment strategies. This software enabled rapid evaluation of the fabric form and its structural behavior, determining its performance in relations to wind loads and weathering conditions. Given the simultaneity of design and engineering analysis, the engineers were able to consolidate the design development process while researching and evaluating material properties of the fabrics under consideration.

Computer-Aided Production of Fabrication Pattern

The fabric manufacturer contracted the engineers to translate the design into a precise description of the fabric structure with quadrilateral configurations. Given a 4-meter width as the maximum fabric cutting pattern dimension, the shape was finalized within these dimensional constraints. The membrane panels' welded seams were configured to emphasize the vaulted roof rather than minimizing material waste.

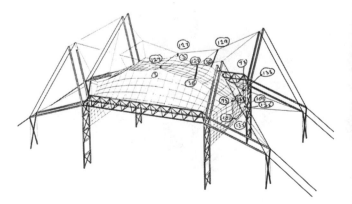

Figure 3-13 This digital model of the Schlumberger roof structure incorporated computer-aided design, engineering, and manufacturing to generate the fabric roof structure's form and cutting pattern. (Source: Reproduced with permission from Arup.)

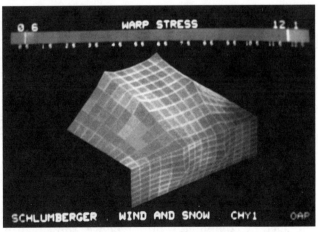

Figure 3-14 A wind and snow stress test on the Schlumberger fabric structure. (Source: Reproduced with permission from Arup.)

The engineers produced cutting patterns for the fabrics. It allowed for a detailed oversight guiding the design from concept to production. In this process, the engineers worked in the mode of the master builders, combining and extending their contribution from design and engineering to fabrication.

3.5 SAGA GROUP HEADQUARTERS (FOLKESTONE, KENT, UNITED KINGDOM, 1996–1999)

The SAGA project, designed and engineered by the team from Michael Hopkins & Partners and Ove Arup & Partners, further expanded their collaboration to produce a more complexly engineered and erected structure, with a tightly fitted membrane to steel roof. This allowed the team to learn from each project and advance the levels of technical difficulty incrementally.

Form-Finding Boundary Conditions

The SAGA design consists of a series of circular steel tubular arches, supporting double-curved fabric roofs enclosing the spaces with faceted clerestory glazing above. Each roof's curved boundary conditions require a precise and complex weather-tight seal securing the fabric to the steel. The engineers digitally modeled early hand sketches and spandex models at the concept design phase to precisely generate the geometry of the building. (See Figures 3-15 and 3-16.)

The search for form evolved from diagrammatical studies to a digital model of the structure. Initially, the edges of each membrane panel were defined by the center line of the adjoining arch framework. Upon the confirmation of the form and budget, the design was again modeled using Fablon, producing precise fabric panels and intersections of forms. At the schematic design stage, the design team took into consideration the fabrication and erection constraints of bent steel, fabric, and glass. The analysis of feasibility complemented their innovative design of a challenging geometry.[21] (See Figure 3-17.)

Combining Full-Scale Mock-up and Digital Modeling

During design development, the architect took the lead in detailing the connections, mocking up numerous steel details with corresponding digital modeling by the engineers. The engineers studied and tested the torsion effect of the fabric attachment to the steel tubes. The challenge was to limit rotational forces applied to it, and to develop a fabric weather closure detail to cover the steel members. A simple pivot steel detail was first modeled by computer. A prototype was subsequently fabricated and physically tested at full size. The fabric

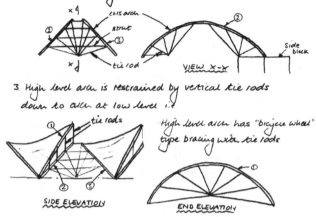

Figure 3-15 The engineers' notes for the inclined arches point out that the high-level arches are restrained by the vertical tie rods down to the low-level arches. (Source: By permission of Arup Engineers.)

cladding is stressed axially to the steel tube; a separate cover strip attaches to the structural fabric and conceals the joinery between the two. The intersections of the arches and columns were first mocked up, detailed in a 3-D model to generate precise steel fabrication drawings. The team expanded this to a mock-up of the integration of the curved gutters and fabric joints. Throughout the process, the team continued to work alternatively with physical mock-ups and models, complemented by digital modeling and engineering analysis. The smallest of the physical models measured 3 to 4 inches in size with 1:50 scale. Some full-scale mock-ups of the detail were built, and modifications generated; design revisions were fed back into the 3-D model

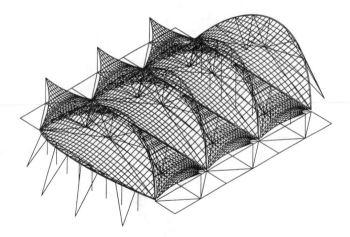

Figure 3-16 Using Fablon, the engineers created a SAGA digital model that produced precise geometry and intersections of forms. (Source: Reproduced with permission from the OASYS engineering division of Arup.)

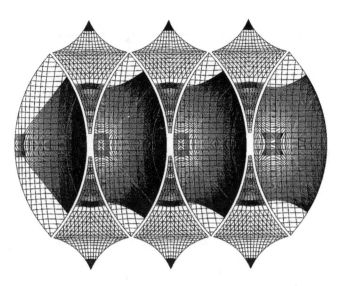

Figure 3-17 Engineering analysis and digital model of SAGA roof. (Source: Reproduced with permission from the OASYS engineering division of Arup.)

process. The 3-D model was then used to produce 2-D templates through shop drawings for steel fabrication.

Fabric Fabrication

The engineers had the ability to generate cutting patterns for the fabric as translated from the Fablon program. However, the team decided to put this project to tender and requested that the fabricator take the responsibility to generate the geometry for the project and reconfirm the stress analysis for the fabric. Unlike the earlier Schlumberger project, the winning fabricator would be responsible for generating its own cutting pat-

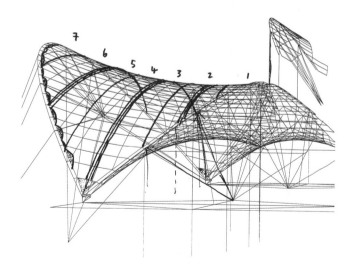

Figure 3-18 The design team sketched the proposed cutting patterns' dimensions and shapes to reconfigure the final line of joinery on the surface model. (Source: Reproduced with permission from Arup.)

terns. In this project, the engineers' digital data was not given to the fabricator. This engendered a peer review through the separation of the data.

Koch-Hightex was the wining fabricator through tender. Tensys, an engineering group, reproduced the stress analysis and refined the cutting pattern configuration. The fabricators set up their own geometry based upon given displacements within the project's tender documents. David Wakefield at Tensys was able to run parallel programs to simulate a setup pattern and to run analysis verifying engineering calculations. This complex geometry was redeveloped via form-finding software for the fabric and steel elements. The fabricator's shop drawings were then generated independently by Tensys and given to the architect and engineers for review. The design team hand-sketched over the proposed cutting patterns' dimensions and shapes to reconfigure the final line of joinery. In this manner, they were able to reconsider the engineers' simulation of weathering, ponding, and staining patterns of the fabrics to determine the final seam patterns. Thus, the surface model was useful for engineering, weathering analysis, and fabrication. (See Figure 3-18.)

Fabric Pattern

The manufacture of the fabric roof panels began with the computer plotting of individual paper patterns (see Figure 3-19). They were laid on the fabric and cut from the fabric. In contrast to fabricators such as Birdair, the patterns are printed directly on the fabric, with a computer-automated cutting process. Other companies use computer-driven laser cutters to cut patterns on PVC or polyester. The engineer configured the quadrilaterals to minimize material waste and optimize pattern configuration. In light of differences in the competing manufacturers' methodologies, the winning fabricator would refine the engineering and configuration of the fabric pattern to match its production. This competitive bid process encouraged value engineering and allowed for manufacturers to suggest revisions to further optimize the design for production. The panel seams, alignments, and erection sequence remained to be finalized by the winning fabricator. They are adapted to the fabricator's production requirements in order to obtain a more economical pricing. In this manner, the design's parametric modeling facilitates these adjustments with the fabricator.

Steel Assembly

The steel arch structures were digitally modeled in three dimensions, including details of the tubular spliced column cap joinery. This CAD was complemented by axial structural analysis model for CAE. This combination of

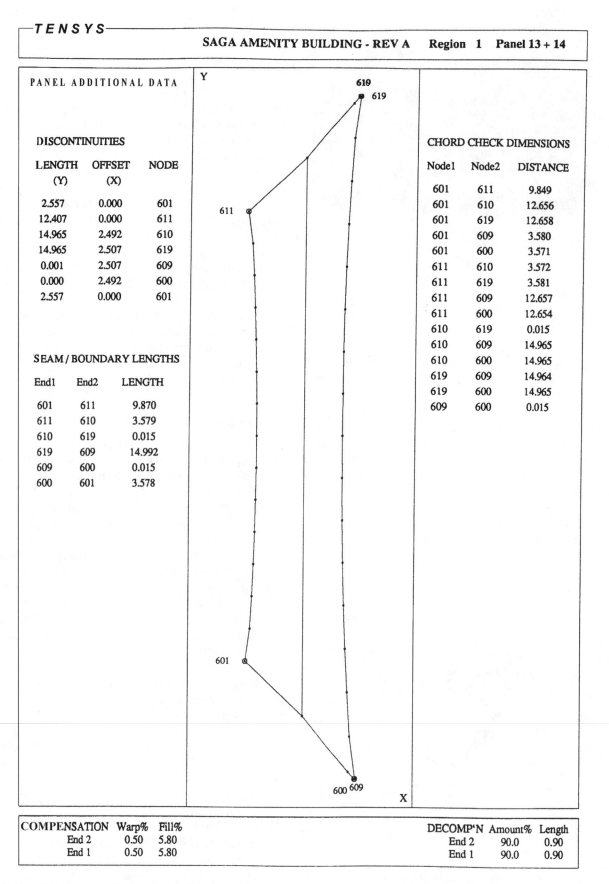

T E N S Y S

SAGA AMENITY BUILDING - REV A   Region   1   Panel 13 + 14

PANEL ADDITIONAL DATA

DISCONTINUITIES

LENGTH (Y)	OFFSET (X)	NODE
2.557	0.000	601
12.407	0.000	611
14.965	2.492	610
14.965	2.507	619
0.001	2.507	609
0.000	2.492	600
2.557	0.000	601

SEAM / BOUNDARY LENGTHS

End1	End2	LENGTH
601	611	9.870
611	610	3.579
610	619	0.015
619	609	14.992
609	600	0.015
600	601	3.578

CHORD CHECK DIMENSIONS

Node1	Node2	DISTANCE
601	611	9.849
601	610	12.656
601	619	12.658
601	609	3.580
601	600	3.571
611	610	3.572
611	619	3.581
611	609	12.657
611	600	12.654
610	619	0.015
610	609	14.965
610	600	14.965
619	609	14.964
619	600	14.965
609	600	0.015

COMPENSATION	Warp%	Fill%
End 2	0.50	5.80
End 1	0.50	5.80

DECOMP'N	Amount%	Length
End 2	90.0	0.90
End 1	90.0	0.90

Figure 3-19 Individual patterns for the fabric roof panels were first computer-plotted. These patterns were laid on the fabric, and the fabric was cut according to the patterns.

digital models facilitated the production of precise shop drawings for steel fabrication. Although the computer-driven cutting and welding of the steel has been in use by other fabricators, in this instance the steel was cut conventionally. The complex intersections of the steel tubes were initially hand mocked up and tested before production by the fabricator. Cardboard templates were made, wrapped around the tube, and then hand ground down to the precise fit. This produced the templates for the final steel fabrication. Thus, the desire for full-size templates and mock-up parallels the digital testing and reconfirmation of digital fabric production.

Glass—Water Jet

The clerestory glazing was positioned between the upper and lower steel curved tubes, which are faceted with vertical panel joints and curve at their top and bottom edges. A computer model generated the glass geometry. The glazing displacements were then given to the glass fabricator, who produced the shop drawings. The geometric data was useful in translating to a digitized format into a glass-cutting pattern. The computer-guided water jet cut the glazing panels, producing the tight dimensional tolerances from the digital model.

The success of this project resulted from the integration of concept design, translated digitally and mocked up in various scales and levels of detail to ensure that the final fabrication and construction were sufficiently studied and detailed before the production of the construction document. Consultant feedback during the design phase allowed the competitive bidders to offer advice that shaped the development of the project details. The independently produced digital fabrication files reconfirmed the design and engineering team's work, reinterpreted in the fabricator's optimizing methodology. Finally, the architect and the engineer reviewed and modified the fabricator's shop drawings to ensure the translation of the concept design into construction.

3.6 THE VILA OLÍMPICA—THE GREAT FISH OF BARCELONA (BARCELONA, SPAIN, 1989–1992)

Frank O. Gehry's large fish sculpture at the Vila Olímpica Hotel in Barcelona is the focal point of a larger hotel, office, and commercial real estate development built for the 1992 Summer Olympic Games.[22] The sculpture is approximately 180 feet long and 115 feet tall, and is constructed of woven steel strips connected to an exposed steel structure. The steel strips are coated with an interference pattern, a crystallized structure on the surface of the steel, which produces a gold color in bright sunlight. They are woven together like a basket over a supporting substructure of steel tubes.[23] This project initiated a series of collaborative CAD/CAM explorations by Gehry's team

with fabricators such as Permasteelisa, and it demonstrated the potential for managing complex geometries with the application of computer-aided technologies. (See Figure 3-20.)

The Physical Models: The Process and the Problem

The fish project began with a series of sketches and study models by Frank Gehry. The last physical model, used by the office as the control model in the initial attempts to translate the project into built form, was approximately 1 meter long. Following the completion of the model, the task was to find a way to accurately reconstruct its curves and to communicate them to the contractor in order to build the fish at full scale. In past projects in the office, this translation was done simply by measuring the physical model and making two-dimensional drawings from these measurements. The office drew a series of sections of the fish model by sampling points from the physical curves. This process was time-consuming and often inaccurate. The severe time constraints of the Olympics led the staff, under the direction of Principal James Glymph, to seek computer software that could describe the complex three-dimensional form.

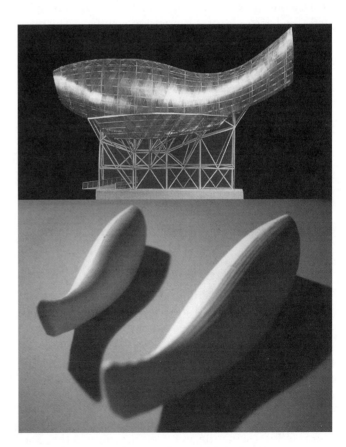

Figure 3-20 Design and concept form models built using a new digital model. (Source: Top photo courtesy Gehry Partners, LLP)

Initial Computer Modeling

This search led them to the Harvard Graduate School of Design. Working with William Mitchell and assisted by Evan Smythe, the sectional drawings prepared from the physical model were used as the "ribs" of the fish, over which the skin was stretched to create the final surface shape in order to create a computer model. The first step of the process took the existing 2-D drawings and used a Hemite curve editor to create smooth curves that approximated these digitized ribs from the physical model. The file was then exported to Alias, an off-the-shelf rendering program with sophisticated curve and surface editing features. The resulting model—a form appreciably different from their own physical model—convinced Gehry's team that their initial rib/section drawings were flawed. A new computer model was re-created and approved by Gehry.

Further Needs Lead to CATIA

Although the new representation was accurate, it could not be used to convey dimensional information directly to the contractor. Alias defines surfaces as a "grid" of polygons, rather than in the mathematical terms that define lines and curves in a way usable by fabricators. Also, at this time, Gehry was planning to build the surface out of two-dimensional material—sheet metal—deformed across a three-dimensional surface. The team did not know exactly what pattern would result on the surface, and it wanted to be able to fold and unfold surfaces on the model without distortion, in order to isolate and form the material in the same way as sheet metal. Alias could not meet these needs. The solution was found in a program designed for the aerospace industry called CATIA, which was developed for the design of the Mirage jet in France. CATIA had all the necessary modeling capabilities and allowed for interface with structural programs. Since it models curved surfaces with complete numerical control, meaning that one can define precise locations of every point on a CATIA model, it was perfect for the fish application.

Mock-up and Construction

With the aid of consultants, the architects created a CATIA model of the fish and tested its accuracy through the construction of a laser-cut paper model based on the CATIA data. The entire structure was then modeled in CATIA and converted into the AES software format for structural engineers at SOM. The engineers further developed the structure and converted the data back into CATIA to study the transition between the structure and skin. "Working from the skin to the structure, 'form follows skin,' the architects determined the exact dimensions of each strake and produced paper tem-

plates that were used to cut and bend each steel piece."[24] These were formed by slightly bent strips pinned together with a single connection to a system of pipe strakes that formed an intermediate structure offset with short struts from the primary structural steel framework. Flat strips wove in and out among the pinned strips to form the basketlike fish skin. The ability to bend the strips without kinking them was critical. The team made a full-scale mock-up to test and determine the maximum flexibility of the strips and the allowable curvatures of the surface itself.

Initially, Permasteelisa tried to build the mock-up component by component. It quickly discovered that almost every connection required a different offset dimension. No two tubes were alike. After this initial mock-up attempt, Gehry's office sent Permasteelisa detailed dimensional data of the components digitally. Using this information to locate and adjust the length of each strut, the fabricators quickly completed the mock-up. From predetermined points on the steel structure, the builder evaluated each fastener point from the CATIA model and adjusted each measurement x millimeters and adjusted the strut out z millimeters. The pipe ribs were then fitted from strut to strut and the skin woven over them. (See Figure 3-21.)

The CATIA model was used for all dimensional control in the fabrication and site assembly. CATIA was also used to detail the connections on the base, as well as the more complicated connections in other parts of the sculpture. These details were developed by Permasteelisa, sent via modem, and reviewed on-screen by Gehry's office. Upon approval, the project went into full construction. Because of the time constraints, the steel structure and the skin were erected simultaneously. Then the overall tiling pattern and the weaving of the strips were installed by hand on-site.

The CATIA system made an extremely complex form possible to understand and to build quickly and efficiently. It was a period of six months from the preliminary design to the time of completion, and the project

Figure 3-21 The team decided to make a full-scale mock-up to test the construction process and to determine the maximum flexibility of the strips and the allowable curvatures of the surface itself. (Source: Drawing courtesy Gehry Partners, LLP; photo by Martin Bechtold)

came in under budget. Even more impressive was that even without drafted construction documents, the final construction was remarkably accurate. While the process began with traditional physical models, the computer was embraced as a means to facilitate the design and construction process, in Gehry's words, to "get closer to the craft"—closer to the physical reality of the forms.[25]

3.7 "FRED AND GINGER" RASIN BUILDING (PRAGUE, CZECH REPUBLIC, 1992–1996)

For the Rasin Building in Prague, Frank O. Gehry & Associates further developed tools and techniques learned from the Great Fish project to model complex curved building elements on the computer and to fabricate portions of the building which could not be described through orthogonal plan and section drawings. Detailed consideration of several complex curved building volumes required the integration of computer-aided design and manufacturing techniques into the design process at an early stage. This was especially true in designing the part of the building nicknamed "Ginger" for the curved glazed tower at the corner of the site. The computer model of the entire project allowed the architect, contractors, and fabricators (who, together with the client, represented seven countries) to closely control building construction.[26] The nine-story building, which opened in June 1996, consists of office space, a cafe and shops at ground level, and a restaurant on the top floor. (See Figure 3-22.)[27]

Computer-Aided Schematic Design Process

The design of Fred and Ginger evolved through a series of sketches and physical models, whose shapes were translated digitally by means of a three-dimensional

Figure 3-22 Fred and Ginger under construction, August 1995. (Source: Photo by Andrea Lamberti)

digitizer. The computer rationalized the forms, ascribing geometry so that points on the model may be located mathematically. The digital model is used to digitally fabricate a physical model to verify the rationalized design before proceeding with further iteration of design development.[28]

For Fred and Ginger, the architects used CATIA software on IBM RISC6000 computers and Pro/ENGINEER software on the Sun platform. CATIA is based on surfaces instead of polygons. This capability allows curved surface to remain curved on the screen and to retain a mathematical description of all points on the surface; the same surface in other CAD programs would be reduced to a series of facets and would not sustain a precise definition of the curvature. The computer modeling of the glazing allowed Permasteelisa to reduce the budget for the glazing from $200 per square foot to $135 per square foot.[29]

The initial design process of Fred and Ginger was similar to previous projects that incorporated use of the three-dimensional digitizer. However, this project marked the first time that Frank Gehry and his associates used milling technology to build a physical model derived from the computer model. Once the shape of the building was determined, the architects made a plaster cast model at 1:100 scale of the Fred and Ginger towers and the façade; this model was then digitized to create a surface model in CATIA. Information from the CATIA model was then translated in order to build a new physical model at 1:50 scale using numerically controlled milling techniques. The larger scale allowed the architects to study the tower details, including the tee-section mullion structure. The second physical model also permitted the architects to verify the design of the surface, which acted as a physical and conceptual substrate for the mullions. Although Gehry and his associates often make a second confirmation model in order to verify design changes made in the computer, in this case revisions subsequent to the 1:50 scale model were minor and were made only in the CATIA model.

Design of Ginger's Exterior Glazing Wall

The surface defining the Ginger volume, which contains complex curves in both plan and section, created a design problem of integrating doubly curved structural steel tee supports with an enclosed building envelope. This problem was solved in part by separating the glazing into two layers—an exterior wall of glass panels whose supports consist of steel tee sections that bend along a three-dimensional curve, and an interior wall of double-pane glazing set into a concrete surface that forms the weather barrier. Defining the exterior wall of glazing and a method of constructing it became the challenge for the architects and the fabricator, Permasteelisa, with whom Gehry's office had worked to construct the fish sculpture for the Vila Olímpica Hotel in Barcelona. The design for Ginger's external glazing developed to become an array of flat glass planes supported by a steel mullion system. This mullion system consists of curving galvanized steel tee-section members, which run vertically, and steel tubes, which run diagonally across the tees to provide lateral support. (See Figure 3-23.)

The issue of connecting a surface to the curving ribs is a problem, which both Frank Gehry and Permasteelisa fabricators addressed when building the Barcelona fish. This was resolved by bolting glass panels to the tees in an overlapping shingle configuration. These bolt connections, as well as the short tee sections connecting the vertical tees to the floor slabs, vary in length and angle of orientation at every point on the building. This did not present an insurmountable design problem, though the designers could focus on detailing two

Figure 3-24 A mock-up of the curving steel tee-section members provide lateral support for the faceted glazing wall. (Source: Photo by Martin Bechtold)

kinds of connections for the bolts and the short tees, or strakes, and use a grid on the CATIA surface model as an index to determine each connection's location, angle of orientation, and length (see Figure 3-24).

Fabrication and Assembly Process for the Ginger Tower

Because the design for the Ginger volume was dependent on the behavior of the structure supporting the glazing wall, the architects sent digital design information to the steel subcontractor, Permasteelisa (who began using CATIA at the time the Barcelona fish was constructed), and sought consultation from them even before the contract was signed. At a later meeting, the designers realized that an early fabrication proposal, extruding the tees along a path defined by the surface grid, would not work because no machine existed that could produce tees that curved in two directions. The subcontractor then proposed making tees out of two steel strips, a web and a flange, both of which could be bent separately and then welded together (see Figure 3-25). This proposal was accepted for the fabrication method. CATIA allowed the fabricators to separate the web from the flange in the computer, and from this information, Permasteelisa was able to produce full-scale plots representing the curve paths of each tee.

The plots were constructed according to a flat reference plane that corresponded to the floor of the Permasteelisa shop. The plots were used to guide the bending of the initially straight flanges with a pneumatic hammer on the floor of the shop. Through the use of registered plates placed at key points along the

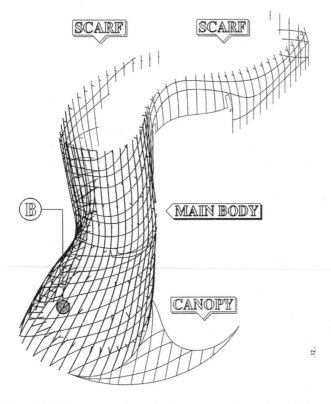

Figure 3-23 The surface defining the Ginger volume, illustrating doubly curved structural steel tee glazing supports. (Source: Project realized by Permasteelisa Group)

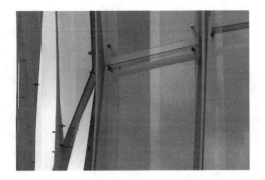

Figure 3-25 A detail of the faceted glass panels bolted to the tees in an overlapping shingle configuration.

curved plots, each metal strip was bent first in one direction and then laid against a second plot with registering plates to achieve bending in the second flange. The same approach was used to bend the web. The web strip began as a straight piece and was then bent to align with its curvature; a plot and multiple registering plates were used as guides. To bend it in the second direction, the team set the web on top of the curved flange and pulled the web down to align with the flange (see Figures 3-26 and 3-27).

Because the tees were to be constructed using galvanized steel, a process that precluded on-site welding, the entire structure of Ginger's external wall was preassembled in Permasteelisa's shop in Italy. In addition, the tees were not capable of self-support during this preassembly process because they were on the building through their connections to the floor slabs and via lateral steel support tubes. The preassembly issue was addressed by constructing a series of templates that together represented the exterior profile of the Ginger tower against which the tees could be set during assembly. Because each tee was fabricated in three sections, and because the overall structure had to be erected in full prior to galvanizing each piece, the template system acted as a necessary reference surface that supported the mullion system. Corrections and adjustments were made, and then the entire structure was disassembled before each piece was galvanized to a minimum of 18 microns. The tees were then packed into trailers, according to the order of assembly, and transported overland to Prague for erection.

Design and Construction of Concrete Panels for Fred

Construction of the concrete panels forming the Fred tower and the wave wall did not require the use of CATIA or the development of a unique fabrication system. The panel fabrication process did, however, utilize three-dimensional computer modeling to rationalize wall surfaces that curved in both plan and section. Even though the surface curved in two directions, the surface

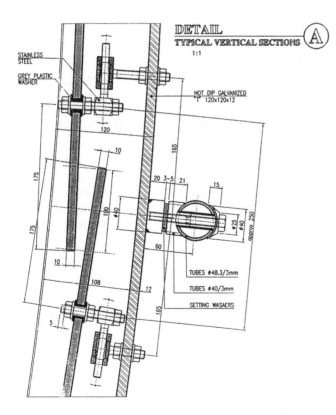

Figure 3-26 Shop drawing of a typical vertical section shows how the glass panels were bolted to the vertical tees. (Source: Project realized by Permasteelisa Group)

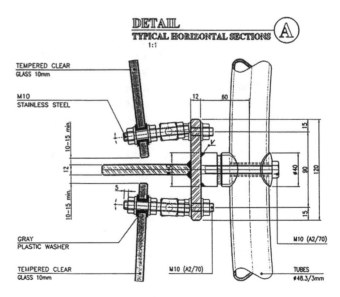

Figure 3-27 The subcontractor proposed that the tees be made out of two steel strips, a web and a flange, both of which could be bent separately and then welded together. (Source: Project realized by Permasteelisa Group)

Figure 3-28 The construction of a window opening ready to have concrete cast. (Source: Photo: Besix Construction)

Figure 3-29 The completed construction mock-up of a window opening in which the wall changes in plan and section. (Source: Photo: Besix Construction)

was regular enough to be described by a wireframe model in the AutoCAD environment. In addition, Gehry and his associates knew in advance that the concrete panel subcontractor used AutoCAD and not CATIA. The resulting wireframe model was developed by placing a 30-centimeter-by-30-centimeter grid on the wall in AutoCAD, from which plan and section cuts of each panel could be used to determine the shape of the formwork for the panels. (See Figure 3-28.)

The panel subcontractor, Kappa S.R.O. of Prague, then subdivided the surfaces of the Fred tower and the wave wall façade into grids measuring 3 meters by 3 meters. Dimensionally this organization corresponded to the design. Each panel contained one window, and the windows varied only by their vertical placement within each panel. To construct the panels, Kappa staff built a formwork box at the shop. Using information from the computer model and the orthogonal sections taken at 30-centimeter intervals, the formwork for each panel was built using bent wood strips 30 centimeters wide. Because the curvature of each panel was slight, the strips could be bent along the curves of the

plans taken at 30-centimeter intervals through each panel. To conserve materials, the panels were cast one by one corresponding to their adjacency in the façade so that tangent information could be utilized (see Figure 3-29).

Although computer numerically controlled equipment was not used to produce some of Fred and Ginger's most complex components, computer-aided design and manufacturing principles were integral to the design and building process from the project's initial stages. The project illustrates that computer-aided manufacturing techniques can inform and aid a fabrication process that involves significant manual and physical work in the shaping of the Ginger tower tee mullions. The fabrication process of both Ginger's mullions and Fred's panels were dependent on the integration of CAD/CAM techniques with traditional approaches. In other words, many steps in the process were not automated and were driven by a creative approach to the tools available. One aspect of this integration is the use of an orthogonal reference plane as a device useful in grounding an irregularly curved geometry so that the form it describes may be built.

CHAPTER 4

Complex Architectural Forms

Architects and other designers have long had a fascination with large-scale complexly shaped forms with curvilinear members or surfaces that exhibit compound curvatures or other more involved geometries. There are long-standing roots to this interest. The opening sections briefly review developments in this area, with particular reference to issues of representation and constructional and structural imperatives. A series of case studies are then presented.

4.1 A LONG HISTORY

Historically, the appearance of curved and complex shapes can be traced far back. Gothic architecture, with its dramatically shaped vaults, provides one obvious example. In terms of more recent design thinking, the products of many movements—the Art Nouveau, Arts and Crafts, Jugendstil, German Expressionism, American Organicism, and even some aspects of Modernism—began to relate formal design expressions involving complex geometries to more fundamental design philosophies. Many movements were based on the adaptation of biomorphic or zoomorphic principles that had little to do with functionally driven reasons for using complex geometries. Examples of works by Ferdinand Cheval, Hector Guimard, Antonio Gaudi, and Victor Horta provide familiar examples to students of architecture of projects that invoke design languages that rely on complex geometries. The works of the German and Russian Expressionists, such as Otto Bartning's "Sternkirche," or works by Bruno Taut, Hans Luckhardt, Hans Poelzig, Karl Hartung, J. J. Leonidov, Paul Goesch, and others reflect similar interests, as do works such as the Götheanum by Rudolf Steiner. The Modernist movement provided works by Le Corbusier—especially in the Notre Dame du Haut in Ronchamp (see Figure 4-1) and projects by architects such as Hans Scharoun and Eero Saarinen. Much more recently, a fascination with complexly curved members and surfaces is obvious in the work of Santiago Calatrava (see Figure 4-2) and in recent works by Frank Gehry. Reasons why these various architects have chosen to use complexly curved members and surfaces, of course, vary dramatically. Clearly, the use of curved members and surfaces is an integral part of historical and contemporary design thinking.

Early Representation

In terms of the profession of building as we now understand and define it, there is a general relationship among the development of tools for representing design information, the development of technologies for making complexly shaped members, and the specific kinds of architectural designs that were enabled by the relationships that existed at a specific point in time. It is not without interest to note that historically many highly evocative shapes envisioned by designers were simply never built (such as works by Hans Luckhardt, Herman Finsterlin, J. J. Leonidov, and others). While attracting great interest, some designs remained simply utopian and were visualized with sketches and physical models only. Few tools were available to represent these design intentions precisely. Descriptive geometry, to be sure, provided a powerful way for dealing with many shapes and was indeed widely used in the area of stone cutting (stereotomy). It was not widely used to describe general design intentions, and hand techniques were extremely cumbersome for extremely complex curves. The mathematical development of differential geometry and related general theories of curved surfaces, as based on the work of many mathematicians and further developed in works by Karl Friedrich Gauss and G. F. B. Riemann, provided the needed theoretical basis for understanding complex surfaces, but their formulations remained beyond the reach of design practitioners.

With the development of advanced digital design systems, many of the historical obstacles in representing complex geometric shapes and conveying design information are no longer problematic. Today's digital design environments are based on sophisticated mathematical formulations of curves and curved shapes (see Part IV).

Figure 4-1 The Ronchamp chapel by Le Corbusier.

Fundamental Constructional and Structural Considerations

In historical terms, buildings with complex geometrical forms that were actually built, such as works by Victor Horta, exploited the technology of the day in ways that respected its limitations. The designers of these same buildings also respected the need to share design intent—as expressed through precise and rational descriptions and representations—over time and with a number of different participants in the design and building process. Many of the following cast-iron forms of the nineteenth century demanded this kind of definition, since the processes by which elements were made were essentially industrialized. Even designers associated with seemingly nonrepresentable form making began seeking ways to simply describe complex geometrical forms in a way compatible with construction imperatives. Antonio Gaudi—known for his wonderfully shaped structures in Spain—faced the situation of having to provide a rational and transmittable description of a highly complex shaped structure. Originally, in the Casa Mila or the Park Guell, masons literally sculpted forms sketched by the architect while under his close supervision, and thus reflected historic practices. In the Sagrada Familia in Barcelona, Spain, this personalized method failed to be feasible because of the sheer size and complexity of the project. During the period from 1914 till 1926 in which he worked on the Sagrada Familia, Gaudi developed a set of rules that masons could follow. He generated the geometry of the principal architectural elements on the basis of "ruled surfaces," including the hyperbolic paraboloid and the hyperboloid of revolution. These surfaces are doubly curved and nondevelopable (see the next section); they can be formed by sweeping a straight line between two edge curves. The presence of straight-line generators greatly eased the work of masons, much of which could then be done without the direct supervision of Gaudi.

(Interestingly, recent efforts directed toward the completion of the Sagrada Familia have extensively utilized computer-based 3-D models.) The same conceptual approach of using specific surface types to facilitate construction can be seen in the later works of Felix Candela and Pier Luigi Nervi (see Figure 4-3). Both of these designers made extensive use of these kinds of surfaces in their reinforced concrete structures because of the direct way that formwork could be made with normative flat planks.

There were, of course, many examples of structures with complex forms that used whatever construction techniques were expedient, whether they were rationalized or not. Erich Mendelsohn, for example, proposed his astrophysical observatory and tower telescope, known as the "Einstein Tower" in Potsdam, Germany (1920–1924), as a monolithic concrete structure. Ultimately, it had to be built of brick with thick layers of plaster on its interior and exterior faces to define surface continuity. Eero Saarinen's TWA airport terminal in New York (1960) is a modernist building well known for its curved structures (see Figure 4-4). A close look at the concrete work, however, reveals just how crudely made was much of the formwork.

Just as construction imperatives have always been a consideration explicitly considered or not in the shaping of complex building forms, so have considerations of structural action. Many of the driving forces behind the works of many of the architects noted previously may or may not be responsive to structural or technical efficiency, a characteristic that stands in contrast to many civil engineering structures that also involve complex geometries (e.g., dam structures). Simply because a shape is curved, for example, does not mean that it inherently possesses positive virtues of structural efficiency. The issue is far more complex than this simple view would indicate. It is well known that classic doubly curved shapes such as portions of spheres or the

Figure 4-2 TGV station in Lyons, France, by Santiago Calatrava.

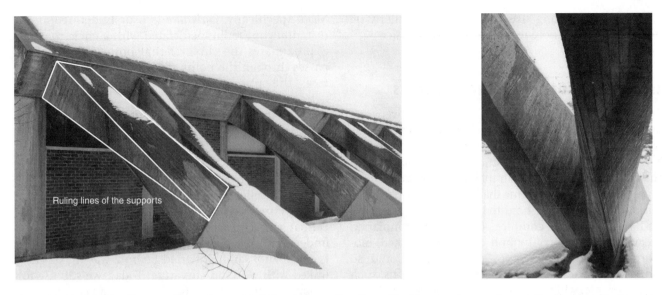

Ruling lines of the supports

Figure 4-3 Pier Luigi Nervi's gymnasium at Dartmouth College, Hanover, New Hampshire. The concrete supports are defined by a combination of ruled and triangular surfaces.

hyperbolic paraboloid shapes noted previously can exhibit what is known as "membrane action," wherein internal forces are efficiently transmitted through the surface of the shell in an in-plane manner. When this action occurs, internal stresses are low and surfaces can be made extremely thin. Just because a surface is curved, however, does not mean that membrane action occurs. Membrane action depends on the existence of particular combinations of surface shapes and types of loading conditions. When these specific combinations do not occur, undesirable bending moments can develop in the shell and resulting internal stresses can be extremely high—thus necessitating dramatically increased thick-

nesses or special reinforcements. The naïve belief that curvature automatically equals structural efficiency is one of the terrible misunderstandings surrounding today's often exuberant use of complexly shaped surfaces, especially when structural efficiency arguments are used as justifications or rationales. Only in carefully thought out circumstances that are in turn supported by structural analysis activities does this efficiency occur. There are, to be sure, a great many positive examples where complex geometries having specific shapes have been used for structural systems because of advantages stemming from structural performance. Historically, the works of Pier Luigi Nervi, Felix Candela, and Eduardo

Figure 4-4 Eero Saarinen's TWA Terminal in New York.

Torroja have a strong structural rationale underlying them, as does the more recent work by Heinz Isler.

4.2 NOTES ON DEFINING SURFACE SHAPES

In the preceding section a number of examples were presented in connection with the general idea of "complex geometries." What kinds of forms are exactly meant here? Some sense of the difficulties associated with answering this seemingly simple question can be seen from the multitude of terms that in one way or another summon up images of hard-to-imagine geometries. We find words such as complex, curvilinear, nonplanar, irregularly shaped, compound, freeform, sculpted, biomorphic, anthropomorphic, expressionistic, and so forth. Many words do have specific connotations, such as biomorphic, which relates to the attributing of biological shapes to inanimate objects, or anthropomorphic, which similarly relates to the attribution of human shapes. Other words, even those broadly used in this text, have meanings that are suggestive only. These terms stand in marked contrast to more easily imaginable geometries (e.g., cylindrical, spherical). Interestingly, Michael E. Mortenson in a book on geometric modeling establishes two primary categories: the namable and the unnamable.[1] For the moment we will continue to use words such as "complex geometries" or "compound curvatures." Generally, we are interested in surfaces that are nondevelopable and cannot be generated by moving a straight line through space, are branched or have multiple axes, or are otherwise intricate.

To further the discussion, however, one of the most useful distinctions is the one between surfaces that are *developable* and those that are *nondevelopable*. A nondevelopable form (exemplified by a sphere) must be cut, stretched, or distorted, if it is to be flattened out into a planar sheet. By contrast, developable surfaces (such as a simple conical shape) are those that can be flattened out into a planar sheet without any such distortions. These latter shapes can always be generated by moving a straight line through space; they are "ruled surfaces" (note that not all ruled surfaces are developable; a hyperbolic paraboloid, for example, is a ruled surface but nondevelopable). This distinction is particularly important from an implementation or construction technology viewpoint. Developable surfaces are relatively easy to make; nondevelopable ones are considerably more difficult. To make discussions even more specific, however, it is necessary to introduce the mathematical concept of "curvature," which is broadly a measure of the amount of bending of a curve at a point along its length. A curve with a constant amount of bending along its length forms all or part of circle. Variations in this bending produce other types of curves.

More specifically, *curvature* is usually defined as the instantaneous radius associated with a circle that best approximates the curve at that point and that both passes through the point and is tangent to it. For surfaces, the "principal curvature" or other concepts are defined in Chapter 11.

Getting to these concepts of curvature, however, was historically no easy task, and it is not surprising that applications to architecture lagged so far behind emerging theories of surface shapes. The study of how curves twist in space has occupied the minds of some of the greatest intellects in history. Without going too far back, we see the names of Johannes Kepler, Pierre de Fermat, and René Descartes associated with the quest to understand curvature. The development of calculus by Isaac Newton and Gottfried Leibniz was inextricably linked with work on curvature. Today, we still use formulations proposed by Karl Gauss as a way of understanding and defining surface curvatures. In particular, the concept of *Gaussian curvature* is fundamental to today's understanding of surface curvature.

Gaussian curvature analyses are widely employed in many advanced digital environments used within the CAD/CAM world as tools for understanding many different kinds of surface properties. These digital technologies and curvature analyses allow designers to understand the smoothness properties of a curved surface, including where kinks or folds might exist. Similar techniques are invaluable to designers in the automotive and shipbuilding world, where the fairness of a surface is of extreme importance. These technologies are discussed in detail in Part IV of this book. Chapter 11, in particular, looks at surface analysis techniques.

The remainder of this chapter generally looks at the problem of designing and making large-scale curved members and surfaces. The opening section presents different computationally based design approaches. The next section broadly reviews primary structural and constructional issues involved. Following sections look more specifically at issues in relation to specific material choices (concrete, wood, etc.).

4.3 DIGITAL FORM-FINDING TECHNIQUES

Recent Trends in Computationally Based Design

The development of sophisticated digitally based design environments has led directly to a preoccupation with their use in developing forms and shapes involving highly complex geometric forms and manipulations. Many of these computationally based design approaches focus on form finding, with only marginal attention paid to the world of manufacturing, construction, and structural efficiency. This section reviews several different conceptual approaches to computationally based design. Part IV discusses specific digital design techniques in much greater detail.

Approaches and rationales to developing shapes vary as widely as attitudes toward architecture itself. The general digital tools described previously, on the whole, do not literally generate designs but are a way of developing and representing shapes envisioned by the user. Designers seek inspiration for developing shapes that are subsequently developed and represented from many different sources, ranging from direct responses to programmatic requirements through often seemingly elusive metaphors. Different common digital design environments may then be more or less appropriate for representing and further developing these variant approaches, but are not in themselves providing the initial inspiration. In other instances, however, designers have sought to develop computational environments that in one way or another actually generate shapes according to prespecified rule structures or other principles. Many of these computational approaches have little to do with normative software environments commonly used by the profession. In the following, we briefly review both common and uncommon approaches to computationally based approaches to determining architectural form as a prelude to a discussion of more specific software-based applications.

The most common approach used by designers in practice is to generate shapes through the direct use and manipulation of computational tools (points, lines, splines, lofts, sweeps, etc.) found in common digital modeling environments of the type described in the previous section. A large number of different software environments can be directly used in this way (e.g., form-Z, Rhinoceros, MicroStation, CATIA, and so forth). In using these digital design environments, designers may or may not explicitly consider the influence of traditional (e.g., spatial use programs) or a rich set of nontraditional interests or concerns during the development of surface shapes. Extreme positions lie with exacting programmatic fits on the one hand and, on the other hand, creating shapes a priori and then seeking to imbue them with architectural meaning. Various ways of achieving more directed design intents lie in between. In general, many different software environments commonly used in the architectural and design world can be used to represent and develop design ideas of this type. Perhaps the biggest difference lies in relation to their respective roles in the overall design, design development, and implementation process. Thus, some environments are better for preliminary design thinking and others for design development.

Visually oriented computational tools based on descriptive geometry or on other ways of mathematically defining lines, curves, and surfaces may also be used in the direct manipulation process to generate shapes. Related software environments are rarely those developed and targeted for the architectural profession but are rather more broadly based mathematical tools (e.g., MathCAD, Mathematica).

In recent years, there has been an interest on the part of some more speculatively oriented architects in using one or more of external factors as a "direct generator" of a building's shape, or in using some reference metaphor (e.g., the "frozen waves" of Bernard Franken's BMW Pavilion in Germany, described later). In these situations, the curved surfaces assume (automatically within an appropriate computational environment) shapes in response to a prescribed forcing function of one type or another. Here, use is invariably made of special software environments, for instance, Maya, which directly enable these kinds of variations.

In yet other cases, shapes may be generated according to sets of predefined rule structures that lead to controlled parametric shape variations. The data sets and algorithms driving these approaches can vary widely; they may have a strong construction rationale to them or may be driven by different programmatic or conceptual intents. The digital environments that are widely used in CAD/CAM applications (e.g., CATIA, SolidWorks, Unigraphics) inherently provide these capabilities. A common approach here is to define a building envelope in terms of a series of parametrically defined elements such as the structural ribs. When their shapes are parametrically varied—for example, by associating key dimensions to a design table—the resulting geometric variations define the building envelope. External forms are thus shaped from variations of internal elements. A contrasting parametric approach would be to define measures that control the geometric definition of the outside envelope directly and generate the supporting structure subsequently.

Another track also based on rule structures but that takes a quite different approach are "shape grammar" formulations. Versions of these grammars have been used for the generation of plans but can be more widely used as well. Typically, the computational environments are specially written.

Other approaches that also normally involve rule structures seek to generate designs via various forms of growth and/or repetition algorithms (see Figure 4-5). Pattern tessellations and fractals that are the joy of many mathematicians, for example, are based on complex rule structures. Cellular automata approaches also rely on rule structures. While many of these approaches require specially written algorithms, some more general mathematics and related function visualization programs are of great use here.

Additionally, there are approaches that seemingly abandon any kind of formal approach to shape genera-

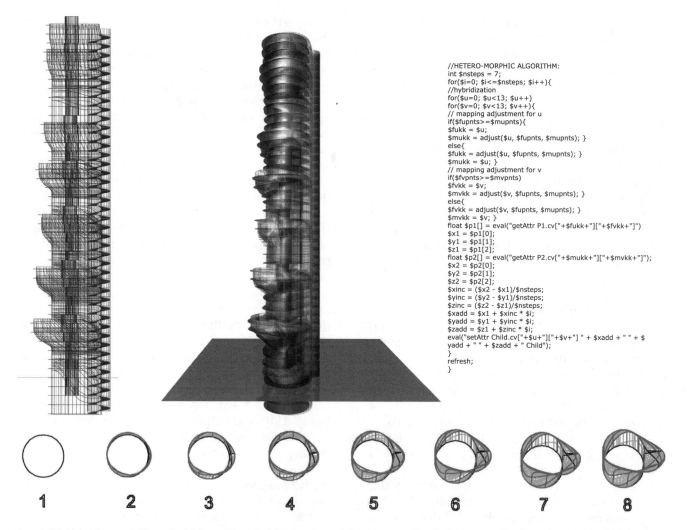

```
//HETERO-MORPHIC ALGORITHM:
int $nsteps = 7;
for($i=0; $i<=$nsteps; $i++){
//hybridization
for($u=0; $u<13; $u++)
for($v=0; $v<13; $v++){
// mapping adjustment for u
if($fupnts>=$mupnts){
$fukk = $u;
$mukk = adjust($u, $fupnts, $mupnts); }
else{
$fukk = adjust($u, $fupnts, $mupnts); }
$mukk = $u; }
// mapping adjustment for v
if($fvpnts>=$mvpnts)
$fvkk = $v;
$mvkk = adjust($v, $fupnts, $mupnts); }
else{
$fvkk = adjust($v, $fupnts, $mupnts); }
$mvkk = $v; }
float $p1[] = eval("getAttr P1.cv["+$fukk+"]["+$fvkk+"]")
$x1 = $p1[0];
$y1 = $p1[1];
$z1 = $p1[2];
float $p2[] = eval("getAttr P2.cv["+$mukk+"]["+$mvkk+"]");
$x2 = $p2[0];
$y2 = $p2[1];
$z2 = $p2[2];
$xinc = ($x2 - $x1)/$nsteps;
$yinc = ($y2 - $y1)/$nsteps;
$zinc = ($z2 - $z1)/$nsteps;
$xadd = $x1 + $xinc * $i;
$yadd = $y1 + $yinc * $i;
$zadd = $z1 + $zinc * $i;
eval("setAttr Child.cv["+$u+"]["+$v+"] " + $xadd + " " + $
yadd + " " + $zadd + " Child");
}
refresh;
}
```

1   **2**   **3**   **4**   **5**   **6**   **7**   **8**

Figure 4-5 Hybrid Tower: A 50-stories-high apartment building constructed through a morphing/hybridization algorithm. The algorithm blends a cylinder (step 1) with a deformed NURBS surface (step 8) in six in-between steps. The resulting hybrid components form the pieces of the building. (Source: Courtesy of Kostas Terzidis)

tion but that seek to allow designers to "discover" meaningful shapes that exist within more complex geometrical patterns and to extract these shapes from the larger whole (with or without the aid of algorithmic shape-finding functions). Most of the approaches using formal shape-identification algorithms require specially written computational algorithms and remain largely in the research domain.

Yet other ideas seek to incorporate a fourth dimension (time) into the definition of a geometry. Here the shape changes in time according to some external forcing function or in some prescribed or rule-driven manner. These approaches argue that temporality has largely been ignored in architecture. An unbuilt project by Kas Oosterhuis and Ole Bauman, for example, seeks to have a building whose skin changes shape with time. Again, digital environments that focus on animation or motion representation (e.g., Maya) are useful here. Other approaches seek to completely dissolve the usual boundaries between virtual and physical worlds.

From Physical Models to Digital Forms

In the previous section, computationally based design approaches were discussed in which the design was initially developed within the computer environment itself. Obviously, there are many other ways design ideas are generated. The use of physical models has especially been a long and valued technique for conceptualizing and developing design ideas. The physical models of cathedrals, churches, and other buildings used during the medieval and Renaissance eras remain marvelous testimonies to the value of this approach to designers seeking to develop and represent design ideas.

Many current designers still work with physical models. The advent of digitally based scanning and computationally based design tools has greatly enhanced how they can be used. Frank O. Gehry is well known for his use of physical models as a basis for generating and exploring design ideas. In many works by Gehry's office, models have been developed by hand and subsequently digitally scanned with the objective of developing a digital model of the physical model. Output from the scanner is imported into a digital design environment for subsequent editing and data smoothing. This data is then used to build a new digital model of the design. Often this new digital model is used as the basis for creating a new physical model that is in turn further manipulated by hand. The process is an iterative one that continues until design intent is satisfied. The digital model is then used for all subsequent design development work.

Structurally Oriented Form-Finding Approaches

In all of these examples, computational tools are used in one way or another to generate complex three-dimensional geometry. They are all alternative ways of generally approaching the historic problem of how to conceptualize and generate architectural form. The forms generated, however, are not necessarily intrinsically viable from manufacturing, constructional, or structural imperatives. Techniques for finding shapes that are structurally viable to work as load-bearing, continuous surfaces differ significantly from the more visually oriented approaches discussed before, and so do the affiliated construction techniques. Physical, experiment-based methods as well as computational methods exist for finding the geometry of complexly shaped load-bearing surfaces. The structural behavior and construction of the resulting systems are discussed later in this chapter.

Historically, most structural form-finding approaches were based on accurate, physical models, such as the network of hanging chains or minimal surface experiments with soap films or stretch fabric. These techniques remain viable today, especially since 3-D scanning techniques can now efficiently transfer the model shape into a digital modeling environment for further design development. Heinz Isler, a Swiss engineer, continues to use pneumatic scale models and hanging-fabric systems to define the shapes of rigid concrete shells. More recently these physical modeling techniques have been complemented by computational approaches to define the shape of structural surfaces—techniques that should not be confused with the computational design approaches described earlier in this section. The two most commonly employed computational techniques include the *force-density method* and the *dynamic relaxation technique*. Both are ultimately designed to minimize the forces present in a system through the optimization of the shape of the system itself. The optimum shape represents the one that achieves equilibrium between the external loads and the internal forces in the surface with the least amount of material. In both physical as well as computational form-finding techniques, shape manipulations are only possible either through changes in loading or by modifying the support and boundary conditions of the system (see Figure 4-6). Each loading and support condition correlates to a unique shape. In membrane structures the curvature of the shape can also be influenced by the degree of prestressing.

4.4 STRUCTURE AND ENCLOSURE

General Strategies

There are several primary options for making a large surface that has compound curvature. Several fundamental approaches are diagrammatically illustrated in

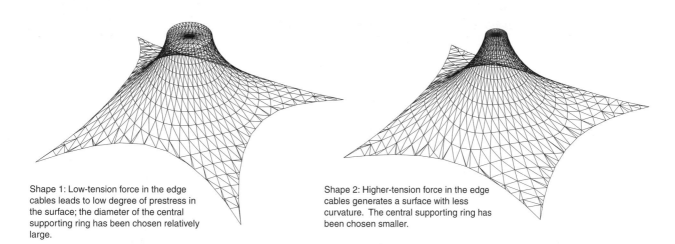

Shape 1: Low-tension force in the edge cables leads to low degree of prestress in the surface; the diameter of the central supporting ring has been chosen relatively large.

Shape 2: Higher-tension force in the edge cables generates a surface with less curvature. The central supporting ring has been chosen smaller.

Figure 4-6 Form finding for a membrane structure using the force-density method: Variations in cable sag along the boundaries generate different shapes. The choice of the central ring diameter is independent of the degree of surface prestress.

the accompanying figures. While a discussion of all relevant design factors is beyond the scope of this book, several primary technical considerations that affect choices can be noted. Important factors include the role of the surface as primary structural element or not. This factor involves a consideration of whether the surface serves as a load-bearing or non-load-bearing function with respect to gravity live and dead loads, and its role in relation to wind or earthquake forces. For purposes of this discussion, many of the structural issues resolve themselves into the primary question of whether or not the complexly shaped surface itself provides needed structural capabilities, and if not, how the surface relates to a supporting primary structural system. Shaped reinforced concrete surfaces, for example, might inherently provide such capabilities, while a surface made with copper sheathing would invariably need its own subframing, which would in turn have to be connected to the primary structural system of the building. Other important surface design factors include the location of the element, transparency and/or porosity issues, energy issues, and the many other factors traditionally considered in enclosure design.

An important initial consideration is whether there are both external and internal surface definitions to the building volume, or whether the external surface inherently defines both the external shape and the internal building volume as well. When there is a single defin-

ing surface, both enclosure and structural functions must be accommodated. One approach would be to make the whole surface inherently structural and capable of carrying all forces induced within it. Many materials, such as reinforced concrete, can serve as both structure and enclosure and further can provide a smooth and continuous surface of the type often desired from a larger architectural perspective. When there are both external and internal surface definitions, choices are extended because the structure can potentially occupy the interstitial spaces between the two surfaces.

One approach is to subdivide the surface, place lines of structural framing following the surface division lines, and employ lighter enclosure surfaces with smaller spanning capabilities between. Depending on how the surface is subdivided, the structural framing elements would often need to have compound curves, and connecting surface zones would be doubly curved. Alternatively, the surface can be represented by a series of planar facets (normally irregular in shape) in which bounding structural framing members are linear and enclosure surfaces are planar. A bar network typically results.

Another frequently used approach is to pass sectional planes at regular intervals through the whole shape and use the geometry of the intersection to define the shapes of structural members. These members would be planar but normally curvilinear. So-called egg-

B: Orthogonal egg crate system: shorter ribs are often assigned primary structural functions. The example shows a BMW pavillion by Bernhard Franken / ABB Architekten.

D: Primary structural ribs support a secondary compound surface. At Gehry's Experience Music Project in Seattle, curved steel ribs support a cast-in-place concrete surface. The image shows the mesh reinforcement prior to the application of the concrete.

F: Slab support system for a multistory building: this approach was employed in Gehry's MIT Stata Center, where story-high panels were connected to the slab edges.

Figure 4-7 Strategies to support complexly shaped surfaces. (Sources: (A) Harold Kloft; (C) Harald Kloft; (E) Shiro Matsushima)

crate structural framing patterns result when sectional planes are passed in orthogonal directions. In some cases where multiple floors are present, the floor planes themselves become sectional planes that are in turn normally supported by typical column or wall grids. Envelope surfaces are essentially draped over the successive edge contours of the floor planes. Many other variants and combinations are possible. (See Figure 4-7.)

In all of the preceding strategies, the implicit assumption is that the external shape has somehow been a priori determined. Structural attitudes and shapes are then derived from these a priori shapes. As noted earlier, however, alternative design strategies exist wherein the shapes of internal elements are first defined, for example, through the parametric variations of supporting structural elements, and the external shape results as a consequence of these variations.

Usually, the achievement of smooth surfaces requires approaches in which the surface is directly equated with the structure, or structural elements and connecting surfaces are curved. The use of framing patterns with linear elements and flat connecting planes generally creates faceted surfaces that conform to the overall surface configuration but do not replicate it exactly. Adoption of one or another of the general approaches noted has implications on the specific shaping and subsequent fabrication of all structural and enclosure surfaces. For example, in some cases structural members would have to be shaped into compound curves, while in other cases they might be linear. Resulting fabrication and construction implications are enormous.

Surface Constructions: Relations Between Structure and Enclosure

In the previous section, we have seen that the role of the surface in relation to the primary force-carrying structural system is crucial in the design of any large surface, whether the surface is part of a building (a wall or roof) or the hull of a boat. Surfaces may be capable of carrying structural forces or not, and, consequently, additional primary structure and subframing may or may not be required. In some cases, the structural role of the surface is dictated by the adoption of one or another of the strategies noted previously. In other cases, the a priori adoption of a particular way of making a surface with compound curvatures may ultimately dictate whether or not it is capable of serving a structural role. Figure 4-8 briefly summarizes some primary approaches to making a surface with compound curvatures. Generally, surfaces of varying thicknesses can either be made directly from a single material that is more or less homogeneous (e.g., concrete), built up in a series of layers that have been molded or deformed, or built up as a series of smaller aggregated panels that in

Continuous Smooth Surfaces:

Molded volumetric materials
    (e.g., concrete; formwork needed)
Molded layered materials
    (e.g., glass-based and other composites,
    molded plywood; mold needed)
Shaped solid materials
    (e.g., stone, foam)
Formed materials
    (e.g., stamped or planished metal sheets)
Aggregated materials
    (e.g., masonry units)

Continuous Smoothly Bent Strips

Thin, bendable strips of various materials
    (e.g., metals, wood, plastics)

Single-level or multilevel crossed strips

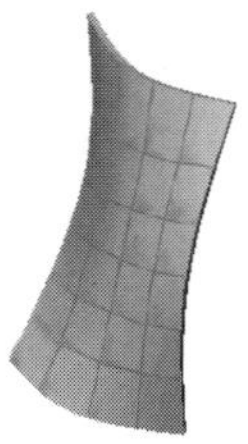

Faceted Planar Surfaces

Various panel shapes
    (e.g., rectilinear, triangular)
Various nominal panel dimensions
    (nonidentical size)
Various materials
    (e.g., fiberglass, metal, wood, cement-based
    materials)
Panel connections dependent on material

Figure 4-8 Typical ways of making large surfaces with compound curvatures out of rigid materials.

turn may be individually homogeneous or layered. Actual final surfaces may be continuous and smoothly varying, made up of thin bendable strips that provide surfaces that appear smooth and continuous, or made of a series of faceted planar faces. As will be seen, not all approaches can provide a structural function.

Figure 4-9 extends the review of basic approaches previously illustrated and focuses especially on wall systems and the relation between structure and enclosure. The figure distinguishes between primary and secondary systems. It first illustrates a structural surface, in this case a load-bearing wall, in which the structure and enclosure are identical. The following figures illustrate walls in which the surface is nonstructural and related to a primary load-carrying structural system.

Structural Surfaces
Large Continuous Surfaces

In general, effective structural surfaces can indeed be made using a variety of different materials, ranging from reinforced concrete to different laid-up composites and structural fabrics. Smooth, continuous surfaces can be made using a variety of materials and techniques. Many require the extensive use of formwork of

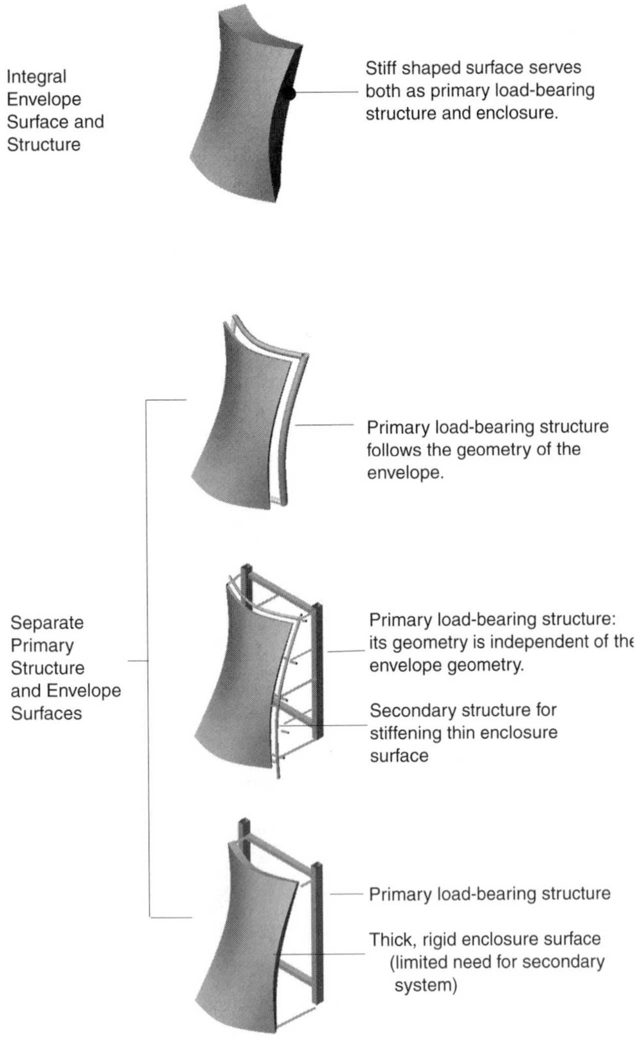

Integral Envelope Surface and Structure

Stiff shaped surface serves both as primary load-bearing structure and enclosure.

Primary load-bearing structure follows the geometry of the envelope.

Separate Primary Structure and Envelope Surfaces

Primary load-bearing structure: its geometry is independent of the envelope geometry.

Secondary structure for stiffening thin enclosure surface

Primary load-bearing structure

Thick, rigid enclosure surface (limited need for secondary system)

Figure 4-9 Basic relationships between rigid compound-curved enclosures surfaces and primary structural elements in buildings with complex external geometry.

one type or another, or rely on direct material shaping via cutting, carving, or molding.

A classic approach that has been historically used by designers since age-old times is the use of small masonry units such as are found in the complexly shaped vaults of ancient cathedrals. For large surfaces, the small planar faces of most masonry units are largely indistinguishable, and surfaces can be covered with smoothed plaster or cementitious material. In today's industry, this approach remains entirely feasible. The central issue is one of making the supporting formwork on which the units are placed. Creation of formwork for surfaces with compound curvatures is inherently difficult. The same techniques developed for reinforced concrete, however, could be used here. These include the use of large CNC machines to mill foam surfaces to exact curvatures (see Chapter 6).

Equally dominant historically is the use of cut and carved stones. Stones have long been individually shaped by master carvers to produce surface shapes of exceptional complexity. On the construction of St. John's Cathedral in New York City, new life was breathed into this ancient craft by the advent of large CNC cutting, milling, and routing machines. In today's industry, it is perfectly possible to use large CNC machines to cut stones that can be rationally stacked but have outer surfaces that have compound curvatures. While load-bearing wall systems can indeed be made in this way, however, current economic practice tends more toward using the CNC milled stone in a thin veneer fashion, which in turn requires subframing and associated structural systems (see the section on stone veneer and masonry).

Reinforced concrete has obviously attracted the interests of designers for large structures because of its inherent fluidlike state during casting—which allows it to conform exactly to formwork of any shape—and the smoothness of resulting finishes. As was noted in the opening of this chapter, the advent of the Modern Movement in architecture renewed interest in the potential of concrete for creating complexly shaped geometries. The essential technical challenge, however, was always how to create the shaped formwork. This challenge remains with us today. There are, however, new methods for making complexly shaped concrete formwork via techniques such as the direct CNC cutting of foam and the use of solid free-form fabrication technologies. The advent of CAD/CAM technologies also holds promise for revitalizing the use of ferrocement structures (see Chapter 6).

Various kinds of components made from wood products can be used as well to make large structural surfaces. Wood has long been shaped into curvilinear elements or made into planar sheets. The use of glued-laminated timber has further extended the range of shapes possible with wood, and digital models have been used to provide the precise geometry data needed to set up the laminating jigs (see Figure 4-10). Generally there has been less success in making wood products into surface elements with compound curvatures. There have been, however, some recent developments in this area that utilize CAD/CAM technologies to produce complexly curved roof surface elements made out of wood (see Chapter 6).

Panelized units made of materials such as thin sheet metals or sheet polymers are much more difficult to make work structurally without secondary stiffening systems. Surfaces made of thin bent strips typically cannot work alone unless multiple bonded cross-layers are used. The use of structural fabrics such as Teflon-coated fiberglass or PVC fabrics is an exception to this rule. Large structural membrane surfaces can be created by prestressing the fabric and thus balancing the external loads. As shown in Chapter 3, structural fabrics were at the very beginning of architectural use of CAD/CAM

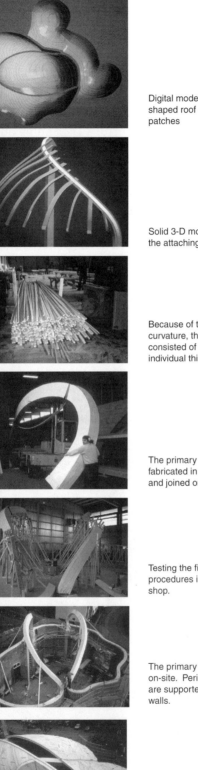

Digital model of the complexly shaped roof surface using Coons patches

Solid 3-D model of a primary and the attaching secondary beams

Because of their extreme curvature, the primary beams consisted of up to 5,000 individual thin wood strips.

The primary beams were fabricated in several segments and joined on-site.

Testing the fit and assembly procedures in the carpenter's shop.

The primary beams are installed on-site. Perimetral ring beams are supported on curved masonry walls.

Prefabricated surface segments were hoisted into place and connected to the supporting beams.

Figure 4-10 Complexly shaped timber roof for a building in Maulbronn, Germany. Primary glued-laminated timber beams support curved surface segments made from secondary beams and several layers of wooden boards. (Source: © 2001 Klaus W. Linkwitz)

technologies, and they remain a viable strategy today for enclosing larger spaces. The traditional use of plotted templates has now been replaced by the CNC cutting of fabric panels, which then can be joined by numerically controlled welding robots in highly automated production settings.

Smaller Continuous Surfaces

There have been a whole host of recent developments in other materials that lend themselves well to making compound curved surfaces with some structural capabilities suitable for smaller structures. They are, however, rarely adequate to carry the larger forces associated with many major building configurations.

Certainly, familiar fiberglass has long been used to create large, stiff surfaces (recall early fiberglass boats or Corvette sports cars). Construction processes typically involve placing the material in strips or sheets over curved formwork and impregnating it with resins. The final hardened material can have excellent rigidity and surface qualities. Surfaces may be made in situ over a large prepared mold or made in a factory setting offsite. This approach has also been applied successfully to small structural roof shells designed by German engineer S. Polonyi. There are now many other composite materials that can be worked with similarly. Many extraordinary applications have been developed in the boat-building industry for making complexly shaped hulls that could be adopted. Again, CAD/CAM technologies play their primary role in shaping the formwork that ultimately gives these materials their final form.

Many layered or built-up approaches use composite materials that can be made with directional strengths that are oriented along the lines of the principal stresses in the surface to increase overall strengths and stiffnesses. (Directions of these lines of principal stresses must be determined from a finite-element analysis of a digital model—see Chapter 11). Often, components are made up in sandwich panel fashion, with distinct core and surface materials that serve different purposes.

The use of shaped metal has always had a special attraction for designers. While many smaller objects can be directly cast or stamped, the making of larger surface shapes has always been more problematic. Many processes usually begin with large, flat sheets, which are inherently nondevelopable. The sheet material must be cut and/or deformed to create a compound curve. Various cold-forming techniques are possible with sheets of limited size. The general act of "planishing" involves rolling or hammering appropriate metals to cause them to deform into appropriate shapes. Large rollers, for example, can create curved steel sheets. While other processes are available, such as large stamping, they are often cost-prohibitive for many common building applications. Resort is often made to various simpler cold-forming operations to produce curved surfaces (see Chapter 14).

Other inherently continuous materials, such as glass, can now be shaped into compound curves. This can be done through various kinds of draping operations that normally involve the use of shaped molds (see the discussion on the glass walls of the Condé Nast project in Chapter 5). Nonetheless, sizes remain limited and support conditions are extremely crucial.

Enclosure Surfaces

Basic Approaches and the Role of Secondary Systems

When the surface itself cannot handle required primary structural forces, it is necessary to introduce a primary structural system capable of doing so. The surface envelope then becomes largely non-load-bearing and of only sufficient strength and rigidity to carry localized forces. The primary structure is usually made internally within the overall volume of the form and is typically made up of some sort of skeletal framing system. In building construction, the most typical approach followed to date is that in which the primary structure is shaped according to its own inherent logic and practical construction considerations—factors that normally mean that the primary structure consists of a braced framework of linear or curvilinear members. This framework carries all major dead and live loads (including earthquake and overturning wind forces). It also supports the weights of all non-load-bearing surface elements. The non-load-bearing surface envelopes are periodically connected to the primary structure. Depending on how the surface envelope is made, there may or may not be a need for a secondary framing system that mediates between the envelope and the primary structure. If the surface is thin and relatively flexible, a secondary system is invariably needed that provides a series of distributed support points to the envelope. This system serves to stiffen the external envelope and to transfer surface loads to the primary structure. (See Figures 4-11 and 4-12.)

One of the most famous examples of the approach just discussed is the Statue of Liberty, which has a primary structure designed by Gustave Eiffel and a complex secondary system that serves to position and maintain the shape of the thin, shaped copper sheets that create the external surface of the statue. Here the

Figure 4-11 Metal façade panels at Gehry's Experience Music Project in Seattle are connected to the primary surface at discreet points. Each panel is stiffened by smaller members. (Source: Harald Kloft)

Figure 4-12 Interior view of the Experience Music Project: The primary ribs are braced; they support the curved concrete slab that effectively separates interior and exterior thermally.

secondary system is specially designed to allow the external sheathing to easily expand and contract without restraint. Any restraints caused by attaching the skin to the structure would ultimately cause buckling or tearing in the external sheathing as temperature-induced expansion and contraction took place. The well-designed secondary system allows necessary movement.

Secondary systems can be designed in many ways. In today's practice, secondary systems for thin or flexible surface envelopes often have a series of stiff but still readily bendable elements—such as pipes—that can be shaped into compound curves that in some way follow the shape of the envelope and periodically attach to it around the periphery of the skin and at several internal points. A series of rigid offset connectors of varying lengths then connect the secondary shaped members to the primary structural system. This general approach has already been seen in several structures (see the discussion in Chapter 3 on the fish sculpture in Barcelona by Gehry Partners, LLP). Faceted panels normally require points of attachment to stiffening systems at each primary nodal point. Surfaces made up of bent strips are typically subdivided at periodic intervals.

One of the problematical design and construction aspects of this general approach of attaching a complexly curved non-loading surface to a secondary and primary structure has been the exact numerical determination of controlling distances between the shaped skin and the normative structure. These determinations are crucially necessary for designing and dimensioning the secondary framing system and its offsets, and for finally positioning and installing and constructing the whole system. This whole activity has been rendered much easier via the use of advanced digital modeling technology that incorporates complete numerical definition and control of surface forms (not all digital mod-

eling environments, however, provide this numerical definition capability—see Chapters 10 and 11). A digital model of a surface can be created and then numerically related to any other type of reference plane or surface. The reference surface plane can represent the normative geometry of a standard structural system. Alternatively, the reference surface can have its own specialized geometry.

Thin Sheet Surfaces—General

Thin non-load-bearing surfaces with compound curvatures may be made in a variety of ways. It was noted in the previous section that materials such as fiberglass and many different kinds of composites can be used to create compound curvatures via the use of CNC-produced molds. There it was also noted that metal sheets can be shaped into compound curves. Single curvature metal sheets are easy to obtain via direct rolling techniques. Compound curvatures may be obtained by various cold-forming techniques (see Chapter 14). These and other techniques are especially suitable for smaller-size sheets but become increasingly difficult when large sheets must be made. Creating compound curvatures in metal is also always expensive.

Thin sheets, including sheet metal, are naturally easy to use when surfaces are planar or singly curved. Large sheets of materials such as sheet metal, however, do have a limited capability to naturally twist and conform to minor out-of-plane curvatures. In some instances, the minor deformations achievable are sufficient for the needed curvatures and the material can be used directly over a secondary system to give it shape. The thinner the sheet, the easier it is to obtain surface conformation.

In all of these approaches, the use of a thin sheet stock typically means that the material is not to be subjected to compressive forces, which would immediately cause buckling. Thin sheet material can carry some bending due to out-of-plane forces, but spans are intrinsically limited. Consequently, a closely spaced secondary stiffening system must normally be used to keep the surface material from bending or deforming excessively. As sheets are made thicker, stiffeners in the secondary system may be placed farther apart. How the secondary system is made depends on the material used. For materials such as laid-up fiberglass, it is perfectly possible to literally make secondary stiffening ribs directly integral with the surface itself. In metal sheets, elements such as pipes, strips, or other easily bendable materials are used.

Thin metal cladding is common. Cladding may be made of aluminum, copper, or other materials. Traditional sheet metal approaches have also been widely used. While sheet metal has been used for a long time, it has recently undergone a true renaissance because of the adoption by leading fabricators of advanced

CAD/CAM technologies for both modeling and CNC machines for fabrication. Many of the most acclaimed recent architectural works have utilized sheet-metal technologies to make their external surfaces. (See Figure 4-13.)

Glass has been used successfully in complexly curved envelopes, mostly in the faceted systems described in the text that follows, rarely as doubly curved complex sheets. Flat sheets of glass can be shaped by heating and slumping them over molds. Again, CAD/CAM techniques serve in defining the mold geometry and fabricating molds (see the case study on the Condé Nast cafeteria in Chapter 5). The same is true for the use of acrylic sheets and other thermo-formable materials, where CNC-milled foam molds have been successfully used in forming sheets to compound curvatures (see the case study on the BMW pavilions).

Bendable Strips

Builders have long made beautiful surface shapes by bending thin strips of rigid material over a mold or series of cross-sectional profiles. Many age-old boat-building techniques have used bendable wood to make graceful hulls. Indeed, the origin of now familiar "spline curves" in digital modeling arenas is traceable to the kinds of mechanical devices used to plot hull shapes, wherein a thin strip naturally bends into a certain shape when held in place at ends and other specific points.

The proportions of strips are usually based on issues related to the ease of bending to the desired radii, ease of installation, and appropriate surface definition. Wood, metal, or polymeric materials have been used for strips, usually attached to a restraining framework in order to maintain desired shapes.

While curvatures obtainable generally restrict surfaces to those with broad, flowing, continuous forms, it is exactly these forms that often prove highly appropriate and desirable for large-scale surfaces—be they hulls of ships or walls of buildings. The intrinsic properties of bent strips to "smooth out" undesired dimples or minor raised points also make them desirable for use in making complex surfaces. When surfaces have reversed curvatures, care must be taken to properly hold down strips to a restraining framework. Very sharp curvatures may or not be obtainable depending on actual curvatures and strip materials and dimensions. Strip surfaces may be placed as single layers or as multiple crossed layers. Unless edges of strips in single-layer systems are continuously connected, the resulting surface has little in-plane stiffnesses (shear or racking resistance is limited). Multiple layers that are bonded to one another can be very stiff.

Digital surface models are especially useful in designing surface shapes to accommodate strips. Surface curvatures can be determined at any point on the digital model and compared with those limiting curvatures associated with the type of strips used. Where cur-

Figure 4-13 (A) At Gehry's Fisher Center for Bard College, New York, the façade panels are prefabricated metal stud constructions complete with insulation and waterproofing. (B) They attach directly to the primary structural steel members (C) and (D). Over the panel surface a rain-screen cladding is applied manually on-site. (Source: Image Courtesy of A. Zahner Company, used by permission)

vatures are too sharp, the surface model must be adjusted to flatten specific problem areas. In some digital environments, surface curvatures can also be limited to specific values during model construction. Digital models are further useful in making finite element models that determine principal stress directions, which would allow critical strips to be aligned in a structurally optimum way if desired.

Aggregated Faceted Panels

The intrinsic problems involved in constructing very large nondevelopable surfaces out of available flat materials has historically led architects and other designers to modeling continuous surfaces as a series of smaller flat shapes, generally called facets. Various shapes are possible depending on the nature of the compound curved surface. Faceted panels that make up the surface can be triangular, essentially rectilinear, or polygonal shapes. Obviously, smaller facet dimensions relative to the overall size of the surface will appear to make a "smoother" surface than coarser sizes. There are trade-offs, however, between facet size and related ease of construction and installation, and the appearance of surface smoothness.

Virtually any surface can be modeled as a series of small triangular facets. The use of triangular facets is particularly interesting because the three points of a facet in turn define a bounded surface that is intrinsically flat. Digital models are, of course, useful in translating a complex compound surface into a series of triangles. When this is done, there is no a priori assurance that all triangular facets will be of identical size and shape. In a digital production world, these variations may not prove problematic, since cutting different-shaped pieces from the same general geometric family is usually not difficult. Alternatively, it is possible in some software environments to impose a common triangular element over the whole surface. Some adjustment in surface shape, however, may then be required.

Other facet shapes are possible. If a compound surface is overlaid with a square mesh, any individual mesh unit looks rectilinear but may or may not contain a surface that is actually flat. The mesh unit might necessarily consist of a warped plane. Other basic polygonal shapes, as well as combinations of polygonal shapes (e.g., the squares and hexagons of a soccer ball pattern) may be used as well. Indeed, there is a whole branch of mathematics devoted to the general problem of how to subdivide surface shapes according to various criteria. The domes of Buckminster Fuller assumed a series of criteria of inherent conceptual interest, but arguments about size repetition were always strained and, in today's digital production world, of limited interest.

Faceted surfaces may be made of many different kinds of panels, typically produced in an off-site con-

text and assembled on-site. Panel materials include a variety of metals and polymeric materials. The design of panel joints and connections is particularly important. Subframeworks may or may not be required depending on surface geometry panel sizes and connection types.

Stone Veneer and Masonry

Shaped stone veneer surfaces cut via CNC machines invariably require special attention. When stone is used in a non-load-bearing way, the actual stone is usually made relatively thin and is periodically supported by a secondary system. (See Figure 4-14.)

Special problems may be encountered in some large surface areas because of earthquake movements. Large stone expanses can be quite rigid and prone to cracking and buckling in seismic events. One approach is to subdivide the surface into zones that are allowed to move relative to one another via the use of special expansion joints. The zonal definition and design of the secondary system are obviously linked.

In complexly shaped masonry surfaces, the role of CAD/CAM technology is primarily to design and fabricate the systems that serve as formwork or guiding elements for the masons. Issues of formwork for vaulted systems are similar as for concrete construction, but masonry formwork does not require a continuous surface; hence, the use of thin bendable strips spaced apart over CNC-cut frames is feasible. Masonry can also be attached via steel connectors to shaped concrete panels. For Frank Gehry's "Zollhof" office building in Düsseldorf, Germany, flat steel guiding profiles were CNC-cut from geometry generated by the CATIA model. These elements—spaced apart regularly and fixed to the floor and ceiling slabs—served as guiding elements for on-site construction of complexly curved masonry walls.

Shaped Primary Structural Elements

The general approach noted previously, in which a secondary system mediates between a complexly curved surface envelope and a more normatively shaped primary structural system, is surely complex and, to many designers, less than satisfying. An alternative approach is to shape the primary structural system in a way that is fundamentally congruent with the shape of the complexly shaped surface. Doing so minimizes the need for secondary framing systems or greatly simplifies them, while at the same time opening up new possibilities for the shaping of internal spatial volumes. Accomplishing this objective initially appears easy—primary structural elements just need to be shaped into any necessary compound curves. For smaller-scale structures, doing so is indeed possible, as is witnessed by many examples of this approach in automobile and boat construction. Doing so in major multistory buildings, however, is

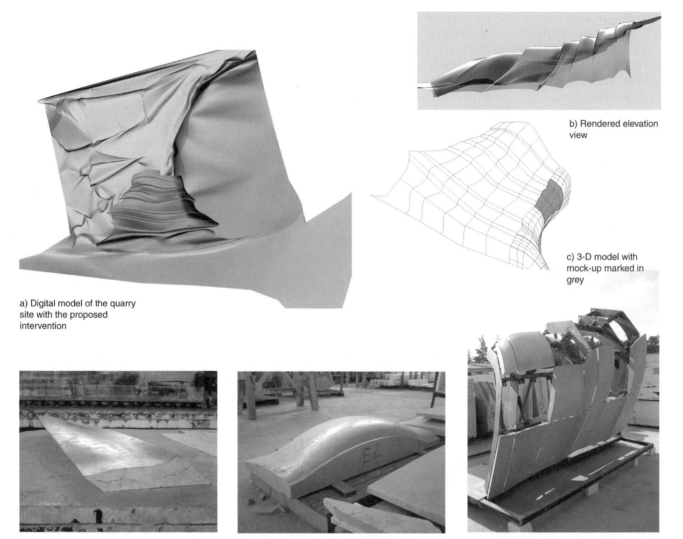

a) Digital model of the quarry site with the proposed intervention

b) Rendered elevation view

c) 3-D model with mock-up marked in grey

d) and e) Natural stone shaped on a CNC-milling machine.

f) Façade mock-up showing the supporting steel ribs.

Figure 4-14 Complexly shaped building envelope using stone: "La Grotta" by Pongratz Perbellini Architects, Verona, Italy. (Source: pONGRATZ pERBELLINI)

considerably more difficult. The members that must be shaped into compound curves are typically quite large and difficult to shape.

The use of reinforced concrete is an obvious approach to making curved members with complex curvatures. Here the problem is almost purely one of formwork. CAD/CAM technologies can be used to create the complex formwork that is necessary. Negative shapes can be milled directly, or various templates used in connection with fiberglass to make formwork that eventually receives the concrete (see Chapter 6). All of this is feasible with large amounts of patience and expense. Similar formwork systems can also serve for structural masonry systems.

Some relatively simple metal structural shapes can indeed be cast or bent into basic curves that lie in one plane fairly readily. Members with curved shapes that lie in a single plane have been made by traditional

metal casting techniques ever since the famous bridge at Coalbrookedale in 1756. Truly wondrous shapes have been cast many times since, but when members are large, the curves lie within a single plane. More recently, various kinds of rolling mills can be used to induce simple curvature into extremely large steel beams. While the curves obtainable via rolling can be quite elegant, they must inherently remain fairly simple. Laminated timber has long been used in simple curved beams that lie in a single plane. Nonetheless, fairly complex external surface shapes can be made using curved members that lie in a single plane.

When a member cannot be conceived of as lying within a plane and thus twists in space, there are severe limitations imposed by available bending technologies. Few members, and among them pipes, are relatively easy to shape into complex curvatures of this type using today's commonly available technologies, but they

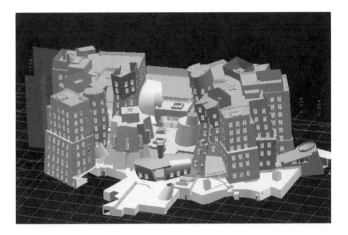

Figure 4-15 CATIA model used to describe the complex shapes. (Source: Gehry Partners, LLP)

often lack the requisite strengths and stiffness. They are frequently used as secondary members, as for example in Gehry's Bilbao Guggenheim Museum. When pipes are used as primary structures, they are much larger and used as linear elements. Structural optimizations, such as varying the cross-sectional shape of a member as it curves in response to varying internal force states, are beyond easy reach.

Given today's recent advances in manufacturing technologies, there are some bright spots on the horizon for complexly shaped structures. Particularly interesting are some of the new soft-tooling casting techniques developed for low-volume production (see Chapter 15). These approaches may indeed allow the efficient and cost-effective fabrication of members that twist in space and vary their cross sections along their lengths. Other approaches that may prove viable include making members out of composites and other kinds of new materials. These materials have different fabrication technologies than those commonly used in building construction to date and lend themselves well to the problem of making curved members.

4.5 CASE STUDIES IN COMPLEX GEOMETRY

The case studies in this section illustrate different approaches to designing and building complexly shaped architecture. The selected projects demonstrate benefits and problems associated with the use of advanced digital design and manufacturing techniques. The motivations for the complex shape vary significantly, starting from a sculptural approach in Gehry Partners, LLP's Stata Center to the use of animation software borrowed from the film industry for Franken's BMW pavilions, and a combined study of the interrelation effects of sunshading, geometry, and program for Michael Wilford/DP Architects Center for the Performing Arts. In all cases a primary support structure needs

to be devised in order to support the complexly shaped envelopes that by themselves would be insufficient to carry the building loads. These support systems are the column and slab structure of the Stata Center, and the aluminum ribs and steel frames of the BMW pavilions. The steel space-frame of the Performing Arts Center in Singapore relies on the interior concrete structure for support.

The MIT Ray and Maria Stata Center[2]

The Massachusetts Institute of Technology's Stata Center, designed by Gehry Partners, LLP, houses various computer-based research groups, the artificial intelligence lab, and the department of linguistics and philosophy. The building provides a total gross area of 710,000 square feet. Two clusters of sculptural buildings of up to nine stories surround a lower base building of lecture halls and a public plaza. (See Figures 4-15 and 4-16.)

Design Process

In Gehry's office the design starts with a physical model that consists of basic program elements in the form of simple, mostly rectangular volumes. In the case of the Stata Center, the functional requirements of the program were complex and necessitated a lengthy process of coordination between the clients, the architect, and various consultants (code, acoustics). During this phase, the architects also studied the massing on an urban design level. Together with Beacon Skanska Building Inc., the general contractor, it was decided to design the building with a primary concrete structure. The material seemed to offer advantages over steel because curved and irregular slab edges that would define the complex outer envelope could be created relatively easily in concrete. The building was structured into regularly spaced floor plates for offices and lab

Figure 4-16 The variety of volumes is covered with metal cladding, glass-aluminum curtain walls, or brick. (Source: Image courtesy of A. Zahner Company, used by permission)

spaces, and there were relatively few higher spaces that would have been easier to construct in steel. In later design phases, it was decided that some parts of the building, especially towers and certain sculptural elements, were to be designed with a steel frame instead of concrete.

As the design evolved, the basic volume model was refined sculpturally, creating the types of complex curved and irregular geometry that Gehry's work is generally known for. The sculpted physical design models were digitized using a medical 3-D scanner originally designed to record the shape of the human brain, as well as with other digitizing instruments. The resulting point clouds were brought into CATIA, where they could be converted into surfaces. Further design development would occur in the digital model, until this model was again used to construct physical scale models using a combination of rapid prototyping, CNC milling, and hand-building techniques. On the physical models, the architects would verify the shapes and spaces and make

alterations that were then again digitized and further refined in CATIA. This iterative design process continued until all functional, aesthetic, code, and other requirements had been met. Beacon Skanska controlled costs, while façade consultants studied and contributed to the construction feasibility of the external envelope.

CATIA Model

The design architects at Gehry's office, together with local associate architect Cannon Design, created the 3-D digital model of the project using CATIA's version 4, operating on Unix-based IBM workstations. The CATIA model was an integral part of the contract documents and served as the central reference for overall dimensions and geometry (see Figure 4-17). The model was structured into five major parts that were each updated individually but could be displayed together in a single master model. The five part models were the geometry, the framing, the pattern, the concrete, and the steel models. Except for visualization of interior

Figure 4-17 The CATIA geometry model defined the exterior surface of the building, including the openings. In this view, the layers with panel subdivisions are turned off. (Source: Image courtesy of A. Zahner Company, used by permission)

spaces and furniture layout, the interior was generally not included in the CATIA model.

The geometry model essentially represented the external shape of the building enclosure and also included openings; this model was—chronologically speaking—the first one to be created. All other CATIA models were ultimately derived from the geometry model, since the shape of structural or façade elements obviously needed to relate closely to the overall shape of the building as described in the geometry model. The framing, pattern, concrete, and steel models, however, were not digitally associated to the geometry model in the way a part model may be associated to a base part or other reference geometry. Changes to the geometry model were not automatically reflected in other models; instead, those models needed to be updated manually using the geometry model as a reference.

The framing model primarily included the ruling lines of metal studs in the exterior metal façade. This model was created by Gehry's office as a design guide for the façade contractors. These firms eventually would create their own, more detailed CATIA models that were also ultimately used to support manufacturing activities. Closely related to the geometry and the framing model was the pattern model. It consisted of a grid of lines and curves that represent the subdivision of façade segments into metal panels. The concrete and steel models included the primary structural system of slabs, columns, shear walls (concrete model), and steel framing (steel model). This structure of the master models facilitated work on a specific aspect of the design and also addressed the division into the basic building trades and construction phases. Representing the concrete structure in its own part file, for example, enabled the concrete contractor to easily extract the overall concrete volume for the purpose of cost control and procurement.

The five 3-D CATIA models were not developed exclusively by the architects. Instead, portions were contributed by subcontractors such as A. Zahner Architectural Metalwork (metal façade panels), the steel subcontractor Capco Steel, or Architectural Skylight Co., Inc. (curtain walls and skylights). The work of the façade subcontractors inevitably affected the adjoining elements of the project. Once Zahner had worked out the detailed panel design and the connections of the panels to the slab, they issued a set of rules—depending on the façade inclination, a 10- or 12-inch offset between the slab edge and the outer envelope geometry had to be maintained. The modification of the slab edge in the concrete model was the responsibility of the architects, since they were the ones in charge of the overall project coordination, in this case through the CATIA model.

2-D Construction Documents

The project employed a mix of 2-D and 3-D construction documents, depending on the needs and on the capabilities of the contractors directly involved in building the various parts of the project. Approximately 1,800 general-arrangement drawings and a similar number of construction details were prepared as 2-D AutoCAD drawings and lists. For the general arrangement drawings—plans, sections, and elevations—the CATIA model was cut and a 2-D section line generated. These 2-D line shapes were then imported into AutoCAD, where they formed the basis for the drawing. The association with the CATIA model, however, was lost in this conversion process, and changes in the 3-D model would not propagate automatically to the 2-D plan and section views.

Details were keyed in the general arrangement drawings much as in a conventional project. Two-dimensional detail drawings generally included CATIA reference points and axes that were present in the 3-D model (see Figure 4-18). For a curtain wall detail, for example, the typical detail shows only one angle between two adjacent segments, as opposed to the various angles that occur throughout the project for this type of detail. For the complete understanding of all geometric conditions, reference needs to be made to the latest CATIA model. Consequently, most 2-D drawings included a series of notes that point out the necessity to refer to the 3-D CATIA model for any accurate information on dimensions, orientation of elements, and their position in the assembly context. These notes also point to Beacon Skanska's responsibility of updating all related elements of the CATIA model if the geometric relationship between the components shown in a particular drawing and the 3-D CATIA model is to be changed.

Design-to-Manufacturing Process

The CATIA model served different purposes for the various parts of the building. The extent to which 3-D CATIA data could be processed directly by subcontractors and fabricators varied greatly.

Concrete Structure. The concrete subcontractor did not make extensive use of the CATIA model, other than for setting out the geometry on-site and for calculating concrete volumes. The setting-out points were supplied by the general contractor Beacon Skanska, because the concrete subcontractor had no capability of working with the 3-D CATIA concrete model (see Figure 4-19). The concrete drawings were essentially conventional 2-D documents, albeit with reference to the CATIA model through inserted CATIA reference lines and points.

Steel Structure. The steel contractor relied heavily on a steel detailing software (SDS) for the detailed design of the steel structure. An IT specialist from Gehry's office wrote a program that allowed the easy conversion of

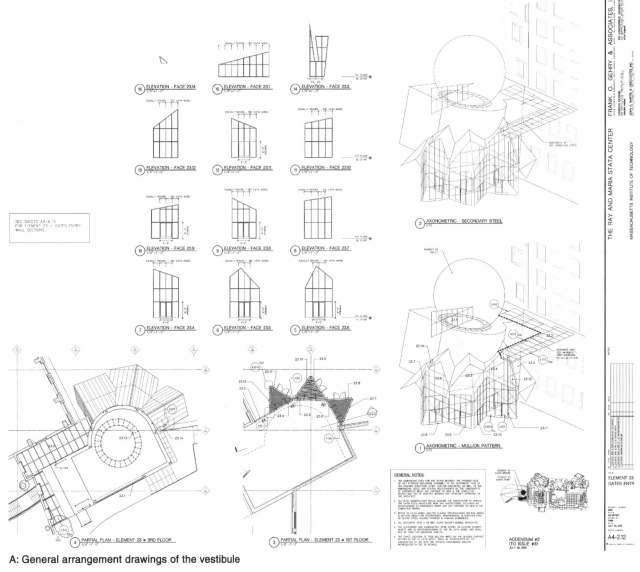

A: General arrangement drawings of the vestibule

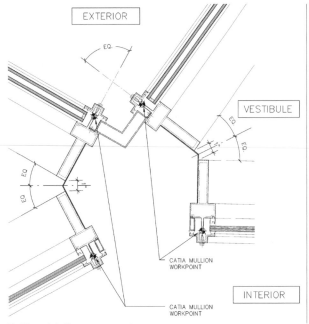

B: Plan detail

Figure 4-18 Two-dimensional construction drawings were derived from and referenced to the 3-D CATIA model. The drawings show details for the glazed entrance vestibule (under construction in the lower right). The CATIA reference lines are clearly marked in the detail on the left. (Source: A, B: Gehry Partners, LLP; C provided by author)

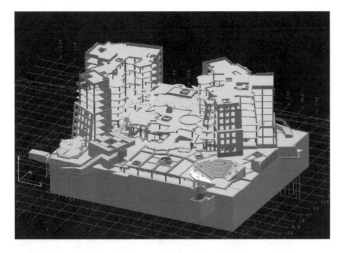

Figure 4-19 The concrete CATIA model included slabs, shear walls, columns, and other elements. (Source: Gehry Partners, LLP)

native CATIA files into a format useful for the SDS system. Bringing the refined steel design data back into the CATIA model—as was deemed necessary in order to fully coordinate the steel with adjacent elements—could only be accomplished through a multilevel process whereby the SDS files were first converted into DXF files, imported into AutoCAD, and then exported in Initial Graphics Exchange Specification (IGES) format in order to import the data into CATIA. (See Figure 4-20.)

External Envelope. Digital modeling by the subcontractors was, in the case of Zahner, based on CATIA, whereas Architectural Skylight employed their proprietary, object-based environment but were able to exchange data with the CATIA model efficiently. Zahner's team had extensive CATIA modeling capabilities. Starting from the geometry, the framing, and the pattern model, they employed the digital 3-D model from detailed design development through to production and installation. Once the approximate shape of the exterior envelope had been defined, Gehry's office employed physical cardboard models to simplify the overall geometry into a series of ruled surfaces that could be built more readily. (See Figures 4-21 and 4-22.)

Once the geometry model showed the revised ruled geometry, the office modeled the studs in the framing model along the ruling lines of the exterior envelope. Initially Gehry's team had conceived the envelope as a stick-built construction. Zahner, on the other hand, proposed a highly prefabricated approach and developed a sandwich panel that could be clipped onto the edge of the concrete slab. This solution was eventually pursued. Zahner's team subdivided the architect's geometry and pattern models and extracted the individual ruled surface patches for each prefabricated panel. These panel files were then no longer associated

through parent-child relationships to the architect's model. Zahner's team positioned intermediate stiffeners along the ruling lines by locating the isoparms of the surface patches. Most of the sheet metal was fabricated on punch presses. A CATIA workstation, set up on the shop floor, allowed shop personnel to easily obtain additional dimensions as needed during the fabrication.

Architectural Skylight's (ACS) approach differed significantly. This company employs an object-oriented modeling approach based on AutoCAD, and the digital model, through certain intermediate steps, is then directly used for the manufacturing of parts. ACS first imported the CATIA pattern model via IGES files into their proprietary software environment.

For the curtain walls and skylights, the pattern model contained the centerline of the members along the exterior surface of the envelope (see Figure 4-23). The design and engineering team at Architectural Skylight created custom profiles that were then inserted into the 3-D wireframe model—these custom profiles were the extrusions designed and engineered specifically for this project. Cuts, holes, and all other features needed for manufacturing were created in the same 3-D model, thus resulting in a very detailed model that included all parts needed for the finished component. This large model needed to be transferred back to the main CATIA model for design coordination. The steel detailing file format SDNF (Steel Detailing Neutral File) was chosen, because it resulted in manageable file formats since it did not include the same level of detail as the fabrication model at Architectural Skylight. The library of profiles could be converted into an equivalent CATIA library—on importing the ACS model, CATIA automatically retrieved the correct sections and built the 3-D model of the component. Along with the 3-D

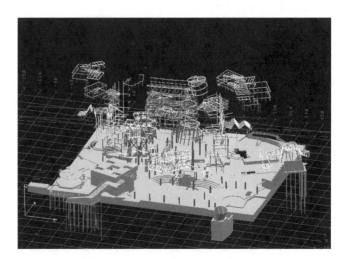

Figure 4-20 Highly curved elements were constructed in steel—shown in the CATIA steel part model. Some concrete elements are shown for reference. (Source: Gehry Partners, LLP)

Figure 4-21 The façade panels were prefabricated and connected to brackets that were bolted to the edge of the concrete slab. Some panels included openings, and panels generally followed developable shapes. (Sources: A and B: Image courtesy of A. Zahner Company, used with permission. C: Shiro Matsushima)

model, ACS also sent 2-D detail drawings, so the shop-drawing phase was both digitally and paper-based.

Mechanical Systems. Most of the mechanical system was designed in 2-D environments, but the 3-D CATIA model was extensively used to coordinate the routing of ducts, pipes, and wiring. The associate architect Cannon Design directly employed the CATIA model to lay out certain rain drainpipes.

Site Work. To transfer reference points of the CATIA model to the construction site, a multilevel system running several software programs was set up (see Figure 4-24). The system allowed 3-D points derived from the CATIA model to be ultimately located in the x-, y-, z-coordinate system on-site. The 3-D model was first sliced and cut at the desired level or plane in order to generate a 2-D section profile. Coordinates of this 2-D geometry could be transferred through AutoCAD into the surveying software Eagle Point. From here coordinate points were transferred to a system called Survey Link in order to convert the data into a format recog-

nizable by the site surveying system. A total station's laser surveying system and a Tripod Data System of wireless handheld computers in the field enabled any point to be located accurately in the field, or alternatively to feed as-built conditions back into the CATIA model. This approach proved extremely useful here because it enabled the façade contractor to design the façade according to the as-built rather than the as-designed conditions.

IT Structure and Project Management

All CATIA and AutoCAD files were kept and managed through a central FTP site to which the architects, engineers, and Beacon Skanska had access. Chronologically ordered folders were created for each issue of documents. Beacon Skanska also set up a local area network (LAN) in their extensive site office. Here, two members of the associate architect CannonDesign would permanently work, and members of Gehry's office joined them occasionally for shorter periods of time. Beacon Skanska was responsible for uploading the most recent drawings from the FTP site onto the site server, making

Figure 4-22 With the base panels in place, the stainless steel rainscreen cladding was mounted. Each metal sheet was numbered, and many had individual shapes.

sure that everybody worked from the latest digital models and drawings. (See Figure 4-25.)

The client, MIT, also hosted a commercial extranet (Citadon), the central clearinghouse for questions and memos that also included access to the various documents issued to the FTP site. It helped coordinate communication between the client's representatives, the architects, the engineers, and the construction manager. Subcontractors did not have direct access to this site; instead, Beacon Skanska set up a separate FTP site to communicate with the subcontractors.

The project team also employed a CATIA-integrated visualization tool called 4D Navigator in addition to the 3-D CATIA model and the 2-D drawings in AutoCAD. This environment enabled fly-through simulations, the visualization of construction stages, and simple markup and annotations; it did not allow for the modification of data.

BMW Pavilions

Architect Bernhard Franken (in a joint venture with ABB Architekten, Frankfurt, Germany) has designed and built several pavilions for Germany's BMW car

company, each time collaborating with Harald Kloft and his team of structural engineers at the Office of Bollinger & Grohmann GmbH (see Figure 4-26). All BMW commissions resulted from winning architectural competitions. These pavilions were used to display BMW models at international automobile fairs. Aspects of three pavilions are presented in this case study, with a general introduction to the design approach and a project-specific description of how digital design supported CNC fabrication techniques. As a main form-finding tool, Franken uses Maya, an animation program initially developed for the filmmaking industry. During the design development and design for production phases, the architects employ a mix of CAD tools that include Rhinoceros, CATIA, and AutoCAD.

Design Approach

Franken's approach to design is strongly driven by an interest in techniques of digital shape definition using animation software. The design process usually starts with a briefing, during which questions of program and the desired marketing messages are discussed with the client. The design team then tries to translate the client's marketing approach into the starting point for the dynamic form-finding process in Maya. In the example of the "Bubble"—a small pavilion designed for the 1999 International Motor Show in Frankfurt—BMW's concept of the hydrogen-powered car led the designers to experiment with the shape of water drops. Franken's team generated the final shape by simulating the merging of two water drops in Maya (see Figure 4-27).

The pavilion for the 2000 auto show in Geneva, Switzerland, again took the BMW hydrogen technology as an architectural theme. A wave was generated by simulating impulses on a water surface. This pavilion was to be installed inside an existing listed building, so the enclosing geometry provided additional parameters in the final shaping of the design. The design of the 2001 Frankfurt BMW pavilion was derived from the simulation of Doppler effects of a car driving through a matrix of parallel lines. To add a place-specific component, the designers also brought the built context of this much larger pavilion as a shaping parameter in the Maya model. The different volumes of adjacent buildings were translated into force fields that distorted the initially regular shape into a curved form. The final geometry represented both the dynamics of driving and a satisfying response to the architectural context; it was referred to as the "Dynaform."

An intense collaboration with engineers and fabricators begins once the master geometry is defined by the architects. During design development and construction, all members of the design team need to refer to this geometry as the governing shape for all design

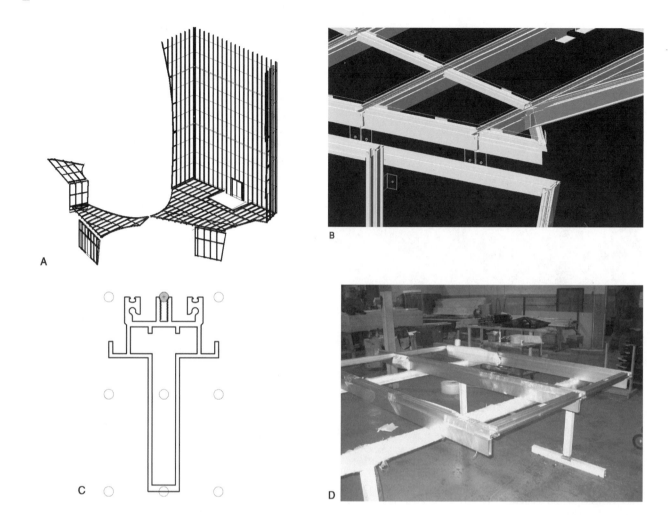

Figure 4-23 Curtain wall design and manufacturing for the MIT Stata Center. (A) 3-D overall model using an object-oriented modeling approach. (B) Detail of the same model. (C) Custom mullion designed and extruded for the project, with CATIA reference marker highlighted. (D) Assembly of curtain wall segment in the shop. (Source: Architectural Skylight Co., Inc.)

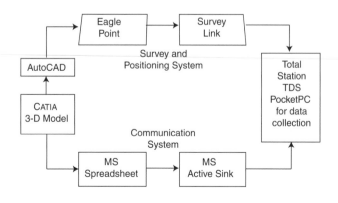

Figure 4-24 Data flow using the 3-D model to support site work (adapted from Matsushima, S.: Collaboration in Architectural Design: An IT Perspective. Thesis, Harvard University, 2003).

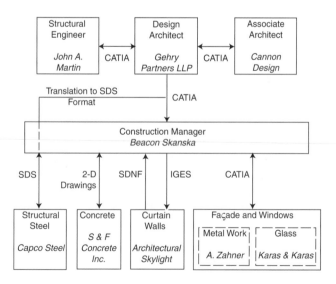

Figure 4-25 IT structure of the Stata Center (adapted from Matsushima, S.: Collaboration in Architectural Design: An IT Perspective. Thesis, Harvard University, 2003)

Figure 4-26 The BMW pavilion "Bubble" for the 1999 trade fair show in Frankfurt. (Source: Fritz Busam)

work. Alterations as may be desired to optimize the structural or other systems are generally not permitted.

Design to Manufacturing: "The Bubble," Frankfurt, 1999

The complex shape of the building was imported from Maya into the CAD programs Rhino and CATIA. The structural engineers performed finite-element analysis to predict the structural behavior of the pavilion, and to determine the thickness and grade of the acrylic to be used. Over 300 individual acrylic sheets were derived from the master model.

The designers had initially designed the pavilion to be constructed entirely of acrylic sheets as the primary load-bearing structure, glued together off-site and lifted in place with a helicopter. A full-size mock-up was produced to test assembly procedures and evaluate the structural integrity of the envisaged construction. This

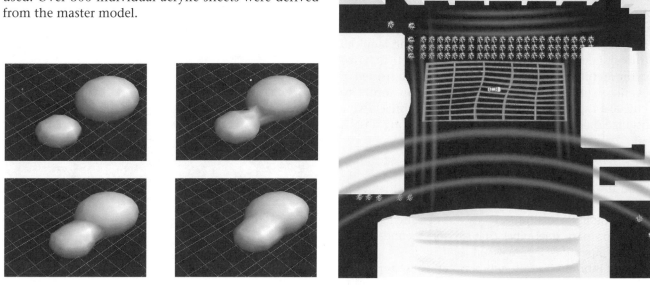

Figure 4-27 Digital form finding for Franken's BMW pavilions: In both cases, Maya software was used to simulate forces that, in an iterative process, would deform the initial shape into the desired geometry. (Source: A: ABB Architekten; B: ABB Architekten/Bernhard Franken)

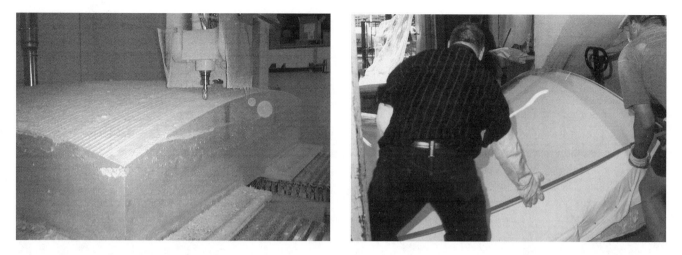

Figure 4-28 Molds for thermoforming the acrylic sheets were shaped on a large CNC milling machine. (Source: Bernhard Franken)

mock-up revealed difficulties in the adhesive connection between sheets and problems in the timing of this procedure. Only six weeks before the opening of the pavilion, the design team decided to abandon the idea of a load-bearing acrylic surface structure and introduce an eggcrate-like system of supporting aluminum ribs. The acrylic sheets needed to be formed from flat sheets into the doubly curved shapes that accurately fit the network of aluminum ribs. The NC code for the milling toolpaths were generated from the CATIA models of the individual sheets. Polyurethane foam molds could be CNC-milled and the sheets, heated to 150 to 160°C, were formed over these molds. Each mold was used several times, each time shaped once more to represent yet another individually shaped acrylic sheet. After the forming process the edges of the sheets were trimmed on the same CNC machine. (See Figures 4-28 and 4-29.)

The geometry of the ribs was generated by intersecting the complex surface of the Bubble with an orthogonal system of planes. The resulting intersection lines were offset toward the inside to provide the required structural depth. The ribs were CNC water-jet-cut based on the architect's model geometry. Each rib consisted of several segments, joined with bolted lap joints to achieve a rigid structural shape. The acrylic sheets were installed on-site over the aluminum supporting ribs.

Design to Manufacturing: "The Wave," Geneva, 2000

As an interior trade fair stand, the structural issues in the Wave were less demanding. The curved skin that covers the BMW exhibition area was designed as a system of primary steel pipes that support secondary aluminum pipes. (See Figure 4-30.)

A membrane is stretched between these pipes. All pipe sections are curved in two directions, thus posing a complex manufacturing challenge. The digital model

of the primary steel pipes was adjusted such that each pipe was subdivided into up to 100 segments. These segments were curved in only one direction and could be easily manufactured on a CNC pipe-bending machine. Individual pipe sections were aligned according to the digital model on a variety of jigs. Segments were then welded together to form the overall complex spatial curve of the main steel pipe. (See Figure 4-31.)

A different process was chosen for the aluminum pipes which, since smaller in diameter and less stiff, were CNC-bent only in one direction. The curvature in the second direction could be achieved during the installation by simply forcing the aluminum pipes into place on-site. This process was only possible because the secondary pipes generally have a pronounced curvature in one direction and much less curvature in the second. (See Figure 4-32.) With the metal skeleton in

Figure 4-29 The mock-up assembly with its temporary support structure made from plywood. (Source: Bollinger & Grohmann)

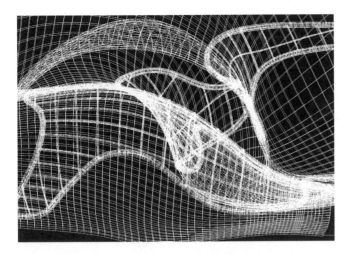

Figure 4-30 The structural engineer's geometry model was ultimately used to drive CNC pipe-bending machines. (Source: Bollinger & Grohmann)

place the prefabricated (CNC-cut) membrane segments could be connected to the custom-designed nodes on the structural framework.

Design to Manufacturing: "Dynaform," Frankfurt, 2001

In the case of the Dynaform it was clear from the beginning that its master geometry did not lend itself to serve as a structural surface. Instead, the design team chose to create a steel frame structure over which a membrane could be stretched. The frames were derived from the digital form-finding model in Maya. Intersecting planes were set up according to the line matrix used earlier in the shape animations. (See Figures 4-33 and 4-34.)

The exterior shape was offset and the intersection lines between the offset surface and the planes found. The exterior member follows the master geometry, while the interior member represents a reversal of this geometry. Both members are connected at regular intervals, and the system works structurally as a Vierendeel frame.

The steel contractor, Seele GmbH & Co. KG, commissioned an external engineering office to provide the final construction documents and digital shop drawings that would be used to generate the machine code for the fabrication of the steel frames. All frames were designed with hollow square and rectangular members according to Bollinger & Grohmann's structural specifications. The curved sides of members were cut on a CNC plasma cutter—the cutting cost was calculated by volume, and there was no cost penalty for cutting many individual shapes. (See Figure 4-35.) The inner and outer flanges of the member were bent to the required radius and manually welded to the curved side pieces. Despite the extensive use of digital design tools, 2-D paper drawings were still needed. Workers in the

Figure 4-31 Pipe segments were CNC-bent and welded together into the doubly curved members. (Sources: A, C, D: Harald Kloft; B: Bernhard Franken)

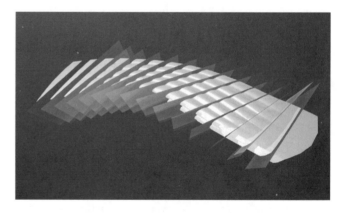

Figure 4-33 Rendering of the scheme during the conceptual design phase. (Source: ABB Architekten/Bernhard Franken)

Figure 4-32 Once the bent-pipe structure was assembled, the membrane could be stretched over it to provide the enclosing surface. The lower image shows a similar project in Munich. (Source: A: Harald Kloft; B: Bollinger & Grohmann)

Figure 4-34 (A) Planes intersecting with the envelope; (B) defined the shapes of the structural frames. (Source: A: ABB Architekten/Bernhard Franken; B: Bollinger & Grohmann)

shop and on-site did not necessarily have access to the digital models, and ultimately over 5,000 paper drawings were necessary to deliver a complete description sufficient for fabrication and installation.

The outer skin of the pavilion can be understood as a lofted shape with changing cross sections—the frames discussed previously. The geometry of the Dynaform is unusual for a membrane surface, since it is only single-curved—as opposed to the typical membrane structures that are always doubly curved with principal curves in opposite directions. The membrane specialist Viktor Wilhelm was commissioned for the detailed design of the skin. To faithfully follow the master geometry, the architects did not accept any double curvature in the skin, as it would visibly deviate from the smooth shape present in the Maya model. Instead, Wilhelm designed

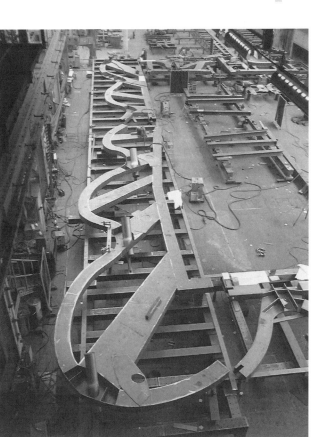

Figure 4-35 Fabrication of the steel Vierendeel frames. (Source: Harald Kloft)

all membrane segments to be single-curved, necessitating very high prestressing forces in the order of 8 kilonewton per meter. The membranes were CNC-cut and welded to form larger fabric segments. Over 8,000 steel connectors were needed to tension the membrane between the steel frames. A full-size mock-up of one bay with two structural frames and the membrane served as a test for assembly procedures and also ensured that the desired smooth visual appearance of the skin was achievable. (See Figure 4-36.) The pavilion was delivered just in time for the motor show (see Figures 4-37 and 4-38).

Figure 4-36 The full-size mock-up demonstrated that the system was feasible and produced the desired smooth surface. (Source: Harald Kloft)

Figure 4-37 Specialists connected successive bays of membranes to the steel frames on-site. (Source: A. Covertex; B. Harald Kloft)

Figure 4-38 The finished pavilion opened just in time for the 2001 trade fair. (Source: Harald Kloft)

The Esplanade: Theaters on the Bay, Singapore

The competition for the Singapore performing arts center "Esplanade" was won in 1992 as a joint entry of London-based Michael Wilford and Partners (MWP) and local architect DP Architects. The project houses a 2,000-seat concert hall and a 1,600-seat theater arranged to connect to a public concourse space. The performance spaces are complemented by the necessary back-of-the-house, practice, and administrative facilities. Both large performance spaces are regular, rectilinear volumes that are each enclosed with a unifying, complexly shaped envelope, the part of the project that this text focuses on. The minimum size and proportions of these two envelopes are dictated by the height and shape of the large theater with its fly towers and the auditorium with its reverberation chamber.

Shaping the Envelopes

The architects wanted the envelopes of the two main volumes to be as transparent as possible, to enable views toward the ocean, and, at night, allow a reading of the enclosed volumes of the theater and the concert

Figure 4-39 The early model still shows a flat area in the center of each envelope. The shape was eventually changed to a more evenly curved geometry. (Source: Vikas M Gore, DP Architects Ptc Ltd)

Figure 4-40 Rendering of the sunshade elements. (Source: Vikas M Gore, DP Architects Pte Ltd)

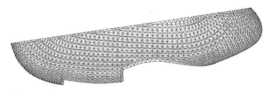

Figure 4-41 Final space frame geometry. (Source: MERO, Dr. Sanchez for the grid design)

hall (see Figure 4-39). The tropical climate dictated an efficient sunshading strategy, and the architects sought to combine vernacular and natural sources in its design. Two engineering teams were brought in to complement the design team for the development of these structures, Atelier One as structural engineers and Atelier Ten as environmental engineers and façade consultants, both based in London. The iterative design process of envelope shape and sunshading system was greatly facilitated by the fact that both DPA and Atelier Ten used the same CAD package for design—Bentley's MicroStation. This common platform enabled the team members to exchange native drawing files without losing data because of file conversion problems. The

design team investigated several types of sunshades and eventually settled on a mesh system that supported triangulated metal sheets as sun protection. The mesh had sides of constant length. Any curved geometry would consequently distort the mesh, resulting in mesh openings varying between square to rhomboid sections, in the manner familiar from industrially produced kitchen sieves.

Seeing the geometric possibilities of the mesh, the design team explored new shapes for the overall envelopes. In an early design proposal the envelopes had been rather regular shapes, with flat surfaces as cap. The architects, in collaboration with the engineering offices, used 3-D NURBS (Nonuniform Rational B-Splines) surfaces in MicroStation to shape the two large spaces.

Different envelope shapes would also impact the orientation and size of the sunshading elements. Studies of the overall shapes were thus always informed by the engineer's sunshade mapping on the façade. Eventually the team decided on an irregularly curved geometry with a relatively flat upper portion and smoothly curved sides (See Figure 4-40.) A diagonal element was added to the mesh pattern, resulting in an overall triangulation of the surface that could be built from flat sheets of glass. Because of the irregular geometry, approximately 5,000 different triangles were needed to describe both envelopes. The two main enclosure volumes are at an angle to each other and orientated differently with respect to the sun's path. The structural grid—being closely associated to the sunshading strategy—consequently takes on a different orientation on each of the two main volumes.

Design Development

Initially the structure of the envelope was designed as a single-layered welded steel structure, with tubes of 200 to 250 mm diameter. Several companies tendered for

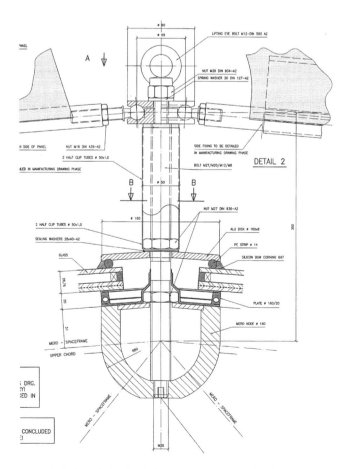

Figure 4-42 Mero's detail solution uses the outer cord of the space frame as support for the glazing. (Source: MERO)

Figure 4-43 The appearance of the building intentionally evokes cultural and natural references of Southeast Asia. (Source: Vikas M Gore Architects Ptc Ltd)

the construction of the envelope, and Mero GmbH & Co. KG was awarded the bid because of the significant cost savings they offered. The company proposed to replace the single-layered tubular grid structure with a three-dimensional space frame consisting of much smaller steel members. Apart from a significant cost advantage, there were a number of other factors that favored the Mero system. Smaller member sizes meant that the space frame was visually lighter, thus enhancing the architectural notion of transparency. Eliminating on-site welding and relying heavily on prefabrication was also expected to decrease tolerances and improve the overall construction quality. (See Figures 4-41 and 4-42.)

The geometry of the space frame now needed to be generated based on the shape supplied by the architects. Mero uses proprietary software to design and analyze space frames, and for the Esplanade project the company wrote a translator program to allow the import of the envelope geometry (MicroStation) into this system. All mesh edges were fixed to a length of 1.5 m, with angles between these bars varying to accommodate the curvature present. The second, inner layer of the space frame was generated at an offset of 0.9 m to the outer surface.

Mero's design-to-manufacturing process of systemized space frames is highly integrated. A single software environment is used for design and analysis, and this same software allows the optimization of frame members with respect to their structural requirements. Bar sizes for the Esplanade envelopes ranged between 48.3 mm and 88.9 mm in diameter; these bars connect to nodes that vary between 110 mm and 200 mm in diameter.

During the generation of the final geometry, all nodes and connecting bars were color-coded—the same color coding eventually helped to organize production, transport, and assembly procedures on-site. The envelopes consist of a total of 8,300 nodes and 34,500 bar elements. The outer cord of the space frame was rectangular in cross section in order to directly support the enclosing glass panes on custom gaskets. Since the system could accommodate a 2.5-mm tolerance for the glass, the number of individually sized glass sheets was reduced to approximately 1,500. (See Figure 4-43.)

Manufacturing and Construction. Mero's design and analysis software is devised to generate all data needed for manufacturing. The highly automated process of translating geometry and cross-sectional data to CNC-machining centers via various post-processors enables the production of individual nodes and bars without differences in bar or node sizes impacting the economics of the manufacturing process. Each node is machined individually from forged steel blanks on a CNC machine, and the bars are prepared on equally automated CNC equipment from standard-size structural tube sections.

CHAPTER 5

Architectural Elements and Components

The exploration of architectural form and the reshaping of individual building components has been greatly facilitated by the application of computer-aided design, engineering, and manufacturing activities. Digital collaboration between architects and fabricators has changed the nature of shop drawings, and CNC technologies have raised issues of craft while expanding the potential for the design of building components.

Various models of digital design collaboration with fabricators have transformed the conventional sequence of design, construction contract documentations, bidding shop drawing, and fabrication. Historically, the shop drawing process began after the signing of the construction contract between the general contractor and the component fabricator and supplier. Through the drafted shop drawings, the fabricator translated and reinterpreted a designer's intentions to take advantage of each fabricator's expertise and machinery. Prepared by drafters familiar with the fabrication process, these shop drawings most closely depicted the final component design.

A master model illustrates the overall 3-D geometry of building forms and spaces, while an element model consists of numerous 3-D modeled components, describing each part's fabricated shape in detail. Individual part models can be integrated with their CNC fabrication codes and instructions, and associated with material and installation specifications, part identification, and pricing. Increasingly, design can be parametrically modeled to retain key parameters and relations, while facilitating rapid design modifications. CAD/CAM technologies are used as improved fabrication tools. More significantly, they can lead to changing the roles of designer and fabricator and the nature of collaboration.

The following case studies illustrate various approaches to digital design and fabrication: complexly curved glass panels and titanium partitions for Condé Nast by Gehry Partners with Permasteelisa, C-Tek, and TriPyramid; cast steel glazing fasteners by TriPyramid for BMW Headquarters designed by Albert Kahn Associates; and a barrel-vaulted skylight and suspended glazing supports designed by Rafael Viñoly

Architects collaborating with Dewhurst Macfarlane with Goldreich Engineering, Architectural Skylights, and TriPyramid. These studies illustrate the incremental innovative nature of design collaboration with digital technologies.

5.1 CONDÉ NAST EMPLOYEE CAFETERIA

At the Condé Nast employee cafeteria, Gehry Partners realized compound-curved glass panels and titanium partitions with unprecedented geometric complexity and precision. This was achieved through the use of digital design and fabrication tools in collaboration with fabricators. "The cafeteria project represented, due to its interior nature, the first time that we developed compound-curved glass panels and found someone who was willing to work with us to succeed at it."[1] (See Figure 5-1.)

The design responded to the client's demand for a " . . . dramatic space in which the identity of the various independent magazines owned by the Condé Nast could be blended by creating a group identity that

Figure 5-1 Condé Nast Employee Cafeteria's interior view. (Source: Photo reproduced with permission from Condé Nast Publications)

everyone would want to be a part of."[2] The 8,000-square-foot design created intimate dining alcoves and islands surrounded by 52 hanging complexly curved glass panels in the cafeteria, and 25 frosted glass panels in the private dining rooms (see Figure 5-2). Made of ¾-inch-thick compound-curved clear laminated float glass, the panels varied in height from 11 to 16 feet, and in width from 3 to 5 feet.[3] In addition, curved titanium panels were introduced in the interiors, extending through the adjacent corridors.

Design Modeling

Gehry Partners' design process integrated physical and digital modeling, repeated through numerous iterations until a precisely controlled 3-D design was finalized. The physical modeling allowed for rapid sculpting and form making in a tactile and physical environment. The digitized model served as a surface controller to translate the rough physical form into precise, smooth digital surfaces. The scaled mock-ups, fabricated from the 3-D digital model, facilitated detail evaluation and refinement. From CATIA, 2-D data was transferred into AutoCAD; building sections were gen-

erated to build larger-scale mock-up studies that were later translated into construction drawings. The physical mock-up was an important means for studying the design, materials, and methods,[4] while the space and form of the interiors was refined and confirmed in a final master model designed in CATIA. This surface geometry model became the design reference for each respective fabricator and installer.

Conceptually, the forms of curved glass and titanium panels evolved from the Gehry team's understanding of the proposed materials and methods of working. Based on past experience, the Gehry team had an understanding of the proposed risks, costs, and design potential of developing the large complexly curved glass as well as the titanium panels in a high-tech CAD/CAM environment. To ensure successful execution, a low-tech backup execution plan for these components was also devised as an alternative to the proposed CAD/CAM glazing design.

In our office we always try to develop at least two methods for getting a job done. In this case our high-tech method included using computer-aided machining to make molds for the glass, while the low-tech method included taking the 3D digital

Figure 5-2 Design phase model for Condé Nast interiors. (Source: Courtesy Gehry Partners, LLP)

information and transferring the data manually in [a] more hands-on approach.[5]

Gehry's team's consulted directly with fabricators such as C-Tek, from design development stage through fabrication and installation.

Detail Mock-up and Development

The architect and the fabricators explored numerous design options, led by the Gehry team's vision. Permasteelisa was invited to develop the titanium wall and coordinate the geometries of the spaces and components. TriPyramid mocked up and tested numerous stainless steel fasteners to suspend and stabilize the curved glass panels being researched by C-Tek.

The Gehry team combined hand sketches and models with 3-D computer models and 2-D computer drawings. Full-scale mock-ups were created during the design phase to study and test the various materials, fabrication, and installation complications. This extended the time frame for design experimentation. Based on the refinements gleaned from the mock-up studies, a 3-D master surface model was issued to the collaborators (see Figure 5-3). It modeled the titanium panels, floating glass panels, curved seating alcoves, and sculpted ceiling. The surface geometries provided each fabricator with the data needed to model individual elements and components, as well as the basis to develop the necessary substructure and assemblies in sufficient detail for their fabrication. A mock-up of these building elements was tested during the design development or construction document phases, allowing the test results to inform the refinement of components for production.

Curved Titanium Wall Panels

The titanium panels, each modeled in tightly curved ruled surfaces, were joined along their 3-D curved edges (see Figure 5-4). The small and highly articulated curves demanded a geometrically complex corner joint and higher level of precision than previously achieved. During design, both nonruled and ruled curved surfaces were considered. The added complexity and expense for nonruled surfaces led to a decision favoring ruled surfaces for the titanium panels. In contrast to the large scale curved walls of Bilbao, the Condé Nast metal curved walls and the ceiling's small and intimate scale's tight curves and precise panel detail joinery presented a new opportunity for the collaborating team of Gehry and Permasteelisa.

> By involving Permasteelisa in the development of the panel, and having a direct line of communication between the architect and the fabricator, fostered early tests of the means and methods of fabrication and assembly. The surface CATIA model was used by Permasteelisa to study the geometry of the walls and ceiling to anticipate the difficult areas of fabrication and construction. This master model became the basis for geometric coordination between various component fabricators and the site geometry. This allow[ed] the diverse parts to be prefabricated off-site, and reconfirm their fit on-site.[6]

Permasteelisa took the lead in supplying thousands of coordination points for the project, translating the architect's geometric model, identifying key displacement points for on-site installation, and updating them for the fabricating team throughout the process. Per-

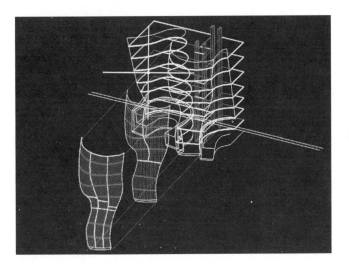

Figure 5-3 Titanium panel geometry shape model in CAD. (Source: Courtesy Gehry Partners, LLP)

Figure 5-4 Installed titanium panel, cut from a single sheet, curved ruled surfaces, with 3-D panel joints. (Source: Photo reproduced with permission from Condé Nast Publications)

masteelisa determined the shape of the single curved sheet, cut and shaped to form.

A pattern for the titanium sheets was then developed through physical models and then refined in Catia. Each sheet is different, and almost every edge of every sheet has some curve in it. This would have been impossible if we didn't believe that our computer information was going to be used to cut the titanium sheets directly through CAD/CAM technologies. Our digital files were sent directly to Permasteelisa, who cut the titanium sheets with a laser-cutting machine.[7]

The titanium panels are layered with perforated panels and acoustic substrates, set over a subframe assembly of horizontal ribs spaced every 18 inches, transferring the load back to a series of vertical structural supports. The titanium panel assembly was held to a 1/32-inch tolerance, with a minimum corner clip detail. This precision was only possible working with the digital model and CNC machinery. Alberto de Gobbi of Permasteelisa recalled:

It is important to note that the computer does not do it all. It is a tool, essential to design, but it only works when you go back and forth with the manual, the samples, the mock-ups and the digital model.[8]

Each titanium panel was cut from 4.5-feet-by-9-feet titanium sheets, perforated and shaped. The titanium was riveted and high-bonding taped onto the substrate and clamped with steel wires hooked into the panel backs, attached over a Teflon pressure plate. Each panel was joined by a corner clip, formed to match the three-dimensional curves, allowing the bends in each panel to engage each other, forming a tight connection.

Compound Curved Glazing

C-Tek consulted with the Gehry team and confirmed the feasibility of the glass shape and form. Each glass panel dimensioned approximately 4 feet, 6 inches by 9 feet. It thus demanded a highly customized glass fabrication process with a high degree of precision.

As an example of technology transfer, C-Tek translated its predominant work in the fabrication of windshields and custom automotive bodies to architectural applications. By using a large-scale CNC milling machine, they were able to produce the necessary mold for the two layers of slumped 3/8-inch glass, laminated with a liquid resin. A 3-D digital model of each of the glass panels with fastener hole locations was further modeled by Gehry's team and coordinated with the fabrication team. The surface models were transferred digitally to C-Tek. (See Figure 5-5.)

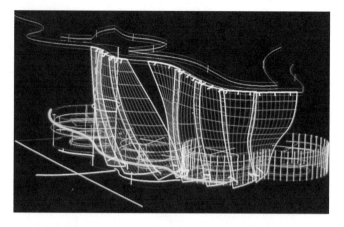

Figure 5-5 Compound curved glass panel CAD model. (Source: Courtesy Gehry Partners, LLP)

The curved panel forms were then translated to direct the CNC milling of the formwork for glass. C-Tek experimented with various methods of articulation and pressure application to produce a 100 percent continuous mold, with a high degree of accuracy, to 5/1,000 of an inch. C-Tek changed their large ovens to accommodate the large Condé Nast glass panels.[9]

To achieve a suspended expression of the glass panels, holes along the top for suspension and along the bottom edges were specialized. The holes are high-stress load transfer points, typically made with high-strength tempered glass. Because of the nature of the glass form, tempering of this glass with holes was not possible. C-Tek was able to fabricate the annealed glass panels with the required holes, located at 1/8-inch dimensional tolerance along the curved surfaces. Working closely with the architect and TriPyramid, the support of these panels and the detail characteristics of the holes were studied in mock-ups to find an optimum solution for the least visible means of support. (See Figure 5-6.)

Numerous revisions of the detailing of the glass supports and testing of the glazed panel mockup led to modification that eliminated glass failure while retaining the design intent. At that point, the glass panels were able to be individually made. C-Tek then aided the shipping and installation procedure by using the digital

Figure 5-6 Glass panel. (Source: Photo-Kimo Griggs LLP)

surface model to design and fabricate a 3-D steel support frame for each unique glass panel.

Stainless Steel Glazing Support

TriPyramid fabricated the glass connectors and developed them together with Gehry's design team during the design phase. Based on previous details at Bilbao, a top and bottom connector system was conceived to suspend the glass panels from above and brace them at the bottom. This scheme resulted in holes on the glass panels, each unique in its curve and displacement.

> The location of the holes in the glass was done in the Catia glass surface model, along with the connector locations on the walls. The location coordinates were transferred to AutoCad, and were then printed out for use at the site by the survey team to locate all the connectors. A similar process was used to set the curving walls as well as other building components within the Condé Nast project.[10]

Based on the design geometry and support points, TriPyramid further detailed and engineered the connectors and supports. The CATIA 3-D model allowed the engineer to run finite element analysis directly from the model, saving substantial CAD time. With frequent design discussions between the architectural and fabrication teams, a design was finalized and a full-scale mock-up was made to allow for potential glass installers to test-hang pieces of glass.[11]

> The four or five eventual mock-ups provided information on the glass panels, and proved crucial. Some panels worked well and proved very durable, while others cracked almost instantly. This led to further development of the connector to resolve the problems of glass cracking at the top-hole locations. The cracking was caused not by the vertical load as might be expected, but by a moment induced in the glass by the coupling of the connection point to the glass surface. TriPyramid resolved this glitch in the final mock-up.[12]

The full-scale mock-ups tested the connectors, allowing the team to reassess and redesign the detail to successfully support not only the loading of the glass panel but its installation and possible in situ movements.

> The original connector detailed a bracket with pivot point outside of the plane of the glass, with limited dimensional flexibility and adjustment. Its mockup yielded excessive stress; the glass hole cracked at the suspension holes, necessitating a redesign.[13]

The failures prompted redesign efforts. Randy Jefferson, from the Gehry team, suggested the repositioning of the spherical ball joint in the plane of the glass, thus reducing out-of-plane stresses at the glass holes (see Figure 5-7). This allowed the movement of the glass panels to tip in and out of the plane pivoted at the ball joint, suspending the panels from the top holes. Meanwhile the bottom holes were designed to provide substantial movement and cushioned against impact loading from use. (See Figure 5-8.)

This collaborative design, mock-up, test, and refinement process benefited from frequent discussions amongst the architect, engineer, and fabricators. The coordination for the site installation of the concealed supports, the stainless steel connectors, the glass panels, and the concealing ceiling and bench claddings benefited a great deal from the digital model, allowing all forms and connections to be updated and revised as the details of the building components and their assemblies underwent testing and revisions throughout the detail design and construction document process.

Fabricators' Collaboration

The Gehry team maintained extensive dialogue with the fabricators and builders from early design to completion. Often confronted with a construction industry hesitant to try out new means of fabrication and building, they engage collaborators interested in exploring new forms and technology. The team shares the goal of striving for a new level of expertise in the use of digital tools in design, fabrication, and on-site building.[14] "It was such a team effort where we could propose an idea, they would take the idea and really run with it and then bring it back to us. It was really a dialogue. But we always brought our initial idea to the table: Okay, here is how we think we should start this thing—what do you guys think?"[15]

Many of the collaborators for the Condé Nast project echo Tim Eliassen's view of the digital medium's value for collaboration. "The benefit of the digital environment is that it fosters collaboration. It does not replace collaboration in any way, shape or means."[16]

> Fundamentally, any worthwhile design and manufacturing project is a collaboration amongst a large number of people, which is something young architects can miss, thinking the computer alone can get them from here all the way to there. That was never possible, and it is no more possible now, especially if you want to do special things.[17]

The use of a digital medium fosters a more dynamic and more precise means for collaborators to share data. Each fabricator worked off the same master model to develop his or her complementary systems of assemblies. This facilitated updates and revisions, transmitted and coordinated through various phases. Mercier noted:

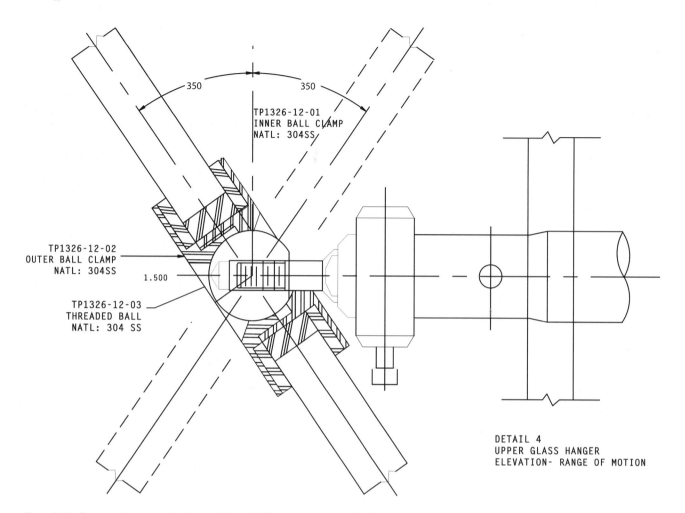

350   350

TP1326-12-01
INNER BALL CLAMP
NATL: 304SS

TP1326-12-02
OUTER BALL CLAMP
NATL: 304SS

1.500

TP1326-12-03
THREADED BALL
NATL: 304 SS

DETAIL 4
UPPER GLASS HANGER
ELEVATION- RANGE OF MOTION

Figure 5-7 Glass panel support detail from TriPyramid. (Source: Courtesy Gehry Partners, LLP)

The use of the computer as a design tool is quite restricted in our office. It is used to refine and control the design, which is created and checked in physical models made in the workshop. The computer acts as a manager, if you will, helping to build the project by pulling together the loosely set parameters of the various physical models through digitizing, surface modeling and building coordination. We use the computer to set limits, provide accuracy and ensure that our physical design models hold together—at the same time providing a complete set of 3-dimensional information for everyone from consultants to contractors to subcontractors.[18]

The collaborators' ability to transmit and share data through the digital design and fabrication process sponsors greater complexity with precision and timeliness.

Our office believes strongly that, in the near future, the construction industry will be revamping itself to better utilize the advantages that computer technology is already providing. We push forward in every project we do to encourage contractors to find ways to use our digital information directly in their manufacturing processes.[19]

Successful collaborations foster continued collaborators' development from project to project. A framework for experimentation is thus developed to enable this incremental innovation process to be supported within the context of a building commission.

5.2 KIMMEL CENTER FOR THE PERFORMING ARTS

The Kimmel Center for the Performing Arts, designed by Rafael Viñoly Architects, houses a 2,500-seat concert hall and a recital theater for the Philadelphia Philharmonic Symphony and other performing arts groups. The smaller theater, its layout inspired by that of a cello, has a revolving stage to accommodate flexible configurations for dance, drama, and opera performances.[20] A nine-story-tall skylight-clad barrel vault

for the engineer to study various structural options. They proposed a series of pre-cambered arches. The structural deflection and vibration analysis were generated to study the impact of its movement on the weather-tightness of the building envelope as well as its vibrations and acoustic ramifications.

> We used computer analysis extensively to determine the deflections under self-weight, and we actually provided that model to the steel fabricator so that they fabricated the members. The principle arches were fabricated to the pre-cambered curved shape—based on our computational deflection analysis.[21]

BLD of Canada modeled the steel structure in 3-D. The model details steel members and connection details. "They designated each structural member and added the reactions on them in order to design the end connections. The member geometry was then sent to the CNC-machines of the steel fabricators, where the steel was cut and drilled to close tolerances."[22] Each steel Vierendeel arch and end wall glazing design was digitally modeled for structural engineering. The steel arches measure 30 inches deep in sections spanning 160 feet. (See Figure 5-10.)

Each arch was "built in five sections: the first one was cantilevered up, the next one was braced off some temporary supports, and then a final one was the keystone that went in at the top."[23] The pre-cambered arches were built according to their own weight, and the anticipated skylight loading deflected the pre-cambered arch geometry into its theoretical geometry. This shape was anticipated via the use of digital simulation, allowing for a higher precision in the final installation of standardized skylight module dimensions.

Figure 5-8 Glass suspension detail above, and flexible bracing detail below. (Source: Courtesy Gehry Partners, LLP)

spans 187 feet by 350 feet, enclosing the performing arts complex and its large urban plaza in downtown Philadelphia. (See Figure 5-9.)

Conceptually, Viñoly proposed a highly transparent glass enclosure over the concert and theater halls. To achieve this intention, the architects worked with the engineering team of Dewhurst Mcfarlane and the fabricator Architectural Skylight to develop a barrel-vaulted Vierendeel-structure-supported skylight. To maximize its sense of lightness and transparency, the design and fabrication team strove to innovate a design with minimum structure. Cable-net-suspended mullionless glazing encloses both ends of the vaulted enclosure over the concert and theater halls. National Glass supplied the glazing installed with TriPyramid's steel glass fittings.

Structure and Cladding Design

The initial hand sketches from the architect, translated into a 3-D digital model, provided the master geometry

Figure 5-9 A computer rendering of the Kimmel Center at night. (Source: Rafael Viñoly Architects)

Figure 5-10 Steel Vierendeel barrel vault structural analysis, fabrication, and erection. (Source: Reproduced with permission from Dewhurst Macfarlane and Partners and Rafael Viñoly Architects, P.C.)

Skylight

The skylight was designed, engineered, and fabricated by Architectural Skylight. They are set up to produce vertically integrated digital CAD/CAM services for customized skylight assemblies. They offer Web-based "interactive skylight design online," allowing for a user-designed 3-D model that is intelligently associated with parts tracking and CNC milling and assembly instructions. They also integrate digital design with fabrication and material ordering functions to provide a digitally transformed fabrication process. For the Kimmel, the Architectural Skylight team proposed an innovative narrow-profile skylight system in a design-build contract.

The Kimmel barrel vault skylight consists approximately of 6,000 identical pieces of glass and 1,500 assemblies of unitized skylight system. They are high-strength structural silicone glazed on a series of arched ridges and valleys spanning 180 feet, in rows covering 380 feet. To achieve the aesthetic demanded by the architects, Architectural Skylight created customized extrusions to fit within 2 inches above the steel arches. The narrow-profile aluminum extrusions were five-axis-milled in their factory in Maine, and shipped in 7-feet-by-14-feet assemblies.

Each 6,000-pound arch segment was crane-lifted into place with its customized section in situ.[24] The prefabrication minimized site work while maximizing the factory prefabrication. The panels were installed in "overlapping shingles effect" with silicone field joint.[25] The assembly is detailed to accommodate for thermal expansion gap, customized valley, and ridge extrusions.

Architectural Skylights developed its own proprietary CAD/CAM software, integrating its engineering and fabrication operations. The skylight design is created in a 3-D model with associated database of each part's complete information and CNC machine language instructions. Its design layout is set up using centerline wireframes, before the full parts models are inserted into the assembly. The engineering department creates the assembly digitally; the model parts' database contains its corresponding operations to tap a hole, cut, drill, mill, notch, countersink, and perform other fabrication procedures. This database includes material supplies, bills of quantities, and referenced costing. It also contains instructions to installers. This digital operation fully incorporates all facets of their services, from concept design to installation completion. Its video capability shows the process simulation, illustrating details of each individual component graphically.

The program works with real-time operations, integrating changes parametrically with updated dialogue information. As each part is modeled, its fabrication plan routine is evaluated for toolpaths and nesting combinations. Its five-axis milling machine is capable of multiple parts work on 28-foot extrusions, making the operation more cost-effective. Each part is individually labeled and tracked in real time, from digital model to fabrication, shipping, and site installation. Each project's materials are ordered precisely to match the designated order generated from the program, thus minimizing the need to overstock. The program automatically optimizes material utilization and schedules the tooling and machining process to maximize efficiency.

For construction simulation, Architectural Skylight modeled the steel arches' deflection and digitally test-installed the skylight panels to confirm dimensional tolerances, comparing theoretical and actual deflections. The construction revealed joint dimensions to have varied only within 1/16 of an inch from the theoretical deflection.[26]

Glazing Fasteners

A suspended cable-net-supported glazing was designed using cast-steel weights suspended from stiffened arches to enclose the barrel-vaulted skylight space. The end wall glazing was engineered for "a system that allowed the glass to rotate between six degrees and nine degrees, and also to accommodate a lot of different sideways and vertical movements because of the curved shape."[27] The glazing was detailed to accept movement. A mock-up was assembled and tested at Architectural Testing Institute in York, Pennsylvania, prior to fabrication.

TriPyramid translated the architect's design intentions, addressing engineering and fabrication concerns. The design of the glazing fasteners began with the architect's sketches and developed its shape further in a 3-D AutoCAD model with greater precision.[28] Transmitted as a 3-D file, the detail CAD model could be dynamically evaluated, rotated, zoomed, and manipulated as needed by each of the collaborators. TriPyramid translated this detail model into a parametrically configured 3-D model, detailing each discrete component of the fitting assembly, evaluating its material, fabrication, and engineering concerns.

> SolidWorks allows us to parametrically change the model as we move along, and on the other hand, it allows us to communicate directly with the architect and with our casting vendor who is going to produce the tool to pour the metal into. The engineers in our office can perform a finite element analysis on each of the components from the SolidWorks model, helping them to decide whether the components are going to work as they are intended to.[29]

During the development of the wall's glazing detail, engineering evaluations and manufacturing concerns increased from 3 to 5 inches. Its dimension subsequently expanded to 7 inches. TriPyramid's parametric detailing accommodated changes in a timely manner and obviated time-intensive efforts to rebuild the digital model. It readily adjusted the detail for dimensional updates and revisions. TriPyramid further detailed the model's component parts, including its gaskets and fasteners.

TriPyramid's parametric model is dimensionally driven. It supports cross platforms for access by other collaborators in design, engineering, and CNC fabrication. (See Figure 5-11.) For structural evaluation, TriPyramid employs the digital model for each component detail's finite element analysis.[30] This process ensures that each part is optimally engineered, detailed for ease of fabrication, and priced. The nature of collaborative design is iterative and cyclical, reflective of multiple perspectives. TriPyramid's parametric modeling exemplifies the efficacy of this method of digital design collaboration.

The ownership of the digital file is an issue when the nature of the collaboration becomes increasingly dynamic and the boundary of responsibility is blurred. For this innovative suspended cable-net glazing, engineered to allow for large glazing deflections, the design team assumed the responsibility.

Figure 5-11 This series of images shows the process of refining the design for the assembly. (Source: Reproduced with permission from © TriPyramid Structures, Inc.)

Normally the design-build responsibility for a typical curtain wall is given to the manufacturer. The construction of the end wall of the Kimmel Center is so unique that no one that we could afford would take responsibility for it. This situation ultimately led to the structural integrity of the wall being guaranteed for by the design team![31]

Dewhurst Macfarlane provided the glazing wall's engineering analysis, detailing suspended cable glass support. The architect at Viñoly set the design intention, TriPyramid detailed and engineered the parts for fabrication, the casting vendor produced the fittings, and National Glass ensured the glazing's integrity. The digital file produced by TriPyramid was shared extensively with its collaborators and was modified through various cycles of refinement.

For rapid prototyping, the digital file was 3-D-printed and sent to the architect for review and approval. The mock-up reconfirmed the part's details and allowed the team to check the file for errors and inconsistencies. This rapid-prototyping method supports distant collaboration, allowing for precise 3-D reproduction output. The 3-D printing process saves time and allows for rapid generation of detail variations for physical evaluation. A thermojet 3-D rapid-prototyping detail output was forwarded to the caster for consultation. (See Figure 5-12.)

The caster uses CAE software to simulate the flow of the casting material, allowing it to evaluate the performance of the molten metal through the form. Its ability to diagnose the shape through the digital emulation process further minimizes failure at the prototype phase. The mock-up and trial casting process further extended the digital model's use. The glazing net cable suspension system was installed and tuned with cast-steel weights, tensioning the cladding with the minimum structure to preserve the transparency design objective set forth by the architects. (See Figures 5-13 and 5-14.)

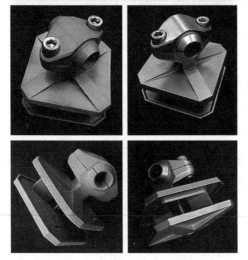

Figure 5-12 Glass fastener components and casting. (Source: © TriPyramid Structures, Inc.)

Figure 5-13 Glass fastener's clamp and cable connection, installation in situ. (Source: Reproduced with permission from Rafael Viñoly Architects, P.C.)

Figure 5-14 The interior of the Kimmel Center vault. (Source: Reproduced with permission from Rafael Viñoly Architects, P.C.)

5.3 TRIPYRAMID AND BMW PLANT—SOUTH CAROLINA

TriPyramid collaborated with the architects at Albert Kahn Associates to design, engineer, and fabricate steel brackets for a glass security fence. Their parametric design process led to a more precise understanding of the potential of collaborative digital modeling. Eliassen noted:

> . . . parametric design can allow you to look at more designs in a given time frame. Ultimately, it might allow you to shorten the time frame. Now, shortening the time frame is a matter of human discipline, which is very difficult and has nothing to do with the computer. The ability to look at different iterations and to fully evaluate them is certainly enhanced by the computer.[32]

When properly configured, parametric variations enable a range of designs to be readily transformed and evaluated between the designers.

Railing Design

The development of the BMW glass fasteners reveals the value of parametric modeling and the need for a greater understanding of its potential in the various stages of design. (See Figure 5-15.) Working closely with the architect, TriPyramid interpreted the early hand sketches of the glass fasteners into a 3-D model of the complex curved bracket (see Figure 5-16).

The early concept sketches by Vaughn Lamer at Albert Kahn Associates outlined the ideas for the glass support using flat steel bars and plates. Starting with these hand sketches, TriPyramid's engineers and designers began to outline the glass support geometry in CAD using the SolidWorks program. By working nonparametrically, Michael Samra of TriPyramid quickly generated digital 3-D sketch models showing various component shapes. This format revealed detailing challenges at the support arm's connection to the vertical support and at the glass fastener plate.

The connection problems encountered in the sketch 3-D model delineated the necessity for parametric design (see Figure 5-17). The designer was able to assess the location of the component requiring greater investigation by organizing the component geometry to be parametrically modeled in varying degrees of precision.

Parametric Modeling

Theoretically, parametric modeling configures a design to be varied within the designated characteristics of the model, without the need to fully reconfigure and re-model. Pragmatically, it is most effective when the

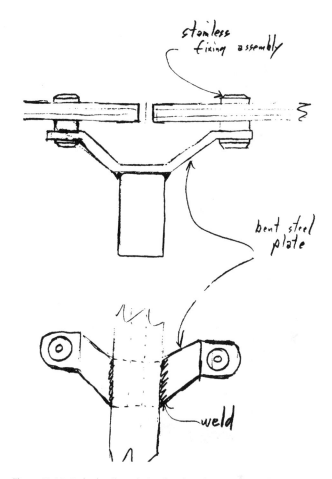

Figure 5-16 Early detail study for the glass fastener assembly. (Source: © TriPyramid Structures, Inc.)

design has been conceptually approved and the specific design variables have been identified for further development. This concentrates the time-intensive parametric modeling to support the scope and nature of further refinements.

TriPyramid produced a detail parametric model of a pair of curved support brackets, transformed from a circle into an oval cross section (see Figure 5-18). During design, the shape changed through angular segmentation, differing cross sections, and surface articulations. The circular support joins a glass support plate, while the oval section is fastened to the vertical stainless-steel rail structure. These variables were studied in the digital model iterations shared between the architects and the fabricators. The team was encouraged by the capacity of digital tools to model the more complexly curved shapes with precision and its facility to manage changes in a time-effective manner. The digital medium allowed such realistic modeling of the detail design that it was approved without a full-scale mock-up.

For structural analysis, finite element analysis was used to study the 3-D model's structural behavior. For

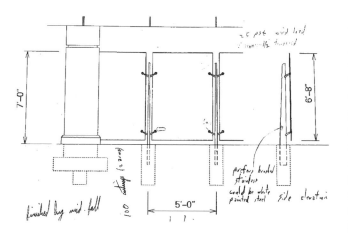

Figure 5-15 The BMW glass wall, initial design sketch. (Source: © TriPyramid Structures, Inc.)

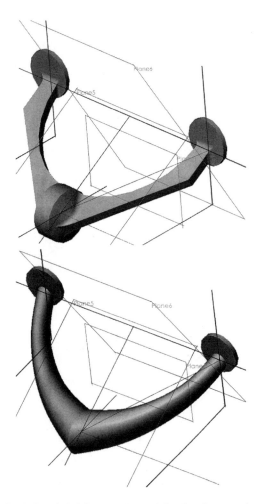

Figure 5-17 Two digital design variants of the glass fasteners. (Source: © TriPyramid Structures, Inc.)

Figure 5-18 Parametrically modeled bracket arm, with finite-element analysis model and detail assembly model. (Source: © TriPyramid Structures, Inc.)

working drawings, TriPyramid generated 2-D plans, sections, elevations, and axonometric drawings directly from the 3-D model. These conventional drawings and the 3-D digital model file were sent to bidders to price the prototypes, fabrication, and installation. (See Figures 5-19 and 5-20.)

Rapid Prototyping

The digital model, developed for design and structural analysis, was sent to the fabricator for pricing. Upon its contract award for production, the digital model was translated into CNC milling instructions to produce the mold for the lost-wax process. The fabricator cast wax into the milled formwork to produce the wax patterns for the casting of the steel brackets. The selected fabricator tested surface finishes on the early prototype units for approval. Although this final finish level can be represented in graphic form digitally, replicating and matching the reality of prototype samples is difficult. In employing parametric design, Eliassen felt that "we were able to look at a lot more options. These things

never take less time—you just get to do more work in the same time. That is still a great benefit."[33] By modeling an architectural component parametrically, a team can expeditiously study various options for design, engineering, and fabrication.

Through the selective use of parametric modeling process, TriPyramid designers are digitally collaborating with geographically remote architects and fabricators. The handcrafting process is transformed using a digital prototyping process combining sketching, digital modeling, and 3-D printing, to increase accuracy while promoting design flexibility.

The digital model is versatile, facilitating analysis with engineers performing finite-element analysis. These studies are formatted parametrically to analyze a variety of solutions, concurrent with their formal eval-

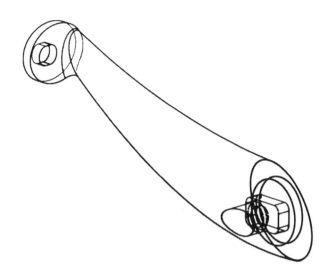

Figure 5-19 Final digital model. (Source: © TriPyramid Structures, Inc.)

uations. The digital model enables fabrication process software to evaluate the casting procedure to analyze the flow of the casting materials. It is able to graphically simulate the fluid flow of the molten metals within the casting formwork.[34] The value of modeling an architectural component parametrically, whether by a prototyping designer/fabricator or by the architect, expands its application and viability to expeditiously accommodate changes to develop various design, engineering, and fabrication refinements.

Figure 5-20 Bracket arm component prototype and finishes' study. (Source: © TriPyramid Structures, Inc.)

CHAPTER 6

Building Systems

Previous chapters have explored the potential of CAD/CAM technologies by looking at specific examples. In this chapter, we look at building systems in a more general way. A fairly classical approach is taken wherein structure, enclosure, and mechanical systems are looked at in turn.

As will be seen, enormous development strides have recently occurred because of the advent of CAD/CAM technologies. For example, there are packages of considerable power for activities such as steel detailing and subsequent fabrication. This is not to say, however, that all of these many capabilities have yet been integrated into comprehensive CAD/CAM environments. Many digital environments that support the design of specific systems were not originally intended for use by designers and continue to be used primarily by fabricators. Many still exist in stand-alone form—sometimes linked to primary digital models, but not yet fully integrated.

Apart from environments primarily geared toward structural analysis and design programs, there have been a host of developments aimed at expediting many activities that directly relate to manufacturing or fabrication concerns—for instance, the modeling of structures or steel detailing for fabrication. These latter environments are necessarily based on the results from primary analysis and design activities, but they go beyond them to address how structures of different materials are actually made—in a real way they represent the "CAM" (computer-aided manufacturing) part of the CAD/CAM spectrum.

We should emphasize that to date there is no single digital design environment that comprehensively addresses all needs in relation to analyzing, designing, and determining manufacturing information for the full range of structural systems found in building and civil engineering applications. Many of the needed capabilities are present but are not yet intrinsically integrated into CAD/CAM environments of the type developed for use in the automotive, aerospace, and product design industries. Interactions among these different environments can and do occur through neutral data exchange formats, albeit with losses of information and control (see Chapter 12).

In the following, each section briefly reviews current analysis and design software relevant to the building system studied and then focuses on related digital environments that specifically address issues of importance in a manufacturing and installation or erection context. For each system, the current use of CAD/CAM technologies for normative systems will first be reviewed, followed by emerging or even speculative approaches.

6.1 STRUCTURAL SYSTEMS

The primacy of structure has long given it a special place in influencing the form of buildings, towers, and bridges. As noted in Chapter 2, the need to analyze and design structures was fundamentally instrumental in the evolution of computer technology itself via the work of Konrad Zuse, who wanted to automate what he termed "the awful calculations" associated with structural analyses. The development of structural analysis capabilities within a computer environment continued to evolve over the years, with great spurts of development occurring in the 1960s and 1970s. Subsequently, more design-focused programs were developed, as were more direct linkages to fabrication and other manufacturing-related activities.

By now, the field of structural analysis has matured. A number of different approaches are used to first analyze structures and then to design members and systems of different materials. Common capabilities include the calculation of sectional properties of members (centroids, moments of inertia, etc.), reactions, member forces and moments, member stresses and deformations, as well as overall deflections. Many current approaches are based on finite-element techniques that are particularly appropriate for analyzing complex solid objects of the kind commonly found in a mechanical engineering context, but also in many building design situations. In a finite-element analysis, an equivalent mesh of nodes and connecting elements replaces a continuous structure and allows the calculation of stresses or deflections (see Chapter 11 for more detail).

Much of architectural construction is based on skeletal frames, and the structural analysis of these systems can be efficiently carried out using analysis environments that employ bar networks. Engineers can either create geometry with these programs themselves or can import geometry created elsewhere. These structural analysis programs do not allow the direct association of data with solid or surface models created in design development environments. Integrated solutions for bar-type structural analysis and geometric modelers exist for certain component-based programs and some entity-based drafting programs.

Usually the centerlines of the skeletal structure members are modeled and cross-sectional shapes and materials assigned. Connections between members and the support restraints need to be defined according to the desired conditions of the physical structure. After the loads are applied, the system is analyzed, and output such as reactions, deflections, internal forces, and stresses can be displayed. Among several underlying mathematical approaches, the matrix stiffness method is one of the most commonly used. Here, a stiffness matrix is formed for each member of the structure, and the system of simultaneous equations solves first for the deflections of the system, based on which reactions, forces, and stresses can be calculated. In some cases these types of analysis programs are already integrated into the environments that specialize in the detailed design of steel or timber systems.

Steel Modeling and Detailing Systems

There are many aspects to designing a steel structure. Working with architects, the engineer's role is fundamentally to ensure that member placements and dimensions are adequate to carry expected loads safely and without excessive displacements. This activity involves using analysis and design programs of the type discussed in the preceding text and in Chapter 11. Following these initial analysis and design steps, it is then necessary to design connections and deal with specific fabrications issues, both of which are closely related. In current practice, different groups often do these steps: The engineers might do the structural analysis, and the steel subcontractor may do the steel detailing. The latter step includes developing connections that transmit the required forces, are easy to fabricate and assemble, and comply with applicable codes and standards. A typical output for a part of a structure, for example, would include a definition of members meeting at a connection, an exact definition of the connection type used (including number, type, and exact geometric placement—spacing, edge distances, etc.), block-outs, clearances, and other necessary information. Supporting software environments must not only be responsive to these issues but also accommodate erection information, production needs such as material listings, workshop management, and so forth.

In general, both 2-D and 3-D steel detailing environments are currently in use. Simpler 2-D environments have been developed for use with commonly used drawing packages, such as AutoCAD. Data exchange usually occurs via DXF formats. Libraries of standard members and standard connection types are subsequently used. Outputs are simple listings and 2-D drawings that can be exported as DXF files. As such, these environments are simple and useful for many normative and simple structural designs, but are not useful for complex structures.

As buildings and civil engineering structures increase in complexity, more robust detailing packages are needed and find application. Several have capabilities for creating a complete geometric 3-D solid model of the steel structure that includes a complete definition of a structure's geometry, dimensions, member properties, connections, and materials. Drawings, bills of materials, CNC fabrication information, and erection information can all be derived from the basic model. (See Figure 6-1.)

These models normally have object-oriented characteristics and allow parametric variations of design objects such as beam or column elements. They behave similarly to the assembly models discussed in Chapter 11. Dimensional changes will propagate throughout the model. Increasing the size of columns, for example, might affect the length of connecting beams because the center-to-center spacing remains unchanged. Stored libraries of common member sections and connecting elements are invariably present. Some systems include automated functions to design systems such as simple stairs in a parametric way.

When coupled with geometric layout tools, a schematic layout can be quickly obtained. More advanced systems have graphical user interfaces that allow a user to create construction lines that define basic framing plans (layout geometries). These same interfaces normally allow a user to place different steel sections in all beam and column locations. For example, in a common grid system consisting of multiple bays, it is necessary to define the exact steel section used at each column location. A user could pick a column section, say, a W 12 × 55 or some other shape, and place it at a particular location, or, alternatively, create an array of one type or another. Additionally it is necessary that a particular steel section, such as a wide-flange, be oriented in the proper direction. Hence, tools are available for rotating placed sections. Similar tools exist for beam placement (including elevational data). Various kinds of additional elements, for instance, diagonal braces, can also be inserted and specified (member type and specific section, member end definitions, etc.).

More advanced systems also allow a user to specify

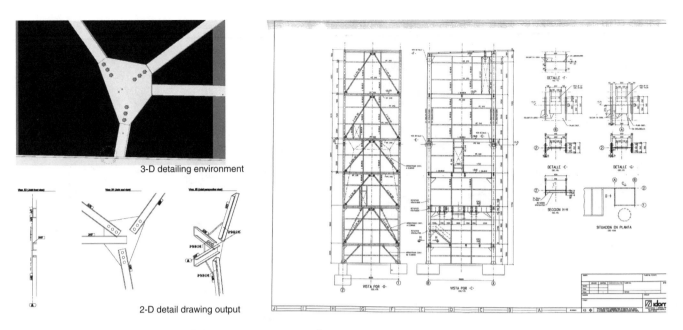

3-D detailing environment

2-D detail drawing output

Figure 6-1 Steel detailing software (SDS). (Source: Courtesy of IDOM)

common connection details. Thus, in the graphical interface, a "WF beam to column" connection might be specified, or a "WF beam to tube" connection of one type or another. Specific steel details (bolt and/or weld locations) are then generated that are appropriate for the specific member sizes and loads previously specified. Various types of member ends can be specified. Prior to the generation of specific details, the user typically has to set detailing criteria. These criteria can assume many forms, including basic dimensional criteria, bolt types, hole types, clip angle characteristics, material specifications, detailing symbols, and many other criteria that constitute the world of the structural steel detailer and fabricator.

Output data includes various kinds of framing plans, erection drawings, material and component lists, and, perhaps most significantly in the context of this book, data that directly supports CNC operations. Output data is updated when a user changes part of the structure. Structural models may be exported in various neutral file exchange formats, for instance, IGES. If a model is brought into an environment such as CATIA or Pro/ENGINEER, however, it becomes a "frozen" model that cannot be parametrically varied.

Research Investigation—Complexly Shaped Metal Structures

Designers often look back with delight at the metal structures of the late nineteenth century—such as the wonderful Art Nouveau Paris Metro stations of Hector Guimard or the roof structure of the Maison du Peuple in Brussels by Victor Horta—and then wonder what happened to the building profession's ability to cast complex shapes out of metal. While still common for small building components, the tradition of casting large-scale structural elements with complex geometries has struggled over time. Notable recent examples include the great castings of the gerberrete beams of the Pompidou Center by Renzo Piano and Richard Rogers or some of the works of Nicholas Grimshaw. These works, while excellent, made no or little use of digital design and manufacturing technologies.

There has been a resurgence of interest in designing and making cast-metal structural elements by utilizing CAD/CAM technologies. Patterns or molds have been made using CNC milling machines for many of the current examples of small castings derived from solid digital models. The task of making large complexly shaped structural elements, however, remains problematic. A critical issue involved in making large castings appropriate for building use is that of identifying an appropriate casting technology for the sizes and number of pieces involved, understanding clearly what kind of negative mold is needed for the particular casting technology chosen, and determining how to efficiently make the needed molds (see Chapter 14). Large-format and high-speed milling machines provide a key technology for actually making molds, as documented in the work by Dr. Kevin Rotheroe at Free Form Research Studio. (See Figures 6-2 to 6-5.)

Reinforced Concrete Systems

As with steel systems, the development of reinforced concrete systems via computer-assisted techniques can be generally categorized into analysis and design sys-

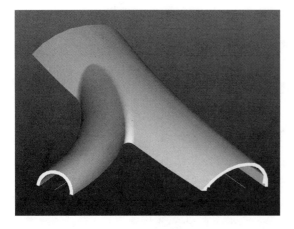

Figure 6-2 Pro/ENGINEER model of a complexly shaped steel part. (Source: Dr. K. Rotheroe, Free Form Research Studio)

Figure 6-4 Rough, unfinished castings made from CNC-machined molds. (Source: Dr. K. Rotheroe, Free Form Research Studio)

tems and those related to prefabrication or in-place construction. The related issues of formwork and reinforcement each deserve to be discussed in this context, since those are the two elements in concrete construction that need to be shaped to the desired geometry in order for any concrete construction element to be built. The formwork relates directly to the outer appearance of the system through the casting process, whereas the reinforcement bars address issues of deflections, stresses, and cracking control, to just mention a few.

Advanced analysis and design modules for members, frames, and plates have been developed that can be used to create designs according to code regulations governing reinforced concrete structures. Many modules are based on finite element techniques, since various kinds of continuous structures (e.g., floor slabs) are used in reinforced concrete construction. General layout plans can be generated, as well as slab reinforcement layouts. Reinforcement schemas and management tools are provided (predefined details, lists, bending schedules, cut diagrams). Several offer three-dimensional modeling to aid in positioning and colli-

sion control. Changes in basic model geometries or loadings can be quickly made with all drawings automatically updated.

This section looks at basic formwork systems first and then briefly considers reinforcement. Specialized design and manufacturing tools for precast concrete are introduced next, followed by a discussion of computer-

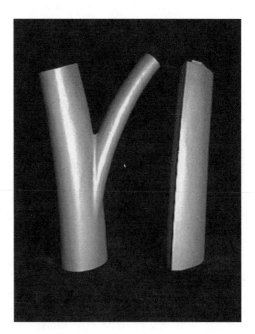

Figure 6-5 Finished prototypes. (Source: Dr. K. Rotheroe, Free Form Research Studio)

Figure 6-3 Milling of a mold using a high-speed CNC milling machine. (Source: Dr. K. Rotheroe, Free Form Research Studio)

driven approaches to the making of formwork for concrete systems with complex shapes.

Basic Formwork Considerations

Before we look into how new technologies can be employed in making precast concrete elements or to facilitate the making of complex formwork, it is useful to review some of the fundamental issues regarding formwork design. In doing so, remember that the use context of concrete formwork is extremely demanding. Unless the formwork is left in place and becomes part of the structure, it must be designed to be removable in a rational and easy way after the concrete has cured. During the casting process it is often subject to large lateral forces by the fluid mixture and the vibrators. The surface quality of the concrete is directly dependent on the surface quality of the formwork. Reuse of formwork causes formwork surfaces to degrade, and overall sheets begin falling apart when repeatedly stripped. These and many other factors make the actual design of formwork extremely complex for any but the simplest of shapes.

In terms of basic types of formwork, the most fundamental difference is that between in situ (or cast-in-place) concrete, and precast concrete of one type or another. The latter includes the use of thin reinforced concrete elements that are used as lost formwork, but that may actually contribute significantly to the structural capacity of the final element. The size and shape of members, the number of units to be made, transportation, and assembly issues typically dictate which approach is used. In typical cast-in-place construction, there are ready-made modular forms commonly available for use that are relatively small and adaptable to many configurations, standardized forms made for repetitive use in forming common elements (e.g., floor pans), or unique custom-made forms that can be made for a single job (albeit desirably reused many times). Software tools that facilitate the design of modular formwork systems are available. On inputting the external dimensions, the pour sequence, and construction joints of the concrete elements, most programs are capable of automatically generating a suitable formwork layout according to a preset, proprietary modular system. Some programs allow the import of CAD data via common data exchange formats. Bills of materials are subsequently generated. Currently these tools are mostly stand-alone systems and are often associated with a proprietary modular system. Other formwork design environments are described in the section on precast concrete systems coming up in the chapter.

Concrete Reinforcement

The automated production of rebars—applicable for both on-site construction and precast concrete—includes the cutting to length of standard stock, the bending of bars, and the automated welding of reinforcement cages and mats. Digital support systems for these automated production environments are common. Many of the structural design and analysis programs mentioned earlier can output bend tables and lists of rebars, but direct data transfer to systems used for the control of the actual production remains problematic.

An interesting example of an integrated approach to structural design and production of reinforcement is the Bamtec® Reinforcement System for slabs. Reinforcement of slabs has traditionally been executed on-site using standard, mass-produced reinforcement mats or bars. An integrated CAD/CAM approach enables the automated manufacture of customized reinforcement mats that can be transported in rolls and rolled out on the formwork. BAM AG, a Swiss specialty fabricator for reinforcement mats, integrated a finite-element analysis tool for the calculation of slab reinforcement in concrete slabs with the computer-numerical control of automated mat welding machines (see Figure 6-6).

The analysis tool outputs the machine code, layout drawings, and traditional reinforcement shop drawings for the design engineer. The CNC welding machine reads the machine code and automatically fabricates custom reinforcement mats whereby reinforcement rod length, diameter, and spacing can be varied (see Figure 6-7).

These custom reinforcement mats are engineered to correspond precisely to the stresses and deflections present in the slab. A separate custom mat is produced for each principal direction of the slab. The rods are

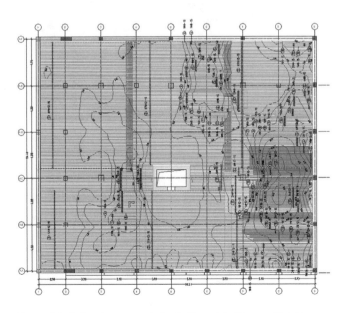

Figure 6-6 Finite-element analysis of a floor slab. (Source: All rights reserved by BAM AG/Häussler Planung GmbH)

Figure 6-7 A CNC mat welding robot for slab reinforcement mats. (Source: All rights reserved by BAM AG/Häussler Planung GmbH)

Precast Concrete Systems

For many years, development has been away from built-in-place formwork that retains craftsmanship components, however vestigial, to large-scale, prefabricated, modular assembly units. Emphasis has been on prefabricated formwork for easier and faster assembly, overall construction sequence, maximum formwork reuse, transportation issues, and so forth. These systems are invariably best suited to simple linear or planar forms, and sophisticated design and production methods rely heavily on specialized CAD/CAM applications and CNC production processes.

Typical digital tools for the design of precast systems enable contractors and fabricators to generate the data necessary for CNC production machines. The architect's or engineer's design models can be imported via neutral file exchange formats (DXF and others), or else the geometry of the concrete system can be generated using the common functions of a CAD system. Component-based systems are available that facilitate the parametric design of standard elements such as walls, columns, or ceiling slabs. There are also precast design environments that form part of integrated, component-based architectural design environments. Here, the system usually recognizes the concrete components that have been designated in the design mode (through use of a consistent *building information model*), granting thus a more seamless flow of information between designer and fabricator. Structural analysis modules may also be integrated into the same environment. (See Figure 6-10.)

welded to flat steel bands that allow finished mats to be rolled up for ease of transportation. Each roll is dimensioned such that two workers can easily unroll it on the formwork. (See Figures 6-8 and 6-9.)

The higher per-unit production costs of custom mats compared to standard reinforcement mats are offset by material savings and labor savings on-site. The analysis and design environment can be integrated in an architectural design package that includes a component-based CAD environment as well as structural, mechanical, and other specialized applications.

Figure 6-8 Rolling out a prefabricated custom mat on the formwork. (Source: All rights reserved by BAM AG/Häussler Planung GmbH)

Figure 6-9 Irregularly shaped slab edges can be accommodated by the system, thus largely eliminating cutting and trimming operations on-site. (Source: All rights reserved by BAM AG/Häussler Planung GmbH)

Once the overall geometry of the structure is established, users can determine the sizes of elements, position construction joints, and design different types of joints. Output includes the traditional layout drawings (plan, elevations, sections, or other views), detail element drawings, reinforcement layouts, loading instructions for pallet transportation, as well as bills of quantities. Most systems also generate the NC instructions for automated production processes and may be communicating data to a company's internal *product data management* system (see Chapter 12).

Sophisticated plants for precast production are usually organized along an assembly line, whereby specific steps are performed at designated stations. The mostly planar precast elements (ceiling slabs, walls) are usually produced on steel formwork. Three-axis CNC machines place magnets on the flat steel base plates and attach the edge boards to them that form the limits of the precast elements. Crane lifting anchors, small ductwork, wiring pipes for later electrical installation, and other equipment are usually installed manually. CNC machines are employed for the placing of reinforcement bars and mats according to the structural requirements prior to the pouring of the concrete. Controlled curing processes and quality control are the final steps before elements are transported to their destinations.

Formwork for Reinforced Concrete Systems with Complex Shapes

Today's architect's renewed interest in complex shapes has challenged concrete contractors and formwork fabricators alike (see Figure 6-11). The struggle to achieve a desired design complexity within a framework of practical construction and cost restrictions has been an interesting area for the application of new digital design and production tools, especially in countries that rely largely on concrete construction.

The use of complexly curved geometries invariably demands *custom-made* forms. Custom-made forms can consist of expendable, temporary, or permanent forms. *Expendable forms* such as some carved foam or plaster molds are used once and destroyed during the stripping process. They tend to be used only in more expensive work with highly intricate forms. *Temporary forms* are stripped and reused as many times as possible. *Permanent forms* are left to stay in place after casting and become an integral part of the structure (see Figure 6-12). In their most desirable form, they contribute to the functional performance of the element and are not merely left-in-place shells.

There are several basic approaches to making custom molds. Basically, there are *shaped molds* made from block materials with one face cut as part of the mold negative, *backed molds* that normally consist of sheeting and backing parts in the form of ribs or filling, and *shell molds* where a shaped sheeting that has sufficient internal strength and rigidity to carry all forces is used. The design approach and materials used are based on a consideration of the size, shape, and number of pieces to be cast, along with the casting environment (on-site, off-site).

Milled Formwork. Direct *surface shaping* of large blocks provides a widely used approach. The digital design model is used as the basis for either creating a negative or a positive mold via the use of CNC milling machines.

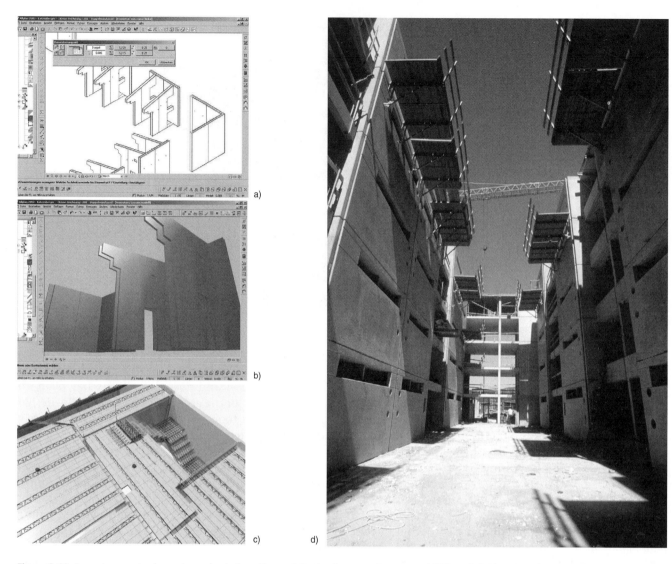

Figure 6-10 Precast concrete elements can be designed in specialized software environments. (A) The subdivision into elements is parametrically driven through a series of dialog boxes. (B) 3-D models of precast panels can be rendered. (C) Complex configurations including stairs, inclined roof elements and semiprefabricated elements are possible. (D) Compared to cast-in-place concrete, precast elements save construction time and are often more accurate. (Sources: A to C. Netmetschek, AG, Munich; D. Firma Oberndorfer, Österreich)

a) The primary concrete structure is covered with either plaster, stainless steel, or a brick façade, each in combination with external insulation.

b) The load-bearing concrete walls guide the masons in the construction of the brick facing.

c) A prefabricated panel on-site. Panels were cast in CNC-milled foam formwork

Figure 6-11 Frank O. Gehry's "Neuer Zollhof" project used a combination of precast and cast-on-site concrete elements for the complexly shaped primary structure.

The scale of the pieces that require cutting, however, is considerably larger than is commonly the case in typical manufacturing applications. The use of recently developed large-format, high-speed milling machines that operate on easily machinable materials, however, makes this approach quite feasible.

Prefabricated concrete units have been made using various milling operations for some time. In 1992, a Finnish-based company used multiple-axis milling machines to cut shapes out of rubber or metal material for repetitively used concrete molds. Nonstructural concrete façade elements have been made in this way. "Reverse engineering" applications based on three-dimensional scanning technologies for replicating existing parts (particularly in historic buildings during renovations) are possible and have been done as well. Available sizes are quite large.

Large-size milled foam negatives have been used in a number of uniquely designed reinforced concrete wall systems, including Gehry's "Neuer Zollhof" project in Düsseldorf, Germany, and a concrete sculpture by sculptor Eduardo Chillida. (See Figure 6-13.)

Milled foam negatives can be laid out horizontally in an off-site setting, as was done for some of the prefabricated elements of the Zollhof project. Reinforcing steel can then be put in place and concrete cast. Units are transported to the site and erected in place. On-site milled forms can also be used wherein milled forms are placed vertically as is commonly done with normal formwork for walls. Here, however, the milled foam is generally supported laterally by mounting the foam onto rigid elements that are designed to contain the pressures from the poured concrete. Reinforcing steel must be placed in the interstitial space before casting takes place. Since the concrete is enclosed by a highly insulating formwork, specially formulated low-heat types of concrete mixes are often employed to prevent overheating during the curing process.

Variants of this approach for big, complexly shaped surfaces include making a basic shape out of normal framing, spraying the surface with foam to create a thick coating, and then milling the easily machinable foam into the final surface shape.

Template Techniques. Generally, template-based processes employ a series of sectional profiles derived from digital models and cut via CNC technologies—such as a CNC router—from thin, flat sheets to define the shape of sheet materials. The templates serve as guides in forming complex contours or shapes with thin deformable strips or sheeting placed over the template edges. Various kinds of thin planar strips or limited-size sheet material can be used. Materials in use include lumber in various forms, wood-based sheet products, steel, or aluminum. Thin strips can be easily elastically bent to form complex curves, but only certain degrees of curva-

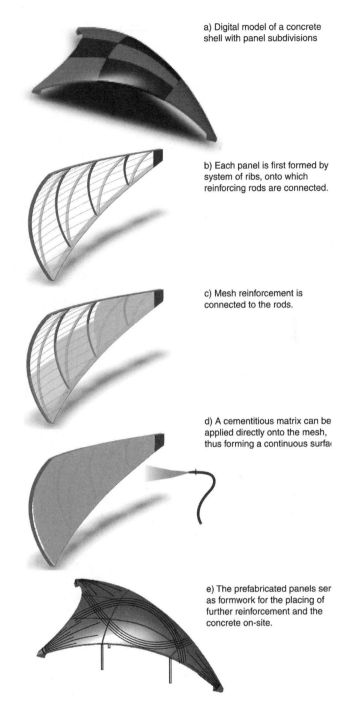

a) Digital model of a concrete shell with panel subdivisions

b) Each panel is first formed by system of ribs, onto which reinforcing rods are connected.

c) Mesh reinforcement is connected to the rods.

d) A cementitious matrix can be applied directly onto the mesh, thus forming a continuous surface

e) The prefabricated panels ser as formwork for the placing of further reinforcement and the concrete on-site.

Figure 6-12 A research investigation by M. Bechthold on the use of prefabricated ferro-cement elements that serve as permanent formwork in the construction of complexly shaped concrete surfaces.

ture are possible. Sharper curvatures require thinner materials and often more backing.

Even when supported by digital technologies, the template-cutting process still involves a lot of tedious manual work, and a good deal of experience and skill is necessary to make high-quality forms. Nonetheless, large-scale building elements can be made in this way.

Figure 6-13 The formwork for a sculpture was milled on a CNC milling machine and mounted onto a standard modular formwork system. (Source: Courtesy of Grunewald)

A variant to the template approach described uses various filling materials such as plaster or foam between templates. Here the template edges are used as a guide to shape the resulting volume (typically by hand).

Laminated Forms. A process that is well supported by digital tools is generally referred to as *laminated forms.* The process is similar to template cutting, but here successive sectional profiles are placed directly in surface-to-surface contact with one another. Sheets are first cut into profiles, aligned, and then joined to make a continuous solid (either a positive or negative shape). Normally, the resulting object has "steps" corresponding to sheet thickness. As with template cutting, digital techniques have made the profile definition and CNC cutting process quite straightforward. Resulting forms can be very rugged and reusable. The stair-stepping effect can be mitigated by finishing and/or infilling and smoothing the surface. Some more sophisticated CNC tools do allow cutting at specified "angles" or "bevels," which could be determined to provide exact conformance with the desired surface shape. Doing so, however, introduces a great many digital and machine control issues. Leaving the stair-stepping in place and casting concrete into the form directly can leave a pattern potentially attractive to some architects. The small

steps, however, are rarely precisely cast and are easily subject to honeycombing, deterioration, and breaking.

Negative Molds from Positive Master Molds. Multiple negative molds may be made from a single positive mold. Thus, in a large project, several master models of complex objects might be made and negative fiberglass shells taken off of these models. These shells would then be used in the actual casting processes. This approach obviously involves multiple steps that can be expensive, but it can be warranted in some cases (e.g., replication of existing objects, intricate shapes, need for extremely high quality finishes). Glass fiber reinforced plastic (GFRP), introduced in the 1950s, is now widely used to make negatives from positives. Complex shapes can be made that include limited pockets or undercuts. The master positive molds can be made in many different ways. Some positive molds are made with laminated sheets over carefully cut profiles. Backing is often required for stiffness. Some newer approaches rely on shaping the positive mold directly via large CNC milling machines.

Future Systems—Reconfigurable Molds. Processes based on *adjustable* or *reconfigurable molds* have significant future potential. These approaches typically rely on a field of adjustable pins that slide back and forth. Their ends define a surface shape that may consist of a flexible skin. In a fully automated system, the adjustable pins could be driven by servomechanisms, which can in turn be linked to coordinate data extracted from a digital model of the surface to be made. These technologies have been explored in connection with sheet metal forming for the aerospace industry and for the lamination of high-performance sails. Mold costs are extremely high and have so far inhibited the use of such systems as formwork. There can also be no undercuts and other complex shapes. As the cost of CNC technology keeps falling, they might prove quite interesting in the future. (See Figure 6-14.)

Timber Systems

A variety of systems specifically address the design, analysis, and automated production of timber systems. Functionalities of these specialized digital environments are remarkably similar to those of steel design software, albeit tailored to the typical construction elements and joints encountered in timber structures. Systems that are ultimately geared to supply data for CNC manufacturing processes are more frequently employed in countries that rely extensively on heavy timber construction. In light timber construction, as practiced in the United States or Canada, most trimming and joining operations of frame construction are executed on-site. Since member spacing is small, member sizes are correspondingly small and the forces to be transmitted in the joints can be dealt with by simple nailed or screwed connections. Heavy timber construction, with its fewer but larger members and higher forces present, often relies on geometrically complex joints that more readily justify an automated design for production process. These setups invariably depend on costly machines and highly skilled personnel, and rely extensively on maximizing prefabrication and minimizing on-site work.

The design environments that support the design for production and eventually output machine instructions for various CNC manufacturing activities are geared toward carpentry companies and the production environment. They are not readily compatible with structural analysis or architectural design environments, but usually have a limited capability for importing data via neutral file formats such as DXF. To enable automated design functions and the support of CNC manufacturing operations, imported data often needs to be edited and refined. Alternatively, users can input all geometry themselves, aided by macros (or specialized stand-alone applications) that automate the design of complicated elements such as stairs or dormers.

The solid modeling technology of timber design systems enables users to determine the exact length and shape of each individual member—inclined members may be cut off at an angle; members may be notched or designed with other features in order to connect to the remaining structure. Collision detection functions are often present. The design modules frequently employ object-based, parametric approaches. Standard details such as connections, corners of timber frames or roof, and others are provided in libraries that then can also

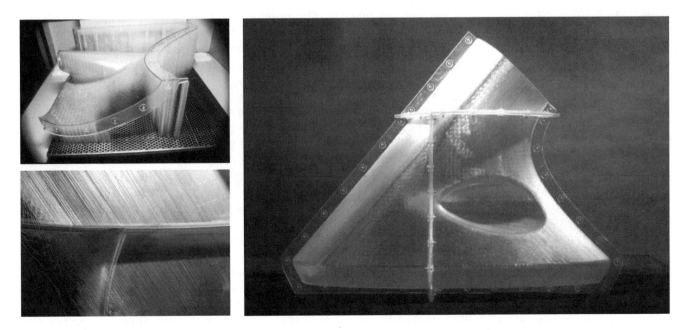

Figure 6-14 Complexly shaped formwork generated on a stereolithography 3-D printer. (Source: Volker Ruhl)

be refined and built up by the user. Sophisticated environments include typical steel elements that connect the timber members. Two-dimensional drawing views and bills of quantities can be directly generated from the 3-D solid model. Some systems also support price calculations, based on volume calculations and input of per-unit costs. Changes to the construction are automatically reflected in all output modes. Post processors can usually generate and compile machine instructions for industry-typical CNC machining centers.

Timber detailing systems, by their nature, are devised to automate the design-for-production process of polygonal timber structures with relatively simple geometry. Curved elements—for example, curved glued-laminated timber beams or arches—are rarely supported, and the design of complexly shaped timber elements is beyond their scope. A recent example demonstrates that extensive digital modeling can provide invaluable support for the manufacturing of complexly shaped glued-laminated timber beams (see Figure 6-15).

The design and construction of a timber grid shell for a spa relied extensively on digital form finding and solid modeling. The design process started out with a conceptual physical model that represented the approximate overall shape. This model served as the basis for an iterative process of digital form and structural analysis. Form finding was based on the force-density method—a computational method used to find equilibrium shapes such as minimal surfaces. Manufacturing constraints such as minimum bending radii were incorporated early during this shaping process. Once the geometry was finalized, each rib was modeled as a 3-D solid model including all features such as notches and slots for connections. On the shop floor, manually adjustable steel jigs were set up according to the digital model coordinates. All ribs were premanufactured off-site and assembled into the complex shape of the grid shell without any need for reworking.

Research Investigation—Complex Shapes in Wood
There are obvious restrictions in the kinds of shapes that can be achieved for architectural elements made in timber. A specific use context where this is most apparent are structural roof shells—material-efficient systems that rely on a structural surface to carry loads without further curvilinear members. These systems depend on sufficient surface curvature for their structural efficiency and pose major manufacturing challenges in timber. This research investigation proposed a multifunctional wood-foam sandwich panel as the structural surface for roof shells. The load-bearing surface thus forms the insulating enclosure of the space and provides all structural capabilities. First, a larger roof shell is subdivided into a series of segments, each

a) The overall shape consists of several surfaces of revolution that are smoothly joined. The structural ribs are covered with several layers of wooden boards that provide in-plane stiffness.

b) Prefabricated beams.

c) Shell assembly using slotted beam connections on-site.

Figure 6-15 Construction of the timber shell in Bad Dürrheim, Germany. (Source: © 2001: Klaus W. Linkwitz)

of which is then fabricated separately and joined with structural connections into the overall complexly curved surface.

The system is based on CNC milling the molds for the lamination of thin wooden strips. Instead of disposable molds, the foam quality is chosen such that the mold can become an integral part of the sandwich as its shear-resistant core. By milling pockets and grooves, wiring and other functions can be embedded into the core and the roof itself. Wooden strips can be oriented according to the principal stresses in order to use the material efficiently—a treatment similar to the lamination of advanced composites. The lamination of multiple layers of strips to the core results in a stiff panel element. Various types of joints allow the structural connection to adjacent elements into the larger roof shell.

The sandwich section permits variations in the core and facing depths to respond to different structural conditions in the shell. Because of its stiffness, this process is also feasible for free-form shapes that were not strictly conceived as structural surfaces. As such, the use of this system in walls, envelopes, or interior elements is possible. (See Figure 6-16.)

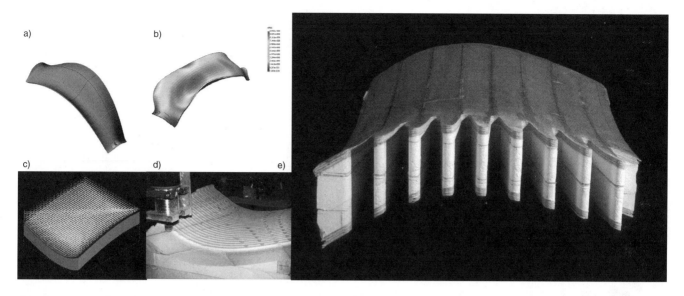

Figure 6-16 Research on wood-foam sandwich shells by M. Bechthold. (A) Parametric, solid shell model with subdivisions into prefabricated panels. (B) During manufacturing thin wood elements are aligned with the principal stresses identified with finite-element analysis. (C) A prototypical panel was extracted from the master model in order to generate the milling toolpath. (D) CNC milling process shapes a foam block/core. (E) Prototype.

Masonry Systems

Masonry construction is traditionally a labor-intense activity, and there are few dedicated masonry design environments apart from those for structural analysis and code compliance checks. One of the few areas that new computer-driven technology has impacted significantly is the design, production, and erection of large-scale masonry blocks. Larger blocks are faster to lay, but they also require more cutting and splitting of blocks on-site, because wall dimensions can no longer be multiples of the modular brick unit. This dilemma is addressed in the custom manufacturing of large-format block sets by the German manufacturer Xella Kalksandstein GmbH (Xella), an international producer of masonry blocks.

Load-bearing masonry construction is a popular construction method for small- to medium-sized projects in Germany. In the late 1990s Xella introduced the integration of partly automated design of masonry walls and the custom CNC cutting of large masonry blocks. As a first step the masonry contractor submits the architect's construction documents, the concrete shop drawings, and a construction schedule to Xella. Here trained technicians subdivide the wall elevations into standard and custom blocks using a specialized software tool. This program also outputs traditional sets of shop drawings that can be sent to the contractor for approval. Once these drawings are released for production, the project-specific sets of blocks are manufactured on CNC circular saws and other machines. Each set includes the required number of standard blocks as well as the custom-cut blocks. Installation drawings, a reference plan, and elevations of each wall are also included. All blocks are code-marked, allowing the masons to reference the appropriate layout plan during installation. Options for custom blocks include length variations, angled elevation cutoffs, recesses for installation, and many more. (See Figure 6-17.)

Sets of blocks are delivered to site on the day a particular wall is to be constructed. This "just-in-time" delivery reduces storage needs and frees up valuable space on-site. Since the blocks are too heavy to be lifted manually—typical dimensions are up to $3 \times 2 \times 1$ feet—they are lifted by small, mobile cranes that are placed directly on the floor slab.

Xella's business model closely resembles mass customization, but it does not allow the customer—here the contractor—to directly configure sets of blocks for production. The digital block configurator is only used by trained technicians. Typical lead time from the contractor submitting the original wall geometry to delivery of the first batch of blocks to site can be as short as 11 working days, depending on demand and available production capacity. The system largely overcomes the modular limitations of large masonry block construction by transferring the cutting and customizing activity from the job site to the factory. The resulting improvements in on-site productivity, wall quality, and reduction in site waste usually outweigh the increased material cost of customized sets of blocks compared to standard blocks.

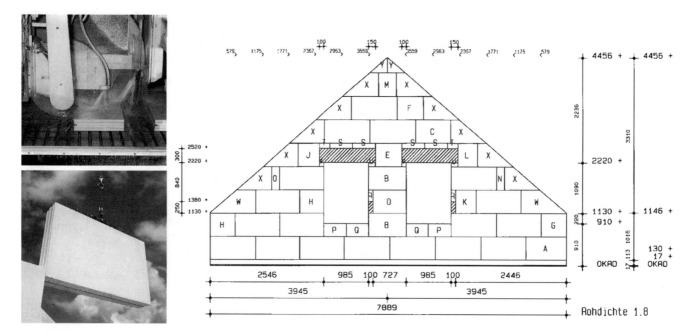

Figure 6-17 Custom-made sets of masonry blocks are CNC-cut and delivered to site. (Source: With kind permission of XELLA Kallsandstein, Duisburg, Germany)

Stone Systems

The natural stone industry is relying heavily on CNC machines for the cutting and shaping of stone. Software solutions for this industry, again, are devised for use by fabricators, not by designers. They include specialized systems for the design of stair and paved stone layouts or stone façades. These environments typically include a graphical design interface through which the design is created. Capabilities for file import vary greatly. Traditionally these types of programs produced bills of materials, installation drawings, and plot files that were used by stone masons as full-size cutting templates. More recently, sophisticated systems generate NC code for the wide range of CNC tools employed for working natural stone.

Manufacturers of the raw material—mining and quarry companies—employ a different set of programs to facilitate the design, analysis, and site control of quarries. These are sophisticated 3-D modeling tools for the design of the quarry that includes functions to replicate the geological layering of the site. They allow realistic renderings, a function particularly useful if the design of a quarry needs to be visualized for the purpose of permissions in public approval processes. The 3-D model provides the basis for the derivation of the cut-and-fill volume calculations that are essential to quarry planning and operations. Quarry operators can be equipped with Global Positioning System (GPS) units that feed back information into the digital model, updated in real time. This data in turn enables precise work instructions for the personnel on the ground, and

has also decreased the need for more expensive airborne survey methods.

6.2 ENCLOSURE AND INTERIOR SYSTEMS

Previous chapters have provided a number of case studies on how CAD/CAM technologies have been used to make both simple and complexly shaped enclosure systems. As was seen, the process of making a complexly shaped enclosure system consisting of a series of individually designed and shaped pieces typically involves the close coordination between the architect, the subcontractor fabricating the enclosure assemblies, and the contractor. While fascinating, it is good to remember that CAD/CAM technologies have also been widely used in the development of a large array of other kinds of enclosure systems and related fenestration elements. Some window and skylight systems provide fine examples of how CAD/CAM technologies are used to efficiently produce high-quality customized products. Indeed, these systems provide some of the best architectural examples of the principles of mass customization discussed in Chapter 18.

Exterior Systems
Doors and Windows

A large range of digital design tools supports the design and manufacture of doors and windows. These include performance evaluation tools as well as environments geared to support design and production. Common performance evaluation tools are covering detailed design studies that address wind loads or thermal behavior. Specific programs support the design of metal frames, with particular focus on producing satisfying thermal designs of the frame profile that minimize heat losses.

Performance evaluation tools are mostly devised for use by engineers, façade consultants, or fabricators. Environments for design and production support are primarily geared for fabricators; they are usually parametric, object-based environments that allow for a range of standard configurations (frames, door leaves, etc.) to be inserted that then can be modified to meet individual needs. Simple modeling interfaces also allow the user to design without such templates. Basic data import/export functions allow some file exchange to occur, but for any useful parametric design activity to be supported, users normally need to edit and change the imported data. Standard details such as hinge holes, lock cases, and accessory parts are normally supplied in libraries. Once the design is complete, part lists, overview, and detail drawings can be extracted easily. Specific output includes overview drawings of glass panels that need to be ordered from and cut to size by external vendors.

The design interfaces usually link to an integrated CAM module that generates machine instructions for CNC production. This data is post-processed to comply with requirements and setups of specific machine environments. Frequently performed machining operations can often be stored and recalled as a whole each time a project requires the same operation. The geometry created in the design mode is normally associated to the machine instructions. In case of last-minute changes to the design, the toolpaths can be updated automatically.

Common programs are specifically designed either to create doors or windows with a specific frame material or to allow for a selection of a material. Material properties not only impact the detailing of the element but also determine the machining instructions that are needed for any CNC manufacturing activity.

These types of integrated design and manufacturing (CAD/CAM) solutions for windows and doors can be used to support manufacturing activities ranging from small shops to full-scale industrial production. Some large corporations have set up systems of mass customization that rely on extended versions of these basic design tools. To facilitate the design of system-conforming windows, digital configuration tools are usually provided that allow architects or the end user to specify the desired design within the production limitations of a given company. (See Figure 6-18.)

Some of these window configurators are merely visualization aids; others can generate specific ordering

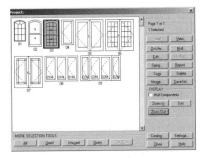

a) Users can select amongst different window types.

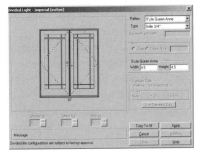

b) Within each window type a number of parameters can be specified.

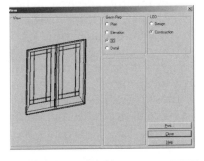

c) Based on the user input the program creates a 3-D model of the design.

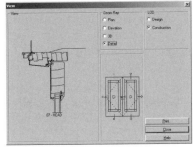

d) Detail drawings of the window can also be generated.

Figure 6-18 Product configurator for a window. This particular software does not currently connect to production processes. (Source: Marvin Windows and Doors)

information that may or may not be used directly in digitally supported manufacturing systems. By integrating these and other tools with a flexible production line of modular products, customized windows can be manufactured at prices comparable to those of standard ones (see Chapter 18 for further details).

Shopfronts, Curtain Walls, and Cladding

Similar systems as for windows and doors are available to support design and manufacturing activities of larger systems used as shopfronts, curtain walls, and cladding. Performance evaluation tools encompass similar functions of structural and thermal analysis but are rarely integrated into these CAD/CAM environments. Specialized tools facilitate the design of custom extrusions as used in custom curtain walls. As mentioned in the previous section, CAD/CAM tools that support activities in this sector are generally devised for fabricators and only interact with the architect's design models rather crudely through basic data exchange formats.

The design of cladding systems in particular, but also of shopfronts and standardized curtain walls, can also be supported by proprietary software that is catered to a company's product line. These systems may or may not be part of an actual mass customization strategy and therefore might or might not interact in any useful way with the underlying production process. Other software products frequently in use are packages that primarily support estimation and bidding processes. To facilitate the specification of a company's products, CAD detail drawings can often be downloaded. Architects can incorporate these detail drawings in their project drawings, but these drawings do not normally contain any information beyond CAD entities such as lines, polylines, and text. As concepts such as the *building information model* or *product modeling* become implemented in the future, it is conceivable that the nature of these CAD files may change from pure geometry to a more in-depth description of components.

Roofs

Roof construction is a complex design task combining structural issues, insulation requirements, and the need to properly drain water. For timber construction the timber design and CAM packages provide extensive support for the design of standard roof frames, with extensions available that process the design data for a CNC production setup. Typical design tasks such as dormers can be largely automated—these structural applications were discussed earlier in this chapter.

Specialized systems that facilitate the design of flat roofs are available, but they are not normally tied into any automated manufacturing activity. Some are stand-alone applications; others are plug-ins for commonly used CAD tools. Automated design tasks include the creation of drainage slopes, drainage points, and valleys and ridges on flat roofs. These systems can be particularly useful if the drainage slope of the flat roof is achieved through a variation in thickness of the exterior insulation. Upon completion of the design, the output can include the complete layout drawings and related list of all necessary insulation boards, with individual thickness and slope to match the drainage plan. Openings as might be necessary for roof lights can also be incorporated. Part list and layout plan are cross-referenced, so changes in the layout immediately affect the part lists.

Interior Systems

As with many other building products, interior fit-out manufacturers are among those that tend to provide architects and customers with easy ways to generate a design that is consistent with the available product line. Recent years have seen a surge of either online or offline (stand-alone) approaches for products such as interior partitions or suspended ceiling systems. Specific packages for the estimation of floor finishes offer data input through laser-supported survey techniques.

A field that is characterized by a high degree of integration between digital design and manufacturing systems is the design and production of cabinets (see Figure 6-19). These systems are for use primarily by fabricators, not by designers. They include simple 3-D design interfaces that often provide automated functions for inserting doors or other standard features. Models can be displayed rendered or in conventional 2-D views, and fabrication drawings for assembly and installation are derived from the 3-D design model. Integrated post-processors can be configured to generate machine code for a wide range of CNC machines. Parts can be tracked throughout the production process with barcodes that are generated within the same system. The code—read by barcode scanners at the various machines—contains all information necessary for manufacturing and installation. Sophisticated setups allow the machine controllers to be connected to a local area network and a database server, and the part-specific machine code can be called up from the server simply by scanning the barcode at each station.

6.3 MECHANICAL SYSTEMS

Digital design environments have been developed to vertically integrate the design and fabrication of mechanical and plumbing systems. Others support the fabrication of elevator systems or the analysis and design of artificial lighting.

Drawing upon an extensive library of 3-D digital component models, the mechanical systems focus primarily on sheet-metal fabricated parts, while the plumbing systems create an assembly of pipes and connectors. These systems incorporate a high degree of process automation and specification-driven design. Their 3-D modeling environment supports on-site coordination and checks for collision and interferences with base building structure, enclosure, mechanical and plumbing systems. Expert knowledge is embedded in the software environment, informing the detailing of these assemblies with technical recommendations. The individual part tracking extends from the digital model to on-site installation, associated with information such as materials, costs, instructions for fabrication, shipping, installation, and maintenance.

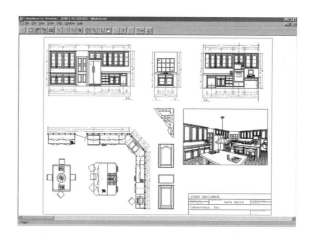

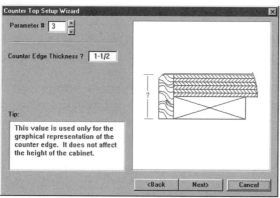

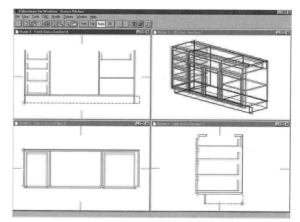

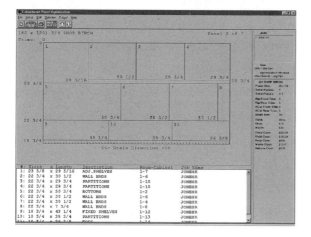

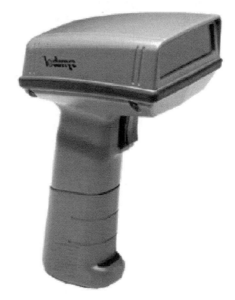

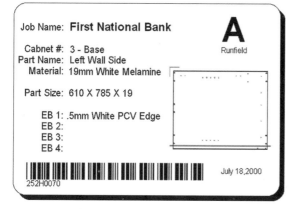

Figure 6-19 Cabinet design and manufacturing software. (Source: Copyright 2002: Cabnetware: A planit solutions, Inc. product)

Sheet-Metal Components

Proprietary software and procedures for design and fabrication for CAD/CAM have been developed for HVAC and plumbing systems. Traditional methods of the HVAC system layout, shop drawing, and fabrication have been codified into proprietary expert software by companies such as East Coast CAD/CAM Inc., Metamation Inc., or Shopdata. Developed from the fabricators' perspective, these digital environments aim to automate the design and fabrication tasks, minimize labor, optimize material use, and apply expert detailing and specification instructions to produce a higher-quality mechanical assembly. The digital translation of the handcrafted manufacturing procedure, as exemplified by East Coast CAD/CAM, includes functions such as specification-driven design, parametric design, multi-dimensional design, multi-database, and object-driven product database detailing.[1] It vertically integrates conventional operations such as 2-D shop drawing, specifications, bills-of-quantity accounting, cost estimating, component identification, and fabrication into a relational database with its 3-D model. These programs support the flexible combination of standard HVAC and plumbing kits of parts, customized for each project through parametric configurations.

HVAC System Layout and Modeling. The HVAC layout begins with the import or modeling of a 3-D building structure, exterior enclosure, interior partitions, finish ceilings, and the mechanical spaces. Conventional 2-D system layout diagrams can be translated with automated 3-D model duct generations, connecting specified devices and machinery (see Figure 6-20). Three-dimensional HVAC system models can be directly inserted and reconfigured. Proprietary HVAC-specific programs such as E-CAD generate solid or surface models, convert them into 2-D fabrication patterns, and generate the necessary operating instructions for CNC sheet-metal fabrication.

Parametric Duct Variations and Library of Parts. The digital design and fabrication environment have been configured to draw upon databases and library of parts, to optimize the detail design and fabrication customized for each project (see Figure 6-21). Mechanical system components include ventilation/exhaust systems, parametric ducts and joints, particle/fume management systems, and all manners of ductwork. Other sheet-metal components are also possible.[2]

Each parametric component is configured with automatic alignment points, ensuring precise connectivity and generating transitional duct geometries to flow from part to part automatically. The selection and placement for the supply, air distribution, intake devices, and returns are specified and located three dimensionally (see Figure 6-22). As an example of parametric design strategy, 3-D models of these devices and their associated databases set up the targets for automatic routing of ducts and their start and finish cross-sectional dimensions, while the lengths of individual

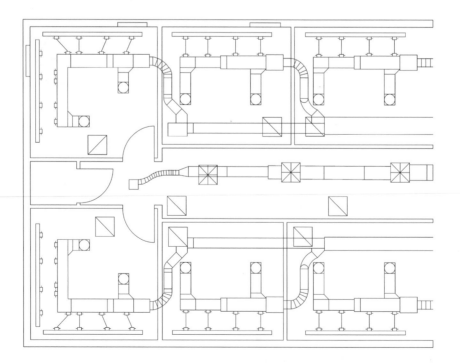

Figure 6-20 The ducting can be sized and laid out with all the sheet-metal parts identified. (Source: Drawing redrafted by author—courtesy of East Coast CAD/CAM)

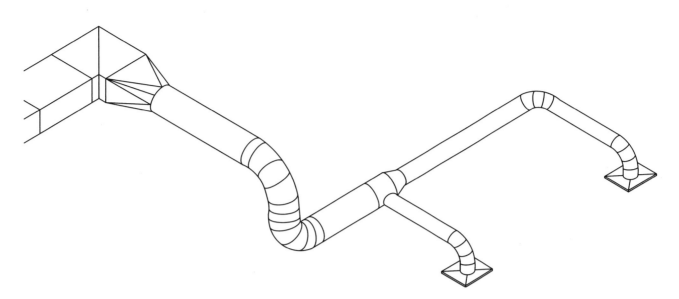

Figure 6-21 The designer determines where air devices should be installed, the lines are laid out with fittings, and a 3-D model is generated. (Source: Drawing redrafted by author—courtesy of East Coast CAD/CAM)

duct segment are determined by the specification of the stock material sizes and property.

The device and duct placements are specified with conditions of heights, clearances from structure, and enclosures. The automated route layout is checked for collision and interference, based on a predetermined dimensional tolerance.

Specification and Detailing. Configured in a specification-driven format, each sheet metal component is 3-D-modeled with associated identification and specification for fabrication and installation. The system or part's specification, as entered by the operator, defines its material properties, manufacturing, and installation constraints. Its material selection automatically determines the appropriate fabrication procedure and tool selection, and activates its corresponding detailing library. The specification also produces a pricing database, which is expandable to include the handling and shipping expenses.

Bills of Quantity and Cost Estimate. Bills of quantity and cost estimate are integral functions for each project. With each part identified and its database integrated, bills of quantity and associated cost estimate can be produced from the associated database, expediting value engineering and design modifications. The integration of the 3-D model, bill of quantity, and pricing allows for simultaneous modification to the design, specification, and unit prices.

For example, an HVAC bend in the duct can be detailed with a straight, radius, or chamfer corner. Specific detail typology can be changed, thus translating and changing all the specified corners with the selected

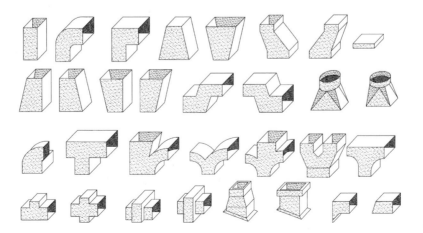

Figure 6-22 Various duct-fitting typology exists in the software's parametric parts library. (Source: Drawing redrafted by author—courtesy of East Coast CAD/CAM)

detail. This impact on cost can be evaluated individually or as a total systems cost and value engineering.

Nesting. For fabrication, the nesting operation of the sheet-metal patterns is automated to minimize the material waste. The layout can be composed with intelligent parts rotation and irregular filler parts placement. (See Figure 6-23.)

Remnant materials are also tracked for future use. If needed, the nesting can also be operator-configured.[3] The fabricator can schedule jobs and track available new and remnant material inventory and update the project status. "The powerful layout sequencer has several optimization switches to minimize machine run time, and the graphical sequence review table can be used to easily edit the sequence of the most complex of layouts."[4] The optimization of workflow combines the scheduling of nesting patterns and material selections with the simplified selection of tools and processing. "The scheduler module can take a set of punch layouts that are ready to process and suggest the optimal process sequence to minimize the overall tool remounts into the turret."[5] To expedite fabrication and simplify workflow, the program automatically maps the tool use sequence, minimizing the time and frequency of tool changes.

CAM Process Planning and Simulation. In a digital design environment, traditional sheet metal shop drawing is replaced by a 3-D model and instructions for CNC fabrication. By transferring most handcrafted operations to digitally driven operations, this procedure expands the efficiency through automation and mass production while producing highly customized designs. HVAC component manufacturing includes operations such as laser cutting, high-definition plasma cutting, CNC punching, water jet, shearing, conventional and CNC press brake forming, welding, bending, and assembly.[6] Toolpath simulators dynamically illustrate the fabrication procedure and allow an operator to optimize each operation.

Parts Identification and Tracking. Each component is digitally identified from its design to installation. This facilitates parts tracking, and just-in-time planning for shipping, on-site staging, and installation. Identical parts can also be classified and identified in batches. The parts are individually barcoded with a referenced full-information database. Assembly instruction can be digitally referenced, providing on-site directions for the installer. Problematic intersections or tight tolerance locations can be identified early during design and tracked by the general contractors to ensure precise on-site execution. (See Figures 6-24 and 6-25.)

The product identification allows for life cycle tracking of its performance, extending from its material to its replacement. Each part's identification, stored with

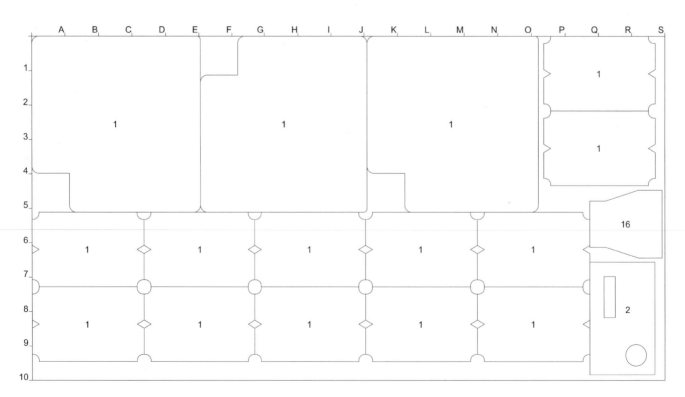

Figure 6-23 The software enables best-fit nesting, reducing waste, and saving material. (Source: Drawing redrafted by author—courtesy of East Coast CAD/CAM)

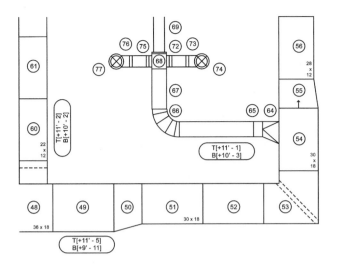

Figure 6-24 Each part is numbered and bar-coded with an associated database. (Source: Drawing redrafted by author—courtesy of East Coast CAD/CAM)

its 3-D digital model and specification, readily allows for detailed diagnostics, repair, and replacement. Its data includes its CNC fabrication instructions, accessible for refabrication.

Plumbing System

The CAD/CAM plumbing programs are vertically integrated digital design environments, configured for the layout and fabrication of piping systems. They have similar functionalities as the mechanical programs, but the plumbing programs fabricate from an inventory of pipes and fittings, CNC cut, threaded, welded, and fitted to its assembly.

Piping Layout. The plumbing systems are typically configured and concealed within the floor, ceiling, wall, and chases. The building structure and enclosure model can be imported or generated to define the dimensional boundaries for each installation. The plumbing engineer diagrams the piping layout's start and destination points. Once the fittings, machines, and instruments are specified, a 3-D piping network is automatically generated, yielding specific pipe lengths and offsets for fittings and welds. Individual parts are identified digitally, barcoded, and documented in bills of quantity reports, cost reports, and inventory reports. Each system is specification-driven, requiring the definition of its material properties and performance parameters, such as the minimum slope to drain for waste lines and fire suppression systems. The program can initiate a collision or interference test, ensuring clearances around structures, ductwork, and key drainage lines.

Plumbing Kit of Parts. A plumbing system is a combination of a large quantity of standard components with

site- and building-specific detailing and coordination. Typically, the pipes, elbows, and fittings are selected from industry-standard material stocks. If necessary, customized connectors can be identified and their specifications generated for customized one-off fabrication. The available pipe lengths are specified for each project. The automated material database allows for the optimization of the layout routes. (See Figure 6-26.) The prefabrication of various subassemblies can be produced within the factory to minimize site work, increase accuracy, and improve the economy of the project.

Site Construction Coordination. The location and displacement of the engineered mechanical and plumbing systems need to be site-verified. The 3-D design model allows collaborating disciplines to coordinate between theoretical and site dimensions.

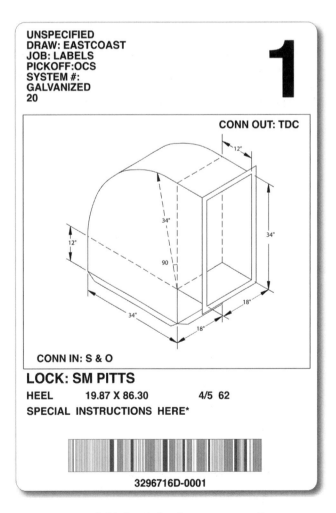

Figure 6-25 Barcode label applied to duct components. (Source: Drawing redrafted by author—courtesy of East Coast CAD/CAM)

Detail Design and Project Pricing. In a conventional design-bid-build process, the responsibility for the accuracy of material accounting rests with the competing mechanical subcontractors. There is an incentive for the bidder to minimize the amount of labor invested to win the contract, while it demands a thorough calculation for quantity and cost estimate.

In an alternate model of practice, the mechanical and plumbing system may be engineered and modeled in 3-D for a construction contract. In this format, the engineering documents gain greater 3-D precision, beyond the line diagrams, symbols, and specifications. With the associated specifications database, the model would enable the fabricators to translate the design into their digital environment, readily generating accountings of materials, labor quantities, and costs.

The competitive advantage for each fabricator resides in its ability to translate each project demand into its specialized fabrication capacity and cost structure.[7] The ability for each fabricator to adopt and adapt various digital programs and systems into its specialty demands the customization of these off-the-shelf systems. This is reflected in the fabrication details and value engineering of the system through the fabricator's pricing and shop drawing evaluation process. The model of a vertically integrated digital practice has been adopted partly by manufacturers, thus transforming their ability to digitally collaborate with the architects and engineers.[8]

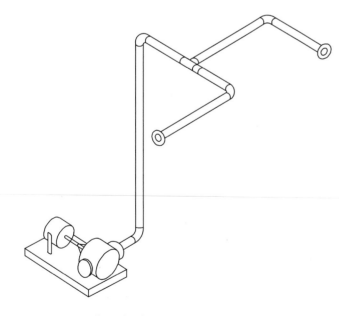

Figure 6-26 Similar to the sheet-metal software program in terms of its layout capabilities in three dimensions, the piping program tags connections and lengths of pipes so that pipes can be cut in the shop, reducing on-site labor and waste. (Source: East Coast CAD/CAM)

Elevator Systems

In any major building there are a whole host of subsystems that perform specialized functions. Architects are involved in their selection, placement, and integration with other building systems; but they often do not actually design them in any detailed way. Elevator systems are a prime example here. Elevator companies have long provided a series of types and models to choose from. The interesting development in this field is that CAD/CAM technologies have been adopted by companies as a way of improving their own product offerings, which in turn is of great benefit to the practicing architect. Elevator systems are highly complex assemblies of many elements that involve multiple manufacturing and assembly steps. It is not surprising that the benefits of high-end CAD/CAM applications would be found to be particularly appropriate. (See Figure 6-27.)

The digital model shown was made using Pro/ENGINEER and is a complex assembly model that can be parametrically varied. Elevators are a typical example of building elements that consist of one or more basic types that are then customized to suit a particular building. Customization includes the number of floors an elevator must serve, floor-to-floor heights, various types of drives, cabin sizes and lifting capacities, door types and sizes, as well as cabin interior design. The Kone Corporation, a Finland-based company that specializes in elevators, escalators, and material handling equipment, uses parametric models to facilitate the design of customized elevators.[9]

Puro used Pro/ENGINEER to set up a complex assembly model with a mix of surface and solid elements based on a top-down modeling approach. The types and sizes of all individual components are associated either to the desired cabin capacity or a given shaft size. The digital model is structured in an object-oriented way. Modularized components have behaviors assigned to them to ensure that the correct component type and configuration is automatically selected upon input of the driving dimensions of cabin or shaft. These component behaviors are largely derived from macros that were programmed by Rand Finland as part of a Pro/ENGINEER implementation project.

The modularized parametric model is capable of supporting automated manufacturing operations, but it is not currently used in that way. The parametric model is employed to quickly determine all necessary parts and part configurations for a custom elevator. Once the design is finalized, engineers and designers at Kone rely on a traditional, paper-based process when preparing an elevator for production. Bills of materials, for example, are not generated directly from the parametric model.

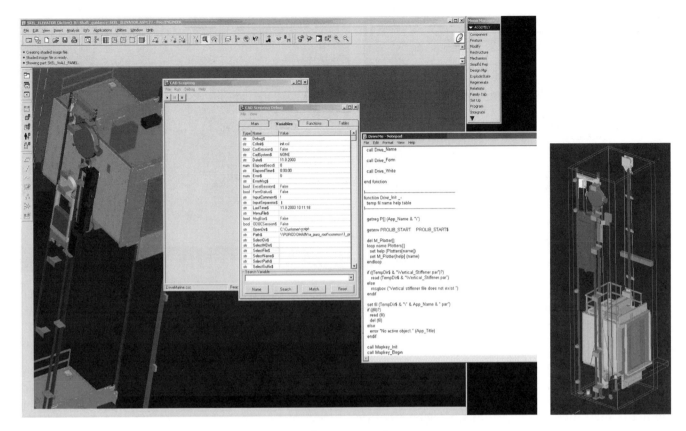

Figure 6-27 Pro/ENGINEER assembly model of the Kone elevator. (Source: Puro Oy)

Instead, the component data is transferred to a separate corporate business support system that includes a product data management module. Currently all further operations are controlled from here, disconnected from the original Pro/ENGINEER model. This digital elevator model could potentially lend more extensive support to automated manufacturing operations, assembly, and installation.

Lighting Systems

A variety of tools supports the analysis of spaces with respect to natural and artificial lighting (See Figure 6-28). Even concept modeling environments for use by architects often allow approximate studies, but their output is usually geared more toward convincing visualization than precise analysis. Other tools, for use by specialists, are devised to support more accurate types of analysis.

Both types of environments allow a variety of parameters to be specified by the designer, including surface materials, textures and colors, strength and direction of natural and artificial light sources, and others. Some architectural CAD programs can write file formats specifically geared for use in lighting simulations and analysis packages. A more complete data

transfer makes for a much more efficient analysis process, since without it all geometry information needs to be generated from the beginning by the lighting designer.

Manufacturers of light fixtures frequently provide extensive information online to designers—this currently represents the only direct link between manufacturer and designer. Of special interest in this particular context are performance files that incorporate the particular lighting characteristics of individual light fixtures. These files are often available in a variety of formats readable by commonly used standalone analysis tools. They allow designers to test the effect of specific lighting products in the context of the design, potentially improving the accuracy of the analysis and of the predicted effects. Some lighting simulation programs can generate bills of materials—essentially counting the number of light fixtures used—that support design development and design-for-construction processes.

Even more sophisticated analysis systems are used by the manufacturers themselves in the detailed design and analysis of reflectors and lenses. These high-end systems are frequently based on solid-modeling techniques and can connect to the company's CAM system and its related CNC-driven manufacturing technology.

Figure 6-28 Lighting analysis of a chapel design. Rendering (left) and illuminance analysis (right), with the illuminance scale in footcandles displayed below. In this case, the architect created a lightscape export file in form-Z that could be directly imported into Lightscape. (Source: rendering/analysis by revolverdesign, architectural design by Pfau Architecture)

The custom design of light fixtures is a specialist's task, and these environments are currently disconnected from the design tools used by architects. Future developments may include closer links between lighting manufacturers and independent lighting designers, potentially bringing custom manufacturing of reflectors and lenses within the budgetary limits of a wider range of projects.

CHAPTER 7

Project Implementation

7.1 3-D MODELS IN PROJECT IMPLEMENTATION

We have already seen that over the years there have been many attempts to improve the ways that buildings and other structures have been both designed and constructed via the use of computer-assisted techniques. A vast array of technologies have been developed that assist in the implementation of design ideas. Rather than attempt to cover this broad field in detail, we will focus on the use of 3-D digital design models during the project implementation processes. These techniques broadly and nonexclusively fall into several categories: (a) design development, documentation, and project planning (including construction process simulation systems); (b) on-site information provision and utilization; (c) site information and component location approaches; (d) the direct on-site computer-assisted fabrication of components; (e) the use of construction automation techniques, including robotic devices, to fabricate or install components; and (f) inspection and subsequent maintenance and repair. A whole host of different techniques exist in each of these areas. The potential value in the development and use of three-dimensional digital models has reenergized interest in how designers relate to others in the design and building process. It has created opportunities, but also a lack of clarity in how relationships among participants are best structured.

This chapter examines these and other issues. In the first part of the chapter, we review how the use of 3-D digital models can be used in various phases of the design and implementation phases of a project. The final part of the chapter speculates more on how these same applications either affect contractual relationships or demand new forms of interactions.

7.2 APPLICATIONS IN DESIGN DEVELOPMENT AND PROJECT PLANNING

General

This extremely broad area includes how all participants in the design and construction process utilize digital design models in relation to collaboration, communications, and data exchange among participants. The construction of any major building project requires the collaboration and close coordination of many participants. A large number of tools have already been developed to facilitate these processes, including many different kinds of intranets and extranets, but the advent of 3-D models is providing new approaches.

Of particular interest here is the idea of the three-dimensional "shared model" to which all participants have access, and from which two-dimensional views and other information needed by project participants can be extracted. Critical issues include how the shared model is developed and managed, how it is structured in relation to supporting different design development and construction activities, and, of course, its level of detail. Here we should note that since major building projects consist of literally thousands and thousands of individual elements, construction of a fully detailed three-dimensional model is commonly neither sensible nor particularly feasible. Hence, selections and abstractions must be made. Related issues include defining what components are developed in full 3-D. What representations remain in 2-D? How are these decisions made and who makes them? How is the design model modified and subsequently distributed in response to ever-present needs for design changes generated from either programmatic need changes or construction imperatives? Where does primary responsibility for maintaining the model lie? What are the characteristics of the network model and system supporting this whole process? Who pays for all of this? The discussion of integrated design environments, product modeling, data exchange formats, and other topics in Chapter 12 is likewise relevant here. Here we will only outline major uses.

Common Model Uses

There are many specific uses of 3-D models, and 2-D drawings may be extracted or derived from 3-D representations (see Figure 7-1). In a robust system, 2-D drawings

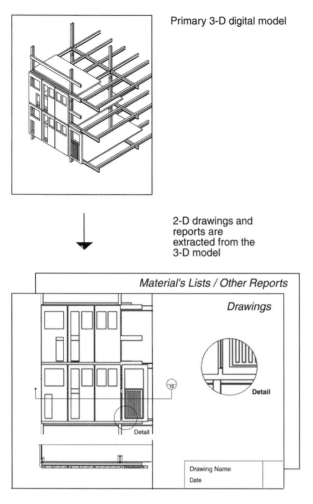

Primary 3-D digital model

2-D drawings and reports are extracted from the 3-D model

Material's Lists / Other Reports

Drawings

Detail

Detail

13

Detail

Drawing Name
Date

Plans, elevations, sections, broken sections, clipped views, details, other drawings, and reports (bill of materials, other) may be generated and exported in a variety of file formats.

Figure 7-1 Standard two-dimensional drawings (plans, elevations, sections, details) may be derived from a three-dimensional digital model.

are automatically updated as the 3-D model changes. Since 3-D models in architecture can only be rarely constructed at the level of detail necessary for full documentation, traditional 2-D drawings may in turn be developed and linked to the governing or master 3-D model (see discussion on this topic in Chapter 12 and the case study of the Stata Center in Chapter 4). How this exactly happens can vary. While a largely unexplored topic, the essential characteristics of the 3-D master model are normally dependent upon the specific design approaches and attitudes of the design architect and normally differ from group to group. Traditional two-dimensional drawings can be coordinated with the 3-D model via established reference points. Three-dimensional and two-dimensional models made by other groups participating in the design process (e.g., engi-

neers) may also be directly incorporated or otherwise linked to models generated by the primary architectural group. Text-based documents, including specifications, may also be connected to the 3-D model via hot links and bill-of-material outputs that can be readily derived from the 3-D model (also see the "Design Collaboration Interchanges" section later in the chapter).

Three-dimensional models may also be used in preliminary cost estimating. The use of computer-assisted techniques for cost estimating is a huge field with a long history. A large number of computer-assisted cost estimation programs useful in preliminary design stages have been developed that make use of area-or-volume measures and associated unit-based material and labor cost estimates. These kinds of area and volume take-offs are normally quite easy to obtain from a robust 3-D modeling environment. The need to use a digital model to support preliminary cost estimating can influence the way the whole digital model is initially structured and built. If the model is intended to be used in this way, cost categories should be carefully thought out a priori and used in the model-building process.

Understanding Design Models

A normal and often problematic part of any design development process are the interactions that occur among the primary design architects, engineers, contractors, suppliers, and others. Simply having all groups understand the primary design model is often a primary issue in itself. Digital design development environments offer a number of tools that greatly enhance the process of understanding and investigating a design. A sampling of some of these tools is illustrated in Figure 7-2.

Any participant with access to the primary design model may navigate through it in a number of modes, including 3-D fly-throughs. Particular components can be automatically located and zoomed in upon. Specific views of controversial details may be generated, marked up with text and sketches, and individually saved for future discussion. Via dynamic sectioning tools, cuts may be made anywhere in the model and at any angle, and then annotated and saved. Gross interferences may be checked for (e.g., between structural beams and HVAC ducts) and recorded. Changed or updated items can be highlighted. A highly interesting aspect of this kind of dynamic investigation is that it can be done collaboratively with multiple participants (see "Design Collaboration Interchanges" coming up in the chapter) and results saved in the form of annotated views. The tree structure of many design development modeling environments also allows these participatory actions to be recorded in order, and thus become a new form of meeting notes.

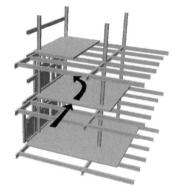

Navigation through model

Magnification of details and interference checks

Dynamic navigation through 3-D models and recorded animations (fly-throughs), detail analyses

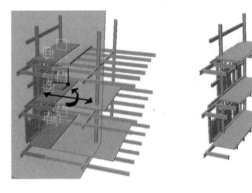

Dynamic section manipulation

Cutaway sections

Dynamic section views while navigating

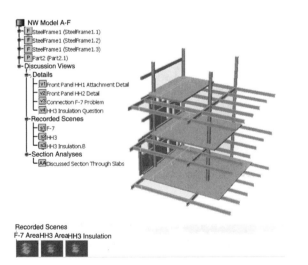

Recorded Scenes
F-7 AreaHH3 AreaHH3 Insulation

Recording of details discussed during design collaboration meetings (visual documentation of "meeting notes")

Figure 7-2 A 3-D model may be used to facilitate interactions among building design and construction participants via fly-throughs, detailed views, dynamic sections, and a variety of annotated notes and hot links.

Construction Planning Simulations

Any manufacturing or construction process is inherently time-dependent. This time dependency is well understood and reflected in many of the tools used to plan and execute projects. Process-oriented computer-assisted scheduling and resource allocation techniques have been used for a long time—dating back to the early development of critical path methods (CPM) and other project evaluation methods (e.g., program evaluation and review technique, or PERT). These techniques basically break the construction process down into a network diagram of a series of dependent and independent tasks (e.g., position bracket, weld connections, attach light fixture) that have time durations and human and material resource needs attached to them. Various optimization techniques can then be used to determine the best work order, expected start and finish times, places where the delay in completion of a task would slow down the whole project, and places where a task can be delayed with little problem. Output is normally tabular or in the form of network diagrams or bar charts. Normally, these abstract representations are not directly linked to the kinds of graphic representations contained in CAD models. This disassociation is not only conceptually undesirable; it also contributes to misunderstandings among participants who should be communicating clearly during the design and construction process.

The desirability of building model elements in view of their time-dependent manufacturing or construction steps has proven valuable in other industries, and its potential value in the building construction world is evident. Models of this general type have long been used in manufacturing sectors to visualize the different manufacturing stages of a product. A simple simulator in manufacturing might show only the product being manufactured (e.g., from stock, through various manufacturing stages such as machining, through to finishing). A better simulator would show not only the piece being made but the actual equipment used as well (including work envelopes), with a full animation of the overall process resulting. Interferences and other problems can then be identified. These simulations allow controllers to redesign processes.

The same general approaches already in widespread use in the manufacturing process sector are now being explored in relation to the construction of major building projects, and for primarily the same reasons. Recently there has been an interesting spate of developments of so-called 4-D process simulators that are based on 3-D digital models (albeit usually simplified ones) and that spatially show construction processes over time as dependent on network analyses. Some initiatives are simple sequences of captured views or non-time-controlled animations that only marginally reflect the actual temporality of the construction process. Better developments have linked 3-D model components to one form or another of construction scheduling approach (e.g., a critical path method or PERT approach). The latter provide the structure and information base for establishing the sequencing and timing of how different components in the 3-D model are displayed. This same structure allows the display model to be updated to reflect real-world issues of changes, delays, and so forth. The optimization features of the scheduling and resource allocation programs impart capabilities to these approaches that go beyond simple animation. (See Figure 7-3.)

Experiences to date with the temporal visualization of the construction process is useful in allowing the design and implementation team to not only understand different implementation steps—often no small feat in a building project with highly complex geometries—but also in rapidly assessing different alternatives.[1] A communication and facilitating role is thus served. Problems with this approach largely hinge around questions of the structuring of model components and related level-of-detail questions, who builds and maintains the model, how it is updated, how it is used, and how it is paid for (see the discussion in the next section). At the moment, models have to be specially constructed in a fairly laborious way. Again, the level of detail of 3-D model representation is an obviously important consideration that affects both the time and the cost of making the model. Models with a relatively high level of abstraction and simplification are feasible, but their value is consequently inherently limited. More detailed models are time-consuming and difficult to make and keep updated. This overall process also requires, of course, that all participants using the model have access to necessary software environments and the expertise to use them (a situation only occasionally achieved by groups that frequently work together). Still, there is every indication that more and more use will be made of 4-D models during the construction process.

Design Collaboration Interchanges

As noted, how participants in the design and construction process interact is both critical and often problematic. To many, there are many positive virtues to so-called teamwork models involving collaborative interchanges. A typical teamwork scenario utilizing 3-D models might be one wherein the primary architectural group develops a master 3-D model and related reports, which is in turn shared with other participants in the design and construction process (engineers, consultants, manufacturers, suppliers, contractors, subcontractors, etc.). These other participants help identify problems and develop and/or refine parts of the base model (or related text documents such as specifications) relevant to their specialties. As changes are suggested

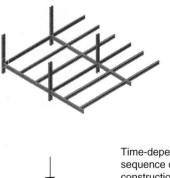

Time-dependent sequence of primary construction events (captures or animations)

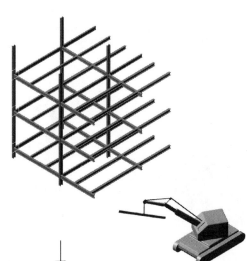

Paths and actions of primary construction equipment may potentially also be shown.

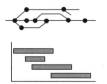

In a well constructed 4-D model, 3-D models of elements appear in the time sequence generated by a network analysis.

Figure 7-3 A 3-D model may be used to facilitate construction planning by showing animations of time-dependent activities.

and accepted, the 3-D master model and associated reports is updated and redistributed to all participants. Here it is assumed that all participants have similar software environments and expertise levels.

Given that participants in the design and construction process are rarely geographically near one another, implementation of the teamwork scenario just noted invariably involves *remote design collaboration sessions*. A 3-D model is remotely shared among participants during a design collaboration session. Currently, remote sharing often involves special structuring of software and hardware environments. When projects are very large, for example, digital models (parts, assemblies) might be located on one server while reports and other text-based information are located on another, with connections managed by special software. The design collaboration session itself requires special software and hardware itself to facilitate remote exchanges. The latter can even involve a user in one location "taking over" a design model or report that resides on another participant's machine (if permissions are granted, of course). (See Figure 7-4.)

During a typical session participants may engage in various communication and discussion activities such as described previously (fly-throughs, detail analyses, interference checking, and so forth) or in the following sections. Actual models are uploaded for all to look at and study. If a design change suggested by a participant is suggested and accepted, the change can be immediately made by the group in charge of the master model.

In an alternative structuring of the process, the master model might not be fully detailed with sub-groups (e.g., engineers or fabricators) charged with developing detailed part models for their own system or component responsibilities. The master model would contain registration points for coordinating these independently developed models. During a collaboration session, an independently developed model of this type could be reviewed and, if approved, uploaded and sent to the group that maintains the master model. This group would then incorporate it into the master model. In some cases this might be as simple as "replacing" one component with a newly modified one. On a simpler note, a contractor or supplier might just update text-based specifications files developed on the format supplied by the primary design group. In all cases, all revisions and updates would be immediately redistributed.

There are many variants to this process, and many different technological environments designed to facilitate it. Critical issues clearly include how the basic model is developed and structured with sharing in mind. Problems of allowable "read/write" access are surely present. Also looming on the horizon are critical issues of liability—who is ultimately responsible for what change and who has to foot the bill when errors are made. Lines of responsibility can be less clear in highly interactive settings. This latter problem is surely resolvable but simply harder to deal with than in traditional—but more sluggish—methods of interaction (e.g., an architect marking up shop drawings prepared by and submitted on paper by a steel fabricator).

From the pure technology viewpoint, the more interactive and real-time interactions seek to become,

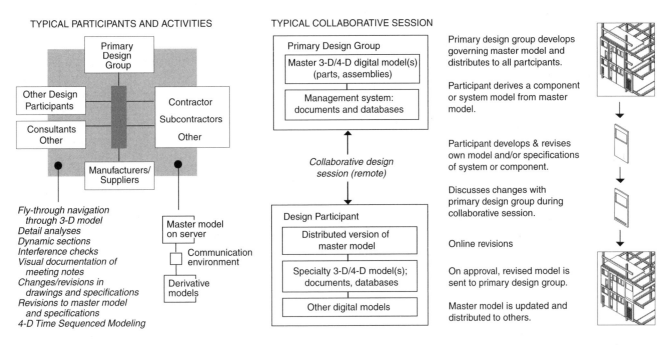

Figure 7-4 Three-dimensional models and associated communication environments can be used to support collaborative design sessions where digital models, reports, or other information are examined in real time and immediately updated if changes are made.

the more specialized the hardware and software environments needed to support the interactions. In general, however, the technology for supporting these kinds of collaborative sessions is constantly improving.

7.3 ISSUES IN MODEL DEVELOPMENT AND USING SHARED MODELS

Model Characteristics and Structure

An ideal scenario *might* suggest that digital models for the detailed design of all architectural elements and components—that often normally involve consultants or others outside of the primary architectural office—should be directly derived from a governing or master digital model of the whole building that is solely developed and maintained by the architect. In this scenario, the digital master model becomes directly used by engineering consultants, general and subcontractors, and others. Here one might imagine that all elements are fully detailed within the master model itself. A truly heroic 3-D model exactly representative of the final building would result. This approach implies, however, a level of detail and model complexity that is fundamentally questionable. The amount of time and labor required to develop such a model is dubiously sensible at best. Technically, models of this complexity are currently cumbersome to use if they are fully parametric and dimensionally driven. The scenario does suggest, however, that many basic questions about the appropriate level of the 3-D model detail and level of abstraction of geometric representation for subassemblies are largely unresolved. It also raises the question of strategy, including, for example, what is usefully represented in 3-D and what is best represented in 2-D and how these representations relate to one another.

Instead of using a massive shared 3-D model as a sole and exclusive mode, the basic master model could be used as a basis for generating derivative submodels associated with each participant's or subdiscipline's focus. A master model would reflect design intent, but specific subsystems would not necessarily be modeled in great detail. They would initially be represented in a simplified or abstracted form of representation. The architect's master model would be referenced for alignment and coordination throughout. However, each submodel would have a complexity and characteristic database specialized for the needs of each discipline, and tuned accordingly for materials and methods, dimensional tolerances, detailing, modeling interpretations, and so forth. These submodels—developed and maintained by the specialist groups—have to be dimensionally and functionally linked to the master model. Ideally, these models would be made using the exact same digital software as used to develop the master model; otherwise, the by now well-acknowledged problems of software incompatibility and the need to exchange data via neutral file formats with all their attendant problems remain present (a situation that is now all too common). In an ideal world, submodels would be directly uploadable for incorporation into the master model that was initially represented at a reduced level of detail. Clearly, interface points would have to be clearly thought out. Methods for coordination and control of these different models, and updating of the primary model, are of paramount importance.

In practice, however, the feasibility and reality of submodels developed by consultants or subcontractors actually being incorporated into a fully functional and detailed master model remains doubtful from both technical and utility points of view. This brings up the interesting question of what, exactly, is the final "master model" or if there is actually a single model at all. Rather, individual submodels normally remain linked and derivative of the master model but not always tied directly into it. Conceptually, the broader question of what defines the design-oriented nature of the master model becomes extremely interesting, including what is parametrically variable and what is not. Is it an abstract geometry, building surfaces, structural frameworks, or even something potentially surprising like circulation networks? These issues are discussed in more detail in Chapter 12. These issues are also important in relation to contractual issues among participants (see Section 7.4).

Model Development

We have seen earlier that in practice the model abstraction level and the inevitable need to coordinate with 2-D drawings are extremely problematic. We can note, however, that the needed level of the model detailing is highly dependent on the uniqueness of the design. If the design is more normative, the construction documentation model can be more abstract and specification-dependent. An unconventional design may need a more detailed 3-D model.

In situations where project types are normative or at least similar, large firms may have the advantage of being able to create detailed 3-D model libraries of common parts through its economy of scale—a process that could require converting essential existing 2-D libraries into 3-D parametric designs that offer the project team the ability to customize its design work. Alternatively, third-party-supplied models could be used (see next paragraph). Larger practices may also be able to engage specialists or consultants who can combine in-depth digital modeling knowledge with CAM-related knowledge. Even with the embedded expert systems and built-in knowledge bases in sophisticated CAD/CAM environments that aid the design and manufacturing process, the artistry of the technology and craft of using

CAD/CAM techniques still demands a thorough and highly skilled knowledge of physical fabrication.

As the field evolves, small practices may ultimately design with third-party-generated building component models. The trend toward fabricator-supplied digital models of components or subsystems is of great interest here, since off-the-shelf products are increasingly offered that have parametric variation capabilities (see Chapter 6)—with all of the problems that these uses and dependencies might involve. Digital model compatibility remains a central issue here (see Chapter 12). The potential of combining these models, however, with in-house-designed 3-D architectural models remains an expected course of development. Major parts of more conventional buildings could then be modeled from suppliers' parts libraries.

Integrated Digital Design and Information Models

The complexity and difficulties of sharing digital design models and sharing information among different participants in the building design and construction process—who often use different software environments—has led to many efforts to provide structured or more seamless ways of digital interaction. Chapter 12 addresses many of these approaches in detail, including the use of product modeling approaches in general, different information exchange protocols (e.g., STEP) based on international standards, product data management (PDM) systems, Web-based process management systems (extranets), and various emerging approaches.

Recently, the term "building information model" (BIM) has been promoted by many vendors as an overall descriptor for the general idea of a parametric 3-D model as being the central vehicle for the generation of everything from 2-D drawings, materials lists, other reports, and various kinds of analyses (e.g., cost, structural), and further serving as the primary basis for interactions and information exchange among all participants in the design and building process. Many of the capabilities described in previous sections—for instance, deriving 2-D drawings from 3-D models—are implicit in this idea, as are others. This central idea is, of course, far from new. It has long been a fundamental tenet of many integrated digital environments now widely used in other industries (e.g., Pro/ENGINEER and CATIA, along with their extensions and related collaboration environments) and long a goal of other initiatives. In the specific BIM terminology, however, most attention is now focused on environments that are specifically "object-oriented" (see Chapter 13). Critical to this implementation is the idea that objects that reflect geometrical and text-based characteristic descriptions or attributes of real building elements (e.g., windows or trusses) are succinctly described

in a highly structured database. In several current constructs of the BIM model, objects are ideally described only once in a single database. In other implementations, a distributed form of linked databases is used. Unlike other approaches relying on international standards, in the BIM model, software vendors are defining proprietary product structures and descriptions. Communication to external systems relies on neutral file exchange formats with all of their attendant problems and limitations.

Current BIM implementations are clearly directed toward common or normative building types, and thus objects are often items such as "doors" and "walls." A door may be inserted into a wall, which accepts it and reconfigures itself. The way the 3-D model is created is typically similar to those of other digital environments. Currently, most implementations are directed toward normative conceptions of buildings where they can be most successfully used. Thus, in some implementations, a "door" object may only be inserted into a "wall" object. Some allow for more robust designs of typical components, for example, curved walls.

For a user wanting to go beyond conventional norms, or for those skilled in using design development environments of the types discussed in Chapter 11, the modeling and other limitations currently imposed by current BIM formulations are highly restrictive, to say the least. Many of the highly sophisticated design development environments described elsewhere also commonly exhibit object-oriented characteristics but may be differently formulated and have related information sharing and collaboration environments that are widely used in other industries. Also, keep in mind that in other design development environments, more flexible models of items like "windows" may be created as well—albeit normative definitions and standards are either not used (or less used) and use operations are less formalized. Characterizations of items like "windows" can be correspondingly more flexible. Communicating with external systems can be difficult because of the vendor-specific nature of these environments.

Many general problems involved in developing and using a 3-D model of a complex building have been already discussed—for example, level of detail and type of representation, complexity of the model, how it is structured, and where does responsibility for maintaining the whole model lie. The problem of who pays for integrated approaches remains paramount. These problems remain present in both BIM implementations and other types of integrated design environments.

7.4 PRACTICE AND RELATIONSHIP ISSUES

As is evident from the preceding discussions, the digital continuum is now being extended all the way from the design model, through engineering analyses and design development, and to project planning and control. Later you will see that on-site project layout, on-site information, and construction automation are also impacted. Within this remarkable sweep, the different roles and responsibilities of various participants in the design and building processes that practice within this context are rapidly changing from those evident in normal practice. Certainly, the old and well-known triangular relationship between owner, architect, and builder is strongly affected. There are more variations in professional responsibilities, and differentiations in project-specific scopes and services. Irrespective of the size of practices, skilled designers versatile in both CAD and CAM are poised to extend the design involvement and responsibility. Given the still evolving nature of the field, however, the question remains of exactly how relationships and responsibilities are structured.

In theory, CAD/CAM environments offer a digital continuum from design to fabrication and subsequently through digitally assisted on-site installation and construction. In practice, the extent and scope of an architectural firm's ability to expand its responsibility beyond normal design phases to include the production of CAD/CAM documentation and other services depends on the expertise of its team members. If the team possesses sufficient working knowledge, skill, and experience in this domain, it can be capable of extending responsibility to computer-aided manufacturing services, and ultimately through all phases of the process. Acquiring this full expertise, however, is neither an easy matter nor necessarily the best model for all firms to pursue.

We have already seen in the case studies presented in earlier chapters that a successful model used to date is that of a "team learning" model—wherein different groups with expertise in various areas form teams that progress from job to job—all the while gaining experience both working with the technologies and in working together. A form of negotiated bid approach is used to structure relationships (see upcoming discussion). Projects are also typically large scale and of high value. This model, based as it is on positive team building and nurtured relationships between participants, is a truly welcome approach in today's difficult professional environment but may not ultimately provide the most feasible model for industry-wide adoption of this kind of process model. Consequently, we should look at how other existing models might work.

Open Bid

The conventional design-bid-build contract preserves the separation of design from fabrication and general contracting of a project. In this configuration, the architectural and engineering contract document conveys the design intentions with building details. The bid-winning fabricator retains the sole responsibility for the 3-D fabrication model and related production procedures. In this format, normative designs may best benefit from this contractual framework. The more experimental and complex designs may be most susceptible to be significantly altered and hard to implement in this format, because of the greater amount of unknown factors in the detailing, methods, and costs for the fabricators. This process also often leads to the formation of new teams of architect, general contractors, and subcontractors for each project. Without continued collaboration opportunities, the knowledge base and collaborative dialogue gained from each project is lost at the completion of each project. This approach makes implementing the positive advantages of the full digital design continuum difficult in complex projects or when participants have limited experience with the digital continuum.

Negotiated Bid

In most forms of the negotiated bid model, the general contractor and/or selected subcontractors are involved in the design development process itself and help shape the final design. In CAD/CAM-related initiatives, the detailed development of highly specialized building assembly or systems can then become the responsibility of knowledgeable fabricators acting as subcontractors and in collaboration with the design team. They would work from a master model defined in limited detail by the architect's office. The question of which trades or subcontractors might be initially involved in the initial negotiation design development process is dependent on project type, size, complexity, and so forth. The negotiated contract can come about in many ways, including via responses to requests for proposals. Once contracts are negotiated, this approach can bring together the key architect, engineer, and fabricators into a design development process that proceeds into final construction. Depending on the project, a general contractor could be involved as well via the same negotiation process. As the process nears completion of the design development phase, general contractors (if not already involved) come into the picture vis-à-vis different normal approaches. Depending on the situation, a general contractor coming in at this point may or may not ultimately team up with subcontractors previously involved in design development and, indeed, might even open requests for new bids from different subcontractors. Leading fabricators acting as subcontractors in the design development phase who have gained special expertise, however, are normally ensured of very limited competition for highly challenging scope of works. This provides incentives for these practitioners to further expand their innovative works to continue their exploratory practices.[2] Repetitive collaborations can afford the team members the opportunity to incrementally learn and improve from project to project.

Design-Build Practices

Design-build groups combine architectural with general contracting services. The 3-D architectural model may be used for design as well as for construction planning and systems coordination. There is a long tradition, however, of this model being associated with highly normative building types and design restraint via imposed cost controls. Ideally, this need not be the case. Specialized CAD/CAM-oriented design-build practices could integrate design and production by combining expertise in digital modeling with digital fabrication methods. This could extend the design effort to experiment, develop, and fabricate assemblies and components—and thus can expand the architect's immediate involvement with the art of making, while allowing the fabrication characteristics to be fully considered during the design phase. The success of this model is more a question of practice orientation and will than of a problem in model structure.

Fast Track

Fast-tracked projects require that a building design be submitted for construction in phased packages, without waiting for the full completion of the project documentation. Three-dimensional modeled projects could benefit a fast-tracked process, allowing each system to be created with an enhanced ability to coordinate with the earlier phased work on-site. The 3-D models enable each construction package to be coordinated digitally, and modifications issued as each phased design is developed (also see the discussion on 4-D models earlier in the chapter).

Packaged Building Systems

Complete building structure and enclosure assemblies are generated with fully integrated digital environments. They are proprietary systems translating their traditional practice, automating design, engineering, and pricing functions through simplified user-designed processes. Here only abstractions of the 3-D building design are needed. A simplified graphic interface can be used by technically trained builders to guide the clients through the design. The design is then forwarded to produce the bills of quantity, detailing, material selection, fabrication details, and so forth.

7.5 ON-SITE PROJECT INFORMATION AND LAYOUT

Part of the design and construction process invariably involves activities such as determining exact information about site conditions, using this information to inform the design of the project, and laying out the locations for soon-to-come construction activities. Traditional surveying techniques, including the use of theodolites and levels, have long been used to both gather information and for subsequent layout work. The advent of digitally based surveying techniques has literally revolutionized in recent years the ancient field of surveying in general, and building-related site surveying in particular. Laser-based surveying equipment can measure and locate points with unprecedented accuracies, in short times, and with little labor. In a typical system, an optical transmitter sends a modulated beam to a physical target placed at the point of interest. The beam is reflected from the target and picked up by an optical receiver. Measurement of the phase differences between the sent and reflected beams allows the distance to be precisely measured. Data is stored in typical microcomputers. Wireless technologies can be used. Any point can be measured in three dimensions.

This sophisticated equipment is typically used first to gather site data—such as boundary or terrain data—which subsequently serves as input into the governing digital model for the building project. During construction, this same equipment can be used to precisely measure and locate what has actually been put into place. Plans may call for a slab top to be at a certain elevation, for example, but only an after-the-fact measurement will tell if the top as actually constructed is located exactly where it was intended. These activities thus also serve an inspection and control function. In cases where dimensional problems have arisen with recently constructed elements, and the design and construction team decides to accept the situation as is, the same dimensional information can be used as a basis for adjusting the dimensions of other elements built upon the problematic one so that fits can be obtained.

At this time, most surveying systems utilize their own software and digital design environments. Normally, typical 3-D CAD environments do not connect directly to surveying environments. A series of data transfers and exchanges must take place. As described in Chapter 4, this approach was utilized in making connections between a 3-D model and a site surveying system for the Stata Center at MIT. In addition to aiding in locating new construction, exact locations of as-built components can be relayed back as well. In a normative building consisting of orthogonally placed components, this kind of approach is rarely needed. In complex projects, it can be essential.

On-Site Applications

On-Site Task Information

Ultimately, project information must be conveyed to the sets of individuals who actually do real construction activities—a process that has long been based on voluminous paper documents (plans, sections, specifications). Feedback from the site has also frequently caused revisions to project plans because of unexpected conditions, misfits, or unanticipated conflicts between components. Since construction progress takes place in specified sequences done by designated workgroups, it is also commonplace knowledge that not all information is needed at all times. Providing the right information at the right time and in a usable way is always a concern.

These and other site-related activities have become prime targets for innovation vis-à-vis digitally based technologies. Clearly, the use of a vast array of communication devices has expedited general information flow and feedback. Of specific interest herein are the increasing numbers of digitally based tools that provide capabilities for sending designated information derived from the governing digital model to a specific field work group and subsequently having this information displayed graphically and as text in portable field devices. The information sent can be as specific as tailored work orders containing dimensioned drawings and other information for the specific daily task of the work group. Capabilities for specialized annotations are common. Feedback concerning task completion can be returned to the central construction management group.

On-Site CAD/CAM Component Manufacturing Facilities

CAD/CAM technologies are widely used in the building products industry in the off-site production of components such as windows, doors, bar joists, timber trusses, wall assemblies, and so forth, with these products subsequently being transported to a site and installed. Unlike other industries, however, the fact remains that much of the time and cost involved in a major building project goes far beyond what can be implemented and controlled in a factory circumstance, but takes place on actual construction sites. Are there opportunities for actually bringing CAD/CAM production facilities onto the actual work site?

The idea of bringing mechanized component production facilities to a site is an old one (recall the building processes of Paxton's Crystal Palace in 1851 to 1852). Many advantages over strictly off-site production seem clear. Only raw or basically processed materials are shipped to the site, saving transportation costs for large or bulky components. There are no size limitations imposed by transportation vehicles. Members can be more easily adjusted or fitted to meet real on-site

field measurements. Expensive inventories need not be maintained. Because of these and other benefits, there are now many devices currently used on-site that transform raw or bulk processed materials into actual building components. Thus, there are many on-site machines used for cutting to length or fitting various metal and wood members. Nonetheless, on-site manufacturing operations have been fairly limited to date. Still, many that are in use are quite suggestive of an interesting future, including, for instance, the common gutter-making machine that uses adjustable rollers to shape profiles from a large roll of sheet metal, or the sheet-metal-forming machine with adjustable pin arrays that can be used to make surfaces with double curvatures. These machines, however, are not normally controlled via a governing digital model and thus are not truly CAD/CAM machines. The same is generally true for many others currently used on-site machines for producing components.

It is possible to imagine how many of these same currently used on-site machines could be converted into CNC machines, which could in turn receive instructions derived from a governing digital model. Likewise, it is possible to imagine how many, but surely not all, CNC machines currently used primarily in workshop settings could be made transportable and used on a site (e.g., in a traveling trailer). Whether doing so is sensible is another question.

Despite interesting future scenarios, however, the use of on-site component production facilities remains in an early development stage. The use of off-site-produced elements with their own many attendant advantages and economies of scale has dominated current building construction and will undoubtedly and correctly continue to do so for the bulk of many common building components (e.g., it is hard to imagine the value of on-site fabrication facilities for common door hinges, faucets, lighting fixtures, and hundreds of other ubiquitous building elements). Considerable research work needs to be done to differentiate the respective values of both off-site and on-site approaches. In particular, there is a need to identify exactly where on-site approaches are truly both viable and valuable.

Construction Process Automation

The process of assembling a building shares some aspects with the process of assembling an automobile, yet the distinctions that are indeed present are enormous and significant. In an automobile assembly line, we see organized assembly paths surrounded by many different types of machines, including industrial robots, that seemingly assembly an automobile with minimal direct human hands-on labor. On a typical construction site we see a vast array of relatively unique process tasks accomplished by individuals or groups of individuals using a variety of tools and mechanized assists, but the primary role of human labor is inescapably obvious. The reasons for these differences clearly have to do with size and scale, uniqueness of product, product value, and general industry structure.

Construction activities consist of many different kinds of processes. Some activities directly alter the shape or forms of materials; others are assembly-oriented. Many of these activities have already been automated to a greater or lesser extent. Some approaches focus on improving the overall construction setting, such as automated construction platforms that rise with a building. Other approaches focus on the development of highly mechanized machines that are designed to accomplish specific tasks. The lure of using robotic devices has led to several experiments in this latter area. In the robust construction era of the 1980s, several construction firms (notably in Japan) developed prototypes for several different kinds of machines to aid in common construction activities (e.g., installing spray fireproofing) that attracted wide attention—albeit they never achieved widespread use or acceptance. Still, it is necessary to view this field as one that is an early stage of evolution.

The development of on-site automation techniques has been hampered by both technology limitations and by the lack of clear development goals and an understanding of primary barriers to innovation. The broad reasons for pressing to introduce more and more on-site automation vary. These include the prospect of economic return via increased productivity, especially in labor-intensive activities; the desire to improve workforce safety via the use of automated devices in activities that are particularly hazardous or unhealthy to workers; the desire to improve working conditions by using automated devices for tasks that are dirty, boring, or repetitious; the need to address vanishing skill capabilities; and the need to provide or improve precision capabilities commensurate with changing building technologies. Broad social changes, such as the changing demographic makeup of workers in the construction industry, can also contribute to the need for automation.

While needs are clear, there are many difficulties that must be overcome and development goals to be achieved before automation on the site is truly a reality. Among the more salient barriers to innovation—particularly for robotic devices—include the following: construction sites are extremely hostile and ill-defined environments (e.g., dusty and dirty environments, clutter, ever-changing conditions, needs to change levels frequently, etc.); many construction activities are non-repetitive or one-off; and many construction materials and components are often poorly suited to manipulation by automated devices (e.g., big, delicate sheets; long flexible lines). There are also many basic techno-

logical feasibility questions that must be addressed in either adopting technologies from other disciplines or in developing new ones. Standard requirements for load carrying, force exertion, precision, and so forth are quite different in construction than they are in other production circumstances; and it is difficult to simply borrow technologies from other fields.

In considering field automation, one of the first objectives is to define what activities or processes could be usefully automated. A first task in developing goals is to define what activities or processes are common on the construction site and, of these, which are the best targets for automation. Grouping the many and varied activities that take place on a construction site into a series of broad process categories is an often-used device for considering field automation issues, for example, material and component movement and manipulation, and surface preparation and finishing. While this approach is useful, it can blur the amazing complexities and subtleties of the various processes that are actually conducted in the field, and, also, it does not immediately bring into focus critical automation questions of scale, complexity, repetitiveness, and so forth. Even more critically, it tends to suggest that a "goal" for field automation research should be the dubious one of somehow creating robots or other automation forms that are capable of performing generic processes (e.g., a fully autonomous robot that does every possible surface preparation and finishing activity imaginable). Often the less generic and more specified the task, the more it is possible to automate effectively. For these reasons, far more specific lists may prove more useful, such as "tile laying," "pipe laying," "slurry walls," or "rebar installation." It is this more specific targeting of tasks that is commonly used as the driving force behind construction automation today. It implies, however, that the goal is to automate normative processes that are in turn derived from normative design approaches.

Applications

Construction invariably involves some form or another of site shaping, foundation work, installation of underground utility lines, and so forth, which involve the use of heavy equipment. The operating environment is large and unstructured. Precision requirements vary but are not high for many common applications. Some conventional equipment has long been equipped with various kinds of sensors (load, position) to aid equipment operators, but the state of the art here is improving daily. The use of newer means of measurement and location control—for example, laser technologies and Global Positioning Systems (GPS)—is a major development. Many earth-shaping machines, for example, now commonly incorporate GPS devices directly into them. These devices can provide not only general locational information but levels as well. They can be used to literally guide a machine along a specific path to create grades of specified slopes. Reference data is obtained from the sophisticated site surveying systems mentioned earlier.

Several different approaches have been explored to aid in the lifting and placement of building components. One of the early examples of automation was a teleoperated system that aided in the lifting and general alignment and placing of major structural steel members. There has been a lot of interest recently in automating the steel construction process, with a lot of attention focusing on off-site automation in relation to preparation for site erection, including rethinking connections to facilitate self-alignment and adjustment.

There are many finishing and enclosure elements (curtain wall components, doors, windows, etc.) that can be cumbersome to move and place, and that would seem to be candidates for some type of automation. While various types of mechanized devices have been developed to assist in these tasks, they have largely been resistant to robotic automation. Reasons are many (cluttered environments, limited lifting power of robots, installation instructions, etc.).

More success has been achieved with specific processes found more amenable to automation. Early experiments by the Shimizu Corporation, a major Japanese construction company, focused on labor-intensive tasks that involved little lifting power (e.g., spraying fireproofing material on beams) but were repetitive tasks. Recently developed automated shot-creting machines that use laser scanning systems to map anticipated work areas provide a positive example of what can be done.

Some progress has been made in commonplace finishing tasks such as finish surface grinding for concrete floor by utilizing control and obstacle detection technologies that are surprising similar to the robotic lawn mowers that creep across many of today's suburban lawns.

Summary

Despite the paucity of successful examples of practical robotic construction devices, the increasing need for improved productivity in this field is undoubtedly going to continue to drive exploration and innovation. Still, many of the fundamental problems noted remain. It is interesting to note that most current approaches seek to automate current construction activities. The introduction of new technologies in the building industry has typically followed the path of initially using new materials or technologies to mimic and replace existing ones. A more exciting possibility is that of rethinking the whole construction process paradigm on the basis of what might be technologically possible from an automation viewpoint. A rethinking by teams of designers, manufacturers, and contractors is needed of fundamental attitudes about how buildings are built. This rethinking should involve designing basic building components in relation to anticipated automated site construction processes. Architects need to imagine and develop innovative designs that facilitate the use of on-site robotic assembly techniques. This would involve rethinking how specific elements are designed, made, and assembled. As a simple example, a common internal wall might cease to be made in conventional ways. The use of big sheets of semiflexible gypsum wallboard screwed onto metal studs—a conventional technology that is difficult to mimic with robotic devices—might be replaced by panelized systems involving smaller clip-on surface units that allow one-sided push-on assembly (see Chapter 16). Ultimately, these operations could be linked to and driven by a 3-D model, which would first govern unit manufacturing—perhaps on-site—and then the subsequent assembly process.

At this point, however, most technologies that have been introduced seek to automate existing processes. A preferred approach is to rethink all processes with automation in mind.

THE PRODUCT AND INDUSTRIAL DESIGN CONTEXT

These two chapters focus on the world of industrial and product design. They are intended for architects interested in understanding the industrial design process and, similarly, for industrial designers interested in overlaps with architecture. The topic is examined through several product design and development examples, and, in the process, the application and impact of CAD/CAM tools in this area is illustrated.

CHAPTER 8

Introduction to Product Design and Development

8.1 INDUSTRIAL DESIGN AND PRODUCT DESIGN

Industrial Design

Industrial design deals with the design of industrially manufactured commodities and services developed and delivered to consumers, clients, and customers. Historically this has meant mass-produced goods, from automobiles to toothbrushes.

The industrial design umbrella encompasses such specializations as product, graphic, packaging, or transportation design (such as train and aircraft interiors), each one with its own subspecialization. Within product design, for example, we find specialization for medical, consumer, and industrial products. Less familiar dimensions of the profession may include other specializations, such as food design, which addresses the demands of an ever-growing industrially based food industry. It is clear that these areas require specialized sets of skills and in-depth knowledge of the market. As a result, industrial design has tended toward an ever-growing professional specialization.

Product Design

As a subspecialization, *product design* is, fundamentally, the development of the aesthetic, formal, and "use" language of products. This process occurs mostly in the conceptualization and design refinement phases of a product development process. The term *product development,* on the other hand, refers to the larger process, from the identification of market opportunities, inception of a product idea, schematic design and refinement, electrical and mechanical engineering, to manufacturing, assembly, and packaging. As such, the designer involved in product development works and interacts with different groups:

- *Marketing.* Typically comes up with product specifications based on the identification of specific market opportunities.
- *Engineering.* Develops, among other things, the electrical and mechanical design of products.

- *Manufacturing.* Ultimately produces the product or parts for the product. This includes parts manufacturing and assembly.

8.2 THE PRODUCT DESIGNER: A HISTORICAL PERSPECTIVE

In a history of the creation of artifacts, the designer represents a break from the tradition of craft, whereby planning is conceived of as a separate body of knowledge and is separated from the act of making. Industrial design is understood as a specialized task that involves the coordination and planning of various specialized skills in an environment of mass manufacturing and serial repeatability. Historically, this newly born need to plan and coordinate, in turn, created the need for the representational tools of drawing and model making. This question of representation is critical, as it directly colors the role and impact of CAD/CAM tools.

Design and the Industrial Designer

Although the industrial revolution is generally regarded as the birthplace of industrial design, we can find earlier examples. The Gutenberg press has been argued as one such example. It is, however, undisputable that it was the industrial revolution that created the full-fledged technological and social conditions that truly characterized the profession. The designer was needed to create and manage the planning of these new products. The impetus was multifold: creating aesthetically pleasing industrial products that would be assured of large-scale acceptance while creating consumer identities for products that had not previously existed. What should the first toaster look like? (See Figure 8-2.) The first radio?

The production of goods was not only fueled by newly found industrial capabilities and the demand for products, but also by the large-scale retail and distribution infrastructure that made the marketing and sale of such goods possible. In 1865, Paris's Bon Marché

Figure 8-1 The Nokia 7600 model mobile phone. (Source: image courtesy of Nokia)

opened its doors and became one of the world's first department stores. New architectural technologies facilitated the conception of such a large-scale building. Alexandre-Gustave Eiffel's use of cast iron gave the large block-sized building skylights and interior courts, and it freed up "window displays" around its perimeter. In an intricate web of causes and effects, the very forces that had powered the industrial revolution had brought about the newfound structures of the department store, which in turn facilitated the sale of the goods, fueling the economic engine behind industry.

Nature of Industrialization

Industrialization occurred in different countries at different times and impacted different industries. This had a large impact on the nature of products produced, the future development of various industries, and the ideological slant of products.

In the United Kingdom, industrialization began with the simple crafts (such as textiles), while the United States started later, by industrializing more complex, three-dimensional mechanical devices. As a result

Figure 8-2 First GE toaster, 1909. (Source: image courtesy of GE)

of its particular historical and social context, many in the United Kingdom saw a moral imperative for industrialization—an opportunity to "bring art to the people." For the first time, quality design could be reproduced and made accessible to a large segment of the population. In the United States, on the other hand, the industrial mandate was seen differently. In a young and sparsely populated country, where labor and the Calvinist work ethic were at the core of a young nation, the imperative for industrialization was through "utility for the people": mechanical time-saving devices for large segments of the population.

Historically Based Models

The following models are used—with latitude—to illustrate some key developments and concepts in the historical development of the profession. We take a closer look at four of the many great contributors of the profession—each one contributing a valuable set of ideas or strategies, many of which are still used today.

Wedgwood: Mix and Match

Born in 1730, Joshia Wedgwood was a talented potter whose pottery is one of the first examples of a mass-produced consumer product. The success of his product is owed to at least three key factors:

1. The application of fundamental principles of division of labor and specialization of tasks to the production of ceramic goods
2. The development of a business model to support his business, whereby he divided the production into tableware and ornamentals (the first being mass-produced and utilitarian and the second being high-margin "art").
3. The application of principles of scientific experimentation to perfect the science and technology of glazes and clays. Wedgwood's quest and final discovery of Jasper alone (considered by many the greatest technological leap in pottery since the Chinese invention, almost a thousand years earlier, of porcelain) involved more than 10,000 different experiments.

The scientific, experimental, and methodical nature of his work allowed him to develop proprietary technologies, giving his product the consistency and appeal necessary to differentiate himself from other ceramic products on the market. He developed, for example, precise technologies to control the firing temperatures of his kilns. Thermometers had not been able to sustain the high firing temperatures. Temperature was gauged by looking at the color of the flame, which resulted in highly inconsistent products and frequent failures.

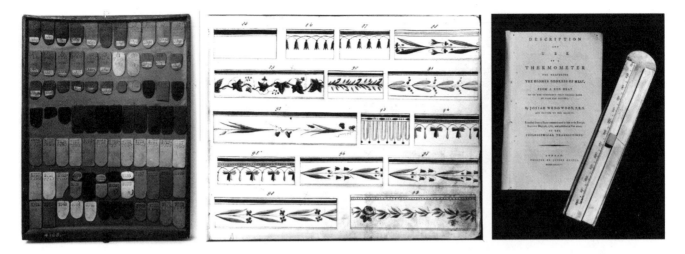

Figure 8-3 Wedgwood's innovation included the development of a high-temperature thermometer to guarantee firing consistency and (A) exhaustive experiments to perfect his ceramic and "Jasper" mixtures. (B) Wedgwood pattern books used by consumers to customize their tableware: Selected patterns could be mixed and matched with tableware patterns. (Source: Images courtesy of the Wedgewood Museum Trust, Barlaston, Staffordshire, England)

Wedgwood devised a thermometer based on the principle that clay shrinks when fired to accurately measure firing temperature. This ultimately allowed him to streamline his manufacturing process and ensure a consistent mass-producible product. Further, to appeal to a diversified clientele, plate and pattern books could be consulted and variations derived by a mix-and-match approach. This enabled him to produce an exceedingly wide range of designs to satisfy the highly diversified English consumer. (See Figure 8-3.)

Colt: Interchangeable Parts

Samuel Colt represents one of the great American success stories in manufacturing industrialized products. Based on his model for a new, rotating drum mechanism, Colt opened a business to design and manufacture firearms. Following the order of thousands of "Walker" firearms by the U.S. Ordinance Department, Colt opened a new factory in Connecticut. The factory had state-of-the-art metalworking machinery, turning out 5,000 finished handguns in the first year. Colt developed interchangeable parts, 80 percent manufactured by precision machinery. This enabled him to easily adapt his designs to respond to consumer needs.[1]

Colt was significant in the development of a product strategy that relied on complex, three-dimensional, interchangeable mechanical parts (see Figure 8-4). He was also significant for his connection with users: He closely monitored user response, perfected his weapons based on customer feedback, and customized his weapons for customers based on a mix-and-match approach and ornamental embellishing.

Kodak: Total Service for the Masses

In 1878 George Eastman set out to simplify—and thus ultimately bring to the populace—the process of pho-

tography.[2] He developed a camera that was ready-loaded with a negative stripping film, and provided developing and refilling services as an extra. He simplified the camera, marketing it with the slogan "you press the button, we do the rest." The camera box had a lens with a short focal length, so that everything beyond the immediate vicinity would be in focus. It was a point-and-click camera. (See Figure 8-5.)

His innovation was also in splitting photography into two activities: taking the picture and developing

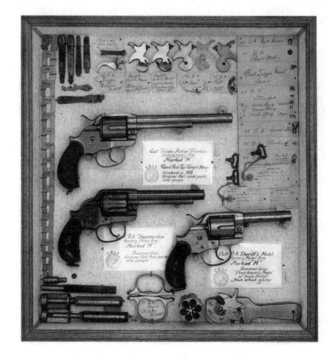

Figure 8-4 Colt's innovation was in his ability to manufacture complex mechanisms with interchangeable parts. This allowed for variation, customization, and universal interchangeability. (Source: © 2004 Colt Archives LLC. All rights reserved.)

Figure 8-5 Kodak Brownie brought—for the first time—photography to the masses. Photography had been simplified to Kodak's motto "You press the button, we do the rest." (Source: Image courtesy © Eastman Kodak Company. KODAK is a trademark.)

the picture. These two realms helped simplify the process (by taking the technologically demanding processing of film out of the user's responsibility) and provided the consumer with an affordable camera to start taking pictures—all marketed and conceived as a full product/service package. This enabled him to offer an affordable camera (for $1) while generating profits from the developing and film replacement (totaling $1 per 6 photographs).

Eastman also recognized the consumer segment as a diversified one and recognized the possibility of market segmentation to include children and women. Children were a clear consumer target: He would be preparing future generations of amateur photographers (ensuring future sales of his products) while illustrating to the larger market that if it "can be operated by any school child, boy or girl," it would surely be simple enough for anyone else. Women, on the other hand, represented a new market of consumers that was growing with the emergence of leisure time.

Thonet: Bentwood Furniture

Cabinetmaker Michael Thonet (1796–1871) was, by the 1830s, experimenting with bentwood techniques as a way of making chair backs. After further refinement—notably, introducing steel inlays at critical points—Thonet brought out one of his most famous chairs:

Figure 8-6 Thonet's classic Chair 14. Reduction of components to easily reproducible elements was a key to Thonet's success. (Source: Images courtesy of Gebrüder Thonet Gmbh, Germany)

Chair No. 14, the *Konsumsessel,* or "consumer's chair." This chair was one of great simplicity and directness. (See Figure 8-6.)

Through the development of specific yokes and a heat treatment process, Thonet was able to serially manufacture consistent bentwood components (see Figure 8-7). This work was based on exhaustive wood-bending experimentation developed into a consistent, reliable process (see Figure 8-8). By combining previously discrete chair members into single bentwood parts, the chair was designed with a reduced number of components. The use of formwork to produce identical components ensured consistency of the chair at a mass manufacturing scale. This reduced not only the labor required to make a chair but also the number of parts required in its assembly. The invention was not so much in the design itself, but rather in the techniques that enabled such ideas to be mass-produced.

Originally supplied in kit form, the chair could be used anywhere, and it was. (By the 1930s, over 50 million of this basic model type had been produced, and it is still being made today.) One of the critical successes of Thonet's was the ability to ship the chairs in compo-

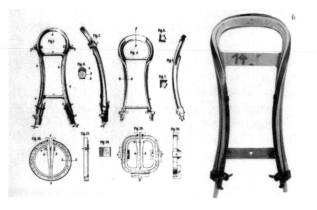

Figure 8-7 Yokes for molding solid wood. (Source: Image courtesy of Gebrüder Thonet Gmbh, Germany)

Figure 8-8 Thonet's experimental wood bending developed new techniques for furniture manufacturing. This experimental chair was based on a single solid bent wood plank. (Source: Image courtesy of Gebrüder Thonet Gmbh, Germany)

nents (thereby reducing shipping volume) and have them assembled on-site. The reduced number of components meant an easier assembly sequence and a reduced number of manufacturing steps. Complete components for 36 chairs could be shipped in a 1-meter cubed shipping container (see Figure 8-9).

Designer Models

The Consultant Designer—1929

Up until 1929's Great Depression, consumer products were, generally speaking, produced by "anonymous" designers. With the 1929 crash of the stock market

Figure 8-9 A 1-meter cubed crate could hold all parts for 36 chairs: Ease in transportation made it an easy global product. (Source: Image courtesy of Gebrüder Thonet Gmbh, Germany

came a poorer consumer, who, as a result, was a more discerning consumer. With little money, the average consumer sought out value. By the 1930s, many accepted products had reached technical parity, and little distinguished them from each other. Struggling for survival, companies looked to bring down costs while differentiating their products from the competition. Recognizing their internal inaptitude to turn things around, many companies looked outside. A new generation of designers—known as consultant designers— emerged. The new cadre was that design should include not just the product but the whole process: from inception to manufacturing. Innovation, aesthetic appeal, market needs, industry capabilities, and costs were forever intertwined by the newfound rigorous conditions imposed by the Great Depression.

Consultant Designers

The new consultant designers gave appeal and identity to products but also streamlined the manufacturing and marketing processes, helped identify market needs, and created brand identities. This full-service product development approach reflected the principle that the industrial product could not be conceived of as a solitary entity but had to be considered through a complex, and interconnected, web of interdependent agents. Part businesspeople, these new designers not only gave identity and flare to products but expanded their scope to cover company identity, branding, and advertisement. These pioneers established the basic practice models and standards that are still followed today. Dreyfuss's ergonomic studies, for example, are still considered an industry standard (see Figure 8-10).

Designers—National Models

Geographic, cultural, and historical differences have characterized other industrial designer models, which in turn have colored the practice, roles, and responsibilities of design and designers in other regions. Although stereotypical, these models do help explain the impact of cultural circumstances and their effects on the idea of the designer:

- *Consultant designer.* Brought about by the need to manage the interdependencies of business, manufacturing, and design, this model emerged primarily in the United States.

- *Craft/industrial artist.* A Scandinavian model, this was fundamentally brought about by the late arrival of industrialization to the region and the strong tradition of craft associations.

- *Architect/artist.* This Italian model grew out of Italy's postwar educational and social structure, along with the tradition and pervasiveness of small-scale craft-based businesses.

HAND MEASUREMENTS OF MEN, WOMEN AND CHILDREN

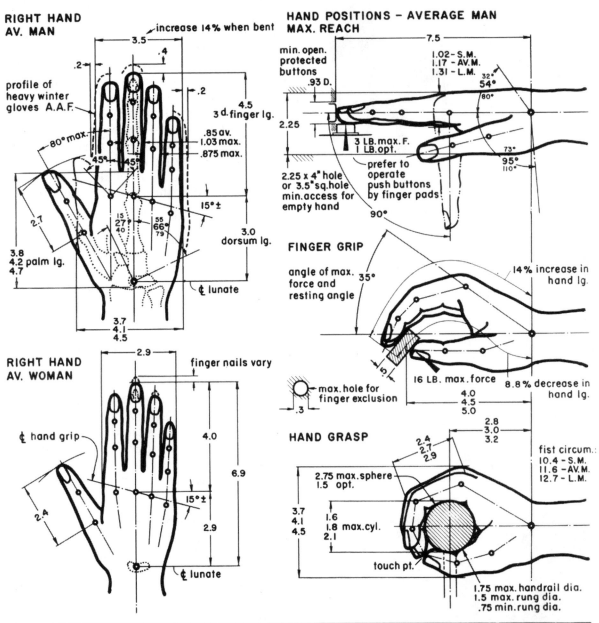

HAND DATA	MEN			WOMEN			CHILDREN			
	2.5%tile	50.%tile	97.5%tile	2.5%tile	50.%tile	97.5%tile	6 yr.	8 yr.	11 yr.	14 yr.
hand length	6.8	7.5	8.2	6.2	6.9	7.5	5.1	5.6	6.3	7.0
hand breadth	3.2	3.5	3.8	2.6	2.9	3.1	2.3	2.5	2.8	—
3d. finger lg.	4.0	4.5	5.0	3.6	4.0	4.4	2.9	3.2	3.5	4.0
dorsum lg.	2.8	3.0	3.2	2.6	2.9	3.1	2.2	2.4	2.8	3.0
thumb length	2.4	2.7	3.0	2.2	2.4	2.6	1.8	2.0	2.2	2.4

Figure 8-10 Henry Dreyfuss's ergonomic standards were the basis for modern ergonomics. (Source: *Designing for People,* by Henry Dreyfuss, New York: Simon and Schuster, 1955, and New York: Allworth Press, 2003. Copyright John A. Dreyfuss and Gail Dreyfuss Wilson)

- *Engineer/designer:* This German model was defined by, among other things, the impact of the Hochschule für Gestaltung (Ulm School of Design), which led to the philosophy behind Braun and other successful companies where design was seen as a science-based discipline.

8.3 PRODUCTS

The Economics of Products

As we've seen, design and technological innovation can help differentiate products. However, other factors such as market launch timing, distribution, and manufacturing can also significantly impact the success of products. Consider that every added expense, error, and distribution/communication hiccup is multiplied by 10,000 for low-volume products and, say, 1 million for high-volume products. This certainly implies that high-volume products need to be tuned to a much higher degree. A 10-cent cost difference for a part, would be in an architectural context negligible. For a high-volume industrial product, that would mean at least a $100,000 difference. Consider that a product may have hundreds of parts, and each cost decision is multiplied innumerably. Costs may be direct (e.g., the cost of a part) or indirect (e.g., the cost of installing a part) and need to be cross-examined against the whole product development process.

Given today's highly competitive markets, even the slightest fluctuation in time and costs can make or break a product's success. As such, great amounts of time are spent in marketing, design, and engineering to cost out and develop optimal product approaches. *Cost analysis* (COGS), *cost reduction engineering,* and *design for high volume* are just some of the engineering tools at the product development team's disposal. In addition, other factors affect a product's economical picture. One factor is *agency approval,* which refers to the approval required by products that require governmental or other agency approval; these may include consumer electronics, such as cell phones, radios, or even simple heaters. Many full-service product development companies offer these engineering-based services to their clients.

Product Types

There are several ways of thinking about the factors that characterize a product. It may have to do, for example, with the production volume, the end user, or the manufacturing complexity. We will identify product types by looking at them through the perspective of the end market, consumer type, and the company.

Product Characterizations

What kind of product is it? Although the terminology varies considerably, we will use it—with liberty—to characterize three large categories:

1. *Consumer products.* Products conceived, produced, and purchased without a specific industry slant for the general public. These are the general products that anyone purchases and that one would commonly find in the household. They might include cameras, pens, and suitcases.
2. *Professional products.* Used to refer to a broad category of products that are driven by the specific circumstance of profession-driven industries. These include medical products, which are characterized by the need of in-depth knowledge and experience in the practice and use of tools, agency approval process, and industry standards. In the context of the medical profession, for example, this might include defibrillators, MRI equipment, and stethoscopes.
3. *Industrial products.* Used to characterize those products used by industry and not intended for end users, these tend to be subcontracted products that are assembled (with other products) into a larger product. In the automotive industry, for example, industrial products are purchased as subcomponents to be assembled into cars. In the architectural context, these would include building systems, ceiling systems, and plumbing components.

Product Context

Here we look at the very useful conceptual approach that has been clearly defined in the work of Ulrich and Eppinger.[3] These authors have articulated different product design and development processes in relation to a firm's context, resources, and fundamental mission. Hence, we have market pull, technology push, platform product, process-intensive, and customized product characterizations.

A *market pull* is where a market opportunity is identified before any design work is done at all. A product concept and its enabling technologies are only subsequently developed in response to this identified need.

A variant model is that of *technology-push* products, wherein a company starts with either a proprietary technology or particular technological capability and then looks for a market in which these technologies could be effectively employed in creating a responsive product. In this age of rapid technological development, many individuals and organizations find themselves possessing unique and seemingly valuable technologies before actually knowing what to do with them. Experience indicates, however, that the general technology-push process must be carefully done to ensure that the resulting product does indeed meet a market need at a competitive price.

Many companies find themselves with existing technologies termed *platform products* developed for one application that they seek to apply elsewhere (see Chapter 9 for more on platform design). In comparison with new technologies associated with technology-push products, these platform products generally have proven performance and customer acceptance records. Normally, their use is explored in connection with variant products intended for an allied market. Often they are essential components—for example, some sort of control mechanism—that normally form an essential part of many product lines.

Many products can be described as being *process-intensive*. In these cases, the manufacturing and production processes involved are so intensive, and often expensive, that product characteristics are highly determined by them.

Customized products are slight variations on standard products that are made specifically upon the request of a customer. These products can be components of other products or end products themselves. Thus, a company producing a line of textured panels might respond to another company's request for panels with a specific texture for use in one of their own products. In these cases, design parameters that can be varied are very closely established, since not all conceivable variations are possible within the context of a given manufacturing facility and process setup.

Product Appeal

A *user-driven* product is one in which the primary value of a product depends on the visual appeal of the product, or on the perceived functionality of how a user would relate to it or use it. Many consumer-oriented products that lie within the "market-pull" category described tend to be user-driven. Industrial designers are frequently engaged at an early stage in products of this type.

The converse is true in a *technology-driven* product. Here, the primary value of the product lies with its technology or the functional capability of the product to accomplish some specific task. User perceptions of the technical performance dimensions of the product influence selections more than appearance or even ease of use.

Obviously, many products are both technology- and user-driven simultaneously or fall somewhere on the spectrum between the two extremes. Many companies, for example, market products to attract different user types: They may have a "professional" (or technically driven) product as well as "easy-to-use" products designed for a broader but less technically demanding market.

Product Volume

Another broad and traditional way of characterizing products has to do with long-made distinctions between high-, medium-, and low-volume production quantities—considerations that are best made in relation to the cost of the product, its technical sophistication, and its manufacturing process determinants. In this context, 1 million units would be a high volume, while 10,000 would generally qualify as a low volume.

Clearly, many common "high-production/low-cost/low-sophistication/process-intensive" products are produced with great economy of scale in huge numbers by strongly deterministic manufacturing processes. The humble stamped pie plate provides an example. In terms of the preceding discussion, these are process-intensive end products where care must be taken in ensuring that a competitive advantage would accrue before any even seemingly minor design variations are undertaken. (For example, is there really a market for elliptically shaped pie plates?) "Customized products" for special customers are indeed possible, but only when the needed number of units is quite high. By contrast, "low-volume/high-cost/high-sophistication/low-process-intensity" products can typically be easily customized and there is relatively little overhead investment in capital-intensive production facilities.

8.4 PRODUCT DEVELOPMENT

There are many specializations associated with the general field of industrial design: product design, graphic design, packaging, transportation. *Product development* refers to the overall process ending in the sale of products. This includes the identification of market opportunities, product concept and design, and delivery of the product. *Product design* refers to those activities that impact the designer's role and decisions: working to produce designs for products by identifying design concepts, manufacturing processes, and cost and time considerations. Given the multitude of companies, industries, and cultures that fall under the larger industrial design umbrella, many concepts are expressed using general terms.

Although each process and product is different (and hence development strategies, paths, and organizations differ), the general product development process fundamentally includes the five basic phases (organized, loosely speaking, in order) that are shown in Figure 8-11.

The product development team will make use of several design, engineering, and marketing tools at their disposal. These tools and skills might include those shown in Figure 8-12.

We will examine in more detail the overall process and interdependent tools, steps, and tasks through the

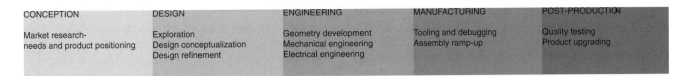

CONCEPTION	DESIGN	ENGINEERING	MANUFACTURING	POST-PRODUCTION
Market research-needs and product positioning	Exploration Design conceptualization Design refinement	Geometry development Mechanical engineering Electrical engineering	Tooling and debugging Assembly ramp-up	Quality testing Product upgrading

Figure 8-11 The product development phases.

Pingtel case study later in the chapter. This will illustrate more detailed considerations and ramifications. The case study will also illustrate standard uses of CAD/CAM technologies in design.

We will focus primarily on design, but there are, as illustrated, many other activities that ride in parallel. Marketing is a major component of the overall process: from the product market conceptualization, to market research, to the advertising and packaging. Many other activities occur. Packaging, for instance, which is also a subdivision of industrial design, may sometimes occur in conjunction with marketing but as a separate designing endeavor in itself.

Product Design Tools

Many of the tools used in the product design and development processes are similar to ones used in the architectural process. These would include 2-D representational tools (such as orthographic projection), illustration tools (such as rendering), models, prototypes, and mock-ups. The biggest difference may, however, be in the way in which some of these tools are used.

Specifically, the greatest difference is in the use of models. While the design process in architecture tends to proceed though changes in scale (from small to large), product design tends to maintain the same scale while changing in detail (from rough massing to refined visual and mechanical models). Architectural models are almost always to scale, while product design models tend almost always to be life-size. Much of the operations of design can only occur at a one-to-one scale and sometime needs to be larger than true scale. Questions of textures or details at $\frac{1}{1,000}$ inch cannot be scaled down.

Following is a quick characterization of general modeling phases as they occur in the product design and development process. There are fundamentally four physical modeling steps used in the product development process:

- *Schematic models.* Also know as "blue foam" models, these are quick, schematic models generally made by hot-wire cutting of blue foam. This is quick but rough modeling method. The ease and quickness in making them allows for many basic concepts or ideas to be explored.

- *Refinement models.* Two general kinds of refinement models are generally used: ergonomic and visualization. They help the team better understand geometry, ergonomics, and general detail considerations.
- *Ergonomic models.* A higher detailed version of the schematic models, these models include true weight, shape, and feel. They generally tend to be neutral in appearance so as to facilitate the exploration of their ergonomic attributes. This might occur through ergonomic testing, with test participants using and evaluating the models under (simulated) "true" conditions.

PRODUCT DEVELOPMENT DESIGN AND ENGINEERING TOOLS

Analytical modeling
Product architecture
Product engineering
3-D CAD
Cost reduction
Optimization
Prototyping
Testing
Agency approval
Manufacturing engineering
Packaging
On-site tooling debug
Product engineering
Small parts design
Functional prototype
Design for high volume
Design for automated assembly

Figure 8-12 Product development, design and engineering tools

- *Visualization models.* These are more detailed models that incorporate weight and feel considerations as well as more detailed and refined visualization. They generally do not have working parts. Traditionally these models have been made of clay or wood. It's become common practice to use quick and inexpensive 3-D printing techniques such as starched-based printing or laminated object manufacturing (LOM™) fabrication. Visual appearance is more important than dimensional accuracy.

- *Appearance models.* These are highly detailed visualization models that include color and final textures. An appearance model may be based on some of the same modeling techniques as the visualization model, although frequently thermojet processes are employed for their accurate and more dimensionally stable end process. This model is primarily used to judge the final appearance of the product. As a "realistic" guide to a product's appearance, it may include some final materials, such as glass. This facilitates its use as a visual prototype. These models may be used in focus groups to determine specific, detail-oriented questions, such as color or final texture. These models are also very important from a marketing perspective and frequently will be photographed for the final packaging of the product. Given the time-sensitive nature of product development, waiting for a final product photo would delay the graphic and package design too much.

- *Engineering models.* Much more detailed and elaborate models of the final product, these are made when the overall geometry of the design has been finalized and are used to test part fit, mock-up assemblies, and so on. They are fabricated via dimensionally stable processes with good mechanical properties. This facilitates their use as functional prototypes. Thermojet or stereolithography (SLA) processes are frequently employed in their fabrication.

Digital Models

The use of digital models within the design and engineering phases is similar to techniques and practices employed in the architectural profession. These include 2-D scaffolding, surface modeling, solid modeling, parametric modeling, CAE activities such as finite element analysis (FAE) mold-flow analysis, and various other analytical and simulation tools. These tools are covered in depth in Part IV of the book (Chapters 10, 11, and 12) and briefly discussed in the engineering section of the Pingtel case study later in this chapter. It is clear that these tools have significantly impacted the product development process, allowing for quicker iterative design processes and refinements. These tools have given greater analytical capabilities (frequently replacing time- and cost-intensive physical prototyping) and enable the product development team to identify and refine opportunities at a far greater rate, frequently with greater precision.

CAD/CAM in Product Development

CAD/CAM tools are extensively used throughout the product development process. We've already touched upon some of the modeling tools used: model making in the design and engineering phases relies on quick 3-D printing techniques (mostly for visualization) and more precise and dimensionally stable 3-D printing techniques (such as SLA) for dimensionally accurate and functional prototypes (mostly in the engineering phases). In addition, both design and engineering use numerous digital representation and CAD tools. Visual renderings are used by the designer to check appearance, while 2-D CAD tools are used to establish preliminary geometries in preparation of the more elaborate 3-D and parametrically dependent models used for the more rigorous engineering tasks.

CAD tools are also extensively used in various analysis tasks: from mold-flow analysis to finite-element analysis to collision and impact simulations. These simulation and analytical tools enable the designer to foresee critical issues that may impact the complex and time-sensitive interrelationships of design, engineering, manufacturing, and marketing.

In manufacturing, CAD tools are used in both the tooling (in plastic-based manufacturing, these are generally injection molds) and debug (modifying existing molds) phases. In the debug phase, for example, CNC milling is used to shape the electrode used to modify the mold (discussed in greater detail in the Pingtel case study to follow) in a process called electrical discharge machining (EDM).

CAD/CAM tools have greatly impacted the development of products. In addition to time-saving benefits (through the ability to simulate or accurately foresee), they've become vital in managing the complex relationship between the various parties that come together and, in the process, they ensure quality. The ability to share and manage complex data has also geographically unfettered the various process participants while enabling companies to leverage the opportunity for mass customization (responding to different market and user needs). CAD/CAM processes have undoubtedly allowed for the design and manufacturing of products of greater complexity to be developed in ever-demanding contexts.

The following case study explores the relationships between design and the product development process and identifies some of ways in which CAD/CAM tools are used.

8.5 THE PINGTEL BUSINESS PHONE

The objective of the case study is twofold:

1. To introduce the product development process and its constituent phases, responsibilities, tasks, and tools. The case reflects a "typical" product development process for a consumer product.

2. To introduce Altitude's product development work from conception to implementation. The case study explores some of the specific design and engineering questions and solutions that emerged in this specific case.

Introduction

The case study explores the development of the Pingtel xpressa™ business phone from conception to completion. Boston-based strategic design firm Altitude undertook the product development. Commissioned in 1999, the design development occurred over about 10 months, with the product launch occurring in the spring of 2000. Altitude's role continues to date with product updates and quality control.

About Pingtel

Founded in 1999, Pingtel develops product for Internet-based (or Internet Protocol-based) telephony solutions. Based in Woburn, Massachusetts, the company's products integrate Session Initiation Protocol (SIP)—the standard for integrated voice, video, and data communications—as well as other leading industry standards, including Java, Linux, XML, and VoiceXML. Targeted toward medium-size to large multilocation enterprises, its products provide IP-based telephony solutions for businesses. Its products are not sold through retail but are delivered directly to the customer.

About Altitude

Based in Boston, Altitude, Inc. is a strategic design firm providing research, product visualization, and industrial design and engineering services. Taking an integrated approach to product development, it employs researchers, strategists, engineers, and designers, specialized in consumer, commercial, and medical products. Its vast product portfolio includes, among other items, familiar consumer goods such as the Black & Decker SmartBrew (which is the number-one-selling coffeemaker in its price range), Brita's Cascade Filter

Pitcher (Brita's all-time best-selling pitcher), and conceptual brand extension for Compaq's iPaq.

Altitude promotes itself as providing high-tech solutions for companies seeking to compete through innovation, differentiation, quality, and a strong connection with their customers. It offers the ability to identify opportunities that clients may not see, to think beyond what is immediately familiar, and to have the capacity to assemble teams that execute quickly and effectively. Taking an integrated approach to product development, Altitude offers services from design to engineering to marketing to packaging.

The prestigious firm has been recognized for its high excellence in design with, among other accolades, 18 Industrial Design Excellence Awards in seven years.

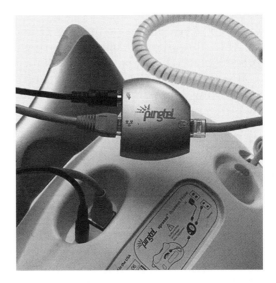

Figure 8-13 (Source: Pingtel®)

About the Product

Conceived as an Internet-based business phone, the xpressa addressed issues of usability and functionality distinct to business phones. The phone was targeted for large business with an already existing IP network, thus allowing them to leverage their existing capabilities at no extra cost.

Current business phones are not designed for the average user to do anything but the most basic functions (person-to-person call, transfer, and hold). Anything beyond that followed a complex set of multiple instructions/steps. As such, Pingtel wanted to develop an IP-based telephony product that could support both low-end and high-end users. The product had to be easy to use and allow intuitive advanced programming and customization for added functionalities.

Imagined as a high-design product, the new phone was to be sold directly to businesses within a targeted price range of $200 to $300. A low-volume product, it was targeted for an initial run of 10,000.

The Product Development Process

In June of 1999 Pingtel contacted Altitude and set up a meeting to initiate the development of its product concept. Pingtel had selected Altitude for its excellence in design and its extensive knowledge of product development with consumer electronics. The project was to be undertaken with a quick turnaround, so good communications and geographic proximity were also important factors in the selection process.

Pingtel had never developed a product, so having Altitude's expertise was critical to the success of the product. The objective of the first meeting was to review the design brief and establish the parameters for the first phase of design conceptualization.

The design development occurred over about 10 months, with the product launch occurring in the spring of 2000. Overall, the product development time (from conception to completion) would end up including the following approximate time distribution. (See Figure 8-14.)

Product Brief—Phase 0

This is generally the first step that engages the product designer. A description of the product objectives, the brief might define such things as market needs and targets. The brief generally comes from a company or entity interested in producing and selling a specific product. A common practice is for the marketing team at the enterprise to study the potential market, customer, consumer, or end client, along with their needs, competing products, and forces. The team then determines a product specification. This specification includes a target price, an analysis of the competition, a description of the market, and a development time frame.

The product brief may vary considerably. Some companies may approach a product design team with a highly determined set of parameters; others may approach the team with general aspirations. Pingtel, for example, approached Altitude with a general notion that the product should instill a sense of advancement, technology, sophistication, and "business-ness." Altitude in turn helped develop a set of specifications and rewrote the product brief. It is not uncommon for the product design team to be involved in developing the brief. Terminology varies from place to place. At Altitude, this "Phase 0" refers to the design team's work developing the specifications for the product brief, before design (in the conventional meaning) begins.

In developing the product brief, Pingtel identified three challenges:

1. Develop a telephone architecture that would enable a simple and intuitive interface with unlimited opportunity for customization.
2. Create an embodiment that boldly distinguished the phone from other business phones.
3. Bring the phone to market without ever having developed a product before.

Exploration or Design Conceptualization—Phase 1

Once the design team has received (or developed) a product brief, it is ready to develop those specifications into preliminary design ideas. The exploratory nature of this phase is to open up the opportunities suggested by the brief. Schematic in nature, this phase sets out to explore the range of possible design variations, strategies, and interpretations suggested by the brief. It is a moment of design breadth rather than depth: Ideas are represented very abstractly and with little resolution. The team works quickly, developing variations and exploring varied strategies. The objective is to get a rough but vast sense of all of the possible outcomes of the brief and of their possible implications. (See Figure 8-15.)

Altitude developed five to six primary concepts with numerous variations. Strategies included upright and horizontal configurations, and many of the variations

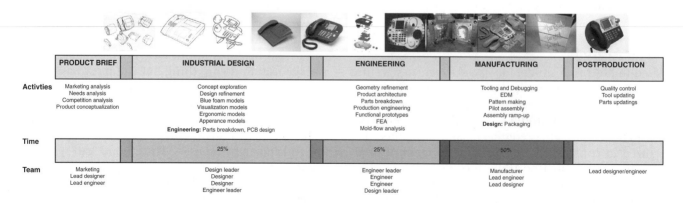

Figure 8-14 The product development process for the Pingtel phone.

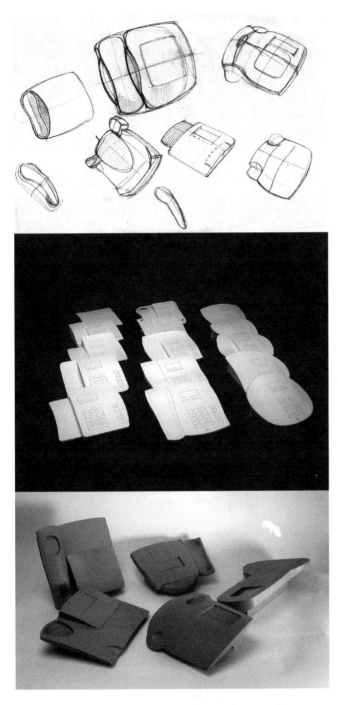

Figure 8-15 The product of Phase 1 was the development of conceptual sketches (above) leading to quick model studies (middle). The team ultimately narrowed the field of design strategies into preliminary "blue foam" models (below). (Source: Pingtel®)

explored ideas of display arrangement, general form, receiver type, and keyboard variations. Quick models give a sense for approximate dimensions, appearance, and massing. As mentioned earlier in the chapter, these schematic models are frequently referred to as "blue-foam" models (after the easy-to-cut foam frequently used to make them). The design team works through intensive review and design sessions, working together

as a way to stimulate interactions that lead to different approaches and perspectives.

While the design team was hard at work conceptualizing designs, the engineering team began to establish some basic project parameters: parts breakdown, basic printed circuit board (PCB) design, and defining geometry. These would be the initial engineering parameters which the designer had take into consideration:

- *Parts breakdown.* These had mostly to do with basic component logic (part number and strategy). For example, Altitude determined that the receiver would be a two-part receiver, with a top and bottom (as is common on most receiver designs). (See Figure 8-16.)

- *Basic PCB design.* The other task that the electrical engineering team developed was a first—schematic—design for the printed circuit board. This is the electrical circuitry for the phone. The objective at this point was to determine the basic architecture of the board and in the process determine the basic size and shape of it. A three-dimensional PCB "terrain" was passed on to the design team to help them understand possibilities and limitations in the exterior shape of the phone. This terrain represented a minimum build volume that the team had to respect. As the process and the interchange of ideas developed, both engineering and design models were updated accordingly. (See Figure 8-17.)

Figure 8-16 The engineering team determined a parts breakdown strategy based on experience. (Source: Pingtel®)

Figure 8-17 The engineering team determined the phone's PCB (printed circuit board). (Source: Pingtel®)

- *Defining geometry.* Following this lead, the engineering team broke up the schematic design into various components and gave them basic attributes and relations. In addition, basic geometrics were determined. This was done in 2-D CAM environments: basic plan geometry for the phone and critical sections. Later on a finalized version of this CAD data will be used to generate the full 3-D surface model.

Phase 1 produced a wide range of preliminary design strategies:

- Quickly explore the range and implications of design possibilities.
- Establish basic breakdown of parts (how each scheme might be broken down to its various constituent parts).
- Generate a rough sense for costs.
- Create PCB design.
- Determine component specifications.
- Determine approximate size and feel of the phone.

Design Refinement—Phase 2

After the conceptualization phase, the most promising concepts are examined at a more refined level. Gener-

ally speaking, this includes selecting or defining a design concept to pursue. Sometimes the team may decide to concurrently develop a few concepts, leaving the selection of the final approach for later. This may be in part influenced by the desire for further verification through market research—with more elaborate appearance models—before committing to the final design approach.

In general, this phase includes more detailed exploration of form, material, and evaluation of manufacturing implications. At this point the engineering team determines the specific materials and manufacturing process employed.

After the preliminary design phase (1), the more successful strategies were further developed and synthesized into a first design proposal. The team developed the desirable design attributes at a more refined level and selected a basic design strategy. The concept selected was a horizontal orientation, with a clear user interface and adjustable phone legs. (See Figure 8-18.)

To achieve the targeted users, the team had to explore the development of an intuitive navigation system for the sophisticated, customizable menu. After numerous alternatives, the team developed a scroll knob. This allowed for easy navigation through the numerous application pages. The concept also relied on the general office familiarity with the Rolodex.

Handset Design. One of the main efforts in this phase was the development of the handset. Several questions related to its design attributes:

1. That it have good acoustical properties
2. That it fit comfortably

By far the greatest questions were raised by the acoustics of the handset (see Figure 8-19). Pingtel wanted a product with high-fidelity sound reproduction. Any deterioration in sound compared to traditional phones would be seen as a reflection of IP's ineffectiveness and might sway customers toward a traditional phone solution. The acoustical question fundamentally revolved around two issues: the quality of the electronics and the shape of the receiver. To ensure good acoustical feedback, effort was made to ensure that the receiver made a good seal around the ear. The comfort issue had two aspects: that it have good weight distribution and feel, and that it have a comfortable contour so as to be easily straddled between ear and shoulder (for a hands-free operation). These questions were schematically defined and refined through a series of free-form solid fabrication models (narrowed to about 10 types) that were tested for feel and fit. Further refinement of these issues were addressed in engineering, through acoustical tests and further refinement of parts models. (See Figure 8-20.)

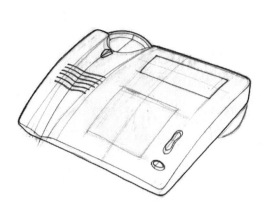

Figure 8-18 A final design strategy is selected. Sketch (left) and "blue foam" model (right). (Source: Pingtel®)

Application Interface and Navigation. Altitude's team recognized the difficulty with the usability associated with traditional advanced business phones. As mentioned, current business phones were not designed for the average user to do anything but the most basic functions (person-to-person call, transfer, and hold). Anything beyond that required a complex set of steps. The design of the interface was deemed by the team as a critical area of focus. To fully leverage its IP capabilities, the phone had to have high-end capabilities but be intuitively accessible to the average user. A traditional touchpad approach was first tried. Although it was possible to take this route, it was soon evident that it would either clutter the phone with many buttons or require numerous steps. After exploring numerous alternative solutions, the team developed a scroll wheel interface that would function much like a Rolodex. This allowed a single point of contact allowing the user to easily scroll through the numerous menu options. (See Figure 8-21.)

Ease of use and cost would be critical factors in specifying the component that would enable the scroll wheel. After searching various options, the team had a breakthough: It cannibalized a computer mouse and used the interior component as a scroll. The fit was good, leaving the team to search for the submanufacturer of the part. Not only would the team need to find the manufacturer, but it would also have to ensure that the part could be made at such low volumes within the targeted price target set. The team was able to find the vendor and successfully developed the part.

General Appearance and Color. The phone was to be marketed as a high-tech-based product, with a contemporary-design feel (see Figure 8-22). The high-tech dimension was in part reflected in the IP-based tele-

phony solution. Continuously trying to break from the "anonymous" conservative office product culture, color became one of the ways to differentiate the product and easily add to it a contemporary dimension. Color was explored in depth. After initial swatch-based studies, colors were further tested through paper-based illustra-

Figure 8-19 Final handsets. (Source: Pingtel®)

Figure 8-20 Handset design required particular attention. Acoustical and comfort concerns required further exploration. A wide range of ergonomic receiver models were made using starch-based 3-D printing techniques. (Source: Pingtel®)

tions. This would give an approximate sense of the appearance of colors on the phone. Finding the right color, however, was fundamental. Based on infinite nuances, it was not possible to completely verify the various color choices through paper-based representations. To further study the questions, 12 appearance models were created, each one with a different color. These were used in trade shows to generate field test data. Visitors were asked about color preferences, which further helped determine the end consumer's color appeal. Of the 12 initial colors (which included lime green and other colors that were pushing the office product color boundary), 5 were selected for the product launch (dark brown, charcoal gray, ivory, apricot, and blue).

Engineering. The engineering phase refers to the first phase in which the selected design strategy is put

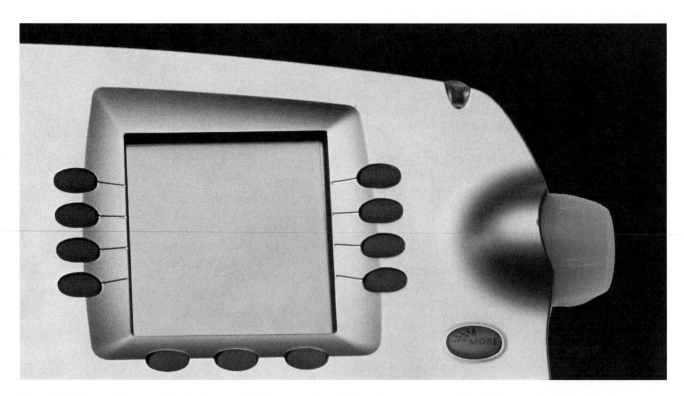

Figure 8-21 The scroll bar navigation tool was a particularly innovative solution using components to simplify the complexity of navigating a programmable phone. (Source: Pingtel®)

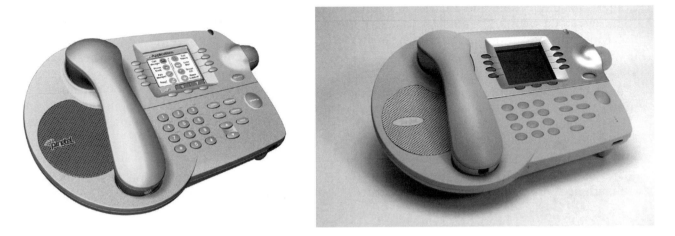

Figure 8-22 Digital renderings allowed the team to work quickly through variation (left). Appearance models were developed for interaction with potential customers and for use in final packaging photography (right). (Source: Pingtel®)

through the first rigorous engineering test. At this point in the product development phase, it's the engineering team that takes over the primary responsibility of developing the product. The design team may become smaller at this point. In the Pingtel project, only the lead designer continued, while the engineering team grew from one to three.

Geometry Development—Phase 3

Note: An in-depth discussion of the principles appears in Part IV (Chapters 10, 11, and 12).

The initial defining 2-D CAD geometry developed by the engineering team early in phase 1 is now brought into a full 3-D digital environment. Generally speaking, these are parametrically based, solid modeling environments that give the engineering team complete control over material thicknesses and analytical tools. At this point the basic design strategy has been selected and the work proceeds in refining the design.

The 3-D geometry generally holds the actual material thicknesses and assembly details all in a parametric environment. This allows the team to keep track and control changes as they accrue. A change in one component will automatically adjust in another part based on the specific parametric relationship. The ability to manage change and maintain critical relationships is essential when dealing with products composed of numerous parts that are all dependant on each other with very tight tolerances.

Generally the geometry development process follows the following steps:

- *Concept sketches.* These are the first, quick, preliminary representations of the design. Frequently these are pencil-on-paper and tend to be a visualization of the product rather than a complete representation of it.

- *2-D scaffolding.* This is a first digital representation of the concept sketch and consists of two-dimensional line elements forming the cross section of the overall geometry. This is a quick step translation of the initial two-dimensional sketches into a three-dimensional representation. It is the underlying structure of a three-dimensional model, without the time and analysis expenditure required for those more time-intensive endeavors.

- *Surface modeling.* The 2-D scaffolding model is brought into surface modeling environments and developed into a surface. This enables the teams to better understand and evaluate the nature of the product's complex surfaces. These models are also helpful for presentation visualizations of the product to the client.

- *Solid modeling.* Here the three-dimensional model has wall thicknesses. These built-up thicknesses allow the engineer to begin modeling not only the shape of the product but its cross section as it relates to materials and manufacturing processes. At this point the 3-D model is being built up parametrically: Overall geometry is set, parts breakdown has been determined, and the task of developing relationships between parts based on manufacturing parameters allows the teams to further explore and refine the model in manufacturing with ease (see Figure 8-23).

Production Engineering—Phase 4

Phase 4 encompasses the following:

- *Solid modeling.* The solid modeling phase in the production engineering further develops the solid model in preparation for production. This includes finalizing wall thicknesses, drafting angles for production, and analysis to optimize process/product/costs. The model becomes a critical tool for the various finite element analysis (FEA) analyses and simulations.

- *Data acquisition.* In preparation of refining the production model, the engineering team generates a whole range of data to help it evaluate successful solutions. The data is generally generated through digital analysis or experimental setups.
- *Acoustic.* This was done employing an artificial ear and mouth. Test frequencies were fed into the mouthpiece and the speaker response evaluated.

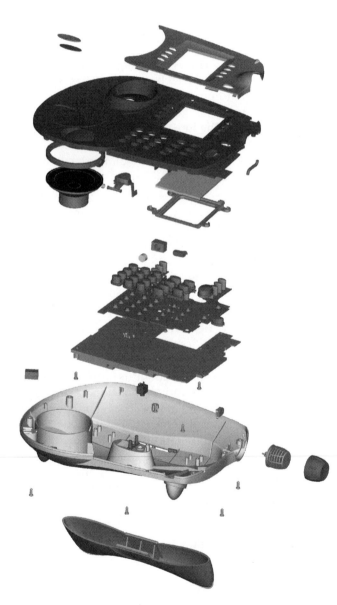

Figure 8-23 The engineering team begins by developing the design geometry and building a parametric model of the complete phone. (Source: Pingtel®)

- *Infrared imaging.* Imaging attempts to identify heat-generating potential hot spots within a product. This is of concern for products such as processing chips and heaters with heat-generating parts. Imaging helps identify areas of concern, where heat may produce problems in the final product. Generally the development team opts to either change the product's internal airflow or add vents at the sites of concern.

The analysis and simulation portion of phase 4 includes the following:

- *Mold-flow analysis.* CAD-based mold-flow analysis allows the engineer to examine the manufacturability of a part in relation to plastic injection processes (see Figure 8-24). It helps identify potential flow problems and the optimal placement of gates.
- *Finite-element analysis.* This CAD analysis is done to evaluate the mechanical properties and performance of parts, for instance, whether a part will be flexible enough to snap on in assembly or rigid enough to hold and act as a self-fastening part.
- *Impact and drop test analysis.* Complex analysis can also yield information about a product's ability to sustain impact (being dropped, etc.). Most low-volume products (such as the Pingtel phone) will acquire this data through drop tests rather than computational analysis, which is performed in the debug round of manufacturing and is time-consuming and expensive.

Instead these were tested in the debug phase. Drop tests were preformed on the phone and it passed with flying colors. The phone was found not to have any problems.

Tooling and Debugging—Phase 5
Tooling. This phase takes the final specifications, models, and geometry of the final parts and begins by developing the tools for the manufacturing of parts (see Figure 8-25). Most consumer and office products have plastic components. For these, molds are made that are then used in the injection molding of plastic. This is a very expensive and time-consuming endeavor. The molds are generally at least two-part (see Figures 8-26 to 8-28) as they must be able to release the part once it's ready. Also they must include intricate means to ensure that the molted plastic flows to the right places at the right time. To withstand the hardship and resist the wear and tear of manufacturing, the tools (or molds) are of hardened steel and built to very exacting standards. (See Figures 8-26 to 8-28.)

The debug phase refers to the process that the tools

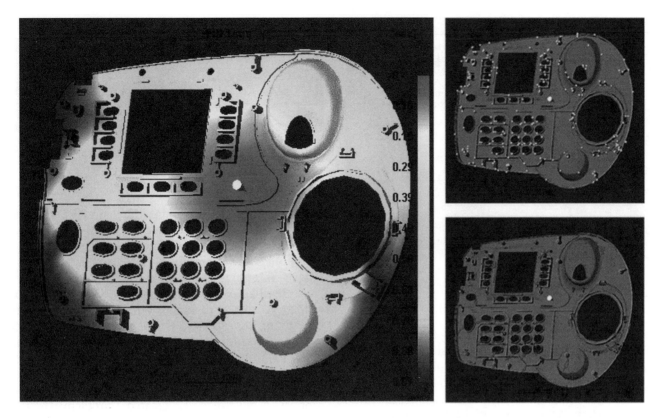

Figure 8-24 Mold-flow analysis allows the engineering team to determine the location of gates and understand the flow of plastic in the injection-molding process. (Source: Pingtel®)

undergo after they are first made. A preliminary parts run is made and each part is tested for dimensional accuracy. If discrepancies are found, the mold is corrected accordingly. Anticipating that there will inherently be a need to fine-tune tools, the engineers overdimension the tool, as it's easier to make adjustments by removing material than adding it.

Other things to consider in tools are the dimension of the parts being made. Small parts require little amounts of plastic and short cooling time and may be manufactured at a rate of every few seconds. A large part may require more material and cooling and may take up to a minute to make. The added time and material required may also produce difficulties that need to

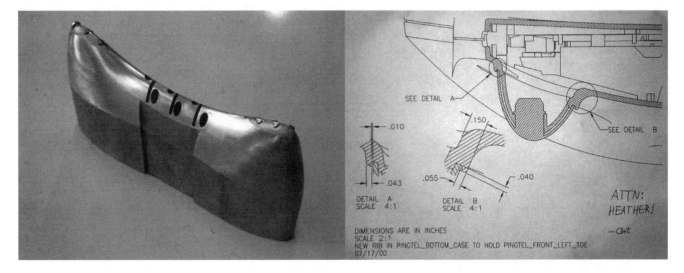

Figure 8-25 Tool part for the adjustable footrest. Manufacturing drawings are to scales larger than life: Details can be developed with $1/5000$-inch precision. (Source: Pingtel®)

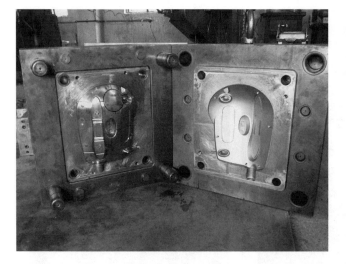

Figure 8-26 Tool fabricating shop showing a two-part mold. (Source: Pingtel®)

Figure 8-28 The fit for part is quickly checked in the shop: The adjustable foot is tried in both orientations to check for fit. (Source: Pingtel®)

be taken into consideration in making the tool. Ideally, this will have been taken into consideration in the engineering phases through the mold-flow analysis.

Altitude bid the manufacturing to five companies. Cost was one of the major factors in selecting the manufacturer. However, assurance of the quality and experience of the manufacturer was also important. After a visit to the manufacturer to see its facilities and tool shop, to talk to the tool makers, and to review previous projects, Altitude selected a Chinese company. They were confident that the manufacturer's aesthetic finish of parts, toolmaker experience, previous product experience and attention to detail would meet the demands of the task at hand.

There were a total of 15 tools (for 15 different plastic parts) required by the phone design. Approximately nine weeks were spent making the tools, at a cost of about $150,000.

Debugging. A first run of 10 phone parts was made and delivered to Altitude's studio. The development team tested and assembled the parts. Dimensional accuracy and consistency were evaluated. Part fit and assembly were also closely examined. After an extensive review and testing session, the manufacturer was contacted

Figure 8-27 Base lid tool and first component. (Source: Pingtel®)

and the results shared. Some dimensional issues had crept up, and the manufacturer made appropriate changes to the tools. One of the major debug issues was the phone's rear footrest part. (See Figure 8-28.) The initial part was too flimsy and the rear foot easily snapped back off when pressure was applied to the phone. The initial strategy was to add wall thickness to the part, in turn giving it greater stiffness. There had been a debate over this part previously. How flexible should it be? Initially it was made flexible enough to facilitate an easy assembly. However, the debug test round had proved that the added flexibility had made the assembly of the foot easier, but it had also created a problem: The legs easily snapped off when minimal pressure was applied to the phone. The team argued that it was more important to have a stable phone than ease of assembly. Further supporting this decision was the realization that the rear foot would be a one-time deal, so certainly stability of the phone far outweighed the assembly debate. At this point the team corrected the problem by opting to reduce the flexibility of the part, which would prevent it from accidentally snapping off.

Working as a negative, material would have to be removed from the mold to make the part thicker. As a hardened steel (or die-cast metal) part, this is not an easy task. Given the hardness of it, this task cannot be achieved by traditional milling operations. Rather, it is done by electrically removing the material, or electrical discharge machining (EDM). This had to be done carefully so as not to remove too much. A first pass of removing $5/1,000$ inch was made. It finally took four $5/1,000$-inch passes to get the desired wall thickness. To further ensure part rigidity, the team opted for an additional strategy: adding interior ribs to the part. This would ensure both wall and added part rigidity.

Electrical Discharge Machining. This process uses an electrical discharge between an electrode and an anode to burn away a desired amount of metal from a mold. In this case the mold part acts as an anode and a CNC milled copper electrode of the desired shape is inserted. Heat generated in the electrical discharge between the two literally burns away the steel. By making the electrode the positive of the desired modified shape, EDM can burn onto the negative the required amount with great precision. The complexity in this process lies, among other things, in the ability to make a precisely shaped electrode, imparting precise corrections to the tool.

When debugging the rear foot part, the copper electrode was milled with a 3-D CNC milling machine. The new geometry for the part determined the electrode's shape. Once milled, the electrode was inserted into the tool, a current applied, and the desired material consumed.

Assembly Ramp-Up—Phase 6

In preparation for the start of production, the product development team meets with the product manufacturer and evaluates the assembly process. This generally involves making a closer inspection of the assembly environment and determining the exact assembly line layout. Stations—and their sequence—are determined, each point responsible for a specific task. Once determined, the manufacturer meets with the development team and assembles a predetermined number of pilot—or sample—products. The number may vary tremendously. For high-volume products where production volumes and profit margins may be critical, the pilot run may take several days until the assembly process has been perfected to an absolute. Given the low-volume (10,000 units) nature of the Pingtel phone, the pilot run was limited to a few hours—this was enough time to assure the team that the assembly line setup was satisfactory.

Pilot Run. In anticipation of the pilot run, the development team made a short run (approximately 20) to test the assembly sequence under factory conditions. In anticipation of a full production run, assembly instructions and minor modifications were reviewed at this point. The pilot run took approximately one-half day. (See Figures 8-29 and 8-30.)

Packaging. Although not strictly part of the assembly ramp-up phase of the product development process, packaging comes into play at this stage. It is here that both product and packaging are examined in the assembly context and issues of product assembly sequence and packaging sequence are examined closely. The packaging design process (frequently done by graphic designers or designers with packaging expertise) begins early on. Because of the time-sensitive nature of product development, photographs of appearance models (from the earlier design phases) are used for packaging. Waiting for final product photography would delay time to market too much. Other design considerations factor into the packaging design, such as retail conditions and the consumer "out-of-box" experience. (See Figure 8-31.)

Figure 8-29 A first run of components was sent to Altitude's office. There the design and engineering team assembled 20 phones to check for part fit and debug possible errors in parts. (Source: Pingtel®)

Quality Control and Product Upgrades—Phase 7

This phase fundamentally includes quality checks in manufacturing and upgrades of the product design throughout the product life. This may include randomly purchasing sample products to test quality. The design development team may randomly purchase products through retail centers and test for quality. Over time, changes may occur to the quality of the product. Tools, for example, will wear down over time, and sporadic quality checks enable the development team to make appropriate corrections. Another frequent post-production issue is upgrading the product. There may be modifications that the client requires. These may be based on user feedback, they may be modifications to upgrade the appearance of the prod-

Figure 8-30 The assembly line: A pilot run was made to verify assembly sequence and technique at a manufacturing scale. (Source: Pingtel®)

Figure 8-31 Packaging for the phones. (Source: Pingtel®)

Figure 8-32 The phone was offered in multiple colors and customizable browsers. (Source: Pingtel®)

uct, or they may involve an upgrade in the mechanical or electrical components.

Altitude has recently upgraded the PCB to accommodate some new electronic components selected for the phone. This has imparted some changes in the body design.

Conclusions

The benefits of Pingtel's phone are that the system enables users to easily share complex information, such as telephone configuration or address/phone books. In addition, the simplicity and intuitive nature of the interface and graphic simplicity allows low-end users to easily engage the phone, while the intuitive Rolodex-like hardware roller allows heavy users to scroll through menus and easily adapt the phone functions to their needs.

Once the team defined the hardware/software relationship, the rest of the phone began to take shape. Form, color, and detail choices were all intended to break the business phone paradigm. The concave top surface is inviting and provides a clean interface surface, while the bottom is soft and animated. As a result, the phone appears to levitate, supported on four pod-like feet. The "soft underbelly" also contributes to the acoustic integrity of the high-fidelity speaker by focusing all of the internal speaker sound toward the speaker grill. The rear foot can be repositioned, allowing two angle settings. The handset, being a primary interface point, went through much iteration and user testing to achieve a very high level of comfort. In addition to being comfortable no matter how you hold it, the final handset solution is well balanced and has a high-quality feel. (See Figure 8-32.)

In the process of reinventing the traditional business phone architecture, Pingtel and Altitude improved usability and enabled unlimited customization. The design won the IDEA/BusinessWeek Gold award in 2002. In addition, Altitude's design helped Pingtel secure $17 million in venture capital.

CHAPTER 9

Industrial Design in Architecture

While there are undoubted commonalities among how design takes place among these allied disciplines, there are also significant differences. Grossly speaking, there are questions tied to the nature and expectations of clients and target users or audiences, as well as the way products are marketed, distributed, and financed. In addition, the nature of the use environments vary dramatically.

Historically these allied professions have gained much from the notion of technology transfer. Certainly there are many precursors: Crystal Palace—with its standardized and mass-produced components—is a good example in the argument for crossover between product design and architecture.

9.1 GENERAL CONTEXT

While there are undoubted commonalities among how design takes place in the allied professions of Industrial Design and Architecture, there are also significant differences. It is within their operating contexts that we find one of the most fundamental differences: the financial context. Decisions in the industrial design realm inextricably bind themselves to business plans, created to promote the success of a company, which is generally defined in terms of revenue return from the sale of a product that supports the primary mandate of the corporation. The same cannot be said about architecture. It is arguably this fundamental difference that creates significantly different demands and roles for design.

In an age where many products and industries have achieved technological parity, differentiation (in cost, in appeal to specific market segments, and in appearance) becomes critical for survival. Henry Ford had a clear competitive advantage with his Model T, but what do you do when more and more products offer the same undifferentiated value? Many companies have opted to find new markets and customize existing products to address a diversified consumer. Differences exist, but it is clear that companies have had to reckon with very sophisticated and discerning "on-demand" con-

sumers in an environment of ever-increasing efficiencies of time and money.

The need for increasingly sophisticated products and market segmentation strategies has increased pressure for more efficient and flexible design-to-manufacturing processes. Design decisions potentially tie a company into specific business strategies that may in turn either ensure its success or failure. With large financial investments at stake, design and manufacturing integration in most industries is a fundamental prerequisite for success. Furthermore, design decisions may lock companies into long-term strategies. Their ability to adapt designs for future demands and changes is critical. Design should be seen as a planning and strategy tool to develop and precisely tune products before large amounts of money are invested. Manufacturing is still for the most part a very resource-intensive activity. As such, being able to reduce decisions to their most efficient state before manufacturing is brought in can make or break the success of a product and, in turn, the company itself. Architecture, with its highly fragmented industry, tends to produce services for one-time projects. As such, the financial implications are generally limited to a single project and generally do not have such intensive setup costs as in the manufacturing of a product.

CAD/CAM has impacted both industries, the industrial design profession leading the way. Computer-based processes have reduced product time to market and supported flexible manufacturing and marketing strategies. Overall they have made the industry more flexible and lean. The whole idea of customizing products for specific market needs or segments is a reflection of industry's increased capacity to adapt and respond flexibly. In the architectural realm, computer-based processes are tying architecture closer to manufacturing principles, allowing architects to embed themselves into processes and models in ways previously unimagined. Within these changes we can certainly see a significant overlap emerging between the professions.

We will explore these issues in greater detail, but they can be characterized as the following:

Figure 9-1 Prefabricated aluminum façade elements being installed in the Alcoa building. (Source: Permission from the Library and Archives Division of the Historical Society of Western Pennsylvania, Pittsburgh. ALCOA Company)

1. From an industry-wide perspective, buildings are becoming more and more an assembly of products. These include "high-end" products (such as ceiling systems) and "low-end" products (such as material products).

2. Mass customization is beginning to cross the traditional divide between the industries of *one of a kind* (*architecture*) versus *mass production* (*industrial design*).

3. Interdependencies are developing among products, services, and environments.

All in all, a different kind of relationship between architecture and product design is beginning to emerge. As illustrated, there are many ways of making an argu-ment for the relevance of the overlap between industrial design and architecture. This interaction is, however, frequently limited, mostly because of the specialization required in each discipline.

Given that there are many topics that have been already covered in previous chapters, we will focus on specific issues not yet covered, with a particular emphasis on CAD/CAM-related implications. We begin with a quick historical overview of the professional context and then focus on two fundamental topics.

First, we examine the fundamental question of volume, which has traditionally been one of the divides between the professions: one of a kind versus many of the same. Within this we will look at the general body of thought gravitating around the topic of mass customization, a topic made popular by the business community. The topic is covered in Chapter 18, so here we focus on specific industrial design implications. We examine different technology transfer models and their impacts on the development of products. A look at the architectural world helps us identify some of the emerging operating models. Here we explore the Stala kitchen manufacturer and Piikkio prefabricated ship cabin manufacturer.

Finally, we end with a particular focus on a traditional area of overlap: furniture design. Here we look at two different projects to explore two notions: the Vecta chair to understand how CAD/CAM processes affect the development of a complex chair product, and the Permobil wheelchair to explore how CAD/CAM enables new material-based processes, which in turn enable a new chair conception to emerge.

9.2 A BRIEF PROFESSIONAL PERSPECTIVE

The development of the overlap between Industrial Design and Architecture has historically been effected by both professional and educational circumstances.

- *Architects in industrial design.* Traditionally most of the overlap has occurred in furniture design, because it evolved out of ideas of "total design" whereby the relationship and considerations among architecture, furniture, and its use were all interdependent. Alvar Aalto, Le Corbusier, Mies van der Rohe, and Frank Lloyd Wright, to mention a few, are examples of architects working as furniture designers. Aalto's Paimio Sanatorium design—at the time a very progressive architectural solution—included every aspect of the building, including furnishings. Most notable is the Paimio chair, a result of Aalto's molded plywood collaboration with furniture manufacturer Korhonen. A product of its time, this "total design"

approach established an aesthetic and syntactical consistency between architecture and furniture design.

- *Industrial designers in architecture.* On the industrial design end, we find people like Norman Bel Geddes, famous for his visionary ideas and breadth of work. In the 1939 New York World's Fair, he designed General Motors' Futurama pavilion, an exhibit that showcased his vision for the city of the future. Based on his ideas of the Magic Motorway, the proposal reconsidered the architecture and urban form of cities as impacted by the arrival of the automobile. (See Figure 9-2.)

- *Traditions in education.* The overlap between the professions can also be found in other traditions. In Italy, the relationship between architects and product designers is very tight. Because schools in Italy did not offer formal Industrial Design education most industrial designers were trained as architects and gained their professional knowledge through practice. The roster of Italian designers is crowded with architects, from Ettore Sottsass to the flamboyant Carlo Mollino.

9.3 ISSUES IN PRODUCT VARIATION AND STRATEGY

Differences between architecture and industrial design have generally been discussed in terms of *volume* and *repeatability*. Traditional means of industrial production have relied on mass-production processes. Architecture, on the other hand, has generally been characterized by "one-of-a-kind" uniqueness and customization. Although significant differences still endure between the two practices, the notion of customization and interchangeability does suggest an arena of overlap. Let's explore this topic with a specific eye toward architectural implications.

Figure 9-2 Norman Bel Geddes' vision for the city of the future at GM's pavilion at the 1939 New York World's Fair. (Source: "Magic Motorways" by Norman Bel Geddes: Random House, New York, 1940)

Variations and Customization

Mass customization (also discussed in Chapter 18) has become somewhat of a buzzword, its meaning suggested by the term: meeting customized needs of customers and consumers on a mass-market scale. The term has been given a lot of airtime; the advancement of computer-driven technologies and their inherent potential for flexibility has further awakened a sense of the arrival of a new era in industrial production. Ford's motto of "you can have any color you want as long as it's black" does not reflect today's complex market structure.

Perhaps not surprisingly, the strategies that give the greatest true customization are the "simple" products: paints, textiles, and operations of a one- or two-dimensional nature. Printing, for example, with desktop publishing, achieved true customization long ago. The more complex products (such as cars and consumer electronics) have adopted strategies that might be more correctly referred to as "personalization," whereby a series of options allow users to personalize predetermined configurations. Unlimited customization, however, is of course inherently impossible, as it would defy the whole idea of a type or product type.

The need for product variation is currently addressed by a variety of strategies. We will refer to two helpful models, *modularization models* for customization and *project strategies* for platform strategies, and adapt them to the context of this book.

Modularization

Here we look to Joseph Pine's helpful work on mass customization and his manufacturing and marketing strategies for customization.[1] Using his terminology, we highlight the fundamental models outlined: component-sharing, component-swapping, cut-to-fit, mix, and bus sectional modularity. We will take some liberties in adapting the terminology to design-specific context.

- *Component-sharing modularity.* Product variations may be made sharing the same fundamental componentry. In this context we further define this as a product range that uses the same functionality but with a different appearance. Swatch watches are a good example: The fundamental functionality is the same (given the same fundamental components), but the appearance (color, pattern, or material) of the watch can be varied.

- *Component-swapping modularity.* Product variation is achieve by being able to swap—or change—fundamental componentry. In this context we define this a product that has the same appearance but different functionality. The personal

computer industry is a good example of this. You can purchase similar computers (in appearance) with significantly different and customized performance.

- *Cut-to-fit modularity.* Product variations in this context are achieved by varying length. This applies particularly well to industries that manufacture fundamentally 2-D or extruded products (or products with limited shape complexity, that are not finite in at least one axis). Jeans are a good example of a product that, based on a model, can be cut to size. Piping, electrical wire, and many simple products adapt well to these strategies. Bicycle manufacturing employs this kind of modular approach as well.

- *Mix modularity.* Product variation in this context is achieved by mixing predetermined elements. Generally these elements are not complete products in themselves and are not bound to specific shapes. Paints are a good example. You can have a custom color mixed, based on a palate of predetermined base colors.

- *Bus modularity.* Product variation in this context is achieved by the use of a standard structure that can support a number of attachments. This is a common strategy in the automotive industry, which uses a *platform* (described in the text that follows) approach to car manufacturing. Platforms are the time-intensive frames of automobile. Multiple car models frequently share the same platform, thus reducing time to market and recourse while maintaining product variation.

- *Sectional modularity.* Product variation is based on the principle of a common interface. Parts can be of any nature as long as they share a commonly shared interface. Legos are a classic example. A part can be of any shape or color as long as it maintains the same common interface on at least one of its sides.

Platform Design

The automotive industry has long leveraged the idea of platforms in the development of new car models. As the term suggests, a platform is the frame around which a car is built. The development of the frame is not only very time- and resource-intensive, but it is critical in determining subsequent decisions in the process of developing a car. It is the heart and soul of a car, employing—to use Pine's terminology—a *bus modularity* strategy. How you design the bus or platform in turn determines what you can and cannot attach to it and how the overall system performs. A platform will fundamentally lock in a series of decisions that have to be closely evaluated and accounted for.

The development and use of platform strategies has become common practice in the industry. It has been a way to reduce costs while allowing companies to maintain a high number of car models, or even increase their model offerings. Different car manufacturers may chose to share resources and develop common or concurrent platform designs. This locks companies into similar strategies and is commonly used to streamline processes and costs in mergers. Some Volvo and Ford models, for example, already share common platforms. This is not visible from the consumer's perspective but helps companies develop sustainable business strategies while maintaining their competitiveness in increasingly challenging markets.

We now turn to Cusumano and Nobeoka's insightful and in-depth work on the automotive industry.[2] We use their helpful definitions for new design, concurrent technology transfer, sequential technology transfer, and design modification.

- *New design.* A project begins with the design of a new platform. A new design is generally used when a company wants to depart from the available platform's strategies. The design of a new platform allows for significant liberties, limiting restrictions on the design team. It is, relatively speaking, the most resource-intensive strategy, but it can produce the most radical innovations.

- *Concurrent technology transfer.* A project begins with the adoption of a platform while it's still being developed for another application. It may mean that Ford adopts or develops (for its own purposes) a Volvo platform while it's being developed. As the term suggests, there is a benefit in the technology transfer by allowing projects to work concurrently. Teams might learn from concurrent developments, applications, and modifications and in the end produce a more effective platform. This is also a good opportunity for companies to share and develop their technologies in effective ways. Concurrent development is also helpful from a team perspective, as it enables engineers on both projects to share knowledge. This model does, however, require a high degree of coordination and communication.

- *Sequential technology transfer.* A project begins by inheriting a platform from a previous team that is then modified to adapt to current needs. This is an efficient means of developing a new project, by leveraging a company's previous investment. Modifications to platforms in a sequential technology transfer model frequently need to occur, but they are limited by the platform's strategy. Furthermore, modification or optimization of resources can be hampered by difficulties of communicating with the original engineering team; they may have dispersed, the knowledge may have been lost, and/or team members may have left the company. This can be a very efficient and successful model for producing variations or new models, but it is contingent on a careful examination of the platform's suitability and fit.

- *Design modification.* A project begins by inheriting a platform from a previous team, but unlike the sequential technology transfer model, it is not—or cannot be—modified. Team members inherit and are locked into decisions; they have to live with the limitations of the platform and adapt their design to it. This is a fairly quick and inexpensive means of upgrading or creating a new product, but it tends to limit the possibility for innovation and may not produce an optimal product. It is well adapted to creating design refinement, but it is limiting in creating new design. This is the least resource-intensive model.

The automotive industry has leveraged these strategies and has been able to produce an ever-growing number of models, to an increasingly diversified consumer base, while controlling (or even reducing) the expenditure of resources. The design of a new platform is very resource-intensive (it might run in the millions of dollars) while also being very time-consuming. Consider that the engineering of a frame accounts for a significant amount of resource-intensive analysis and testing. Being able to share or modify a platform enables the production of more flexible model ranges in shorter times for less overall cost. As such, most cars are developed leveraging either concurrent technology transfer, sequential technology transfer, or design modifications models.

Of late, however, there has been an emerging reluctance to share platforms across brands, as it can tend to work against differentiation and potentially undermine brand identity. Some multibrand companies are opting to develop brand-specific platforms while sharing knowledge and components across the brands. For some automotive companies, this may prove a good balance between efficiency, flexibility, and variation within the company while maintaining a differentiation of identities across its brands.

If we examine these platform models from an architectural perspective, we quickly recognize that most architectural endeavors would fall under the new design model. Time- and resource-intensive activities, which reside at the core of each design, are generally done from scratch on a project-to-project basis. Parametric modeling and the emergence of knowledge-based networks suggest related opportunities for the architectural context. Although the transfer of these models cannot be direct or literal, there could be fruitful opportunities to explore.

Case Overview: Platforms and Interchangeable Parts in Cell Phones

Producing variants, offering different models, or customizing products to specific market segments have become commonplace. We see this especially in large-scale consumer products where the "design appeal" of a product is important but the design of new products is time- and resource-intensive. Customization techniques allow companies to tailor their products to specific market segments or niches while leveraging existing technologies and platforms (thus reducing costs and time to market). Cell phones are a classic example of this. Phones (as in Figure 9-3) may appear different: Perhaps the model on the left is targeted to appeal to a younger, more athletic consumer, while the phone on the right might be targeted to appeal to an older business-oriented clientele. Upon closer inspection, however, we realize that these phones have much in common. The exterior appearance may be somewhat different, but they still maintain some fundamental parametric similarities (dimensionally, in touchpad alignment).

On the inside we find the same platform, which is fundamentally where most of the expensive engineering and manufacturing efforts go (see Figure 9-4). Shape variations and the development of subsequent models can leverage the existing knowledge base. This approach allows industry to address a variety of issues:

- Producing a wide variety of variants or models based on the same platform technology. This cuts costs and time to market while addressing specific—custom—needs of a highly diversified and segmented consumer base.

- Allowing the consumer to further customize appearance by marketing additional interchangeable parts (such as the colored shell commonly available in stores).

- Allowing for flexible production management, whereby a common platform may be easily customized for regional needs while maintaining time to market and keeping costs down. The platform and interchangeable approach supports just-

Figure 9-3 Aesthetically different cell phones based on the same platform.

Figure 9-4 Interchangeable parts: Different appearance, similar components allows for variant models to be made. Visible on the far right is the cell phone platform.

in-time platforms or platform upgrades in a complex global setting.

- New variants can be easily manufactured by retooling existing manufacturing setups.

Case Overview: Parametric Variations in Kitchen Counters

Kitchen manufacturer Stala developed, with the assistance of Puro of Finland, an online interface for client-based customization and automization of kitchen design. The interface allows users to custom-define their kitchens based on interior spatial conditions and user needs.

The Stala Modules allow the user to select from a variety of worktops, sinks, waste sorting systems, material finishes, and so on (see Figure 9-5). The models are based on parametric relationships that allow the user to identify component types or finishes and define them within preset ranges or variations. As the user makes a dimensional selection for the worktop, the model parametrically defines the limitations that this imposes on the subsequent range of possible selection for the sink. Simple visualization of the context combined with a point-and-click set of options allows the user to effortlessly make decisions.

The interface is questionnaire-based, starting with defining the various basic configuration. It works from the large-scale parameters (such as worktop size) and branches down the tree structure (from sink type and size to color and finish). Included is an ever-evolving

axonometric model of the configuration for quick visual inspection. Upon completion, customized kitchen specifications are produced for manufacturing while simultaneously a set of plan representations is produced to be incorporated into the architect's work. (See Figure 9-6.)

Case Overview: Prefabricated Ship Cabins

Piikkio Works is the world's leading manufacturer of prefabricated cabins and bathroom modules for ship owners and shipyards. The company has manufactured

Figure 9-5 The Stala stainless steel kitchen counter can be customized by the consumer/architect. (Source: Image courtesy of Puro Oy)

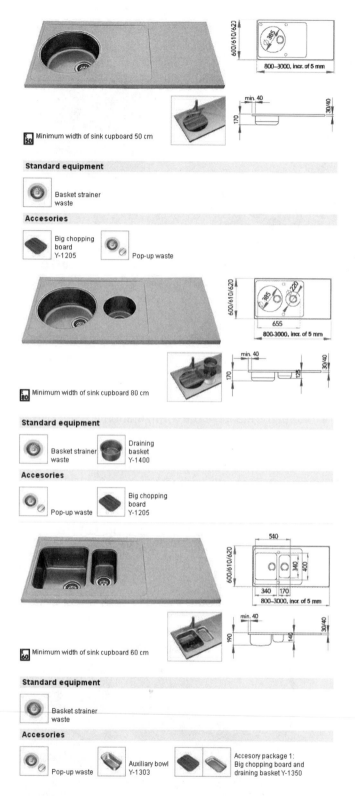

Figure 9-6 The customization process. Note the component and dimensional options. (Source: Image courtesy of Puro Oy)

more than 60,000 custom-made modules for delivery in a variety of environments: luxury cruise liners, cruise ferries, car/passenger ferries and RoPax ships, as well as for offshore platforms and hotels. These cabins are prefabricated to include the full layout, including furnishings, plumbing, and electrical systems ready to be installed into the ship frame, leaving only the systems connection hookup (between the module and shipwide systems). (See Figures 9-8 and 9-9.) Prefabrication facilitates the management of the overall ship construction by reducing construction times, range of construction trades needed on site, and construction on-site. (See Figure 9-11.)

Piikkio specializes in the concept of prefabricated cabin, from mock-up to ready-installed cabin.

- The design of the cabin units is completely customized, including layout, interior design, and materials.
- Modules are prefurnished, reducing on-site shipyard production times and costs.
- Modules are also suitable for semimodular installation. (See various strategies in Figure 9-8.)
- Product's high quality is achieved by, among other things, serial production in factory conditions.

In addition to the modularization and prefabricated strategy to ensure quality, serial reproducibility, precision, and cost-effectiveness, Piikkio has developed proprietary solutions. These include

- The floorless modular cabin solution
- Ultralight bathroom unit based on aluminum construction
- Low floor, low sill height bathroom design
- New cabin wall construction of better quality and higher noise absorption
- Seamless wall panels

Figure 9-7 Section of a cruise ship under construction in the shipyard. Cabins are inserted into the frame and slid into place. Prefabrication reduces on-site construction times. (Source: © 2004 Kvaerner Masa-Yards Inc. and Piikkio Works Oy)

Figure 9-8 Cabin modularization strategies. (Source: © 2004 Kvaerner Masa-Yards Inc. and Piikkio Works Oy)

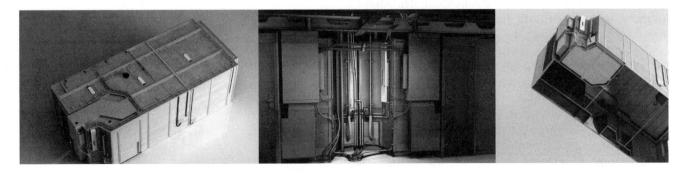

Figure 9-9 Digital model of cabin complete with interior finishes. Systems hookup between two cabins (center). Bathrooms are back-to-back to bring systems closer. (Source: © 2004 Kvaerner Masa-Yards Inc. and Piikkio Works Oy)

Figure 9-10 Cabin in the factory being hoisted and moved toward ship for installing. (Source: © 2004 Kvaerner Masa-Yards Inc. and Piikkio Works Oy)

9.4 ISSUES IN FURNITURE DESIGN

Furniture design evolved in response to specific industry traditions, developing into a specialization of its own. Knowledge about regulatory standards, techniques, and processes has contributed to the specialization of knowledge and skills. The design process has its own particular variants and is highly dependent on full-size mock-ups and prototypes to test critical dimensional variations. Because some furniture, such as chairs, are highly dependent on ergonomic factors, models provide significant feedback regarding look *and* feel.

Certain high segments of the industry have benefited significantly from digital design technologies. Ergonomic data, for example, can be used to model and test seat prototypes. Analysis can provide digital representations of weight distributions and help identify pressure points. Such data may be less significant for a chair for occasional and limited use, but it becomes critical in a high-performance seat—such as aircraft seating, where users may be seated for 8 to 16 hours at a time. CAD/CAM integration into the industry has allowed companies to visualize and respond to problems with greater accuracy and develop more complex and sophisticated solutions. (See Figure 9-11.) German-based Recaro, a leader in aircraft and car seating, has leveraged this technology to a great extent. They have an integrated design unit that includes an *ergonomics designer* (who researches, tests, and evaluates the use context and develops scientific data for the team), an *industrial designer* (who designs and manages the different regulatory agency needs and approval), a *CAD specialist* (who helps visualize concepts and performs analysis for comparison with the ergonomics data), and a *prototype designer* (who constructs working prototypes to test ergonomics and overall design).

Although there has been an increase in specialization, furniture design, as mentioned, has been a traditional area of overlap between the architectural

Ergonomically driven aircraft seating

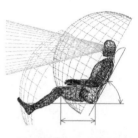

Digital pressure mapping analysis

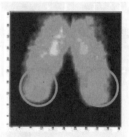

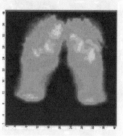

3-D visualization of pressure points

Figure 9-11 Ergonomics in aircraft seating: pressure mapping. (Sources: Top and bottom images courtesy of Ergonomic Technologies Corporation (ETC); middle two images © RECARO Aircraft Seating Gmbh & Co. KG.)

profession and the industrial design profession. Given this tradition, it seems appropriate to include a glimpse into furniture-design-related issues.

In the following sections we look at two different projects to explore two notions: the Vecta chair, to understand how CAD/CAM processes affect the development of a complex chair product, and the Permobil wheelchair, to explore how CAD/CAM enables new material-based processes, which in turn enable a new chair conception to emerge.

9.5 THE VECTA KART CHAIR

The Vecta Kart chair is an innovative new type of stacking task chair. In this case study, the whole design concept is reviewed and the subsequent design development process is explored.

Chair Description

The Vecta Kart chair, a high-quality nesting task chair, was conceived to provide a comfortable and flexible seating solution that could be easily stored (see Figure 9-12). At the time when the Vecta Kart was conceived, most current designs for stacking or nesting chairs did not provide comfortable seating for extended periods of time, such as the normal eight-hour workday. Their usefulness as task chairs was thus impaired. Good task chairs of the day, however, could not be stored easily.

In response to these needs, the Vecta Kart chair was conceived as an "eight-hour" chair that is comfortable enough for use all day long but capable of being easily put away and stored when not in use. The initial idea was eventually developed into a comfortable task chair that nests with others in a manner akin to the way shopping carts fit together. Eight of these new chairs can be stored in the space of two and a half standard chairs. The company involved, Vecta, is a Steelcase Design Partnership Company that already produced a variety of chair products for niche markets.

The initial industrial design team, 5D Design Studio, developed basic concepts for the chair and presented them to Vecta in 1996. The basic chair responded to two sets of users: the sitters and the individuals charged with putting away and storing the chair. For sitters, comfort is determined by standard features such as back tilt, swivel bases, height adjustments, and so forth. For the second group, the storage process had to be made simple. This meant limiting the number of actions required in order to nest the chairs. As in any design responding to different user groups, the possibility of conflicting design requirements was ever present. For the Vecta Kart, an explicit rule was established to avoid any features necessary for nesting that would be considered negative by a sitter. Priority was thus given to making the chair comfortable and attractive to the sitter. The basic chair ultimately proposed by 5D Design Studio to Vecta at this meeting was truly unique. It had fixed arms, an unusual four-leg base with front legs lower than the raised back legs, and a tilt-up seat that allowed the chair to be nested.

Steelcase had recently acquired IDEO, a full-service design and design development and engineering firm. Consequently, individuals from IDEO attended the early design review where 5D Studio presented its proposals to Vecta. The initial design proposal was undoubtedly exciting, but it was clear that a good deal of development work needed to be done to go beyond initial design work, particularly with the mechanisms involved. Initial proposed mechanisms were highly complex. By the second design review, the industrial design part of the work being done by 5D Studio was fairly far along. Full-size drawings, foam-core models, and different prototypes for the nesting base (even preliminary castings) had been made and presented. At this stage, detailed design development and engineering work was assumed by IDEO.

IDEO's primary charge was to further develop the initial concept proposals and bring them to manufacture. Specific charges included incorporating back tilt with adjustable tension, including height adjustability, and developing a range of production versions. Additionally, production versions had to meet or exceed governing ANSI (American National Standards Institute) and BIFMA (Business and Institutional Furniture Manufacturers Association) standards for durability, adjustability, and safety. Designing to meet aggressive cost targets was also a clear priority. A target of 27,000 units per year was established (a small number in comparison to any of Steelcase's more common products). An accelerated schedule was anticipated. An aggressive time frame of nine months was also established so that the chairs could be featured at the next NeoCon show, a highly important event for generating sales. Final production runs were to occur shortly afterward. (Eighteen early chair models were eventually presented at NeoCon. This event, and the need to have so many working models, was a decisive and influencing factor in the design and development process.)

After receiving the final 5D Studio design, a kickoff meeting was held at the Vecta plant, which included a tour that allowed the IDEO design team to assess Vecta's assembly plant and production capabilities. Subsequently, the design team began developing and refining the original 5D proposal and identified three things that needed to happen for the chair to nest properly:

- The base piece must be properly oriented with respect to the seats and backs.
- The seat bottom must be rotated or flipped upward.
- The chairs must be at their maximum heights.

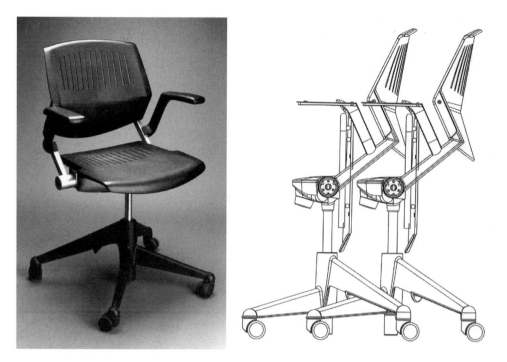

Figure 9-12 The Vecta Kart (Source: © IDEO)

Additionally, these operations need to be combined into a process that is easily performed with as few steps as possible. The design that ultimately evolved provided a simple and elegant solution for meeting these conditions. A latch is pulled that unlocks the seat bottom and raises a gas cylinder to its maximum height. When the seat is flipped up, a slot on the underside of the seat bottom engages a tooth on the base that aligns the seat with the legs. The motions are simple: pull the latch, lift and spin the seat, and it is ready to nest with other Vecta Karts. Simple and elegant solutions like this, however, require intense development to make them actually work.

Within a month of the kickoff meeting at Vecta, the IDEO team presented at a review three basic options for the chair's architecture: "Go with the Flow," which continued the basic strategies started by 5D design studio; "Gas in Back," which moved the gas cylinder used for height adjustment to a location behind the seat's axis; and the "Offset Rubber Pack," which moved the back-tilt spring to one side of the cylinder as a way of conserving space. Also addressed at the same review were general issues of design for manufacturing and assembly, materials, and process selection. Specific problems were also addressed. In the original model, with the gas cylinder located where the tension knob is now placed, grease could potentially get on the seat. (See Figure 9-13.)

The initial industrial design team had earlier suggested the use of a self-centering gas cylinder that rotated the seat into alignment while at the same time raising it to its maximum height. Thus, as a sitter would rise, the chair would rotate and raise as well. This feature might be useful for the maintenance person stacking chairs at the end of the day, but it is truly an annoyance for the primary user—the sitter. Hence, it violated that basic and explicit rule established earlier to avoid any features necessary for nesting that would be considered by a sitter to be negative. In addition, self-centering gas cylinders were also found to be about three times as expensive as normal gas cylinders. IDEO then looked at using regular gas cylinders with additional mechanisms directly targeted for making the chair easy to adjust by the end user.

At the same time, the design development team looked very closely at Vecta's core competencies. As noted previously, Vecta had long been addressing niche markets that involved relatively low production volumes. The target volume of 25,000 units per year is not large compared to other more common chair products. The team looked carefully at Vecta's assembly plants and production capabilities in detail. It became clear that the development of unique pieces (particularly those involving new dies) solely for the Vecta Kart chair would be an expensive proposition. The approach that evolved was to seek to modify part designs already used with existing chairs (e.g., Steelcase's Criterion) that were already being successfully produced in volume at relatively low cost. By making some relatively simple modifications, critical parts for the Vecta Kart, notably

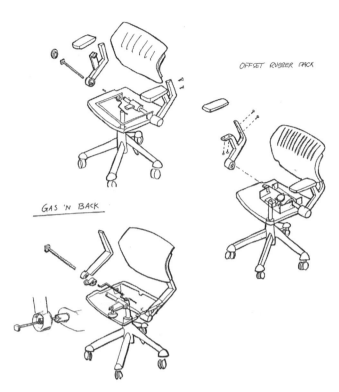

GO WITH THE FLOW

OFFSET RUBBER PACK

GAS 'N BACK

Figure 9-13 First approaches to the chair design. (Source: © IDEO)

the offset rubber pack, were thus able to be economically produced in relatively low volumes.

The detailed design work done by the IDEO team is best described relative to each of the primary individual chair components: the base, the tilt-back mechanism, the seat, the base tooth, the seat latch, and the height adjustment mechanism. This division into subsystems is also the way IDEO organized the design and development process. Teams were charged with developing specific major components within an overall framework. As with many industrial design teams, their processes involved traditional representations, including two-dimensional, handcrafted models and prototypes. It was evident that IDEO needed to immediately introduce digital modeling techniques for many reasons. Not the least of these is that in going from two-dimensional models to three-dimensional models, there is invariably a lot of interpretation by others that must accompany the process. A model maker (typically not the original designer) necessarily interprets the exact shape of a complex or volumetric form. Precision is also an issue. Many shapes are axisymmetric. Getting these shapes exact by hand is a difficult process. Obviously, going from handcrafted models to models useful in a production environment is also problematic. Digital models were needed to support anticipated produc-

tion processes. These models became part of the design development process. As will be seen, however, the process also involved significant materials investigations, prototyping, and testing.

The Base

The unique base design involving staggered leg heights so essential to nesting was largely in place from initial design proposals. The immediate task at hand was largely design development, including materials and manufacturing process selection. 5D Design had developed the design to a significant extent, including providing prototypes made via sand-casting techniques. The IDEO team explored a number of alterations to improve nesting. These included minor changes in the angles and heights of the legs. The team then explored a number of different materials and manufacturing processes that might be appropriate for the unique base configuration. Castings for the base were anticipated as being expensive given the fairly low production volumes anticipated. Castings also had to be specially painted. Various other techniques were explored, including a weldment with rub strips. The anticipated distortions from a welding process were decided to be problematic (the distortions would not be a problem in a three-legged chair but could cause the four-legged chair to rest unevenly on a level surface). For welding to be feasible, a robotically assisted procedure would have to be used—a process again prohibitively expensive in view of the low production volumes anticipated. A form of an injection-molded plastic base was considered, since materials would be relatively inexpensive. Problems with "creep" (deformation over time) were anticipated, however. The tooling for this approach was also anticipated as being quite expensive, in this case because of the peculiar shape of the legs (with one pair raised above the other). This form caused the tooling to be quite deep and injector pins quite long. Die casting in aluminum was also explored, and after numerical cost quotes were obtained for various processes, it was chosen as being the best alternative. Painting was needed for pieces produced in this way, as were special polypropylene shields to prevent scratching from contact with other bases during nesting. Tooling costs were reasonable and piece prices not excessive, and, importantly, risks were low (particularly in regard to hitting the schedule). Costs for basic processes were first roughly estimated via an internal procedure, with each team member making estimates for comparison with others (with surprisingly close agreement obtained). Improved costs were obtained by getting initial quotes from vendors. Once the database was transmitted to vendors, accurate cost data could be obtained. (See Figure 9-14.)

Parallel to the preceding investigations, the team also performed a detailed BIFMA analysis to ensure that the base exceeded mandated stability requirements. In any radial-legged chair base of this kind, overturning from someone sitting off center or on a chair arm can potentially occur about a line joining the extremities of any two legs. The critical design factor in preventing overturning is the distance from the center of the chair to this line (i.e., the moment arm). The lengths of the legs had to be made longer than those proposed in the original design to ensure adequate stability. A finite-element structural analysis was also made using a variety of different materials to verify the basic strength and rigidity of the proposed base design. By this time, the team had settled on die casting for the base. Wall thicknesses, therefore, were intended to be quite thin. The finite-element analysis verified that the thicknesses selected were indeed appropriate.

The Base Tooth

As noted previously, for the chair to nest, the chair must not only adjust itself to its maximum height, but the legs and seat must be aligned. The alignment function was originally met by the self-centering gas cylinder that subsequently proved problematic. The proposed use of a lower-cost regular gas cylinder then necessitated that an additional alignment mechanism be developed. Ultimately, a tooth was incorporated into the base that aligned to a pocket in the seat when the seat was rotated upward for nesting. While simple in concept, this feature required extensive prototyping and testing to determine a shape and related material that worked every time. (See Figure 9-15.)

The Tilt Mechanism for the Back

To lean back properly, there must be a controlled tilt resistance to the back. The first option explored was via the use of a torsion spring contained within a housing or yoke beneath the seat. The moment causing the back to rotate was determined (i.e., the horizontal force exerted by the user's back times the associated moment arm as measured from the location of the force to the resistance mechanism) and an appropriate torsion spring selected. During the tour of the Vecta plant, however, team members observed that a torsional rubber pack was used in many Steelcase chair products. (The rubber pack is essentially a tube within a tube. The tubes are separated by cast rubber. When one tube is twisted with respect to the other, a torsional resistance is generated as the interstitial rubber deforms.) Around 1.2 million rubber packs have been produced. Given their high volume, rubber packs could be produced inexpensively en masse via a 24-cavity tool. These rub-

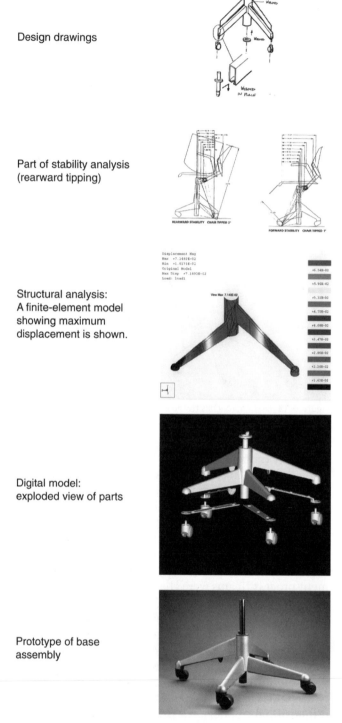

Design drawings

Part of stability analysis (rearward tipping)

Structural analysis: A finite-element model showing maximum displacement is shown.

Digital model: exploded view of parts

Prototype of base assembly

Base of Vecta Kart

Figure 9-14 Base of Vecta Kart. (Source: © IDEO)

ber packs, however, came in specific lengths that were too long for the Vecta Kart chair. After looking at costs of changing lengths within the primary production environment, however, the team decided on a much

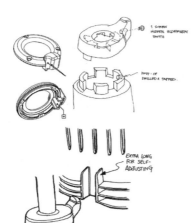

Design sketch for tooth and pocket in seat

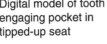

Part prototype

Digital model of tooth engaging pocket in tipped-up seat

Final mechanism

Figure 9-15 Base tooth for aligning chair legs and seat. (Source: © IDEO)

simpler alternative. Standard rubber packs were simply hand-modified to the correct length (via elementary bandsaws and similar equipment). Given the low production volumes, needed units could easily be pro-

duced in this way. A similar approach was used for the tension knob.

The housing or yoke containing the rubber pack axle assembly necessarily had a complex shape. The first housing designed was a sand-casting and was the housing used for the 18 chairs presented at NeoCon. The sand-casting solution, however, presented many problems. Some secondary machining for tolerances was required with each of these housings. Further design studies indicated that it was possible to ultimately eliminate bearings and go directly to a metal-on-metal axle-to-housing system (the number of expected uses was judged relatively low). Ultimately, a die-cast housing was devised. Accommodating the axle proved extremely difficult in this design, however, because of both tolerances and the needed specific shape of the tool itself. (Thin internal fins would have been required in the die-casting tool that were difficult to cool and would wear out quickly.) The casting was eventually designed to accommodate a bent sheet-metal insert that attached to the housing at either end. Holes were punched in the sheet metal, and then the metal was bent to shape. The insert attached to the housing at only two points on either end. This general strategy enabled good tolerance control (via the inserts) while at the same time greatly simplifying the die-cast shape. Assembly was simplified as well. The yoke could be dropped in place and attached with only two screws at either end.

Seat

The seat and back of the chair were intended to have desirable "bounce" to them. In the original prototype, the shaped seat was cast from polyurethane. It had small, rectangular hole patterns. A U-shaped bent metal tube was used underneath the seat to provide necessary strength. Metal "ears" were welded to it for necessary attachments to other parts of the chair. The open end allowed the seat to deform to obtain the desirable bounce. Initial impact tests, however, revealed that cracks were opening up around some of the rectangular holes. This already troublesome problem was heightened by the fact that release of the final database—as dictated by the master schedule—was only two weeks away. The seat was immediately redesigned to have raised material around the holes. The seat was machined directly from ABS. This was an improvement, but additional support at the back seat edge was still needed. Simply continuing the bent tube around would solve the problem, but the desirable bounce would be eliminated. A series of studies were quickly made to see if the whole underside of the seat could be better designed. Eventually, a casting approach evolved. There were problems, however, in how to easily and inexpensively provide the needed metal "ears." In exploring this problem, a metal caster observed that it was not so difficult to insert metal plates directly into a casting. A new design was quickly evolved that resembled the older bent tube, but that was redesigned as a die-cast member that incorporated special steel plate inserts. The latter were to be laser-cut to the necessary accuracy. The shape control enabled by using a casting process allowed designers to simply extend the shape around to the back edge to provide strength, but to lower it very slightly at the back so that a space existed between the seat and the strengthening member. Thus, a user would experience bounce as the seat edge deformed, but the member beneath would prevent seat deformations from getting so large that cracking would again be induced. A rough prototype was quickly made. Physical load tests were made to make sure that all worked as intended. The final database was released on time.

The Seat Latch

The need to flip up the seat for nesting introduced the need for a latch to lock the seat in place and to release it upon demand. This need was unique in the world of task chairs, since no existing task chairs had ever used flip-up seats before. The designers also kept in mind that seats are invariably used as stools at one point or another, so the locking mechanism must be totally secure. While the technical requirements were clear, the human interface issues were more subtle. The look and feel of the handle must clearly convey to the user its basic function and be easily accessible when called upon for use, but it should be largely invisible under normal conditions. A series of designs were developed and prototyped so that these conditions could be met.

Height Adjustment

The basic rule that the chair should have no negative features needed for nesting that are apparent to the sitter necessitated close attention to the problem of height adjustment. The user should be able to adjust the chair to his or her preferred setting and leave it. Only when the chair is readied for storage should it assume its needed maximum height. The solution finally determined allows the user to adjust the chair and leave it in its preferred setting, but the seat automatically assumes its maximum height when the seat is flipped upward in anticipation of storage. Here, the whole complex of components comes into play. When the seat latch is released and the seat is flipped upward, the base tooth is engaged when the seat is spun and aligns the leg and the seat, and the regular gas cylinder is enabled to raise the seat to its maximum height. (See Figure 9-17.)

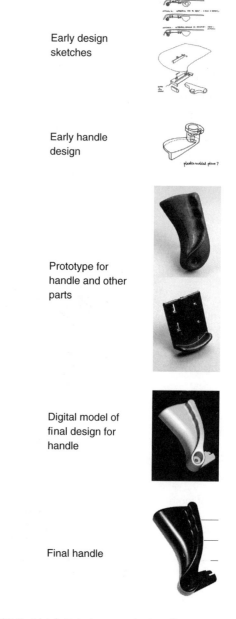

Early design sketches

Early handle design

Prototype for handle and other parts

Digital model of final design for handle

Final handle

Figure 9-16 Seat latch and release mechanism. (Source: © IDEO)

Summary

In reflecting on the project, IDEO engineer Alan Vale noted that three primary factors always affect the design development process—appearance, cost, and schedule—and that only one of these factors typically drives a project. In the Vecta Kart, he noted that cost and schedule were the primary determinants for IDEO's contribution, with schedule being probably the most influential. (The chair's underlying concept and appearance were already largely fixed by the industrial design team.) These factors drove many of the specific decisions. The adoption and modification of a standard

Early design sketches

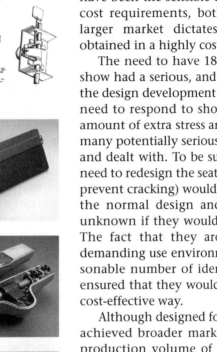

Part prototype

Mechanism

Digital model of chair with seat in flipped position showing the location of the adjustment mechanism

Prototype of chair with height

Figure 9-17 Height adjustment. (Source: © IDEO)

rubber pack from Steelcase provides a good example here. An entirely new element could have potentially been designed and produced (that conceivably might have even possessed better design features, although this remains unclear), but surely doing so would not have been the sensible choice in view of schedule and cost requirements, both determined in response to larger market dictates. Needed functionality was obtained in a highly cost-efficient way.

The need to have 18 working units at the NeoCon show had a serious, and ultimately positive, impact on the design development process. While at the time, the need to respond to show demands created no minor amount of extra stress and was seemingly a distraction, many potentially serious issues were quickly uncovered and dealt with. To be sure, these same issues (e.g., the need to redesign the seat and supporting tube system to prevent cracking) would have surely been uncovered in the normal design and testing process, albeit it is unknown if they would have caused schedule delays. The fact that they arose within the context of a demanding use environment and a need to have a reasonable number of identical units present, however, ensured that they would be dealt with in a timely and cost-effective way.

Although designed for a niche market, the chair has achieved broader market appeal. The original target production volume of 25,000 units per year proved inadequate to meet demands. An 80,000-unit-per-year target was quickly identified.

The chair is widely regarded as a fine example of how an innovative idea was technically well developed within a short time frame. The Vecta Kart chair has been widely acclaimed. In 1998, the chair was awarded the "Best Innovation Award" by NeoCon. In 1998, it received the "Most Excellent" award from Officeinsight, and the 1998 APEX award for task seating. It won the IIDA, Southern California Chapter; 1999 ACCLAIM Award; and the "Most Innovative of Show" Award. From IDSA/BusinessWeek, it received the 1999 IDEA Gold and "Designs of the Decade" Bronze awards.

9.6 THE PERMOBIL WHEELCHAIR

The Design Context

In the following case, we look at a recent example of a new bentwood chair that at once remains in the tradition of prior bentwood furniture and yet is strikingly new in form—a newness that is at least partly due to the way the designer(s) exploited recent computer-aided design and manufacturing technologies in the design and production of the chair (see Figure 9-18).

Permobil, a Swedish company, has been a leader in manufacturing motorized wheelchairs. The company

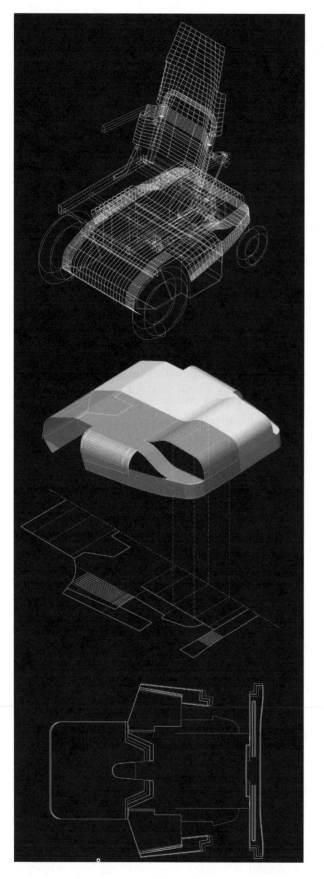

Figure 9-18 The unfolding process: from shell to unfolded veneer pattern.

was conscious of the strong Scandinavian tradition of using wood in mass-produced products and also well aware of the intrinsic consumer appeal of these same products. The company was interested in exploring shaped plywood's potential for a wheelchair, particularly as a way of maintaining their leadership as a wheelchair manufacturer and further differentiate their product lines from competitors. Consequently, the company commissioned Marco Steinberg, an architect and designer at the Graduate School of Design at Harvard, to design and fabricate a full-scale prototype of a plywood prothesis for a motorized wheelchair.

A broad design goal was to inextricably link the positive aesthetic and tactile qualities of a bentwood product with a high level of performance vis-à-vis the chair's functioning as a wheelchair. The immediate design environment, however, was severely constrained. The company mandated that for the first prototype an existing metal frame, wheels, and all accompanying electronic and mechanical elements (motor, drivers, etc.) were to be used directly. Only seats, backs, and other covering elements could be redesigned. The bentwood—in this case normally in the form of formed plywood sheets—also had to achieve the strength and rigidity of existing plastic elements, albeit not necessarily reflecting their same shapes. (See Figure 9-19.)

The studies and prototyping that took place occurred with a general framework wherein it was anticipated that the plywood chair would be built upon the fine tradition of bentwood technology, but updated with newer computer-based technologies. A specific technological approach was also anticipated and formed part of the argument that design innovation within the context of a by-now-familiar and widely used material was indeed still possible and could effectively help the company position itself in a new way, albeit a way that was nonetheless consistent with the fine Scandanavian tradition of design with wood. (See Figure 9-20.)

Specifically, it was anticipated that needed compound curvatures (surfaces that are nondevelopable and that can curve differently in different directions, for instance, saddle shapes—see Chapter 11) could be made via initially translating three-dimensional surface forms into flat cutting patterns. The shapes of the cutting patterns would have to be such that when formed over carefully shaped molds, the resulting shapes would have the desired compound curvatures. (See Figure 9-21.) It was anticipated that cutting each laminate layer to a specific shape *before* any kind of forming or pressing would ultimately enable a far richer vocabulary of compound curves to be made than would be possible with any attempt to shape previously laminated stock material. Individual laminates already cut to a pattern would thus be layered, glued, and pressed into the desired shape over an appropriately shaped

Figure 9-19 The final base shell.

mold. Given the probable precision required, the normal "laminate stepping" anticipated to be associated with this bending approach was considered to be problematic. This stepping can occur as a consequence of making a thick element from individually bent laminates, much like occurs at the edges of a deck of cards when collectively bent prior to shuffling. The need for a nonstepped edge suggested that each laminate would have to be shaped slightly differently from its adjacent neighbor. (See Figure 9-22.)

The need for this kind of precise shaping in turn suggested the need to use numerical control technologies in the design and fabrication of the chair. (Given his point in time, Thonet could not avail himself of numerical control technologies despite his own needs for precision in cutting patterns. Perhaps he would have been very quick to adopt them had they been available.) Within the framework of this anticipated process framework, design work for the chair was undertaken. (While described in the text in a linear way, it was an iterative process).

Basic Chair Design

As ultimately designed and prototyped, the resulting design consists of an integrated assembly of individually shaped plywood components. The backrest has three fundamental portions. The upper portion cups in for shoulder blade support and better sectional rigidity.

A center portion bends back and has slits for connectors for future sets of attachments (telecommunication devices, etc.). Simple pinholes click into pin connectors. The lower portion cups inward for lower back support. Side connectors bolt to pneumatically controlled side levers for chair tilting. A headrest plate is stabilized by a lapped vertical brace. (See Figure 9-23.)

The seat and footrest also follows a three-part sequence. The back portion cups up to provide bottom support, the center folds up at the sides for lateral support, and the front creases in the middle for leg support. Beneath, the seat is supported by three ribs connecting it to the frame. Side louvers can be raised to provide further side support for flailing legs or can be pushed down to create a flush seat surface for easy user movement out of the chair. These side louvers are formed as a series of S-profiles that fold in from the frame and support the sides of a user's legs. The footrest is connected via nylon sleeves laminated within a thick L-profile. They may be folded up.

The base shell shields the chair's driving mechanisms and computer (see Figure 9-24). It is a two-part assembly, with the front capable of being slipped off for maintenance access to the driving mechanisms. The top portion follows the contours of the chair's computer. Acrylic panels that provide space for rechargers and other devices cover side apertures. Triangular corner inserts provide both locking mechanisms and external input connections (a recharge plug, data, and voice

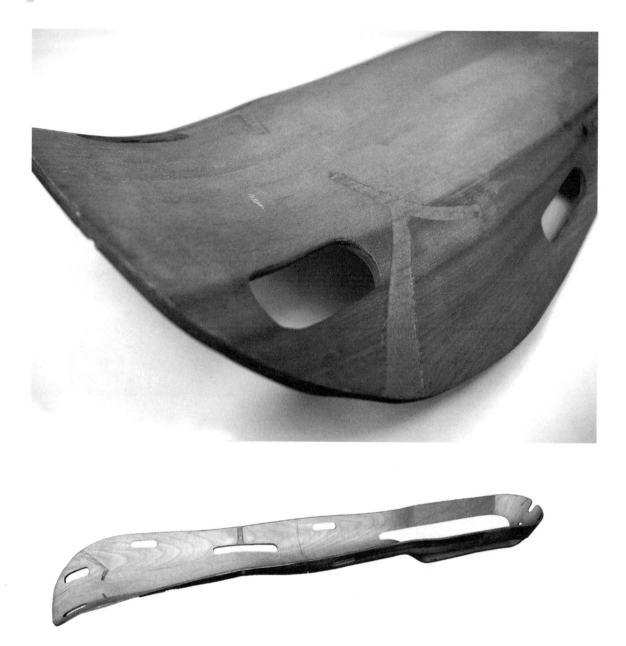

Figure 9-20 Traditions in complexly molded plywood from—such as the Eames' leg splint—provided some of the precedents to the approach. Visible is the cut pattern on the veneer to relief material, enabling it to be formed into a compound curve.

connections). The back is connected via a plate to the chair's steel frame. The plate also has embedded lights that make up the chair's rear brake light.

The armrests cup the user's arm in place. Side connector plates curve slightly outward for increased lateral support after attaching to the steel frame. They are in turn tabbed into the armrest in an exposed end-grain connection that with humidity expands and further tightens. The armrest for the control panel splays to allow for a laminated tubular metal sleeve and pin pivot connection. Thus, the control panel can pivot outward to an orthogonal position so that the chair can be

brought closer to tables. The control panel itself is of a smooth wood finish only and has a varying sectional shape. The initial portion undulates to support the wrist. A raised portion then contains function button outlines etched into the wood surface. A final portion contains wiring and bottom support of the joystick. Inserted into the laminates under the function button outlines are internal membranes and wiring. A user pushing against a "wood" button outline makes a closed internal electrical connection that activates the desired mechanism. Thus, the user only touches wood. (This feature is one of several in the chair that really

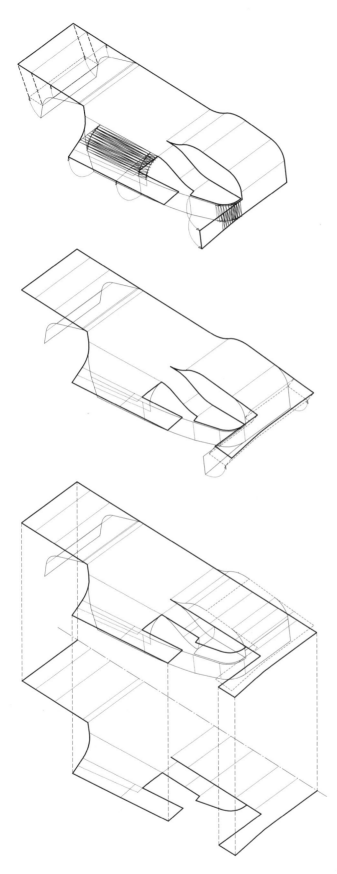

Figure 9-21 Unfolding half of the base shell.

makes use of the tactile qualities of wood and the positive feelings that users have when touching wood. Compare this effect to traditional buttons and/or electronic touch pads.)

Design and Prototyping Processes

Design goals were first established through compilation of a *program performance matrix*. Performance demands for the wheelchair and each of its discrete components (e.g., armrests) were established. The wheel covers, for example, normally must provide user protection from the wheels, serve as splash and mud guards, and, at the designer's choice, conceal hardware.

A *material performance matrix* was also compiled that defined plywood's unique physical properties (e.g., its bendability or tactility) and related design potentials as they exist independently of any direct application. A series of tests were made for various laminated wood products to determine minimum bending radii in relation to thickness (clearly, wood products cannot be simply bent into any arbitrary shape without material failure). Other tests addressed fundamental questions regarding to what extent were surface deformations possible, and thus to what extent could different laminates be shaped into compound curvatures. Additionally, explorations were made of alternative finish types, how other materials could be laminated to the basic wood product, and so forth. (See Figure 9-25.)

Program performance demands were subsequently matched with performance attributes of bent plywood. Thus, "tactility" properties were associated with armrests but not necessarily directly with casing components intended primarily for hardware concealment and components where specific types of compound curves were needed.

At this point, and within the framework of a general design image, specific elements were prototyped and tested. The seat, for example, was initially configured within a digital environment and a preliminary folding strategy devised. Central arch and side profiles, with associated key locking points, were modeled and subsequently fabricated. Actual use tests were then conducted, and the design revised as needed to meet demands for comfort or to achieve an improved physical artifact. New models were made and tested until a positive congruence between shape and process was obtained.

In these processes, a digital model of a chair element was first made. A compound curve was subsequently "flattened out" into a planar shape. This process necessarily involved specific shaping knowledge as dependent on the properties of the plywood, which had been determined before, as previously noted. Broadly, the process involved a digital "unpeeling" and flattening of a surface form. Given the complexities of the shapes

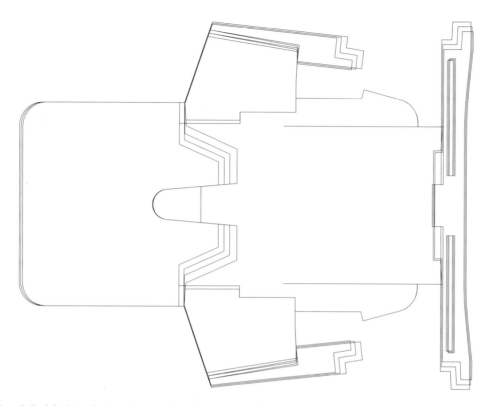

Figure 9-22 Overlay of all of the base sheets. Offsets at the edges ensure a 90° alignment throughout the edge of the final piece. Stepping between parts is for connective "dovetail" joinery between veneers.

involved, the process used herein involved a process of triangulation and faceting to fold curves into the cutting plane.

Ultimately, during the fabrication process, these shapes were made of molded plywood components built up from 1/16-inch aircraft grade plywood sheets. As previously noted, each of the laminates for any given component had to have a slightly different shape than its adjacent neighbor, so that end edge "stair stepping" could be avoided. Thus, each laminate had to have a different cutting pattern. This was accomplished digitally via a series of offset views.

In addition to general shape adjustments for stair-stepping avoidance, specific geometric features, for instance, relief cuts (see Chapter 11), often had to be introduced in order to achieve specific compound curve shapes. Additionally, the bendability of a designated layer was locally controlled or enhanced via a scoring technique. In this technique, a laser cutter was

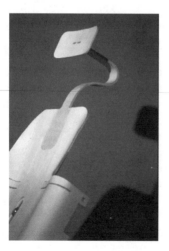

Figure 9-23 The complete backrest. Note the flat "dovetail" joinery to the headrest.

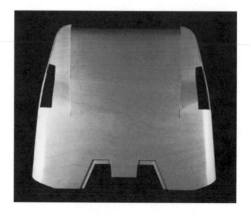

Figure 9-24 A first wheelchair base with continuous wood grain.

Figure 9-25 "Crumple" tests (left). On the right: The control panel, from veneers, formwork, and first prototype to the final control panel prototype.

Figure 9-27 Backrest prototypes and formwork—the overall process (note flat veneer in the foreground).

used to score a pattern onto a laminate. The associated thickness reduction enabled the sheet to be curved in a different way than was possible with a constant thickness sheet, yet still provide a continuous surface with positive tactile qualities.

Because in many cases there had to be "joints" or splices in individual laminates because of the restrictions in available stock sheet sizes, a system of overlap joinery also had to be devised that also affected final laminate cutting patterns. Alignment guides were also cut into place in anticipation of the vacuum-forming process to be subsequently used.

The same digital models were used to make the molds for the basic shaping processes. Molds were made by making a series of parallel fiberboard panels with cut edges that collectively defined the needed curve (rather like a loaf of sliced bread). Digital descriptions of sectional profiles were extracted from the base model and subsequently cut from flat fiberboard sheets via the use of a CNC router. Additional orthogonal pieces had also been modeled so that all individual pieces could be fit together as an interlocking eggcrate-like assembly. The grid resolution of the mold was determined so that small undulations of the plywood in unsupported areas was not problematic.

Cut veneer elements were placed over the molds and pressed into shape via a vacuum press. (See Figure 9-26.)

Interior surfaces of laminates were skim-coated with glue and put into place. Alignment guides not only allowed correct placement but were needed to hold sheets in place during the vacuum process. In a vacuum process, the air in a vacuum bag over the surface of the series of laminates is then extracted. As the bag shrinks down, it presses the laminates down and forces them to conform to the shape of the underlying mold. In this case, pressure was applied to the glued laminates for about three hours while the glue set. Upon removal of the bag, pieces were taken out and minor finishing done.

The general processes previously described were used to produce a initial prototype. To demonstrate that the process was "repeatable"—a particularly important point given the notorious variability present in the properties of wood elements—several identical prototypes were produced. Further demonstrated was the potential of developing unique shapes for some elements such as the backrest that could easily conform to user-driven needs or specifications. (See Figure 9-27.) Thus, using a parameterized version of the basic digital model, cutting patterns and mold elements could be generated for a family of differing shapes.

Ultimately, the chair was considered a highly successful prototype (see Figure 9-28). Exhibited at several shows, the chair challenged prevailing notions of what a wheelchair should look and feel like.

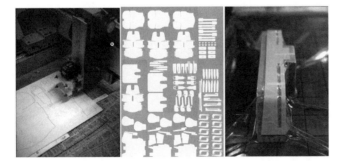

Figure 9-26 The process: CNC router-cutting the veneer (left) the flat template (middle). Veneers in a vacuum press against the CNC-manufactured formwork (right).

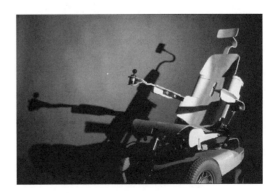

Figure 9-28 The final wheelchair prototype.

PART IV

THE DIGITAL DESIGN ENVIRONMENT

These three chapters describe the kinds of digital design environments that are used to support CAD/CAM applications. The initial chapter reviews the general types of digital design environments in current use, and then looks at the fundamentals of digital modeling. The next chapter addresses capabilities of robust design development environments, such as dimensionally driven design, parametric design, feature-based design, assembly modeling, and other topics. The final chapter looks at issues related to digital design in practice.

CHAPTER 10

Fundamentals
of Digital Modeling

10.1 INTRODUCTION

This chapter provides an introduction to digital design environments and the way they are used to support different design activities. Basic characteristics of digital design environments are introduced first, followed by an overview of the broad differentiations between concept modelers, renderers, animation programs, entity-based drafting, component-based CAD, and design development environments. These categories provide the context for the more detailed discussion of design development environments in Chapters 11 and 12. Understanding the way three-dimensional shapes can be represented is closely related to what software can or cannot do. Section 10.4 introduces the characteristics of representational elements such as splines, wireframes, surfaces, and solids and directly leads to a brief discussion on fundamental modeling techniques using these same elements in the following section.

10.2 DIGITAL DESIGN ENVIRONMENTS: GENERAL CHARACTERISTICS

In this day and age of seemingly endless and constantly changing software systems that each purport to meet virtually all imaginable needs, there is little wonder that some designers spend enormous amounts of time seeking to understand whether one system or another is best to use for a specific purpose. Others, frustrated by the rapid and continuous change of digital design technology, resort to what they already know and thus might miss out on some of the exciting new possibilities. There is currently no clear, generally accepted way of classifying and describing software environments in a way that is meaningful to users who are not computer scientists but need to perform in their professional design activities. Software is invariably designed to meet specific perceived needs or to serve defined roles within the overall design and implementation process. This section begins unraveling some of these issues and places different digital design environments into a general perspective.

There are many ways to classify digital design environments. Broad approaches to description and classification can include the following perspectives:

- Primary user industries (e.g., entertainment, architecture, aerospace, industrial design)
- Design phases (e.g., conceptual or schematic design, design development, design for production or construction)
- Primary-use applications (e.g., 2-D graphics, geometric modeling, rendering, animation, structural analysis)
- Model types and modes of representation (e.g., wireframe models, surface models, solid models)
- Internal data structures and object-oriented capabilities, which include the nature of basic database structures (e.g., whether relational or object-based data structures are used) and the way a digital model is structured (feature- and component-based design, parametric design capabilities, dimensionally driven design)
- Communication/dissemination/collaboration capabilities

This list is not meant to be exhaustive but merely to provide a basis for organizing a discussion of how to think about digital design environments.

User Industries

Given the huge amount of cross-industry use of different computational environments, the first classification by the target industry is only marginally interesting. It does, however, give an indication for what might be expected of specific software and partially explain the wide variety of ways that even a basic three-dimensional shape can be digitally generated and represented. Predominant geometry, design processes, business models, and other characteristics all factor into how exactly a software is devised and what possibilities it might offer to support activities such as engineering, visualization, simulation, cost estimation, and others. CATIA, an environment developed originally for the aerospace industry, can surely be expected to support not only complex surface and solid modeling but assembly modeling and engineering applications as well. On the other hand, it is less likely to be useful for high-end photo-realistic renderings or animations where programs such as 3D Studio Max or Maya are more applicable. (See Figure 10-1.)

Design Phases

Many digital design environments were created specifically to support activities in certain design phases. Conceptual design especially is very different from design development or design for construction and production, and few if any environments provide adequate support throughout. The relatively unstructured phase of formulating the basic characteristics of a project during conceptual design relies on quick feedback from (digital) sketches, 3-D models, and renderings, with an emphasis on visualization rather than mathematically precise modeling. Design development, the detailed study and technical development of a concept, is a more structured activity involving the quantitative and qualitative evaluation and development of the design intention. Supporting this highly collaborative phase is the primary objective of tools such as ProEngineer, CATIA, or SolidWorks—environments that are equally valuable during design for production.

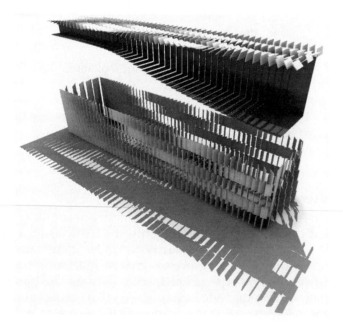

Figure 10-1 Maya, a software initially conceived for the movie industry, has recently attracted the attention of digitally well-versed architects. Apart from animations, users can also create shapes through direct input of algorithms, as shown in the example. (Source: Project by Andrew Saunders)

Primary-Use Applications

This category is of basic use in relation to conveying a sense of what different digital environments were designed to primarily do. For a given industry this primary use is closely related to the specific needs in different design phases. A fundamental differentiation can be made between purely 2-D graphic design environments and those geared toward generating more or less accurate model geometry to support the design of three-dimensional objects. Programs such as Adobe Photoshop or Illustrator—pixel versus vector-based—are primarily used for graphic manipulations such as image control or graphic layout work.

Geometric modeling environments can generally create two- or three-dimensional representations of shapes, and many support some degree of rendering for visualization purposes. Individual programs may be optimized for high-end rendering or lighting studies (3D Studio Max, form-Z, VIZ, AccuRender, etc.) or animation (Maya, Premiere, and others). Others primarily support traditional drafting activities of 2-D drawings (AutoCAD, VectorWorks, and many others). Animation programs may allow for a convincing visual representation of dynamic objects subject to forces such as gravity, but they are not based on exact mathematical and physical models. The results may be inaccurate in a physical sense but are still perfectly useful for their intended user groups and purposes.

Model Types and Modes of Representation

Applicable only to geometric modeling systems, here we enter into basic ways geometric models are created via points, lines, surfaces, various primitives, voxels, and so forth. Of fundamental importance here is the common distinction between wireframe models, surface models, and solid models—discussed in more detail in the following section. Many modeling environments support more than one type of element. Extensive surface modeling capabilities are found in many design tools that are employed primarily for visualization purposes, but high-end surface modeling remains the preferred way of modeling the highly complex surface shapes found in application domains such as industrial design, aerospace design, and automotive design. Some environments allow surfaces to be converted into solids, which in turn support a broader range of engineering calculations such as calculations of mass or centroid.

Closely related to model types is the question of how elements are represented. Of primary importance here is the distinction between environments that represent curves and surfaces as a series of straight-line segments or equivalent meshes and those that use explicit mathematical expressions to define these entities. The latter approach has become widely used in geometric modelers (Maya, CATIA, Rhinoceros, SolidWorks, Unigraphics, etc.), but some, for example CATIA, offer mesh-based alternatives as well. Explicit mathematical representations are often referred to as "parametrically based," whereby the word "parametric" is used in connection with the mathematical description, not as a way of manipulating shapes. This concept is briefly outlined in the following section.

Internal Data Structures and Object-Oriented Capabilities

Ultimately, what one can or cannot do with a digital design system depends on how the underlying program is written and structured, what programming language is used, and what type of application database stores the information the user inputs during the design process. This is a comprehensive subject beyond the scope of this immediate discussion, and it is closely related to the degree of object-oriented capabilities that software may or may not include. The ability to define classes of objects, create instances of objects, assign behaviors, and have objects inherit such behavior is only fully present if sophisticated object-oriented programming languages and databases are employed. Object-oriented programming characteristics are implemented to various degrees in programs such as MicroStation or Revit, as well as in high-end design development environments such as CATIA, Pro/ENGINEER, or SolidWorks, but they are not necessarily referred to in those terms.

What exactly is object-oriented design? Originally a method of computer programming, *object-oriented design* borrows its name from the object-oriented data model—a way to describe complex information through discrete but interrelated components. These units of data, or *objects*, contain both attributes as well as methods. *Attributes* are properties, for example, the "width" of a "sliding door" object, and *methods* are bodies of programming code that contain operative or behavioral descriptions. Objects also contain a set of messages that an object can respond to. *Messages* are requests between objects to execute a particular method, such as "adjust the 'width' attribute of the 'brick wall' object to match the 'width' attribute of the 'sliding door' object." Objects that share the same methods, respond to the same messages, and have attributes of the same type are grouped together in *classes*. The "sliding door" object could be one instance of a class called "doors," with other instances being "swinging doors" or "folding doors." These objects all share certain attributes such as "width" or "height," and they can be differentiated by the values that are assigned to these attributes.

Closely related to the concept of object classes is the principle of *inheritance,* an elegant way to create new classes based on the attributes and methods of existing classes. When additional attributes and methods are specified, these new classes can correspond to more requirements. Classes can also inherit attributes and methods of multiple classes (*multiple inheritance*). The "door" object class, for example, clearly shares attributes with the class "window." On deriving the class "door" from the class "window," "door" can inherit attributes such as geometry as well as methods such as how to calculate the relative position of the object within a "wall" opening. On changing the attribute thickness of "wall," the "wall" object would send the message "thickness" to both "door" and "window" objects, and their relative position would be recalculated based on the particular algorithm. (See Figure 10-2.)

Objects are manipulated by having messages sent to them, but an object can change or be manipulated only if the message belongs to a set of allowed messages and to the extent that this manipulation corresponds to the methods assigned to the object. By inserting a "door" object into a "wall" object, "door" would send a message that triggers the creation of a suitable opening in "wall." Inserting "door" into a floor slab would not invoke any methods, since the message "make opening" would not be allowed for "door" in the context of a "slab." This structuring allows the object to be used in certain ways by the system, but at the same time, it can be changed or extended without affecting the way the

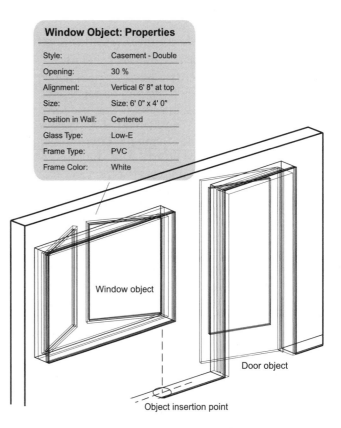

Figure 10-2 Architectural objects in a component-based program: Properties such as position, geometry, materials, and others can be modified at any time, usually via dialog boxes.

object is already being used. Objects can be built up and reused, and they can be refined over time. When the "door" is inserted during schematic design, for example, the corresponding wall opening may be the exact size of the door. A good object-oriented system would allow the opening to be enlarged during design for construction by the user adding attributes and methods to "door" that take into account the particular way the door will be connected to the wall—information that is irrelevant in early design but essential for construction. Objects such as "window' or "door" can encapsulate a method for computing the location of the object with respect to the wall thickness—for example, at the geometric center of the wall or flush with one side of the wall.

There are obviously many ways to organize the description of a design based on objects. The definition of attributes for width and height in both classes "window" and "door," for example, results in multiple attributes that deal with essentially the same type of information. This redundancy can be reduced by creating a separate object class called "geometry," and by defining appropriate messages and methods in all three classes. Object-oriented modeling attempts to capture not only geometry but also design intent by adding content semantics to what otherwise would be simply digital representations of shapes.

Communication/Dissemination/Collaboration

The environments noted in the preceding text are all directed toward representation and digital model building. Ideas concerning data transfer, shared digital models for collaborative design activities, and so forth have not yet been explicitly considered but are intrinsically important in the use of any digital environment in a complex design process setting. Most building design, for example, invariably involves the interaction of multiple groups of individuals with different kinds of expertise. The use and role of digital models varies accordingly, but the need to share information, model revisions, and so on is always present. Many of the digital environments noted previously are essentially stand-alone systems (e.g., Rhinoceros, form-Z) that allow certain tasks to be executed well, without being part of any organized approach to communication, data sharing, or model sharing. Many CAD vendors such as Autodesk or Bentley are integrating platforms to interchange data more effectively—either through Web-based environments between geographically separated members of the design team or through company-internal computer networks (intranets). High-end design development environments—often used in collaborative and concurrent design processes of participants that all use the same platform—provide tools for explicitly dealing with these needs (for example, Enovia

in relation to CATIA). See Chapter 12 for a more detailed discussion.

10.3 GEOMETRIC MODELERS: BASIC CATEGORIES

Differentiating digital design environments by the characteristics mentioned is useful in understanding individual aspects of these programs. In practice it is useful to combine these characteristics in categories of geometric modeling software for design professionals. This grouping largely reflects the need for specific applications in discrete design phases. In this more practical approach of looking at geometric modeling software, it is also useful to include the basic modeling aids and different output modes. Modeling aids in this context are all tools such as basic snap and grid functions or construction planes that facilitate the creation of shapes without themselves having any intrinsic representational purpose. Output modes clearly relate to what a user needs to accomplish with a given design environment—they include a range from paper plots to 3-D renderings or various types of material or part lists. The grouping of geometric modelers includes five basic categories:

- Concept modelers and rendering programs
- Animation programs
- Entity-based drafting programs
- Component-based programs
- Design development programs

Concept Modelers and Rendering Programs

Three-dimensional visualization during the early design phases is the principal use of these environments. They include a fairly wide range of stand-alone sketching programs, geometric modelers, and renderers. Sketching programs are, for example, SketchUp, Alias SketchBook Pro, or PlanDesign. Geometric modelers primarily used for conceptual design include programs such as Rhinoceros, and conceptual modelers with strong emphasis on rendering are, for example, Form-Z or 3D Studio Max. Certain programs such as AccuRender are pure rendering environments. During conceptual design, emphasis is invariably on initial shape generation. For direct manipulation approaches, the primary consideration in selecting a tool to use largely hinges around whether it can be used as a kind of "visual thinking tool," much like architects have historically used, and are still using, sketches on paper. These environments must be simple to learn, easy to use, and not impose limits. Since many users find data input through mouse and keyboard cumbersome,

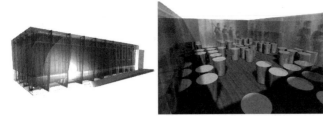

Figure 10-3 Modeling and rendering during conceptual design. Textures and images can be mapped onto model surfaces to produce special effects. (Source: Courtesy of Chung-Ping Lee)

sketching programs often enable users to input data by drafting on interactive tablets in a manner similar to sketching on paper.

The conceptual modelers are typically hybrid modelers in that they rely on a mix of surface and solid model elements. Sketching programs also employ line elements to facilitate the transition from traditional hand sketching to digital modeling. Grids, snap functions, and construction planes are typical modeling aids in conceptual modelers, and layers organize digital models into manageable units. These modeling aids do not require extensive planning on the structure of the digital model itself; users can focus on the design itself, and the models can be easily changed at any time. Model revisions require deleting the outdated portions and replacing them with revised ones—there is no built-in intelligence that would point out conflicting geometry as can be found in some component-based programs or in the design development environments. Primary outputs of these environments are 3-D views in various projections and perspectives, easily rendered to communicate a design idea. (See Figure 10-3.) Some environments also possess a capability for animations. Many of the geometric modelers and rendering pro-

grams are also used to generate realistic 3-D views in later design phases, inevitably relying on file import options using commonly supported formats such as DXF, DWG, and IGES (see Chapter 12) to import geometry data from other applications that needs to be visualized. Concept modelers do not necessarily produce the kinds of "watertight" models that are ultimately needed to support computer-controlled manufacturing operations.

Animation Software

Animation software, initially developed for the entertainment industry, finds increasing use in product design and architecture. Fly-through simulations or visualizations of construction sequences can be equally useful on many scales but are particularly effective for larger and complex design projects ranging from buildings to urban design. Programs such as Maya or Softimage are also used for the creation of complex forms based on dynamic model animations during conceptual design (see Figure 10-4). These environments have parametric capabilities, let the user define key frames and animation paths, and generate animations by interpolating the transition between frames and along paths. The outputs are commonly supported video or proprietary movie formats as well as static 3-D models.

Entity-Based Drafting Programs

These widely used environments represent what until recently was commonly understood as computer-aided design: AutoCAD, VectorWorks, and a number of other tools are universally useful drafting tools and remain popular in architecture and product design. These environments are used in all design phases but primarily

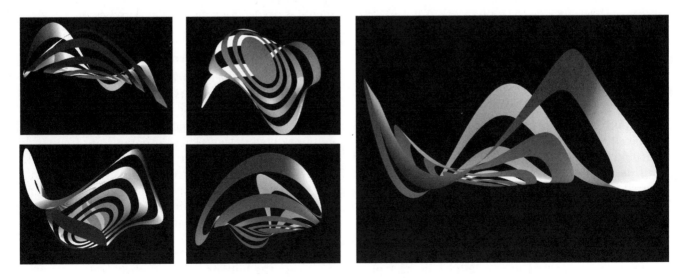

Figure 10-4 Sequence of animation studies using Maya. (Source: Allen Sayegh—INVIVIA—Studies for SAMSUNG Electronics)

facilitate the creation of 2-D design documentation such as projected views, section, elevations, and plans. Even though some 3-D modeling and even rendering capabilities are now commonly integrated, 2-D drawings remain the principal use of entity-based CAD. In architecture and product design, the notion of using only 2-D means to describe a 3-D object is still not only a commonplace but also a useful way of thinking about many issues because of its abstracted nature. Initial 2-D representations have historically been used to conceptualize 3-D objects. This approach does not mean, however, that any 2-D information thus produced is internally consistent or fully descriptive. The age-old problems of plans and elevations not matching or consistently describing the same 3-D object, or a change in a plan not automatically leading to a change in the elevation, are inherent conflicts that design professionals are frequently struggling with. External references and drawing blocks—geometric models generated and stored in separate files—can be inserted for reference purposes in the effort to reduce such inconsistencies.

Entity-based drafting programs rely, as their name suggests, on drawing entities such as lines, polylines, arcs, splines, and others to model shapes, with surfaces and solids being also supported to a lesser degree. Modeling in these programs normally starts from 2-D geometry. Modeling aids and the organization of data is similar as in concept modelers, but proprietary or open-source scripting languages often allow knowledgeable users to customize functionalities and adapt the software to the requirements of a certain industry or company. The output of these programs has traditionally been the paper plot, and automated layout functions, extensive text editing, as well as comprehensive dimensioning features are usually present to support this type of documentation. The ability of entity-based drafting programs to represent shapes in a 2-D line format is also useful for many manufacturing processes such as CNC cutting of sheet stock or 2-D router work. AutoCAD and similar programs are still widely employed to prepare the 2-D representations needed to generate G-code for CNC machines.

Component-Based Programs

This group of 3-D geometric modelers was developed to specifically support architectural design activities from conceptual design through design development and even design for construction. This approach is also referred to as *building information modeling* (BIM). Commonly used software includes Autodesk's Architectural Desktop and Revit, Bentley's MicroStation, Nemetschek's Allplan, or Graphisoft's ArchiCAD. These systems rely extensively on 3-D components or "objects" to represent major elements of a design scheme, replacing or supplementing drawing entities such as lines,

arcs, or surfaces in entity-based drafting. Using 3-D objects generates consistent and nonambiguous models from which 2-D views such as elevations and plans can be generated subsequently. A change in the 3-D model leads directly to a corresponding change in the extracted 2-D view. Some tools permit users to start with a conceptual massing model and incrementally refine this same model by assigning internal spaces and eventually construction objects such as walls, windows, and others. Other environments let users begin by constructing 2-D geometry and then allow the transformation of these drawings into a 3-D object-based model by assigning attributes that specify heights and other properties. Many component-based environments rely on extensive libraries of predefined component or object classes (such as walls, partitions, windows, doors, or stairs).

Objects in these environments can be annotated with information about materials, construction types, tolerances, and many others. This relative richness of data provides additional value in professional practice because the actual modeling package often can be combined with other tools that support cost estimation, site management, structural analysis, facility management, and others. Component-based programs normally offer a convenient means of deriving bills of quantities (amounts of certain construction elements, for example, *x* square feet of masonry wall 4 inches thick)—useful information during cost estimation and bidding.

While convenient for regular and planar geometries, users may find the modeling of complexly shaped buildings or building elements challenging. There are also limitations to the detailed 3-D modeling capabilities for the design of architectural components. Few component-based programs support any kind of CNC manufacturing activity. They are mostly geared toward early design development. Parametric capabilities are often limited and do not extend to the preparation of detailed documents as needed for construction purposes.

Design Development Programs

The name *design development programs*—the primary focus of the book—points to their principal use in phases where an existing basic scheme needs to be developed into a functional, aesthetically, and technically resolved design. These programs are frequently used in product design and, increasingly so, in architectural design. Since they are not originally conceived for the building industry, users should not expect to find specific architectural functions or model libraries, although some standard data such as steel sections and others might be available.

In terms of time and effort, design development makes up the bulk of a design office's role, especially when the design for production or construction is

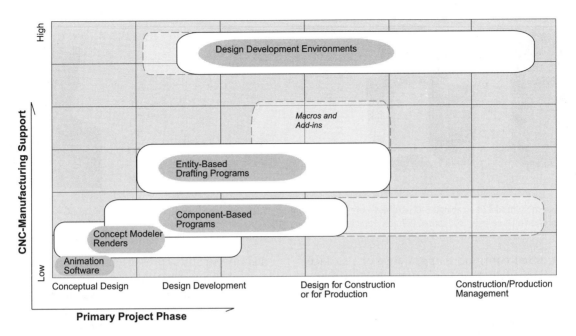

Figure 10-5 Simplified mapping of geometric modelers: Extensive support of CNC manufacturing processes generally can be expected only of design development environments.

included. The more structured, planned procedure in this design phase is reflected in the hierarchical way design development environments such as CATIA, Pro/ENGINEER, or SolidWorks themselves are structured. Design development programs (see Chapter 11 for more detailed description) are feature-based and dimensionally driven, and they visually show the way a model is internally structured in a treelike display of text and symbols. Their principal modeling elements are features made from surfaces and solids, with line-type elements being largely supported as construction or reference geometry. Part models consist of features such as extrusions, cuts, and fillets, and parts may be combined in an assembly model. Even though related to the components of the previously discussed component-based programs, features are distinctly different in that they do not have semantic content—design intent—attached. Instead, several features form components and thus represent the building blocks that allow users to construct components or parts. Only once the latter are assembled into assembly models can these represent the design intention and reflect the way a design would eventually be physically put together. (See Figures 10-5 and 10-6.)

The nature of design development is a collaboration of specialists, and these programs often incorporate extensions or add-on modules such as structural analysis, computational-fluid dynamic analysis, mold-flow analysis, and other application-related modeling techniques such as sheet-metal functions or piping. The design models can also serve directly in the generation of machine instructions by integrating applications for the programming of CNC machines. (See Figure 10-7.)

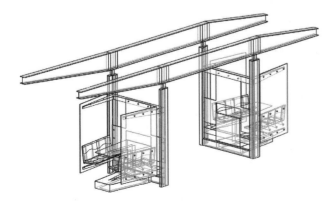

Figure 10-6 Detailed study of a construction assembly modeled in a design development environment. (Source: Courtesy of Scott Snyder)

10.4 DIGITAL REPRESENTATIONS OF THREE-DIMENSIONAL SHAPES

In any digital modeling environment, the ability to precisely define constituent lines, surfaces, and solids is of paramount importance. Accurate representation of model entities becomes a key issue in the CAD/CAM context, since the digital model not only serves as a design tool but also drives rapid prototyping devices or CNC-controlled machines during the manufacturing process. Any inaccuracy of the digital model thus directly translates into an undesired built component or condition. When a design is modeled for the purpose of representation or rendering, it is often irrelevant and even hindering to enforce this same accuracy. Whether

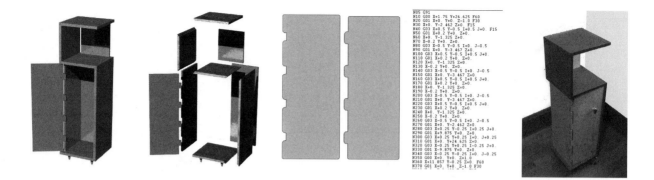

```
N05 G91
N10 G00 X+1.75 Y+26.625 F60
N20 G01 X+0. Y+0. Z-1.0 F30
N30 X+0. Y-2.462 Z+0. F15
N40 G03 X+0.5 Y-0.5 I+0.5 J+0. F15
N50 G01 X+0.2 Y+0. Z+0.
N60 X+0. Y-1.325 Z+0.
N70 X-0.2 Y+0. Z+0.
N80 G03 X-0.5 Y-0.5 I+0. J-0.5
N90 G01 X+0. Y-3.467 Z+0
N100 G03 X+0.5 Y-0.5 I+0.5 J+0.
N110 G01 X+0.2 Y+0. Z+0.
N120 X+0. Y-1.325 Z+0.
N130 X-0.2 Y+0. Z+0.
N140 G03 X-0.5 Y-0.5 I+0. J-0.5
N150 G01 X+0. Y-2.462 Z+0.
N160 G03 X+0.5 Y-0.5 I+0.5 J+0.
N170 G01 X+0.2 Y+0. Z+0.
N180 X+0. Y-1.325 Z+0.
N190 X-0.2 Y+0. Z+0.
N200 G03 X-0.5 Y-0.5 I+0. J-0.5
N210 G01 X+0. Y-3.467 Z+0.
N220 G03 X+0.5 Y-0.5 I+0.5 J+0.
N230 G01 X+0.2 Y+0. Z+0.
N240 X+0. Y-1.325 Z+0.
N250 X-0.2 Y+0. Z+0.
N260 G03 X-0.5 Y-0.5 I+0. J-0.5
N270 G01 X+0. Y-2.462 Z+0
N280 G03 X+0.25 Y-0.25 I+0.25 J+0.
N290 G01 X+9.875 Y+0. Z+0.
N300 G03 X+0.25 Y+0.25 I+0. J+0.25
N310 G01 X+0. Y+24.625 Z+0.
N320 G03 X-0.25 Y+0.25 I-0.25 J+0.
N330 G01 X-9.875 Y+0. Z+0.
N340 G03 X-0.25 Y-0.25 I+0. J-0.25
N350 G00 X+0. Y+0. Z+1.0
N360 X+11.857 Y+0.25 Z+0. F60
N370 G01 X+0. Y+0. Z-1.0 F30
```

Figure 10-7 Assembly model of a cabinet: 2-D part files were translated into drawing files, which were then used to generate G-code for the cutting of individual parts on a three-axis CNC router. (Source: Courtesy of MM Design)

or not the desired continuous appearance of a surface, for example, is actually based on a digitally continuous *representation* is not important as long as the surface looks convincing. These same minute discontinuities of surfaces would, however, inevitably generate enormous problems in the generation of toolpaths for CNC production.

This section presents basic modes of representing three-dimensional shapes using wireframes, polygonal meshes, parametric surface patches, and solids. Many geometric modelers, especially those used mostly for conceptual modeling, support a mix of these entities, allowing users to choose whatever best suits their representational needs. Design development environments mostly rely on parametric surface patches and solid representations. Those offer the highest degree of accuracy with respect to numerically controlled manufacturing operations that such models are ultimately meant to support.

Parametric Representations

There are two fundamentally different manners of describing model entities in a digital modeling environment: parametric and nonparametric. Many earlier CAD tools employed a nonparametric mode of representation. Here all shapes are ultimately derived from conic sections such as lines, arcs, ellipses, parabolas, and hyperbolas. These sections (circles, ellipses, parabolas, and hyperbolas) are simply derived from intersecting a plane oriented in different ways with a cone. While conic sections allow a wide range of shapes to be modeled, they are insufficient to describe the complex surfaces present in many everyday objects. The need to digitally model airplanes or car bodies spurred the development of parametric representations. These are now widely employed, and all design development tools inevitably rely on them. Typical parametric entities are spline curves and Nonuniform Rational B-Spline (NURBS) surface patches. (See Figure 10-8.)

Parametrically represented curves and surfaces are described through polynomial expressions that allow the calculation of shape parameters at any point of the entity. In spline curves and NURBS patches, these expressions enable the local modification of shapes while leaving the overall geometry unchanged. Joining curves and surfaces in a smooth way—thus with a continuous curvature—is thereby facilitated: A shape can adapt to join an adjacent shape smoothly without the local curvature affecting the overall shape, as would be the case in arcs or sphere segment, where changing the tangential relation with an adjacent shape inevitably changes the geometry of the whole entity. Parametric representations are not only extremely useful in modeling complex shapes. The currently used splines and NURBS are equally capable of representing simple geometries based on conic sections—overcoming thus a shortcoming of earlier parametric representations such as the Coons and the Beziers patches. A parametric surface patch often allows the positioning of points and curves according to a relative u-v coordinate system on its surface. (See Figure 10-9.) Typically the four edges of a patch will have respective u and v—values of 0 and 1. To locate a point on the patch, users specify a u and v coordinate between 0 and 1, thus specifying a relative or parametric rather than an absolute position of the entity on the surface (see Section 11.1 for practical implications).

It is still useful to remember that the "spline curve" discussed has historical antecedents in the draftsperson's

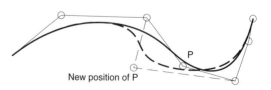

New position of P

Figure 10-8 B-Spline: Dragging control point P locally modifies the shape of the curve.

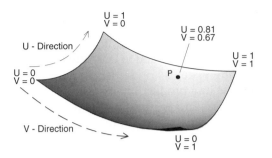

Figure 10-9 NURB surface patch: The local *u-v* coordinate system can be used to define the relative positions of entities on the parametric surface.

or loftsperson's flexible drawing aid made of thin wood or metal that was long used in the boat-building industry. Because of the natural elastic behavior of the thin member, which is forced to conform to a set of defined control points, a spline inherently describes the smoothest curve that can pass through the control points (i.e., it forms a minimum-energy curve). The mathematical equivalents that underlie spline curves and NURBS patches are approximations of these profiles.

Three-Dimensional Representations

Wireframe Models

The wireframe is a simple form of three-dimensional transparent model. Model edges are created with straight or curved lines in three-dimensional space. Sweeping, extrusion, or rotation operations facilitate the development of wireframe models by enabling a user to extrude or push a shape specified in a simple two-dimensional environment out of its two-dimensional plane. Any polyline, for example, may be translated orthogonally to its plane or rotated about an axis in its plane to create an image of a complex volumetric entity. Polygons may be created and extruded, rotated, or swept to form complex shapes. The wireframe model is efficient for conveying and extracting approximate geometric information about an object without taking storage space to describe it in greater detail.

Wireframe models may be projected onto a two-dimensional picture plane with a variety of techniques to create a three-dimensional image. Locations of picture planes and projection types may be easily specified in most systems. Orthographic and axonometric projections are common. Oblique and perspective projections are also widely used. Wireframe models, however, do not support the kinds of manipulations and numerical operations typically needed in integrated computer-aided design and manufacturing environments. Since only bounding edges are used to make up the model, actual surfaces are not numerically defined.

Commonly needed capabilities, such as the merging of complex surfaces to form new surfaces, are not possible.

Polygon Meshes

Polygon meshes are simply connected polygonal surface shapes. The mesh is defined in terms of edges, vertices, and various types of polygons. Triangular shapes are frequently used, since any three nodal points can be used to define a planar mesh element. Other shapes are possible as well. Various ways of defining and manipulating a mesh are in use, such as representing each polygon by a list of vertex coordinates, or using pointers to a vertex list or to an edge list. A significant issue is to know when the mesh is internally consistent—that is, when all polygons are closed, there are no gaps between them, or there are no unconnected vertices.

Even when successfully implemented, a surface out of planar segments can only be an approximation of the actual shape. Clearly, there can be significant errors introduced in the shape definition. The surface is also not well controlled in a numerical sense; critical exact dimensional information—for instance, the exact distance from a point on a curve to a reference plane—is unavailable. Making elements smaller and smaller certainly improves the approximation but at the cost of increased memory and execution time. Still, this approach remains widely used.

Parametric Surface Patches

The bounding lines of a wireframe model may be used to form two-dimensional surfaces that in turn create a three-dimensional surface model. A *surface model* thus employs two-dimensional elements to describe a three-dimensional object in space. These kinds of models are widely used for visual display purposes, since surfaces may be colored, shaded, and given textures; they are also used for high-end applications such as automotive body design. Surface models can produce views that approach photo-realism when rendered. These views may have hidden surfaces. Surface properties (color, texture, etc.) may be assigned, lighting sources specified, surfaces shaded, shadows cast, and so forth. (See Figure 10-10.)

Surface models are widely used for visualization of designs. As with wireframes, surface models may be visualized via a number of different projections (orthographic, oblique, axonometric, and perspective). To enhance a three-dimensional view of a surface model, surfaces not normally visible from the point of view of the observer are hidden. A variety of simple and more complex hidden surface algorithms exist for calculating and displaying planes in a visually realistic way, with back planes being covered by front planes. Hidden-line algorithms have been developed that are quite precise and can be used to calculate where lines are cut by

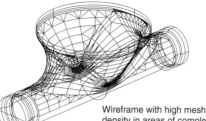

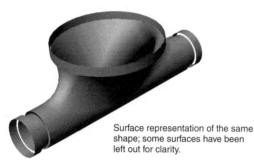

Wireframe with high mesh density in areas of complex shapes, and low mesh density for simple shapes such as the cylinder element at the bottom

Surface representation of the same shape; some surfaces have been left out for clarity.

Solid model complete with fillets and other details: this is the most complete type of representation and supports analysis techniques such as mass calculation or finite-element analysis.

Figure 10-10 Representations of a cast steel connector (see Figure 11-28 for a finite-element analysis of the same model).

polygons. Intersection coordinates are developed. Less computationally intensive hidden-surface algorithms are also available. A typical algorithm sorts polygons by depth and then draws polygons from the back forward so that the latter polygons are drawn over earlier ones. Procedures of this type are not computationally difficult, since intersections are not actually calculated. But when complex geometries are present, the simple sorting approach can lead to failures in terms of a logical and/or realistic display of the three-dimensional object. Many different types of hidden-surface algorithms are available that trade off accuracy with speed.

While surface models are the workhorses of the visualization industry, they do have limitations. Since the volumes are defined by bounding surfaces only, they cannot support many kinds of applications. Properties such as mass or moment of inertia cannot be assigned,

which limits the use of surface models in the engineering world. Analysis tools such as finite-element analysis often cannot be used in a meaningful way with surface models. While in many CAD/CAM situations more precise modeling systems are needed, surface models still find wide use in a production environment. Most software that is used to write CNC toolpaths can import surface models directly, and limited surface models can serve as the basis for the CNC milling of a complex surface shape from one face of a block of material without necessarily defining the whole volumetric solid.

Solid Models

The most complete and accurate digital representations of a shape available are solid models. These take into consideration the volumetric space contained within the bounding surfaces and are based on data structures far richer than simpler wireframe or surface models. Complex geometrical manipulations involving intersections of solid volumes may be performed, and the same models may be used to support volume, mass, center of mass, and other calculations. The latter properties are extremely important in an engineering context. It is often difficult, however, to get the same richness of surface shaping in a solid model.

Since solid models represent real volumetric objects, they necessarily must be unambiguously defined and topologically well formed. The bounding surfaces must form a closed volume, and some environments do not permit dangling lines or floating surfaces. These and other characteristics make the use of solid models imperative in many applications where *any* ambiguity is problematic, particularly those involving sophisticated computer-aided manufacturing operations. Many manufactured objects are, after all, necessarily actual volumetric objects that must be unambiguously defined and topologically well formed; otherwise, they could not exist as holistic physical objects. Isolated lines or floating surfaces may be depicted visually on a screen and may be highly useful during early design stages to help form an image of the final object, but ultimately they cannot be made.

The final applications of solid models are many. Only solid models allow the calculation of mass-related properties such as the moment of inertia or centroid. Other uses for solid representations of single components include the generation of the mesh required for the finite-element analyses (structural, thermal, vibration, and so forth; see Chapter 11), the generation and checking of particularly complex numerically controlled (NC) cutter toolpaths, the pre-teaching of industrial robots to recognize certain shapes, and many other applications. The geometric interactions of parts in both assemblies and workplaces can also be modeled with solids. Unwanted interferences among parts can be anticipated by solving for intersections. Human interaction with machines can be crudely modeled, and the movements of industrial robots can be coordinated using solid models to describe their motions.

10.5 GENERAL MODEL BUILDING

Here we briefly review some of the primary ways of building geometric models from a user-oriented perspective. The methods described are applicable to the creation of surface and solid shapes in both conceptual modeling and design development environments. (See Figure 10-11.) It is assumed that the reader has, however, a general exposure to common acts such as point, line and curve creation, general editing, and manipulation of entities (insertion, moving, copying, rotating, mirroring, scaling, deleting, etc.)

Reference Geometry

Most common software environments require that an active reference plane (also referred to as a construction or sketch plane) be initially specified for the purpose of modeling. (See Figure 10-12). Such planes may or may not be visible on the user interface. Typical *x-y*, *x-z*, and *y-z* planes are commonly used in the global (Cartesian)

Reference Plane R 2 was used to model the upper circle of the lofted shape.

The rectangle for cutting the hole was modeled using the circular model face directly as a reference plane.

R 2

R 1

Reference Plane R 1 was used to model the lower circle.

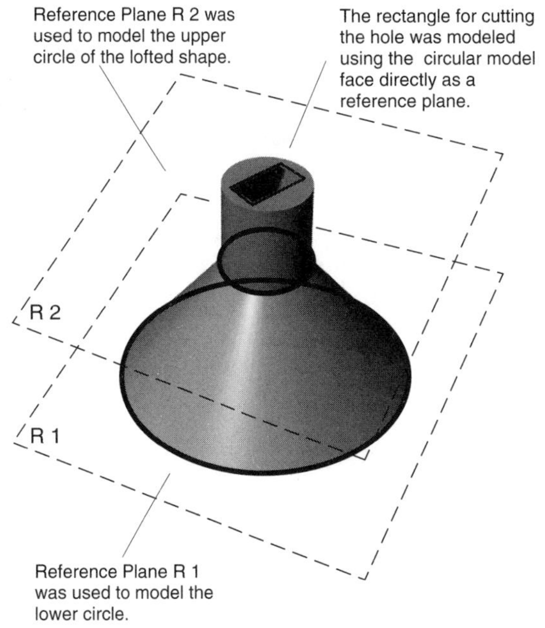

Figure 10-12 Reference planes for the model of a lampshade: The conical element has been lofted between two circles; the cylinder is an extruded shape.

x-y-z coordinate system, but planes may also be offset or rotated from some other plane.

Alternatively, model entities such as points and lines or model faces can be used to define reference planes. In some systems, even complex surfaces that have been created may be used as reference surfaces. In design development environments, using model entities to define planes creates a dependency between the model and the reference planes. Changes of the model lead to an update of the reference plane that in turn affects those parts of the model that are dependent on this plane.

Coordinate systems may be global or relative to model elements. Relative coordinate systems—defined by the user—are often useful when exporting model geometry in a specific orientation, such as might be suitable for a particular application. A typical example is the export of the design geometry from a design development environment into a manufacturing applications program. Here, users may desire to orient the digital model in a specific relation to a machine environment that may be different from the orientation in the design model.

Extrusions and Sweeping Operations

A common way of making an object is to initially draw entities on a reference plane and extrude them or sweep them along a path. An extrusion is generally executed perpendicular to the reference plane of the initial entities, while sweeping allows the definition

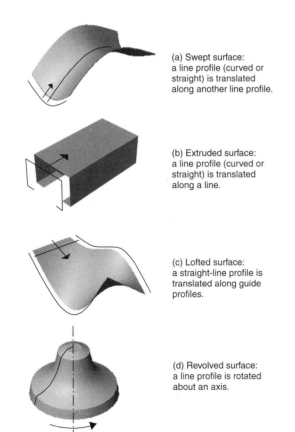

(a) Swept surface: a line profile (curved or straight) is translated along another line profile.

(b) Extruded surface: a line profile (curved or straight) is translated along a line.

(c) Lofted surface: a straight-line profile is translated along guide profiles.

(d) Revolved surface: a line profile is rotated about an axis.

Figure 10-11 Basic ways of creating surfaces.

of a linear or curvilinear guide path at any angle to the reference plane. Extruding or sweeping an open profile such as line or curve entities along a path obviously makes a surface, while performing the same operation with a closed profile (e.g., polyline, curvilinear shape) generates a three-dimensional volume. In many environments, the latter creates a solid model, since the resulting object is inherently a closed, nonambiguous volume. Voids may often be created by extruding a "hole" (e.g., a polygonal/curved shape) instead of a solid either through the whole object or to some specified distance from a reference plane. This activity is essentially a Boolean operation. When extruding or sweeping closed profiles into solids, users of design development programs can often specify a tapering angle. This functionality is especially useful for modeling parts that eventually will be manufactured with a molding or casting process, where tapers are useful to facilitate the removal of parts from the mold. A subset of extrusions is the *radiating* technique of mostly circular profiles or lines. It generates surfaces or solids by radiating entities from a center outward instead of extruding entities in a linear manner.

Sweeping operations offer additional capabilities in some systems (see Figure 10-13). Entities may be twisted or otherwise altered along the length of the sweep, and different systems supply a variety of tools to control such alterations.

One way to control the shape of the swept geometry is to define supplementary guide paths that essentially scale the initial profile along the primary guide path. Another method of altering a swept shape is to adjust the relative orientation of the profile with respect to the guide path. Options may include the restriction to a given angle between the reference plane of the profile and the guide path, as well as keeping the profile always parallel to its initial orientation. Certain software environments offer special capabilities for creating different kinds of end tangencies for swept shapes. These may include keeping the surface normal or at a specific angle

(a) A rectangular profile is swept and twisted along an arc. The transitional stepping is exaggerated for clarity.

(b) A sweep is defined with a square on one end of the sweep and a circle on the other end. Transitional shapes are automatically computed between. The transitional stepping is exaggerated for clarity.

Figure 10-13 Types of swept surfaces.

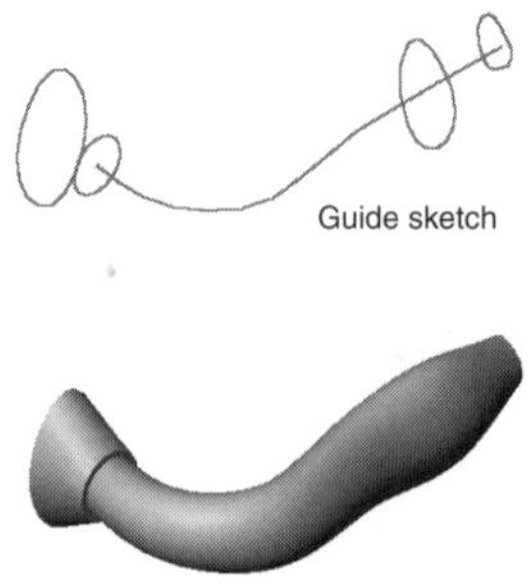

Guide sketch

Lofted surfaces can be specified to follow guide lines or centerlines. In this case, the profile always remains perpendicular to the guide sketch.

Figure 10-14 Use of guides in lofting.

to the sectional profile. The way the end direction of the surface is specified can have a large impact on the shape of the resulting model.

Lofting Operations

Many systems allow one profile to be specified at the beginning and another at its end. The resulting model transitions from the initial to the final shape and is commonly referred to as a *lofted shape* (See Figure 10-14). Translating a line or spline along two or more open profiles can create lofted surfaces. A volumetric object can be obtained by lofting closed profiles that may or may not be on parallel reference planes. In cases of more than two profiles, the lofted shape is typically shaped from cross section to cross section by using spline curves. The resulting shape is smooth from one end to another.

Many complexities can develop when the path along which the profile's transformation occurs is irregular or if it does not occur within a consistent plane or parallel sets of planes (a complex space curve). In such situations, the possibility of involuntary folding or creasing arises. These may often be avoided by prescribing specific end tangencies or by using guiding paths that control the interpolation between opposite profiles. In general, conceptual modeling environments tend to be more forgiving than design development environments. (See Figure 10-15.)

Other Operations

Virtually any shape can be modeled with a combination of extrusion, sweeping, or lofting techniques (see Figure 10-16). In many cases, one identical shape can be created with several different techniques. In conceptual modelers, the technique of choice is often motivated by individual user preferences. Design development environments offer powerful ways of editing shapes after the initial process of modeling. Users thus have to carefully plan digital models, because each modeling tech-

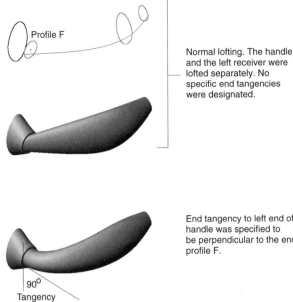

Normal lofting. The handle and the left receiver were lofted separately. No specific end tangencies were designated.

End tangency to left end of handle was specified to be perpendicular to the end profile F.

90°
Tangency

Figure 10-15 Preliminary design for a door handle. Influence of end tangency specifications on lofted models.

nique enables a specific range of editing options—usually identical with the shape control functions available with each of the modeling techniques.

For axisymmetric shapes, extrusion, sweeping, and lofting techniques are often found unnecessarily cumbersome. Here, *revolving techniques* can offer increased modeling speed, though at the expense of more limited

shape control. Rotating an open or closed profile around an axis creates surfaces or solid shapes. Control is mostly limited to the angle of rotation of the profile around the axis.

In addition to these approaches, other model-building techniques exist as well. Some of those specifically important to design development environments will be addressed in the next chapter. Here it is important to note that the techniques of extrusion, sweeping, lofting, and revolving can create both surface and solid models. In many conceptual modeling environments, it is not always obvious what kind of model is obtained after a series of operations. A model might look like a volumetric object but not actually be a solid model. A general rule of thumb is that any true solid object must be a "watertight" volumetric object. There must not be places where two boundaries do not exactly meet, nor can there be floating surfaces that do not make up part of a volumetric form. Many very good surface modelers can be used to create complex configurations that visually look like solid models but actually contain discontinuities or other problems that prevent the configurations from being truly watertight. This is often the case when complex surfaces are intersected. Whether or not watertightness results in such an instance depends largely on the quality of the underlying algorithms used. In other situations, the volumes formed are inherently watertight and are often automatically interpreted by the system as solids. This is often the case with simple extrusions or well-formed volumes of surface revolution.

A union operation simply joins two overlapping individual solid models and combines them into a single overall solid volume.

A difference operation or subtraction identifies the volumetric overlap between two individual solids and removes it from one or the other of the overlapping solids, thus leaving a single solid with the removed sector.

An intersection operation defines and extracts as an identifiable solid only the volumetric overlap between two overlapping solids.

Figure 10-16 Boolean operations underly many modeling activities in digital design environments.

CHAPTER 11

Design Development Environments

In this chapter we look at digital design environments that have evolved primarily to support the design development and the design for production or construction—a particular subset of the whole design process. These design development environments, including software such as CATIA, SolidWorks, Unigraphics, or Pro/ENGINEER, are primarily intended to support the detailed design of actual objects and assemblies in relation both to their use and their ultimate production environment. As a consequence of this orientation, the precise way in which models are built and manipulated is surprisingly different from other digital design arenas. The designer must initially have a clear understanding of the envisaged design before he or she sets out developing it within the digital environment. These are not tools for conceptual design thinking but for design development. Typically, important base features that govern the characteristics of the whole object must be consciously preselected. Subsequent building of the model and the definition of key dimensions must frequently anticipate design changes that inevitably occur during the development process.

Once a basic understanding of the intent and structure of these digital modeling environments is gained, however, their power becomes quite evident. Capabilities such as *parametric modeling, feature-based design,* and *dimensionally driven design,* discussed in the text that follows, are invaluable when a conceptual scheme is developed into a design that can be manufactured or constructed.

This chapter assumes that the reader is familiar with the general model-building techniques reviewed in Chapter 10. Based on these operations, Section 11.1 discusses advanced techniques for the modeling of curved and complex surfaces—one of the prime domains of design development environments and historically one that triggered much development in this area, particularly in the aerospace and automotive industry.

Surface models by themselves may be sufficient to represent certain design projects, but solid models offer possibilities that go beyond a surface representation mode. Section 11.2 addresses this field in some detail, with particular emphasis on the multiple levels of internal associations among portions of a solid model. Central to all solid modeling activity in design development environments is the notion of the *model feature—* the basic building block of a good parametric model. Users can control the internal relations between part features through constraints and dimensionally driven modeling techniques. These multiple control options are particularly powerful when generating instances or configurations of a basic part model in the explorations of type variations or design options. Specialized features are available in many systems for application-oriented modeling techniques such as sheet-metal design, mold design, or piping. These features are reviewed in Section 11.3; they are automated functions that, to some extent, allow designers to consider material properties or process characteristics in selected design activities.

Most objects that surround us are ultimately assembled from numerous individual components. Designers frequently need to replicate the dependencies and relations of assemblies. Multiple parametric parts can be arranged in *assembly models* (Section 11.4) that allow for their geometrical and dimensional coordination in the larger design context. Assembly techniques are also useful when parts need to be modeled based on an overall design concept or shape.

A robust design development environment also includes capabilities for conducting various kinds of technical analyses (e.g., structural, thermal) on the part or assembly being developed. The results can then inform the design of the object itself, thus potentially increasing the efficiency for certain design processes. Section 11.5 summarizes the most commonly used types of analysis such as mass properties, centroids, and finite-element analysis.

11.1 CURVED SURFACES: ADVANCED MODELING AND ANALYSIS

One of the greatest liberating contributions made to the design field by the advent of sophisticated digital modeling systems has been enabling designers to create, control, and manipulate truly complex geometric forms. Nowhere is this more evident than in the many special capabilities developed for working with complexly curved surfaces. (See Figure 11-1.)

All of the basic modeling techniques, such as extruding, sweeping, lofting, and revolving, are applicable to the modeling of surfaces. Often, users start off with a surface model and then convert it into a solid model at a later point. Many modeling packages are quite good in allowing users to create highly complex surfaces, but it is sometimes not possible to generate solid models based on those same surfaces. Likewise, some good solid modeling systems have restricted capabilities for the generation and manipulation of complex surfaces. While capabilities are always being extended and the issue may soon disappear, users still frequently run into difficulties in this regard.

Several techniques are available to convert a highly complex surface into a solid—and thus allow for the calculation of properties such as volume, weight, and centroids. Simply extruding surfaces normally does often not have the desired effect, because varying thicknesses result for curved surfaces. A more useful way of generating a solid shape is the technique of "thickening" surfaces. The specific underlying algorithms differ from the extrusion process in that the thickness of the resulting solid is constant in the direction perpendicular to the initial surface. This approach is particularly important in the context of modeling in design development environments, because the ultimate goal is to obtain an accurate geometric description of a part that can be used directly for various types of analysis and for manufacturing. In the architectural design context, a thickened surface might be part of an external wall enclosure assembly, thus representing real materials and manufacturing processes such as metal pressing or stamping.

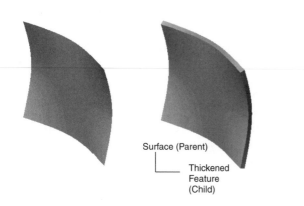

Surface (Parent)

Thickened
Feature
(Child)

Figure 11-1 From surface to solid model: The surface on the left has been uniformly thickened by a user-specified amount. In a design development environment, the thickness becomes the child feature of the parent surface.

Understanding Surface Curvatures

The generation of highly complex surfaces can be an easy or a difficult task, depending on the nature of the surface and the modeling tools of a particular software package. It is often more difficult to actually understand what has been created than to generate the surface itself. Complex surfaces can have reversals of curvature in them (from concave to convex), zones of extremely sharp curvature, and zones of relatively flat or no curvature at all. Complex curvature gradients can be present that differ in different directions; even crimps and foldbacks can occur. It is absolutely imperative that the exact nature of the curvatures present in a surface be well understood if the intention is to transform the digital model of a curved surface into a physical reality. This is especially true since these considerations have a strong influence on the choice of materials and manufacturing processes used, or alternatively, the choice of materials and processes to be used can dictate the kinds of surface shapes and accompanying curvatures that are allowable.

This section examines some of the basic ways surface curvature can be represented and understood. We start with some simple geometric considerations and then explore more complex formulations.

Simple Surfaces Based on Conic Sections

First, recall that the underlying geometry of many basic curves and curved surfaces is really quite simple and straightforward. For curves, conic sections are frequently used. The resulting shapes—most of which can be generated with pen and paper using classic descriptive geometry—are well understood mathematically and intuitively graspable. These same conic sections can be used to produce curved surfaces via the common operations described in the previous chapter: surfaces of revolution (revolving technique) or translational surfaces (sweeping and lofting techniques). A circular arc can be rotated about an axis to produce a domical shape, or a parabolic curve can be rotated about an axis to produce a similarly shaped parabolically curved surface. Likewise, circular arcs can be translated along a straight line to produce a barrel shell form; or a parabolic curve can be translated (sweeping technique) along another reversely curved parabolic curve to produce a hyperbolic paraboloid surface. The important point in the context of this discussion is that the resulting shapes and curvatures are relatively easy to comprehend without resorting to the curvature analysis tools described later in this section. Simply thinking about how a specific shape was generated will yield enormous insights into what the screen image of the shape actually means.

Ruled and Developable Surfaces

Certain of the shapes that are based on a manipulation of conic sections can be generated by more than one process. Translating a straight line over two other lines having inclinations with respect to one another, for example, can also create the hyperbolic paraboloid (HP) surface. In a similar manner, both the rotation of a hyperbolic curve and of an inclined straight line around an axis can generate an identical hyperboloid surface. Any surface that can be generated by the translation or rotation of straight lines is called a *ruled surface*. These include developable surfaces such as sections of cylinders, cones, and conoids, as well as nondevelopable surfaces such as hyperbolic paraboloids and the hyperboloids. Ruled surfaces are historically particularly important in architecture, since they are simple to represent and easily constructed. The formwork for complex concrete shapes, for example, can be built by following the orientation of the ruling lines with straight-edged wooden planks. Well-known examples are the formwork for Felix Candela's HP concrete shells or the twisted column shapes of Pier Luigi Nervi's sport stadiums.

Many but not all ruled surfaces are also developable surfaces (see later section on Gaussian curvature). The question of whether or not a surface is developable is of crucial importance in the design to manufacture process. Developable surfaces can by definition be converted into a planar form without cutting or stretching any part of the original surface. A cylindrical shell, for example, could simply be flattened out into a planar sheet and can consequently be constructed from planar sheet materials such as plywood. All flattening procedures involve only bending in a single direction for any given part of a surface. For the sake of simplicity, we are here neglecting the fact that physical sheet materials, unlike mathematical surfaces, always have a thickness. Naturally, some minor degree of stretching and/or compression will occur on bending even in a single curvature. A nondevelopable (mathematical) surface, by contrast, requires cutting and/or stretching if it is to be flattened out into a planar sheet. The classic example here is a spherical shape. It cannot be simply flattened out–a problem encountered by early cartographers seeking to make maps of the Earth (remember the maps with their sliced segments or other projections based on a stretching of the North and South Pole regions).

Complex Parametric Surfaces

The surface modeling capabilities of current design environments far exceed the restriction to surfaces based on conic sections. All basic modeling techniques described in the previous chapter are equally applicable to complex, parametrically defined curves such as B-splines and NURB curves. The resulting shapes may look similar to those generated from conic sections on the screen, but the difference in terms of the surface curvature can be significant. There is an obvious need for more rigorous ways of defining and understanding surface shapes and curvatures in more complex forms. Ultimately, the treatment and understanding of surface shapes is the province of quite advanced fields within mathematics. In this text, we can only introduce some primary notions. We will first look at basic mathematical principles of describing curvatures and surface curvature, and then review how information on curvature can be represented in modeling environments.

Surface Curvature

What is *curvature*? While the general idea is familiar to us, and, indeed, we have already been making frequent use of the term itself, the word actually has a very precise definition that is necessary to understand fully. Any basic mathematical treatment of curved lines suggests that at any point the shape of the curve can be defined in terms of an "instantaneous radius" *(R)* and an associated "curvature" defined as *1/R*. The instantaneous radius is that associated with a circle that best approximates the curve at that point and that both passes through the point and is tangent to it. Curvature, in turn, is the reciprocal of this value. Usually the curvature is symbolically noted as $k = 1/R$. Note that small radius values imply large curvatures, and large radius values imply small curvatures.

For a simple circular arc, the application of these definitions is trivial. A circle has a single radius defined by some value *R*. The defining characteristic of a circle is that the value of *R* is the same at each point along the arc length. Since the instantaneous radius *R* at any point along the arc length is constant, the curvature (defined as *1/R*) is also constant along the arc length. Thus, the circle looks and is "round." If a circle has a radius of 50 mm, its curvature is given by $k = 1/R = 1/50 = 0.002$ mm^{-1}. Note that a perfectly straight line, which evidently has no curvature, has an indefinitely large radius value ($R = \infty$). Hence, its curvature is zero (i.e., $1/R = 1/\infty = 0$).

If we look at a parabolic curve, the instantaneous radius of curvature varies from point to point along its length. At the apex of the curve, the instantaneous radius is small; hence, the curvature must be quite large. At the ends of the curve, the instantaneous radius values are quite large, since the curve is clearly flattening out. There is an ever-changing curvature gradient from point to point along the curve. The same is true for most curves other than the extremes of the simple circle or the straight line.

Most curved surfaces—with the exception of the sphere—are characterized by constantly changing curvatures. Values of curvature thus can only be obtained for infinitesimally small points on the surface; they are *instantaneous curvature values*. If we look at a point of a general surface in space—let us call the point A—we can always construct precisely one line that is perpendicular (or normal) to the surface in A. We can now imagine a plane that passes through this point and that contains the line normal to the surface in A. This plane is called a *normal plane* because it is normal or perpendicular to the surface at point A (see Figure 11-2). If we extend the normal plane so that it intersects the surface, we obtain a particular curved line called the *normal section* or normal curve at that point. The instantaneous curvature present at A is called *normal section curvature.*

It is evident that the normal plane in A can be rotated around the line in any way desired; thus there are an indefinite number of normal sections possible, each with a different normal section curvature at the point of interest. There necessarily exists, however, a specific normal section curvature that has a maximum value, denoted by k_{max}, and another that has a minimum value, denoted by k_{min}. They can be found by rotating the normal section plane until extreme curvature values at the point are obtained. These particular values, k_{max} and k_{min}, are called the *principal curvatures* of the surface at the point in question. For continuous and nondevelopable surfaces, principal curvatures form an orthogonal net.

Gaussian and Mean Curvature

Based on the principal curvatures we can also understand the concept of *Gaussian curvature* (after Karl Friedrich Gauss, whose early and fundamental work on the theory of surfaces laid the groundwork for current approaches) and *mean curvature*. These are two other widely used ways of understanding surface curvature. In its simplest sense, Gaussian curvature is defined as the product of the two principal (greatest and least) normal section curvatures at a point, or $k_G = k_{max} \times k_{min}$. Mean curvature k_m is simply the average of these same two values.

When the Gaussian curvature is positive ($k_G > 0$), the surface is referred to as a *synclastic surface*. The normal section curvatures have the same sign in all directions. Common concave and convex surfaces have this property, including the ubiquitous sphere. These surfaces are not developable into flat sheets without cutting and/or distortion. One type of measure for positive Gaussian curvature is if, at any point on the surface, a plane can touch the surface and all parts of the surface lie on one side or the other of the plane. Even if the exact magnitudes of the principal curvatures vary somewhat, this property remains.

When the Gaussian curvature is negative ($k_G < 0$), the surface is referred to as an *anticlastic surface*. The principal curvatures are of opposite signs. These surfaces are normally not developable into flat sheets without cutting and/or distortion, even though some classify as ruled surfaces. Saddle-shaped surfaces such as hyperbolic paraboloids or hyperboloids have this property. A plane touching any point would cut the surface into parts on each side of the plane. If a normal plane is rotated about a point on one of these surfaces, the normal curvature has a value of zero at two instances during a half rotation.

When the Gaussian curvature is zero ($k_G = 0$), the surface can always be developed into a flat plane without cutting or distortion. Cylinders and cones are common examples. At least one of the principal curvatures must be zero in order for the product of the principal section curvatures to take on the value of zero.

Curvature Analysis and Display

Most advanced surface modeling environments have some way of numerically analyzing surface curvature. Most commonly, mean curvature and/or Gaussian curvature can be displayed, whereby different hues of colors represent the curvature values, including negative and positive values. Some environments allow the definition of a color range for certain curvature values, since the range of values can be quite high and designers might be interested in a particular zone of the sur-

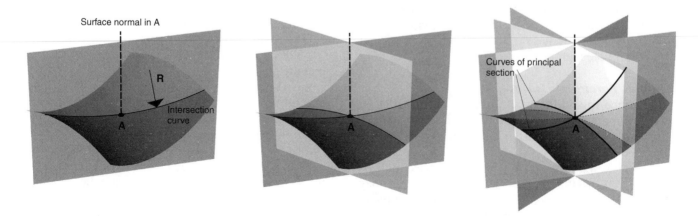

Figure 11-2 Curvature of surfaces: normal curvature and related principal curvature values of a synclastic surface.

face. By color-coding the curvature values, users can normally see whether a surface follows the desired shape, or whether any unintentional shape features occur. This quantitative analysis of curvature is supplemented by qualitative visualization techniques such as the wireframe display or shaded views. By frequently rotating the model, the designer can obtain some degree of judgment as to the approximate shape of the object.

Figure 11-3 illustrates some examples of graphical depictions of Gaussian curvatures.

Graphical depictions for Gaussian and principal curvatures are superficially similar, but their meanings and interpretations are quite different. When surface curvature with respect to manufacturing processes is analyzed, Gaussian and mean curvature are often found appropriate for parts that will be manufactured from isotropic materials such as metals. For nonisotropic materials such as wood products or reinforced plastics, users are often interested in the normal curvature for a certain direction. Some design environments, especially those originally conceived for fields such as the

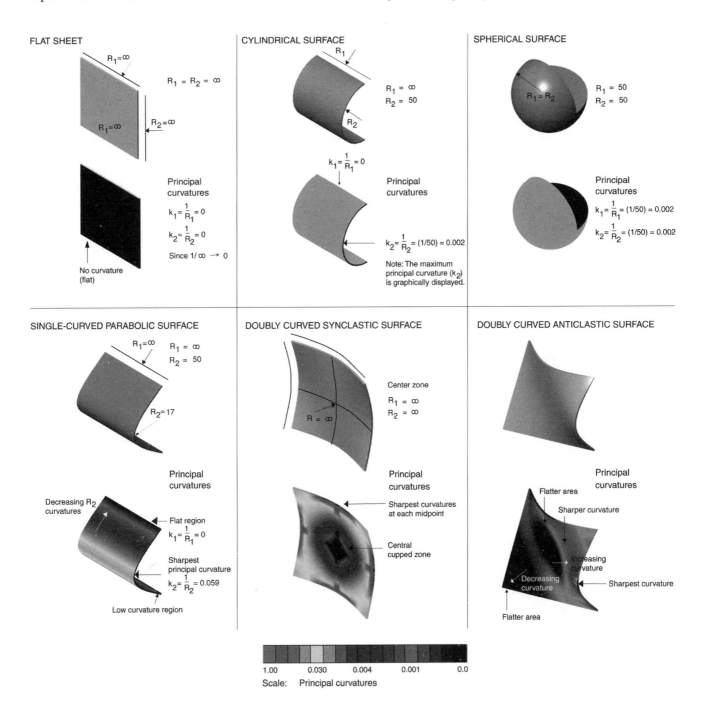

Figure 11-3 Principal curvatures for different simple and complex surfaces.

marine industry, allow the direct display of normal surface curvature for a user-specified direction. See Figures 11-4 and 11-5.

Advanced Surface Manipulations

Once a surface has been created, it can be subjected to a number of manipulations. During these operations, it is crucial to remain in control of the shape, or, in more quantitative terms, of the surface curvature. The following section reviews advanced techniques of surface manipulation such as shape editing, joining, trimming, and splitting.

Editing Shapes

Design environments for advanced surface modeling are normally based on parametric surface representation such as NURBS patches (see Figure 11-6). The shape of such patches can be edited by changing the boundary curves—usually the spline curves that constitute profiles and their lofting or translation paths. Some environments allow users to move individual control points of the patch surface itself, either by redefining their position in a purely qualitative manner (dragging points on the screen) or through a more accurate numerical definition that grants a higher degree of quantitative shape control.

Edge tangencies that have been defined on creation of the surface are usually kept during these manipulations. Some modeling environments focus on the use of meshing techniques to both represent surfaces and as a fundamental way of creating and manipulating them. These kinds of surfaces can often be manipulated with a fine level of control by moving sections of the mesh or individual mesh segments or points to alter the mesh

Figure 11-5 Different ways of visualizing surface curvature: mean curvature and zebra stripe display for the same shape. The latter simulates the reflection of a regularly striped image in the surface and can be useful in determining whether or not a surface is smooth.

shape. The resulting shape, however, is often not a smooth, continuous surface.

Connecting and Separating Surfaces

Many design projects contain multiple surfaces, which may need to be connected smoothly to other surfaces. Often designers focus on the geometry of the major surfaces, and only connect these in a second modeling step. There are several techniques for connecting surfaces, including extending and knitting (stitching). When a surface is *extended* its shape is extrapolated by a defined amount in a manner similar to extrusions. Typically, a surface can be expanded until it touches a second control surface. This technique normally depends on the extending surface to fully meet the control surface that forms its boundary. (See Figure 11-7.)

The geometry of the extended surface is usually extrapolated from the characteristic of the base surface, and shape control is more limited than with modeling techniques such as sweeping or lofting. Improved shape control can be gained by creating surfaces large enough to generate overlaps, and then using trim or cut functions to remove the portions that are not needed. During the removal operation an intersection curve is first calculated, which then becomes the new edge curve of the trimmed surface patch.

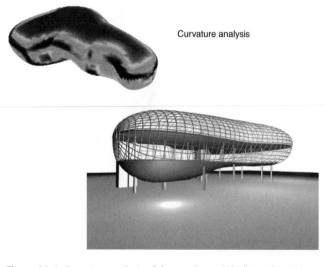

Curvature analysis

Figure 11-4 Curvature analysis of the envelope of the "Kunsthaus" in Graz, Austria, designed by architects Peter Cook and Colin Fournier. (Source: Bollinger & Grohmann)

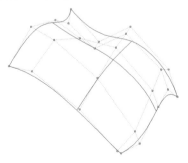

Figure 11-6 NURB surface patch: Control points can be individually moved, and the surface shape can be manipulated locally.

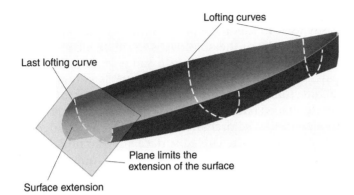

Figure 11-7 A boat hull has been lofted over several curves. The rear end of the hull on the left needs to be continued beyond the outermost lofting curve, so the surface is extended up to an inclined plane. For clarity, only one side is shown extended.

fore means that the derivatives along the boundary of adjacent surfaces are equal. Some systems allow users to specify the degree of continuity desired, whereby higher degrees of continuity generally result in a smoother transition. The lowest degree of continuity is a simple point condition, generally referred to as *G0 continuity*. Higher degrees of continuity (G1 to G3) refer to the degree to which higher derivatives of surface algorithms are used to define the surface shape in the transition zone. These subtle differences are extremely important for designers who deal with complex shapes such as car bodies or boats that eventually will receive a highly glossy finish. Automotive designers and naval architects need to be extremely aware of

Another way to connect surfaces is by *stitching* or *knitting* individual surfaces that share common boundaries into one single surface. In some environments the original surfaces are kept and a new "stitched" surface is created; other environments merge the original surfaces into a single surface or allow users to convert the surface model into a solid model (see Figure 11-8).

For these manipulations it is important to remember that surfaces in advanced digital environments are really parametric surface patches defined by their boundary curves and control points. Any place on a patch can be described in terms of its relative *u* and *v* coordinates, with the edge curves possessing the extreme values of *u* and *v* equal to 0 and 1. On removing or adding a portion of a surface patch, the parametric algorithms that initially described the shape can no longer be validated. Some systems allow the rebuilding of patches, which effectively results in a redefinition of the boundary curves and the regular redistribution of control points according to certain algorithms. Such patches are then again fully parametrically defined.

Surface Transitions

There is a frequent need to connect surfaces smoothly to each other, thus without any visible edges. Standard functions such as filleting of surfaces effectively create such connections (see Figure 11-9). Certain systems allow the definition of changing fillet radii along the length of the surface intersection. Some filleting functions are combined with trimming operations, allowing users to trim and fillet at the same time. When dealing with surface transitions, it is important to remember that the mathematical description of the surface inclination is obtained through the derivation of the equation that describes the surface geometry—just like the derivation of a 2-D curve describes its inclination. Smooth in the mathematical sense there-

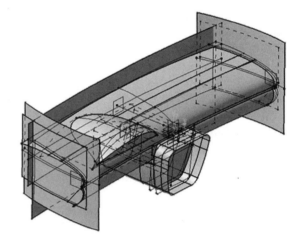

The surface model is "curve-based" and involves a series of sweeps, fills, extrusions, and intersection and joining operations that are generated from curved lines to create the basic surface shape. Unwanted surfaces are removed by a series of trimming and splitting operations.

In a "surface-to-solid" operation, the trimmed and split surface model is converted into a solid model by a "close-surface" operation.

Figure 11-8 Converting a surface mode into a solid model. (Source: Kihong Ku, Doctor of Design candidate, Harvard Design School)

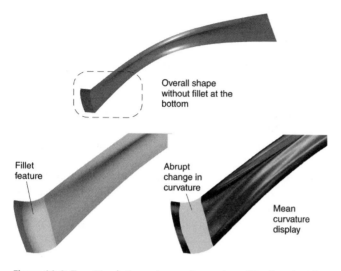

Overall shape without fillet at the bottom

Fillet feature

Abrupt change in curvature

Mean curvature display

Figure 11-9 Transition between two surfaces using a fillet function. The connection might look convincingly smooth on the screen, but the curvature analysis on the right reveals an abrupt change in curvature. Choosing a higher degree of continuity along the edges would result in a smoother transition.

what degree of continuity will generate the desired appearance.

Surface Subdivisions

Most industries have an extensive need to subdivide surfaces. Many building envelopes are assembled from smaller panels of identical or similar size, and most car bodies, airplanes, and ships consist of individual sheets or plates that are derived as subdivisions of a larger digital surface model. Subdividing a flat surface is obviously a straightforward task and one that most design development environments greatly facilitate through pattern functions or equation-driven modeling techniques (see Section 11.2). Equivalent automated design techniques are rarely available for the subdivision of a complexly curved surface; instead, designers need to execute a series of steps that may or may not lead to useful results. There are three basic techniques for subdividing surfaces: projections, intersections, and the direct parametric definition of curves on the surfaces to be subdivided. Any of those techniques usually results in the splitting of the original base surface—a subdivision into individual pieces whereby all pieces are kept as separate surface patches.

Projection techniques normally rely on the projected lines or curves to be modeled in separate sketch or construction planes. Users can often specify the projection path, including paths orthogonal to a selected construction plane or model face. *Intersection* techniques rely on the subdivisions to be generated by surface penetrations. Planar or curved surfaces are modeled and then intersected with the surface to be subdivided. The resulting intersection curves become the boundaries of smaller surface patches on the subdivided shape.

Both intersection and projection techniques can be easily used to subdivide planar surfaces. They are difficult to employ if the objective is to subdivide a curved or doubly curved surface into same or similar sized patches. (See Figure 11-10.) This task is common in architectural applications such as the cladding of complexly shaped buildings. The size of subdivisions is hard to determine beforehand because of the changing angles between the curved surface and the projection path or the intersecting surfaces. Only through iteration can a regular subdivision be approximated, and projection or intersection techniques are not normally used whenever accurate repetitive subdivisions are needed.

A conceptually different way of subdividing a surface is to define parametric curves directly on the surface using a relative u and v coordinate system on the parametric surface patch. Thus, a spline curve on the surface can be defined by locating a series of points that are each offset by $u = 0.1$ from one of the edge curves,

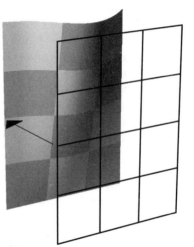

(a) Projecting a regular grid onto a curved surface results in panels of varying size.

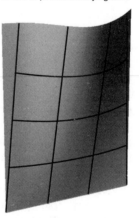

(b) A surface is subdivided to generate surface panels of similar size.

Figure 11-10 Surface subdivisions.

and have *v* values stepping in 0.1 increments between 0 and 1. These coordinates generate a curve across the surface patch that interpolates the shape of the edges *u* = 0 and *u* = 1 at an offset distance 0.1 *u* from the *u* = 0 edge. This spline curve would be redefined according to its relative coordinates on editing the length or shape of the edge curves. Although the parametric definition of curves can generate regular subdivisions, it cannot easily generate regularity in absolute terms. (See Figure 11-11.) For that purpose it is necessary—and possible in some environments—to specify absolute instead of relative offset values for the curve. Complex hierarchical structures can be set up, with multiple relations between entities driving the geometry of the subdivisions. Many design environments allow users to model isoparametric curves directly on the surface. These curves—often referred to as isoparms—are curves with constant *u* and *v* values.

Automated functions to regularly subdivide complex surfaces are still rare. Professionals such as Gehry & Partners LLP that rely heavily on subdivision techniques have developed and programmed proprietary macros that supplement off-the-shelf functions of CATIA or other environments.

Geodesic curves, albeit different in their underlying mathematical description, are a related concept. They describe the shortest distance between two points on any mathematically defined surface. Historically they found their most prominent architectural application in the design of geodesic domes—structural systems based on regular subdivisions of spheres by geodesic curves. For a sphere, geodesic curves are the arcs of the great circles—intersection curves between the spherical surface and planes that contain the center of the sphere. Geodesic curves for complex curved surfaces remain a powerful way to subdivide shapes, but design development environments do not normally permit the direct generation of such curves for the user.

Other Techniques

A useful functionality found in many systems is the flattening of developable surfaces. (See Figure 11-12.) Thereby a set of surface patches is "unrolled" onto a predefined plane. This process is normally based on the meshing of the surfaces and the computation of the positions for each mesh point in the original and flat configuration. Flattening of nondevelopable surfaces involves stretching and/or compression of material; the maximum strains and stresses of the material and the envisaged manufacturing process need to be factored into the digital flattening process. These techniques are described briefly in Section 11.3 on application-oriented modeling techniques. Other useful techniques include the error analysis of surfaces that detects defects and inaccuracies that may be impossible to see in the graphic model display. A common problem is, for example, the discontinuity along common edges of adjacent surface patches.

11.2 FEATURE-BASED MODEL BUILDING

As previously noted, in comparison to general modeling environments, there are fundamental differences in the way models in a *design development* environment are built and structured, and they hinge around the *feature,* the basic building block of design development environments. As might be expected, there is no one way to build a successful feature-based model. Parent-child relationships, the chronological and logical connections among features, must be clearly thought out in advance of building the model. The same is generally true for many of the dimensionally driven features of a

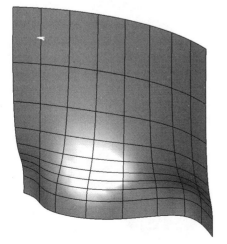

Figure 11-11 Isoparametric curves on a surface: *u* and *v* values are constant, but the absolute size of panels usually varies.

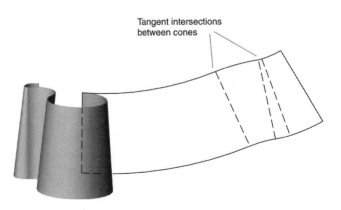

Figure 11-12 Flattening a developable surface: A series of tangent cones or cylinders can be developed into a plane without any stretching or compression of the surface.

model. Critical variables must be carefully considered before jumping in to build a model.

Primary features are used to create shapes through extrusion, lofting, sweeping, or revolving techniques, as well as by thickening surfaces into solids. Note that some primary features can also be used for the subtraction of shapes in the manner of Boolean operations—holes, for examples, can be cut-extruded circles. Features thus can be solids as well as voids. The model building usually begins with the *base feature,* a primary feature that, as its name suggests, becomes the basis of a part or component. Secondary features are essentially used to modify primary features; they include fillets, chamfers, or shelling features, as well as a number of more specialized modeling techniques for scaling, shaping, mirroring, and patterns. Application-specific functions, as for example sheet metal or mold making, are described in Section 11.3. As previously mentioned, all features are listed, usually in order of their dependencies, in a treelike graphical display that visualizes the internal structure of the model. Users can normally suppress selected features temporarily—those are retained in the model but are neither visible nor active. The model is generally evaluated for internal logic without the suppressed features. Error messages previously caused by those features may temporarily disappear, while others now appear because certain dependencies of model features can no longer be validated. Feature suppression is also a core element of the *part configurations,* discussed later in this chapter.

Base Feature

Selecting an appropriate primary feature as the base feature is of crucial importance. As the design evolves the digital model—and often the base feature—needs to be frequently updated to reflect the latest design iteration. Unfortunately, not all changes are equally possible with all base features. Instead, each base feature allows for certain changes to be easily accomplished, while others may be difficult to do without major rebuilding of the model. This need for thorough planning of the digital model is probably the most prohibiting factor in the use of feature-based environments during earlier design phases, with their unpredictable design changes.

The base feature is the all-important framework that all other elements are built upon and in turn depend upon for their existence. To understand some of the issues involved in selecting an appropriate base feature, consider the model of the steel connector shown in Figure 11-13, a simplified component of a structural tension member that connects a steel tension rod to a steel plate. The steel plate can be inserted in the slot of the connector and be fixed with bolts, whereas the rod is to be screwed into the threaded hole on the other side. The base feature of the component shown has the

shape of a truncated cone; it can be modeled using a revolving, extrusion, sweeping, or lofting technique. The choice of the appropriate technique depends on which dimensions or part features will have to be modified throughout the design process. In this case, the selection of the base feature must anticipate that different versions of the connector need to accommodate plates of different thicknesses and rods of varying diameters.

In a first modeling strategy, the base feature is the tapered extrusion of a circle. The dimensions that drive the shape of the feature are the radius R_1 of the circle, the length L_1 of the extrusion, and the tapering angle α. Each of these dimensions can be modified indepen-

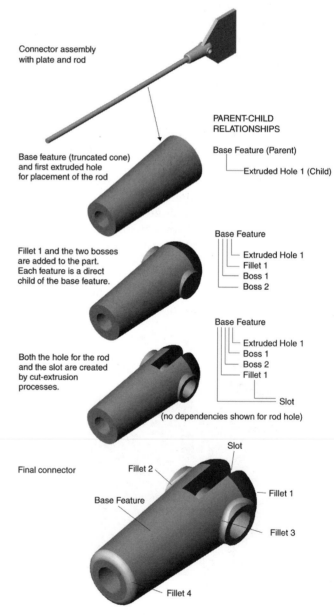

Connector assembly
with plate and rod

PARENT-CHILD
RELATIONSHIPS

Base feature (truncated cone)
and first extruded hole
for placement of the rod

Base Feature (Parent)
└─ Extruded Hole 1 (Child)

Fillet 1 and the two bosses
are added to the part.
Each feature is a direct
child of the base feature.

Base Feature
├─ Extruded Hole 1
├─ Fillet 1
├─ Boss 1
└─ Boss 2

Both the hole for the rod
and the slot are created
by cut-extrusion
processes.

Base Feature
├─ Extruded Hole 1
├─ Boss 1
├─ Boss 2
├─ Fillet 1
└─ Slot

(no dependencies shown for rod hole)

Final connector

Slot
Fillet 2
Fillet 1
Base Feature
Fillet 3
Fillet 4

Figure 11-13 Feature-based connector model.

dently and at any point in the design process, but it is cumbersome to alter the radius of the truncated cone on one side without affecting the other side. Increasing the radius R_1 as may be necessary to accommodate a larger rod automatically enlarges the diameter of the cone on the slotted end unless the tapering angle α is modified at the same time. This modeling strategy is undesirable if the designer wishes to adapt the base feature to changing rod diameters without affecting the slotted side of the connector. The alternative lofting technique consists of drawing the two end circles on parallel construction planes at each end of the base feature and lofting the truncated cone. Both ends of this base feature can now be modified independently by changing the radii of the circles. This model can more readily accommodate changes in plate thickness or rod diameter.

The base feature is round and axisymmetric—would it not be easiest to use a revolving technique? Here the designer first creates the sectional profile and then revolves it fully around the centerline of the cone. The edges in the sectional profile can be rounded to incorporate the fillets of the final design into the base feature. Is this modeling approach better than the two previous ones? Doubtfully, since it is evidently now cumbersome to edit the model to allow for the desired variations. To make any changes, the designer needs to modify the sectional profile.

In general, designers tend to distribute the dimensional control of the base part between the 2-D sketches and the dimensions that directly drive the feature. The distance between the construction planes in the second modeling approach, for example, is a feature dimension that conveniently allows for the length of the model to change but does not affect the cone in any other way. The rotation angle of the revolving feature remains unutilized, because no connector will be missing a slice of the truncated cone. While it is conceivable that the desired alterations of this simple component could be achieved with any of the three modeling techniques, successful feature-based modeling for more complex projects may require one specific modeling approach in order to implement the intended variations. (see Figure 11-14.)

In practice it is not uncommon to rebuild a model completely as the design progresses, because detailed technical questions necessitate changes that were not initially anticipated. Fortunately, building the same part based on a different primary feature, and possibly incorporating other changes, is usually accomplished in a fraction of the time needed for the first version. Sometimes users may be able to reorganize the internal dependencies of features by altering the position of individual features in the graphic display of features. Doing so may enable the types of changes to be made that would have been impossible with the original feature organization.

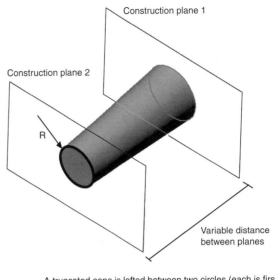

A truncated cone is lofted between two circles (each is first "sketched" on a construction plane). The radius of the circles and the distance between the two construction planes can be parametrically varied at any point during the design process.

Figure 11-14 Modeling the base feature: lofting.

Parent-Child Relationships

The logical links between features are generally referred to as *parent-child relationships*. A parent feature—for instance, the base feature of the connector in the previous example—can be augmented by child features such as fillets. Generally, parents can exist without children, but children cannot exist without parents. Deleting the base feature of the connector obviously removes the shape to be rounded off with the fillet, thus making the existence of the fillet feature 1 impossible. The hole for the rod is dependent on the existence of the flat face onto which the circle for the cut-extrusion process was drawn.

A child feature can have several parent features, each of which must exist in order for the child to exist. Deleting any of several parents will also delete the dependent child. Fillet 3, for example, intersects with the base feature, the boss feature, and with fillet feature 1. These three features are considered parents of fillet 3. Deleting one of them, for example, the boss, will immediate delete the child feature fillet 3, even though the other two parents still exist.

Parent-child relationships also play an important role when changes are made to a model. A dimensional change in a parent feature can affect any of its children, and changes to a child feature may affect its parent. Features that are not linked through parent-child relationships can be changed without any mutual effects. It is partially through parent-child relationships that the internal logic of a feature-based model is checked. Changes in a fillet may be incompatible with either its children, or vice versa. In the example of the connector, users may attempt to specify a fillet 1 radius (child feature) that is larger than the radius of the truncated cone (base and parent feature); this conflict would be detected and the dimension not be permitted. Changing the parent feature can generate a similar conflict: On attempting to reduce the cone radius, users may need to also reduce the radius of fillet 1, or this feature can no longer exist and error messages are generally displayed. These types of dependencies obviously reflect real dimensional conflicts of physical objects and are consequently essential to detect in a design development or design-for-production process.

Parametric Design

When changes to a design do not alter its basic characteristics, these changes are referred to as *parametric variations* (see Figure 11-15). The width-to-height proportion of a subdivided window, for example, could be varied, all the while retaining its familiar image; or the number of panes in the window could be varied from six to eight. This general concept, though not originally conceived in the context of geometric modeling, is particularly powerful and useful considering the built-in functionalities of design development environments. Changing a feature-based model by editing key dimensions is possible at any point, and parent-child relationships between features let changes affect dependent model features. As long as no logical errors are detected, the model rebuilds according to the rules and relations set forth in the links between features. Parent features drive and determine the nature of their dependent children features.

In the example of the connector, it was mentioned before that the same basic part could be designed for different situations (e.g., incorporating different rod diameter and plate thickness), and a good parametric model would allow the designer to easily create these parametric variations within a single digital model (see Figure 11-16). Editing the key dimensions that generate these different versions is simply done by actually changing the original model. Good design development environments generally offer additional functionalities that further automate and streamline design processes based on parametric variations. These include dimensionally driven modeling techniques and the generation of part configurations through the use of design tables, both to be covered in the following section.

Dimensionally Driven Design

Closely allied to parent-child relationships and parametric design is the concept of dimensionally driven modeling. Here certain dimensions of the model (driven dimensions) are expressed as functions of other key dimensions (driving dimensions) through equations that the user defines. A designer may specify an equa-

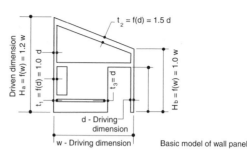

Typical relationships or formulas - f(x)

1. f(x): H_a = 1.2 w   Formulas defining relationships among
2. f(x): H_b = 1.0 w   parameters may assume many forms, including
   and others   algebraic, trigonometric, Boolean and others

Design Table			Typical simple design table
Variation Number	Panel Width w	Edge Distance d	
1 •	2800	130	
2	3200	130	
3 •	3600	130	
4	2800	400	
5 •	3200	400	
6	3600	400	

Values in design tables defining different variations may be directly specified, algorithmically calculated, or linked to external data sources.

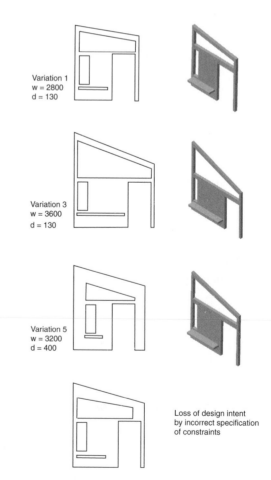

Figure 11-15 Parametric variations of window openings in a wall using the dimensional control of a design table.

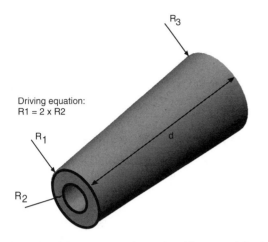

Driving equation:
R1 = 2 x R2

R$_3$

R$_1$

R$_2$

d

The radius of the cut-extrusion feature (hole) R2 can be defined
as driven by the radius of the base feature on the same side.
Further dimensional dependencies could be introduced using R3 and d.

Figure 11-16 Parametric variability of the connector base model using
simple equations.

tion, for example, that lets dimension X always be three times the value of dimension Y. Driving dimensions can be modified through the user interface; the program then calculates the driven dimensions and the model is rebuilt accordingly.

Obviously these kinds of interdependencies are fairly simple to achieve computationally for single objects. Interdependencies become more difficult to handle in complex shapes or when assemblies of shapes are involved. More sophisticated systems support capabilities for dealing with not only the parametric variation of single objects but also the relationships between objects. The parameters of one shape may be made dependent on the parameters of another shape. The diameter and center location of a hole, for example, might be dependent on the length-to-width ratio of a surrounding rectangle. Constraints may be further introduced to set limits on the extent a parameter may be varied. These same operations could, of course, be accomplished by a series of step-by-step constructed operations in virtually any system. Parametrically driven environments, however, allow the user to make these manipulation strings directly and transparently as single operations, and with various kinds of model consistency checks.

Consider the example of the steel connector. In a traditional modeling approach, the user can independently specify all dimensions, since no dimension depends on any other. In a "dimensionally driven" approach the radius R_2 of the hole for placement of the rod can be defined in relation to the radius R_1 of the base feature. The hole could be always half the size of the overall diameter of the component ($R_2 = 0.5\ R_1$). Many other dependencies are also possible. Dimensionally driven modeling can avoid some of the obvious

logical errors in parts that are being parametrically varied. In the connector example the radius of fillet 1—the rounded end of the base feature—could be driven by the radius of the base feature itself, ensuring thus that the fillet radius is always equal to or a certain percentage smaller than the radius of the base feature. Note that some design development environments restrict the use of dimensions that may be utilized in equations to those present in 2-D sketches, and do not allow, for example, the depth of an extruded feature to be either a driving or a driven dimension. These software-specific restrictions need to be carefully considered when setting up a dimensionally driven model.

Constraints

Constraints are a series of mathematically defined relationships that help to define the geometrical and dimensional characteristics of a model. Normally, these relationships apply to points, lines or faces within a single sketch or solid part, but they can be structured between multiple elements in an assembly model as well. Most programs can generate constraints automatically as the user defines entities: A snap-to-grid function in sketch mode, for example, often implies that entities are automatically constrained. Alternatively, users can add constraints after the model is built. Without any constraints points, lines or faces in the initial model can be freely moved, but little precision is associated with these movements, nor is there a capability to return to previous configurations. Constraints can be defined, edited, or deleted at any point during the design process, and changes are propagated throughout the entire design because of the associativities present.

By setting up constraints in part models, users normally embed characteristics of the model that are not expected to change frequently during the design process. Some software environments restrict the use of relations to entities in sketches; others allow a more extensive use of constraints. Simple *geometric constraints* are relations such as parallel, perpendicular, or tangential; others relate sketch entities to a coordinate system and restrain, for example, lines to be horizontal or vertical. *Dimensional constraints* define the distance between or the length or radius of entities. Entities can also be fixed to prevent them from moving on changes to the model.

A frequently employed modeling technique is the setting up of sketches that are partially based on existing geometry; for example, the edge of a model feature is projected onto the sketch plane and forms the basis for the 2-D sketch. (See Figure 11-17.) These projections normally imply the "on-edge" or "projected" constraint: When the model feature is changed the dependent projected edge updates automatically in the sketch. These constraints are particularly useful if com-

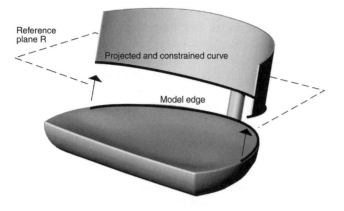

Figure 11-17 A model edge was projected to reference plane R in order to extrude the backrest. The projected curve is constrained to be "on edge" or "projected" with respect to the original model edge. In the example shown, the backrest will update once the seat shape changes in plan.

plex geometry needs to be derived from the model as a basis for a dependent feature.

Patterns

Many design development environments automate modeling techniques that are frequently used and would involve a significant number of individual steps. One example of these types of automated modeling techniques is the pattern feature. Patterns are linear or revolving arrays of one or more model features. Users can specify distances or angles as well as the number of features to be arrayed, and some environments allow certain instances of the array to be skipped.

Figure 11-18 shows a *pattern* of holes for the buttons on a simplified cellular phone design. The hole is actually a combination of three different features—a boss that connects via a fillet to the faceplate and the actual cut-extrude feature of the hole. Since it would be cumbersome to model all 12 buttons individually, this group of three features is arrayed as one object in a pattern feature. Users specify both the number of instances to be copied and their relative distances in each direction. A modification of any feature of the feature group (parent) will be reflected in each instance of the group. After the pattern has been generated, designers may desire to round off all holes to allow for the insertion of a rounded button. Upon modification of this original feature group, this change will propagate throughout the pattern. Moving the position of the parent feature group also displaces the pattern—its position is only defined relative to its parent.

Patterns are also useful if the features share some but not all properties. In that case the features to be copied and arrayed only represent the shared properties, and all individual variations are modeled subsequently. In the example of the cellular phone, it is possible to change the shape of the opening for a single button by

adding fillets to this particular instance of the pattern. The changes to one instance do not affect the remaining instances of the pattern; pattern instances are children of the parent group of features, and adding to one child clearly has no effect on the other children features.

Part Configurations and Design Tables

The exploration of parametric design variations is an obvious domain of design development environments, enabled by the parent-child relationships of features and the possibility to embed design knowledge dynamically through dimensionally driven modeling. These techniques would be of limited usefulness if each variation would have to be stored in a new file, as is commonly the case for the entity-based drafting programs and the component-based programs discussed in the previous chapter. Design development environments allow users to store different configurations of a single parametric model in the same file and actually generate new instances of the basic model by modifying its key dimensions using a design table. The cells in these design tables are linked to the key dimensions of the model, and editing the dimensions in the table will update the model accordingly. When dimensions are named and multiple values for them are specified, different instances of the parametric model are generated and stored. Many environments permit more extensive functionalities of design tables, such as adding comments, suppressing or resolving parts, and many more. Users can choose to display any one instance at the time without having to switch between different files. The model is treated in much the same way as an object class, with different model configurations representing individual instances of this class. Once a number of

Figure 11-18 Cellular phone housing: parametric pattern feature.

instances have been generated, users can still modify the parametric model but will have to specify whether a modification should be valid for all or only a selected range of model instances. Features that are not activated for certain instances are generally suppressed.

Part configurations are well suited for the parametric design of repetitive elements or components that share some but not all characteristics, such as the ribs in the structural frame of the design project shown in Figure 11-19. Here, all ribs have the same cross section, but the angle between the vertical portion and the upper inclined portion varies. These ribs are instances of a single parametric model, dimensionally controlled through a design table.

Derived Parts

It is frequently necessary to model a part based on dimensions and shapes present in an existing part. In that case the reference part can generally be inserted into a new file; it serves as the base part from which the subsequent model features are derived. Updates in the existing model are reflected in the inserted part in the familiar manner of external references in entity-based drafting programs. Note that some environments do not allow disjoint bodies, while others allow multiple disconnected solids in a single file. Deriving parts from others is closely allied to certain aspects of assembly modeling (see Section 11.4). The difference between part models with external reference parts and a true assembly model can be subtle and depends much on the individual options within given software. It is generally possible to initially insert an external reference model, but if it forms the base part, it must remain part of the new model because all new features will be dependent children of the base part. Assembly models generally allow for individual parts to be removed.

Macros and Rules

Many of the modeling techniques described in this chapter may be extremely powerful but inevitably require a certain amount of time to implement. To avoid having to perform the same sequence of modeling steps repeatedly, the user can record any number and sequence of modeling steps as a macro, thus automating the task. Examples of user-created macros include the modeling of typical connections in steel members, the insertion of chamfered holes, filleted bosses, or any other modeling task that combines sev-

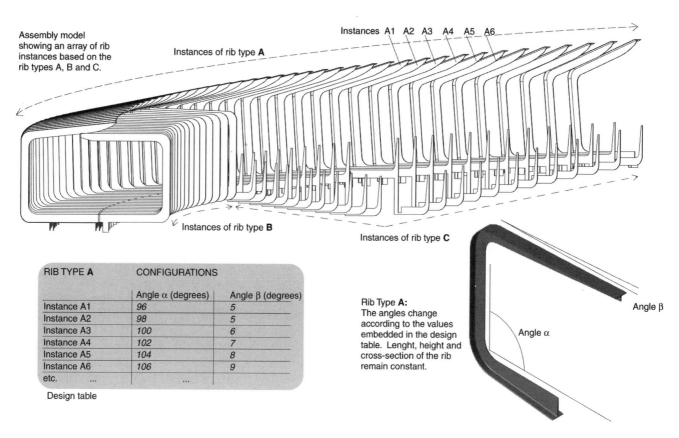

RIB TYPE A	CONFIGURATIONS	
	Angle α (degrees)	Angle β (degrees)
Instance A1	96	5
Instance A2	98	5
Instance A3	100	6
Instance A4	102	7
Instance A5	104	8
Instance A6	106	9
etc. ...	...	

Design table

Rib Type **A:**
The angles change according to the values embedded in the design table. Lenght, height and cross-section of the rib remain constant.

Angle β

Angle α

Figure 11-19 Part configurations and design tables: The structural ribs of a small building have been generated as instances of three basic rib types. (Source: Courtesy of John Nastasi, Architect)

eral modeling steps. Most sophisticated design development environments allow users to create macros directly within the user interface by recording the desired sequence of modeling steps and saving a macro file. Macros can also usually be created by programming directly in a separate environment according to the conventions set forth for a particular application. Typical programming languages used include Visual Basic, C, and C ++.

Related to macros are design rules—instructions that govern the relationship between several parameters of feature-based models based on conditional statements. A typical rule-based concept would be to add studs automatically in a partition depending on its total length. Rules can trigger the running of macros, or simply determine dimensions or other properties of parts. By enhancing macros as behavioral responses instead of merely automated modeling steps, a company can partially automate complex tasks, with the promise of improved productivity. Rules can serve to enforce a company's design or engineering principles, because individual users can download rules and macros that have been created as shared resources within a networked computational environment.

From 3-D to 2-D: Paper Documents

Despite the obvious tendency to communicate electronically, there is a persistent need to generate 2-D views from 3-D feature-based models. Much of manufacturing starts with flat stock, and toolpaths for the CNC machining inevitably need traditional 2-D projections as a useful basis to generate the code that eventually drives a machine. Drawings also remain useful documents to accompany personal interactions between designers, and they are frequently sent along with electronic files to verify that the electronic information is complete and no data was lost in the electronic transaction.

Any 2-D view of a digital model in design development environments is normally generated directly from the 3-D model. When this model is changed, the 2-D views update accordingly. Drawing views can be generated from part or assembly files, and users can normally select standard views such as plan and two elevations, as well as custom views. Many environments allow the adding of annotations and explanatory dimensions in a drawing—the latter are normally driven dimensions that cannot be used to directly manipulate the model. These detailing techniques are evidently useful in communicating the design intention. The associations between drawing view and 3-D model extend beyond merely graphic representations. Users can normally display the design tables that drive and generate configurations of the 3-D model. For parametric design projects it can be sufficient to graph-ically show the basic configuration with its key dimensions and clarify the individual dimensions of each configuration through the dynamically updated design table.

11.3 APPLICATION-ORIENTED MODELING TECHNIQUES

Many design development environments support modeling techniques that are closely related to the way objects are actually made. These techniques include shelling, piping, sheet-metal bending and flattening, as well as casting and mold-making techniques. Material properties and manufacturing variables can be incorporated to varying degrees. Such predefined modeling routines, when complemented by the necessary technical expertise, facilitate the building of digital models that can be directly suitable for manufacturing and prototyping activities.

Shelling

A great many common consumer products can be characterized geometrically as volumetric objects having thin-shell surfaces. Many common toys, for example, are made in this way via a variety of different pressing or die-casting operations that yield thin-walled structures. As described in Chapter 14, these processes make use of several types of materials (e.g., plastics, metals, metal powders). Historically, the development of a digital model of a thin-shelled object was extremely difficult. Recent systems, however, now readily allow the easy creation of these kinds of digital models through what are typically called "shelling" operations. Shelling operations convert a solid model to a similarly shaped object with thin walls and internal voids. The thin walls are still solids in a digital sense (as opposed to a surface or other models), but their thickness is by magnitudes smaller than all other dimensions of the same structure. Fundamentally, a shelling operation creates a series of offset internal surfaces from the existing set of external surfaces. Planes and curved surfaces are mimicked. Whether or not all surfaces in a volumetric object are shelled largely depends on the order in which the shelling operation and creation of additional volumetric shapes occur. Figure 11-20 illustrates a typical shelled piece.

In more advanced systems, the thin walls of a shelled piece can be given a specified draft angle that subtly causes the thickness of a wall to vary from a thinner to a thicker wall section. This capability is extremely useful when a designer is creating pieces that are ultimately to be made via casting operations when the presence of a draft angle is often vital to support removal of the piece from the mold.

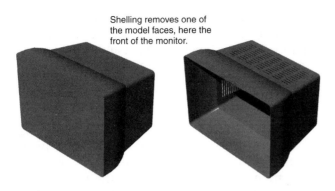

Shelling removes one of the model faces, here the front of the monitor.

Figure 11-20 A preliminary design for a monitor housing. The initial model on the left is a solid that was then shelled to obtain the thin-walled part on the right. The pattern features for the ventilation slots were added subsequently.

Piping

Complex pipe assemblies can be found in mechanical systems of buildings, cars, or many consumer products. The design of such systems involves the routing of mostly standardized pipes and pipe fittings in often three-dimensionally complex assemblies of components. This tedious design task has been automated in most sophisticated design development environments. Libraries of standard components are supplied, allowing the designer to concentrate more on the system design and routing than on the modeling of parts. User-defined custom components, especially those used repeatedly throughout a project, can often be added to such libraries.

The design of piping and tubing systems is a parametric design activity. The designer initially specifies a path that is typically the centerline of the pipe system. Piping components are then added along the path, and an association between path and pipe components is established. The routing of the pipe network can be changed anytime, and the selected pipe components are updated automatically according to the revised path geometry. This automatic update is essentially a parametric variation of each basic component. Most systems allow interference checks and the extraction of bills of materials.

Sheet Bending and Folding

The creation of volumetric objects by cutting and folding flat sheets has a long and honorable history. The approach remains highly ingrained in today's advanced manufacturing environment because of its simplicity and economy. One of its greatest users is the enormous cardboard box industry. Many common consumer products use housing made of folded sheet metal. In the building industry, common and widely used elements such as joist hangers and cladding panels are made by cutting and folding operations.

Essentially, these approaches involve cutting a two-dimensional shape from a flat sheet and folding it along specified lines to make a volumetric shape. Issues involve determining what is the exact shape of a two-dimensional pattern required such that it can be folded into the shape desired. Conceptually, volumetric objects with planar faces can be "unfolded" and laid out to obtain the flat shape needed to be cut and folded. This process is invariably easier said than done. There is usually more than one way to unfold a volumetric object (consider unfolding a simple cubical shape, for example, and you will note immediately that more than one option presents itself). Assuming that the shape can be conceptually unfolded, the resulting flat shape may or may not yield the exact original shape when folded. This is frequently because of the bending and thickness characteristics of the material. Even a thin piece of sheet metal has a certain bending radius to it. As a sheet piece gets thicker, so does the minimum possible bending radius. Associated with the bend radius is an arc length. The conceptual unfolding previously described typically assumes a "sharp" corner in an infinitesimally thin material where bend radius and arc length have no bearing. In actuality and if precision is required, the effects of these various bend radii and associated arc lengths on the developed model must be taken into account in the cutting and folding process. These same effects also typically throw off the locations of holes or attachments specified in the volumetric shape. While the differences are small, they are truly significant when building precisely dimensioned objects.

In current systems, these problems and others peculiar to folding processes are addressed. They are often called "sheet metal modelers" because of their frequent application to sheet metal products. Figure 11-21 shows two ways current modelers allow a user to create a digital model. In the first model, a flat sheet is laid out first; fold lines are then specified, bend radii inserted, and the sheet then folded (all digitally, of course). In the second model, a profile is drawn and extruded as a thin sheet. Bend radii are then inserted at each of the bends.

Either of the approaches noted is usually supported in a good software environment. The latter approach (profile to flat sheet) is frequently used because it makes designing the resulting final shape easier, particularly when holes or attachments are present. Figure 11-21 generally suggests the importance of bend radii and arc length effects in the development of a simple U-shaped piece, as well as which modeling approach is best used. In the upper part of the figure, the design intent is noted and the shape developed ignoring the effects of bend radii and arc length. Clearly the location of the holes and the height of the object are adversely affected. In the model in the lower part of Figure 11-21, the resulting geometric model that is desired is first

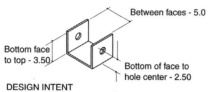

DESIGN INTENT
The intent is to locate the holes 2.50 from the bottom of the plate and to have an internal face-to-face dimension of 5.0.

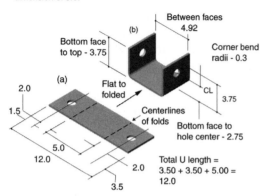

DESIGN REALIZATION "A"
This folded model was naively constructed from a simplistic flat sheet model with no allowances made for plate thickness or length changes due to corner radii. The resulting final positioning of the holes and model dimensions are not as desired.

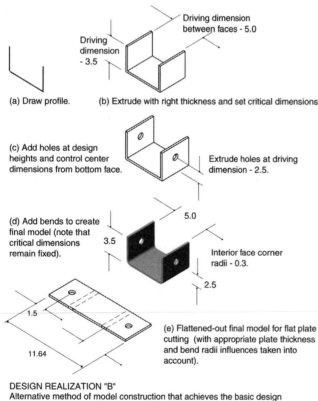

(a) Draw profile.   (b) Extrude with right thickness and set critical dimensions

(c) Add holes at design heights and control center dimensions from bottom face.

(d) Add bends to create final model (note that critical dimensions remain fixed).

(e) Flattened-out final model for flat plate cutting (with appropriate plate thickness and bend radii influences taken into account).

DESIGN REALIZATION "B"
Alternative method of model construction that achieves the basic design intent. Critical dimensions are established and then bend and fold patterns are determined.

Figure 11-21 Implications of alternative thin-sheet modeling approaches.

constructed out of flat, thin sheets. Bend radii are then inserted at fold points. Radii were specified as appropriate for the material involved. The resulting model, with bends, is then unfolded. The unfolded state reflects the changes caused by arc lengths. When folded, the exact shape desired would result.

Other issues involved in actually making physical products out of cut and folded sheets include what happens at corners of one (or more) intersecting planes (e.g., the corner of a common cubical shape). If the planes are made of thick material, the need to have three different folds taking place at the same point can cause crumpling of the material. Common practice is to insert a "relief cut" at this point.

Figure 11-22 illustrates a sheet metal part with a relief. Sophisticated systems automatically incorporate relief cuts where needed. The exact size and shape of a needed relief is, of course, dependent on the type and thickness of the material present (and the geometry of the intersecting planes).

Many special-purpose sheet-modeling environments either incorporate special algorithms for calculating bend radii and the size and shapes of relief cuts or provide more simple lookup tables. Bend radii can be user-specified or extracted from known experimental data that has been tabularized. Sometimes a K factor can be specified. The *K factor* is a ratio representing the location of the neutral plane with respect to the thickness. Bend allowances can then be calculated according to some simple expressions. For relief cuts, various offset ratios can be specified.

Joining of folded sheet products also typically involves the use of common devices such as folded tabs to connect adjacent planes. These tabs must be built into the unfolded two-dimensional shape. Some environments provide for more or less automatic tab generation.

Metal Plate Flattening

Sheet bending and folding are automated modeling tasks that are restricted to developable model surfaces. Bends can only have a single curvature, and material stretching and compression are only caused by the

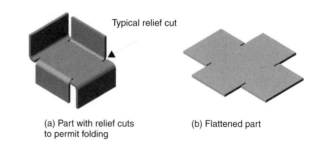

(a) Part with relief cuts to permit folding   (b) Flattened part

Figure 11-22 Relief cuts in thin-sheet models.

sheet thickness itself; they are usually negligible. In certain industries, especially ship or boat building and aircraft and automobile production, performance-driven requirements frequently dictate the use of nondevelopable shapes. The marine industry in particular is faced with the challenge of having to design complexly shaped ship hulls that consist of many individually formed metal plates. For the metal plates to be efficiently assembled and welded together, they need to be shaped and cut accurately. Since all plates are cut from flat stock, special software modules have been developed for the digital flattening of nondevelopable metal plates (see Figure 11-23).

Depending on the characteristics of each forming process (line heating, shot peening, brake forming, etc.), the sheet material can be subject to any combination of stretching or compression. Flattening software can usually be configured such that the digital flattening process more or less accurately reproduces the characteristics of any particular forming procedure. Various algorithms are used in flattening software. Most commonly, the complexly shaped metal plate is subdivided into a triangulating mesh. During the flattening process, the programs then calculate the position of each mesh point with respect to its theoretical position without any stretching or compression. The algorithms of many programs add offsets that take the material strain into account, according to the user-defined combination of stretching or compression. Some systems allow the additional quantitative output of the material

strain that is to be expected in the formed plate. Experienced designers can then judge whether or not the original shape and size of the plate can be fabricated without the risk of crimps or tearing.

Related to plate flattening programs are applications designed to simulate the draping of sheets of advanced fibers such as carbon, Kevlar, and others over complexly shaped molds. Such modules are available as stand-alone and integrated add-ons to comprehensive design development environments.

Models for Cast and Mold Making

As is discussed more extensively in Chapter 14 on manufacturing processes, any part that is intended for casting must be shaped with the intended process in mind. Process variables include whether a one-part or multipart mold is to be used, the nature of the casting material, and so forth. These variables frequently entail shaping a part in specific ways. Repetitive open-faced sand-castings, for example, are normally designed with one flat face that naturally has to exist as part of the fundamental material flow process. Pieces are also shaped so that there are no undercuts or interior voids that would prevent the piece from just being lifted from the mold. Sides of a piece are also typically shaped with small draft angles to facilitate easy removal.

More complex multipart molds allow correspondingly more complex geometric shapes to be cast. In a two-part mold, the negative void for the future cast piece is formed by two mold halves, each containing part of the void that fits together. Gate and sprue channels are cut into the molds to allow material to be poured into the void and for gases to escape. When cast, evidence of where the two molds fitted together is usually present in the form of a small metal bead or discontinuity, called a "parting line," that circumscribes the cast piece. Upon removal, pieces are finished by removing leftover metal from gate channels and, depending on the use of the piece, grinding away evidence of the parting line. Pieces are typically designed with this process in mind. Each half of the piece must be easily removable from its mold half. In many pieces, the surfaces of the piece are given a draft angle away from the parting line to facilitate easy removal. This process accentuates the visual presence of the parting line, and it simply becomes a feature in the final design.

In other forms of casting—for instance, different forms of investment or lost-wax processes—demands on object shaping may not be excessive at all. What is always present, however, is the requirement that metal flow into the mold must occur and that gases are allowed to escape.

Digital design environments that are intended to support these kinds of activities have a number of help-

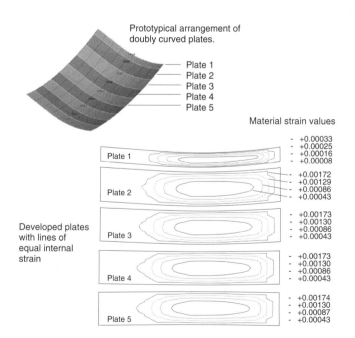

Figure 11-23 Plate flattening needs to take material strain into account. The long plates cover a synclastic shape. Each plate can be developed, and the internal strain (compression and/or stretching) can be predicted more or less accurately.

ful capabilities. In the part design process, most allow features to be given specified degrees of draft. Parting lines can be specified. Good systems also support sizing and shaping modifications that account for the material shrinkage that is encountered in most casting operations. This accounting for dimensional changes caused by shrinkage can be reflected either in the design of the original piece or in the design of the associated mold. Some advanced systems and special purpose systems support mold design more than others. In addition to the capabilities noted, some systems aid the designer in developing gates and sprues. Most, however, still demand that the user possess experience and/or common sense in shaping a part to be suitable for a specific kind of casting process.

Figure 11-24 illustrates the general steps in creating a digital model of a part and a corresponding mold. The example illustrates a number of different operations. A parting line has been defined and a volume created around the line via an extrusion process. A steep draft angle was specified as part of the extrusion process. A mold volume sufficiently large enough to enclose the part was next created. Via a Boolean operation in an assembly mode, an interior void in the block was created that corresponds to the shape of the original part. As part of this process, the mold cavity was enlarged by 2 percent to compensate for expected material shrinkage. In this case, a uniform shrinkage percentage was arbitrarily chosen. Obviously the percentage chosen should be a function of the specific casting material, and the size and shape of the piece to be cast. In many cases, shrinkage may not be uniformly constant, and different shrinkage factors should be used in different directions. Clearly expertise in the casting process is vital in obtaining an accurate end product.

The mold is completed by cutting it into two pieces. Different systems have different capabilities for supporting this act. Simple sectioning is possible. In some systems, the parting line can be picked and projected onto the surrounding mold surfaces. The projected line can then be used to cut the mold into pieces. This process ensures that the mold is cut exactly to correspond to the desired parting line of the part model.

Gates, sprues, alignment devices for the mold halves, and other features could be added to the mold model as well. Obviously, once a digital model of the mold is developed, it can be used as a basis for fabricating the physical mold, perhaps by milling the negative void out of a block of metal.

11.4 ASSEMBLY MODELS

Most artifacts—buildings and products—actually consist of assemblies of smaller discrete components. A

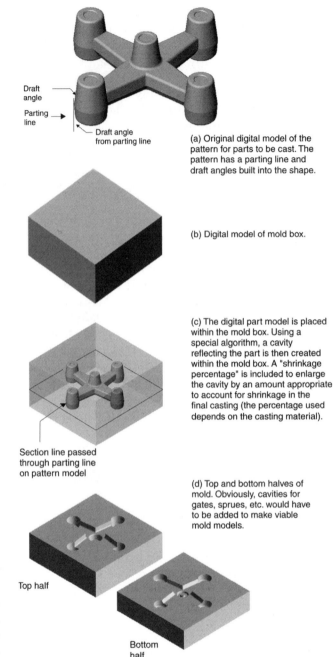

(a) Original digital model of the pattern for parts to be cast. The pattern has a parting line and draft angles built into the shape.

(b) Digital model of mold box.

(c) The digital part model is placed within the mold box. Using a special algorithm, a cavity reflecting the part is then created within the mold box. A "shrinkage percentage" is included to enlarge the cavity by an amount appropriate to account for shrinkage in the final casting (the percentage used depends on the casting material).

(d) Top and bottom halves of mold. Obviously, cavities for gates, sprues, etc. would have to be added to make viable mold models.

Figure 11-24 Creating a two-part mold from a digital part model.

simple switch, for example, with its clearly defined functionality, is often represented in the context of the design of a lighting fixture as an element to be assembled along with other components of the fixture. But it is obvious that the switch itself consists of many subelements and parts. In any design of any complexity whatsoever, basic constituent elements are often made by several distinct manufacturing processes—often in different locations and by different machines—and subsequently formed into subassemblies. These subassemblies are in turn assembled to make final objects. Design development environments have the capability to bring together multiple feature-based parametric models in a single assembly file, and mimic the way these individual parts would be put together in the final product. (See Figure 11-25.) Such assembly models are fundamentally different from arranging a series of geometric models in some visually convincing manner in a single file, because the assembly context allows a more in-depth understanding of whether an envisaged mechanical and functional link is actually likely to work or not.

In a design context, a change to one part of a larger assembly typically necessitates a change in the proportion or configuration of some other part, or a reconfiguration of a part implies a reshaping of a whole. Many assembly models support this reshaping. Certainly, it is common to want to change some basic shape parameter as the design develops—say, varying the diameter of a fountain pen housing to make it feel better in the hand, an act that necessitates corresponding changes to constituent subassemblies such as tip housings. In other cases, it is often desirable to automatically change the physical characteristics of a whole *class* of parts (e.g., changing the diameters or material properties of all baseplate bolts). Having to painfully rebuild each subassembly model each time is clumsy at best. Other needs exist as well. Perhaps it would be desirable to change the final surface finish of all exposed surfaces of an assembled piece while leaving nonexposed surfaces alone. All of these actions and others prove extremely difficult in a modeling environment where all pieces have been separately created and imported and bear no dependency relationships one to another.

In assembly modeling, as in feature-based part modeling, it should be understood that it is necessary to first have a clearly defined design model. The model should be limited to reflect the *fundamental intent* of the designer, which in turn makes operations such as the parametrization of geometric shapes both more feasible and useful. These assembly environments do not design something for someone; rather they make it possible to explore particular design intent. Basic forms and relationships among constituent parts and their related features as decided by the intelligence of the designer must be in place during initial model-building phases.

Basic Concepts: Assemblies and Subassemblies

A basic assembly model not only allows the placement of individual part files in a single file; it also enables the designer to set up geometrical and dimensional constraints and relationships between individual parts, check for interference between parts, and perform vari-

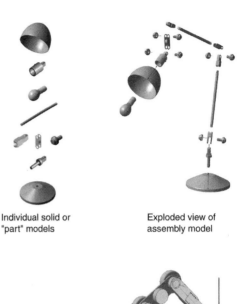

Individual solid or "part" models

Exploded view of assembly model

Section through assembly model—Dynamic section cuts may be made through any part of the model.

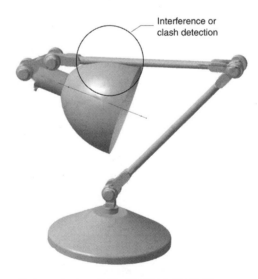

Interference or clash detection

Parts may be dynamically moved in mechanisms—Clashes or interferences between solid parts can be detected.

Figure 11-25 Assembly model of a lamp.

ous types of analysis dealt with in Section 11.5. The part files remain linked to their original source files and can be either modified in the context of the assembly itself or in their own part file. Modification of a part model in its own part file updates the same model in the assembly file and vice versa. One and the same part file, for example, a structural rib, can be inserted many times in the same assembly model in order to represent the overall structural system. It is often useful to create subassemblies that contain a closely related set of part files—for example, a panelized curtain wall element—and then arrange subassemblies and possibly other part files in a larger assembly model. Different environments allow varying degrees of complexity in this layering of the assembly file, and the rebuilding of the model can be cumbersome for large assemblies.

Assembly Constraints

In operational terms, individual parts or subassemblies in assembly models are related one to another via a series of specified geometrical or dimensional relationships—constraints very similar to those discussed previously in the context of parts. Geometric constraints include those of alignment and orientation, and the use of mating surfaces, lines, or points between adjacent parts. Thus, the axis of one round shape might be specified as being "aligned" with that of another, and the bottom surface of one as being "mated" to the top surface of the other. Typical *mating relationships* include aligned, angled, tangent, coincident, or a certain distance between model elements. Combinations of these are possible. Upon execution of these specifications, the individual parts will be brought together, dependency relationships are created, and the changes propagate throughout the assembly model. For assemblies that will be dynamic systems in their final built state, it is important to note that parts can be moved in all but the restrained directions. For rotating parts, the specification of an aligned central axis in combination with a distance between parallel model faces will let users rotate the parts, and allow them to visualize the dynamic behavior of the final assembly.

Interference Checks

Especially important in the assembly context is the ability of most systems to detect part interferences—situations or model configurations in which two parts occupy the same location in the model. This capability is truly valuable in all geometrically complex and spatially tight situations, such as in the design of aircraft and automobiles. There, interference checks in assembly models are also a mechanism of coordinating the part designs of multiple concurrent contributors. Some environments allow the automated calculation of clear-ance dimensions between selected parts, and most programs enable the user to measure distances between parts directly. A graphic display of the overlapping volume from interfering parts is often possible, allowing designers to visualize the situation in order to facilitate design decisions.

Other Functions

During the design process it may be necessary to replace certain parts in an assembly with others. These types of changes are possible at any time but usually require the user to redefine mating relationships, since the associated model faces and entities of the replaced parts are no longer present in the assembly. To exchange parts, users normally update the links to the part files and simply name another part file to replace an existing one. Similar modifications are possible for parametric part files that have been modeled using design tables and configurations. Here users can decide and change at any time which configuration a particular part file should represent. This powerful feature of assembly modeling enables the testing of design options quickly and elegantly.

Many systems also allow the designer to dissolve subassemblies into part files of the master assembly. Individual subassemblies and part files can be suppressed or their visibility simply turned off—both functionalities are useful especially for large assembly models. Suppressing a part usually implies that all related constraints are equally suppressed, whereas turning off the visibility of parts only simplifies the display without any consequences for the internal logic of the assembly model. Useful, especially for larger assemblies, are the simple *assembly statistics* that most environments support. Information such as the total number of components and subassemblies, the number or unique parts, and the currently suppressed or resolved status of its components can be displayed.

Techniques such as patterns and configurations, previously described in more detail in the context of part modeling, are also available in assembly models. The pattern function in assemblies is similar to its equivalent in part mode, but instead of affecting the features of a parametric part assembly, patterns copy and arrange the parametric parts or subassemblies in the assembly model in linear or curvilinear fashion. The direction of the pattern can either be the edge of a part feature or a locally created reference line, curve, or other entity.

Configurations in assembly models serve a similar purpose as part configurations. Assembly configurations allow individual parts to be suppressed, control assembly features such as the patterns, or modify dimensions and constraints. Users can display any desired configurations. Macros and rules as described in the previous section on parts modeling are equally applicable to assembly modeling—indeed, they are probably more useful here because of the usually more complex and demanding modeling tasks.

Modeling Parts in Assemblies

Assembly files do not need to be treated merely as the convenient bringing together of multiple components in a logical and structured way. This *bottom-up* approach—discussed more in detail in Chapter 12–is often complemented or even replaced by the modeling of parts in the context of the assembly. Creating a part model in the context of an assembly enables users to easily refer to higher-order design concepts or geometry while maintaining the functional advantage of assembly modeling. This approach, commonly referred to as *top-down,* is equally useful in product design as in architectural design.

Figure 11-26 demonstrates one possible application, the preliminary design of a small, complexly shaped envelope. Here, the basic surface provides a reference for individual structural ribs. Changes to the surface geometry are directly reflected in the shape of the ribs. A related example is the modeling of a bar stool as illustrated in Figure 12-8.

When parts in assemblies are modeled, the usual modeling aids and structures are normally present, including parent-child relationships, constraints, parametric dimensionally driven features, as well as configurations. Not only parts but also 2-D or 3-D layout drawings can serve as reference in assembly-based part modeling. When setting up the structural frame of a skeletal construction project, it can be useful to define a 3-D grid first and then model parts such that their length and position is derived from the grid. Modification of the grid spacing then immediately affects the actual parts of the frame assembly.

Depending on the degree of sophistication of a program, there may exist a number of other techniques for modeling and editing of parts in assembly models. Some environments allow multiple parts to be joined into a single part, upon which overlapping model elements are trimmed and the two parts merged into a single one.

11.5 ANALYSIS TOOLS

In most computer-aided design systems, the object created has carefully defined geometrical and dimensional characteristics, but the inherent capability for analysis

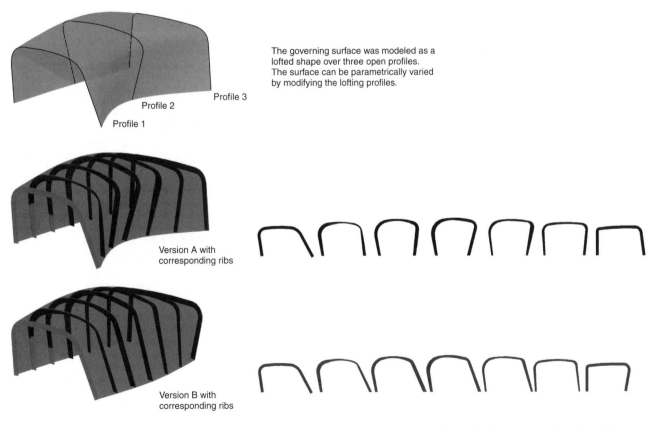

The governing surface was modeled as a lofted shape over three open profiles. The surface can be parametrically varied by modifying the lofting profiles.

Profile 3
Profile 2
Profile 1

Version A with corresponding ribs

Version B with corresponding ribs

Figure 11-26 Modeling parts in assembly files: The external surface is modeled first, and structural ribs are then derived. When the shape of the surface is changed the ribs update automatically. This procedure is a typical top-down approach.

of the digital model varies depending on the type of modeling environment and the mode of representation. Simple types of analysis include dimensional studies that can be readily carried out in any modeling environment. Extracting mass properties and material lists is usually dependent on using solid models to represent the design. Other commonly needed kinds of analyses include structural, vibration, steady-state or transient heat flow, airflow, electrostatic, and manufacturing-related analysis manufacturing techniques. Depending on the results of one or more of these analyses, the object may need to be redesigned via a change in geometry or materials and subsequently reanalyzed. Vendors of design development software typically offer the integration of third-party plug-ins and add-ons for various analysis purposes. This seamless integration of analysis and design environment accommodates the need for reliable and fast data flow during this iterative design process (see Chapter 12, Section 12.4 for a more detailed discussion).

Measurements and Bill of Materials

The need to calculate basic measures of a component or assembly, including dimensions, volumes, and surface areas, is obvious. Virtually all software environments include excellent capabilities for extracting dimensions from basic digital models. In addition to measuring dimensions relative to the 3-D model—for instance, the absolute length of an edge—users can easily create 2-D projected views that can be dimensioned. Dimensions can be formatted according to any of a number of standard dimensioning schemas. Of particular interest herein is that many design development environments support critical *tolerancing* specifications. There are not only tolerances associated with digital model construction; physical tolerances associated with part and assembly manufacturing are also a major concern. Better software environments support established tolerancing standards, such as the ANSI Y14.5 Geometric and True Position Tolerancing guidelines in the United States.

Important surface area and volume measures are easily computed from surface and solid models. Solid models normally allow for a bill of materials to be extracted—essential information for bidding, for cost control, and for a production context. These lists are automatically updated as the design changes.

Mass Properties

Weights of parts and assembles can be calculated by specifying the material density of solid models. Of particular importance in an analysis context are engineering properties of sections and volumetric entities (see Figure 11-27). In any structural design context for a

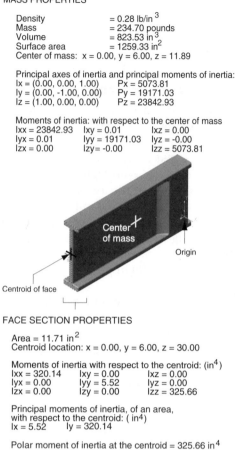

Figure 11-27 Section and mass properties.

simple beam, for example, it is absolutely necessary to be able to determine the location of the *centroid* of the cross section, the *moment of inertia* of the cross section, and related distances from the neutral axis of the member to different locations in the cross section. For column design, you need to know this information about both axes. As analysis demands and needs increase, other information is needed. The *center of mass*, for example, and related inertia values are often needed. Since all of these measures are readily calculated from a digital model, better systems support these kinds of needed analyses directly.

Finite-Element Analysis and Related Techniques

A great many existing CAD/CAM systems utilize structural analysis approaches based on *finite-element* methods. These methods are particularly appropriate for solids or structures with continuous surfaces, although they may be used for other structural forms as well.

Finite-element analysis models are almost invariably the method of choice in relation to the design of complex parts in a mechanical engineering design context.

They are easily capable of handling pieces that have unusual surface geometries or can only be characterized as solid objects. Before the advent of these techniques, stress analyses for such elements were extremely difficult and recourse was often made to experimental approaches (e.g., photoelasticity) or approximations. By now, however, finite-element techniques are common. In architecture, these techniques also find widespread use, although more exact and more efficient matrix displacement techniques often remain preferred for many applications involving frameworks (see the discussion of bar-type analysis at the end of the chapter and in Chapter 6.)

In finite-element approaches, the structure is considered as composed of a series of point *nodes* and connecting *elements* (see Figure 11-28). The elements may be geometrically characterized as lines, polygons, or volumetric units (solids). The mesh is often automatically generated, whereby its characteristics (density, geometric properties) may be varied. For a thin-shell structure, for example, the surface is first modeled within a computer-aided design environment. The continuous surface is then replaced by a series of discrete polygons that are considered connected at specific points (usually nodes but sometimes edges). The discrete polygonal elements are specially formulated to have specified structural properties in relation to specific performance evaluations, such as structural analysis. Distributed loadings that may exist on the whole structure are converted to nodal loadings. A structural model based on one or another of a variety of energy laws is then used to predict internal forces and displacements. Often outputs are graphically displayed.

A similar process is followed for the finite-element analysis of solid structures. A volumetric solid model of the object is first created within a computer-aided design environment. The solid is then converted into a three-dimensional mesh assembly of discrete volumetric elements (e.g., tetrahedral elements). Nodal loadings are again applied. Outputs are obtained that describe internal forces, stresses, and displacements generated by the loadings.

In a few cases, finite-element analyses may yield more or less exact results. More usually, however, finite-element models produce only approximate results. Care should be also taken in developing appropriate assumptions for the physical case present—finite-analysis methods require more intelligence in their proper use than novice users often believe. Similarly, the interpretation of results is often difficult and inevitably requires sound engineering knowledge. All too often, novice users generate multicolored graphic diagrams from tabulated analytical outputs and think that they have "done an analysis" without actually knowing how to interpret the images. Often they are of "lines of principal stress or strain"—concepts that may seem obvious but most assuredly are not without a keen understanding of structural behavior.

The general ability to conduct structural and other kinds of analyses on models related directly from the overall design model has proven to be one of the great attractions of integrated CAD/CAM systems. The exact representation of the object used in the performance evaluation algorithm, however, is typically extracted from the base model and may ultimately look quite different from it because of the need to specify unique boundary conditions and other parameters as inputs. Boundary conditions may be at higher levels of abstraction than physical models; for instance, slope is maintained at a particular angle or there are certain "degrees

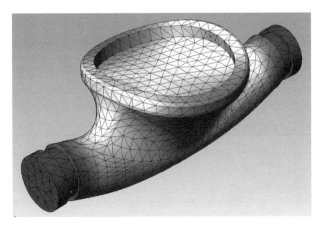

Displacement analysis: The deformation of the joint can be shown exaggerated for the sake of clarity. Here the underlying mesh is also shown.

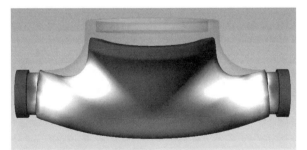

Stress analysis: The undeformed shape of the joint is shown superimposed

The joint is the base support for the pivoting mast of a cable suspension bridge.

Figure 11-28 Finite-element analysis of a solid model.

of freedom" at a particular point. It is generally necessary to extract from the base model an underlying geometric description of the object, create a mesh to support finite-element techniques, and then define various boundary conditions and loading types. This process generally entails the creation of what is commonly termed an *application model* or *view model*. These terms are often used to describe the application-specific representations of data.

A particular employment of finite-element analysis is the study of molding and casting processes for the production of plastic and metal parts. Here, finite-element analysis is used to predict the filling, packing, and cooling stages during various molding and casting processes. Since internal thermal stresses can result in warping and other distortions of parts, these studies are essential to carry out as part of the design process. Again it must be mentioned that only experienced designers can interpret the results in a meaningful way. The design of molds is a highly complex task, and experience can at best be complemented, but not replaced, by mold-flow analysis programs.

Another manufacturing-related application of finite-element analysis is metal-sheet-forming analysis. It calculates the stresses and strains that develop within sheet metal during the forming process, based on the digital model of the forming tool and various process parameters. This type of analysis helps designers understand whether a sheet-metal design is feasible for manufacture. Excessive strains indicate that changes may need to be made to the design or to the process parameters, or that a different forming or manufacturing process needs to be chosen altogether.

Related to finite-element analysis is *computational fluid dynamics* (CFD) analysis. CFD is used to study the behavior of liquids or gases in a given environment. In architecture, it is frequently used to study indoor or exterior thermal behavior, or to predict the performance of buildings subject to high wind-loads.

Much of commonly performed structural analysis—especially in the architectural context—is not based on solid geometry. Instead, bar-type elements are used, connected at nodes and with material and section properties assigned to them. The line-based nature of these environments makes any data exchange with design development programs rather difficult. These popular tools communicate more easily with entity-based drafting programs. See Chapter 6 for a more in-depth description of bar-type structural analysis programs.

CHAPTER **12**

Digital Design in Practice

12.1 INTRODUCTION

As digital design tools continuously evolve, it has become a task on its own for professionals to stay informed about current developments and identify opportunities that new software is opening up. Many practices follow well-proven paths in their digital design efforts but may be unaware of ways to improve productivity and quality. This chapter attempts to provide some basic information on the use of digital design tools with an emphasis on design development environments in practice. These tools offer some exciting new opportunities for design professionals, but getting started with programs such as CATIA, SolidWorks, or Pro/ENGINEER can be a daunting task. Not only is there an inevitable need for training; designers will typically have to integrate these parametric design environments into an existing pool of software and decide on what tools to use when in the design process. Questions like what portion of a project to model parametrically and where to rely on traditional 2-D representations will have to be answered.

At this point selective use of design development environments probably remains the most promising approach in practice. The choice of what to model parametrically depends on design values and objectives that dominate in a particular design phase but is also a function of the complexity present in a scheme. Independent of the type of environment used is the general question of the appropriate level of modeling detail. One of the positive features of older two-dimensional hand-drawing techniques was that the level of detail represented in a drawing changed according to the scale of representation and a certain degree of useful abstraction was present. Only certain features were shown in ⅛ inch = 1 foot drawings, while the level of detail increased in scales such as ½ inch = 1 foot. This not only was done for sound conceptual and contractual reasons but also was dictated by the limitations of hand-drawing techniques. In the digital world, it is perfectly possible to have extremely high levels of detail contained within a model that is subsequently represented at different scales—the enforced abstraction process is eliminated. Determining the appropriate

level of detail to be represented in a digital way is an extremely important task, and it is independent of the type of environment used. More likely, it will depend on the complexity of the design task. Buildings with uniquely designed complex roofs of glass supported by rod assemblies often require all components (rods, nodes) to be modeled down to the last bolt. In other roof design situations involving off-the-shelf skylight systems, only the basic geometry and some conceptual details need be defined, but final details and dimensions can be left to the manufacturer.

Section 12.2 discusses these and other aspects of implementing parametric models in practice. The use of base models to define the governing geometry of a larger project has proven to be a useful approach. Here, the design office furnishes the generic description of the overall scheme that is then developed and refined by engineers, subcontractors, or consultants. Related to the use of such reference models are techniques of assembly modeling known as bottom-up and top-down approaches—digital design strategies.

Designing complex projects is a highly collaborative process, involving any number of design participants. There is an obvious need to exchange information, and an increasingly pressing need to enable collaborative digital design. Currently, these needs are addressed in different ways for stand-alone systems and integrated systems. *Stand-alone applications* (Section 12.3) communicate through neutral file exchange formats and can be managed through Web-based, database-driven systems. This setup is a common paradigm in architectural practice, reflecting on the fragmented nature of the building industry with its small teams that are assembled on a project-per-project basis. *Integrated systems* (Section 12.4), on the other hand, have been extensively implemented in industries such as automotive or aerospace. They combine all needed applications—CAD, engineering analysis, manufacturing, and process management—in a single and consequently more tightly integrated environment. This approach is particularly well suited to the highly structured nature of design development environments, since feature-based and parametric models facilitate the incremental refine-

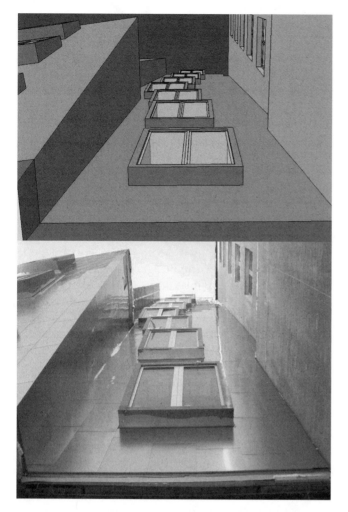

Figure 12-1 The CATIA model and finished façade of the MIT Stata Center by architect Gehry Partners, LLP. (Source: Image courtesy of A. Zahner Company, used by permission)

development environments. A key question is obviously how to find the appropriate tool for the task to be accomplished, and, within the focus of this book, when to opt for a design development environment. There are many factors to be considered that go beyond the immediate discussion of this text—including staffing and training situations, ever-changing costs of hard- and software, schedules, office sizes, collaboration with others, and many more. In a mixed approach including design development and other digital design environments, it is conceivable that key aspects of the overall design are modeled as a parametric assembly or part model, while most details, unless they are spatially particularly complex, remain in the domain of 2-D entity-based programs and hand sketches. Gehry Partners, LLP, Associates have successfully used this combination in complex projects such as the Stata project for MIT in Cambridge, Massachusetts (see Figure 12-1).

The traditional hierarchy of project representations—general-arrangement drawings (plans, sections, elevations) and cross-referenced details (core plan, details, schedules)—can be heavily dependent on and driven by a 3-D parametric model (see Figure 12-2). On the one hand, the 3-D model can be treated as an independent geometric reference that is dealt with and exchanged electronically between design participants. For geometrically complex schemes the 3-D model supplies all dimensions that otherwise are hard or impossible to determine. On the other hand, it can also generate 2-D section lines in plan, section, and elevation that then become integrated into the 2-D general-arrangement drawings.

Designing details, in many cases, will not necessarily entail extensive parametric modeling. It may frequently be sufficient to represent details with traditional 2-D drawings, even though a project may be geometrically complex. When these detail drawings are referenced to an element of the 3-D parametric model—a surface, a centerline—the geometric description resides in the 3-D model, where it can easily be updated. The constructional and technical solution, for example, the joint between a metal cladding system and a glass-curtain wall, is displayed in 2-D drawing views. It is obviously important to develop the detail bearing in mind that the same basic solutions need to adapt to various geometric conditions and underlying shapes. In other cases, especially when subcontractors or engineers are closely involved, it may be advisable to model selected key components using a feature-based design tool.

ment of a scheme as the design progresses. Here, *product data management* (PDM) systems are extensively used to control the design to production process. The systems combine with and extend into concurrent design or engineering techniques, knowledge-based approaches, and virtual prototyping—all efforts to further streamline and accelerate the design process that are currently being used outside the design profession but could become feasible in the near future. Emerging technologies include *virtual reality* and *augmented reality,* which merge digital modeling and user interface into a single immersive virtual environment.

12.2 PARAMETRIC MODELS IN DESIGN

Professionals faced with the design task for complex buildings or products are likely to employ a range of digital tools instead of a single environment. These may include, among others, conceptual modelers, entity-based drafting programs, and since recently, design

Selective Parametric Modeling

In structuring a large assembly model of a complex building or product with parametrically varying components, a first decision to be made is that of deciding

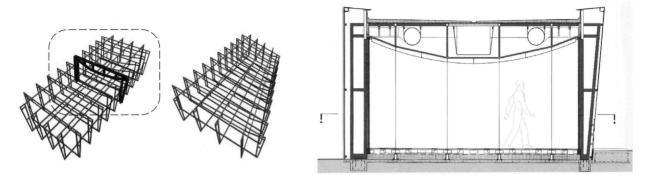

Figure 12-2 Parametric variations of the structural frame for a small building. A section view is generated in the 3-D model, forming the basis for a detailed 2-D arrangement drawing. (Source: Courtesy of Chung-Ping Lee)

what to three-dimensionally model, which elements to define parametrically, and, finally, which specific features of each selected elements should be subject to variation. The designer must thus first determine the intent and purpose of the model, the scope of the model, and the appropriate level of modeling detail.

Buildings and complex products are composed of literally thousands of individual parts and large numbers of subassemblies (a typical lighting fixture, for example, is normally an assembly in its own right). It is neither time-efficient nor sensible to attempt modeling all of these individual parts and create a gigantic assembly model. The digital modeling task alone would be critically time-consuming, and tasks such as modeling hundreds of common bolts in a normative design situation are simply a poor use of a designer's time and expertise. Additionally, many components that are designed and prepackaged to provide specific technical functions are often best left as units with fixed geometries, dimensions, and interface points. From a computational viewpoint, current technologies are such that assembly models with large numbers of elements (more than several hundred) become extremely cumbersome to manipulate and manage even if developed. Many environments provide users with automated functions to create simplified versions of assemblies through a combination of suppression and visibility controls of components, but there is clearly a need to keep the overall size of the models as small as possible.

There are no easy answers to questions of scope and detail of parametric modeling. In general, it can be argued that within the current state of the art in the CAD/CAM world, it is best to be highly selective about what is chosen for detailed assembly modeling and parametric variations. Presumably, this decision would be highly influenced by the design office's own attitude toward the building or product and what is viewed as important. For example, in some situations it might be considered highly important to be able to vary the geometric and dimensional characteristics of the basic structural grid, while in other cases this capability

might be irrelevant. In other cases, the visual characteristics of an external wall system might be considered of such overwhelming importance that it is this system that would be primarily modeled and varied. In a laboratory complex, the mechanical and other infrastructure demands might be so high as to focus modeling efforts on the interactions of mechanical, structural, and internal wall elements, with the external building skin being of marginal interest. Different attitudes toward the question of what to model are discussed in case studies throughout the book.

Parametric Variations and Constraints

Parametric variation, the systematic exploration of different geometric and dimensional configurations that are possible for a given design, is a powerful design tool. Computationally, geometric and dimensional constraints (see Section 11.2) are used to generate shape variants once the primary design intent has been captured in a basic model. These constraints can then be applied at the sketch, part, or assembly level. The computational tools that support these variations have been largely developed for part and assembly manipulations in later stages of the design process. Even though their primary focus is on capturing design intent, they nevertheless can be useful in conceptual or preliminary design stages where approximate shape and massing options are explored.

In terms of direct application within a design context, these computational techniques can be applied in a number of different ways. Figure 12-3 broadly summarizes and provides different examples of applications. In the following, it is assumed that the broader parametric variations typically occur within assembly models.

At the broadest level, the idea of constraints and related parametric variation techniques can be applied to overall building planning and configuration studies (see Figure 12-4). Many digital design environments allow particular dimensional parameters to be linked to

(a) Parametric variations of gross areas and volumes as driven by programmatic requirements.

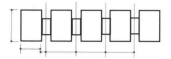

(b) Disposition and/or organization of major spatial elements, e.g., spacings of stair units, as controlled by related dimensions.

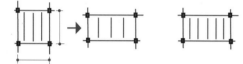

(c) Variations in gross shapes as driven by external factors.

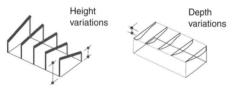

(d) Parametric variations of structural grids. Knowledge to "add" required members normally requires special scripting.

Height variations   Depth variations

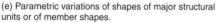

(e) Parametric variations of shapes of major structural units or of member shapes.

Panel and subpanel shapes and dimensions

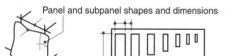

(e) Parametric variations of surface shapes, relations to primary structure, and fenestration patterns.

(f) Parametric variations of small scale elements, e.g., stairs, railings, louvers, fenestration subdivisions.

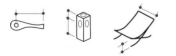

(g) Parametric variations of lighting fixtures, hardware, furniture, and other small elements.

Figure 12-3 Fundamental applications of parametric design principles.

external data sources. Hence, a number of different kinds of data-driven models can be developed. A case in point is simply that of linking gross building areas or volumes to externally stated programmatic area requirements. Several architects have devised overall shape definitions that were determined by other kinds of external driving forces—for instance, traffic movement on adjacent streets. In many situations (e.g., housing) there is a need to explore many variations of basic plan types wherein there are a number of predefined constraints because of functional considerations or building regulations.

Parametric variation capabilities are widely used in application areas that relate to basic building systems and elements. The bay dimensions of common structural grids, for example, can be easily varied. Shapes of individual structural units—frames or members—can also be easily varied. Beams can be varied in shape along their lengths, for example, according to simple rule-based systems.

Changing the bay dimensions of a seemingly simple structural grid does provide an illustration of a basic issue. A simple dimensional variation of an object may not actually result in something that is realistically viable. Radically changing the length-to-width ratio of a rectangular structural bay, for example, may cause internal beam arrays to become inappropriately spaced (too far apart), and in an ideal modeling environment, there might be a knowledge system built-in that automatically adds needed elements or otherwise suggests needed configurational changes. Most digital environments do not commonly support this kind of design intelligence for parametrically varying objects without additional user input through subprograms.

Enclosure systems provide another obvious application domain, and surely one that has received much attention by architects who have seemingly gone wild making curved shapes. Common design acts such as varying size, proportions, and placement of fenestrations (windows, doors) can also be directly accom-

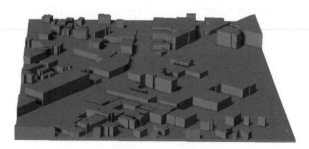

Figure 12-4 Massing model in the urban context: Parametric design environments can be useful for systematic massing studies even though they were clearly meant to be used for modeling mechanical parts. (Source: Courtesy of Chung-Ping Lee and Hyung Moon)

plished. The need to study particular situations, such as the implications of inserting rectangular openings into complexly curved surfaces, can be relatively easily addressed. Once basic fenestration opening geometries are determined, specific fenestration elements such as glass patterns, glass support points, louver systems, and so on can all be varied parametrically. The same is true for basic pattern variations of panelized or modular enclosure systems made of metal or other materials. Overall pattern geometries can be varied, as can patterns of panel features. Subsequently, specific panel instances can then be extracted and used to provide the base geometry for more detailed design development work (see Section 11.2).

Parametric variation studies can be made of most smaller-scale elements commonly found within a building. Stairways provide a common example, particularly since normal safety and related building code regulations often provide a strong external constraint system (e.g., riser/tread dimensions) that can be incorporated into constrained models. Related elements, such as handrail systems, provide another related application domain, as do lighting fixtures and the many other elements that go into the making and furnishing of a building.

Base Models, Governing Geometries, and Related Design Environments

While it is clearly necessary to be selective about the scope and detail of the digital model created, one of the great benefits of current digital modeling environments is that a carefully structured basic digital model can be developed at a manageable level of detail such that it can be used to provide the base geometry for subsequent detailed design development work. The abstracted model is known as a *base model* and provides the *governing geometry* for the whole design.

Base models can be used to support more detailed design activities typically done independently of the base model. In today's professional environment, these detailed design activities are often done by subcontractors or consultants that are critically involved in the design process but not directly part of the originating design office. For example, an exterior wall to be made of panelized sheet-metal components could be fairly simply represented in a base model (perhaps as a simple surface model), and basic pattern subdivisions established within this base model. The geometry of these pattern elements could then be extracted as a separate digital model. The sheet-metal fabricator would use this geometry as the basis for further detailed digital models of the panel, including all of the necessary ribs, stiffener plates, and so forth. The latter level of detail would not necessarily have to be reflected in the base model. If

needed, however, the model developed could be uploaded and become part of the base model (particularly if changes made during the design development process impact the governing geometry present in the base model). The models developed by subcontractors or consultants would not normally be directly associated back to the base model—for example, changes in the base model would not be dynamically reflected in the digitally separate models of individual components. (See Figure 12-5.)

Similar scenarios can easily be imagined for structural and mechanical systems. The base geometry can provide the critical definition of a structural system that is in turn developed in more detail by a structural engineering office that uses its own simulation software to determine member types and sizes. The same model might then be transferred to a structural fabricator to develop connection details via the use of special-purpose software. In mechanical systems, the ductwork might be simply represented and subsequently developed in detail by mechanical contractors using special-purpose software especially relevant to the task. In all cases, however, it should be emphasized that any change made to the base model must be propagated throughout all groups involved. If subcontractors or consultants extract data from one model version and do not remain directly linked to the base model, subsequent changes in the base model might not be propagated throughout as desired. The more models are disaggregated, the greater becomes the human management task to ensure that all changes are made in timely and correct ways.

Determining the characteristics of a base model is again a subject of great interest and largely dependent on the intent of the design office. In the scenarios described, the base model literally provides the govern-

Figure 12-5 Pattern of prefabricated façade panels at the MIT Stata Center: The panel subdivision was designed by the façade contractor in coordination with the architect.

ing geometry for the entire design, and, as such, would typically be developed and maintained by the designer's office. As discussed before, any modeling act implicitly allows certain kinds of manipulations and does not allow others. In the case studies presented throughout the book, it can be seen that some offices well known for their emphasis on the shape of the external skin of a building typically permeate the external enclosure surface of the building as the governing geometry, as shown in Figure 12-6 (also see the case studies on the MIT Stata Center by Gehry Partners LLP and the work of Bernhard Franken/ABB in Chapter 4). Other design offices chose other governing geometries that depend upon both design intent and design attitude.

Top-Down and Bottom-Up Design Approaches

When a building or complex product is being designed, there are inevitably phases during which designers are preoccupied with defining the whole, and individual parts may come into focus later. Once the general design concept and intent is well defined, the focus might shift primarily to the design of individual parts. For some designers, focus on parts comes rather early; for others, it comes later. These personal design styles, combined with the nature of the designed object and the particular phase in the overall design process, determine which of the two approaches is found to be appropriate. In design terms, the process of designing individual parts and assembling them into a whole (with an overall design image in mind) is typically called a *bottom-up* process. Alternatively, a *top-down* process would be to define the characteristics of the whole and then create the appropriate subcomponents. Both approaches have their advantages and disadvantages. In design philosophy circles, the distinctions made between these two approaches are critically argued. Fundamentally, top-down proponents argue

that this approach is the way designers "really proceed," and the proponents abhor the conceptual implications of the bottom-up approach. Pure top-down digital design approaches, however, have been found to be problematic in their own terms, because the nature of individual parts often reflects significantly on the whole. In this discussion, we shall not enter into this particular war zone but instead focus on the more pragmatic aspects of how one or the other approach is actually done in a design development environment.

In a typical operational circumstance involving multiple parts to be joined together, digital models of the parts are imported into an assembly document, alignments and mating relationships are specified, and the assembly is created. Obviously, the process described is a bottom-up one (see Figure 12-7).

A whole assembly can be operated upon as a unit as well. Features or subelements can be added to an assembly model developed as described. A hole might be cut through several parts just previously attached, for example. This latter act is characteristic of a top-down operation, where an action taken at the assembly level affects all of its constituent elements. The top-down process can be taken to a greater extreme wherein the designer starts with a parametric shape model of the whole assembly and then operates upon it to produce needed subcomponents. In sophisticated modelers, critical dimensions of the whole assembly thus created can be parametrically varied, which in turn automatically causes alterations in the geometric attributes of individual parts. (See Figure 12-8.)

In any of these modeling approaches, not all possible proposed geometry changes, of course, are possible within a given assembly model. It is conceivable to envision changes that are topologically impossible or otherwise not feasible. Careful modeling is required to ensure model consistency and integrity, and to be sure that all changes are propagated correctly through the model.

Returning to the question of top-down versus bottom-up, the practical dimensions of the question hinge around the following. In bottom-up processes, the designer has great control over the design of components and their relationships. In top-down approaches, the geometry of the whole is used to determine the geometry of the subcomponents to be made. The reference geometry need not be just that of a physical object but could be entities such as reference sketches or construction planes. This basic reference to model geometry allows the user to better control the overall dimensions and characteristics of the whole.

There is clearly a need for both types of processes in the practical design development world. In design philosophy terms, it is unclear if either of the two extremes really reflects the way design proceeds. Most design development environments allow a combination of

Figure 12-6 The geometry model of the MIT Stata Center defines the external shape of all parts of the building. (Source: Image courtesy of A. Zahner Company, used by permission)

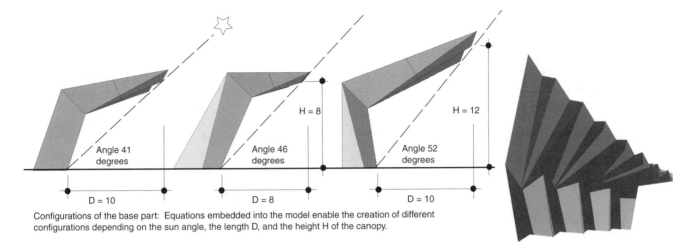

Configurations of the base part: Equations embedded into the model enable the creation of different configurations depending on the sun angle, the length D, and the height H of the canopy.

Figure 12-7 Bottom-up approach demonstrated with the parametric model of a canopy: Configurations of part files were inserted into an assembly model to create a model of the overall system.

these two approaches. A basic skeletal structural frame, for example, can be modeled such that a parametrically defined 3-D grid determines the overall geometry of the frame (top-down) while member sizes are controlled individually (bottom-up). The associative system of member centerlines is inserted or directly modeled in an assembly model, forming the reference for individual structural members that are modeled as parts in the assembly context. Allowing the length of each member to be directly driven by the spacing of the 3-D grid—on

changing the grid these members rebuild accordingly—represents a top-down approach. The cross-sectional profile and its possible variation along the member length are independent of the 3-D grid. Designers need to define them individually—a typical bottom-up approach.

As is typical for feature-based modeling, the designer must decide before the outset to what extent a top-down and/or bottom-up strategy will be pursued. Some design development environments allow the parent-child relationships between driven parts and the driving geometry

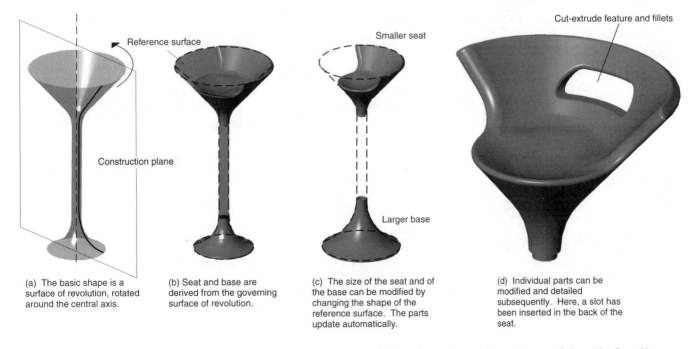

(a) The basic shape is a surface of revolution, rotated around the central axis.

(b) Seat and base are derived from the governing surface of revolution.

(c) The size of the seat and of the base can be modified by changing the shape of the reference surface. The parts update automatically.

(d) Individual parts can be modified and detailed subsequently. Here, a slot has been inserted in the back of the seat.

Figure 12-8 Mixed approach to top-down and bottom-up design strategies. Here the basic design idea was the conelike overall shape. This flowerlike shape was initially modeled in a part file, then inserted into an assembly model in which all separate parts—foot, stem, and seat—were then modeled. Since all dependent parts derive their external shape from the initial part shape, any changes of this master model propagate into the individual part files (top-down approach). The individual parts can then be refined in the part files by adding individual features such as the slot in the backrest of the seat.

to be suppressed, broken, or redefined. Redefining associations such that a top-down approach is reversed into a bottom-up approach, however, is usually not possible without major reworking of the digital model.

Collaboration between the design office and engineers, consultants, or contractors can be structured in the manner of top-down approaches as previously described. As the design office supplies the reference geometry that everybody else works from, the individual models only update to a change in the master geometry if all reference elements remain in the reference model. This approach is likely to be successful only if employed during design phases with changes limited to small adjustments in shape or properties. It only works if the participating offices employ the same application, since data exchange via neutral file formats normally does not allow the internal structure of a feature-based model to be transferred in any way that would be useful for another design development environment. (See Figure 12-9.)

12.3 INFORMATION EXCHANGE BETWEEN STAND-ALONE APPLICATIONS

Exchanging information among different project participants is a constant and common need—and so are

the problems associated with this basic task. The multitude of digital design, analysis, and management tools normally used on a project clearly reflect on the fragmented nature of the building industry. To a lesser extent the same can be said about product design. Current design processes rely predominantly on *stand-alone tools* that store information in proprietary file formats. These tools are widely employed by design professionals; they are optimized for a certain task, such as rendering, 2-D drafting, or animation. The conversion of proprietary file formats into neutral file exchange formats through built-in processors enables the data exchange between these stand-alone systems.

The need to review the design for consistency is constantly present, since the design process essentially replicates a traditional paper-based approach. Web-based systems have been devised to manage the design process more effectively, and to do so also for geographically dispersed participants.

Data Exchange Formats

The need for neutral file exchange formats originates in the fact that design environments from different vendors structure their application domain programs in different ways and use different internal representations for the entities they create. File exchange formats

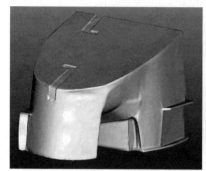
Digital model from scanned physical model

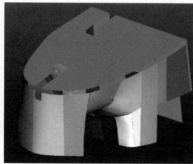
3-D model with subdivision into prefabricated panels

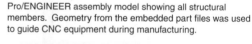
Pro/ENGINEER assembly model showing all structural members. Geometry from the embedded part files was used to guide CNC equipment during manufacturing.

The façade is an assembly of stressed-skin panels that were prefabricated, including the waterproofing

The guest house near completion in the summer of 2002

Figure 12-9 Top-down modeling approach at architect Steven Holl's "Turbulence House," a guesthouse for artist R. Tuttle. The physical model provided by Holl's office was scanned and served as the master geometry for A. Zahner Company to develop the parametric assembly model in Pro/ENGINEER. (Source: Image courtesy of A. Zahner Company, used by permission)

are generally entity-based and support elements such as lines, arcs, surfaces, or solids. Some also support nongeometric information, tables of data (attributes and properties), or annotations. Any data exchange based on neutral formats typically requires several steps. The first step is that of preprocessing—data to be exchanged must be converted to one of these neutral formats. Preprocessed data is next written to a file. It is then read by the receiving system. The last step is post-processing—converting or mapping the data from the neutral format into a form readable by the application program. These are largely offline procedures. The neutral file exchange thus facilitates the sharing of data, but application programs remain largely independent of one another.

One of the most commonly used formats is Autodesk's proprietary *Drawing Interchange Format* (DXF) format, the de facto standard exchange of data from entity-based drafting programs. DXF files can be binary files, but most are standard ASCII text files. They support line entities, surfaces, solids, and text, but cannot contain NURBS. DXF files are structured into tables of entity groups that can include additional information such as line type, layer, model coordinate system, blocks, and more. Some design development environments allow users to import 2-D DXF files, parametrically dimension them, and use them like native drawing entities. This is particularly useful if professionals choose to work with a mix of entity-based drafting programs and design development environments. Exporting DXF files from the latter programs is often possible from the 2-D files that are used to produce paper documents.

The *Initial Graphics Exchange Specification* (IGES) is another ASCII text-based file exchange format—essentially a set of protocols for the display and transfer of graphic documents between different computer-aided design systems. Intended as a neutral format not specifically associated with any vendor system, it was adopted as a U.S. national standard in 1981 and is widely used and supported by most major CAD software systems. IGES files mainly consist of entity-based sets of tables with corresponding protocols. Entities, the fundamental data units of the file, comprise geometry as well as nongeometric entities. Geometry includes points, curves, lines, surfaces, and solids; nongeometry includes information on viewing perspectives for planar drawings, dimensions, annotations, attributes, and others. All entities are divided into sections that are classified by numbers: 100 is a circular arc, 110 is a line, 120 is a surface of revolution, 126 is a rational B-spline curve, 222 is a radius dimension, and so forth. Extended standards allow transfer of NURB surfaces and restricted patches. Files are made up of lines of specified character lengths and specific delimiters. The protocols are essentially descriptions of the relation between the entities. IGES files support a larger range of entities than DXF files and are commonly used, for example, in transferring 3-D geometry from CAD systems to CAM modules. Sophisticated design development environments normally offer the option of configuring the file in ways that allow it to be imported into the envisaged application program without errors such as surface gaps.

Another increasingly used file format is *stereolithography* (STL)—ASCII or binary text files used for special purposes such as data transfer to free-form fabrication machines. STL files, also known as *Standard Triangulation Language,* must be written from solid models and involve the triangulation of a solid's faces (see Figure 12-10). Each triangle is described by its three end coordinates and by a vector that is oriented away from the original solid—therefore allowing the machine processor to recognize the inside and outside of a part. STL files can also be used to import geometry data from a modeling domain into other software applications such as computational fluid dynamics programs. Users can often define the resolution of the STL file—for curved shapes, increasing the number of triangles improves accuracy but leads to larger files.

While data exchange via these and other formats is an integral and invaluable part of today's digital design and analysis world, its inherent limitation is due to exchange formats primarily taking a "lower common denominator" approach to standardization and data formats. Typically, they reduce the information contained in the model to be exported to a basic set of stan-

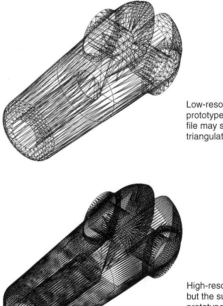

Low-resolution file: a rapid prototype generated from this file may show visible triangulation of the surface.

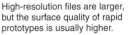

High-resolution files are larger, but the surface quality of rapid prototypes is usually higher.

Figure 12-10 STL file of the steel connector shown in Figure 11-13.

dardized descriptions or entities that may not have the richness of the original model. When importing a parametric model from one design development environment into another one, users are likely to lose vital information such as the hierarchy of features, parent-child relationships, or constraints—in short, the powerful associations between portions of the model. The imported shapes remain static, cannot be edited, and serve merely as reference objects. Support is typically quite good for simple geometric entities but can be more erratic as geometric entities get more and more complex. Some software environments have idiosyncratic characteristics that prevent good data exchange using IGES files. This has even led to a small industry that develops specialized file translators for specific vendor environments.

Product Modeling

As many companies are operating internationally, the need to move from national to international standards has become increasingly pressing. The most significant development in this area has been the emerging STEP standard. To the user, STEP seems just like another file format, and indeed it can be used in that way. There are, however, important conceptual differences in what STEP files compared to IGES or DXF files are meant to accomplish. STEP stands for Standard for the Exchange of Product Model Data, pointing thus to the underlying notion of *product modeling* as the natural extension and evolution of thinking about data exchange formats. Product modeling comprises the geometric information on designed objects, their attributes, and their relations, but it is structured to support data exchange throughout the life cycle of the product. Thus, STEP files may include data for design, analysis, manufacture, and product data management, including information on design versions, tolerances, materials, finishes, quality control, and others. They communicate the design intent as well as the proposed solution. (See Figure 12-11.)

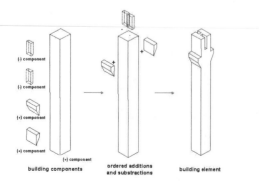

Figure 12-11 Definition of a precast concrete column using application protocol 225 (Source: Haas + Partner Engineering)

The formal designation of STEP is ISO 10303 "Product Data Representation and Exchange." Following the approach of describing products from initial development to the end of a product's life, STEP is based on a standardized data model, capable of describing core product data in a way that is usable for different applications. The basic components of STEP are the object-oriented data modeling language EXPRESS—a description of implementation methods involving an application programming interface—the integrated resources, and the application protocols.

Integrated resources are the abstract logical units of data (*parts*) that contain the actual data about the product. *Generic resources* are those commonly found in a wide range of applications and include general definitions such as geometry, material, or tolerances. Part 501, for example, is an "Edge-based Wireframe"; part 45 is "Materials." *Application-specific* resources are those more specifically used by specialized applications such as structural analysis or process planning. These resources—entities, their attributes, and their relationships, all described in the programming language EXPRESS—are organized according to the underlying product model and not to suit particular application software.

All CAD systems and other software organize data internally in a way that best suits the algorithms in support of a particular application (e.g., rendering, thermal analysis, parametric modeling). For an application to process the generic STEP parts, *application protocols* organize the product data into the application-specific data views. The wide range of available application protocols—with new protocols being developed as new applications require different data views—covers general areas such as "Explicit Drafting" through to specific applications like "Building Services: HVAC." A new application protocol, AP 238, at the writing of this text under development and testing, enables users to embed instructions for CNC machines in a STEP file, thus potentially streamlining the design to production process further.

Some design development environments allow users to select a specific application protocol when converting data into STEP files. The choice of application protocols may impact what data a user can expect to transfer. Not all application protocols for geometric representations support colors or layers—elements that clearly play an important role in many design settings.

Building models are currently defined in AP 225 "Building Elements Using Explicit Shape Representations." This protocol includes the 3-D shapes of building elements and their spatial relations, along with properties such as materials, cost, and order of assembly or as-built configuration. On generating the initial model in a CAD system, the STEP file processed with AP 225 can transfer rich building data to applications of engineers, consultants, quantity surveyors, construction managers, or contractors. Structural elements can be easily isolated to simplify the analysis by the structural engineer. Three-dimensional building elements, for example, are recognizable in HVAC design software, and collisions between ducts or pipes and building elements can be detected without having to re-create the 3-D building model. The same model can eventually be used to support computer-aided facility management applications that control interior climate, security, maintenance, or occupancy.

Major software vendors—including those specifically addressing the needs of architectural design, government agencies, and large companies in the automotive, marine, and aerospace industry—are presently implementing STEP. Many design development environments include the option of importing and exporting a part or assembly model as a STEP file. The possible impact on the building industry and product design remains unclear, even though the need for better mechanisms of data exchange is undisputed. Connecting project team members with their stand-alone applications in seamless ways is vital if advanced digital design techniques are to enhance productivity and quality. Rich data exchange with STEP, however, can only be one aspect of a more collaborative digital design process. STEP does not address the need to manage the design process, neither can it propose a solution to overcome the increasing need for efficient collaboration between geographically dispersed design teams.

Web-Based Process Management: Extranets

The worldwide acceptance of open (nonproprietary) Internet standards such as file transfer protocols (TCP/IP), server protocols (HTTP), and a markup language (HTML) has strongly affected business operations and structures alike. In early years, noting that many internal information and communication needs could be addressed with Web technology, many firms began to look to the Internet as a means of streamlining information exchange within one company. This desire led to the development of *intranets,* company-internal networks based on Web servers and Web browsers for sharing information. These systems are still widely used in corporate settings. Subsequent needs to link both internal and external users led to more complex systems called *extranets.* Typically, extranets are used to allow suppliers, customers, or collaborating consultants to gain access to selected information from the project database. Extranets in the design professions have found limited acceptance as communication platforms between the individual stand-alone applications of designers, engineers, owners, contractors, and manufacturers. They are also available directly from CAD vendors, with a supposedly more seamless integration

into the CAD system's proprietary structure and file format, albeit sometimes at the expense of integrating system-external participants.

At the core of these Web-based systems is the *document database* that stores and archives all information (e.g., digital models, drawings, images, specifications, letters, schedules, etc.) relating to the project on a central database server. (See Figure 12-12.) Once users are authorized by the system through their usernames and passwords, they can read, edit, download, and upload information according to the level of access assigned to them by the project manager. The user interface allows the project participants several modes of asynchronous and synchronous communication. *Document conferencing* enables multiple participants to collaborate on the representation of the same document, normally a drawing or a sketch, sometimes a 3-D model. It involves running one computer application with shared controls and enables the synchronous markup and redlining of CAD drawings, often in combination with integrated videoconferencing and project-specific chat functions. These tools rely on specific data views of CAD data, and it is here that issues of compatibility of different stand-alone CAD systems and platforms can be problematic, since viewing tools often rely on a limited number of supported file formats. *Discussion databases* are invariably present in Web-based extranets. Here users can read and post messages on a topic of discussion; these messages are displayed in a threaded manner, visualizing thus who responded when and how. Systems also typically have applications that manage *workflow*—standardized and sequential organizational tasks such as the writing and review of meeting minutes, issuing a request for proposal, or the routing of documents according to predefined review and approval steps. Notification of current tasks keeps team members informed of project activities and deadlines. Since documents with the same name are inevitably edited during the process, various *auditing* procedures document a file's creation and authorship, and keep track of modifications.

Security issues are invariably concerned. While file security in the database depends partly on whether a Web-based collaborative environment is hosted by an independent third-party vendor or is actually custom-created within a specific, mostly corporate setting, file transfer security is an issue of Internet protocols and encryption features.

Extranets for stand-alone systems address the need to manage the design process, and research shows some positive effects on productivity, especially when participants are located at great distances from each other. The limitations of data exchange using neutral file exchange formats, however, do not yet allow for the kinds of collaborative processes that can be achieved with the integrated approaches described next.

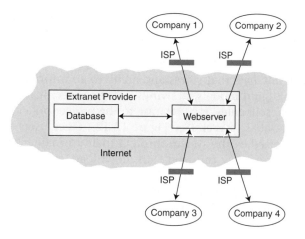

Figure 12-12 Users of an extranet connect to the application through their Internet Service Providers (ISP)

12.4 INTEGRATED DIGITAL DESIGN SYSTEMS: PROCESS MANAGEMENT AND COLLABORATION

The integration of different applications within an overall system has long been practiced in larger corporations, especially in the automotive and the aerospace industries. These turnkey systems offer almost everything a company needs to conceptually design, develop, analyze, and manufacture a product. They are used in many manufacturing companies where most design and engineering work is done in-house. Large corporations may outsource much of their design work, but their market power enables them to require that any collaborating company simply has to employ the same digital environment. This is indicative of one of the major drawbacks of integrated systems—they again rely on proprietary data models and file standards, and usually communicate with other systems through the same neutral file exchange formats described earlier. For this reason they are also commonly referred to as *closed integrated systems.*

This proprietary approach to integration was only much later adopted by software vendors that cater specifically to the building industry. The fragmentation of the building industry does not easily allow the transfer of business models that facilitate the implementation of integrated solutions. But as the international effort to define a common product-modeling standard (STEP) only proceeded rather slowly, some software vendors began to address the need for more seamless integration between the different design disciplines and participants. These integrated, closed systems may not support the range of applications users of design development environments find themselves with, but they do usually integrate design and design management in a more or less seamless manner. In most cases these solutions have evolved from a stand-alone CAD program into this broader support of the architectural design process.

Product Data Management Systems

Digitally speaking, design is essentially the creation and modification of data. During the development of a project, a parametric model can easily undergo hundreds of iterations, many of which will impact engineering, production, and marketing as well. The need to manage this complex process is addressed by product data management (PDM) systems. These are available as stand-alone tools and connect to multiple individual applications, but frequently they are modules of integrated design environments that are geared toward support of design development activities. A central database server stores and manages the information that authorized users access typically through a company's intranet or, for company-external users, by using a virtual private network (VPN—a connection over the public Internet that ensures security through encryption and protocol techniques). Most PDM systems broadly deal with data management and process management.

Data management is the organization of all project data, such as digital part and assembly models, text documents, related communication, schedules, etc. To be accessible, the system must allow for this data to be classified in a way that is suitable for a particular company and project. Attributes of parts and assemblies can be individually defined; some systems can include optional attributes that represent model configurations (see Chapter 11). Data classification—for example, by document type, by project, by author—combined with query techniques allow the database to be searched. It should be easy to retrieve all documents regarding a specific part, or limit the search to data that was created within a certain time frame or by certain authors. Data can also be retrieved by product structure, usually the bill of materials (bill of quantities in architecture) for a project or component. Specialists, for example, structural engineers, can see project-related data according to their particular interests, displaying, for example, all data that relates to structural issues throughout the project.

When a participant downloads a document or digital model from the server, a copy is created that then can be modified locally. Once the data is again uploaded to the secure vault of the server, it is digitally signed, dated, and stored along with the old version. Users can retrieve a previous version at any time (*work history management*).

The organization and storing of data is the basis for *process management,* the control of how people create and modify data. Process management includes *work management* and *workflow management.* Work management functions grant privileges for creation, editing, and viewing of data, ensuring that only one person can modify a document or digital model at the time, while others may be able to view it but not edit. Sophisticated systems notify viewing users that a more recent version of an open document is available as a newer version of the same document is released to the server.

Everybody should be working with the latest information and coordinate their work in order to create a meaningful design. Someone working on a detailed component design must be aware of changes to the assembly made elsewhere in the team, because these changes may immediately impact design decisions. Viewing of related files and notification of updates are essential. A useful feature for such workflow management functions is the grouping of related data into *packets*. Authorized individuals can monitor design processes easily by checking out packets—for example, all data relating to the power train assembly of a vehicle. This procedure facilitates workflow management because logical and complete groups of data easily can be moved between individuals or departments. Various status controls are normally employed to signal the status of a design, ranging from "initiated" to "checked" and "released." Sophisticated PDM systems, especially those integrated into high-end design development environments, for example, can prevent individuals from releasing an assembly model unless all parts have been released individually.

PDM systems are crucial in concurrent design efforts of larger team, and are extensively employed in manufacturing companies, especially when the team is seeking conformance with international quality management standards (ISO 9000 and others). Related systems are knowledge bases that capture specific know-how and make it available through the PDM database to authorized users.

Integrated Systems for the Building Industry

At the core of many integrated architectural systems is normally a *component-based CAD* system (see Chapter 10) that may or may not be a discipline-specific version of a more generic design environment. Specific modules may then address the needs of conceptual design (sketch tools), the incorporation of digital building surveys, the design of mechanical systems, or structural analysis. Other possible modules include bill of quantity tools, cost estimation and control, scheduling and site management, as well as steel detailing software (see Chapter 6). More advanced systems also offer facility management modules.

The underlying concept of *building information modeling* (BIM) is closely related to the notion of product modeling and STEP, with the major difference being that each software vendor tends to define a proprietary product structure and semantic description of the design instead of relying on international standards. Since these systems inevitably rely on proprietary file formats, they normally communicate with external systems through neutral file exchange formats. Collaborating users of the same proprietary system can usually expect the transfer of comprehensive building information, thus geometry, attributes, and other properties. Definitions of structural elements, for example, columns and beams, should ideally transfer between the CAD environment and the structural analysis module, but they do not always do so successfully. Many application modules were initially designed as standalone software, and changes in the design model do not always propagate to the model used by other applications. To avoid input errors, some structural analysis applications allow users to open the architectural drawings or models and use them as a reference to define an independent model of the structural system. A closer integration is usually achieved with tools for bills of quantities and cost estimation. These recognize the 3-D objects such as walls, doors, or suspended ceilings in their calculation of quantities.

The often-limited associations between individual application models and the underlying CAD system imply a persistent need for managing the design process. Management modules are normally available that support this task. They usually include a range of functions similar to those encountered in product data management systems, albeit usually not at the same level of sophistication. All data is stored on a central server, sometimes supplemented by local servers to provide storage space for local workgroups. Up- and downloading of files may be possible from within the LAN or through a secure Internet connection (virtual private network).

Integrated Design Development Systems

Compared to the current status of integrated architectural design environments, users can generally expect a more complete level of integration from high-end design development environments, albeit at inevitably much higher cost. Major systems such as CATIA, Pro/ENGINEER, and SolidWorks fully relate application-specific modeling functions to the design model. On updating parts and assemblies, these changes propagate through all associated applications. Each application generates the individual representation or view model of the same base data that either is stored locally or, in the case of a network-based system, is accessible through a server/client setup from a central server. As mentioned before, finite-element analysis modules are among those typically encountered in integrated systems; other analysis tools may include motion analysis or CFD analysis. Manufacturing-related tools include mold creation and mold-flow analysis, sheet-metal tools and sheet-forming analysis, piping tools, and modules to generate toolpaths for CNC machines. Production-related tools enable the simulation and analysis of production sequences and procedures.

Larger firms inevitably manage the complex design processes with a product data management system that can be integral part of the digital design environment. A seemingly obvious extension of PDM systems is to enhance corporate knowledge and expertise by capturing the knowledge of the many daily design decisions taken by individuals or teams that might work for the same company but do not necessarily interact. The information can include general documents, project management techniques, team organization, notes of experience, solutions to specific problems, and so forth. Knowledge-based networks seek to organize this kind of information from all individuals and teams in a way that becomes accessible to everyone else who is authorized to access the searchable records in the database.

Concurrent Design and Engineering, Virtual Prototyping, and Other Approaches

It is the nature of design—be it architectural or product design—that multiple design and performance aspects of a project need to be considered simultaneously. Several individuals or groups with specialized expertise usually develop a project at the same time, and larger design tasks are subdivided into manageable related portions that are worked on simultaneously. The need for these design activities to occur in a controlled way—*concurrent engineering or design*—is shared by most industries. In product design, for example, the concurrent design requires the consideration of all elements in the product's life cycle, thus from conceptual ideas to manufacturing and marketing to disposal. The general objective of concurrent design and engineering is accelerated development, reduced time to market, and quality improvement.

On a simple level, concurrent design efforts can be enabled by digitally marking certain portions of a project for certain teams or individuals, excluding access for others except for viewing purposes. The latest version of the base model is downloaded from a server, and the central database registers this particular data as currently locked to the particular user. These reservations of work zones can be allocated for various time windows, ranging from hours to the duration of the project. Functions of this type are possible through PDM systems, as well as for team-working platforms available for entity- and component-based CAD systems.

More sophisticated approaches to concurrent engineering are online environments that allow geographically dispersed users to collaborate simultaneously using a secure Internet connection. A large variety of viewing and redline tools are available and, as previously outlined, may be part of an extranet. High-end design development environments allow multiple users

to view, mark up, and even modify digital part and assembly models. These concurrent design platforms usually enable large model files to be compressed using streaming techniques. Parametric assemblies are evaluated in 3-D views; they can be rotated, exploded, or shown in section views. Some systems allow for assembly motions to be simulated, enable users to "fly through" complex areas of the design, conduct interference and collision tests in real time, and study human-centered design issues such as operability or reachability. These activities, also referred to as virtual mock-ups or virtual prototyping, are commonly used in product design or manufacturing companies, especially by those that deal with complex products such as vehicles or airplanes.

Virtual reality (VR) and *augmented reality* (AR) environments are at the high end of concurrent design and visualization techniques (see Figure 12-13). These interactive technologies permit users to virtually experience a 3-D digital model assembly and to conduct real-time studies of complex designs. VR environments usually require a dedicated cubicle with stereoscopic back-projection systems onto at least three walls and the floor. Users inside these cubes wear stereo shutter glasses to perceive true 3-D images; they navigate the virtual space using head and hand position track devices. VR environments rely on high-end computing power that is currently only available in relatively few dedicated research facilities. This technology has found extensive use in the automotive and the aerospace industries. Here, VR has partially replaced the traditional physical prototypes used to verify decisions during design development. Architectural applications include the visualization of airflow for urban design projects and other complex 3-D visualization tasks. With the rapidly falling price of computing power, VR can be expected to become more broadly accessible for design professionals in the future.

AR technology is a related concept, albeit comparatively simpler. Its objective is to overlay a virtual 3-D image over a real physical object. Users wear a *head-mounted display* (HMD) with a stereoscopic video camera attached to it. The camera captures the physical object, which is then displayed in the HMD blended into the virtual model. AR environments are being developed for use with standard desktop computers and could be usable for design professionals within a relatively short time. Networked versions, whereby several users experience the same AR model, can enable collaborative design using 3-D technology.

A different area of interest in this context is the development and emerging use of haptic devices for input of data in digital modeling. Extensively used by the animation industry, these are instruments that react to the 3-D movement of a stylus by the user. When the user moves the stylus such that the digital

Figure 12-13 Augmented Reality and Virtual Reality: The head mounted display (upper left) enables users to see a virtual model overlaid onto a physical model (lower left). Markers in the physical model (middle left) provide reference points to align physical and digital model. The same combination of models can be experienced in a remotely located CAVE in real-time. (Source: High Performance Computing Center Stuttgart (HLRS) / FH Wiesbaden)

tool touches a surface or the face of a solid in the digital model, the device translates this encounter into a force feedback of the stylus: Users "feel" the digital model in addition to merely seeing it in the display. Various modifications to the digital model can be carried out that resemble traditional sculpting techniques. Portions of the model can be removed by drilling, chiseling, or other operations borrowed from the physical world. The models are generally solid models that can be exported to and imported from other applications using neutral file exchange formats. A current limitation is the relative lack of dimensional control. Similar systems are used for the remote control of machines and robotic devices.

Open Integrated Systems—Emerging Approaches

Vendor-specific integrated systems clearly share the disadvantage that seamless integration, if at all, exists only within these closed, proprietary environments. A need for *open integrated systems* is identifiable. Several concepts are being explored, some based on Internet-related technology, others investigating new approaches to the use of networks and client/server constellations. The emerging world of open integrated systems and distributed computing is still faced with multiple unresolved issues, many of which are currently being addressed by

researchers in several development communities. While thorny problems still exist, and will undoubtedly continue to exist, the evidence is such that the promise of robust distributed computing capable of supporting design and production applications may well be fulfilled in the near future.

VRML

An Internet-related technology is the Virtual Reality Modeling Language (VRML), an open standard markup language primarily designed to graphically represent 3-D objects in Web browsers. Ongoing research for building related applications explores the use of VRML to represent construction elements in an objectlike way. Such objects can encapsulate details about how they are to be implemented—such as how a steel beam is oriented and connected to a column or an adjacent beam. VRML technology is particularly suitable to create 3-D models dynamically on Web sites. It potentially allows for more interactive teamwork in synchronous viewing and collaboration environments, such as the simulation of dynamic assembly and construction processes, and the incorporation of real-time collision detection. Experiments with VRML as a visual control interface for robotics are suggesting future areas of study. VRML can also visualize STEP files directly, and potentially plays a role in the communication between STEP conforming stand-alone applications.

Distributed-Object Technologies

The standards of distributed-object technologies are promoted and developed by the Object Management Group (OMG), a vendor-independent group founded in 1989. Distributed-object technologies create networks of computers whereby a computer can represent a client for one request and can act like a server for the request of another computer. The notion of centralized data servers is replaced by distributed computing in a cross-platform network. *Middleware* programs are needed to enable the communication between participating computers and applications that were not originally designed to exchange data with each other. The key enabling technology of OMG's standard for distributed-object technologies is a platform-independent data model created with the Unified Modeling Language (UML). This generic core model communicates through platform-specific modules with middleware software such as OMG's own CORBA (Common Object Request Broker) and vendor-specific ones (Microsoft's .NET or Sun's ONE). Through the middleware, data objects can be exchanged across platforms, enabling a distributed network of communicating computers.

XML and Java

Another approach to open systems is the combination of Java, an object-oriented programming language with particular capabilities for Web-related applications, and the *Extensible Markup Language* (XML), a machine- and human-readable markup language. Again, the underlying idea is to facilitate the communication of stand-alone applications over the Internet. Java (originally developed by Sun Microsystems) enables software to run on any computer equipped with a Java interpreter. This concept makes it possible to write software once and use it with all Java-compatible applications, such as standard Web browsers (with built-in Java applets) and Java-based stand-alone applications.

As an object-oriented programming language, Java enables programmers to represent complex data structures and object-oriented models. XML, on the other hand, is well suited to represent such hierarchical data. Both XML and HTML are electronic tagging languages. HTML uses predefined tags to define how content is displayed in Web pages, whereas XML allows users to define individual tags and attributes to describe content. It does not contain instructions on how this data is displayed, but it allows for the nested document structures indispensable in an object-oriented approach to data modeling. Mapping techniques have been developed that enable STEP files to be easily represented using XML. It is conceivable that commonly used objects in architectural design and construction could be exchanged between different platforms using XML, and that different applications communicate over the Internet. The combination of both Java and XML is considered by many to be a core part of future developments in Web-based distributed computing.

PART V

THE PRODUCTION ENVIRONMENT

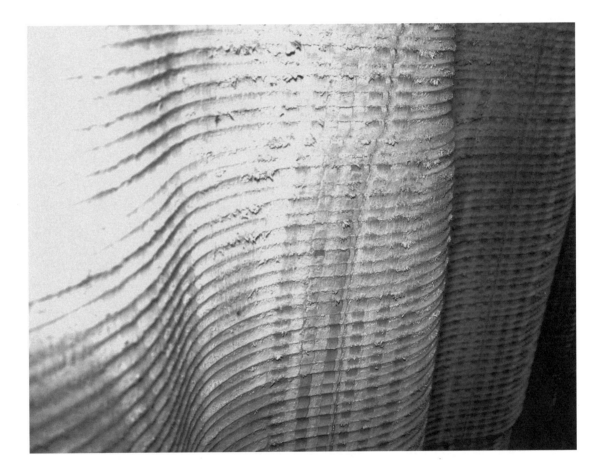

The initial chapter in this part gives an introduction to computer numerical control technologies (CNC). The following chapter provides a broad summary of primary manufacturing processes used in relation to CAD/CAM technologies. Subsequent chapters look at issues such as prototyping and designing in light of manufacturing and production considerations.

Computer Numerical Control (CNC) Technologies

13.1 THE MACHINE ENVIRONMENT

In Chapter 1 the historical, conceptual, and technological elements leading to the development of computer numerical control (CNC) technologies were examined. Some changes to the design of machine tools as well as the use of punched paper cards and tapes to control a variety of mechanisms via numerical control (NC) set the stage for the emancipation of universal machine tools from direct, hands-on control.

While the development of servomechanism control and a standardized numerical control language made possible the initial development of NC machine tools, parallel developments in digital computer technologies during the 1950s established the basis for the CNC technologies used today worldwide in virtually every field of production. Since that time developments in actuator design, control software, and digital visualization tools have allowed the applications of CNC technologies to expand, while their cost has been dramatically reduced (see Figure 13-1).

This chapter outlines the major characteristics of CNC technologies. The first part of the chapter outlines some general characteristics of CNC as it applies to machines that make things. The second part of the chapter quickly examines the nature of numerically controlled machines—how they work and why (this is found in greater detail in Chapter 14). The third part of the chapter looks at how CNC programs actually work—the basics of how machines can be instructed to do things using simple numeric instructions. The final part of the chapter gives a broad introduction to how the increasingly broad spectrum of computer-aided design and manufacturing activities are brought to bear on some specific manufacturing applications, from drawing to production.

Chapters 14 and 15 look more closely at the specifics of some manufacturing processes and applications that use CNC technologies, as well as how they are being used in the design and manufacture of components, from the prototype stages through low- and high-volume production.

13.2 GENERAL CHARACTERISTICS OF COMPUTER NUMERICAL CONTROL

Numerical control technologies allow automated equipment to be controlled and operated in real time through the use of a symbolic language—another way of saying machines can be told what to do at any time (and at any speed) by using numbers and letters (or holes or bits that represent those letters and numbers) arranged in a regular way. The information may be contained on a punch card, a continuous paper or mylar tape, a magnetic thread, a tape or cassette, or any of the many computer storage devices available today. The now relatively old concept of NC, coupled with computers to produce CNC, is at the heart of today's robust computer-aided manufacturing industries, as well as robotic manufacturing and a host of other enterprises. Drawings are plotted, shirts and hats are embroidered, commercial signage is cut, memorial stones are lettered, automobiles are produced, and the chair you are sitting in may have been assembled using CNC technologies.

The first machine tool equipped with NC control was a large universal milling machine with three axes of movement originally designed for hands-on control using hand wheels (see Chapter 2). It was very large, but in most other ways it was similar to milling machines around the world in shops large and small. Numerical control of the machine was made possible by substituting servomechanisms in place of hands to turn the screws controlling motion along x, y, and z axes. The servomechanisms were accompanied by an array of electromechanical devices that fed back the position and the acceleration of the work as it moved so that it could be "controlled" by the motors in a predictable, repeatable manner. The instructions were given via a paper tape, punched with holes representing letters and numbers. The tape was read by the "Director," a processor that read the instructions and turned them into electrical impulses directing the motors that drove the three axes individually (see Figure 13-2). In retrospect, the idea seems as simple as pie, but there were substantial obstacles to overcome.

Instructions for the Director had to be typed by hand—without mistakes. This alone was a forbidding

Figure 13-1 CAD/CAM technologies are used worldwide to produce work at all scales in virtually all materials. Examples here include a bronze cathedral door in Los Angeles, cast from a wax original that was machined on a large milling machine; lettering in stone created by sandblasting through a rubber mat cut by a CNC knife cutter; a wood component being cut with a CNC three-axis router; lost-wax and die-cast metal components; sheet-metal cladding systems; wood cabinetry parts; and milled complex shapes in foam for laying up composite materials.

task. The information to be typed was first taken from drawings and physical models by direct hand-measuring—another forbidding and time-consuming task. Once appropriate calculations had been performed and results tabulated, small, incremental movements in the *x, y,* and *z* axes were typed onto the tape, one at a time, describing the entire shape to be milled out of solid material. Programming and tape preparation took significantly longer than the actual machining so that, without the development of substantial computing resources, today it is hard to imagine NC having much of an impact outside highly specialized markets. The mind-numbing, time-intensive task of determining numerical values to represent any reasonably complex shape would make the technology inappropriate for anyone other than producers of extremely expensive or very high volume goods.

Of course, substantial computing power is not an issue today. We can also rely on sophisticated CAD programs that were not in existence at the dawn of numerical control to define complex shapes and keep track of all of the parameters of those shapes without our having to know what they are. But to understand computer numerical control today, it is important to remember that it was developed during the early years of computer technology, and continues to exhibit many characteristics made necessary by the limitations of technologies used during those early years.

CNC tools can be more accurate, faster, and lower-cost to run than conventional tools controlled by hand, although any good machinist knows this is not always the case. They can produce work more uniformly and with greater versatility. CNC tools may also look quite different than their conventional counterparts, and with increasing frequency, conventional counterparts simply don't exist as tools as such, as lasers, electric discharge machines, shape-cutting machines, water jets,

and electron beam welders were not conceivable without computer numerical control. (See Figure 13-3.)

Some basic shared characteristics of CNC technologies include the following:

- The preparation of instructions describing the work to be done in a digital format
- Reading those instructions via a controller, which "decodes" the instructions to convert them from a digital format to a stream of electrical impulses
- The machine tools themselves

Another shared characteristic of many CNC technologies are the languages used to describe work to be done. When Automatically Programmed Tools (APT) language was developed for NC in 1959 (and announced by MIT in 1962), the context was one in which hand labor, calculation, and other time-consuming concerns naturally led the designers of the language toward an efficient, simple, easily modified set of basic instructions. When many of the same concerns were later addressed during the development of G-Code for CNC tools, the concern was perhaps less about hand labor and more about computer processing ability and the cost of storing additional bits of data at a time when processing time was slow and data storage was very expensive. In both cases, there was good reason to find a way to describe three-dimensional things that needed to be made with as few keystrokes as possible. The same could be said for the later development of Hewlett-Packard Graphics Language (HPGL), an efficient language for controlling plotters that has been applied to many tools within the CAD/CAM world, such as laser cutters, water-jet cutters, plasma cutters, routers, vinyl cutters, and the like.

These shared characteristics are well understood. In addition, while under constant incremental improve-

ram, saw blade, etc.), and some method to affect the movement to actually do useful work such as a handle, lever, actuator, or feed mechanism. CNC machine tools incorporate all of those features, as well as motors or other actuators to control the movement devices, a controller (also called a machine control unit, or MCU) to direct the motors, and a computer to send instructions to the controller. Two types of motors are generally used: stepper motors (usually with open-loop systems) and servo motors (with closed-loop systems). See Figure 13-4.

It may be useful to place CNC machines or tools into general categories, based on shapes and processes, to describe their general characteristics—despite the many exceptions and special cases such categorization will

Figure 13-2 Section of a typical numerical control paper tape, with reader.

ment, they are stable enough so that the manufacturing world is able to match a complex part made in one environment with another part made halfway around the globe with allowable tolerances as low as zero. This is done simply by using the same geometric model from which to prepare instructions for CNC tools.

13.3 GENERAL MACHINE TYPES

Computer numerically controlled machines and tools include a bewildering array of varieties and shapes. Many CNC tools are virtually identical to manual or automatic predecessors, with a few added components. Other tools are similar without appearing to be so, while others bear little or no resemblance to tools previously designed or built.

A "conventional" machine tool might incorporate a base or chassis, a power source, mechanisms to cause movement in directions necessary to perform work, the actual tool itself (a drill bit, milling cutter,

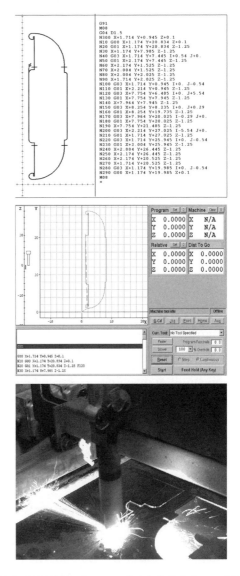

Figure 13-3 CAD/CAM software producing G-Code from a 2-D drawing (top), the controller interface showing the shape to be cut and tool positioning information (center), and the plasma cutter cutting the actual shape from steel (bottom).

Computer with Controller, adjacent to plasma cutting table

Plasma cutting tool

Stepper motor assembly

Figure 13-4 A conventional CNC plasma cutter showing the components typical for CAD/CAM machine tools, including the computer, controller, and the tool itself.

produce. The next chapter provides a fuller understanding of the true capabilities of these tools.

Shapes

For designers, these categories might be determined by the shapes able to be produced by families of tools. For example, many CNC tools are designed to make flat, outline shapes to be used directly, such as for glass, metal, or wood panels. Traditionally based tools such as saws, routers, milling machines, oxyacetylene cutting torches, and plasma cutters produce such work, as do newer technologies such as water jets and laser cutters. Many of these tools are designed to move primarily in the *x* and *y* axes, with limited control of the tool head in the *z* axis. (See Figure 13-5.)

Many flat shapes undergo further transformation into complex open forms such as boxes or embossed panels. Such transformation requires tools that can bend, fold, or deform using molds, punches and stamping dies, or bending tools. Wire, tube, and sheet-metal bending and punch tools with CNC controls are readily available for much of this work, although stamping dies themselves may have to first be made with CNC milling and grinding tools. Bending tools may have any number of heads to create simple 2-D bends of different radii or complex 3-D shapes to satisfy the demands of

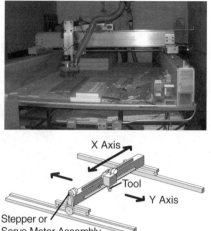

Figure 13-5 A three-axis CNC router, with limited vertical motion in the Z-axis, used primarily for work on flat sheet stock.

hydraulic engineers (tubing for aircraft, automotive or air conditioning, for example), structural engineers (individual reinforcing bars or entire mats), and anyone requiring wire or tubular parts and assemblies.

Shapes with complex solid geometries can be created using a variety of CNC tools. Milling machines (see Figure 13-6), machining centers, lathes, drills, routers, and grinding machines can work directly on real building materials by mechanically reducing large pieces of stock to smaller finished pieces. Electrical discharge machining (EDM) wire-cutting or sinking tools may also be used on electrically conductive materials to remove material. So-called free-form fabrication tools can build up solid models from 3-D digital models of pieces at actual size from plastic, wax, powder-based substances (including some metals), paper, and other materials, often for use in indirect manufacturing processes such as casting or mold making. This is a

Figure 13-6 A tabletop three-axis CNC milling machine, with roughly equal motion in all axes.

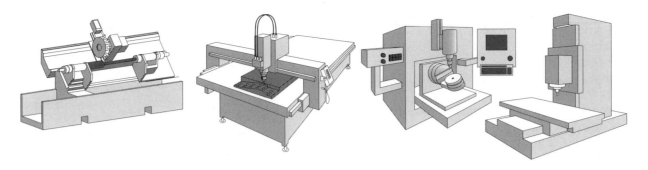

Figure 13-7 Typical CNC tools for material removal.

rapidly developing field that uses layering techniques to first divide solid digital models and to then reconstitute them by depositing material in layers.

Processes

Another way to think about the variety of CNC tools that exist is to divide the world of making things into three broad, process-based categories: machining or material removal processes; deformation, molding, and casting processes; and fabrication or additive processes. There is a good deal of overlap within these categories, especially as a great deal of casting and molding work requires that molds or waste pieces be produced using other processes first.

Machining or Material Removal

In this category material is removed from a piece of stock to produce a useful item. Milling or mechanical cutting, drilling, chipping, burning, grinding, punching, electrical, electrochemical or thermal removal, or any of a number of other methods may do this (see Figure 13-7). The basic idea is to conceive of a useful thing and to carve away all the material from a piece of stock until only that thing remains. The underlying material removal technologies are well understood—tables of cutting speeds, appropriate tool geometries, and their capabilities have been published for well over a hundred years, and they continue to be augmented with values for new cutting techniques. (See Figure 13-8.)

These values have been entered into databases within CAD/CAM software, making it a relatively simple matter to program machine tools to carve out even the most sculptural shapes from a variety of materials. The plethora of modern automobiles exhibiting closely fitted, curvaceous body panels, or the overwhelming variety of inexpensive home products with complex or curved shapes, offer direct evidence of these capabilities. The actual manner in which the milling or cutting takes place varies according to the design of the specific tool. In some cases the table to which the workpiece is mounted is stationary, while the tool itself moves in space via straight-line actuators, rotational movement,

or both at once to address different surfaces of the workpiece. Two-axis (sometimes called two-and-a-half-axis) tools such as laser cutters, knife cutters, some routers, water-jet cutters, and plasma cutters often work like a plotter, utilizing only two axes of movement along straight tracks to locate a tool in space. While the tool can cut through material to make flat 3-D shapes, there is limited or no actual movement of the tool in the z axis. Many of these tools are able to be controlled

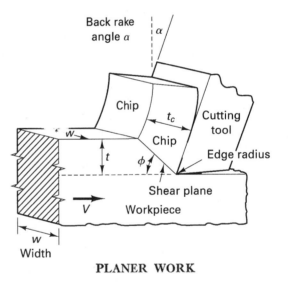

PLANER WORK

Planing Speeds and Feeds. The speeds for planing usually vary from 25 to 75 feet per minute on the cutting stroke, with a return speed two to three times as great. A general idea of planer speeds may be obtained from the following table, representing the practice in some of the best machine shops:

Cast iron (roughing)	40 to 50 ft. per minute
Cast iron (finishing)	30 to 40 ft. per minute
Cast steel (roughing)	40 to 45 ft. per minute
Cast steel (finishing)	30 to 40 ft. per minute
Wrought iron (roughing) . . .	30 to 45 ft. per minute
Wrought iron (finishing) . . .	20 to 25 ft. per minute
Bronze and brass (roughing and finishing)	50 to 75 ft. per minute
Machinery steel (roughing) . .	40 to 50 ft. per minute
Machinery steel (finishing) . .	30 to 40 ft. per minute

Figure 13-8 Typical early twentieth-century table and diagram illustrating cutting geometries and recommended feed rates and cutting speeds.

using Hewlett-Packard Graphics Language, a plotter control software that provides greater ease of use. Where a plotter will direct a pen to the "down" position in order to make a mark and the "up" position to move in space without making a mark, a cutting tool will interpret the same commands as instructions to raise and lower its knife, or to turn on and off its laser, plasma stream, or water jet.

A three-axis milling machine tool is perhaps the most common CNC machine tool, moving the work or the tool up and down in the *z* axis, while the work is carried in the *x* and *y* directions by a moving worktable (see Figure 13-9). At larger scales the worktable is often stationary while a carriage and a gantry move the tool in the *x* and *y* axes above the work. For shapes requiring that material be removed from different sides to deal with undercuts, for example, more axes of movement may be added to allow the tool itself to rotate out of the *z* axis. (See Figure 13-10.) Alternatively, the workpiece itself may be rotated manually or via an additional, CNC-controlled axis to address a new side (see Figure 13-11).

Other tools may operate differently—a lathe operates only along the *x* and *z* axes, for example as the rotation of the workpiece itself obviates the need for *y* axis control (see Figure 13-12). Milling centers may include aspects of both mills and lathes in order to produce complex shapes beyond the capabilities of standard milling machines or lathes alone (see Figure 13-13). Descriptions of specific aspects of these machines appear in the next chapter, but it is worth adding here that while the most obvious aspect of the numerical control of these tools is the automatic movement of tools or material to create work in response to defined geometries, the utility of the tools is greatly enhanced by features such as the ability to change tools in the middle of a job, turn cooling systems on and off, adjust the rotational speed of cutting tools, and run in either incremental or absolute spatial coordinates, all using the same controller software.

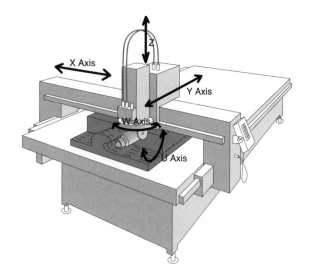

Figure 13-10 A five-axis gantry-type CNC router, showing major axes of movement.

Deformation, Molding, and Casting

These methods describe ways in which material can be cast directly into a mold as a liquid; pressed into a mold as a "plastic" material; deformed under pressure using dies, forming tools, or molds; or otherwise made into shapes different than that of the original material without directly removing or adding material. Many of these techniques originated in ancient times, and modern methods continue to exhibit characteristics of their earliest manifestations. Ancient sand-casting and lost-wax casting methods are used at the craft level and industrially to efficiently produce metal objects despite the development of other methods. Forging, bending, and drawing, too, have stood the test of time as efficient ways to produce strong, precise, useful metal components. The development of reinforced concrete,

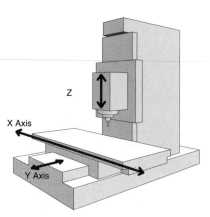

Figure 13-9 The three axes of movement on a typical three-axis milling machine

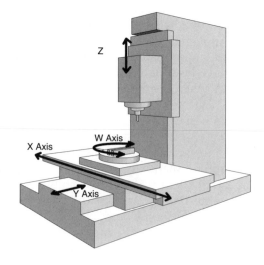

Figure 13-11 A milling machine with an additional fourth axis supplied by a rotating CNC turntable to allow greater part complexity without refixturing a workpiece.

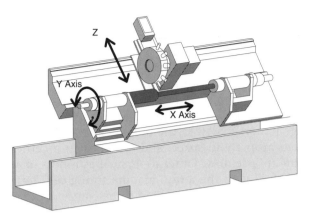

Figure 13-12 A CNC lathe, indicating the major axes of movement and control.

plastics such as acrylics and resins, and engineered or composite materials such as plywood and glass- or fiber-reinforced plastics, among other materials, has led to the need for tools to make molds suitable for shaping them. CNC machines have helped some of these materials to find useful applications at a reasonable cost. CAD/CAM software and CNC manufacturing tools have forever changed plastic casting and molding endeavors in particular, as well as the design of products utilizing those technologies. Metal molds used for injection molding of plastic are created on milling machines almost directly from 3-D digital files. The ease with which this can be done, relative to traditional pattern and mold making, has allowed for the design of products using fewer, more complex parts at lower cost. This allows designers to produce sophisticated designs that are simple and cost-effective to assemble. CAD/CAM technologies are also embraced by pattern

makers. It is a an easy matter to produce digital models of metal objects that take shrinkage into account, as well as the removal of the pattern from the mold, while also calculating the thickness of elements and the volume of metal required. Once a pattern has been sized appropriately for the metal from which it will be cast, patterns can be made using both CNC tools and traditional hand bench-work techniques. Rough castings may be clamped onto CNC tools to mill and finish specific surfaces as determined by the designer (see Figure 13-14).

In such a case the CNC tools are used before the casting takes place and again after the casting has been produced, but they are not used to directly create the casting. Similarly, specially shaped foam blocks may be cast using molds made with CNC tools, and those blocks used in the "lost-foam" casting process, but the casting process itself, while perhaps automated, is not required to be digitally enabled. The same holds true for "lost-wax" casting in which a wax model produced by machining processes, or using one of the many types of rapid prototyping machines is melted from within a ceramic shell or investment mold to produce a hollow mold into which metal is poured. This is also true for other casting methods such as shell casting, injection molding, die casting, and extrusion—many details of which may be found in the next chapter.

Molding and deformation tools have benefited from CNC controls, although not in the same manner as other types of machine tools. Actions such as bending, folding, stretch-forming, and stamping may be imprecise by nature because of the characteristics of the materials being acted upon. Sophisticated metal tubing benders, for example, may utilize feedback mechanisms for accurate work in order for the bending tool to make the constant adjustments required to produce regular bends in metal supplies that vary to some degree in hardness, thickness, and working characteristics. The

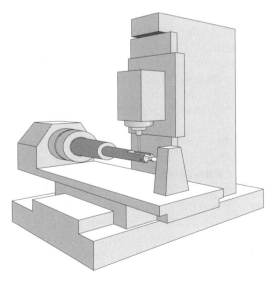

Figure 13-13 A schematic machining center, combining aspects of both milling machines and lathes to produce extremely complex parts without refixturing.

Figure 13-14 A rough casting being machined to final tolerances.

same applies to machines that deform structural shapes, and even wire. A machine that uses both wire rod and wire from a spool has to compensate for the "memory" of the shape of the wire coming off the spool. In the same way, steel or aluminum plate being fed through a three-roll press may need to have the downward pressure on the top roller adjusted to account for differing thicknesses and hardnesses of material coming from different suppliers or from different lots (see Figure 13-15).

The manufacture of stamping tools has benefited greatly from CNC technologies. EDM machines are capable of machining accurate dies directly from hardened blanks, thus saving heat treatments and the deformation risks associated with them. More conventional tools may be milled using CNC machines at great speed and with accuracy equal to or greater than that achieved by hand work. The dies for simple shapes to be stamped out of metal, for example, may be cut directly from hardened steel using a wire EDM machine. In such cases both the die and punch can sometimes be cut from the same blank by canting the angle of the cut so that the bottom of the punch closely fits the top of the die. Prior to the development of CNC EDM equipment, such work was virtually impossible, and certainly not cost-effective. Again, more detail related to these technologies is found in the next chapter.

Fabrication or Addition of Elements

Fabrication processes occur when material is added to a base element, layers of material are built up, or small elements are connected to one another to produce a larger item. This may be done by welding, screwing, riveting, squashing, gluing, mechanically engaging (like a puzzle), or using any number of other methods. The basic idea is to use small pieces specifically designed and created to make larger, more complex ones. The individual elements may be made from different materials to incorporate different strength, wear, or performance characteristics in the larger component. Automotive construction is a good example of this, as are many building components such as stairs, railings,

light fixtures, cabinets, windows, and doors. For the most part, the small elements required to make a larger one have been made using machining or casting methods—panels, wire parts, structural components, rubber pieces, steel or aluminum tubing, and castings of all kinds are examples of these. CNC tools such as welders, riveting or nailing machines, punch tools, rollers, and edge joiners may take the individual elements, locate them properly in space, and fasten them together to form an assembly. Other tools such as robots may be organized with them into manufacturing cells to fully automate these activities, but some components such as sheet-metal boxes may be produced within one machine in their entirety. Larger components such as metal trusses and space frames can be custom-designed and produced and shipped entirely within a CNC setting. Smaller custom elements such as metal enclosure elements for buildings or detail components are often produced using a combination of CNC tools and other methods.

A growing variety of free-form fabrication, or rapid prototyping, tools are available to build three-dimensional models in real materials at a modest scale for visual and mechanical testing, for use in indirect forms of manufacture such as casting or—occasionally—actual long-term use in a real setting. These tools are discussed in detail in Chapter 14, but it is worth noting here that these tools are unique in that they are capable of producing volumetric shapes with hollows and undercuts without the necessity for more than three axes of movement.

13.4 CNC MACHINE CONTROL AND OPERATION

All numerically controlled devices have some type of machine control unit, and some form of interface for the input and interpretation of the program. CNC control is recognizably similar to even early Jacquard looms that incorporated a control mechanism using wire pins to read punched cards at an interface, yet it is the specific machine control unit (or controller) and its computer interface that distinguish CNC control from other forms of NC.

Tools sold with CNC controls today make up over 70 percent of the machine tool market. They are generally sold either with cables leading to a fully operational minicomputer or with an attached microprocessor capable of receiving and storing parts programs but not able to produce much beyond the simplest of programs on its own. Developed from early, freestanding machines that received programs via punched paper tapes, this latter type are now usually purchased with the intention of connecting them to a network from which part programs may be received if sent, or

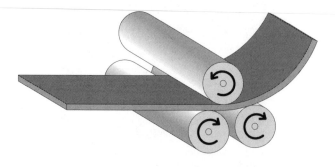

Figure 13-15 A three-roll machine bending metal sheet or plate.

retrieved from a common server as desired. In either case, a CNC machine is usually put to work through the following steps:

- A digital design is produced within the CAD portion of a CAD/CAM program using Cartesian coordinates to create geometry, or it is received from another source (perhaps drawn elsewhere) and opened within the CAD/CAM program (see Figure 13-16).

- A toolpath is defined within the CAD/CAM software that will produce the desired shape using the previously created geometric model (see Figure 13-16).

- The toolpath is post-processed by the CAM portion of the CAD/CAM software to produce a G-Code or similar text file (these may be saved in any number of generic or vendor-specific formats such as TAP, NC, and CNC). This is the part program that may also—in the case of simple shapes—be entered directly by hand using text editing software (see Figure 13-16).

- The part program file is sent to the controller (usually attached to the tool itself), where it is opened (see Figure 13-19). The toolpath may be visually verified on-screen and perhaps modified to suit the parameters of the specific machine tool. As the part program is read by the controller, the instructions written in a symbolic language are converted into a digital format to communicate with motors or other actuators that make the tool move. The information may be saved in random-access memory in its entirety, or if insufficient memory is available, it may be buffered.

- The machine tool is commanded to run the program, at which point the translated toolpath commands are sent to the tool itself and it begins to do its work. Most tools incorporate a display screen showing the tool position as it moves while also displaying the line of code being machined at that moment—information such as tool speed, coordinates of the tool relative to the machine zero position and the local zero position of the job, the status of coolant, the tool bit being used, how long the job has run, the time to completion, and so on.

While many tools utilizing paper tapes, cassettes, and diskettes for direct input are still in use, the technologies are rapidly growing obsolete for obvious practical reasons. A hardwired machine using tape files must run the tape through every time a part is to be machined, for example. A metal chip accidentally lodged in a punched hole may ruin a workpiece by causing the tool to move to the wrong location, not to mention what a tear in the delicate paper tape might cause. Even though plastic and aluminum reinforced tapes have helped cure some of these problems, the reigning method for transferring digital design files is completely within the digital environment through networked computing, FTP, e-mail, and Web-based solutions. It is also the current trend to load part programs onto increasingly powerful and intelligent local control systems associated with individual tools, rather than attempting to run multiple machines from one central networked computer (the latter is referred to as DNC, or direct numerical control). Local control allows individual tool operators to respond to specific conditions such as unanticipated vibration of the tool, loss of coolant, discovery of program errors, and so on. The lack of DNC does not eliminate the possibility of communication between tools or other resources, however, allowing data to flow to computers controlling other phases of manufacturing in computer-integrated manufacturing (CIM) environments. (See Chapter 17.)

13.5 SPECIFICS OF MACHINE CONTROL WITHIN THE CAM ENVIRONMENT

While it may be unlikely that readers of this book will be programming machine tools directly, some knowledge of how G-Code and other control languages work will allow a better understanding of the capabilities of CNC technologies. An introductory discussion here will also aid understanding of material related to manufacturing application environments or computer-aided manufacturing software later in the chapter.

The key to understanding CNC operations lies in understanding how controllers work. Controllers are situated between the computer and the machine tool itself, in essence taking the place of a human operator translating drawings to know how to directly control tooling to do the required work. Controller hardware is combined with controller software residing in the computer that permits it to "think" like a lathe, or a milling machine or bender or any other tool for which the controller is configured. This allows the computer to verify that a part can be manufactured by "reading" a parts program to manufacture the resultant part within virtual space, respecting the parameters of the specific tool.

The purpose of a controller is to manage information by translating and converting one binary language to another so that language understood easily by humans may be easily understood by machine tools. G-Code, HPGL, and other text-based languages are universal in nature, while instructions understood by machine tools are specific to each tool. Controllers are often also universal in nature and must be configured

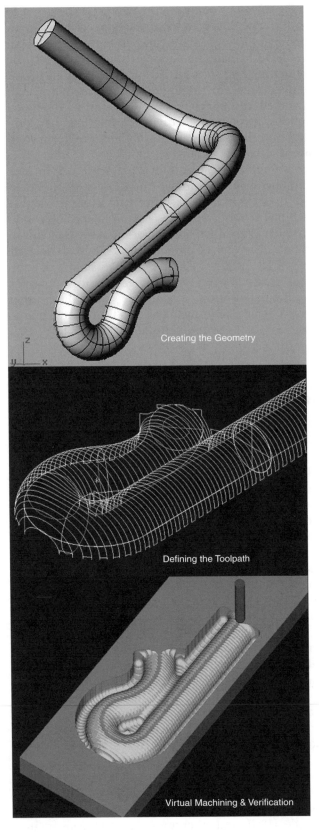

Creating the Geometry

Defining the Toolpath

Virtual Machining & Verification

```
N114G91
N116Z-.75
N118G1Z-.25F6.42
N120X.0086Z.0709
N122X.0126Z.0343
N124X.015Z.0389
N126X.0206Z.0312
N128X.0299Z.043
N130X.0054Z.0054
N132X.0349Z.0331
N134X.0348Z.0309
N136X.0061Z.0052
N138X.0284Z.0178
N140X.0342Z.0202
N142X.0341Z.0185
N144X.0339Z.017
N146X.0015Z.0007
N148X.0323Z.0117
```

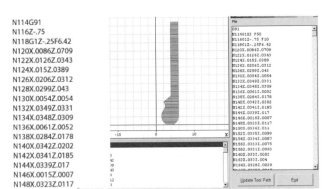

Sending the Toolpath to the CNC Machine Tool Controller

Cutting the Stair Component using a 3-Axis CNC Router

The Completed and Installed Stair Component

Figure 13-16 A complex handrail element designed within a digital solid modeling environment and produced using CNC tools.

for the parameters of each specific tool at some point, often before or upon delivery of the tool by the manufacturer.

CNC machine controllers generally respond to the numerical code defined as RS274D, a standard developed by the Electronic Industries Association (EIA) in the early 1960s. The language has been updated to account for the obsolescence of paper tapes and needs that have since developed within the realm of machine tool design and manufacturing, but the basic underlying rules and structures of the standard remain in use. An updated dialect of the standard, RS276NGC, has been produced for an enhanced machine controller (EMC) by researchers at the National Institute of Standards and Technology (NIST), and efforts continue to improve the capabilities of what may be generically referred to as "G-Code."

G-Code is an elegant way to define movement in space along defined axes, either when the tool simply needs to move from one place to another to begin a new operation or while work is actually being done. It is a form of "Word Address Programming," following many common rules of computer programming: Instructions are written in the form of "blocks" (a single line of text), which contain "words" (a letter followed by a number, representing a setting to be made or a function to be performed, and the value of that function). Each block is a self-contained command to the tool. Simple moves or operations require fewer blocks, while complex operations generally require many.

The following sample of G-Code will introduce what is involved. The code is written to drill a hole at located 1.5 inches in the *x* axis and 1.5 inches in the *y* axis from a starting point, as illustrated in Figure 13-17. The following limited number of commands will suffice for now:

- *N* signifies the number of the line the block is on.
- *G0* signifies a move to a position at as high a speed as possible, usually in preparation for doing useful work.
- *G1* signifies movement at a controlled feedrate (*F*) while doing useful work.
- *M3* turns on a spindle in the clockwise direction.
- *M5* turns the spindle off.
- *F* signifies the speed at which the tool will move, in inches per minute.

G-CODE FILE REQUIRED TO DRILL A HOLE 1.5 INCHES FROM AN ORIGIN IN BOTH X AND Y AXES

N00	G91	This informs the machine that the code to follow is incremental.
N01	G0 X1.5 Y1.5	The tool moves quickly 1.5 inches in the *x* and *y* axes.
N02	M3	The spindle turns on, rotating in the clockwise direction.
N03	G1 Z-1.0 F5	The tool moves downward 1 inch at a rate of 5 inches/min.
N04	G0 Z1.0	The tool moves upward rapidly.
N05	M5	The spindle turns off.
N06	G0 X-1.5 Y-1.5	The tool returns to its starting point, retracing its first move.

It can be seen that for simple operations, typing this text directly—"Manual Data Input (MDI)"—may be faster than taking the time to go through all the steps required to draw a shape, place a point on that shape, use the drawing to define a toolpath that will complete the drilling operation, and then produce a G-Code file to be opened in the controller software environment. In fact, a great deal of useful work is done through MDI without resorting to sophisticated CAD/CAM software programs. Manual editing of G-Code is also often necessary or desired once a numerical control file has been produced through CAD/CAM software, or once a toolpath for a part has been verified at the tool. For that reason, even some relatively simple controller microprocessors are capable of MDI.

G-Code is capable of telling tools to move in either absolute coordinates or incremental coordinates. Each has its advantages, and the two locating systems may be used within the same file. If the preceding simple file were run in incremental coordinates (G91), the tool will behave as described. If, however, you were to type "G90" at the top of the file, the tool would operate in an absolute coordinate system. While the simple file will still cause the tool to do the required work of drilling the hole, after drilling the hole, it would retract at line N04 to a point 1 inch above where it is meant to, to +1 in the *z* axis, and would then move at line N06 to a point that was −1.5 inches from the origin relative to the zero *x* and *y* coordinates. In all cases the tool simply moved to the discrete absolute points in space it understood it was meant to travel to according to absolute programming. During the first few moves, those positions corresponded with the directions used in incremental programming. (See Figure 13-17.)

More sophisticated work will simply go awry if a tool is not directed to run in the correct coordinate system. G-Code properly written to do the same work using absolute coordinates would appear as follows:

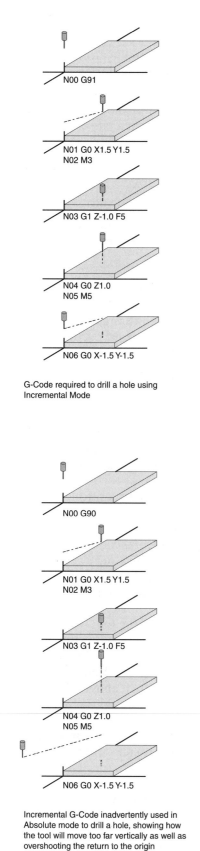

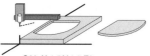

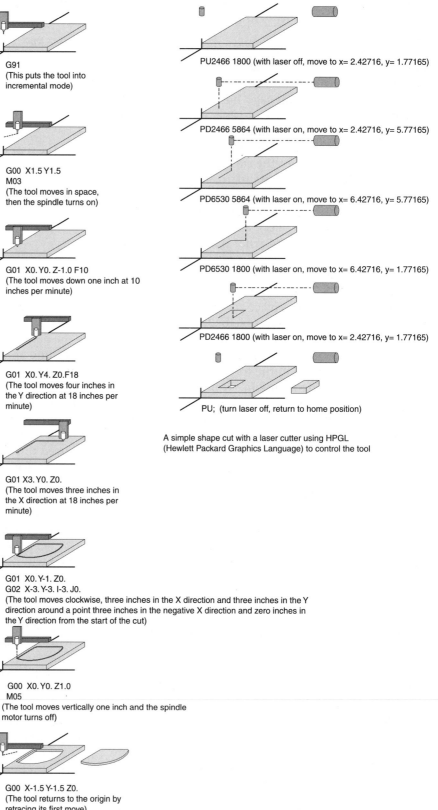

G-Code required to drill a hole using Incremental Mode

Incremental G-Code inadvertently used in Absolute mode to drill a hole, showing how the tool will move too far vertically as well as overshooting the return to the origin

Using G-Code to cut a flat shape with a curve

A simple shape cut with a laser cutter using HPGL (Hewlett Packard Graphics Language) to control the tool

Figure 13-17 Diagrams of CNC tool control using G-Code and HPGL languages.

N00	G90	This informs the machine that the code to follow is absolute.
N01	G0 X1.5 Y1.5	The tool moves quickly +1.5 inches in both the x and y axes.
N02	M3	The spindle turns on, rotating in the clockwise direction.
N03	G1 Z-1.0 F5	The tool moves down to –1 inch at a rate of 5 inches/min.
N04	G0 Z0.0	The tool moves upward rapidly to the height of the z axis origin.
N05	M5	The spindle turns off.
N06	G0 X0.0 Y0.0	The tool returns to the 0,0,0 origin, retracing its first move.

(See Figure 13-17.)

The standard list of letters used to delineate specific program elements follows:

O	Program number
N	Sequence number
G	Preparatory functions
X,Y,Z	Coordinate axis function command
R	Arc radius, corner radius
F	Feed rate
E	Thread lead
S	Spindle speed
T	Tool number
M	Miscellaneous on/off toggle functions

The EIA standard originally provided for 99 G-Code values and the same number of M-Codes. Other, miscellaneous letters were also defined with functions as seen previously. A full listing of G-Codes and M-Codes and their application is shown in Figure 13-18. Most controllers recognize only those codes applicable to the specific machine they are associated with, and many of the codes are unassigned by the EIA to be used by tool manufacturers for unique or specific control functions. The use of those numbers may vary from tool to tool so that G-Code understood by one machine may not work for another.

The simplest G-Code motions are the same as those available on manually controlled machines—an operator could easily move a workpiece in two axes with pre-

G00 positioning (rapid traverse)	G54 work conditions system 1 select
G01 linear interpolation (feed)	G55 work coordinate system 2 select
G02 circular interpolation CW	G56 work coordinate system 3 select
G03 circular interpolation CCW	G57 work coordinate system 4 select
G04 dwell	G58 work coordinate system 5 select
G07 imaginary axis designation	G59 work coordinate system 6 select
G09 exact stop check	G60 single direction positioning
G10 offset value setting	G61 exact stop check mode
G17 XY plane selection	G64 cutting mode
G18 ZX plane selection	G65 custom macro simple call
G19 YZ plane selection	G66 custom macro modal call
G20 input in inch	G67 custom macro modal call cancel
G21 input in mm	G68 coordinate system rotation ON
G22 stored stroke limit ON	G69 coordinate system rotation OFF
G23 stored stroke limit OFF	G73 peck drilling cycle
G27 reference point return check	G74 counter tapping cycle
G28 return to reference point	G76 fine boring
G29 return from reference point	G80 canned cycle cancel
G30 return to 2nd 3rd & 4th ref. point	G81 drilling cycle, spot boring
G31 skip cutting	G82 drilling cycle, counter boring
G33 thread cutting	G83 peck drilling cycle
G40 cutter compensation cancel	G84 tapping cycle
G41 cutter compensation left	G85, G86 boring cycle
G42 cutter compensation right	G87 back boring cycle
G43 tool length compens'n + direction	G88, G89 boring cycle
G44 tool length compens'n - direction	G90 absolute programming
G49 tool length compensation cancel	G91 incremental programming
G45 tool offset increase	G92 programming of absolute zero pt
G46 tool offset decrease	G94 per minute feed
G47 tool offset double increase	G95 per revolution feed
G48 tool offset double decrease	G96 constant surface speed control
G50 scaling OFF	G97 constant surface speed control cancel
G51 scaling ON	G98 return to initial point in canned style
G52 local coordinate system setting	G99 return to R point in canned cycle

M00 program stop	M21 tool magazine right
M01 optional stop	M22 tool magazine left
M02 end of program (no rewind)	M23 tool magazine up
M03 spindle CW	M24 tool magazine down
M04 Spindle CCW	M25 tool clamp
M05 spindle stop	M26 tool unclamp
M06 tool change	M27 clutch neutral ON
M07 mist coolant ON	M28 clutch neutral OFF
M08 flood coolant ON	M30 end program (rewind stop)
M09 coolant OFF	M98 call sub-program
M19 spindle orientation ON	M99 end sub-program
M20 spindle orientation OFF	M19-M28 used for maintenance purposes)

Figure 13-18 Typical standard G and M codes.

cision and then drill a hole just as effectively as with a machine using the sample G-Code we looked at earlier. With the engagement of just two additional G-Codes, however, a CNC tool is capable of generating precise, repeatable shapes considerably more complex than those able to be produced using hand control. G2 and G3 command the tool to move in two axes simultaneously around a centerpoint, generating arcs in a clockwise or counterclockwise fashion, respectively. With only G0, G1, G2, and G3 commands, virtually any shape may be defined. (See Figure 13-17.)

For even greater productivity, "canned cycles" may be employed. An example of a canned cycle is a predetermined drill pattern in which a machine tool will move to a place rapidly, feed the drill down at a programmed speed to the required depth, withdraw from the hole, and then move to another position, where the cycle may be repeated. The canned set of instructions defining only the downward drilling movement can be copied and pasted into a program listing hole locations to make the drill repeat the movement at each of them, or G-Code can be written to pull the instructions from memory at each hole location. A repeated milled pocket shape or a number of identical flat cut-out shapes might also employ canned cycles.

Hewlett-Packard Graphics Language is sometimes used to control tools that are configured like plotters, such as laser and plasma cutters, water-jet cutters, and engraving or routing machines that engage *z* axis movement by using only one cutting depth. The plot files that are used to control the machines are seldom seen by users—much less edited—but such a thing is indeed possible, if daunting. HPGL language was not intended to be edited on a regular basis and is not an easy language to understand, beyond the basics. The programming manual is large and extensive, but to most users this presents little difficulty. Tools controlled using HPGL generally incorporate a seamless interface allowing users to use a mouse click or Return key to energize the tool to complete the task at hand.

HPGL generally works in an absolute coordinate system, but incremental commands may also be understood. The default measurement is 1,016 plotter units (PLU) per inch, but some machines can be programmed to accept different values.

Four HPGL instructions may be used to control a laser cutter, for example:

PD (Pen Up)	May be used to turn on the laser beam to cut a shape
PD (Pen Down)	May be used to turn something off
SP (Select Pen)	May be used to adjust the amplitude of the laser beam

| VS (Velocity Speed) | May be used to control the speed of the laser beam |

An operator needs only to direct the tool to a location or series of locations in order for the laser to work—for example, a 3-inch square would be cut by the set of instructions shown in Figure 13-17.

While HPGL may be attractive within certain markets, editing the code is cumbersome and is not ideal for everyday use; having to enter dimensions in increments of 1016 is, alone, enough to cause confusion, and even consternation. There is, however, little question that it (or languages like it) will remain an obvious choice for controlling certain types of tools, especially for users with little interest or incentive to become engaged in the stream of information used to control their tools.

While languages such as G-Code and HPGL allow the orthogonal movement required by a wide variety of familiar machine tools, they don't meet the control needs of all types of tools. Tools utilizing rotating joints such as robots, some wire and tube benders, and articulated-arm milling machines often use proprietary, specialized software based on languages such as C++, for example. In many cases the users of these tools operate them directly through a graphic interface without having to process the numerical-code files required by users of traditional machine tools.

13.6 MANUFACTURING APPLICATION ENVIRONMENTS: CAM AND CAD/CAM SOFTWARE

Having established some general characteristics of machine tools and the languages used to control them earlier in this chapter, we will now look at a crucial link between the design and CNC manufacturing of the work itself. Any organized CAD/CAM process requires that digital designs coming from a CAD environment into a manufacturing environment be looked at anew. Geometries must be verified to make sure the file transfer from CAD software to CAD/CAM or CAM software is accurate. Parameters must be checked to ensure the designs can be manufactured using available tooling, and manufacturing methods must be compared to find the most appropriate methods for completion of the parts described in the original CAD file—milling out of solid material, turning material on a lathe, cutting flat sheets to be folded or fabricated, or manufacturing a mold into which the piece may be cast, for example.

This is work that takes place within CAD/CAM software environments, as much as possible. CAD/CAM software is based primarily on CAM software, to which a CAD package may be added to provide a design environment compatible with manufacturing parameters.

While many manufacturing choices continue to be made by qualified personnel based on research or experience, as CAD/CAM software continues to be developed, much effort is being made to embed logic and knowledge-based procedures within the software itself to expedite the making of objects. It might be possible, for example, for software to recognize that a box design with very thin walls would be best made from metal sheet, cut in a flat shape and folded rather than milling the box out of a solid block of metal; the software might issue such a recommendation to the user. The portion of the software recognizing how sheet metal can be folded might also incorporate minimum bending radii for different thicknesses of metal so that a bend with too tight a radius would cause a warning that the design was not feasible, and perhaps even recommend a design change. A program might also warn a user if a proposed hole was too close to an edge, or if it would be inaccessible to a tool during fabrication.

Any experienced machine operator knows how to avoid such problems by following rules, but there is a great need to incorporate them into "rule-based" software applications. The need becomes pressing as manufacturing moves to a more distributed environment over the Web and other networks and as designers are further removed from direct access to the reliable knowledge bases they often rely on. It is desirable to have some automated capability to analyze an object to be made to determine the most appropriate manufacturing method. Should the object be cut, machined, or cast? If so, what are the optimal ways to do each of those operations? A cylindrical shape could easily be made by milling it from solid stock, turning it on a lathe, or casting it, for example, but milling or turning would waste material and casting would be an equal if not greater waste of resources. It would be obvious to an operator that cutting off a piece of round stock of the correct diameter would be the most appropriate solution, but having this information at least optionally available at the design stage (even though use of some knowledge-based approaches may obscure what parameters are actually within the control of the designer) could enhance a designer's ability to work effectively.

CAD/CAM software varies significantly, from the very basic to the almost unimaginably complex, with add-on programs that allow all manner of characteristics to be checked and verified, from the smoothness of curves on a design to the volume of material required to cast it in a mold, and even to life cycle costs. The vast majority of work done with CNC tools can be defined using relatively simple programs, but designers will be interested in what can be done in a more sophisticated software environment.

As previously mentioned, CAD/CAM software contains two coordinated software packages that allow drawing and virtual machining operations to occur within the same environment (see Figure 13-19). This strategy came about largely as a result of the problems associated with maintaining the integrity of information shared between designers and manufacturers. Designers working within CAD software environments optimized for design, for example, may unwittingly be using descriptions of geometry that are programmed to maximize the appearance of their designs without defining solid entities that can reliably be transferred through standard "neutral" file formats such as DXF, IGS or IGES, and STL. The algorithms used to describe shapes such as spline curves, for example, vary widely among software used for architecure, engineering, product design, and graphic design. While it is possible to save design work in simplified formats, a great deal of information may be lost while doing so. Formats such as STEP and kernels such as parasolids continue to be developed to transfer comprehensive descriptions of geometry and other features between software environments, while existing neutral formats are updated to ease the suffering of both designers and manufacturers. Many CAD programs (including those that are part of an "integrated closed system") are specially designed to produce solid modeling, feature-based modeling, and so on to minimize the difficulty of transferring data. In any case, the CAD portion of CAD/CAM software allows parts to be drawn directly or (increasingly) reliably imported from other CAD software. If data can be accurately imported to the CAD package, modifications necessary for manufacturing may be made to the model within that environment, and it is likely that the CAM operations will then be able to be successfully completed.

CAD/CAM software is often described in terms of the manufacturing activities they support—for instance, Router, Milling, Lathe, Sheet Metal, or Casting. While there are more similarities than differences between these, each package is optimized for a particular manufacturing activity, and many machine tools are bundled with appropriate CAD/CAM software to provide a nonintegrated stand-alone system that simply

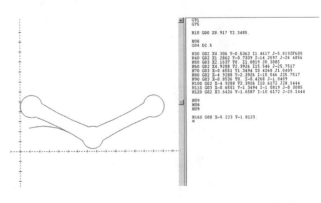

Figure 13-19 A typical CAD/CAM software interface showing both a drawing component and a related numerical-control window.

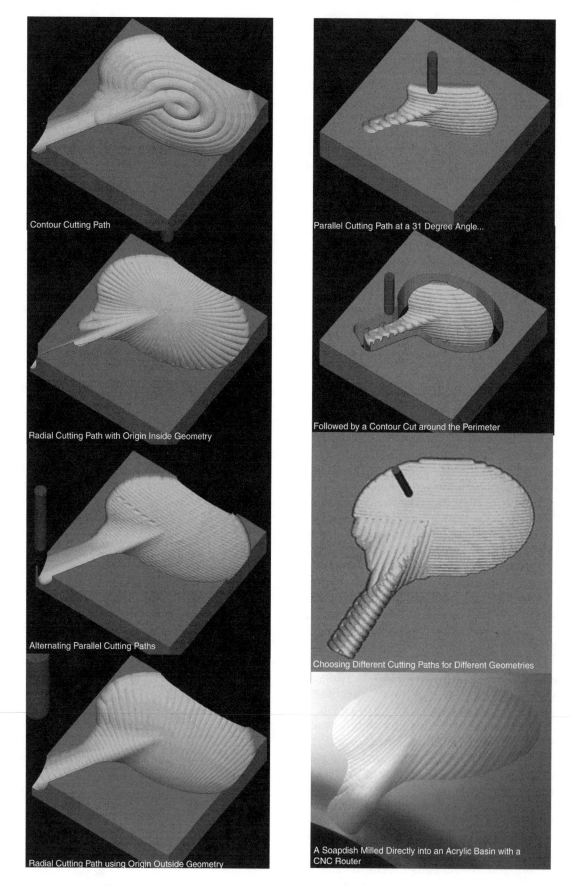

Contour Cutting Path

Radial Cutting Path with Origin Inside Geometry

Alternating Parallel Cutting Paths

Radial Cutting Path using Origin Outside Geometry

Parallel Cutting Path at a 31 Degree Angle...

Followed by a Contour Cut around the Perimeter

Choosing Different Cutting Paths for Different Geometries

A Soapdish Milled Directly into an Acrylic Basin with a CNC Router

Figure 13-20 Proposals for different types of toolpaths to cut the same digitally-generated shape for a soapdish element, followed by the actual milled example.

needs to be plugged in and turned on. Many vendors provide proprietary software systems containing the entire "dedicated" design environment, some of which are quite powerful. A variety of low-end packages are also available, often incorporating more limited design capabilities that are appropriate to a particular tool. Many CNC laser cutters, for example, which are used primarily to etch or cut 2-D shapes from flat sheets, are bundled with simple drawing software incapable of drawing solids, since the final machine environment has no capability to machine them. Minimal packages of this type are intended to be more user-friendly, but once a novice user has learned how to use them, the limitations may be very irritating. For example, it may not be possible to import a complex model from a generic CAD package into the simplified interface without losing some or all of its more exotic features—perhaps curves requiring robust geometric definitions. Bear in mind that this may reflect the fact that the shape is not able to be "manufactured" by the attached tool, but complex models may simply require the use of more complex environments (with attendant higher costs), or the adoption of a clear strategy for making complex shapes using simple methods in a methodical and intelligent manner.

The ultimate application of CAD/CAM software is the generation of instructions specifying tool movements related to the geometry of the object. The steps needed to achieve this goal have already been covered generally, but it is worth noting that certain choices can be made during the definition of the toolpath that may be of interest to the designer. Once the geometric model has been fully defined, choices are made within the software environment to determine the final appearance of the object. When milling a shape from solid material, for example, the user may choose specific tools from a software library (a listing of ball end milling bits, router bits, or drills, for example) or the user may define them. The user may also choose the manner in which the piece is processed by the tool from predetermined types of "paths," such as spiral, zigzag, project, one-way, and contour, or the path may be specifically determined by the user (see Figure 13-20). The order or cuts and their direction may be chosen—cutting back and forth across a solid to create a contoured shape, for example, or at a 31° angle, followed by cutting the entire shape out of a the block. (See Figure 13-20.)

In essence, the user gives virtual directions to the tool, and a toolpath is thus defined. Other instructions may be given—to change to a different tool for part of the toolpath or to adjust the speed of the spindle. The distance between "passes" of the tool can be determined, along with the accuracy of interpolation of curves; these last two features allow for a wide variety of interesting surface textures caused by deliberate manipulation of the toolpath (see Figure 13-20). This may be thought of as a modern-day equivalent to the conscious and artful mark of a chisel on wood or stone, or the mark of the hammer on metal. These kinds of marks have been historically valued as representative of the processes that created artifacts and are reminders that humans do continue to make and control the tools and the ways tools are used to create artifacts.

Once the toolpath has been fully defined and the parameters of the tooling have been chosen, the CAM portion of the software will create a file. In some cases the file is proprietary and is stored along with the drawing file to be post-processed later for specific tools upon command. In other cases the post-processing for a specific tool is immediate, resulting in a G-Code file that may be sent to a machine tool. In either case the file may be machined from a virtual solid in virtual space to ensure the toolpath and the final piece do, in fact, look like they should. (See Figure 13-20.) In the first case the file may be rewritten and updated to correct errors or omissions without having to write new G-Code. In the latter case an entirely new G-Code file will need to be generated to incorporate changes to the toolpath—a task once time-consuming, but thanks to enhanced processing speeds, this is the case only when extremely complex work is being done.

The computer numerical control of tools is now a mature industry, with an increasingly wide range of activities being managed through the digital interfaces that have become ubiquitous in the manufacturing environment. The increased capabilities of CAD/CAM software have begun to obviate the need to use language such as G-Code to control movement, allowing flexible movement such as rotation or output such as pressure to be efficiently controlled—types of actions that G-Code was not optimized for. As the design of tools becomes less dependent on nineteenth-century and even earlier types, manufacturing capabilities controlled through the digital continuum promise to provide us with some interesting surprises.

CHAPTER 14

Fundamental Manufacturing Processes

14.1 INTRODUCTION

The last chapter introduced the essentials of the CNC environment, describing the interrelated digital technologies that have allowed an increasing variety of production tools to be digitally controlled. This chapter reviews manufacturing processes in general, with a special emphasis on those typically coupled with computer numerical control technologies. No attempt will be made here to give more than a broad overview of the field, as it is well documented elsewhere. Also, specific applications within the worlds of design and architecture are covered in other chapters.

Manufacturing processes may be examined by categorizing them from a number of perspectives. Designers may be interested in the geometric characteristics they make possible, or what materials they are capable of processing, or even the final finish imparted by the tool. Shape-making and process characteristics can also serve the purpose of categorizing—it is possible to look at tools and manufacturing processes by simply dividing them into the three broad categories of Machining or Material Removal; Molding, Deformation, and Casting; and Fabrication or Additive Processes. These categories are not intended to be precise—a good deal of overlap exists as to which one a particular tool may properly belong to, for example—and since many processes such as casting or molding require that tools be made by *direct* CNC machining in order to produce a part such as a mold or pattern, some processes may be considered to be *indirect*. In other words, CNC may not be utilized during the final processing of the work despite the use of a fully integrated digital design and manufacturing process up to that point. It should be remembered that many processes are simply difficult to categorize (e.g., should powdered metallurgy be categorized as a molding or a fabricating process?).

Any discussion related to manufacturing processes must also consider material properties. Broadly speaking, industrially produced objects are commonly made from metals, polymers, glass, ceramics, and composites. The specific properties of each material, including qualities such as melting point, malleability, machinability, minimum bending radius, and coefficient of expan-

sion, influence decisions related to what manufacturing processes may be applied to them. Some processes, such as laser cutting or casting, can be applied to a wide variety of materials by taking advantage of their inherent shared properties. Other processes take advantage of properties exhibited by only a few materials. Punching and drawing processes, for example, are used extensively in the manufacture of metal shapes but are difficult or impossible to apply to materials such as stone, most plastics, wood, or ceramics.

Manufacturing processes and tools are usually developed with a specific goal in mind, so it is not surprising that many of the processes that work well at the scale of individual pieces are not appropriate for mass production, and vice versa. In the manufacturing world, issues of scale and repitition can be critical, and lot size is a fundamental concern. The manufacture of a large lot size has come to mean that processes must be geared to the efficient production of massive numbers of elements, often using tools designed specifically for that one purpose. The historical extreme of this condition should be familiar to generations of readers from commonly published images of military components, transportation products, and consumer goods being produced on huge, hard, fixed assembly lines using enormous tools. The extremely high initial capital expense associated with these manufacturing centers is justified by the large lot size. Smaller lot sizes may be made using more flexible or universal-type tools arranged in a less permanent manner and, in fact, this has become increasingly true for large-volume production as well. Distinctions between large and small lot sizes remain critical, with lower production runs typically using a more flexible approach to using machine tools. A variety of techniques continue to be developed that are targeted at the cost-effective production of small lots, from the fitting of CNC controls and flexible tooling to large and expensive multipurpose machines, to the development of inexpensive and accurate molds with short life cycles that allow the casting of metal and plastics without the high cost of a traditional hard mold.

Closely related is the value of the product itself. A small consumer-goods product that commands a good price may allow the use of technologies that are not affordable for the production of low-end products. Camera parts may have a higher unit value than filing cabinet parts of similar size and shape, for example. The value of the small camera parts justifies manufacturing approaches with levels of precision and finish that could never be economically justified for making the filing cabinet components.

Issues of size and scale arise constantly at the junction of design and manufacturing. The large difference between manufacturing many small objects versus relatively few larger objects necessitates an understanding of how different CNC technologies can be appropriately employed. In the world of CNC manufacturing, relatively few machines are utilized for the manufacture of the larger components for buildings, while a great many are geared for small-scale manufacturing of hardware, furnishings, and the like. This reflects manufacturing generally, but it is also the case that some digitally enabled technologies do not scale up for larger work. Small-diameter tubing may be easily formed using CNC tubing benders to a wide variety of shapes, while larger diameters resist similar deformation, for example. Similarly, rapid prototyping using stereolithography is limited by the size of the build envelope, the high cost of the build material, and the slow build speed to relatively small, expensive parts. On the other hand, many technologies do scale up easily—milling shapes or knife-cutting fabrics are activities limited only by the size of the machine workbed, allowing components for buildings (foam inserts for complex concrete forms, or panels for a fabric roof are two examples) to be made as easily as products for a desktop.

Following is a look at some of the general types of manufacturing processes that have benefited from the development of CNC technologies, organized according to the aforementioned categories, with notes related to some of the related production considerations previously mentioned.

14.2 MACHINING OR MATERIAL REMOVAL

Mechanical Removal

Many stock-removal technologies and tools such as saws, drills, mills, routers, and lathes are based on the well-understood ability of a sharp tool to mechanically remove crystalline, granular, fibrous, or other types of materials in a controlled manner, producing chips or shavings much like the action of a chisel. Either the tool or the work must be moving in order for the tool to engage the workpiece in a productive manner. Higher tool speeds will allow higher feed rates or finer finishes, but they may also produce less accurate work, vibration, and heating or even burning of the material. The parameters required for the mechanical removal of material include cutting speed, feed rate, and rake angle of the cutting tool itself—all of which are well understood and easily incorporated within the databases of CAD/CAM software. Tools that employ a simple cutting action capable of removing material in a precise, predictable, and repeatable manner through simple control mechanisms are the workhorses of any machine shop environment. (See Figure 14-1.)

Saws

Saws using circular, straight, and even flexible blades are among the simplest tools controlled via CNC, generally making straight cuts (see Figure 14-2). Blades may have teeth or abrasive edges, but in either case, the width and the diameter (where applicable) of the blade may be precisely defined. Used in conjunction with movement of material in only one axis, saws provide very accurate and effective cutoff tools that are useful in metal fabrication, woodworking, stoneworking, and other activities requiring long lengths of material to be cut down or large blocks to be cut into a series of slabs.

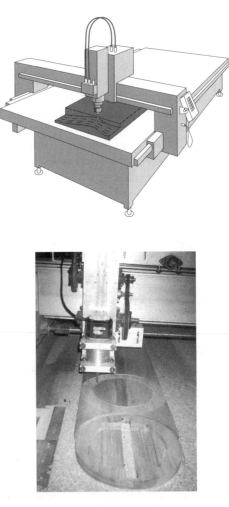

Figure 14-1 CNC routers with three axes of movement.

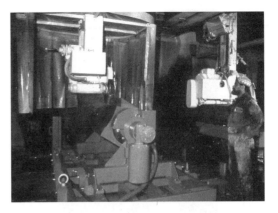

Figure 14-3 A stone column being carved using a six-axis CNC saw.

Figure 14-2 A large CNC saw cutting a slab of stone and stone moldings produced by making many parallel cuts.

Additional axes of movement allow circular saws to make angled cuts and compound angles, and to "mill" complex curves (limited by the diameter of the blade). These types of saws are also very good at making linear elements with complex contours running in only one direction.

Saws are particularly good at cutting along boundaries to quickly remove large amounts of material—often prior to further machining operations—and they are also effective at cutting panels out of sheet stock and solids out of blocks when installed on a four-axis or five-axis gantry-type tool such as that shown in Figure 14-3. Saws are routinely mounted on milling centers to speed the manufacture of metal and plastic components (see Figure 14-4).

Drills

Drills are among the most ancient of tools and are designed to remove material to make holes. While some drilling techniques continue to employ the use of abrasives and slurries used by the earliest toolmakers, drilling today is usually accomplished through a mechanical cutting action while working primarily in one axis, commonly the z, or vertical one. (See Figure 14-5.)

Traditional drilling machines lend themselves to even the most basic CNC control, as they need only to

move efficiently to successive locations to do their job—a type of movement called *point-to-point*—without the need for the sophisticated motion control. Drill bits are available to do a wide variety of work, from making rough holes to the most precise reaming operation. Many drills are also equipped to perform tapping operations subsequent to drilling, allowing one machine to perform all the operations required to make threaded holes in a workpiece. CAD/CAM software and CNC drills take advantage of characteristics of the different types of tools through the control of spindle speed and direction, coolant flow and feed rate, and by drilling successively deeper (peck drilling) or successively larger holes to speed the work, reduce tool wear, clear chips, or improve precision. Location of a hole may be determined by moving the drill head or by moving the workpiece in the x, y, and other axes so that the hole location is brought directly beneath the head of the drill. The "throat" of a drilling machine may effectively limit the distance any hole may be drilled from the edge of a workpiece. Overhead drills are hung from above, as shown in Fig-

Figure 14-4 A sawblade on a CNC milling center, cutting aluminum extrusions for a custom skylight frame.

Figure 14-5 A drill bit cutting into metal, showing the characteristic formation of spiral chips made by the cutting edges of the bit. (The drill is not doing the impossible; it has been pulled back from the workpiece for clarity)

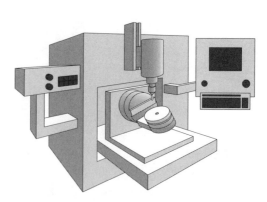

Figure 14-7 Diagram of one type of five-axis CNC drill.

ure 14-6, thus eliminating the support column to allow drilling over a large surface (drilling wings in the aircraft industry, for example). Drills employing more than three axes may be used to drill into the sides of workpieces as well as from above, or at an angle to the workpiece, and automatic tool changers allow a number of related operations to take place without human intervention. (See Figure 14-7.)

Turning

Lathes exist in a variety of forms for a variety of purposes, but they all share the characteristic that the work must be turned around one axis in order for a stationary tool to be brought to bear against it. Particularly appropriate for "turning" round shapes such as spindles, shafts, and knobs, lathes also excel at "facing"—cutting a flat surface on the end of a piece—and spinning, wherein a disc of metal is pushed over a form as the two are spinning together. (See Figure 14-8.)

Lathes are proficient at making tapered pieces and drilling or boring holes into or through parts using a tool fixed in a tool holder or the tailstock. Screw-cutting lathes are designed to cut threads of any size along the length of a piece. Most lathes are universal in

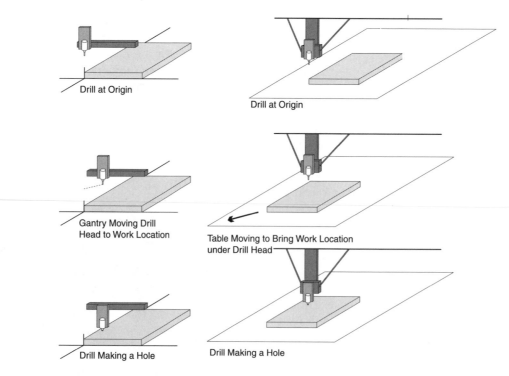

Figure 14-6 Diagrams showing a gantry type drill with a moving tool (left) and an overhead type drill with a moving table (right).

Figure 14-8 Turning (left), facing (right) and spinning (bottom) operations associated with lathe work.

nature; CNC engine lathes, or machine lathes, are found in machine shop environments, and CNC wood lathes are used to turn components in millwork shops. These lathes are available in a variety of sizes to suit most work and are perhaps the simplest CNC tools to program. Lathes may be controlled using only two axes of control, as the turning in the y axis is done by simply spinning the work. On a conventional machine lathe, the cutting tool is attached to a cross slide moving in the x axis, which is itself fixed to a carriage that slides along the length of the lathe in the z axis, both being controlled by lead screws or rack-and-pinion gearing—a type of construction that is immediately suitable to digital control. (See Figure 14-9.) More

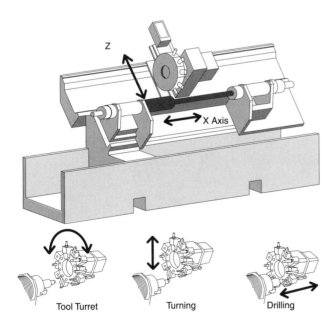

Figure 14-9 A diagram of a typical machine lathe showing the two computer numerically-controlled axes (X and Z) and the CNC tool turret.

sophisticated lathes have automatic CNC tool-changing turrets that allow a succession of tools to be brought to bear on a complex workpiece without stopping, providing flexibility where a variety of operations are required to produce different products cost-effectively.

Lathes also form the basis of digitally controlled tools called turning centers, which have significantly extended the utility of turning technologies through digitally controlled automatic feed mechanisms, among other features. Controls for the y, or spinning, axis allow the rotation of a workpiece to be stopped precisely at any point in its rotation. This feature allows live tooling such as drill heads, milling bits, saws, or grinders to perform machining work while a piece is in known fixed positions, while still on the lathe.

Milling

Shaping and milling machines share a common ancestry dating to the industrial revolution, when the ability to reliably cast large metal components led to the development of new types of large, substantial tools to which human, animal, water, or steam power could be applied. These tools were critical in the development of manufacturing systems dependent on interchangeable parts and remain among the most appropriate technologies for the routine manufacture of precision parts. Shapers in the metalworking world use a fixed cutting tool primarily to produce a flat surface, whereas in the woodworking industry, a different type of tool, also called a shaper, cuts contoured shapes using rotating tools (see Figure 14-10).

Milling machines employ a powered "head" to hold circular-type cutters with multiple teeth or cutting edges. Both shapers and milling machines employ CNC, but mills form a much larger tool group and are closely tied to the rapid development of numerical control. The first numerically controlled tool was, after all, a milling machine. A remarkable variety of three-dimensional shapes can be realized using milling machines. Knee-and-column, fixed-bed-type, and planer-type milling machines are but a few versions of this type of tool, and these may be further classified as horizontal or vertical, depending on the position of the spindle that holds the cutting tool itself. New milling machine types have been developed in association with CNC controls, often called machining centers because of their flexible nature. Most milling machines share the characteristics of traditional, straightforward orthogonal or rotating movement along straight rails or rotational axes. Most work demanded by industry can be done using just three axes of movement, but machines with up to six axes are now common (see Figure 14-11). As the number of controlled axes increases, the complexity of the work that can be produced also increases—along with the

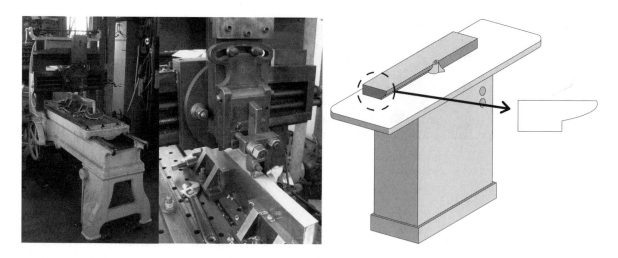

Figure 14-10 A nineteenth-century metal shaper with a cast-iron bed still at work in a punch press tool shop and a diagram of a wood shaper.

programming challenges. A notable exception to machines based on older, traditional models are those based on the "Stewart platform," or hexapod geometry (see Figure 14-12).

Typical smaller milling machines utilize a substantial fixed head with a powered spindle and a moving worktable. Milling centers often move the tools around a fixed workpiece, while larger machines adopt a strong, gantry-type mechanism or even articulated arms to deliver a tool bit to the work. (See Figure 14-13.)

End milling utilizes cutting tools with flat, spherical, tapered and bullnose shapes to produce flat areas, grooves, slots and keyways, pockets, islands of material left when material is milled away around them, and all varieties of contoured shapes (see Figure 14-14). The rotating bit may be angled through the use of an angled cutter or movement in a fourth or fifth axis. CNC tool changers optimize the flow of work by allowing a variety of operations to be performed using different tools to complete a workpiece. Some highly automated and flexible CNC mills even monitor tool wear or breakage to ensure extreme accuracy and to keep expensive projects from being damaged.

Shaping

Wood shapers have also benefited from CNC. Shapers have incorporated digital control to expand their capabilities well beyond their original purpose of producing mass quantities of linear profiles by placing fixed, rotating molding cutters along the path of moving material. Stacked tooling on long powered spindles allows a variety of molded shapes to be made by simply raising or lowering the spindle to the height where a particular cutter can do its work, while multiple spindles allow the accurate shaping of many sides at once (see Figure 14-15).

Routing

CNC router systems are among the most popular of CNC tools because of their ease of use, great utility, and affordability. Routers are distinguished from milling machines largely by the speed of the spindle holding the cutting tool—routers operate at significantly higher speeds of up to 30,000 rpm on a routine basis. Milling operations usually require a more robust support structure as well, but the tools otherwise share many characteristics. Routers are commonly mounted on a gantry, which can be combined with moving beds or multiple workstations to allow work to be loaded while other parts are being completed (see Figure 14-16).

Routers are designed to work to very fine tolerances and are well suited to cutting shapes from flat sheets of wood and plastic, as well as relatively thin nonferrous

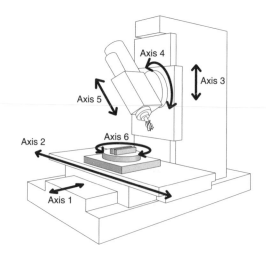

Figure 14-11 A diagram of a typical milling machine with six axes of movement in addition to the rotating tool.

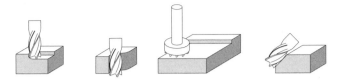

Figure 14-14 Diagram of milling operations such as end milling, face milling and angle milling.

terns and signage. Substantially built, production-oriented industrial CNC routers with vacuum hold-down devices, dust-removal systems, and live tooling such as drills and saw blades have changed the face of modern cabinetry production, while simpler, more affordable flat-bed routers now compete with table saws and band saws as the first major tool purchase considered by woodworkers, small prototyping and design shops, and amateur users.

Abrasive Material Removal

Abrasives may be used to remove material—usually at a slower rate than other mechanical means, but with great accuracy and control of the surface finish. Grinding, sanding, lapping, and polishing use abrasive particles in a variety of media to make a multitude of minute chips similar in most respects to those made by single-point cutting tools.

Grinders

Grinding technologies colonized many standard types of machine tools on their way to becoming machine room necessities, while also engendering the development of a wide variety of specialized grinding tools, including familiar handheld ones. They are used to finish the molds and patterns required by the injection molding, punch press, and stamping industries, for example, and are also used for the important task of providing the pre-

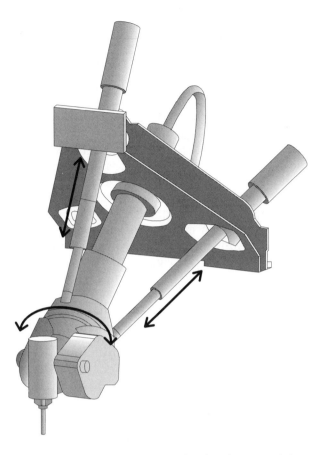

Figure 14-12 A diagram of a milling machine based on one variation of the Stewart Platform, showing three extending arms with a central support structure as well as two rotating axes at the head. This tool moves more like an arm and a wrist than a conventional milling platform.

metals. Routers also excel at making contoured shapes such as those found on wings, boat hulls, or sculpted panels, and they are frequently used to cut foam form inserts for complex concrete shapes, backup support shapes for composite construction, and intricate pat-

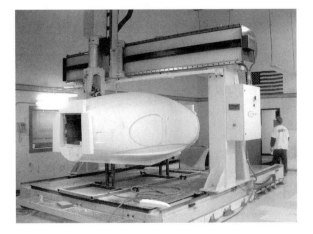

Figure 14-13 A large five-axis gantry-style milling machine used here to create a movie prop.

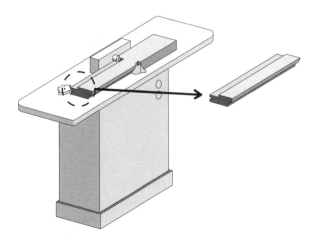

Figure 14-15 A diagram of a multihead wood shaper cutting profiles on three sides of a workpiece in one operation.

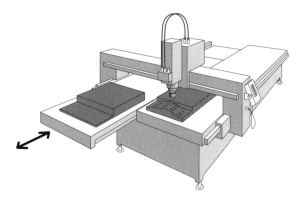

Figure 14-16 A diagram showing a gantry-type CNC router with moving worktables to ease loading of one workpiece while the other is being worked on.

cise, sharp edges on most cutting tools. Surface grinders with horizontal or vertical spindles utilize the same substantial frames, moving tables, and fixed heads that milling machines do (see Figure 14-17). Grinders with lathe ancestry include cylindrical and internal grinders. These tools also use correspondingly similar types of digital control. CNC grinding machines can perform exceedingly precise work on a wide variety of materials, but they are especially useful on metal components. They are frequently used at the completion of other machining operations to achieve final tolerances and finish, but they have long enjoyed particular success in the shaping and finishing of metal too hard to be machined such as tool steels, carbide, and the hardened blanks for punching and drop-forging tooling.

Plain surface grinders perform flattening or tapering work by moving a workpiece in the *x* and *y* axes beneath the edge of a rotating wheel, and tapers are then made by adjusting the axis of the workpiece. Rotary surface grinders work in a similar fashion, although the rotation of the wheel is perpendicular to the workpiece, working like a facing mill. The work table on these machines is generally fixed in the *z* axis, with the necessary vertical movement being controlled by the height of the grinding wheel itself. Wear of the wheel may be compensated for through software or through direct measurement using sensors on the tool itself.

Electrochemical Grinding

Electrochemical grinding reduces the pressure and heat associated with standard grinding by allowing chemical action to do most of the work. The work must be immersed in an electrolyte solution containing positive and negative charges in order for a reaction to take place, but the method can be faster than conventional grinding, and the work may be accomplished with considerably less pressure and less accompanying heat buildup. For these reasons, it is a particularly useful method for finishing parts that are subject to breakage or thermal damage such as thin or otherwise fragile parts.

Blasting and Abrasive Gas-Jet Methods

Abrasives may also be utilized in a loose form by directing the individual abrasive particles en masse against a workpiece to abrade it in a controlled fashion. Sandblasting and bead blasting will be familiar to many, in which a controlled stream of compressed air picks up and projects sharp particles of sand, glass, or other media at a resistive surface, causing material to be broken away. Blasting media can easily be controlled through careful hand-control of the blasting gun or nozzle, or through the use of rubber mattes, which are themselves produced using CNC knife cutters. Adhered to a material such as glass, stone, metal, or wood, the rubber causes abrasives to bounce harmlessly away except where openings have been cut, allowing finely detailed lettering and patterns to be cut affordably. (See Figure 14-18.) Abrasive gas-jet technology carries this method further by using a higher-pressure, high-velocity jet of air or gas (nitrogen or carbon dioxide) to direct abrasives through a nozzle to cut intricate patterns in a variety of thin materials, including brittle, hard, metallic, and nonmetallic ones.

Water-Jet Machining

Abrasive water-jet machining is quite similar to abrasive gas-jet machining, but the significant advantages of water-based delivery of abrasives have led to the rapid growth deployment of this technology among general manufacturers. Water-jet machines use extremely high

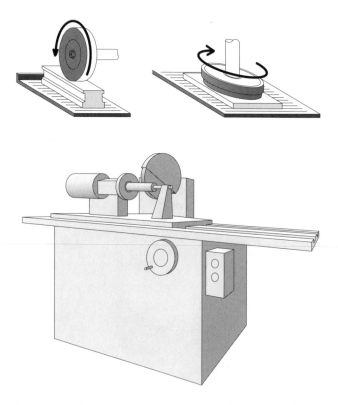

Figure 14-17 Diagrams showing typical horizontal and vertical abrasive wheel configurations.

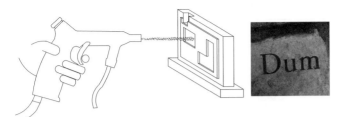

Figure 14-18 A diagram showing a sandblasting gun while sand or bead blasting a surface pattern utilizing a rubber matte cut with a CNC knife, accompanied by an example of lettering in stone produced in this manner.

water pressures to deliver abrasives through hard nozzles made from materials such as tungsten carbide, rubies, and sapphires. The abrasives are chosen, loaded into a hopper, fed through a tube into the already-accelerated water jet, and projected with the water at enormous velocity onto and through a workpiece. (See Figure 14-19.)

Abrasive water-jet technology is very precise and easy to control through CNC, and it can produce through-cuts or etching in a wide variety of materials, including wood products, plastics, metal, stone, tile and brick, composites, and glass. The majority of such machines are controlled like a plotter in only the *x* and *y* axes, but machines with more axes of movement are also used in the creation of complex three-dimensional parts. A major advantage of water-jet cutting is the cooling effect of the water stream, allowing all types of heat-sensitive material to be cut with minimal stress. Advantages include high cutting speeds, the possibility of making cuts in the middle of a workpiece (it is not necessary to start a cut from an edge), and reduction or elimination of fixturing to hold a workpiece in place.

Machining with Water

It is well known that water itself can wear material away or, if under great pressure, break material away in a variety of different ways, and precise, powerful streams of water are indeed used to cut a variety of materials. Foam, paper, leather, and insulation are all cut using water streams with pressures from 400 MPa to 1,500 MPa. The process is generally clean, inexpensive, and does not produce heat, although cutting speeds are not as high as with abrasive water-jet machining.

Ultrasonic Machining

Ultrasonic machining is one other form of abrasive material removal that should be mentioned here. Used to produce holes, cavities, and contours in materials that are hard or brittle (and therefore able to be abraded), this process wears material away much the same way sandblasting might, except that the abrasive particles are projected at high speed against the workpiece in a novel and unexpected way. A shaped tool

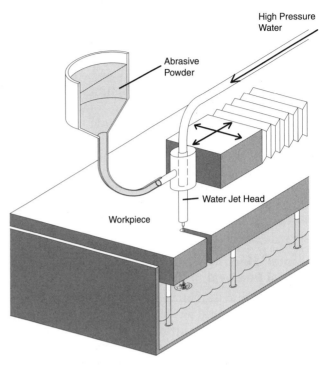

Figure 14-19 A diagram of a typical water-jet cutting machine, shown cutting through thick material over a water bed.

with a shape that is the negative of the desired one is placed very close to, but never touching, the workpiece. The tool is subjected to high-frequency mechanical motion while a slurry containing abrasives is flushed constantly between the tool and the workpiece. Abrasive particles in the slurry are propelled at high velocity into the workpiece by the rapidly vibrating tool, causing a multitude of very tiny cuts. (See Figure 14-20.)

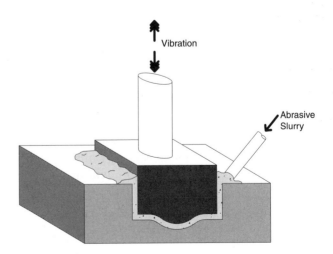

Figure 14-20 A diagram showing a tool cutting into a workpiece through the action of ultrasonic machining. The tool vibrates rapidly while a slurry containing abrasives is flushed beneath and around the tool. The tool will gradually cause the workpiece to be cut precisely to the same shape.

Eventually, a burrless, distortion-free imprint of the tool appears on the workpiece.

Ultrasonic machining is quite similar in effect to electrical discharge machining (EDM) and electrochemical machining, both of which are described later in this chapter, and in fact they are sometimes used for the same purpose. EDM works only on some electrically conductive materials, while ultrasonic machining is applicable to virtually any material that is hard or brittle. Blind holes can be drilled that would be difficult or impossible using lasers, electron beams, or abrasive jet drilling, and the work is not subjected to heat or severe or concentrated mechanical, electrical, or chemical stresses.

Thermal, Electrochemical, and Chemical Material Removal

Material can also be removed through thermal, electrochemical, or chemical means. Oxy-fuel cutting, carbon-arc cutting, metal-arc cutting, oxy-arc cutting, plasma cutting, and laser cutting are among the methods used to thermally remove stock such as sheet metal or plate by melting it, vaporizing it, and blowing it away, or simply through burning. Electrochemical and chemical methods such as EDM and etching remove material by destroying the atomic bonds within the material itself and flushing the loosened material away. Each of these technologies has distinct characteristics relative to its speed and precision, as well as the nature of the materials to which it can be applied, but they all lend themselves to use within a CNC environment.

Oxy-Fuel Cutting

Oxy-fuel cutting has been associated with the building industries since the invention of the oxyacetylene welding and cutting technology early in the twentieth century, and various systems based on templates, tracks, robots, and "magic eye" guidance systems were developed to cut and weld regular shapes prior to the introduction of numerical control—many of which remain popular in the fabrication domain. Oxy-fuel has long offered a simple, portable, low-cost, noncontact method of cutting steel up to 10 inches thick relatively accurately using hand- or machine control. Oxy-fuel cutting was easily augmented with the advent of two- and three-axis CNC gantry systems, and despite being unable to cut nonferrous metals, it has remained popular in the steel fabrication industry. It is an especially practical method for cutting steel over ½ inch thick, and the gas, hoses, regulators, and other necessary equipment owned by fabricators for hand work can also be used for the affordable CNC cutting systems.

Oxy-fuel cutting works by first applying heat to steel (5,000 to 6,000°F) to begin a chemical reaction, and

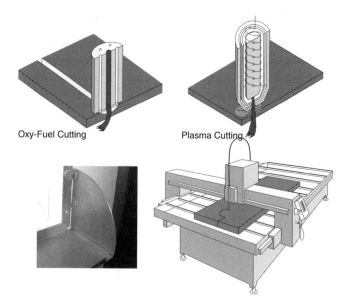

Figure 14-21 Diagrams showing cutaway views of oxy-fuel and plasma cutting torch tips, a sheet metal part, and a typical CNC cutting machine. There are few limitations to the size of these machines.

then introducing a stream of oxygen to oxidize the heated steel, causing it to vaporize. (See Figure 14-21.)

Plasma Cutting

Plasma cutting systems have been developed more recently than oxy-fuel but are used in much the same way. They are as portable as oxy-fuel setups, and a marked advantage of plasma cutting machines is that they can be used to cut a variety of metals, including steel, stainless steel, some copper alloys, and aluminum.

Plasma cutting is a very cost-effective way to cut many metals for the building trades. The plasma stream is narrow and capable of being controlled accurately to dimensional tolerances of hundredths, or even thousandths, of an inch, typically through ⅛-inch- to 1-inch-thick material, but thinner and thicker metal can also be cut—up to 3-inch steel easily and 6-inch if pressed. The concentrated heat produced by the plasma stream will have an adverse effect on finishes and may cause material deformation, making it an unsuitable choice for trimming finished panels or tiny parts, for example.

Lasers

Lasers are perhaps the most compelling and useful of the thermal cutting tool family. Lasers are used for a variety of manufacturing needs in addition to cutting, such as welding, measuring and digitizing, recording information, and inspection. LASER stands for Light Amplification by Stimulated Emission of Radiation. Lasers work via a high-voltage current being passed through specific gas mixtures (gas lasers) or via a solid

Sample of Laser Cut Stainless Steel

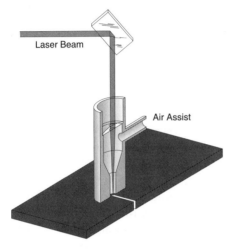

Laser Beam

Air Assist

Figure 14-22 A laser-cut component and a diagram illustrating important parts of a laser cutting tool, including the laser beam, reflecting mirror, focusing lens and air assist (optional on some small machines).

an assisting stream of oxygen or some other gas to encourage a chemical reaction or to blow away the waste material. The air assist also often helps to keep the laser head and mirrors clean. (See Figure 14-22.)

A wide range of materials can be cut or etched, including glass, ceramics, metals, plastics, composites, soft rubber, and even diamond. Since laser light can be delivered in a focused manner to a small area without affecting immediately adjacent material and without mechanical stress, laser cutters can cut weak, fragile, and delicate materials. They require no dies or hard tooling and can reduce or eliminate post-process finishing steps. The constant relation of the focused beam to the surface of the material allows for consistent precision work. In addition, noise, dust, chips, and fumes are minimal when compared to competing technologies.

Gas lasers using helium, nitrogen, and carbon dioxide are responsible for the majority of production cutting and are available in a wide range of sizes and wattages. High-wattage lasers have more power and are capable of cutting thicker material or of faster cutting speeds. Lasers of 25 to 60 watts are sufficient to cut paper and acrylic materials for design, model building, and prototyping purposes, while a laser that can cut inch-thick slabs of steel may be as powerful as 4,000 watts. Lasers easily cut up to ½-inch steel with an oxygen assist, or ⅜-inch stainless steel and ¼-inch aluminum using a nitrogen assist, and thicker material can also be cut.

Lasers offer features in addition to straight cutting. They may be used to make precise markings; etch letters, numbers, or bar codes; or produce perforations. Using an additional rotating axis, tubing may be contoured to make precisely fitting angled connections with any other shape—a feature that has been used to revolutionize the production of space frame and bicycle frame production, for example. While precision and the quality of the finished edge is critical, heat control can be utilized to anneal, harden, or otherwise heat-treat precise areas of transformation-hardenable metal alloys.

The digital control of lasers varies from the very simple to the enormously complex. Small lasers with fixed tables often use HPGL to move a mirrored head in the x and y axis to reflect the beam from a fixed laser down to a workpiece (see Figure 14-23).

lasing medium (solid-state lasers). The high voltage energizes the atoms of the gas, producing instability. The atoms release light in an effort to regain their composure by shedding energy, and the light is then directed into a stream by photons passing by the excited atoms in a consistent direction. Mirrors in a laser assembly reflect the light to amplify it, and when the light becomes intense enough, some of it passes through a partial reflector at the end of a tube, and then a lens, to become the focused beam. While small laser cutters cutting paper and acrylic can cut by melting and vaporizing with a laser beam alone, larger tools employ

Figure 14-23 A diagram of a typical arrangement of mirrors allowing a fixed laser device to provide a consistent cutting beam to a moving head using HPGL.

A moving mirror is used on some large machines, but frequently the laser head itself is held in a moving gantry that controls the *x, y,* and *z* axis movement. Additional axes may allow three-dimensional cutting for different manufacturing needs—trimming complex castings or stampings, cutting profiles in structural or decorative sections to fit other work closely, or cutting curved glass or ceramic components to fit together or into defined frames, for example.

To review briefly, there are a number of commonly available types of thermal removal methods, each with its own advantages and uses. Oxy-fuel and plasma cutting are fast, inexpensive, and easily controlled, especially to make accurate flat shapes, and they are much used in the metal manufacturing industries. Plasma cutting has the advantage over oxy-fuel of greater flexibility, but it is not appropriate for the thick steel plate that oxy-fuel can handle. Laser cutting is even more flexible, considerably more precise than the previously mentioned methods, and is capable of cutting three-dimensional profiles in shapes with thin walls that are beyond the capabilities of the other tools. Water-jet cutting should be included in any discussion of these three methods, as it is comparable to laser cutting in terms of flexibility, being able to cut a wide variety of materials even more precisely than lasers and with no discoloration or distortion from heat. Water jets are slower and noiser, and they require significantly more maintenance, but aside from potential differences in the cost of proposed work, it is unlikely that these considerations will impact your use of the different technologies unless you purchase and use the tools yourself.

Hot-Wire and Electrochemical Machining

Material removal techniques involving the direct use of electrical energy are of interest, such as hot-wire cutting, electric discharge machining (EDM), and electrochemical milling.

Hot-Wire Cutting

Hot-wire cutting is appropriate for cutting shapes from foam sheets or blocks. An electrically energized linear heating element may be used to produce a wide variety of simple or complex shapes. The cutting action is achieved by the heat from the wire heating element rather than direct contact with the wire itself, so the wire needs only enough strength to hold its shape (see Figure 14-24). Straight heating elements will lead to shapes with ruled surfaces, but linear heating elements may be bent to cut other shapes as well—a wire shaped like a column profile may be rotated to cut a "turned" shape, for example. Foam is used directly in buildings for insulation, backing panels, ornamental details, as the basis for exterior façade systems, and for stackable insulating concrete forms, among other uses—all of

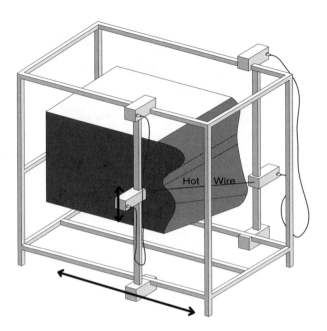

Figure 14-24 Diagram of a typical CNC hot-wire foam cutting tool.

which may be shaped using hot-wire cutters. CNC foam cutters are also commonly used to manufacture foam cores for composite structures such as wings, surfboards, and sailboards. They are used to make lost-foam sand-casting patterns, precast concrete mold inserts, and inserts for in situ concrete forms. While foam is often milled using large, high-speed machines, more cost-effective CNC hot-wire cutting machines can cut profiles and shapes directly through the material without having to remove stock gradually. It is possible to purchase standard hot-wire machines with capacities of $16 \times 16 \times 16$ feet, and larger custom machines can be built, making them capable of producing very large parts. The two ends of the cutting wires may be controlled separately along different axes to allow cutting of complex shapes.

Electrical Discharge Machining

Another use of electrical energy in the removal of material is called electrical discharge machining (EDM). Related to some other methods of removing metal using an electric arc or bimetallic corrosion, EDM has achieved a high standard for the precise linear or shaped removal of electrically conductive materials to produce finished, burrless shapes. Unfortunately, EDM is also a slow method of material removal, rendering the process of little direct use for most designers or fabricators, yet it is worth understanding the important role it plays, especially in the manufacture of tools and dies for the manufacture of innumerable things. Despite the relative youth of the industry, EDM machines are the fourth most utilized tool in machining industries today.

EDM works by bringing an electrode such as a thin wire (wire EDM) or a solid block (sinking EDM) in the shape of the negative of the desired shape very, very close to a workpiece immersed or bathed in a dielectric (nonconductive) fluid (see Figure 14-25). The high-density current then jumps across the miniscule gap, forming multiple tiny arcs of short duration. The arcs dislodge material on the workpiece, and the waste material is flushed away by the fluid, exposing new material to the electrode. The dielectric fluid also functions to keep the temperature of the workpiece constant while also helping to concentrate the electrical pulses. Wire EDM is capable of making precise straight cuts in hardened materials that are too thick to be cut with lasers and too hard to be machined conventionally. Differential control of the two ends of the wire allow the production of shapes with sloped walls, tapers, and ruled curves.

The process is extremely accurate—more so than most other methods covered in this chapter. A 0.0001-inch tolerance is achievable for routine work. The work also takes place with little or no human intervention once the workpiece has been properly located, allowing work to be completed while other tasks are being done. EDM tools can directly shape hardened tools for molding, stamping, and forging, making them important in metal- and plastic-forming industries as well as for the direct production of some usable parts.

Electrochemical Machining

Electrochemical machining shares many characteristics with EDM technologies, although metal is removed by anodic dissolution rather than by minute direct electrical charges. This is, in essence, a purposeful and controlled form of bimetallic corrosion, or galvanic action. A shaped electrode carrying high current density is brought very close to the workpiece to maintain a very narrow machining gap—approximately 0.004 inch. The workpiece may be submerged in an electrolyte solution (contrasting to the dielectric solution used for EDM), or an electrolyte may be flushed constantly over and through the gap, removing ions and other dissolved materials, gas, and heat as the tool is fed in the direction of the workpiece. ECM is particularly useful for machining shapes that are too complex, small, or thin to be machined otherwise. Like EDM, the shape of the tool can be duplicated by simply moving the tool into the workpiece. Complex surfaces may also be machined using a round electrode with multiaxis control. (See Figure 14-26.) Common uses for ECM technologies include the making of tools and dies for punching, forging, and glass making.

Photochemical Machining

This method of material removal is also known as photo-fabrication or photo-etching, while chemical milling is a variation described in the text that follows. While also relying on an electrical charge to remove material, no direct electrical input is used. A precise and

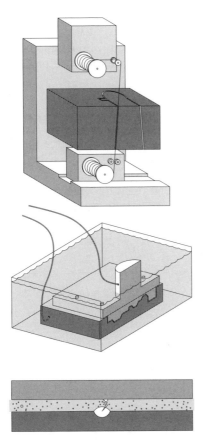

Figure 14-25 Diagrams illustrating wire and "sinking" type EDM tools, showing the electrically charged tool being slowly moved or lowered to eat away at the workpiece. The lower diagram indicates how the cutting action works through tiny electric charges within a dielectric environment. Suspended particles of material are flushed away.

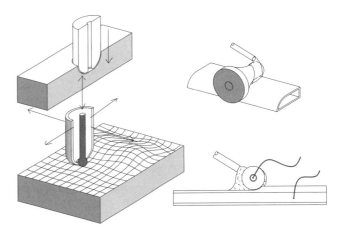

Figure 14-26 Diagrams showing how electrochemical machining is accomplished using a fixed die or a three-axis moving universal head.

stress-free technology, the reaction that causes removal of material is based on chemicals, using reagents and etchants.

The first step in photo-etching is the application of a chemically resistant mask to the metal piece. A photo-curing liquid is applied to the workpiece, after which an image is projected onto it. The workpiece is then rinsed, washing off any liquid not cured by the projected light. Finally, the workpiece is submerged in a chemical bath where chemicals attack all unprotected areas, resulting in a finished product comparable to those made by blanking or stamping. (See Figure 14-27.) The rate at which various chemicals eat away at known materials is well known, so the depth of the machining is simply based on controlling and timing the immersion of the workpiece properly.

The advent of digital technologies has increased the cost-effectiveness and flexibility of metal etching, as the mask may be applied using digital projectors, digitally printing directly onto the workpiece or applying digitally cut adhesive masks. This allows instantaneous changes in the pattern when prototyping or finalizing required dimensioning for a new design.

Chemical Milling

Chemical milling is similar to photochemical machining, but larger amounts of metal are removed and the precision of the patterns is not usually as high. A useful application of chemical milling is metal removal to decrease the weight of the part while maintaining its overall shape. Pockets, grooves, taper ribs, and grid patterns are typical examples of design features well suited for chemical milling. As in photochemical machining, the workpiece is masked (not necessarily photographically) and immersed in an etching solution. The maximum practical amount of metal removal is about ½ inch deep.

Other Material Removal Technologies
Punching

Punching is an important material removal technology. While the basic punching process may appear to belong in the category of deformation, which follows this section, CNC punching technologies compete with milling, drilling, water jet, and laser cutting. Applied to sheet metal, CNC turret punches are among the speediest and most flexible of modern tools, within their limitations. Punches work by shearing material between an active punch and a passive die, causing a shaped hole to be made. Round, square, oval, and triangular hole shapes are common, but any shape of punch and matching die may be mounted in a tool. Typically, the minimum size of a punch is based on being equal to or greater than the thickness of the material it is meant to pierce. Punches of this type are used primarily on sheet metal rather than thicker stock.

CNC punches are capable of making simple punched holes in any pattern over a workpiece, of course, but they are also capable of "nibbling" with extreme accuracy and great speed, enabling them to cut perfect shapes of all descriptions anywhere on a sheet (see Figure 14-28). They are a perfect tool for sheet-metal work of all descriptions, doing their work without producing heat, fumes, or waste that is difficult to dispose of. They are an appropriate choice when prototyping or for small- to medium-scale production.

14.3 DEFORMATION, MOLDING, AND CASTING

This very broad category includes a wide variety of technologies of interest that have benefited either directly or indirectly from the development of CAD/CAM and CNC technologies. Deformation, molding, and casting operations are used at different scales,

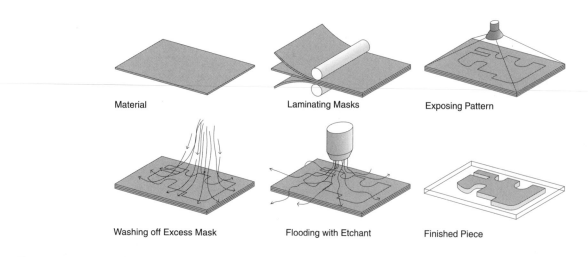

Material   Laminating Masks   Exposing Pattern

Washing off Excess Mask   Flooding with Etchant   Finished Piece

Figure 14-27 Diagram showing the steps required to produce a photochemically machined piece.

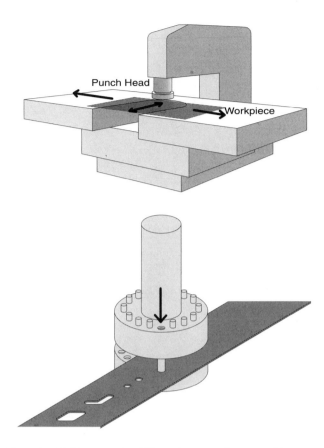

Punch Head

Workpiece

Figure 14-28 Diagrams of a CNC punch press and a turret with a variety of punches of different sizes and shapes making shapes in sheet metal.

from the the initial processing of raw material into useful shapes (casting steel ingots and processing them through rollers, deforming them into rolled shapes, or producing engineered wood products through sheet-forming operations, for example) to secondary production processes and finishing operations. We will not focus on the processing of raw materials, even though digital enhancements and control of many such processes continue to improve the quality, cost control, and precision of the processes related to them. We will, however, examine many secondary industrial processes used to bring designers' ideas to fruition.

Materials may be deformed or molded through the use of single, repeated, or continuous applications of force, distinguishing the processes from casting, in which a shape is formed by pouring or forcing a liquid into a mold. Molding and casting techniques are often faster than material removal technologies that can produce similar products, and may use material more efficiently by eliminating the waste that accompanies material removal processes, such as chips. In many cases, positive material qualities are associated with molding, deformation, and casting, such as greater strength and stiffness, but the technologies may be inappropriate for working brittle and hardened materials. In many cases, designers find themselves consider-

ing the comparative advantages of all these processes during the design development of a new piece.

Deformation and Molding Processes

This is a very broad category. Materials may be deformed, formed, and molded using a multitude of methods, from individual hand-bending to stamping or forging in bulk quantities. Pieces may be simply bent to create products such as reinforcing bar components or simple boxes; stamped using large, expensive tools to create small components or large panels with shapes such as those used on automobile bodies or building envelopes; or forged to create large, solid pieces from bulk stock—and these are but a few of the processes within these categories.

General deformation and molding processes may be divided into those used for *sheet, wire, and tube forming,* which may include compressive forming, tensile forming, shear forming, bending, and others, and *bulk forming,* which includes drawing, rolling, forging, and extruding processes. The processes generally refer to the type of stress to which the workpiece is subjected. Materials to which these processes are applied are generally capable of plastic deformation under high stress, including steel, stainless steel, aluminum, copper, and other metals. Forming processes include both cold and hot methods, and may also be applied to thermoplastics, rubber, and some wood and composite products; however, sheet forming usually refers to the use of sheet-metal materials that are cut, punched, drawn, stamped, bent, or otherwise formed, while bulk forming generally refers to the shaping of geometrically complex metallic components, which may be quite large.

Sheet, Plate, Wire, and Tube Forming Processes
Pressworking—Shearing and Bending Processes

The term *pressworking* generally refers to cutting and shaping sheets and strips between the members of a die. Pressworking falls into two categories. The first involves shearing or cutting processes to make the flat outline of the workpiece that will later be bent, deformed, or used directly. A second category has to do with forming the cut pieces into more complex shapes.

The first category includes several processes. *Blanking* is a process in which the outline of a flat piece is cut, producing a shape that can later be finished by secondary operations. A blanking die with the shape of the desired piece cut out of it is placed below the work while a punch in the shape of the piece itself is pushed against the work with enough force to literally shear the material between the tools (see Figure 14-29). Many metals shear well because of their crystalline structures, and shearing operations can produce very clean cuts when the punch and die have carefully controlled

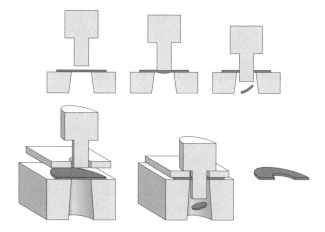

Figure 14-29 Diagram showing a cutaway of the blanking process in which a punch is forced through material against a lower die, causing the material to shear.

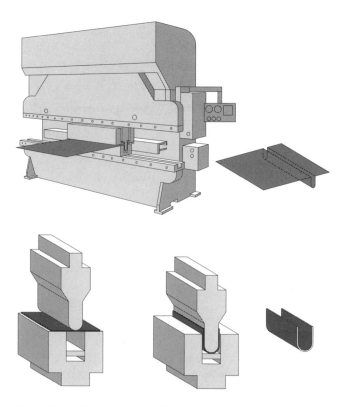

Figure 14-30 Diagram of a typical press brake and the sheet metal shape it is set up for making, including a detail of the dies used to produce the shape.

clearances. *Punching* (or *piercing*) is simply the process of cutting openings, holes, or slots into the workpiece, which may be done at the same time or as part of the same set of operations.

Trimming removes excess material from a workpiece that has been previously formed. *Shaving* is a trimming process, which removes thin shavings of metal in order to increase the smoothness or squareness of the workpiece. Various slitting and nibbling operations are also possible using press tools.

The production of finished blanks is the goal of most blanking, punching, and trimming operations, but blanks may also be produced by other means such as band sawing, EDM, laser, or water-jet cutting—the goal is simply to produce a given flat shape economically so that other forming operations may be performed on them.

The second category includes forming operations, including bending, drawing, and coining. The *bending* process, which includes folding, flanging, or twisting operations in addition to simple bending, is used to create shapes in metal sheet, wire, tube, and sections. These methods do not usually change the thickness of the metal, although hard bends in thicker materials will cause thinning at the bend itself. The shape and configuration of a bent part is largely dictated by the nature of the bending processes used.

Press brake forming is a common way of bending a sheet or a plate. A die and a mechanically or hydraulically assisted ram or press are used to bend the sheet material. Dies can be simple long strips to assist simple bends or have special shapes and profiles to help create desired cross-sectional profiles (see Figure 14-30). Some dies, such as those for creating lock-seams, support two stages of bending. If multiple bends are made on a workpiece, the order in which they are made is often determined by the machinery available and the geome-

try of the piece itself. It is not cost-effective, or even possible, to accurately bend all shapes.

Other forms of bending can be done through various kinds of rolling operations, which create curved shapes. These include the simple three- or four-roll bending process for making simple curves. Sheet, plate, tubing, and structural sections such as angle, bar, and I beams are also bent this way, usually using shaped rollers to support the shape being bent. Sequential roll-forming that forms sheet material through the use of a series of graduated shapes is used to form corrugated roofing and floor pans from sheet metal, as well as common roof gutters made from rolls of metal (see Figure 14-31). CNC technologies have been incorporated in many bending tools that allow software to correct for the constant variation in metal supplies.

The *deep drawing* process, often referred to as *stamping*, enables formed metal parts to be mass-produced economically by utilizing a power-assisted punch to force a flat blank into a preshaped die cavity (see Figure 14-32). Relatively deep parts such as sinks, light reflectors, and containers of all descriptions can be made this way. Shallow parts requiring little deformation are relatively easy to produce, and deep-drawn parts typically leave the machine as finished pieces, alleviating the need for separate surfacing, machining, and drilling.

A wide range of sizes can be accommodated in these processes, but typical stampings are made from sheets of

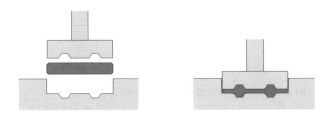

Figure 14-33 Diagrams of the coining process, showing the top and bottom die and the precisely shaped preformed piece. No flash is present on the finished piece.

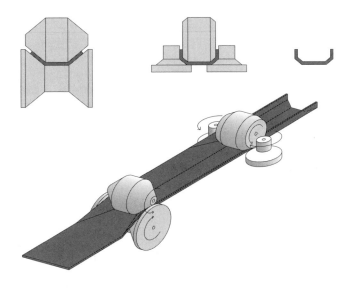

Figure 14-31 Diagrams of typical roll-forming operations.

metal that are ⅜ inch in thickness or less. Presses range from small bench presses to enormous press units. Cold stamping with large presses can accommodate parts up to ¾-inch thickness. Hot stamping can accommodate parts up to about 3½ inches thick. The dies used in these processes are usually made from hardened materials, but rubber and other materials can be used to reduce cost as well as wear and tear on the tools themselves.

Coining is a process used to form relatively small parts by compressing a blank between a confined die and a movable punch (see Figure 14-33). The action of the punch cold works the material into the shape of the dies. This process is often used to make intricate finish parts.

CAD/CAM technologies have had little effect on the basic methods used in presswork because of the very basic nature of the operations—presses simply bring enormous pressure to bear on relatively small areas—but they have affected the design and manufacture of the tooling to a great degree. Most punches and dies are made from hardened steel blanks, which were previously (and often still are) worked by hand in an annealed state by highly skilled die makers before being heat-treated and finished. Complex shapes are difficult to accurately transfer from a drawing to a three-dimensional block, and the heat treatments often cause

the tools to deform. The accuracy of material removal methods and the direct transfer of digital design data to machine tools has allowed new presswork tools to be made directly from hardened stock more quickly, using more complex geometric features.

Stretch Forming

In bending operations, the thickness of the material usually remains unchanged and unstretched. There are special processes, however, for creating complex surface shapes that involve stretching or otherwise deforming the material within its plane. Many common metal pieces made by forming flat stock have bent flanges at their edges. When the bend line is to be curved instead of straight, the flange cannot freely deform but must be bent into a concave or convex shape, causing the metal to stretch or compress. This can lead to tearing, wrinkling, or other breakage. Special *stretch forming* techniques have been developed that plastically deform metals into curved shapes via the application of large forces.

It is also possible to stretch-form larger sheets that have to be deformed into a complex shape (e.g., a spherical surface) by gripping the edges of the workpiece and pulling it over a shaped die using hydraulic rams or other power assists (see Figure 14-34). The

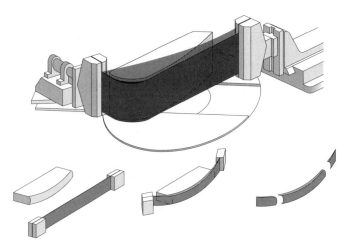

Figure 14-34 Diagrams showing how a complex shape with a curved flange may be formed using stretching techniques.

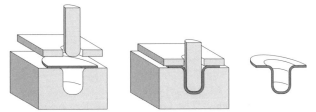

Figure 14-32 Diagram of the stamping, or deep drawing, process.

metal sheet may be heated during the stretching. Stretch forming is widely used in the custom automobile and aircraft industries, for example, to create uniquely formed panels.

Other Sheet-Forming Techniques: Spinning, Hydroforming, Peen Forming, Explosive Forming, Adjustable Dies, Laser Bending

Many hollow round shapes are made by spinning processes that are similar in many respects to turning operations. A circular blank of sheet material forced by a burnishing tool against a hard mandrel while rotating with it on a lathe will produce cost-effective and accurate parts, as long as they are round. (See Figure 14-35.)

Variations include shear spinning and tube spinning, both of which cold-extrude the spinning metal along the mandrel. These spinning processes can be used to generate a variety of finished objects, ranging from cowls for lighting fixtures and ventilation shrouds, to large architectural features. *Hydroforming* has provided both an alternative and a complement to the spinning and pressworking industries by providing a flexible and cost-effective way to make very accurate parts similar to those made using the former methods. Hydroforming includes a number of methods, all of which utilize pressurized water or oil to deform material, usually metal. Hydroform pressing and tubular hydroforming are the most common methods, but panel-type radiators, doorknobs, and other hollow metal shapes have long been formed using these methods.

A major advantage of hydroforming techniques is the reduced need for closely fitted die pairs. Press hydroforming requires just one fixed die, which may be made from softer materials in many cases than those needed to resist the enormous pounding forces of typical press work (see Figure 14-36). Tube hydroforming similarly requires a mold to contain the piece, but no die to force the work into the mold.

Hydroforming presses eliminate the upper, moving die, instead using a pressurized rubberized fluid pressure forming chamber—essentially a membrane—to push a workpiece into a mold, which may also move upward into the membrane for more complex forming. This method is capable of producing complexly shaped parts without the mechanical power and bulk of press

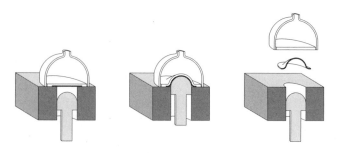

Figure 14-36 Diagrams illustrating the steps involved in making a simple shape using hydroforming techniques.

machines, and with none of the tool marking or material thinning that often accompanies spinning. Tubular hydroforming involves sealing the ends of a tubular shape, placing it in a mold, and expanding the tube within the mold using pressurized fluid. This technique has been eagerly adopted in the automobile industry to manufacture frame components and panels.

Peen forming is used in conjunction with relatively thin sheet metals. The workpiece is hit with a stream of small balls (shot) of steel or cast-iron via either air-blasting or rotating-wheel techniques. The shot creates a thin compressive layer on the surface layer of the metal, which in turn causes the layer to expand and the whole sheet to curve. (See Figure 14-37.) Large sheets can be gently curved in this way.

Explosive forming is a process used for limited-size parts. A blank is usually mounted over a die with a molded cavity similar to those used in press work. A surrounding tank is filled, and the air in the die cavity is removed. An explosive device is detonated over the workpiece, creating a shock wave in the water, which in turn deforms the blank into the die in a manner similar to hydroforming. (See Figure 14-38.) The near-instantaneous nature of this type of forming may allow the making of shapes that are not able to be made using other forming techniques because of unique material flow qualities.

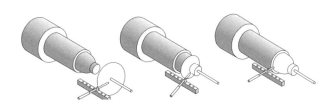

Figure 14-35 Diagram showing how a simple sheet metal piece such as a lamp shade shape is spun over a mandrel on a lathe.

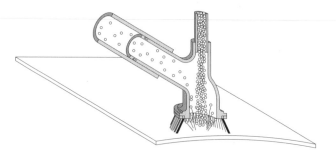

Figure 14-37 Diagram showing a cutaway view of shot peening a sheet, causing it to curve upward through the action of the continuous hammering of the shot.

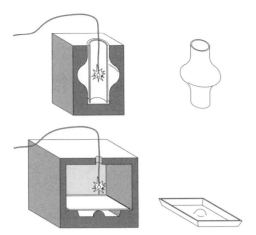

Figure 14-38 Diagrams showing typical explosive forming techniques.

A primary cost in many forming techniques is the high cost of the dies. To change or vary a part configuration, a new machined die, or pair of dies, is typically needed for each variation. There has been a good deal of interest in the development of various types of adjustable dies. This can be accomplished for some simple configurations, but it has proven to be quite difficult for dies that permit changing complex curved surfaces. One approach being explored is the use of a numerically controlled array of hardened rods or pins that slide back and forth against one another to create a complex surface shape over which material can then be stretched. Fixing the rods in place during the stretching and minimizing their size to provide a smooth surface are ongoing challenges for this method. The active control of the shape of the adjustable die is a unique application of CNC.

Laser beams can be used to bend relatively thin pieces of material by the application of laser-beam heat along predetermined lines of a workpiece. When the workpiece is subsequently cooled, local stress and strain fields are induced that define the final bend. The shape of the bend is achieved through programmed computer control, requiring an extensive database on the properties of the workpiece, expert knowledge of the relevant physical effects, and special robotized equipment. The angle of the bend is a function of beam power and spot size, the speed at which the beam traverses the workpiece, the sheet material and thickness, and the bend radius.

Many other specialized forming techniques are used industrially, but they do not vary in meaningful ways from those described. They will be identified by qualified consultants where appropriate, but it is likely a designer will not be aware of the specific processes being used to manufacture a particular piece when a variety of options exist. In fact, different consultants and contractors may use quite different methods to produce the same work, based simply on local capabilities, economies and traditions, availability of appropriate tools and personnel, and personal experience. A contractor with offices down the street from a punch press may well be able to have work done there less expensively than by having it sent to another company that uses laser cutting for flat work or hydroforming for complex shapes despite the apparent savings these technologies should theoretically allow.

Bulk-Forming Processes

Bulk-forming processes are those used to shape materials in forms other than sheet, plate, wire, and tube into useful shapes and products. These are major industrial processes that typically require the application of heat and great force. Like many of the processes already described, they have not been directly affected by CNC technologies for the most part, but within the industries that create the molds and dies necessary to make these technologies, usable CNC technologies have proven to be extremely important, if not ubiquitous. Forging, drawing, and extruding rely heavily on the accurate molds that are manufactured utilizing many of the CNC technologies already covered in this chapter.

Molding bulk materials through forging may be done using hammers, anvils, and other small tools, but in most industrial applications, it is performed using hard, expensive molds and dies that can make shapes repeatedly and reliably, relating these processes to those used in casting. The machines used are substantial and powerful, yet are often capable of producing work with great precision. The high cost of making forming-die tools usually restricts molding processes to the production of large lot sizes, but CNC technologies have allowed for more cost-effective small-lot production in many cases.

Drawing

Drawing is the process in which a rod, wire, or tube is pulled through a die or a succession of dies to reduce its size and to possibly change its cross-sectional shape (see Figure 14-39). The material is typically lubricated and then pulled through the die, either hot or cold. This process can improve mechanical properties through work-hardening. A variety of compact shapes of virtually any length can be produced in this way. Variations of round shapes are common (e.g., fluted shapes), as are other cross sections. A particularly useful aspect of the drawing process is that it is known that every drawn element can withstand at least as much tension as it was under when being pulled through a die. This allows more accurate specification of tension members made of drawn wire or rod.

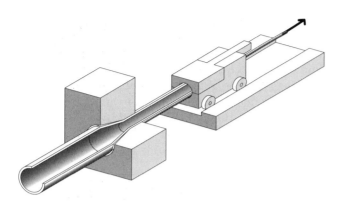

Figure 14-39 Diagram showing a cutaway view of a tube being drawn to a smaller dimension through a hardened die.

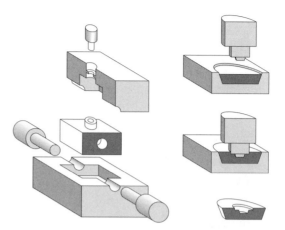

Figure 14-41 Diagrams of closed-die forging of a complex shape and impression die forging.

Forging

Forging is an ancient process used to create metal parts as well as a variety of tools and dies that can also be used to create parts. Essentially a hammering or pressure forming technique, both cold and hot forging are applicable to a wide variety of work. Hot forging generally allows work to be produced using less force and can have a positive effect on the material qualities of metal being worked. Cold forging can also improve material qualities through densification of surface layers and work-hardening, for example. Materials such as steel (automobile components and tools), brass (plumbing valves), tungsten (rocket nozzles), aluminum (an enormous number of uses), and virtually all the other metals can be forged.

Shapes produced by forging tend to not have undercuts, and cavities must be relatively straight and widest at the opening to allow the removal of forging tools. Common types of forging are open-die forging, closed-die forging, and impression-die forging. At the scale of manufacturing components used in buildings, these tools are heavy and receive intense punishment.

The open-die process places the workpiece between flat dies and compresses it (see Figure 14-40). Also known as upsetting or flat-die forging, this is a relatively simple process that produces relatively simple shapes. Internal mandrels are sometimes used to create particular shapes. Closed-die and impression-die forging forces metal into shaped dies that often have cavities in them. In closed-die forging, upper and lower dies are used that allow more precise shaping of parts (see Figure 14-41). The material completely fills the die cavity. Impression-die forging is similar but some material is allowed to spill out, which in turn makes it easier to fill the die cavities. Dies can be quite complex and expensive to make. CNC milling machines are typically used to make them directly from 3-D models.

Press forging puts hot metal under slow but steady

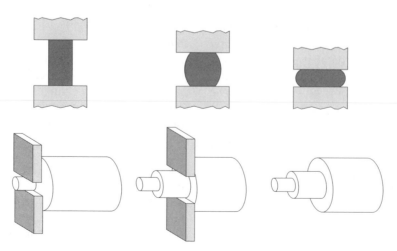

Figure 14-40 Diagrams of open-die forging, showing a shape being flattened by pressure (top) and a workpiece being rotated while being formed to produce cylindrical shapes (bottom).

hydraulically produced pressure rather than the intense and sudden hammer blows usually associated with forging. Huge pieces have been made this way in a controlled manner. A number of specialized forging processes exist, and more continue to be developed to satisfy specific demands, demonstrating the continuing flexibility of this venerable manufacturing method. The forming of bolt heads, threaded fasteners, and tools such as the Phillips screwdriver are good examples.

Extrusion

Many building components—particularly long, straight ones—are formed through a process of forcing metals or other materials through an opening, or die. The die opening is the shape of the cross section of the desired object. As the material emerges from the opening, it conforms to the cross section. Irregular cross sections can be easily accommodated as long as the section is not required to change over the length of the piece.

Extrusions are usually made using a machine that incorporates a ram energized by a screw or hydraulic element, and a hardened die (or set of dies). Material in bulk form is placed in a chamber, and the ram is set in motion to produce the desired part. Die design is sophisticated because of the need to have the material push properly through the die and to not twist or curve once it has left the die. Some dies for common shapes have variable pieces to allow size variations. The limit of the size of the extruded workpiece is based on the equipment and type of material used.

Hot extrusion processes are common, for plastics and aluminum in particular. The force required to extrude these materials is reduced because of the elevated temperatures used, but shrinkage can cause disaster as the extrusion cools upon leaving the die, making die design a critical feature of the technology. Cold extrusion processes are typically used for smaller pieces. Like the drawing process, the cold extrusion processes can actually improve the mechanical properties of the material because of the work-hardening that naturally takes place.

Casting

General

Casting processes have been used since antiquity and remain among our most viable ways for making objects. The general process involves pouring or forcing a basic material in a fluid state into a mold shaped like the negative of the desired shape. We look first at some of the most common casting methods such as casting molten metals that harden as they cool, or materials that harden because of other processes (concrete, for example, hardens because of a chemical curing process).

Common casting processes are typically divided into those using *expendable* molds, and those using *reusable* molds (see Figure 14-42). In addition, various kinds of composite molds are also possible. *Patterns* are frequently developed as an aid in these processes. Patterns are usually the shape of the object to be cast and can be used to develop permanent molds or to make expendable molds as in sand casting. Patterns may be

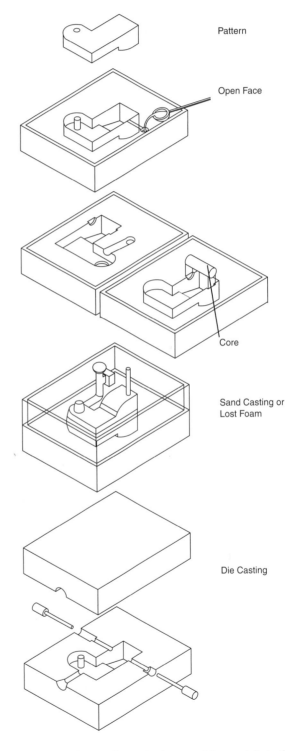

Figure 14-42 Various casting methods appropriate especially to the production of metal components.

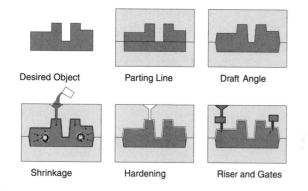

Desired Object   Parting Line   Draft Angle

Shrinkage   Hardening   Riser and Gates

Figure 14-43 Diagrams showing some considerations for the design of cast components.

made from metal, wood, plaster, or other materials depending on how they are to be used. Free-form fabrication techniques are increasingly used to quickly and accurately produce patterns for all types of casting. (See Figure 14-43.)

When expendable molds are used, the mold itself is normally destroyed in the process of removing the cast object, and the patterns may be reusable—as in the sand casting process—or also expendable—as in the investment casting process. The molds can be made of materials such as sand, plaster, or ceramic.

Reusable mold casting methods allow many castings to be made from a "permanent" mold. Die casting is a good example of this technique. Reusable molds must typically be very well made using tough materials to withstand the demands of the casting process, which can involve extremely high heat and great pressure. Metal or graphite molds are common. Negative shapes are often milled directly into the material (along with gates, risers, and sprues for getting the material into the mold, holding sufficient material while the casting cools, and allowing gas to leave the mold as material enters). They must be designed to easily come apart to remove the objects cast within them.

Sand Casting

Sand casting utilizes expendable molds in one of the oldest of all casting technologies that is still common today. In sand casting, a pattern is used to directly form a negative shape of the object to be cast in a bed of sand (see Figure 14-44). Primary components of a sand molding installation include the original *pattern* and the *sand mold* itself (typically made of two halves—the *cope* on top and the *drag* on the bottom); its support (often called a *flask*); a *pouring basin* for initially receiving the molten metal; a *sprue*, which channels the metal downward; a *runner system*, which carries molten metal to different parts of the cavity; *gates*, which provide entry into the mold cavity; *risers*, which supply extra material to the cavity as it shrinks during hardening; *vents*,

which carry off gases generated during the process; and any *cores* (sand inserts to form hollow volumes inside the object) that may be used (see Figure 14-45). The sand that is used is capable of being packed into a shape and staying in that shape until it is knocked or smashed, and it is capable of holding surprisingly fine detail. Once a sand mold has been packed around a pattern, the mold halves are split apart, the pattern is removed, and the mold is reassembled. The cavity is then filled with molten metal and allowed to cool until it solidifies. The sand mold is then removed from the object, usually by breaking it away. The extraneous metal and casting features such as gates and risers are then removed by trimming before grinding and machining operations remove any remaining extra material and bring the part to final specification.

Match plate casting, a method using two matching halves of a pattern mounted to either side of a plate, is an excellent way to achieve a high production of accurate parts, particularly when using casting machines that can automatically add sand to fill the flask, pack it, and imprint the pattern to produce a mold ready to be

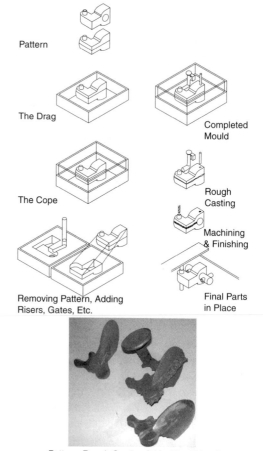

Pattern

The Drag

Completed Mould

The Cope

Rough Casting

Removing Pattern, Adding Risers, Gates, Etc.

Machining & Finishing

Final Parts in Place

Pattern, Rough Casting & Machined Handle

Figure 14-44 Diagram of the sand-casting process, with some typical sand-cast elements.

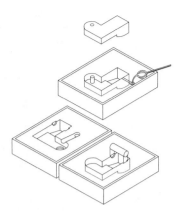

Figure 14-45 Diagrams showing open casting and the use of cores in sand casting.

filled with metal. Sand casting also lends itself well to open-face casting, which does not require sprues, runners, and so on. Open-face casting produces shapes of limited complexity, of course, and the top side of the part may be ill-defined.

The patterns used for sand casting must be the shape of the object to be cast and are usually slightly larger to account for metal shrinkage during cooling. Wood, plastic, plaster, and a variety of rapid prototyping or free-form fabrication tools are appropriate for making patterns that can stand up to the wear and tear of sand-casting methods. While pattern makers continue to employ handcraft techniques for some work, CNC technologies are now used for most pattern making, being capable of automatically scaling complex and highly detailed designs to account for metal shrinkage, required draft, and other clearances.

While common sand casting typically requires designs to be simple enough to use a matching cope and a drag to make up a two-piece mold, additional complexity or size can be supported by using features such as cores and inserts. Plumbing valves and automotive engine components are typical of small-scale complex parts, while locomotive frames or the exterior cast details of the Pompidou Center in Paris are examples of larger components.

Other Expendable Mold Materials—Plaster, Ceramics

A number of other materials may be used in place of sand in the general process previously outlined, such as plaster molds. Many materials may be cast in expendable plaster molds, including metals with low casting temperatures (e.g., aluminum, zinc). Good surface finishes can be obtained. A mold is typically made from a pattern and then dried in an oven after curing. Backing materials are often used to increase strength. Plaster molds have low permeability and do not allow gases developed during casting to escape easily, so

metal is often forced into these molds under pressure or suction.

Expendable ceramic molds share some characteristics with plaster molds—they are typically baked once an impression has been made, and they yield high-quality finishes—but they can withstand extremely high temperatures. They can be expensive, however, and are prone to being damaged.

Lost-Pattern Casting—Investment Casting

A variety of casting techniques rely on the use of an expendable pattern. The pattern is still made into the shape of the object to be cast, but it is made of some material that melts, evaporates, or burns when subjected to heat. Once a mold has been formed around it, the pattern is removed using heat, prior to pouring metal into the now empty cavity. Wax is often used as the expendable pattern material. Polystyrene beads can be used as well (see section that follows), and various plastics and organic materials such as wood can also be used. The use of foam patterns can obviate the need to empty the cavity prior to pouring, as the foam will disintegrate upon contact by the hot metal. Lost-pattern casting can be done using large *investment* molds cast around an object (for traditional lost-wax casting of jewelry, sculpture, and other components), *ceramic shell* molds (which have largely replaced the traditional method of investment molds for lost-wax production), or even loose sand when it is packed around a foam pattern (a production technique used to cast engine blocks, for example).

In *ceramic shell casting*, a pattern is made of an expendable material. Once the pattern is attached to a sprue—or multiple patterns are arranged along a sprue like a "tree"—the assembly is repeatedly dipped into a slurry of ceramic refractory materials to build up a coating around the entire assembly. A continuous one-piece mold results. (See Figure 14-46.)

The mold is inverted and heated. The pattern melts away, leaving a cavity. The mold is then fired for a long time to harden it, to burn out any remaining pattern material, and to drive away residual water. Metal or other materials are then cast into the resulting mold. The mold is broken away to remove the piece or pieces, and the extraneous metal parts such as sprues and vents are cut away. Extremely precise and/or complex parts with good surface finishes can be produced using this technique, which is as appropriate for one-off individual creations such as fine jewelry as it is for the casting of large multiples of relatively low-cost complex components. The ceramic shell casting process has become quite automated in some production environments. In an industrial process, multipart metal dies are made (usually with CNC mills), into which wax or thermoplastic can be injected to make multiple precise copies of the expendable pattern. Alternatively, a soft

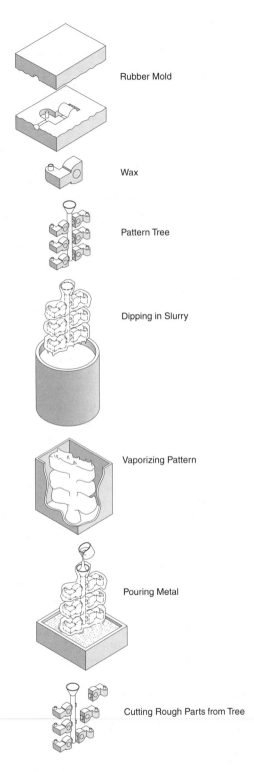

Rubber Mold

Wax

Pattern Tree

Dipping in Slurry

Vaporizing Pattern

Pouring Metal

Cutting Rough Parts from Tree

Figure 14-46 Diagrams of the lost-wax or investment-casting process.

Figure 14-47 A rubber mold used to make wax patterns for lost-wax casting, with a wax and matching rough cast metal component.

Lost-Foam Casting

A variety of other expendable-pattern casting techniques are in use. In the lost-foam process, polystyrene is commonly used for the expendable pattern (see Figure 14-48). Foam shapes can be machined or hand-shaped, but in a highly industrialized process, a die having a cavity the shape of the object is first prepared (typically from aluminum using a CNC mill). The die is preheated and filled with expandable polystyrene beads. More heat is added to fuse the beads together, and the new polystyrene shape is removed. This shape is coated with a refractory slurry, dried, placed in a flask, and surrounded by compacted sand (or another packing agent). Molten metal is then poured directly into the mold as usual, but with the polystyrene shape still in place.

The molten metal completely vaporizes the polystyrene and fills the cavity. A variation of this process is to place the foam directly into green sand, or even dry sand contained within a box. The rapidly expanding gas generated by contact with hot metal combined with the weight of the metal itself keep the walls of the sand mold from caving in as the metal is poured. The environmental concerns associated with vaporizing foam are easily solved with proper filters and ventilation. This method is extremely useful for designers and sculptors who desire to have one piece cast from an original, as foam is inexpensive to buy, easy to shape, and efficient when used as a lost pattern. Unfortunately, the flexibility of the foam allows it to be easily bent or deformed when sand is packed around it, so this is not an ideal method for casting accurate thin and flexible shapes.

Shell Casting

Shell casting can be used to make small elements with good finishes. Two half-shell molds are first made by encasing a pattern with a shell of molding material,

rubber tool can be used to produce the large number of identical patterns to be cast individually or, more likely, in the aforementioned "tree" structure, which is then dipped as a whole into the refractory slurry mixture, often by a robotic or automated system (see Figure 14-47).

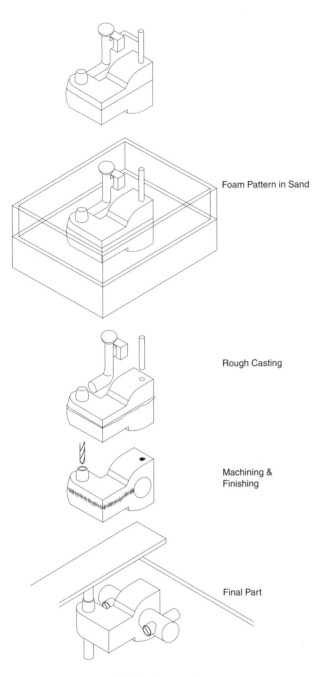

Foam Pattern in Sand

Rough Casting

Machining & Finishing

Final Part

Figure 14-48 Diagram of the lost foam casting process.

removing the mold shells, and then attaching them to one another to form a complete mold. The pattern is made of metal attached to a moveable mounting. The pattern is heated and then coated with a release or parting agent (such as silicone). It is then affixed to a box containing a sand-binder mixture. The binder is typically thermosetting. The box is moved, shaken, or rotated in some way so that the sand-binder mixture coats the pattern. The coated pattern is baked to harden the coating. It is then removed from the pattern via special ejection pins. Resulting shells are joined and casting ensues.

Vacuum Casting

Vacuum casting is a relatively new method for casting metals. The possibility of casting complex shapes, improved base tolerances, the possibility of obtaining very narrow walls, improved surface finishes, the ability to use alloys not commonly possible with other casting techniques, and better control of alloy characteristics (improved ductility, for example) are some of the advantages of this technique. Vacuum casting also produces parts with few air pockets or bubbles—a classic problem for all types of casting—as the material is gently drawn into the mold rather than being forced or poured in a manner that can allow air to mix with the casting material.

The vacuum casting process involves making an expendable mold of sand and a urethane binder that is formed onto metal dies and allowed to set. The mold is removed, reassembled, and then lowered down to the top of a molten alloy, which is then drawn into the mold by a vacuum applied through the top of the mold. To make cleaner castings, heat is cut off prior to the mold being filled to allow impurities to fall to the bottom of the molten material. Once the mold is filled and lifted, the furnace is turned on again. The whole process occurs very quickly and is necessarily controlled by microprocessors.

The technology is currently used in the automotive industry and for fine-art applications, but thus far it has had little application in the building industry. Nonetheless, many smaller-scale products cast using conventional methods could be produced this way. The flexibility of the approach is such that many products produced by machining operations could now be made via vacuum-casting techniques.

Rotary Casting

While many metal casting processes use the weight of the material itself or applied forms of pressure to ensure complete and accurate filling of a mold, rotary casting simply places molds at the periphery of a spinning mechanism so that metal is forced outward into the mold cavities (see Figure 14-49). Used for a variety of casting types, it is utilized in particular for small parts made from metals with a low melting point. Vulcanized rubber molds can be utilized.

Die Casting

Die casting is a process for forming parts by forcing molten metals under great pressure directly into permanent or reusable metal molds (or *dies*). Metals such as aluminum, copper, brass, magnesium, lead, and other alloys are typically die cast. (See Figure 14-50.)

A typical die-casting machine has two heavy platens containing the die halves. One of the platens is fixed and the other is moveable. After cleaning and spray lubrication of the dies, die halves are closed and locked

Figure 14-49 Photo of a small rotary casting machine and molds.

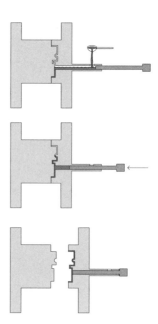

Figure 14-51 Diagram of a cold-chamber die-casting process.

automatically. Molten metal is then driven under high pressure (on the order of several thousands of pounds per square inch) by a plunger into the die cavity. Pressure is maintained long enough to allow the metal to solidify, at which point the die is opened and the casting is removed. (See Figure 14-51.) Inserts of materials other than that of the cast material itself can be placed in the mold to become mechanically fastened to the casting as it is being formed to achieve special properties (sleeves around holes for axles, for example).

Various kinds of die casting machines are in use for different kinds and sizes of part production, as well as different metal alloys. *Hot chamber* systems are appropriate for metals with low melting points, in which the pump can submersed in the molten metal. Hundreds of injections per hour can be achieved with these systems. When the pump could be adversely affected by the

temperatures involved, the pump is placed outside of the molten bath and a transfer or ladling system of some sort is used to bring the metal to the injection system (a *cold chamber* system).

Injection Molding

Injection molding is a form of die casting that is frequently used in the manufacturing industry to mass-produce plastic objects with relatively complex shapes (see Figure 14-52). A seemingly endless variety of products have been produced by this method, including toys, buckets, trays, steering wheels, and plates. These shapes are well suited to being molded between two plates, which determine their exterior and, where applicable, their interior shape. In injection molding, a solid material is melted into a plastic state and forced into a mold, where it is held under pressure until it cools and assumes the shape of the mold.

Most materials used for injection are called thermoplastics. *Thermoplastics* are plastics that can be repeatedly heat-softened, shaped, and hardened by cooling. Once a material has been melted, it is injected into the mold. The basic mold is composed of two plates. The cavity plate (the female portion of the mold) determines the external shape of the object, while the core plate (the male portion of the mold) gives the internal shape. When the two plates are connected together, a space is created between the cavity and core. This space, which is called an *impression,* defines the overall form of the object. The surface finish of the molded product is determined by the surface finish on the cavity and core plates, which can range from very rough or textured to mirror smooth.

Figure 14-50 Typical die cast component and rough casting.

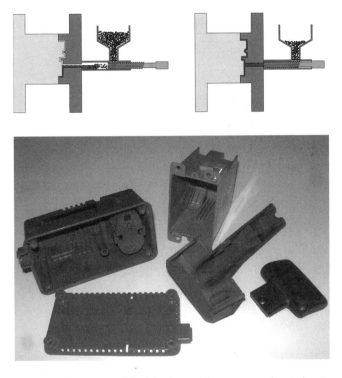

Figure 14-52 Diagram of the injection-molding process and typical parts made using it.

Injection molding also allows the easy insertion of other elements into the mold. Kitchen utensils are a well-known example of this, in which a metal handle or blade is inserted into the mold so that plastic can be formed around it completely.

Centrifugal Casting

This is a process for making parts that are essentially cylindrical in nature. Molds are normally made of metal and mounted on a rotating axis. Molten material is then poured into the center of the rotating mold, and it is distributed throughout a mold by centrifugal action, being forced against the outer surfaces. Long, hollow cylindrical parts of varying cross sections along their lengths can be made in this way. Many of the wonderful cast-iron street lamps made in the latter part of the nineteenth century were made this way, and the relatively simple and inexpensive process is now used for a whole range of parts. Finish quality is good.

Spray Metal Molding

Spray metal molding is an interesting technology for making short run molds for injection, vacuum, and other molding processes. A metal, such as a zinc-aluminum alloy, is applied with a sprayer to a prototype model of wood, wax, plastic, or other materials. The alloy is sprayed directly onto the model, where it cools to form a metal shell between 0.05 and 0.125 inches in thickness. The shell is then surrounded by a stiffening material, such as an epoxy resin or an alloy with a low melting temperature.

The final mold can be used to produce parts from many different materials, such as polypropylene and other plastics. The technique can be cost-effective for short production runs (on the order of less than 500 or so) and is consequently useful in working out problems with prototypes or with evaluating alternative molding materials.

While the original prototype model that is sprayed can be made of virtually any material, it is anticipated that spray molding will find increasing usefulness in connection with models made by stereolithography, fused deposition, or other rapid prototyping systems.

Special Processes for Plastics

Most of the processes previously described are particularly appropriate for metals except where noted, but they can often be applied to plastics, composites, and other materials as well. The unique characteristics of these different materials, however, often make special demands on generic processes or necessitate unique approaches to allow successful production.

Long Sections, Sheets, and Films

A number of plastics can easily be formed into thin sheets or films using extrusion-based methods. In an extrusion process, heated plastic is forced through a die. The die has the shape of the product to be extruded.

The extruded product is then cooled, usually by air but sometimes using water. Long sections with quite complex cross sections can be made in a continuous process in this way. The extrusion process is also used to make pellets that are in turn used in other processes.

Sheets and tubes are also made using extrusion-based processes; many familiar acrylic sheet products are made this way. The extrusion dies have devices for monitoring and maintain exact heats and heat distributions near the die outlet. Sheets may be fed onto a take-up roll or cut and stacked.

Volumetric shapes, such as common bags, can be made by extruding a tube and then blowing air into it. The air outlet is part of the extrusion die.

Thermoforming (Vacuum Forming)

Thermoforming is a commonly used way of forming thermoplastic sheets or films into various kinds of shapes (see Figure 14-53). A vacuum process is typically used to pull the sheet into close contact with the mold. The process involves pulling an easily deformable sheet of heated plastic over a mold, then applying a vacuum while the part is still soft, and simply releasing the vacuum once the part has cooled.

Figure 14-53 A typical thermoforming process.

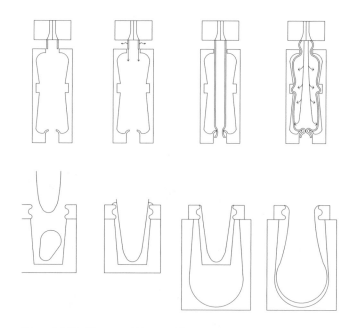

Figure 14-54 Diagram of blow molding.

A mold having the shape of the final object is first made. Metals, wood products, and even foam or wax can be used (depending on the number of pieces to be made). At a series of strategic spots in the mold, holes are provided to ensure that air can be removed. A sheet of heated, softened thermoplastic is then placed in a special fitting above the mold, vacuum is applied, and the sheet is pulled around the mold, where it quickly cools. After release, excess material around the edges of the piece can be trimmed. Parts can be produced quickly and inexpensively using this process, and it has proven especially useful for prototyping activities and packaging.

There are a number of design limitations to the shape that can be made. Surface curvatures must be generally smooth. Complex undercuts generally cannot be achieved, and material thickness is limited. The use of thermoplastic itself as the base material limits product uses. A key process in mold design involves making sure that a complete vacuum can be achieved.

Blow Molding, Compression Molding, and Other Techniques

Blow molding is a process for shaping plastics based on either extrusion or injection principles (see Figure 14-54). In the extrusion-based process, a tube is extruded and fed into a mold cavity, fixed, and then blown out with high air pressure to fill the cavity. Common bottle shapes can be made in this way. Processes can be designed so that these operations are continuous. In the injection-based process, a short tube is first injection-molded and then moved to a blow cavity as previously described.

In cases where objects are to be made of "foam," such as polystyrene, the material is designed in the form of expandable beads that are subsequently fed into an expansion cavity and exposed to high heat. The beads expand enormously in volume to fill the cavity. Common cups and other objects are made in this way.

Compression molding, used largely with thermosetting plastics, is a unique bulk-forming process involving placing a powder or semiliquid material (a molding compound) into a hot cavity and subjecting it to intense pressure. In some variants of this process, various rams or screw feeders are used to force the material into the cavity.

Special Processes for Glass and Ceramics

Glasses and ceramics share a lot of common properties. Both are of ancient origin and familiar to everyone. Who has not eaten from a ceramic bowl? This familiarity, however, belies the fact that these materials are used for highly sophisticated products that are used in a great many circumstances. Ceramics in particular have become highly engineered products with many remarkable physical properties.

In addition to normal flat sheets or plates, rods, and tubes, *glass* can be shaped into complex forms or be made into fibers for a variety of uses, such as reinforcing, optics, and so on. (See Figure 14-55.) Manufacturing processes are dependent on the exact form of material desired. Common flat sheets and plates are made by either floating or rolling glass from a molten mass. In the float method, sheet glass is continuously fed onto a bath of molten tin, where it floats as it cools (this process mitigates surface blemishes and imperfections and yields clear, though not optically perfect, glass). It then moves into a chamber, where it cools and hardens further before being cut and stacked. Rolling is literally done with hot glass drawn into rollers that are designed to size and imprint textures onto the glass.

Complexly shaped glass objects may be made by blowing, pressing, casting, or via a sagging process. Blown glass is commonly used for thin-walled objects (e.g., bottles). While glass can be freely hand-blown, industrial processes make use of a highly automated mold system. A mass of molten glass is put into a blank mold cavity. Blown air expands the glass against the cavity walls. A series of sequential steps are usually involved to create special features such as lips and necks. Resulting surface finishes are not perfect but are generally acceptable.

Sagging, or slumping, techniques are used to make both small and large pieces of shaped glass. For making small pieces, a dish-shaped mold is first made. A sheet of glass is placed over it, heated, and allowed to sag into conformity with the mold. This technique is increasingly being used to make larger sheets as well. For more conventional large pieces, a simple external perimeter shape is sometimes made, but there may be no mold beneath. A large piece of glass is put over the frame, attached to it, and the entire assembly is heated. The glass begins to slowly sag under its own weight. At the desired degree of slump, the glassmaker simply stops the process. The resulting glass is quite clear. While this is an easy and interesting way of making large curved glass pieces, there are obvious limitations on the shapes that can be made in this way and precision is limited. Large sheets of thick, curved glass with precise shapes are also still made by big multistage machines that heat the glass and press it into forms, or by slumping large sheets over simple curved molds made of steel sheet.

Volumetric glass objects can be cast directly into molds (see Figure 14-56). In a simple open-faced mold, glass is ladled directly into a preheated open cavity. It generally hardens quite quickly upon entering the mold. Objects are usually subjected to continued external heating for a while to ensure even hardening. Once hardened, still-hot glass objects are placed in an annealing oven with controlled heating cycles for a long period (several days or more).

The curing steps are necessary in casting glass because the differential cooling of different parts of a glass mass can result in high internal stresses being built up in different parts of the object. Failure in the form of severe cracking can result. All objects must be carefully designed to be easily removed from molds. The shrinkage that takes place during the cooling process can affect both the dimensional accuracy of the piece and the ease of removing it from the form.

Glass can be cast into complex multipart molds, but the viscous nature of the material prevents it from easily filling complex mold cavities. In better installations vacuum-assists can aid in filling the cavity completely. The molds themselves can be made from a variety of refractory materials capable of handling the extremely high casting temperatures associated with molten glass. Sands and ceramics can be also be used as mold materials, but surface finishes may suffer. Graphite molds are frequently used to achieve a high-quality surface finish and are able to be milled easily to close tolerances using CNC equipment. Some ceramics can be similarly treated, albeit milling ceramics is a difficult process.

Glass can also be pressed against the sides of a mold, allowing greater integrity of shape reproduction. Pressing shares characteristics of both blowing and casting operations, except that molten glass placed in a mold is immediately forced against the cavity walls by a plunger.

Figure 14-55 A complex glass shape.

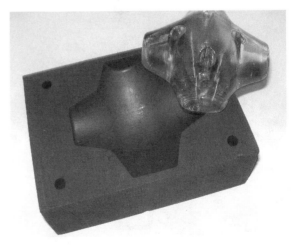

Figure 14-56 A graphite mold and a cast glass component.

The need to extract the plunger requires that the object be designed to allow extraction of the tool. The two halves of most hollow glass blocks are made in this manner, after which they are adhered to one another.

Ceramics are generally made by grinding raw materials; adding various binding agents, lubricants, plasticizers, and other additives; and shaping, drying, and firing them. The additives typically improve mixing, make the mix more plastic, improve mold release, improve water-suspension properties, and control or alter foaming properties. Many ceramics are made using a slip-casting process (see Figure 14-57).

A *slip* is made up of ceramic particles suspended insolubly in water or some other liquid. The slip is poured into a mold cavity, typically made of plaster of paris. The mold absorbs some of the water from the slip, which coats the mold. Excess slip can then be drained off, leaving a thin shell of ceramic to be removed from the mold upon hardening.

Various pressing techniques may also be used. In dry pressing, a powderlike mixture is used and pressed into molds under great pressure. The mix contains additives to aid the compaction process. Wet pressing processes are similar but use a more moisture-laden mix. Alternatively, various extrusion, injection molding, and other methods may also be used with a stiffer claylike mixture to form ceramic objects.

After shaping, a ceramic part is dried in a controlled humidity and temperature environment. The part is then fired at high temperatures, causing it to become strong and hard through vitrification. In the drying and firing processes, considerable shrinkage can take place that must be taken into account in the original design.

While ceramics will continue to be a common mainstay of many typical household goods and products, it must be remembered that they can also be engineered to have remarkable mechanical properties. Properly engineered ceramics can withstand tremendous heat (recall that forms of ceramic tiles are used on the exterior of the shuttle spacecraft). They can also be remarkably hard and are finding uses in bearings and other places where steel used to be the material of choice.

Special Processes for Metal Powders

In society's long fascination with metals, we have become used to thinking of them as being either in a solid or molten state, wherein they can be cut and drilled, or formed in molds to make complex shapes. Powder metallurgy, an unfamiliar technology to most, has become a common way to make many objects. The essential nature of these technologies includes metals in powder form that are compacted into mold cavities in dies and then subjected to a sintering process. The sintering process causes the surfaces of the particles to melt and bind strongly without melting the mass of the object.

A variety of metals or alloys can be used in powder metallurgy. Aluminum, nickel, titanium, copper, iron, and refractory materials are commonly used. Alloy powders can also be made. The powders are made by any of several processes to produce different particle sizes and shapes.

Dies for forming powdered metals are typically milled from steel. Compaction of the powder into the dies is done mechanically or hydraulically, hot or cold, typically under extremely high pressure. Higher pressures generally result in higher powder density and, ultimately, a stronger and stiffer part.

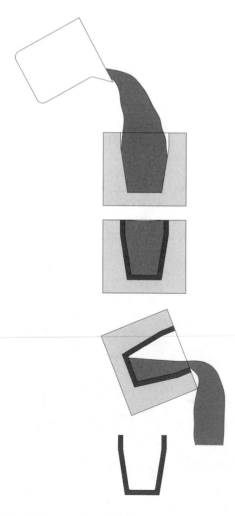

Figure 14-57 Diagram of a typical slip-casting process.

14.4 CONNECTIONS, FASTENINGS, AND FABRICATION

Joining

The design and manufacture of component parts for larger structures is done within a larger context requiring connections to be made between all parts. Connections can be made mechanically, with adhesives or by welding or brazing (see Figure 14-58). Welding and brazing in particular deserve some discussion relative to other CNC-enabled technologies, as they have benefited in specific ways from digital developments. We look at these technologies first, followed by a brief investigation of mechanical and adhesive fastening.

Welding, Soldering, and Brazing

Processes such as welding and brazing allow component parts to be connected without the use of mechanical fasteners. Welding is a process for joining materials by using intense, focused heat to melt the parent material, allowing parts to become one. Various materials can be welded, but the processes described in the following text apply primarily to metals. Brazing, including the low-temperature variations known as soldering, is a process that involves the joining of two metal parts by melting a second material with a lower melting temperature (lead, tin, and silver, for example) to cause a strong bond between the parts upon cooling. (See Figure 14-59.)

Basic Processes

There are five primary types of fusion welding processes: gas, arc, resistance, laser, and electron welding. Gas, arc, and resistance welding are most common. Specialized fusion processes include chemical reaction, thermal, and high-frequency welding. Stir welding is an interesting new process that may begin to have applications of interest to designers.

Common *gas welding,* commonly called *oxy-fuel welding,* relies on the intense combustion heat of a mix of oxygen and acetylene or other gases. The application of heat from a torch is easy to control for a variety of purposes, including brazing, welding, and heating for some hot forging actions. To make a weld, metal elements are heated together to close to melting temperature, at which point a puddle forms at the tip of the gas

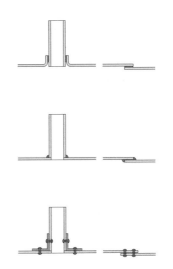

Figure 14-59 Diagrams of brazed (top), welded (middle) and mechanically fastened (bottom) metal joints.

flame. As the torch is moved along a joint, the puddle can be made to follow, allowing the pieces to intermix and then cool as one. If the parts are spaced apart, or there is a need for more metal, welding rods are used in conjunction with the torch to supply filler metal. This can make for stronger joints and can replace metal consumed by the heated reaction. Gas welding is flexible but not desirable for most structural work, as the heat affects a large area, causing severe expansion during the prolonged heating required for welding and subsequent stress as joints cool.

Arc welding is perhaps the most common contemporary welding method, having assumed primacy over oxy-fuel welding during the latter half of the twentieth century for a variety of practical and structural reasons. Arc welding relies on the heat created when a low-voltage, high-amperage electric arc jumps through a gap of air separating an electrode and a base metal (see Figure 14-60). The arc creates an intense, focused heat capable of penetrating deep into metal parts to provide strong joints. Arc welding with a standard handheld electrode, or *stick welding,* uses a ground cable attached to the metal to be welded, along with a second cable attached to an insulated electrode that also serves as a filler rod. When the electrode is brought close to the base metal, an arc jumps to the metal to complete the circuit, allowing welding to begin directly. The electrode is intended to melt away to contribute to the pool of molten metal, pulled there by the electric current, while an outer flux coating melts and vaporizes to protect the new weld.

Methods that have improved on stick welding include *gas-shielded metal arc welding* (MIG) and *gas tungsten arc welding* (TIG). In these processes, the weld is shielded from detrimental exposure to oxygen and

Figure 14-58 Typical fabricated components including a welded structural bracket and stainless steel hardware for tension members (left) and a rail support (right).

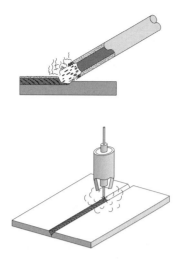

Figure 14-60 Diagram of arc-welding processes.

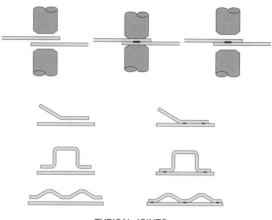

TYPICAL JOINTS

Figure 14-61 Diagram of the spot-welding process.

nitrogen in the atmosphere via the propulsion of an inert gas such as argon or carbon dioxide around the arc itself, protecting the hot parent metal while it is vulnerable to reaction with atmospheric gases. MIG (metal inert gas) welding utilizes a continuous-feed wire electrode to provide the arc and filler material, in a manner similar to stick welding. TIG (tungsten inert gas) welding is similar, but the wire electrode is replaced with a tungsten electrode that conducts the arc without degrading. The MIG process is the most commonly used form of arc welding because of its simplicity, speed, and general-purpose utility. TIG is more flexible and able to be controlled more precisely. Highly developed modern aluminum and titanium bicycle frames are welded with TIG equipment, for example. Finally, *plasma arc welding* is a fusion process frequently used on thinner materials, often without the use of filler rod or wire. All of the arc welding methods have been good candidates for CNC controls.

Resistance welding is a term describing any of several processes in which current passing through the work generates localized, focused heat by exciting electrons past their ability to easily flow. Resistance welding is most frequently used for making spot welds and for welding wire structures together where they intersect. In *spot welding*, pieces are generally joined at a number of different points by relatively small, localized welds to produce a strong overall assembly (see Figure 14-61). Commonly seen images of automobile chassis and body manufacturing include spot-welding robots making weld after weld along the joints where parts overlap.

Spot welding is particularly suitable for thin, ferrous metals. Spot welding large, thick pieces is difficult because the heat is quickly conducted away from the contact points, producing large areas of heat and distortion by the time welding temperatures finally occur. A typical spot-welding gun has a pair of electrodes

arranged like a pincer, while specialized CNC spot welders for wire parts may have large pads to contact many elements at once.

Advanced Welding Techniques
There are many advanced welding techniques, including a number of related welding processes that rely on the use of extreme pressure to make the final joint. *Flash welding* is a resistance welding process in which current is passed across a loosely fitted joint to provoke an electric flashing that heats surfaces to, or close to, the melting point just prior to the pieces being tightly clamped together. *Percussion welding* is similar, but the pressure is more rapidly (percussively) applied to create an instaneous welding heat from the applied pressure alone. *Forge welding*, the only type of welding that existed prior to the advent of torch assisted and arc welding, is performed by hammering, rolling, or pressing sufficiently hot metal parts together so that their surfaces become intermixed.

Laser welding is a "penetration welding technique." This means that the laser beam induces a metal-vapor-filled cavity, or "keyhole," on the workpiece. A "weld pool" is established, in which molten metal is in dynamic equilibrium with metal vapor. This weld pool migrates through the metal being welded.

The laser welding process is capable of a variety of applications, from welding microcircuits to heavy steel. One characteristic of this process is that it requires no filler material—the pieces simply become molten and fuse together. There are several advantages to using lasers instead of traditional techniques, including precision control, small-area coverage, access to normally inaccessible areas, and a small heat-affected zone. A wide variety of materials have been successfully bonded using laser welding, including metals, plastics, glasses, and ceramics.

Stir welding is an intriguing and important new

development that utilizes a spinning tool guided by a CNC milling machine to make friction welds along linear joints (see Figure 14-62). Friction welding has long been a common way to weld parts together that have dissimilar qualities, such as the malleable stem and hardened head of engine valves. By spinning the stem in a lathe while pressing it against a fixed head, enough heat can be produced to cause the surfaces to melt. Bringing the parts to a standstill causes them to cool together, fully joined. Stir welding is a friction-welding method that looks much like a machining action, but no material is removed. The spinning welding tip is pressed against the surface of two parts to be joined, creating heat to soften the parent metal. The tip of the tool then passes horizontally through the softened metal, mixing it together as the metal passes around the sides of the moving tool. The metal reforms behind the tool and cools to provide a smooth, continuous weld. The method is being used to weld alloys that are challenging to weld conventionally, as well as to weld dissimilar metals. Stir welding is currently being used to weld aircraft parts and other critical components, but applications are growing rapidly.

Welding Machines

A variety of spot and arc welding machines with automatic controls have been in use for many years. Most are used in connection with jigs, fixtures, or clamps that bring parts into alignment for welding. In production environments, *automatic* arc welding equipment performs entire operations without continuous observation but is adjusted through periodic operator intervention. In typical assembly work using spot welding machines, the devices can be programmed for complete cycles of clamping, welding, holding, and releasing.

Automated arc-welding machines are somewhat different in that the entire process occurs without operator intervention via the use of sensing devices and programmable controls. The sensing devices feed back

information regarding the work in progress to the control system.

Robotic welders can be used effectively in more complex environments or where economies of scale make them useful. An early major application for industrial robots was to facilitate spot welding in the automobile industry (circa 1969). Robots are also widely used for arc welding operations to create long continuous joints.

Mechanical Fasteners

The world of mechanical fasteners is a vast one. Where simple cylindrical rivets held sway in the not-too-distant past (admire the riveted construction of the Eiffel Tower, for example, or many twentieth-century transportation structures), connections made with common fasteners such as nuts and bolts, screws, blind fasteners, clips, and anchors of various kinds are now the rule.

Common types of fasteners will not be treated here, but it is worth recalling that they must be considered in conjunction with other design criteria. Many of the technologies described thus far are capable of providing holes, seats, slots, grooves, keyways, and other features needed by mechanical fastening devices to contribute to the overall success of a project. Fasteners are humble, but critical.

Mechanical fasteners transfer forces through tension, through shear, or through frictional forces between components joined tightly together. The number and location of fasteners can be a critical design decision—too close to an edge may allow tearing of the part under certain loads, for example. When vibration or regular expansion and contraction occur, special nuts and lock washers can be used to prevent loosening. These are typical of the considerations that must be kept in mind, as components don't magically join themselves—despite the fact that it may appear to be possible in many design development and visualizing software environments.

Rivets have been in use for a long time. Their direct simplicity has long been appreciated. While they are no longer used for assembling large steel structures, they remain in very common use in many manufactured goods. Riveting consists of putting a headed rivet in a hole and deforming the other end. *Blind rivets*—those that can be put in and fixed from one side only—were a major development that facilitated the use of riveting. Common pop rivets are included in this type, as are many specialized rivets used to build aircraft and boats.

Stapling is a familiar method for making light connections in thin materials. Stapling is among the fastest and most economical of connections. Punch-through, looping, and clinching stapler configurations are common, and no hole or particular surface preparation is

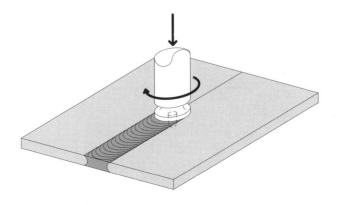

Figure 14-62 Diagram of stir welding.

required for their use. Staples are generally not chosen for transferring forces between materials, but they do allow the joining of a wide variety of materials. CNC nailing and stapling machines have been developed to assist with assembly of fencing, wood frame wall panels, and other components of wood construction.

Mechanical connections made simply through the careful design of components that can interlock to provide discrete support or to create an entire structure using a minimum of fasteners have long existed in building design. Interlocking joints found in traditional construction in China and Japan, for example, or some modern buildings utilizing precast concrete elements that stack or fit together may provide inspiration for activities easily tackled with the aid of CNC tools.

Sheet products may also be connected via shape change and deformation techniques. Seaming and crimping techniques provide obvious examples. In *seaming,* pieces of material are literally folded together to form a seam. Metal roofing is an example of this. *Crimping* is a process wherein simple forms are interlocked through localized deformations, or in which individual complex shapes are made without stretching or shrinking the material itself.

Other connections can be made by *shrink fitting* processes. These processes typically rely on the differential heating of the components being joined. A metal ring might be heated (and thus expanded) and slipped over another ring, for example. Upon cooling, the outer ring would shrink around the inner one to form a very tight fit.

A seemingly simple but potentially exciting way of joining components is through the use of *snap-in* fasteners. Snap-in fasteners are commonly found and vary widely. Many rely upon deforming ductile material into a particular shape that is in turn temporarily deformed out of the way when another shaped piece is inserted into it. At some point in the insertion, the shaped piece springs back to its original shape and locks in the inserted piece. These fasteners are very inexpensive and easy to produce. Like staples, they are not usually a good choice where large forces are expected to act upon them.

Snap-in fasteners are more sophisticated than they might first appear. They are critical in formal approaches to design for assembly (see Chapter 16), since they allow one-sided assembly and are typically self-aligning. Often one or both sides of a snap-in fastener can be made as parts integral to the elements being joined. Snap-in fasteners can be considered for many connections that typically involve screws and nuts, and while normally used to connect small elements, it is also possible to use snap-in fasteners for larger ones—particularly to align elements to be fastened with more substantial hardware, or for temporary installations.

Adhesives

Adhesives of one type or another have long been the method of choice for many joint conditions (see Figure 14-63). Glues have been obtained from animal products or organic substances since antiquity, and many of these are still in regular use—the simple mixture of flour and water is used by bookbinders, for example, and heated rabbit skin glue is still used by some instrument builders and woodworkers. New material advances have allowed a remarkable variety of adhesives to be developed that securely hold together more and more of our world. A look into the future may well reveal a world held together more by adhesives than by welds or mechanical fasteners. Adhesives with high load-carrying capacities, toughness, and resistance to fatigue and degradation from moisture, heat, or chemicals are now common. Adhesives distribute forces via a bonding action at interfaces, which can make the design of part connections easier. Thin pieces can be easily joined, as can materials exhibiting vastly different properties. The inherent ease of use of adhesives coupled with these improved properties and joining characteristics has made them very attractive alternatives for many uses, including larger-scale products.

Many special-purpose synthetic adhesives are available, including those that are chemically reactive, such as epoxies and silicones. Pressure-sensitive adhesives, hot glues, delayed setting, and even electrically conductive adhesives are part of increasingly large adhesive families.

Well-designed adhesive connections often rely on the presence of large surfaces to provide the interface area, much like good brazed connections. They are designed so that a force transfer between connected members results in pure shear, compression, or tension. Joints should be designed to avoid peeling actions, as

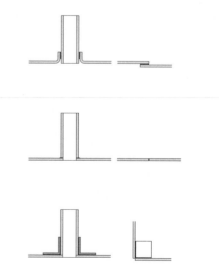

Figure 14-63 A diagram showing typical adhesive joint connections.

adhesives generally work best when a load is distributed over a wide area. Lapped joints work well, and adjacent pieces are sometimes tapered, or scarfed where it is desired that pieces lie in a single plane. Butt joints generally require large surface areas and should be avoided altogether under some conditions, such as when joining the end grain of wood components.

Special Considerations for Plastics and Glasses

While many of the previous connection strategies are appropriate for plastics and glasses (e.g., many plastics can be joined with mechanical fasteners and glass with adhesives), their unique properties have led to some special joining techniques. Adhesives don't work well on some plastics, for example.

Other methods for joining plastics are dependent on their exact makeup. Specific kinds of thermoplastics such as common polyvinyl chloride (PVC) can be joined adhesively or they can be welded using heat, but other thermoplastics, such as Teflon, are difficult to bond adhesively because common adhesives do not stick to surfaces.

For those thermoplastics that allow fusion welding, heat in the form of hot gas or air or a hot metal tool can be used as heat sources to melt the material to make a weld. Welding temperatures are much lower than with metals, of course.

Thermosetting plastics (polyester or epoxy resins, for example) do not soften with temperature and therefore are not appropriate candidates for fusion welding. They are, however, typically quite hard, allowing them to be drilled or threaded and connected using nuts and bolts, screws (often made from the same material), rivets, or other mechanical devices. Alternatively, various solvents can be used to create a bond through the application of the solvent to the surface. The attendant softening of the surface accompanied by pressing parts together and letting them harden again is equivalent to a weld.

Glass is commonly held in place by mechanical devices along the edges such as metal, wood, or rubber channels shaped especially for the purposes at hand. Various adhesives may also be used to hold glass in place and are also often used along the edges to seal an opening and to provide continuous support. Point connections via mechanical fasteners are increasingly common. They must be attached to the glass either with strong adhesives or by making holes in the glass and using specialized headed fasteners. The well-known spider connections used to attach big sheets of glass to a building frame provide an example of the latter approach. These connections are complex, as they typically require precisely dimensioned holes to be made in the glass, and the fasteners must then be designed to hold the glass in place without applying any undesir-

able forces on the sheet, such as twisting or bending. For large sheets of tempered glass, this means that the holes must be made before the actual tempering process is done, since holes cannot be drilled in tempered glass. These processes are commonly done, but they add additional layers to the design, manufacturing, and erection processes.

Solid Free-Form Fabrication Tools

Variously known as solid free-form fabrication, rapid manufacturing tools, rapid prototyping systems, and "fabbers" (short for digital fabricators), as well as by more specific names relating to specific processes such as 3-D printing, a number of beguiling technologies have recently been developed to address the desire to mechanically prototype objects directly from digital models. We will look briefly at the major types of machines now being used, describing the salient characteristics that are likely to be of interest to readers. This is still a rapidly growing and changing field of development with perhaps unimaginable potential. Some systems use readily available materials such as paper and plastic sheet to build substantial solid parts, while other machines require the use of expensive proprietary plastics, powders, and other materials to make parts with competing or different qualities.

The effort to manufacture objects directly from digital models that are capable of being used directly in the real world is ongoing. At this early point, there are relatively few applications for manufacturing real objects using rapid prototyping tools, but that has done little to dampen the enthusiasm of users or to restrict the uses to which these technologies are being put (see Figure 14-64). In particular, some rapid prototyping tools offer the ability to quickly manufacture superb patterns for investment casting to produce parts of enormous complexity. Others allow the direct manufacture of complex molds into which rubber, wax, acrylic, and even metal can be poured.

Much effort is being expended in the effort to create tools that can manufacture objects with the same strength, wearing, and appearance qualities associated with existing technologies, or to improve on them while shrinking the manufacturing envelope to the size of a single tool or a trailer containing a selection of such tools. Portable factories capable of directly manufacturing machine parts, automobile components, or other specialized pieces from a database of all possible configurations would allow every conceivable part to be inventoried without having to provide any storage, solving delivery problems as well. While the production speed of these tools is not likely to threaten fixed manufacturing methods such as stamping and high-speed milling, the number of applications for tools of this nature would clearly be enormous. A drilling com-

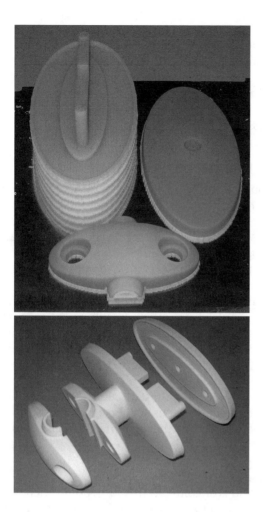

Figure 14-64 Some parts made by rapid prototyping machines.

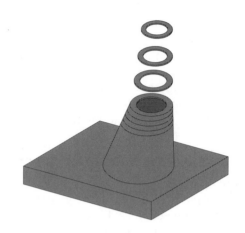

Figure 14-65 Diagram of the layered manufacturing concept.

pany needing to replace a machine part while at sea, an army requiring repair parts during an operation, antique auto enthusiasts looking for parts that no longer exist, a patient needing a custom-fitted replacement hip—there is clearly an immediate market for tools that can provide limited production parts where cost is not the main concern.

There are many types of tools within the rapid prototyping arena. The processes that are utilized to actually produce a 3-D shape include photolithography, laser fusion, laminating techniques, extrusion systems, and modified ink-jet printing.

Rapid prototyping tools are based on layered manufacturing. A solid must be broken into smaller parts in order to then be reassembled. Organizing a 3-D model into layers works well for this process. A solid part is first decomposed into layers representing cross sections equal in height to the build layer of a specific machine. The machine is then guided to deposit, cut, or harden already-deposited material layer by layer until the object has been completely reproduced (see Figure 14-65).

The original file format—called STL—devised to rep-

resent solid models for this activity was based on the first stereolithography machine, built by 3D Systems. The STL format has since become a standard for directly manufacturing 3-D objects. The STL format has been described earlier in this book. Surfaces of solids can be defined through the use of triangles that employ an ordered numbering system to describe the three defining points so that the inside and the outside of a surface cannot be confused. An STL file can be sent to any rapid prototyping system, where it will then be interpreted by the resident software and cut into appropriately dimensioned slices.

Stereolithography apparatus (SLA) uses photopolymerization to build models. A plastic monomer (resin) in liquid form is placed in a tub. A platen is placed just below the top surface, and a laser shines ultraviolet onto the surface of the resin, hardening it where it is exposed (see Figure 14-66). Light is applied only to the area corresponding to the slice of the shape being built. Once one layer has been solidified onto the platform, the platform is lowered slightly, a wiper blade sweeps material across the top to ensure an even layer, and the process begins again. Layer by layer, the laser draws an entire solid shape. The process is slow, precise, and relatively expensive. The models are hard, tough, and usually slightly transparent, making them particularly useful for the study of fluids and gases prior to the development of software that can do the same job. Stereolithography parts expand slightly when heated, which made early models difficult to use for investment casting patterns—a use for which they should have excelled. This problem was solved by the design of software that automatically creates a regular system of interior cavities during the build process to lower material useage, speed build times, and provide an interior structure that will collapse before an investment mold fails. Stereolithography machines are compact and relatively benign environmentally, and the process itself, though relatively expensive, is widely used.

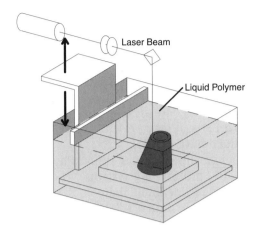

Figure 14-66 Diagram of the stereolithography (STA) process.

Laminated object manufacturing (LOM) is another useful process that produces substantial models similar to those made of solid wood or plastic (see Figure 14-67). The machine itself is relatively simple. A feed roller supplies paper or plastic sheet material to a platform, where a shape representing a layer of the object can be laser- or knife-cut. The shape is then dropped below the material roll, and the roll is advanced. A heated or pressurized roller adheres another sheet on top of the previous one, and the process is repeated until a solid object has been completed. The waste sheet is taken up on a collector roller.

The completed object is surrounded by a block of waste material. This material is sliced as it is being built, so it is usually a simple matter to take the waste apart to expose the finished piece. There is no particular limit to the size of the machines that can be built to make parts using LOM, but normal rolls of paper or plastic are used. Some machines can also feed individual sheets, allowing sheets with different colors or other characteristics to be laminated together.

Laser fusion technology is utilized in *selective laser sintering* (SLS) technology. SLS machines allow parts to be built of a wide variety of hard and soft materials, sometimes in combination. The actual mechanism for doing so is similar in many ways to stereolithography devices, but powders are used for the build material rather than a fluid, and the laser light source makes powders into solids through an instantaneous heating process that allows the surfaces of particles to fuse together in a sintering operation (see Figure 14-68). Metals, plastics, rubber, and other materials can be joined in this way.

The SLS process employs a platen that can be lowered as a part is built upon it. Powdered material is swept or rolled across the platen to make a consistent layer. A laser is then directed at the powder to fuse it together. The platen is lowered, more material is brought across, and the process is repeated. Material that is not fused supports the solidified part, allowing overhangs and undercuts to be built. This is one of the very few technologies that can build useful metal parts directly from a solid digital model. SLS machines themselves tend to be larger than other rapid prototyping tools, but they fit comfortably into most environments.

Fused deposition modeling (FDM) uses an extrusion process to build models with excellent physical properties, typically using a thermoplastic, wax, or nylon material to build solid models for fit-testing or for use in metal casting (see Figure 14-69). Molds for casting rubber, wax, and other materials can be easily made using FDM, but it is a relatively slow process. FDM machines feed a filament via rollers through a relatively small head that heats the material just before depositing in onto the top of the solid shape being built. The head moves in the *x* and *y* axis while the platen is lowered and layers are built up. One superb feature of FDM technology is the ability to extrude more than one material, so that solid shapes with overhangs and undercuts can be supported by a secondary material that can be melted or dissolved upon completion of the build process. FDM machines are modestly propor-

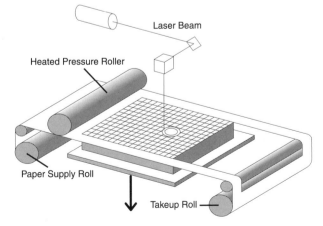

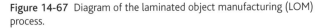

Figure 14-67 Diagram of the laminated object manufacturing (LOM) process.

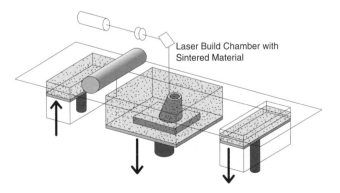

Figure 14-68 Diagram of a selective laser sintering machine.

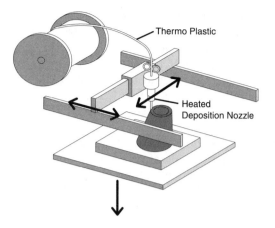

Figure 14-69 Diagram of a fused deposition modeling machine.

tioned and environmentally benign, allowing them to fit into any environment.

Solid ground curing (SGC) is an interesting system that utilizes photolithography (see earlier paragraphs on stereolithography), but using photomasks rather than a pinpoint laser to develop the liquid polymer. SGS machines use an erasable mask produced with an electrostatic toner (like a photocopier) to control ultraviolet light as it is shined down upon the surface of a polymer bath (see Figure 14-70). The light selectively cures the material, and uncured material is then removed to be replaced with a water-soluble wax, as in FDM. Once the wax has cooled, the entire surface is milled flat and the process is begun again using a new mask. Upon completion, the part is removed from the support matrix by simply melting it away.

SGC machines can build multiple parts rapidly because of the large surface area that can be cured at the same time. Building time of a part is not dependent on the size of the cross section, as it is for technologies that

must draw out each and every square micron of a layer before moving to the next layer. SGC builds an entire layer at the same time—it takes no longer to cure a layer of a large part than it does for a tiny one. Finally, SGC machines can actually build parts above one another by using the wax as a platen after the first parts have been built. Height issues may prevent this possibility, but for small or flat parts, it may present a real opportunity to speed production of models.

Ink-jet printing methods are utilized by a number of different rapid prototyping systems. One popular system employs a powder build material that is built up in layers in a manner similar to SLS manufacturing (see Figure 14-71). The powder is brought to a platen, after which a modified ink-jet print head passes over it, releasing a weak glue rather than ink. The glue binds powder that it contacts, leaving the rest of the powder to support the object as it is produced.

Once the object has been printed, the platen is raised and the model is found within the powder support matrix. Compressed air is used to clean the model, which is normally followed by strengthening the part by dipping it in hot wax or through the infusion of glues or resins. Various powders can be used as the build material, including starch and gypsum. Starch models burn out of investment casting molds well. Gypsum

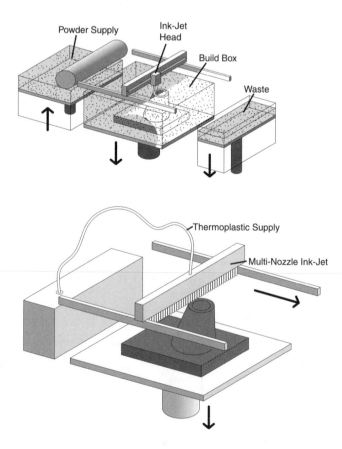

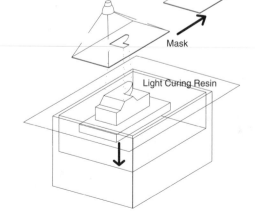

Figure 14-70 Diagram of a solid ground curing machine.

Figure 14-71 Diagram of 3-D ink-jet printing methods.

models are harder and can be used to produce molds into which metal can be cast directly. Colored glue systems allow color to be printed throughout a model, and elastic qualities can be added to powder-based 3-D prints through the use of proprietary methods.

Powder-based ink-jet printing methods are among the least expensive and most rapid methods for making objects from digital models, making them a natural choice for designers and architects interested in immediate feedback. The machines themselves are compact, but the powder can provide some challenges in some environments, as it does have a tendency to get into the air when the powder chambers are charged or when models are being removed and then cleaned. Producing parts with these machines also requires an owner to find room for a small airtight booth and a compressed air system to clean models, a vacuum system for collecting extraneous dust, and a waxing system or some other method to strengthen the models once they are complete. Most competing systems don't require any additional supplies or machines to produce parts, but the low cost, complete absence of support structure (and the attendant need to remove it), quality, and speed of this technology is hard to compete with. Ink-jet technology is used in other 3-D printers as well. Multijet 3-D modelers produce substantial models quickly and with great accuracy. Many small ink-jets are lined up in a row, allowing print material to be deposited directly onto a platen (see Figure 14-71).

An entire layer can be printed in one pass using this method. Great accuracy is achieved by milling the surface of each layer after it has been deposited. The potential problem of one or two clogged print heads producing a fissure through an entire part is solved by moving all of the print heads slightly each pass, so that the resulting deposits overlap one another as a part is built. Relatively expensive proprietary materials must be used in these machines, but they are quite rapid. Again, the process is environmentally benign, so these machines fit easily into even corporate environments. Multijet 3-D modelers produce good patterns for lost-wax and investment casting, more examples of which can be seen in Chapter 15 (see Figure 14-72).

Reinforced or Composite Sheets or Tapes

Most of the materials described thus far are homogeneous, but composite materials are increasingly able to be designed and fabricated using digital technologies to good effect. Reinforced concrete construction has, of course, benefited from the ability to design and engineer within the digital realm, and construction of complex shapes has been aided by the use of CNC tools to cut foam inserts for formwork, for example. Plastics with reinforcing fibers, strands, or mats are also common. (See Figure 14-73.)

Figure 14-72 A multijet 3-D model with the metal component resulting from using the model directly as an investment-casting pattern.

The reinforcing is typically pretreated by impregnation with heat-sensitive resin. Full sheets and tapes are often preimpregnated and left partially uncured for use in subsequent processes. These products are known as *prepegs*. (See Figure 14-74.)

Processes for making reinforced fiber plastics begin with extruding a sheet and then adding chopped-up reinforcing fibers to its surface. A sheet of polyethylene can be created, for example. The chopped fibers are

Figure 14-73 Photo of a light, thin canopy structure made using composite materials.

Figure 14-74 Typical composite materials used in boat construction.

then deposited on a layer of viscous polyester-based resin applied to the surface of the sheet, and the whole matrix is then run through a series of compressive rollers. It is ultimately gathered into take-up rolls like a fabric, or cut into sheets to be stacked. This process produces useful sheet products for general use, but the location and length of the short strands is not likely to be optimal for any specific use. The strength of these materials is limited because of the discontinuous nature of the reinforcing strands.

Tapes using continuous strands for reinforcing are similarly made, in which each of the strands is fed from a separate roll onto the surface of the tape as it is created. They are run through a resin bath, after which some post-processing then takes place. These tapes can be very strong because of the continuous nature of the reinforcing fibers.

Molding compounds for the production of sheets molded over a plug, or for compresson molding between dies, are made up of a viscous mixture of fibers, resins, and other additives. When used in conjunction with sheet molding, the compound is placed between layers of plastic sheets that aid in placement. The latter are typically removed when the material is placed in a mold. Sheet-molding compounds can contain chopped or continuous fibers, or a combination of the two. This allows a designer to choose from the different qualities available.

Vacuum-bag molding is a classic technique used to make molded shapes from this material. Prepeg sheets or tapes are laid into a mold and generally formed into it. The result is overlaid with a vacuum bag (see Figure 14-75). A suction is then created that forces the overlay bag against the prepeg material, which is forced to conform exactly to the shape of the surrounding mold. Internal sheets of different materials may be placed between the prepeg and the bag to absorb squeezed out resin and to aid in releasing the bag from the object formed. After a period of curing, the vacuum is

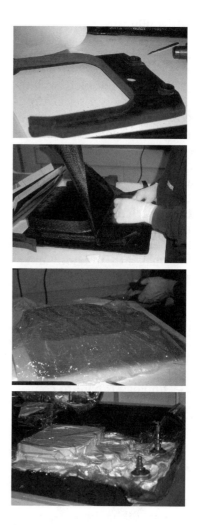

Figure 14-75 Photographs of a carbon-fiber-reinforced component made using hand layup of prepeg materials and vacuum bag molding.

released. Depending on the nature of the composite material, the shape obtained may then be cured further by heating.

An alternative means of making objects relies on a single mold to which layers of wet, recently impregnated material are directly applied. The reinforcing fibers and the resin usually come together at the point of application. The material often comes in strips and is set in place by hand. Spray molding is also used, where chopped fibers are mixed in a gun with resin as it is sprayed onto the mold. Large architectural objects, tubs and showers, boat hulls, and other complex shapes are easily made using these methods (see Figure 14-76). Generally, only the molded side of the product will have a nice surface finish, but the detail on that side can be very fine indeed. Many architectural restoration projects utilize these processes to re-create existing details using one-sided rubber molds that have been cast directly against the object to be replicated.

Figure 14-76 A glass-reinforced acrylic tub.

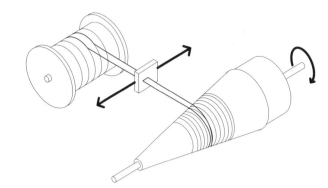

Figure 14-78 Diagram of composite molding over a mandrel.

An interesting variant explored in the aerospace industry and in high-end racing car bodies for making a material that can be structurally optimized is to use a numerically controlled machine to lay reinforced prepeg tapes containing continuous reinforcing strands in a way that optimizes the strength of the final configuration while minimizing weight. Stranded tape is thus laid in directions where stress analyses predict they are most needed, and can be crisscrossed or built up as needed. Special CNC tape-laying machines have been devised for this purpose (see Figure 14-77). The whole is usually then pressed together, using a vacuum bag process, and then heated. Fiber deposition machines are being explored for the same purpose.

A whole series of approaches based on filament winding and knitting processes are also in use. Continuous reinforcing strands are literally wrapped around a form, or mandrel, or they are knit in 3-D

matrices (see Figure 14-78). The reinforcing strands are impregnated with resin just before they are wrapped, or prepegs may also be used. Filament winding machines are capable of producing complex shapes with precisely defined strength characteristics and are especially useful for the manufacture of structural nodes for the joining of tubing, for example. The surface quality of the interior is based on the quality of the mandrel, but the exterior surface is generally rough. Filament winding is not appropriate for forming shapes that will capture the mandrel, not allowing it to be removed.

Bladder molding allows the creation of many of the same shapes as filament winding but also provides a fine exterior surface. Complex parts can be molded through the insertion of a balloonlike bladder into the part. The bladder is then inflated to push the composite material against an enclosing die (see Figure 14-79). Bladders may be made of flexible materials such as latex. They are inexpensive and are often left inside the formed shape.

Other approaches to creating useful composite parts include pulforming and pultrusion. These involve creating a composite by pulling individual reinforcing strands through an impregnation bath and then directly into a two-part heated die that compresses and shapes the composite, much like a metal drawing die. A variety of structural and sheet products can be produced this way in a continuous process. Structural products are produced in this manner to be used in caustic environments that would be unfriendly to conventional structural materials.

The techniques and technologies covered in this chapter are but a relative few of those available when you are considering appropriate methods for completing a project. You may be well served by exploring and comparing local alternatives as well as more distant ones when making choices related to production methods, and especially by speaking directly with the individuals responsible for manufacturing things—an extraordinary, knowledgable, and accessible resource.

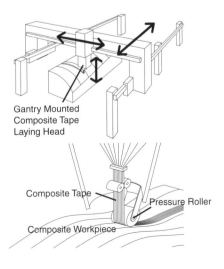

Gantry Mounted
Composite Tape
Laying Head

Composite Tape
Pressure Roller
Composite Workpiece

Figure 14-77 Diagrams showing the general operation of a CNC composite tape-laying system.

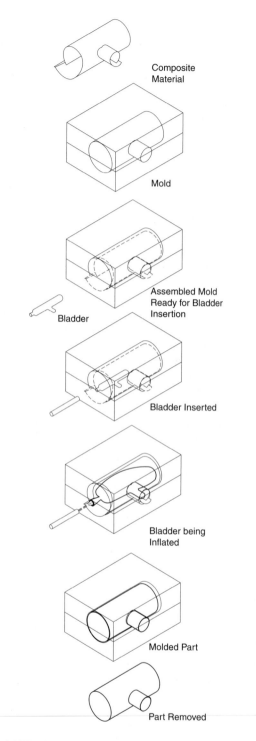

Composite Material

Mold

Assembled Mold Ready for Bladder Insertion

Bladder

Bladder Inserted

Bladder being Inflated

Molded Part

Part Removed

Figure 14-79 Diagram of composite molding using an inflated bladder.

CHAPTER 15

Prototyping and Production Strategies

15.1 INTRODUCTION

This chapter explores how prototypes are used in design practice and how digitally enabled techniques are increasingly used to expand and speed exploration through prototyping. In addition, discussion focuses on the similarities between some new prototyping and low-volume production methods, pointing toward the increased potential these methods provide designers. Finally, some useful information is provided regarding the different considerations designers may want to know before prototyping for low- and high-volume production.

Prototypes have long been an integral part of the design process. They are used during different stages of design development and while production processes are being considered to develop and test ideas and methods (see Figure 15-1). Digital technologies including CNC tools have helped to compress the time required to produce an accurate physical model and have greatly expanded the range of techniques available for making them in a variety of materials to suit differing needs.

The same digital technologies have provided an entirely new family of low-volume production techniques appropriate for making relatively small numbers of actual useful components. Of particular interest are the "rapid prototyping" or "free-form solid fabrication" technologies discussed in the previous chapter. In a few cases, these tools can actually build useful parts. In other cases, they may be used to produce "soft tooling" or even molds into which metal can be directly poured to produce parts of extreme complexity. These rapidly developing techniques are changing the viability of producing individual or short-run components of small to medium scale, and bear watching as they continue to develop.

15.2 PROTOTYPES

Characteristic Types of Prototypes

The advent of new means of making prototypes during the design process is one of the most apparent symbols of the new age of computer-aided design and manufacturing. The term *prototyping* was coined in response to the age-old activity of making prototypes in the predigital era. Today rapid prototyping, or RP, describes a range of activities not to be confused with the family of tools also referred to by the same name. Rapid prototyping is often associated with terms such as "time compression," "accelerated production," "rapid molds," "accelerating time to market," and "better products in less time." In fact, some of these terms apply to only some processes some of the time, but there is little doubt that an upsurge in the making of prototypes has been led by new digital capabilities. Prototyping activities have never been more useful or widespread.

Prototypes take many forms; they are seldom fully functioning and fully finished in the sense that a final component will be. They may be used to quickly test an idea or method of production, or they may be made to look convincing without having any functioning parts. During the design process, they are generally quickly made to provide feedback for further design activities. During preproduction, more time may be spent making them true to the actual materials and shapes of the final parts, using proposed manufacturing processes.

Designers use prototypes to help understand design issues, but they may also be directed toward a larger audience. Initial prototypes can play a key role in communications with clients, management, and other design team members. More developed prototypes can aid in understanding system integration and assembly issues, and can be directly tested or otherwise evaluated. In some organizations, prototypes of various types and development levels are used as milestones, becoming explicit goals in a project schedule. The many overlapping qualities associated with prototypes of all sorts defy their being defined specifically. No uniform terminology is agreed upon by all industries, but prototypes can fairly be described through descriptions of how they are made and how they will be used. The utility of physical and digital prototypes can be examined by means of examples such as appearance studies, look and feel, experimental, design development, prepro-

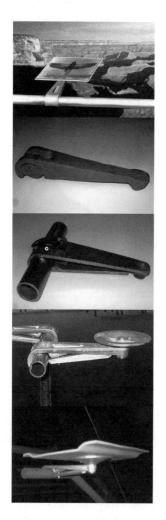

Figure 15-1 Conception and prototyping for a sign bracket, including appearance (clay), functional (steel) and working prototypes (cast aluminum and formed plywood).

duction, and alpha and beta prototypes. We will consider how the various types of prototypes can be made.

In the context of this book, a *physical prototype* is a preliminary, full-scale model of a design. Early design stage physical prototypes typically embody the essential features of the final object, allowing formal and functional characteristics to be judged. Physical prototypes of this nature are often incomplete or minimally defined using inexpensive materials to achieve the sought-for characteristics using a minimum of time and effort.

Historically, most prototypes have been physical models. *Digital prototypes* have recently come into use for design proposals based on solid models built within the digital environment. Many digital prototypes are made for form and appearance studies. In fact, there is often little or no difference between digital models and the so-called prototype within the digital environment—the model simply serves as the prototype. Digital prototypes are used in simulation modeling of all

kinds, allowing them to fulfill purposes for which physical prototypes may not be well suited. Physical and digital prototypes together provide a comprehensive means for testing and judging virtually all characteristics of a proposed design, from its inception to modeling the methods in a digital environment that will be used in its manufacture.

Another way to look at prototypes is in relation to how they will be used. *Form prototypes* are made to explore shape and appearance concerns, and can be useful for exploring ergonomic issues. *Functional prototypes* demonstrate how something is intended to work—through the modeling of a mechanism, for example. *Performance simulation prototypes,* normally digital in nature, can combine 3-D solid or surface models with graphic simulations of phenomena such as heat flow or structural loading. Some of these types of prototypes can combine both formal and functional features, of course, while permitting the exploration of design issues communicating ideas early in a development process.

Some prototypes serve an ongoing overall visual and inspirational role during the development of ideas and products. In some automotive or product design scenarios, for example, form prototypes are often created early on to allow production engineers and marketing departments to provide quality feedback early enough in the design sequence to have a meaningful effect. *Experimental prototypes* made during the early design or design development stages may express only concepts without concern for the size and description of necessary component packages. *Design development* and *pre-production prototypes* may incorporate more of the "real" qualities necessary to the engineering and production staff, but the agility of this system often leads to a visual continuity among the prototypes that would be less usual in other design scenarios, such as one in a typical architecture office.

Prototypes made early in a design process usually fall within the category of experimental form prototypes, mimicking the shape of a proposed product without addressing functional aspects (see Figure 15-2). With moderate experience, a designer can get the feedback needed to move directly to a final design from a relatively rough paper, cardboard, clay, foam, or plastic experimental form prototype. Rapid prototyping technologies are often used to make such prototypes from digital models. Even the more highly developed experimental prototypes typical of the product design industry—an automobile or a toaster, for example—do not possess all needed functional capabilities for the simple reason that they are not necessary when the purpose is to explore the "look" or "feel" of something. Form prototypes at an early stage are often used to evaluate the ergonomic characteristics of a design. Is a chair comfortable to sit in, or does a medical device "feel right" in the hand of the user? These qualities are judged more easily with physical form prototypes than with their digital counterparts, of course.

Early-stage functional prototypes serve to demonstrate the basic functions of a design. These prototypes may show little concern for the appearance or shape of the final object while demonstrating that a basic mechanism will work as intended (see Figure 15-3). Designs involving audio, lighting, or other elements may be roughly prototyped to indicate how these elements function and how the necessary components will be physically arranged, with less attention usually paid to their housings. Naturally, functional prototypes are well suited to the development of technology-driven products in which functionality can dominate the design decision process.

It is not unusual for early-stage physical prototypes to combine both form and functional concerns, particularly when the functional aspects are relatively simple. This is especially true for design development prototypes. Prototyping a common mechanism such as a sliding door lock, for example, would allow the shape to be reviewed while also proving that the mechanism will function properly. Functionality, feel, appearance, and perhaps even production strategies could also be tested, though the prototype would not be useful for strength testing unless it was made of the same materials as the intended final design. In the example shown in Figure 15-4 of a new computer mouse design, the proposed shape is based on the original idea that a more vertical hand position will lead to a less pronated forearm to reduce the physical stress caused by the movement of the mouse—a repetitive activity that has historically led to pain among some users. Preproduction prototypes are made of a solid plastic that is sub-

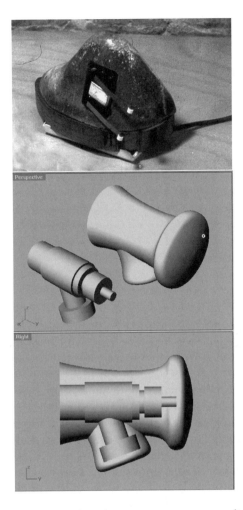

Figure 15-3 Functional physical computer mouse prototype (top) and digital prototype of a water spout (bottom).

stantially heavier than the intended production model, making it difficult to ascertain the success of the new design approach.

Design development prototypes can serve additional functions. A working prototype that exhibits both functional properties and aspects of the intended final shape can be used to ensure that the functions of all subsystems are integrated and to study how physical parts might be packaged into subassemblies even though it may exhibit only the central features of a proposed object. Actual parts from competing precedents or earlier prototypes, different materials, and off-the-shelf components are frequently used at this stage to get results without being bogged down in the details that come, inevitably, later on. Nonetheless, at this stage, the basic form of a thing is defined so that the relations between systems, subsystems, the related geometric configuration of physical parts and subassemblies can be examined and defined.

Preproduction prototypes are specifically made for testing and evaluation prior to actual production. The language used to describe prototypes during this stage

Figure 15-2 Experimental computer mouse form prototypes.

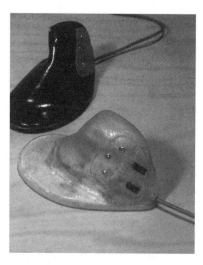

Figure 15-4 Functioning physical computer mouse prototypes.

larly appropriate to a discussion of prototypes and prototyping. During many prototyping scenarios, the desire to learn as much as possible about a given area is best satisfied by first investigating what others have previously accomplished in the same area. Documenting objects and examining or taking them apart—even

becomes very specific and is probably more universally agreed upon, particularly in the realm of product and industrial design where these prototypes are most used. There are two types of preproduction prototypes: alpha and beta. *Alpha prototypes* are built using the final part geometry and intended final materials, but are not necessarily fabricated in the same way, or using the same machines as expected during actual production. Materials have probably been chosen but not finalized. The performance, shape, appearance, look, and feel of the alpha prototype is intended to match the final product so that they can be rigorously tested by the design team. (See Figure 15-5.)

Beta prototypes represent the next stage of development. Beta prototypes normally use parts produced by the actual final production processes. Assembly methods may differ somewhat from those to be used during actual production, but the idea is to test manufacturing expectations while producing things that can be extensively tested to provide accurate feedback prior to final production. Where appropriate, the product will also be given to members of a user community for testing and feedback—a process more usual for small products than for architectural components or actual buildings, of course. The value of testing can be very high, as design flaws or unanticipated manufacturing problems can be uncovered and corrections made before actual manufacturing begins.

15.3 MAKING DIGITAL PROTOTYPES

Utilizing the wide range of available visualizing, modeling, and analysis software, prototyping in the digital environment is an activity suited to many purposes. In addition to activities and strategies described in previous chapters, the field of *reverse engineering* is particu-

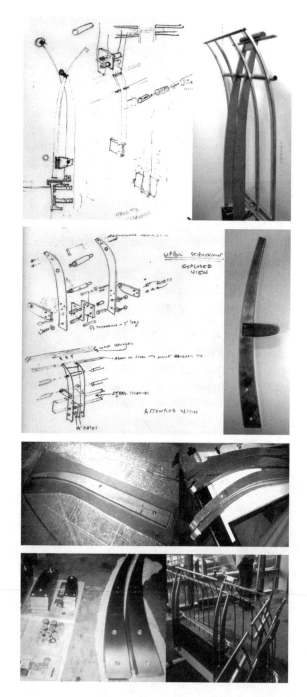

Figure 15-5 Prototyping a new railing design, showing the major steps from hand sketches through installation. Rapid generation of sketches and initial rough full-scale mock-ups led quickly to an alpha prototype of major components that could be reviewed by all parties. Manufacturing of the actual components closely followed manufacturing processes used during prototyping.

to the point of destruction—is a tried-and-true way to gain knowledge.

Prior to the development of digital technologies, digitizing was a completely manual process in which Cartesian points in space corresponding to critical features of an object were measured within the context of *x*, *y*, and *z* coordinates. The recorded points were then utilized to compare objects against one another directly or via graphs and tables—or they could be used to determine the coordinates necessary to produce new three-dimensional prototypes. Digital technologies have provided a more convenient way to model and visualize points in space once they have been measured, but they have also enabled a variety of digital tools to enter measured data points directly into the digital realm. Direct input via manual or automatic touch-type digitizers is now a well-established activity among designers of all stripes, particularly for relatively small objects (see Figure 15-6).

Noncontact forms of digitizing such as laser scanners are also widely used. In all cases, the information gathered is in the form of *point clouds*—nothing more than collections of measured points in space that can be translated through standard file formats to be used in most software environments. Very little can be done with point clouds alone, but they can be draped with surfaces or triangulated to form shells, or the points can be connected to form poly-lines to loft surfaces over or to perform other ordinary drawing and modeling activities. (See Figures 15-7 and 15-8.)

Digitizers may be used to input extremely complex shapes with extraordinary accuracy, and they are useful

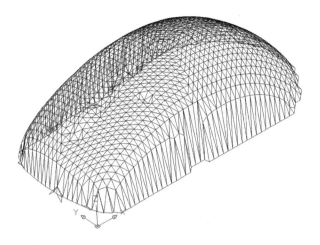

Figure 15-7 A mesh drawn over a digitized point cloud of a computer mouse.

for a variety of prototyping activities at all stages. It is common for a designer who has used a digital model to produce a prototype using a milling machine or 3-D printer, for example, to then modify the resulting physical model and to digitize changes back into a design software environment for a second or third round of development. This is a significantly more accurate method than manually measuring and entering data, and the cost of the equipment is typically quite small.

15.4 MAKING PHYSICAL FORM PROTOTYPES

General Considerations

There is no preferred way to make prototypes, and the materials used for prototypes are dependent on the size, shape, and complexity of the project. Design intention and basic construction (is it a solid, or a skeleton with a wrapped skin, for example) can help determine how a prototype will be made.

Technologies and strategies used to make prototypes also vary widely. Several are based on constructing three-dimensional forms out of two-dimensional tem-

Figure 15-6 A variety of contact, or touch-type digitizers, including a tabletop manually operated articulated arm capable of digitizing complex shapes, an automatic three-axis digitizer, and a large digitizing bed used in the automobile design process. Two digitizing heads are shown, each with its own computer interface.

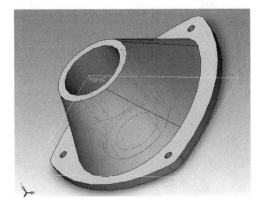

Figure 15-8 A digitized metal bracket, rendered from a discrete collection of points.

plates using computer numerical-controlled (CNC) laser cutters, water jets, routers, or other cutting tools. CNC milling machines and other traditional machine tools are also used to shape solid materials into prototypes. Rapid prototyping technologies such as stereolithography, fused-deposition modeling, and 3-D printing are extremely attractive for some, but not all, applications. Those making complex prototypes will typically use any appropriate and available technique, with an emphasis on getting required feedback as quickly and inexpensively as possible. Despite advances in digital technologies, hammers, soldering irons, screwdrivers, duct tape, glue, and other common tools remain indispensable. Many early prototypes are temporary in nature and are often scavenged for useful parts when later, similar projects come along.

Prototyping activities provide an early way to test different methods for making a final object. Generally speaking, designers can fabricate, mold or cast, or carve an object from solid stock. (See Figure 15-9.) Of course, a combination of methods may also be used, but most objects fall into one of these process groups, and feedback from early prototypes can be critical when making the decision as to which method will be most appropriate for final manufacturing.

Of particular importance in creating a prototype is size. Techniques suitable for making relatively small-scale prototypes in product design may simply not be appropriate for prototyping the large-scale objects used in an architectural environment. Full-size prototypes have an almost irreplaceable value to the designer and should be used if at all possible; they satisfy normal expectations in the product design world, and in that part of the architectural world that deals with components of manageable size. Some architectural objects

are so large that creating an initial full-scale prototype is not feasible. In such cases, only the most complex part of a large object need be built at full scale, with less complicated areas developed minimally, if at all. Nodal elements of a space frame system might be built to full size, for example, but the long rods connecting them might be represented by end pieces only.

If an extremely large assembly must be modeled whole, a scale model can be useful for identifying critical aspects such as connection or assembly strategies, and can be used to identify the specific areas worth full-scale development. Designers know that the useful information embedded in a small-scale model is simply not equal to the information capable of being embedded in a larger-scale model, so scaling up from a small prototype to a larger one can be done in a sequence of steps. With each increase in scale, the designer must resolve different issues and invariably add detail.

Small- and Medium-Scale Complexly Shaped Solid Forms

There are many examples where the prototyping objective is to make relatively small forms that can be conceived as geometric solids, such as computer mouses, cast nodes of space frame structures, and so on. These forms often consist of surfaces with compound curvatures that are inherently difficult to both visualize and prototype.

Design development prototypes for these forms can be made in a number of ways. For prototypes used in very early design stages, various kinds of foam, for example, remain a widely used material for quickly generating complex forms by simple carving, milling, or turning on a lathe. (See Figure 15-10.) In traditional practice, models are often made by hand on the basis of sketches or formal drawings. In some cases, model makers are furnished with a series of cross sections of a complex form and asked to create a three-dimensional model by hand-carving or by using manually operated machine tools. While skilled individuals can readily and quickly make effective models using manual techniques, the approach is often unsatisfactory for a number of reasons. Making a prototype by hand is time-intensive, for example, and is thus both slow and expensive. In addition, when a prototype is made by someone other than the designer, a certain degree of interpretation of the design model is invariably introduced (there are often many different surface shapes that can be made to conform to the same series of cross sections—for example, a traditional model maker has to necessarily choose one). Several iterations may be required to achieve design intent, reducing efficiency.

If the designer has prepared a digital model, prototypes can be made directly from it. Accuracy of design intent is ensured, since there is no intermediary inter-

Figure 15-9 Architectural components made via material removal, fabrication, laminating and casting processes (clockwise from top left).

Figure 15-10 Foam prototypes for testing shape, fit, texture, and manufacturing methods.

pretation by a third party. Early-stage prototypes can be made using several types of CNC tools capable of making complex volumetric shapes. CNC milling machines are frequently used to make initial models out of engineering wax or other soft materials. When the need for a harder material exists, aluminum alloys can be machined relatively easily and quickly. Rarely are hard steels used in making early prototypes with complex geometries because of the difficulty of working with them. For larger prototypes, high-speed, multi-axis CNC milling machines and routers can be used to quickly create foam models. These tools can quickly make surprisingly large objects in a short amount of time. For some larger models involving undulating surface shapes of relatively simple complexity (e.g., no undercuts), CNC wire-cutting machines and limited-axis CNC routers can be effectively used.

Prototypes of great precision can also be made directly from a digital model with rapid prototyping tools using free-form solid fabrication techniques (see Figure 15-11). Chapter 14 described the many different kinds of technologies available, including laminated object manufacturing, stereolithography, laser sintering, droplet deposition, inkjet-based 3-D printing, and others. Free-form solid fabrication technologies may be used to produce a model of the actual object itself, or they may be used to produce a mold containing a negative shape of the object to be used for casting a shape. These technologies have achieved wide acceptance in the prototyping domain.

It must be strongly emphasized that many early-stage prototyping techniques, including solid free-form fabrication concept modeling systems, do *not* produce prototypes from the same material that will be ultimately used to manufacture the object itself. Objects that have been made using these technologies might have the look of the final object and can be used to test some aspects of functionality (how one or more elements generally relate to one another), but they do not share all characteristics of the final production object. The specific mechanical properties (strength, deformation characteristics, durability, etc.), chemical, or other properties of the materials that might be needed in the

final production object simply cannot be modeled accurately. A hammer made out of a solidified polymer does not weigh or feel the same as one made out of steel, for example, and will surely fail if put to real use.

Care must be taken while using solid free-form fabrication technologies to make prototypes, as the possibility of designing an object that will not be able to be made using realistic production technologies is quite real. These tools allow complex parts to be made that may not be possible within a production context because of undercuts, lack of draft angles, impossible folded conditions, and so on.

Despite these limitations, these new solid free-form technologies have gained a deservedly preeminent position within the prototyping arena. They allow designers to quickly produce and visualize complex three-dimensional objects that could only be previously imagined, or obtained only as the result of a long and tedious process.

Preproduction Prototypes

As prototypes near the alpha and beta stages near the end of the design process, the material the prototype is made of must reflect that to be ultimately used in the final product. *Alpha* prototypes, by definition, must use the materials and final processes intended as much as possible, although fabrication techniques may be varied. Thus, a prototype of a die-cast element (a process requiring expensive tooling but that is suitable for very high production runs) might be initially investment-cast or sand-cast to produce a prototype useful for many kinds of testing and evaluation programs at a reasonable cost. As another example, a proposed plastic product intended to be injection-molded could be prototyped using soft rubber tools and fast-curing liquid plastics. (See Figure 15-12.) These and other techniques are especially useful for the short production runs needed to provide a number of evaluation and testing models.

Small- and Medium-Scale Envelope Forms

As objects get larger, designs often don't lend themselves to being prototyped via carving, milling, or solid

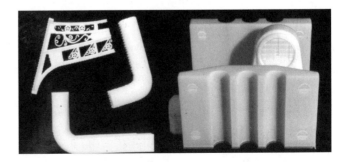

Figure 15-11 Components produced with a 3-D printing machine.

Figure 15-12 Soft rubber tooling for a two-part mold to manufacture small quantities of a plastic computer mouse body.

free-form fabrication techniques. This is particularly true of envelope forms in which a thin skin (made of either rigid or flexible materials) wraps around a skeletal framework. A design for a kayak that can be disassembled and put in the trunk of a car, for example, might have a skeletal framework wrapped with a skin. The prototype should reflect this basic constructive approach—a carved, milled, or cast solid prototype of the same shape will not tell the designer or client very much about the kayak itself. Some parts of the skeletal framework, such as the ribs, could ultimately be cut from flat sheets, while commonly available linear pieces might be used elsewhere. A laser cutter, router, or water jet could quickly cut prototype shapes from flat sheets of different materials such as plywood, plastic, or aluminum. Skins might be made from one of several different types of flexible materials.

Techniques for making these envelope forms with rigid skins vary enormously. Handcraft methods are common, particularly when envelope surfaces are relatively flat. Large foam sheets, cardboard, acrylic, fabrics, and a host of other materials are commonly used to make the surrounding skins. Initial digital models of envelopes or bounding surfaces can be "unfolded" to create a flat profile to be cut and bent. (See Figure 15-13.)

There are typically a number of ways to unfold a complex shape. Often a single edge is chosen as the line around which to unfold a shape. When different edges are chosen, different unfolding patterns may be obtained. Tabs and other connectors may also be inserted.

Doubly curved rigid skins present a particular problem, since many common sheet materials can't be deformed into complex curvatures (see the discussion on curvatures in Chapter 11). Small-scale prototypes of this nature can be made using free-form solid fabrica-

tion techniques. Larger prototypes can utilize laid-up surfaces formed of common fiberglass or other similar materials on top of rigid, shaped molds. It is often hard to control thicknesses and surface finishes using laid-up methods, but these techniques can yield excellent prototypes. A rigid mold must obviously be developed first. These molds can be made using hand techniques, but accuracy can suffer. Forms that more precisely match a digital model can be made using templates derived from the digital model and cut on CNC equipment, or through direct milling of solid materials to create the complex mold surface.

Vacuum forming machines are useful for creating medium-size thin shell skins directly from thermoplastic sheets that are heated and then deformed during the vacuum shaping process (larger objects can be made using vacuum bag techniques and other materials as described later in this chapter). In this process, a heated sheet of plastic is placed over a mold. A vacuum is applied (typically from below), causing atmospheric pressure to push the sheet down over the mold. Releasing the vacuum releases the newly created plastic shell. (See Figure 15-14.) Objects and their molds must reflect the limitations of the process—the single direction of the process makes precise detail and undercuts difficult or impossible, for example. Sharp corners are usually avoided, since it is difficult to pull the heated plastic around such shapes.

As with other molding processes, handcraft and digital methods are equally useful for making molds, although CNC tools will provide truer accuracy from a digital model. Holes are often drilled into the mold at intervals in order to aid in the process of evacuating the air below the plastic sheet in a uniform way, and care must be taken to ensure that holes are placed in sensitive locations such as low points, where the normal air evacuation process might otherwise be cut off. On a continuous surface with a lowered dimple, for example, the dimple might not be formed unless a vacuum hole is placed in the depression to allow the air to escape.

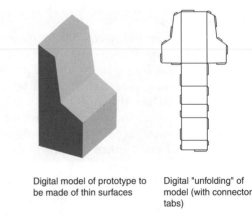

Digital model of prototype to be made of thin surfaces

Digital "unfolding" of model (with connector tabs)

Figure 15-13 Construction of a prototype using flat sheets.

Vacuum forming machine

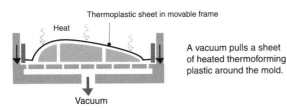

Heat

Thermoplastic sheet in movable frame

A vacuum pulls a sheet of heated thermoforming plastic around the mold.

Vacuum

Figure 15-14 Constructing a prototype of a thin-shell shape using a vacuum forming machine.

Minor undercuts are possible; the challenge is to keep a shape from being very difficult or even impossible to remove from the mold.

Large-Scale Forms

As larger prototypes are desired, many of the techniques useful for making small models become impractical or cost-prohibitive. Objects the size of wall assemblies, boat hulls, or automobile bodies may utilize other prototyping methods. As with medium-sized objects, there are few difficulties involved for prototypes with planar surfaces, or where other elements are straight or simply curved. Complex curved surfaces, perhaps exemplified by a boat hull, remain the primary challenge. Designers have been making prototypes of complex shapes of this type for many years, of course, with the many remarkable models developed in the automotive design process being a good example. The following sections review some of the techniques used for making prototypes of large-scale forms.

Template Technologies

One of the most time-honored and useful methods for prototyping fairly large objects is the use of what are often called "template technologies." Flat shapes can be used directly to make an approximation of a surface (via a surface tessellation approach), or a series of flat planes with contoured outlines can be intersected or joined in some way to define the final outside shape of a form. While the use of very large high-speed CNC machining techniques to shape foam or other soft materials has superseded template technologies in many applications (see discussion that follows), they remain an effective prototyping technique for many large-scale shapes.

Use of the term "template" to describe a variety of approaches is imprecise, but it has long been used to describe any process for creating three-dimensional shapes from a series of flat planes. This type of model has long been used as a way of prototyping complex surface forms. The automobile industry, for example, has historically utilized them to create many of their most interesting products by starting with small,

sculpted clay models whose contours were profiled, increased in scale, and then converted into a series of interlocking contoured planes to define the external boundary of the shape. They have then been used directly as prototypes, or as molds for subsequent prototyping processes.

These techniques have been given a new lease on life with the advent of new digital modeling techniques that allow tessellations and cross sections to be quickly and accurately determined from digital prototypes. CNC tools such as laser cutters, routers, and water jets are widely used for quickly cutting out flat sheets of varying profiles to precisely match these shapes and cross sections.

There are three primary methods for creating large, complexly shaped objects using template technologies. The first approach is useful for objects with surfaces that can be modeled using flat planes. *Bounding surfaces* can simply be modeled, cut, and assembled. As previously discussed, a digital model can be "unfolded" into flat sheet patterns after bounding planes have been determined, allowing them to be cut out.

The pieces are then refolded or otherwise manipulated in a logical way to form the final volume. For objects with inherently flat boundaries, this is a simple task. When surfaces are doubly curved, and smooth and continuous, the surface must first be subdivided or tessellated into a series of flat planes or facets. Reducing facet size improves surface verisimilitude but makes subsequent prototype construction much more difficult. Assembling many differently shaped polygons can then be very problematic. One approach used to simplify the process is to "unfold" a complex tessellation pattern into a flat sheet of still-connected polygons (see Figure 15-15). Determining geometrically possible unfolding patterns can be challenging, but these operations are well within the capabilities of good digital modelers. These larger sheets can then be cut out and

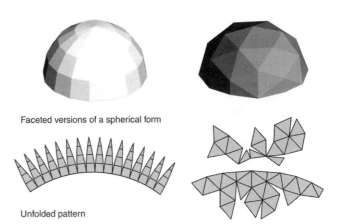

Faceted versions of a spherical form

Unfolded pattern

Figure 15-15 Alternative ways of using planar shapes to form a nondevelopable surface shape.

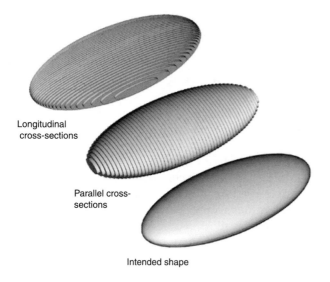

Longitudinal
cross-sections

Parallel cross-
sections

Intended shape

The digital model is subdivided into a number of cross-sections with assigned thicknesses.

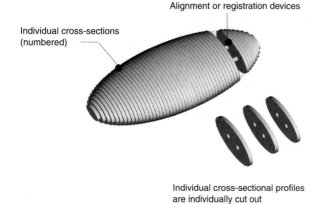

Alignment or registration devices

Individual cross-sections
(numbered)

Individual cross-sectional profiles
are individually cut out

Figure 15-16 Prototypes made using cross-sectional profiles.

subsequently folded without losing track of which planes belong where.

A second approach, often called *cross-sectional prototyping,* is based on the successive layering of closely spaced contoured planes (see Figure 15-16). The digital model is sliced into a series of cross sections, which are then cut out using CNC tools. Alignment of the resulting stacks of cut profiles is made easier by also cutting registration holes or slots, as well as layer numbers. The basic surface shape is defined once the profiles have been assembled. The precision of the shape can be determined by how closely the layers are assembled. Smooth and accurate surfaces can be achieved by filling interstitial spaces with softer materials, such as clay or expanding foam, and then cutting or sanding to the edges of the profiles. Surfaces of slices can also be literally connected to one another without leaving any space between. The "steps" formed by adjacent planes may be an issue, depending on material thickness and

the use for which the model is intended, but such models can usually be sanded smooth or filled if desired.

Another approach is typically called *bulkhead modeling* (see Figure 15-17). This method is based on slicing the digital model in two directions (typically orthogonal). The planar slices are then designed with interlocking notches that are the width of the model material.

The notches then serve as the final assembly guides. This approach can be used for making very large models. Interstitial spaces may be left open or filled with a softer material and shaped (as previously described). Increasing the density of the spacing grid increases surface definition but can also increase the difficulties of assembling the interlocking pieces. (See Figure 15-18.)

Prototypes Based on Template Technologies

The various ways previously described of making three-dimensional forms from planar sheets can be used to make prototypes directly, or they can be used to make molds for making thin shells of fiberglass and other composite materials (see Figure 15-19). They can also be used as forms to cast plaster or concrete against. Smooth surfaces can be produced if the interstitial spaces between the bulkheads are filled and the surfaces then finished by sanding and painting or otherwise treating the surface to enhance appearance or wear characteristics.

The same kinds of three-dimensional template constructions can also be used as molds for deforming or bending rigid sheet material into desired shapes. These processes often use vacuum forming (previously described; see Figure 15-14) or vacuum bag techniques. Vacuum bags allow multiple layers of flexible, thin sheets of veneer and glue, for example, to be laid over a three-dimensional template. The flexible vacuum bag can then be placed over the whole assembly so that, upon application of the vacuum, the bag is pushed against the veneers by atmospheric pressure, causing them to conform to the mold, where they are held until the glue has cured. This process is described in more detail in relation to the Permobil chair discussed in Chapter 7. Dimples and other concave or convex surface deformations can be problematic, as most vacuum

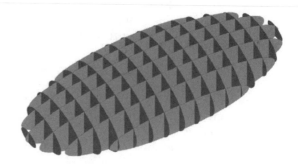

Figure 15-17 Prototypes made using "bulkheads."

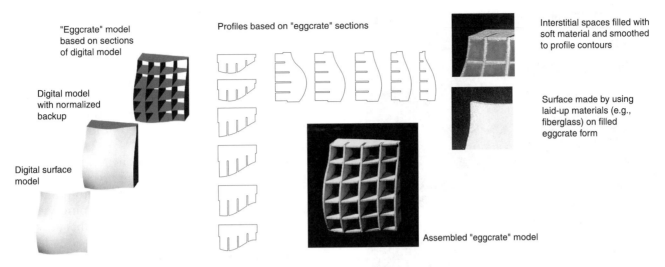

"Eggcrate" model based on sections of digital model

Digital model with normalized backup

Digital surface model

Profiles based on "eggcrate" sections

Interstitial spaces filled with soft material and smoothed to profile contours

Surface made by using laid-up materials (e.g., fiberglass) on filled eggcrate form

Assembled "eggcrate" model

Figure 15-18 Construction of a complex surface via the use of cross-sectional profiles.

forming is done at room temperature using materials that, while flexible because of their thinness, are not capable of being otherwise deformed.

Vacuum bag techniques are also used to form various laid-up materials, including fiberglass, when a smooth external surface is desirable. The action of the vacuum-clamping helps smooth the outside surface.

Laminated and composite materials can also be made using rigid upper and lower molds (see Figure 15-20). Material layers laid up on one mold are pressed against it and clamped by the other. Obviously, inside and outside forms must fit precisely, taking the thickness of the clamped layers into account, as uneven pressures can cause bubbles and other defects to appear in the laminates. Digital modeling and CNC production techniques make such precision routine. (See Figure 15-21.)

Other Techniques—High-Speed Milling

The development of high-speed, large-bed milling machines has been a boon to the making of large-scale prototypes with complex shapes. As previously discussed, these machines are quite different than conventional milling machines designed to produce relatively small objects of great complexity. Large surface shapes

can literally be milled out of materials such as foam in a surprisingly short amount of time. Many of the template-based technologies for making complex forms might well be superseded by the increasing availability, and consequent use, of these tools.

15.5 LOW-VOLUME PRODUCTION TECHNIQUES FOR SOLID FORMS

Throughout this book the relation between form, production process, and the volume of production has been repeatedly stressed. We look briefly here at production techniques intended especially for low-volume production. Many high-volume production techniques are simply cost-prohibitive for producing just a few units—compression molding, blanking, or die casting, for example. In many situations, such as in the archi-

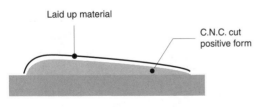

Laid up material

C.N.C. cut positive form

Figure 15-19 Constructing a prototype of a large thin-shell surface using laid-up materials and a CNC-cut positive form. The process is quick, but thicknesses and finish qualities are hard to control.

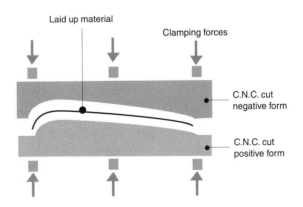

Laid up material

Clamping forces

C.N.C. cut negative form

C.N.C. cut positive form

Figure 15-20 Constructing a prototype of a thin-shell surface using laid-up materials and clamped positive and negative forms. This process is particularly good for slightly rigid materials that bend easily but still need to be forced to conform to the mold surface (e.g., thin veneers).

Figure 15-21 A digitally produced form for making curved formed-plywood shapes.

tectural world, there is simply no need for very many units of a particular product. (See Figure 15-22.)

Custom-designed pieces tend to be used in some way that visibly supports the larger architectural language of a building and are by nature relatively large and few in number. The numbers of needed parts are relatively small compared to what might be expected in the product design world today. Of course, there are many instances in product design as well where relatively few numbers of units are needed—as might be the case for a product (or parts of a product) serving a small niche market, and the increased interest in mass customization is a driving force in the search for new methods to reliably and cost-effectively produce in lot sizes as small as one unit. There is great interest in suitable technologies for low production across many disciplines.

This section looks specifically at techniques that are useful for making relatively small numbers of solid

parts that have complex geometries, where the need for efficient repetition is still a driving concern. Absent any agreed-upon terminology, we will use 25 to 200 similar units as a working definition for "low volume." This level allows for some efficiency that is not found at the lower end of lot sizes, perhaps in the 8 to 10 unit range. At the same time, it is clear that the technologies employed to run off lots of 1,000 or more will not be applicable.

Processes for low-volume production may be conveniently divided into direct and indirect processes (see Chapter 14). Direct processes involve no tooling and include various forms of material shaping via techniques such as cutting or milling, or by what are known as "layered manufacturing processes." Indirect processes involve tooling and typically involve some sort of casting or molding process.

Direct Processes

The most traditional way of making complexly shaped solids is through machining operations, or material removal. CNC technologies allow the accurate production of many multiples of the same design model, but they are not able to eliminate the time-intensive and wasteful aspects attending the reduction of stock material down to a finished part. Indirect technologies such as molding and casting are often more cost-effective. Large elements with complex geometries—where indirect methods may prove difficult to implement—can often be effectively completed using newer high-speed milling, particularly when certain types of easily milled materials are used.

Figure 15-22 A stair design incorporating custom components.

Perhaps the most exciting developments taking place in low-volume production are the aforementioned layered manufacturing processes (see Figure 15-23). The eventual intent of many of these technologies is to directly make final useful parts, and a great deal of active research is being directed toward this end. For the time being, however, they are particularly well suited to a variety of indirect processes such as mold making and lost-pattern casting.

While the future is bright for layered-manufacturing techniques, the difficult issue of production time remains because of the intrinsic nature of the technologies. Even the faster of the very few technologies that do directly produce components are still slow in comparison with other established techniques. As will be discussed shortly, however, some of these same technologies are playing an increasingly important role in indirect processes.

Indirect Processes

A wide variety of indirect production technologies are applicable to low-volume production. A view of casting as an expensive technology is perhaps outdated, being predicated on the difficulties and expense of making both reusable patterns and molds, which in turn required high production volumes to justify initial costs. Digitally enabled production technologies allow some patterns to be made more easily, and innovations in materials have allowed new methods to be applied to making both patterns and molds.

Approaches to low-volume production based on casting techniques discussed in Chapter 14 are briefly reviewed here, with a focus on primary techniques such as sand casting and investment casting. In a typical sand-casting procedure, a rigid pattern or model in the shape of the intended object is made and is then surrounded by compacted sand, after which it is removed and the casting medium is poured into the void. This holds for both open- and closed-mold procedures. Similar processes are used with other mold materials such as resin shell. In investment casting, a sacrificial pattern

is made individually or through the use of a hard mold or tool reflecting the negative shape of the object. The pattern is then coated with a ceramic mixture that hardens to form a thin, continuous mold. Finally, the sacrificial pattern is melted or vaporized, and the resulting void is filled with the final casting medium. The ceramic shell is subsequently broken off to expose the rough casting.

Primary Castings

In the selection or development of a technology for low-volume production runs, attention needs to be focused on the pattern or the mold, or in some cases, both. Critical to the design and material selection for the patterns are the strength and rigidity necessary to resist any forces caused by the process (forces from sand compaction, for example), surface wear, and issues related to the number of times a pattern will be used. Critical to the design of the mold is whether the selected material can handle the high temperatures and other forces caused by the cast materials, as well as the direct costs of making the molds. Reusability is of paramount importance in mold design and material selection.

The use of CNC machining has allowed the rapid and accurate creation of patterns for digitally modeled objects for use in connection with the types of casting methods appropriate to low-volume production. For very small runs of only a few parts (at the very low end of the low-volume production range noted previously), machined *expendable* patterns can often be used. The use of expendable patterns that have been individually machined can become cost-prohibitive when production numbers rise, or when parts become geometrically complex and large—factors that dramatically increase milling time and the associated cost. Expendable patterns can be machined directly from materials such as wax or any of a variety of foams specially formulated for the purpose. Certain kinds of wood products may also be used. Wax patterns made from typical CNC milling machines are typically fairly small.

Reusable patterns with strengths and surface characteristics suitable for multiple sand-casting processes can be made using specially formulated wood products, polymeric materials, high-density foams, and aluminum. These materials can withstand the high forces associated with sand compaction without being distorted. Aluminum is often used because of the speed and ease of milling it relative to its wear capabilities. A variety of dense, hard foams are also used, as are stable wood varieties. Patterns are often made using either rapid or high-speed milling machines. High spindle speeds and feed rates are used to take off most of the material quickly before shifting to a process better able to provide an excellent final surface.

Patterns can also be made using some free-form solid fabrication technologies. The specific technology

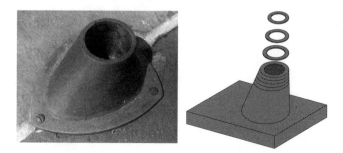

Figure 15-23 A diagram of layered manufacturing techniques, with a cast socket manufactured with the use of a wax original produced by a 3-D printer.

and related type of material used in making the pattern is dependent upon the anticipated casting process. Sand-casting patterns must be made using rigid materials that are strong and stiff, so stereolithography and laminated object manufacturing are useful technologies. For larger sand castings, patterns made with these tools can be subdivided to a size compatible with the available build volume. Patterns made with laminated object manufacturing tools do not have high wear characteristics, so a metal original is usually cast from the pattern to be used for longer production cycles.

In the area of mold materials, technologies such as die casting, forging, and injection molding that use expensive molds—sometimes made of hardened steel and cast iron—are usually employed only for large production runs or very expensive parts because of the cost and time associated with making the molds. The molds do make huge production runs possible, of course, without mold degradation. Less expensive machined aluminum molds are frequently used for low- and moderate-volume production, although they may not be used with high-temperature casting metals. Sand molds are versatile and relatively inexpensive, but surface qualities are relatively poor. Other mold materials, including plaster, resin shell, and ceramic molds, can be used for low- to medium-volume production, depending on the casting media.

An interesting new approach that can make effective use of free-form solid fabrication technologies for pattern making is the V-Casting Technique™. This process is essentially a form of sand casting, but it utilizes a vacuum-packing approach to hold the sand in place. The technique uses very fine, dry sand without any binders. The sand is held in place by placing it between sheets of thin plastic film and applying a vacuum. The process offers several advantages. Since the sand is not mechanically bonded, extremely fine sand can be used, resultings in a high-quality surface finish. The small grain size also has reduced porosity from gas inclusions and has reduced permeability. No draft angle is required when using this process. Importantly, relatively soft initial patterns can be used, since the process does not exert high forces on them—allowing patterns to be made using a variety of free-form fabrication technologies. Patterns must have small vent holes drilled through them. These patterns are then mounted onto specially designed boards, with a wood gating system installed. The assembly is mounted on a hollow pattern holder so that a heated plastic sheet can be placed over the pattern and a vacuum applied to pull the sheet over the pattern. A double-walled flask or box with internal vent holes is then placed above the covering plastic sheet, filled with sand, and a second plastic sheet placed on top. A vacuum is applied, holding the close-packed sand firmly in place inside a vacuum bag. The mold is then removed from the pattern while main-taining the vacuum, and is treated like a normal sand casting mold. The thin plastic film above the pattern is vaporized when hot metal is poured in. Once the object has cooled and hardened, the sand easily falls off the casting.

There have also been some interesting new developments in making sand-casting molds and cores using selective laser sintering (see Figure 14-68). The general approach—typically called rapid tooling—is to use special sand that is coated with binding agents that are in turn solidified by the action of a laser to directly create a mold.[1]

Investment Casting

Patterns for investment and ceramic shell casting procedures can be made using either CNC tools or free-form fabrication techniques, as earlier described. Materials used for patterns include casting waxes and a variety of foam or organic products suited to the purpose. (See Figure 15-24.)

Hard mold tools with the negative shapes required to produce expendable wax patterns can be made by using CNC technologies, typically by milling aluminum blanks. Liquid wax subsequently forced into the molds creates a pattern (see Chapter 14 for more detail). The molds may be used many times to produce large quantities of wax patterns—an important consideration because of their relatively high initial cost. Soft tooling (see next section) allows for similar results in either prototyping or very low production activities, without the prohibitive cost.

An interesting variant of the hard-tooling approach to making expendable patterns makes use of expanded polystyrene beads instead of wax. The Replicast™ process uses hard tooling to make initial mold components.[2] Partially expanded polystyrene beads are then placed into the mold and heated until they fully expand into the shape. The polystyrene pattern is then coated with a ceramic mixture several times before it is

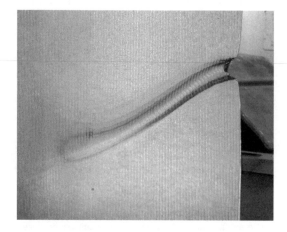

Figure 15-24 A milled foam pattern for lost-foam casting.

baked and fired, vaporizing the polystyrene while preparing the mold for casting. A wide range of alloys can thus be cast, including steel.[3]

An important feature of this technology is that various polystyrene patterns (reflecting different parts of a final component) can be individually made and then simply glued together. The whole can then be coated with the ceramic mixture to create quite large and highly complex castings. Very thin parts can be difficult to cast.

Free-form solid fabrication technologies have also been widely adopted for use in connection with investment casting. The primary objective in investment casting—that the sacrificial pattern has to melt or vaporize completely, cleanly, and without expansion (which can cause the mold to crack and fail) during mold preparation—cannot be met by all free-form solid fabrication tool and materials. Several technologies have been developed, however, that are specifically useful in making prototypes and patterns suitable for use in connection with investment casting processes. These technologies involve both material and software components. The software creates a build structure that is easily melted or burned out of a ceramic mold by allowing the structure to collapse internally during heating, and thus not expand. The material itself is also formulated to melt or burn out fairly completely. Other variations of the investment casting process that rely on free-form fabrication technologies include the general area of "soft tooling" described in the following.

Soft Tooling

This approach has recently received wide acceptance as a viable way of producing low-volume production runs (under a thousand, for example). Patterns produced using digitally enabled tools (CNC-milled aluminum or free-form fabrication technologies, for example) are used to produce a full-size pattern. The pattern is then placed in a box, and a soft tooling material, such as liquid urethane or silicon rubber, is poured in to surround the pattern. Once the rubber has cured the box is removed and the mold is cut (usually by hand) to separate the material into two halves (alternatively, the mold is cast in two parts using registration pins). The cut is rough so that natural rough resulting faces serve to accurately register the two halves. The original pattern is then removed. Gates to supply the mold are added, and the halves rejoined to produce wax patterns in a manner similar to that used with hard tooling. There is no need for special parting planes or the like because of the flexibility of the mold material. Moderate numbers of patterns (20 to 200 or even more) can be produced this way for use in the investment casting process previously described. While the life of this soft tool is not long relative to hard tooling, it is a remarkably inexpensive process, and several molds can easily be made at nominal cost. Very detailed or very large and complex castings with good surface qualities can be made this way.

The processes and activities described have been chosen with a product and architectural design audience in mind. The number of techniques used in prototyping activities is enormous, and it is different for every conceivable field of endeavor. The task of describing them all even generally is well beyond the scope of this book, but it is safe to say that many of the specialized digitally enabled production tools of today will become common tomorrow, just as appropriate technologies have always found their way to interested users. As prototyping activities become more prevalent, staying abreast of production technologies can provide designers with many advantages.

CHAPTER **16**

Design for Production

16.1 INTRODUCTION

This chapter examines how concerns related to manufacturing and assembly can positively affect the design process. The realities of production have concerned designers through the ages—probably inspiring and frustrating them in equal measure. When designs are created that can be easily produced, any number of positive things can begin to happen, including cost being lowered while interest increases among vendors qualified to make the product. Design for production has grown more prevalent as it has become more codified to serve the needs of increasingly industrialized cultures, but much of the general thinking behind it has a solid historical basis.

In the product design world, manufacturing costs are known to be a primary determinant of the success or failure of a product. In the architectural world, if the expected costs to produce a given design are high, the project may never even reach the construction stage. Economically successful design is dependent on affordable production costs, which are in turn dependent upon the characteristics of the design itself. Examples abound in which the failure to coordinate design and production activities has led to design proposals that cannot actually be reasonably produced within the available manufacturing or economic context. This chapter takes the view that a knowledge of general manufacturing and assembly can make a positive contribution to design, that good design practice can result in improved production, and that any number of benefits will accrue to all parties when design-for-production practices are implemented. (See Figure 16-1.)

Formal knowledge of how the shape of a thing is determined by production practices is not widely promulgated in design teaching, and the information has historically not been easy to find. The direct intent of this chapter is to identify and explore how design solutions lend themselves to cost-effective production. This is the realm of experienced designers for the most part, as noted previously. Despite the wealth of practical experience and common lore, little in the way of formal theory is available that elucidates how design principles relate to manufacturing and assembly.

Several formal methodologies do exist that allow positive and negative design features to be identified in relation to a production perspective. Design methods such as "design for manufacturing" are consciously engaged during the early design stages, thus influencing the shaping of artifacts to enhance their manufacturability and assembly. The methods tend to be based on organizing common and tested ways to translate designs into manufactured objects, arranged in a hierarchy such that decisions can be made. It is not always clear how to make the required decisions—trade-offs can be made at any stage to provide higher design "value" at the expense of manufacturing ease, for example. On the other hand, such methods may allow the systematic reduction of parts needed for an assembly, with the potential to increase design value while providing much-appreciated gains in other areas. Digital technologies are providing an increased capability for manufacturing the complex parts that help reduce the total number required for a product, thus reducing manufacturing and assembly costs while potentially enhancing design value—a quick look in any bicycle, kitchen, or electronics store will provide ample proof of this.

Beyond the manufacture of common objects, designers are finding inspiration in the remarkable capabilities of new digital manufacturing technologies. From mass production to the production of individual components, designers and architects delight in the ability to engage manufacturing tools and principles to derive new shapes representative of what are ultimately functional manufacturing realities. The pleasure derived from forms that derive beauty from the way in which they are manufactured is simple, clear, and classic; objects that are created to be at once beautiful and functional through a precise articulation of material, structure, and manufacture have always been held in high esteem.

Despite the obvious reasons that exist for doing so, it is hard to put down principles on paper that relate to design and production. Virtually all design intentions and ideas have production implications, but to fully understand the relationships and causal chains required to bring even one product to fruition, one

313

Figure 16-1 Many steps are involved in the manufacture of even many small components, such as this yoke to support structural stair balusters. In addition to the required tools themselves, various jigs and fixtures may be required to accurately produce multiple parts.

as well, as it might imply a standard to be modified or altered during a production run, whereas in architecture it might have quite a different meaning. Finally, it should be noted that, while digital technologies have greatly improved aspects of design, manufacturing, and assembly, the basic physical and organizational principles are general in nature, not digitally based. They apply to handcrafted as well as mass-produced items, though with obviously different effect.

16.2 DESIGN AND ASSEMBLY

Introduction

Previous chapters included discussions related to larger design strategies that influence manufacturing and assembly issues through their impact on overall shapes, layouts, and relations between assemblies and components. Standardization was also raised as an issue. In this section, we look more directly at specific design principles that underlie the shaping of specific parts and components with the focus on digitally aided design and production techniques.

Design principles in relation to production processes generally fall into several broad categories: (1) the need for nonambiguous design models, (2) the shaping and material selection for individual parts in relation to an anticipated production process, (3) the assembly of individual parts into larger subassemblies or overall configurations, and (4) issues dependent on specific needs such as installation or rapid disassembly. We will review these categories in turn.

If successfully applied, these principles can reduce direct parts manufacturing costs, time to manufacture, and assembly times and costs. These reductions often imply further reductions in supporting activities such as equipment maintenance and stocking. While the primary justifications for employing these techniques are economic, designers find them interesting in other terms. Designs can often—though not always—be simplified, consequently causing other design qualities to evolve that have little to do with economic motivations but more to do with visual appearances and the way users relate to the designs. One reason for formally stating these principles is to structure knowledge gained by experience in a way that can be easily communicated to less experienced designers.

Models and Drawings

Several fundamental guidelines apply to manufacturing a part using industrial processes. A complete geometric description and accompanying dimensions must be available. For digital design models, this means that the geometric model intended to govern a digitally based

would need to understand the entire corpus of design theory while simultaneously being deeply knowledgeable about all aspects of production—a goal well beyond most, and one that is certainly beyond the scope of this book. Principles do exist, of course, and though they are not consistently agreed upon, we will attempt a general outline here.

Many of the discussions in earlier chapters regarding design methods in product design and architecture, standardized and interchangeable components or models, systems and subsystems, assemblies and subassemblies, and the like are part and parcel of any discussion relating ultimately to design for production and assembly. "Interchangeability," for example, might refer to any number of things, including broad geometric or functional qualities, or very specific mechanical characteristics that allow parts to be easily replaced—an obvious tie-in to design and production methods. A "model" in product design has direct implications for production

production process must be unambiguously defined (one that doesn't have floating one-sided planes or unattached lines, for example), and it must successfully characterize the anticipated physical object (one cannot make undefined designs). Use of a robust three-dimensional solid model usually serves this end (see Chapter 11). When traditional processes that rely on two-dimensional representations of three-dimensional objects are used, some agreed-upon three-dimensional interpretation of the two-dimensional drawings must be found. This apparently trivial requirement is not always easily met. In making a prototype of a shape or a pattern for casting, for example, a pattern maker using traditional methods often has to interpret the meaning of the designer when creating a specific surface shape from a series of cross-sectional profiles (several interpretations are often possible). Results may achieve accuracy but may or may not meet design objectives.

Part Shaping: Relation to Manufacturing Processes

Once the intent of a shape is understood, the shape can be modified to suit a specific production process using specific tools or machines, which may impose specific geometric dictates on the part shape. A first step in this process is the selection of an appropriate manufacturing process. In many cases, the size and shape of the design object itself inherently suggest a process—a flat shape might suggest laser cutting, or a small part with a complex shape might suggest machining, for example. Specific material types might also suggest specific processes. Production volume is another important consideration. Injection-molding techniques might be suggested for a relatively small plastic part with high unit production volumes, or a small number of parts might simply be machined.

As part of choosing an appropriate process, a cost model and related production schedule should be developed to make economic driving forces clear. Direct cost comparisons are valuable in choosing a specific process. Costs generally consist of fixed costs that are incurred to enable the process at all (even to make one part), and variable costs that are directly dependent on economies of scale (the more units that are produced, the cheaper overall unit costs become). Schedule considerations such as meeting a tight deadline, however, are often equally important from a broader perspective (e.g., "time to market"), possibly suggesting the use of a more costly process to produce the needed unit numbers in time rather than a less expensive process that takes too long to set in motion. Part IV addresses these issues in more detail.

Once an appropriate manufacturing process is targeted, a design review taking into account constraints imposed by the process—and opportunities afforded by it—can take place. For example, if a simple open-faced sand-casting process is all that exists within a particular manufacturing environment, *all* designed objects must have at least one flat face (the top of the casting), draft (a slope) on the sides, and a relatively simple geometry in which no undercuts exist to keep the pattern from being easily removed from the mold. Even if the designer had some other shape in mind, it would have to be reconfigured to meet these fundamental process-imposed requirements. The process does not greatly limit the size of parts as many other technologies do, however, so opportunities do exist in the face of other limitations (recall one of the great open-face castings of all time: the 70-foot-long ribs of the Coalbrookdale Bridge in England that was built in 1779). If two-faced casting processes were suddenly made available within the same environment, fewer limitations would apply, as geometries could be made more complex, but specific considerations governed by the process would still have to be respected (see Chapter 14).

Many parts are made using several processing steps rather than just one, complicating a variety of factors. A simple part originating from a flat sheet might be cut out by one machine, have holes drilled into it by another, and be bent into a specific shape by yet a third, for example. Each one of these steps requires part handling, setup time, and perhaps even different kinds of skilled workers. The potential for communication problems obviously increases as well. Multiple process steps can add directly to unit costs, as well as increase overall production time, of course, so eliminating as many steps as possible is a primary goal during the design development processes. Making steps as simple as possible is another alternative.

Design of Assemblies

Here we look at more general design considerations relating to the overall characteristics of an assembly—how it goes together and how parts can be shaped to better support assembly processes. There is a distinction between assemblies that are primarily hand-assembled and those that are machine-assembled (using assembly machines and robotic devices). Part handling, part placement, and the type of tools required are issues common to both approaches.

Part handling and assembly issues can impact the size, shape, and weight of objects. In hand assembly, size and weight issues are clearly important, as people have limited strength, endurance, and reliability, not to mention their ability to work together as a team. A question such as whether an individual can position a piece for an assembly operation while at the same time using a tool to secure it in place is an important one, as is whether an assembler could easily recognize how to put a piece in place (how easy is it to put it in place upside down without realizing it, for example?). Interestingly, many of the same broad issues relate to many machine-assisted assembly techniques—the need to have two robotic devices rather than one simultaneously handle and/or operate on a single object introduces surprising complexities, for example.

While the aforementioned observations are valuable, they are much more useful when framed more specifically. Several attempts have been made to establish more formal methodologies with specific criteria, and to subsequently embed them in a software environment. Early well-known developments include those by Ford Motor Company and Westinghouse. A significant breakthrough came with the work of Boothroyd and Dewhurst,[1] who developed a numerically based evaluation methodology specifically targeted for manufacturing and assembly environments. They coupled observations from practice with theory to produce a general method that can be calibrated for specific applications. It targets smaller-scale elements while addressing manual, transfer machine, and robotic assembly practices, and establishes "rules." Other parties have developed less strict versions of these same kinds of methodologies. In the following, we look broadly at the common underlying principles of these methodologies.

Part Numbers and Types

Arguably, the two most important design guidelines in devising assembly forms that can be cost-effectively produced are as follows: (1) reduce part count, and (2) reduce the number of different part types. Implementing these principles can have a significant impact. (See Figure 16-2.)

A reduction in the number of types of parts reduces the time and cost of setting up and producing parts, including eliminating the fixturing costs for parts that are no longer needed. Reducing both the number of part types and the total number of parts can also greatly reduce the number of steps in the assembly process, reduce the number of different tools needed, and reduce error. Assembly time and costs can be greatly improved, and smaller, less complex inventory can result. Production control and inspection can also be simplified, easing management as well. (See Figure 16-3.)

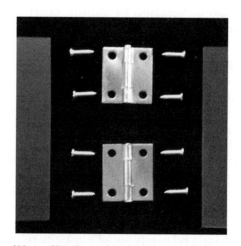

Traditional hinges. Note the number of parts and recall that each piece must be separately handled and aligned.

A "Living hinge." The hinge is part of the box itself, which is produced in a single operation.

Figure 16-3 An extreme example of designing to reduce part counts, handling, and alignment issues. The functional performance of the two systems, however, are not identical.

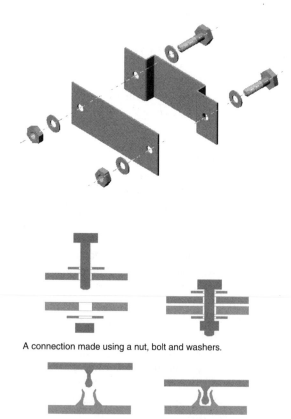

A connection made using a nut, bolt and washers.

Figure 16-2 Part count and part type issues. A connection made using clip angles requires fewer elements than a typical nut, bolt, and washer assembly. It may or may not, however, meet needed mechanical requirements (e.g., force transfer).

These principles of reducing part count and part type are coupled. Various corollaries also support these two fundamental principles, including those of eliminating parts whose functions are neither clearly defined nor can be integrated into another part (thus making multifunctional parts where possible) and arranging parts to minimize additional parts needed for housings or connections. (See Figure 16-4.)

Boothroyd and Dewhurst suggest some criteria for determining if a part is actually needed. Based on their work and others, the following measures can be used to test whether a particular part should remain separate or be integrated with another: (1) In the overall assembly, does the specific part in question have to move relative to other parts in order to accomplish its intended function? (2) Does the part in question have to be made from a different type of material than others in the assembly because of required mechanical, chemical, electrical, or other properties associated with the functioning (not manufacture) of the part? (3) Does the part enable any specific capability or feature of the whole assembly that would not be possible if the part were not present (does it allow other parts to be assembled or disassembled in a needed order, for example, or does it allow access for repair)? (4) In an intensive-use environment, does the part need more frequent replacement than other parts? If the answer is no to these questions, then the part should be eliminated or its function combined with another if possible.

Of course, combining multiple functions into single parts can increase the complexity of the parts and may make designing individual pieces more difficult, but it can also help to simplify the overall design. Increased part complexity raises the cost of production dependent on traditional manufacturing processes, but this is a fact that many of the newer digitally based design and production techniques are challenging. From the perspective of assembly, it is clear that reducing the number of part types and individual pieces is a valuable thing to do, but a cost model weighing the advantages of improved assembly against the cost of manufacturing and the required numbers of parts is often necessary in order to reach a decision regarding reducing part numbers and types.

On a simple level, application of these principles means replacing a number of parts that accomplish a function with fewer parts. A simple nut and bolt can be replaced with a clip or other fastener involving fewer pieces, for example, although direct substitution of this type should only occur if all roles and functions required in the final assembly are adequately served by the substitute part. A clip may not provide the needed force transfer through all connections, for example (it may be too easy to pull a clipped joint outward), but many standard parts such as nuts and bolts are used more out of habit and familiarity than because of careful design.

Figure 16-4 A utilitarian example—variations of the common electrical box. These examples illustrate how the use of increased part complexity can reduce total part count. The top example is made up of five stamped plates and two bent attachment clips. Modifications can easily be made and attachments added, such as the strap in example two. The third box is simplified by means of drawing and stamping operations to allow it to be made of one piece, and the fourth was die cast for similar reasons, but modifications to these boxes are no longer possible. The last two boxes are injection-molded plastic of some geometric complexity. These boxes were formed in a single operation. The example at the bottom takes downstream installation into account by including properly sized nails for fastening directly to wood studs.

Part Placement and Alignment

A critical step in any assembly process is locating a part and aligning it properly at the same time. Several guidelines can help ensure success: (1) ensuring that parts can be readily identified, (2) ensuring that they can be easily located, and (3) ensuring that they can be properly aligned or oriented. Equally important can be ensuring that parts cannot be *incorrectly* placed or positioned. Self-location and alignment are design concepts related to the preceding. Of course, various marking techniques can aid in identifying, locating, and aligning parts, but more fundamental techniques can be based on the thoughtful shaping of parts themselves.

Proper part identification simply involves being able to readily distinguish between different parts. When two parts share characteristics but are not interchangeable, problems can ensue. Increasing visual or physical differences between parts can help, and making sure that parts are truly identical and thus interchangeable elegantly solves the problem. (See Figure 16-5.)

Once a part is correctly identified and brought to its correct location, orientation can be an issue. In the placement of a round washer over a projecting bolt, there is obviously no need to align the washer, as any orientation will work. When a part needs to be reoriented (twisted or even turned over) to achieve the required fit, however, inefficiencies in the assembly process begin to occur. In cases where an incorrectly aligned part can still be installed, failure is likely to result some of the time.

Design responses to these issues include (1) increasing part symmetry so that there is no preferred alignment (e.g., the washer), (2) increasing the asymmetry or nonsymmetry of part features so that clues to part orientation are immediately evident, and (3) introducing various physical features that specifically aide in properly locating and aligning parts.

Figure 16-5 shows some of the difficulties associated with parts that are not quite symmetrical. It is easy to get confused as to how to place and align these kinds of objects. Either increasing part symmetry or increasing part asymmetry aids in placing and orienting the part. Accentuating the asymmetry of a part makes its orientation far more visually evident.

These basic concepts of needs for symmetry or exaggerated asymmetry can be extended in many ways. They can also be used as a basis for evaluating alternative designs and their assembly cost implications. Boothroyd and Dewhurst succinctly present an interesting approach to more precisely defining and quantifying degrees of symmetry and asymmetry in common parts.[2] A coding system is suggested that relates to their suggested evaluation methodology. A typical part is defined as having several principle axes of symmetry. A part can be symmetric about one axis and nonsymmetric about another. Or, it may be symmetric about two axes. In their terms, a part can thus have "alpha" or "beta" symmetries. These symmetries are then considered in relation to how the part would be inserted into another related geometry and the number of operations that could be possibly needed to orient the part properly. A "beta-symmetric" part has rotational symmetry about its axis of insertion and need not be twisted or rotated to be put in place. An "alpha-symmetric" part

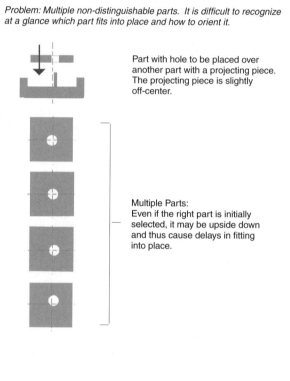

Problem: Multiple non-distinguishable parts. It is difficult to recognize at a glance which part fits into place and how to orient it.

Part with hole to be placed over another part with a projecting piece. The projecting piece is slightly off-center.

Multiple Parts:
Even if the right part is initially selected, it may be upside down and thus cause delays in fitting into place.

Solutions: Increasing symmetry or increasing asymmetry of limited numbers of parts.

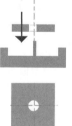

Increased symmetry. It doesn't make any difference which way the part is oriented or which face is up.

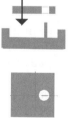

Increased asymmetry. Exaggerating the asymmetry of the two parts makes it easier to quickly tell how pieces fit together.

Figure 16-5 Symmetry and asymmetry in part design.

has rotational symmetry perpendicular to its axis of insertion and describes whether or not a part has to be flipped before insertion. When parts have to be flipped or rotated, the alpha and beta values are defined in terms of specific angles. (According to Boothroyd and Dewhurst, a value is defined as "the smallest angle through which the part can be rotated and repeat its orientation.") The resultant coding then describes how many of these operations are potentially required for correct alignment. Thus, a sphere (alpha- and beta-symmetric) can always fit into a receiving round hole without any need for further orientation about either axis. A long rod with a rectangular cross section might have to be rotated to fit into a receiving rectangular hole. A rod with an odd cross section and different features at either end might have to be both rotated and flipped around before it fits properly into a receiver.

All of these operations require time and handling, and potentially introduce error. The same authors go on to use these characterizations in part of their more extended formal methodology for evaluating how well designs are structured to support efficient assembly. Thus, parts that require extensive handling and reorientation during their assembly process are less favorable than those that require little or no orientation. These techniques are particularly appropriate and useful in higher-volume operations where many repetitive operations occur.

More aggressive design approaches may be taken to incorporate directly physical features that either ensure self-location and self-alignment, or that literally prevent a part from being installed incorrectly. These approaches take many different forms but are often in the form of different kinds of guides. Guides can be designed as obvious physical features whose functions are visually self-evident. Typically they require that the two pieces be simultaneously designed to interact with one another. Common alignment pins provide good examples here. (See Figure 16-6.)

Often they do nothing once an assembly is completed, but they serve invaluable functions during the assembly process. Various kinds of raised guides serve similar functions. These can range anywhere from simple projecting bosses to upturned tabs on a sheet-metal piece. Commonly, the raised element on one piece fits into a specified cavity on another, or in some way wraps its exterior. These kinds of self-alignment features often also serve to temporarily secure a piece during attachment. Care must be taken, however, to make sure that

the use of these guide features does not require such careful placement that a whole series of different features must be carefully aligned at one time, nor should the resulting assembly be overconstrained (see upcoming text on part adjustment).

Self-locating features can also be much simpler and part of the subtler shaping of individual elements. In fitting a cylindrical rod into a close-fitting receiving hole, for example, long-established wisdom suggests that this process is made much easier by simply chamfering the end of the rod, the circumference of the hole, or both (see Figure 16-7). The chamfers obviously help guide the rod into the hole. If looked at more carefully, the chamfers also allow some variation in the angle of the rod as it approaches the receiving plane during installation. In general, the avoidance of sharp edges on mating parts will enhance the ease with which they can be joined. More generally, gently sloping or wedge shapes that fit into comparable receivers are widely used in guiding one piece into proper relation to another (see Figure 16-8).

Another simple but useful principle is to avoid situations where more than one difficult alignment must be made at the same time. The difficulties of making any one alignment are compounded by the added difficulties of doing several at once. In some cases, careful sequencing is required. In other cases, it might be useful to exaggerate dimensions of some features so that some features come into alignment before others.

Securing Parts

Parts can often be initially located and aligned with ease, but then can often fall out of location and/or alignment during further assembly processes. Hence, there is often the need to be able to either temporarily or permanently secure a newly installed part. Depending on the design context, this need can be met by additional parts (clamps or screws, for example). Sometimes alignment devices that might have been used can hold the part in location until the next major piece is added.

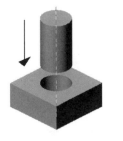

Difficult to insert. The cylinder and hole must be exactly aligned.

Chamfering the edges of the cylinder and the hole makes insertion easier. The chamfers guide the cylinder into the hole.

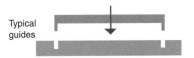

Typical guides

Figure 16-6 Use of special features to aid in locating and aligning parts.

Figure 16-7 Use of chamfers as alignment aids.

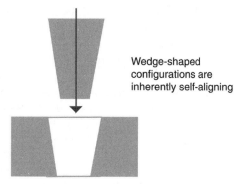

Figure 16-8 Self-alignment strategies.

Wedge-shaped configurations are inherently self-aligning

Part Adjustment

Closely related to issues of part orientation are part adjustment issues. Adjustment devices are needed for a variety of purposes. Some relate to compensating for manufacturing tolerances, while others have a more functional basis. In general, the need to adjust installed parts because of fit and tolerance issues should be avoided whenever possible. In addition to simply being made to work properly, they also often require additional parts and pieces (thereby increasing part types and numbers). A great benefit of digital design and production techniques is the great precision they foster, which can in turn help reduce tolerances and the need for post assembly adjustments. If adjustment devices must be made and used, then they should be designed to have as few parts and to necessitate as few operations as possible. Thus, simple spring clamps might be better

than a complex assembly of yokes, screws, and nuts. Adjustment procedures and mechanisms should also be in line with known kinematic design principles.

By way of analogy, consider the design problem of adjusting the levelness of a table on an uneven floor. Everyone knows the difficulties in adjusting leg lengths to prevent rocking or shaking—it is often a time-consuming and frustrating process. If the same table has three legs, however, it will always sit easily on any floor without adjustment. The same principles generally hold true in part design: There can be so many elements that need adjustment that it is not possible to get all of them adjusted simultaneously (a design can be said to be "overconstrained" by the number of features that restrain its movement). It is easy, for example, to have too many screws for adjusting the positioning of a plate, where tightening one screw will provoke another previously tightened screw to loosen. Adjustment devices should be designed to enable a few positive operations to properly position the whole. (See Figure 16-9.)

Part Access and Handling—General Issues

Part access issues fall into several categories: (1) physical access to the intended part location, (2) part handling access, (3) tool access, and (4) visual access. It is obvious that an assembly can be designed and drawn that is physically not feasible to assemble. Figure 16-10, which shows a nut and bolt connecting closed volumes, is an extreme caricature of this situation. The nut and bolt can neither be placed, seen, handled, nor tightened with a tool, but the drawing itself would not convey these potential problems.

Issues related to physical and part-handling access are closely related and must be carefully thought out. The location and shape of one part cannot physically interfere with how the next part is brought to its proper location and orientation. Tool access issues are related; if a tool is needed to install or secure a part, then the spatial dimensions of the tool as it moves through its nec-

Four-point adjustment - It is extremely difficult to adjust the four leveling screws so that the top plate does not rock on the lower plate.

Three-point adjustment - The top plate cannot rock on bottom plate even if the two plates are not parallel.

Figure 16-9 Basic kinematic considerations in designing adjustments. The minimum number of adjustment points should be used.

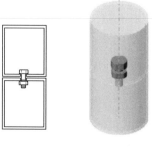

The nut and bolt cannot be located, inserted, or secured either by hand or via the use of tools.

Figure 16-10 An impossible assembly from an "access" point of view.

essary motions must be defined and considered in both the shaping of parts and in the sequence of assembly. Tool access issues can be very precise—not putting a nut too close to an adjacent flange such that a wrench cannot be used, for example. (See Figure 16-11.)

If interference issues such as these exist, then part shapes or the assembly sequence must be altered—or some combination of the two. Visual access is obviously highly useful and can prevent any number of assembly problems, but it cannot be dogmatically stated that it is always necessary, since there are many situations where pieces can be blindly assembled.

An interesting issue raised by the question of tool access is the question of "what tools?" On the one hand, there are many common and familiar hand tools that serve multiple purposes. Designs can be developed with this tool set in mind. On the other hand, some particular assembly requirements might suggest the development of a new special-purpose tool that is designed to enable a particular assembly process. Obviously, developing a new tool just to support a particular process is something that should be carefully thought out, since there are many disadvantages (the cost of developing and manufacturing the tool, for example, which includes increased direct costs, indirect costs associated with tool management, distribution, replacement, etc.). Despite these related concerns, there are many successful examples of special tooling. The decision to go forward with the development of a special tool will include considering what time and cost advantages are associated with the use of a new tool, which in turn can depend upon the number of units produced, where the assembly takes place, and who is doing the assembly.

Part Access and Handling—One-Sided versus Two-Sided Installations

A particularly important series of access and handling issues that have important part and assembly design implications stem from the seemingly simple question of whether one has access to only one face of a part during assembly or access to both faces. One-sided assembly means that the assembler (human or machine) can operate from one side of the object only. Many elements must be assembled from one side. A typical interior panel of a car door, for example, can be installed from only one direction. All of the handling and access issues mentioned in the previous section become accentuated when considering one-sided assemblies. Design responses are correspondingly accentuated as well. For example, the seemingly simple act of attaching two pieces using a nut and bolt must be carefully thought out in view of limited access issues; it is impossible to put a nut and washer on the far side of an assembly if access to that side is not permitted. Alternatively, adhesives, clip connections, or blind connectors

might prove to be a far more preferable design response. Self-locating and self-alignment features are clearly highly desirable here as well. (See Figure 16-12.)

While one-sided assembly designs may seem to generate many problems, they are a useful construct in thinking about any assembly design. Arguably, an assembly designed to have as many one-sided assembly pieces as possible may well turn out to be a highly effi-

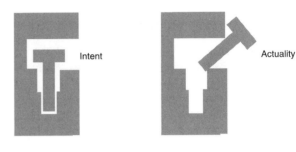

Intent Actuality

Impossible to handle and put into place

Difficult to handle. Cannot hold onto piece while putting into place.

Insufficient tool access

Figure 16-11 Typical location, handling, and tool access issues.

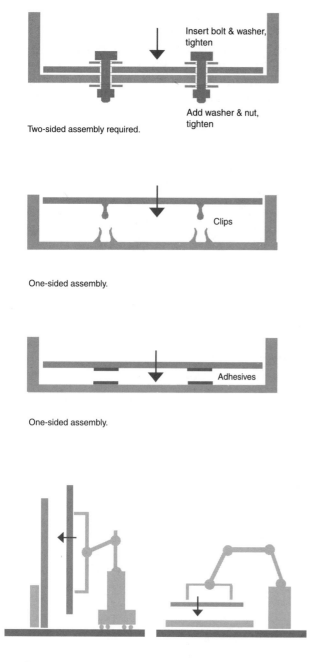

Insert bolt & washer, tighten

Add washer & nut, tighten

Two-sided assembly required.

Clips

One-sided assembly.

Adhesives

One-sided assembly.

One-sided assembly. The need for one-sided assembly is particularly important when pieces are assembled using automated tools.

Figure 16-12 One-sided versus two-sided assembly. One-sided approaches are generally preferable from an assembly perspective.

cient design in an overall sense with respect to larger assembly issues (one that requires as few as possible assembly steps, for example).

Part Handling—Preassembly

In many assembly situations involving high volumes and large numbers of parts, there are invariably stacks of parts awaiting assembly. Quite often, a box of parts can get quite jumbled and individual parts tangled up with one another. The seemingly simple act of removing a part from a box can be surprisingly difficult and time-consuming. In these situations, parts can be designed to be less susceptible to tangling by minimizing projecting sharp features and holes within parts (see Figure 16-13).

Connecting Parts

Many assemblies consist of various functional sub-assemblies or components that are in turn linked by various kinds of linear connecting elements, such as wires or tubes, that also serve critical functional roles. Strict adherence to the earlier principles of minimizing part types and numbers might suggest that these very connectors should be eliminated or their lengths at least minimized—perhaps by directly locating linked elements adjacent to one another and using hard connections. This cannot always be accomplished, of course, and connecting elements still find their way into many designs for a variety of practical reasons.

Assembling these connecting elements in differing assembly designs can be easy or difficult. Issues of size, scale, and function are clearly important, of course, but more important are the connectors. As they become more important, they may need to be treated as primary parts. In other instances, they can be treated less formally. For example, in highly structured design envelopes including modular design environments, the location and placement of these connecting elements is as much a part of the design as are major subassemblies. Chases or open paths are left to pass connectors through, or special conduits are provided specifically for this purpose. In less structured design envelopes, they might simply be

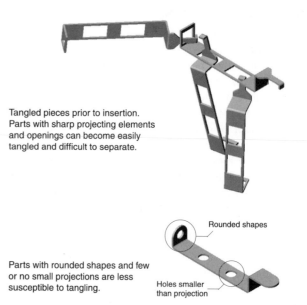

Tangled pieces prior to insertion. Parts with sharp projecting elements and openings can become easily tangled and difficult to separate.

Rounded shapes

Parts with rounded shapes and few or no small projections are less susceptible to tangling.

Holes smaller than projection

Figure 16-13 Part design to avoid tangling.

snaked around as needed to link widely separated functional elements.

At another level, the basic question of whether a connecting element should be made of rigid or flexible materials is an interesting one. We are all familiar with common electric wires housed in flexible insulation. Their flexibility clearly allows them to be more easily installed than some of their rigid plumbing pipe counterparts, raising the question: Why on earth would anyone choose to make connecting elements rigid? There are situations where rigidity is desirable, of course. While no hard-and-fast rules govern the area, some observations can be made. The installation of flexible elements in different locations is an act that is superbly easy for humans to do manually in a normal two-handed operation—you grip a plug with one hand while holding a socket in the other and push them together. Creating and/or using machines to install flexible elements is quite another story. (In a later chapter, for example, it will be argued in more detail that it is much easier for a robotic device to pick and place a rigid piece than a flexible one. The normal deformations associated with handling flexible elements are truly difficult for a machine to anticipate and manage.) In many assembly environments involving very high production levels, and in which machine assembly may be desirable, it is thus often better to use rigid elements that are treated more like small parts than flexible ones. Product configurations have to be designed accordingly. On the other hand, it is equally clear that many products use different combinations of hand versus machine assembly techniques, so one can find many products exhibiting rigid primary pieces assembled largely in a machine environment, including the use of assembly jigs and so forth, with necessary flexible connecting elements such as wires being put in place by hand.

Assembly Order

Broadly, there are several ways of thinking about part assembly order issues. As noted previously, the act of designing should inherently consider the act of assembling individual parts to make the final configuration. The design principles noted in the previous section characterize some of the part design issues that make this assembly thinking possible. These same principles often—but not always—suggest an order of assembly.

When a designer is thinking through an assembly order, digital design models can be extremely useful and can be used to simulate the actual sequencing of part placement as a way of studying the viability of the proposed sequence (see Figure 16-14). The "assembly

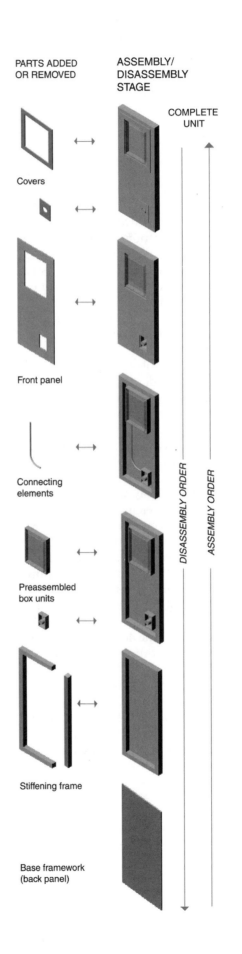

PARTS ADDED OR REMOVED

ASSEMBLY/ DISASSEMBLY STAGE

COMPLETE UNIT

Covers

Front panel

Connecting elements

Preassembled box units

Stiffening frame

Base framework (back panel)

DISASSEMBLY ORDER

ASSEMBLY ORDER

Figure 16-14 Assembly/disassembly order. A useful way of thinking about part assembly order is to determine the order in which a completed assembly can be disassembled (several alternatives are usually possible).

modeling" techniques discussed in Chapter 11 are particularly relevant here. The order in which a digital assembly model is done and the kinds of decisions that need to go into its construction (such as issues of mating parts, the alignment of axes, or making surfaces coincident) can be used to simulate a proposed sequence. Unless great care is taken, however, critical steps can be overlooked in a complex situation (not only would the assembly have to be modeled, but all the tools used and their related operations over time as well). Such models can be extremely complex.

Physical prototypes are always a useful way of testing assembly viability and order. Given that for many product designs, various kinds of alpha and beta prototypes are usually made (see Chapter 15), these same prototypes can be used for assembly studies. (In architectural designs, it is rare that these kinds of prototypes can actually be made because of cost and scale limitations. Small parts are often prototyped, but rarely large ones. Hence, digital models must be used in lieu of large physical prototypes.)

Defining principles that help in establishing an efficient assembly order is a more difficult task. In some instances, the assembly order is implicit in the design itself. When modular design approaches based on regular geometries are used, the assembly order and sequence is pretty well defined during the act of defining the modules themselves and how they relate to a base framework. The base framework is put in place, then major modular subassemblies, and then, normally, connecting elements. Major modular subassemblies may have been preassembled (in which case each subassembly may have its own base framework).

As noted previously, some modular approaches are also defined in terms of what groupings of parts are made by what groupings of machines. Assembly-order thinking naturally applies in such circumstances.

In less structured designs, a specific part is often identified early in the design process to serve as the base part to which all other parts are ultimately added or related. This base part is typically a major physical part able to provide an essential construction framework. It should normally be a rigid rather than a flexible element, and it should be designed specifically to accommodate future attachments in the form of either subassemblies or other individual parts. In many cases,

these base components are self-evident. In a powerboat, the hull is invariably made first and all other components relate to it, for example. In more common products, a typical approach is the use of rigid internal housings of one type or another to provide a base framework, while also using the frameworks to provide other critical functions. In other cases, the base frame is simply that—the glory of many electronic devices, for example, lies in their electronics and not in the often seemingly lowly folded sheet-metal boxes that simply provide a basic framework and housing.

A useful way of thinking about assembly order in less structured designs is to first look at the assembly as a whole and then begin to systematically disassemble it. Reversing this disassembly process can suggest an actual assembly order. Disassembling a configuration usually involves a process of first pulling the object apart into major subassemblies. Any coverings or elements connecting major subassemblies get removed first, followed by removal of the subassemblies themselves. The subassemblies are then taken apart in turn, with major components that are accessible being removed first. The process continues in this manner until finally the base framework is exposed. This "disassembly" process should be done in light of the several part access issues noted earlier, keeping in mind issues such as tool access and noting how they might influence design solutions.

Reversing the disassembly order will suggest an assembly order. Since there are many ways of disassembling an object, it follows that there may be many ways of assembling it. Several disassembly approaches should be explored and various time and tool requirements noted and compared to find the correct solution for a particular situation. Suggested assembly sequences should then be explored more directly, particularly in light of the actual proposed final assembly environment and related machine configurations.

While issues and topics related to design for production may not be regularly taught or consciously discussed in many design environments, attention to the importance that is placed on them when products are engineered and manufactured is advantageous in all design endeavors. It should be abundantly clear that digital technologies can be used to anticipate both the problems and the opportunities that exist within these activities in a variety of useful ways.

PART VI

STRATEGIES

This part takes a broad perspective. Types of overall manufacturing systems and related business strategies are first briefly reviewed. Interesting developments in "mass customization" are next addressed, with specific attention paid to differences in the concept as it applies, respectively, to the architecture and product design industries. The final chapter summarizes salient issues previously identified and speculates on future directions.

Manufacturing Systems and Strategies

17.1 INTRODUCTION

This chapter addresses issues relating to the organization and management of entire systems for supporting design, analysis, and production activities. Earlier chapters have reviewed computer-aided design and engineering systems, the nature of numerical control technology and associated machines, and other topics that are relevant to the fundamental idea of automation. These various capabilities may be linked or otherwise integrated in any of several alternative ways to achieve different levels of desired functionality. Closely linked are specific production strategies that have been developed to increase productivity or to make groups of machines more adaptable for meeting highly varying production requirements—for instance, manufacturing cells or flexible manufacturing systems. (See Figure 17-1.)

The following section briefly addresses manufacturing systems and related specialized equipment in relation to production objectives—particularly volume of production. Many issues are obvious. For example, CNC-based technologies discussed earlier, such as CNC milling, may well provide precision and flexibility but may not be the most appropriate way to produce thousands of similar parts. Injection molding may be fascinating, but inappropriate if the objective is to produce 10 parts. Considerations go beyond just choosing an appropriate manufacturing technique, however, and get into questions about organization of machines and labor forces in response to product types and volumes, information management, job processing, and so forth.

There are also many alternative attitudes and strategies for how different design, analysis, and manufacturing capabilities and larger associated planning activities can be interrelated. Perhaps the most interesting conceptual attitude is the priority that information and information processing can have over other considerations in a production environment. Various approaches have been developed in light of information utilization that are characterized by a plethora of different names (e.g., agile manufacturing, computer-integrated manufacturing systems, etc.) and related catchy-sounding acronyms. The second part of the chapter deals more with larger manufacturing attitudes and strategies that are related to distinct business model orientations.

17.2 GENERAL CHARACTERISTICS OF MANUFACTURING SYSTEMS

The chapters in Part V addressed primary machine technologies and related manufacturing processes. Here we briefly review essential characteristics of manufacturing systems that are composed of simple or complex systems of production machines, material handling systems, and so forth that transform materials into products.

The characterizations presented of job shops, project shops, and flow shops (including assembly lines) are classical in the larger manufacturing world.[1] Manufacturing cells, flexible manufacturing systems, and various combinations and hybrid approaches are more recent. This general approach reflects differences in the volume and variety of units produced. Other approaches reflect different business models (e.g., made-to-order products).

A *job shop* provides small production quantities. A *job* is often considered the smallest production run feasible. More broadly, however, a job shop may also offer other assistance in developing a product for large-volume manufacturing, for instance, machining tooling dies. Job shops may also provide mock-ups and prototyping services, although ones that specialize in these services are often called *prototyping shops*. Shops may specialize in certain areas, such as metal fabrication. Workers are usually highly skilled. General-purpose machines predominate. Many job shops use CNC equipment such as machining centers alongside other more traditional equipment. Some larger shops—particularly prototyping firms—now have 3-D printing or solid free-form fabrication machines. People and equipment are employed flexibly. Jobs are normally unique and setup requirements and times can be high. Costs are consequently high. Job shops may exist independently or be part of a more extensive manufacturing organization. A *production job shop* targets low-volume

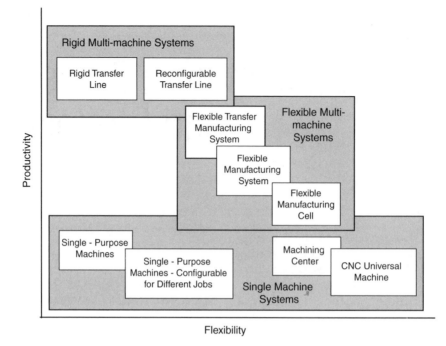

Figure 17-1 General relationships between manufacturing system types, production levels, and flexibility level. Adapted from F.T. Piller, *Kundenindividuelle Massen Production*, (München: Carl Hanser Verlag, 1998), 243.

production (say, 50 to 100) and tends to specialize more. While many machines remain general-purpose, others may be more targeted to limited production runs. In many cases, *manufacturing cells* or simple *flexible manufacturing systems* (see upcoming text) may provide many of these same functions, typically in connection with other general-purposes tools.

In a *project shop,* a product is assembled from parts made elsewhere. Equipment is oriented toward assembly, as are worker skills. Parts may be small and come from job shops. They are subsequently assembled in relatively low- to medium-volume quantities.

A *flow shop* is organized for high-volume production (say, 50,000 to 100,000 units). A repetitive flow shop most resembles the classic image of the assembly line, with parts and assemblies moving through different machine stations. A *transfer line* is a flow shop that has even more dedicated processes and machines. High levels of automation are normally present for information management, materials handling, manufacturing, assembly, and inspection. Machines are normally special-purpose or dedicated types. They are highly organized in stations according to process sequences.

Machines for sorting and limited assembly are common. Industrial robots may be used as well for pick-and-place operations, finishing tasks (e.g., spray painting), assembly tasks, or other tasks. Automated material handling equipment in the form of conveyors or other transfer devices is normally present. Parts typically move from station to station in an automated

way. Capital investment in equipment is high. Tooling costs can be very high. For example, expensive special tooling such as dies required for some high-volume production runs is not uncommon but can be distributed over large numbers of units. Production efficiency is high for large production volumes. Unit costs can consequently be low. Flexibility, however, is low and it is not easy to change product types.

With pressing market-driven needs to be able to respond more flexibly to the need to produce many different types of products and/or product variations and in varying numbers, various systems based on manufacturing cells and flexible manufacturing systems have evolved. These approaches invariably involve some form of computer control and CNC machines but can include other types of machines as well. Both flexible manufacturing cells and systems are generally targeted for low- to medium-volume production of differentiated product lines that are within a family.

A *flexible manufacturing cell,* sometimes referred to as an FMC, is a machine or group of related machines that perform a particular process or step in a larger manufacturing process. A cell may be segregated because of noise, chemical requirements, raw material needs, operator requirements, or manufacturing cycle times. The flexible aspect of a flexible manufacturing cell indicates that the cell isn't restricted to just one type of part or process but can be programmed to accommodate different parts and products, usually within families of similar physical properties and dimensional characteristics.

The important aspect of a flexible manufacturing cell is that among the machines of the cell there is common control.

A *flexible manufacturing system* (FMS) is a programmed system of fully integrated machines, or machining centers, capable of performing a series of operations on different work pieces, within a product group, flowing through the system one piece at a time, with no or minimum setup time required between each piece. A flexible manufacturing system may be one manufacturing machine or multiple machines, which are integrated by an automated material handling system and whose operation is managed by a centralized computerized control system. A flexible manufacturing system can be reconfigured by computer control to manufacture various products that lie within the manufacturing capabilities of the machine grouping.

The general approaches listed are basic types only. Many hybrids and combinations are in common use, as are approaches that don't fit easily within the basic classifications presented. Thus, there are linked-cell manufacturing systems and so forth. Of particular interest in this book are approaches directed toward creating large and complex assemblies of low unit volumes and/or model variations. Perhaps the extreme example of this domain is in the shipbuilding industry, where final units are large in size (to say the least) and total units produced in a year are obviously low. While several approaches are in use, highly efficient yards often create a ship by assembling large sections of hulls and superstructure elements originally made off-site and transported to a single operation focused almost exclusively on assembly. (Also see the discussion in Chapter 9 on modular ship cabins.) This is clearly a special type of project approach.

Other hybrids or variants are possible for large assemblies. In some niche automotive products, for example, the example of single team groups assembling major parts of an automobile at fixed stations with parts, subassemblies, and so on being brought in an automated way to each station is well known (in contrast to more assembly-line-oriented approaches used elsewhere). Model variations are easier to obtain, as well as quality benefits accruing from pride of authorship by the assembly team. This is again a form of project approach but with flow characteristics.

In modular home factories, the basic chassis for each home is completed as a subassembly at a fixed station and then moved along a prescribed path to receive other subassemblies (walls, roofs) made at other fixed stations nearby. Units reflecting different model variations (and thus different subassemblies, finishes, or other components) might follow different branch paths so that a whole line is not held up by the most time-consuming unit variation being produced.

17.3 COMMON COMPONENTS OF MANUFACTURING SYSTEMS

As can be appreciated, manufacturing systems can be highly complex and consist of many component elements, including fabrication machines, material handling systems, assembly machines, inspection devices, and surrounding information systems. Refer to earlier chapters on basic CNC machines and other equipment related to basic fabrication and processing. Here we will only briefly look at some of the components not already touched upon in earlier chapters.

Information Systems

There is a vast array of software specifically designed to facilitate manufacturing system operation and control, including general production control, scheduling, flow control, and machine control. At the floor level, machinists can view prioritized lists and schedules of jobs for their work centers, as well as various job status and completion reports. Software for manufacturing cells and flexible manufacturing systems controls all machine operations and reset operations for new jobs. At larger levels, management systems control most aspects of the flow line. Programs are available that allow entire processes to be analyzed, optimized, and controlled. Visual simulations are possible as well. Many more types of systems are available at a more general level for resource and personnel management, inventory management, material handling, and the like.

Industrial Robots

There are literally thousands of different applications currently performed by industrial robots. They are often used in situations where tasks are dangerous, tedious, or highly repetitive, or, in some cases, where special precision is required. Many types of industrial robotic devices are in common use—including those that have been developed for specific fabrication or finishing applications—for picking, lifting, or moving activities, and for assembly applications. In most of these instances, large volumes of usage are needed to warrant their employment.

There are, for example, a great many robotic welders used for fabrication. A typical automotive assembly line has large numbers of these devices, for spraying, or spot or line welding. There are literally thousands of robots that do various kinds of pick-and-place operations, wherein the robot identifies different parts (typically from mixed batches), picks them up, and places them in a new location. There are also many types of robotics that have been specially devised and programmed primarily to accomplish assembly functions. Common consumer products such as digital cameras, for example, consist of many different parts that must be precisely assembled. Special high-precision robotic devices have been developed and specially programmed to perform a series of precise assembly operations.

Basic Characteristics of Industrial Robots

There are many different ways of characterizing typical industrial robots. The primary components that make up a robot include the basic arm assembly and related manipulators (e.g., wrists), end effectors, programmable controllers, feedback and sensory input devices, a drive unit, and associated servomechanisms. A robot may have differing degrees of mobility (stationary fixed base, track mounted, vehicular mounted, legged). Power sources may be electric, hydraulic, or pneumatic.

There are many common types of jointed assemblies used in robots. Rigid arms are joined to form assemblies of varying types. As shown in Figure 17-2, arm assembly types are commonly defined in terms of their fundamental global coordinate systems: Cartesian coordinate assembly, polar coordinate assembly, cylindrical coordinate assembly, revolute coordinate assembly (jointed-arm), and the SCARA assembly (Selective Compliant Assembly Robot Arm). Robots based on Cartesian geometries can reach large areas, especially when gantry arrangements are used, but they can sometimes be slow, since final end movements are based on extensions and retractions instead of rotations. Cylindrical systems have relatively fast movements. Polar devices can also move very quickly, particularly in the vertical direction because of the location of the lower rotation axis. Articulated configurations can be relatively slow but are highly maneuverable. Reaches are limited, as are loads that can be carried. Many robots used for spraying applications use this kind of geometry because of the subtle movements required. The SCARA assembly is popular and provides a highly rigid horizontal plane that minimizes undesired vertical movements. Arms can move quickly within this horizontal plane. Great precision is possible.

In each of these basic configurations, there can be a wrist assembly that has its own movement possibilities. The *effectors* attached to the ends of the wrist assemblies provide the most popular images associated with robots. Common grippers, hands, or holders may be broadly characterized as *mechanical, magnetic, adhesive, magnetic,* or *vacuum.* Many mechanical grippers are available that use jaw devices that can grasp and hold objects. More dexterous mechanical fingers can also be used to grasp an object from either its outside or the inside. Magnetic grippers of one type or another have wide application in the handling of ferrous materials, particularly those in sheet forms. They can be extremely simple, fast, and capable of handling unusual shapes. Grippers of this type are normally electromagnetic. Vacuum or suction cups are frequently used for handling sheets with flat, smooth surfaces. Glass, sheet metal, and other materials can be picked up using vacuum cups.

Important in industrial robotic applications is the *work envelope.* The work envelope of a robot is the limited spatial volume in which end work manipulations can actually be performed, and is in turn a fundamental determinant of how a robot can actually be used. Work envelopes are also the determinants of the spatial organization of a work cell containing one or more robots or other automation equipment. The size and geometry of this spatial volume primarily depends upon the size and geometry of the arm assembly, movement opportunities, and restrictions associated with the type of arm geometry used, and the nature of the wrist end with its associated end effectors. Cartesian robots generally have rectilinear volumetric work envelopes. Cylindrical robots generally have cylindrical work envelopes. Polar and jointed-arm configurations normally have spherical envelopes. Many production process simulation software packages provide geometric models that not only simulate the actions of a robot but clearly define the associated work envelope as well. More advanced packages extend this capability to geometric modeling of the actual work operation on a part or component.

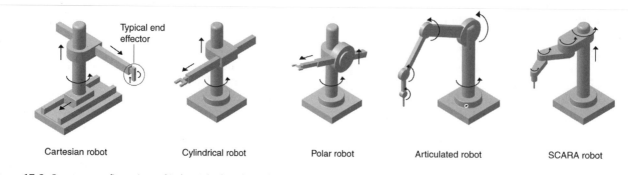

Cartesian robot   Cylindrical robot   Polar robot   Articulated robot   SCARA robot

Figure 17-2 Common configurations of industrial robots have different primary-movement characteristics. Many different types of end effectors with their own movement possibilities can also be utilized.

There are many different ways the complicated motions of robots are controlled or directed, including via mechanical devices, direct programming, teach pendant programming, deriving programming information from a computer-aided design model, and through various machine learning technologies for enabling a robot to react intelligently to a situation or learn from one. Simple learning systems have been devised wherein robots are taught by manually holding a robot arm and guiding it through a series of motions that are then remembered. For many applications, these techniques are being replaced or supplemented by interfacing with a CAD description of the workpiece and work environment. This model provides much of the needed data. Use of simulation models is also increasing. Great emphasis is currently placed on the development of intelligent react/learn techniques that are coupled with robots equipped with sophisticated machine vision and sensor systems.

Teleoperated systems provide a different means of control. In a teleoperated system, the mechanical manipulators are directly controlled by human operators who are normally removed from the actual operation. The devices themselves may look quite like an industrial robot and even utilize similar manipulators and effectors.

Material Handling, Assembly, and Other Systems

A huge number of special collections of machines and devices systems exist for transporting materials, parts, and assemblies to the right place at the right time; feeding parts; sorting and routing; assembling parts; conducting product inspection; and performing other activities. In the context of this book, it suffices to say that the majority are electromechanical machines of wondrous ingenuity and extreme value, but that play primarily supportive roles in the production process. Computer control is common. They are not, however, "CNC" machines in the sense discussed in this book.

Technological sophistication is extremely high, as witnessed by the widespread use of coordinate measurement machines and machine vision systems for inspection and quality control. In a machine vision system, for example, visual captures of products from cameras are analyzed via various object recognition algorithms to assess whether flaws are present, dimensional tolerances are met, and so forth. They can also be used for quality sorting. These analyses can occur while products are literally flying by in front of the cameras. Special machines select and reroute products picked out by the vision system.

In manufacturing building products, many automated machines are used to transform bulk materials into finished products (see Figure 17-3).

17.4 APPROACHES AND STRATEGIES

This section briefly looks at broader manufacturing philosophies and attitudes. These strategies typically focus on more fully integrating all aspects of a production environment via information technologies and/or are closely connected with encompassing business models. At the production level, the ideas of central interest herein relate to such concepts as the *flexible manufacturing systems* (FMS), previously discussed, and to *group technologies* (GT). Full systems integration is sought in *computer-integrated manufacturing* (CIM) systems. The latter approach stresses the full integration of all technologies and information flows, and seeks to embrace all related domains, such as computer-aided design, computer-aided engineering, computer-aided process planning, manufacturing planning and control, factory automation (including robotic devices, etc.), general resource planning and management enterprises, and so forth. *Concurrent engineering* approaches seek to restructure the whole activity of design and production in order to utilize advanced technologies fully and to create a process wherein designers, users, production engineers, and others are involved together

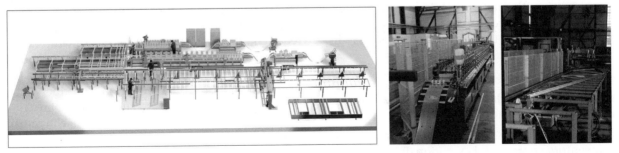

Fabrication and assembly line   Sheet metal shaping   Final truss

Figure 17-3 Trusses are made in a line-assembly process from rolls of sheet metal via a sequence of forming, drilling, and other operations. (Source: Courtesy of Rosette Systems, Ltd.)

from the very inception of a project and communicate in a fully digital way. In addition to how individual machine-based capabilities may be integrated, there are important related issues of design and production planning and management, inventory and process control, quality assurance, and so forth. Many of these approaches have direct implications on how machines are laid out and interconnected. In the *just-in-time* approach described in the next section, for example, the smoothing of production flows may necessitate special machine organization patterns.

Group technology is a manufacturing approach that identifies and exploits the underlying similarity of parts and manufacturing processes. A basic idea underlying group technology is to use (as much as possible) existing work in the design and manufacturing of products. Specifically, GT implies the notion of recognizing and exploiting similarities in three distinct ways: (1) by performing like activities together, (2) by standardizing similar tasks, and (3) by efficiently storing and retrieving information about recurring problems. By grouping similar parts into part families based on either their shapes or their manufacturing process, it is possible to reduce costs through effective design rationalization and design data retrieval. It is also possible to lower stock levels and purchase quantities and improve production planning and control. The approach allows for reductions in programming costs and allows for a more efficient NC machine utilization. In particular, this approach is important to the efficient operation and utilization of the flexible manufacturing systems described in the previous section. One of the many driving forces behind the development of FMS was the desire to extend the benefits of automation to mid-volume and low-volume production quantities. An intent was to combine the advantages of the automated production line with the flexibility of the job shop. Via group technology, the FMS concept allowed much more efficient use of capital equipment, increased productivity, improved product quality and consistency, reduction of work in process, reduced direct labor costs, and reduced floor space. In some circumstances, however, FMS systems have sometimes been found to be very expensive, with many difficulties attributable to the failure to design or redesign products in accordance with group technology thinking for manufacturability in an FMS environment.

Manufacturing Requirements or Resources Planning, Just-in-Time

A number of formal systems support operations planning, inventory control, and execution. Broadly known as *manufacturing requirements planning* or *manufacturing resources planning,* these systems support and coordinate planning and production activities done by different groups within an organization. These groups include high-level planning by senior management, business planning, sales planning, and actual production control and planning. Manufacturing requirements planning tends to emphasize the machine aspects of these activities, while manufacturing resources planning tends to have broader connotations.

The central activity of *production control* involves setting production goals, outputs, and rates; coordinating material delivery and inventory control; directing and controlling the scheduling and movement of elements or components through a series of operations relating to their manufacturing or assembly; and other activities involving any installation done by the production group or shipping. Planning and scheduling functions include considerations relating to machine use, shop capacity, and demand. Many monitoring and reporting functions are included. The general activity of *inventory control* management relates both to the supply of parts and materials needed in the manufacturing process as well as finished products.

The phrase *just-in-time* reeks of hype and jargon, but it actually represents a sound operations philosophy for improving a production process via a number of steps that systematically eliminate non-value-adding activities, eliminate waste, identify process improvements, reduce production cycle time, and so forth. The approach does seek to avoid costly idle inventories by avoiding unnecessary stockpiling of materials to be used in a manufacturing process, but it is also more than simply an inventory control program. Similarly, it does not replace materials resource planning but puts this planning in a broader context. The just-in-time idea applies to any kind of production activity, but it is most clearly implemented in large-flow environments. The approach is most fully applicable in perfecting already well-developed repetitive production processes.

The just-in-time approach is usually implemented through a series of distinct steps. Initial steps are planning- and organizationally oriented, including goal definition and the establishment of various task groups and steering committees charged with implementing goals. Related steps focus on education, responsibility assessment, and definition. Subsequent steps focus on activities such as establishing uniform plant flows, redesigning process flows, and reducing setups. The *uniform plant flow* (UPL) idea is fundamental to the larger just-in-time operations philosophy. UPL is a make-to-demand approach that moves end products directly into distribution and not to stock. This approach usually requires planning systems that reduce manufacturing lead times and that attempt to coordinate all components of the production cycle so that final outputs match demand rates. This objective in turn may require redefining process flows and necessitate changes to the arrangement and linkages of manufacturing cells. Specific improvements to the process follow, which include various kinds of pull strategies for optimum authorization of part initiation and production in view of short-term demand and resource environments. A related activity includes controlling the supply continuum so that materials are delivered only when needed by the smoothed-out production process.

Lean Manufacturing

At first glance, the term *lean manufacturing* is seemingly another jargon descriptor, but it does imply a specific attitude and way of thinking about manufacturing. The concept of "lean" was introduced in the book *The Machine That Changed the World*,[2] which addressed performance gaps between the Western and Japanese automotive industries—particularly the Toyota Production System, which used less human, capital, space, and other resources in production than did their American counterparts of the time. Defined largely in relation to large production volumes, principles generally include the following: producing only what is needed or demanded by the market addressed—and defining production and other processes in relation to them; clearly defining the value chain or value stream present in relation to how production processes and business models transform the product; defining which activities add the most value to a service or product and treating the remainder as targets for removal; creating flows based on value-added steps; and establishing methods for continual improvement in processes and final products. Programs of aggressive waste elimination are of fundamental importance. Implementation of this kind of thinking occurs at many levels, including managerial, and provides a means for identifying value and waste targets, and for improving many technically oriented processes. Software environments have been devised to assist in implementing lean techniques.

Quality

While to many the idea of "quality" may initially seem vague or uselessly abstract, the general issue surfaces again and again as a fundamental design, fabrication, and assembly goal. Systematic efforts have consequently been made in many design and production fields to define, quantify, and refine this seemingly elusive idea and to codify definitions and procedures for ensuring quality in a product or service. In these sectors, terms like quality or quality assurance can thus mean something very specific. In an architectural context, the term quality unfortunately remains less precisely defined.

A first issue is defining what is meant by "quality." A common meaning connotes the presence or absence of faults or defects in an object. An object may be considered as faulty or defective because it does not fulfill its end-use requirements. A fault or defect might arise because of the absence of a critical feature or functionality (i.e., a design shortcoming) or be present within an object because of inadequacies or inaccuracies in the way the object was manufactured or produced so that design goals and specifications are not fulfilled. A simple door may be considered to be defective because it does not have a handle; or if it has a handle, it may be considered defective because it jams or sticks when the door is opened or closed. Not having a handle is clearly and exclusively a design flaw. Jamming or sticking could be the result of a design flaw if the designer failed to specify reasonable use tolerances, or it could be a manufacturing process flaw if specified tolerances are reasonable but the door was cut crookedly in the manufacturing cycle such that design tolerances are not met. Alternatively, the door may have been acceptably manufactured, but it might have been improperly installed (it could have been racked out of alignment during placement because of rough handling).

There are many more formal definitions of the term quality. According to documents promulgated by the influential American National Standards Institute (ANSI), quality in relation to a product or a service is described in terms of the composite set of features and characteristics that are present that will ultimately bear on the ability of the product or service to meet design goals and related end-use requirements. In common usage, this characterization of quality implies that design goals and use needs must be clearly articulated *before* the idea of quality in a product or service can be assessed or even rationally discussed. In relation to products, more specific interpretations of quality include ideas related to issues such as maintainability, safeness of use, and so forth, which are normally more precise descriptions of normal functional or use specifications. These general constructs may be implemented via formal *quality assurance programs*. These programs have defined sequential steps that are implemented during successive phases of the planning, design, and production process. Manufacturing process control can occur via *Total Quality Management* programs. In repetitive part-manufacturing processes, control charts are used to first identify and quantify variations present in the process via statistical methods for characterizing a measured parameter, such as a critical dimension for a part. These and other methods are a crucial part of any large-scale production environment.

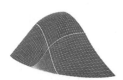

Digital model of roof corner
(K. Vollers)

CNC milled foam mold
(K. Vollers)

Concrete molds (K.Vollers)

Framing for water reservoir
(Exploform)

Explosion above panel
(Exploform)

Typical explosion formed panel
(K. Vollers)

Hydra-Pier, Haarlemmermeer Pavilion, Floriade Exhibition 2002, Haarlemmermeer, The Netherlands
Architect: Asymptote Architecture, New York
Project team: Lise Anne Couture, Hani Rashid
Engineering firm: Octatube Space Structures, Delft
Explosion Forming: Karel Vollers, The Blob & Technology Research Team, Delft University of Technology and www.Exploform.nl, Delft, The Netherlands

Haarlemmermeer in the Netherlands was host to the Floriade World Horticultural Exhibition in 2002. As a result of a competition, Asymptote designed the main host pavilion. Streaming surfaces of water that flow over the building and into a large overhead basin made of laminated glass. The overhead roof is covered by complexly shaped aluminum panels. Making limited numbers of uniquely shaped doubly curved metal panels has long proven difficult and expensive. A decision was made to adopt the use of existing explosive forming techniques to shape the aluminum panels. This process uses the force of an explosion to force a panel to conform to the shape of an underlying mold.

In the process used in the Pavilion, digital models using Maya were made of exact panel shapes. Basic mold shapes were then CNC milled from high-density polystyrene foam. The accuracy of the milling process allowed patterns for adjacent façade panels to be precisely matched and trimmed. Shapes were then finished with a glass fiber and epoxy coating to prevent damage during reuse. Relatively inexpensive concrete molds were then made on top of each of the foam molds. In making a typical panel, a sheet of aluminum was placed over a concrete mold, and both sealed in a plastic bag. A vacuum was then applied to prevent compressed air from the explosion from separating the aluminum sheet from the mold. Both were then placed in a water reservoir. Explosives placed above the panel were ignited, and the panel was forced into a shape that conformed to that of the mold.   The same team that developed this process is now exploring other methods of making the basic molds. Several different groups were involved in this process (see illustrations).

Wood frame for trial assembly (Octatube)

Pavilion

Assembly of adjoining panels (Octatube)

Figure 17-4 Needs in architecture often simply do not support high-volume manufacturing processes. Rather, project-based approaches are frequently used.

CHAPTER 18

Product and Process Approaches

18.1 INTRODUCTION

The demand for the largest possible variety of products, whether architectural, consumer, or industrial products, has clearly increased over the past decades. Products and architectural components can be created in a large variety of ways, depending on the quantities needed; the scale, materials, and performance requirements; and the underlying design concepts. Between the two extreme approaches of individually crafting a one-off artifact and mass-producing a commodity product, there are many processes that are suitable for intermediate quantities (see previous chapter). These relate to the many different ways of characterizing buildings and products. Clearly there are obvious differences between buildings and products in terms of function, size, number of units produced, inherent technologies, complexity, methods of construction or manufacturing production, organization of the design and production team, and so forth.

Product Complexity. Chapter 8 introduced some general characterizations such as market pull, technology push, and platform products, as well as user-driven and technology-driven products. Many of these concepts apply more to industrial consumer products than to architectural products. A more generally applicable way to categorize products is their relative complexity. Elemental products, for example, are only marginally removed from basic raw materials via the addition of a few straightforward value-added processes (e.g., lumber). Other products are highly sophisticated (e.g., automobiles). In between the extremes lie a whole host of products with varying degrees of complexity. Buildings are generally assemblies of products and materials, and as such necessarily relatively complex. This overall complexity can be achieved without highly complex parts and subassemblies, because these latter elements may be standard elements and products that, with minor modifications through simple secondary processes, suit project-specific conditions. The same is true, albeit to a lesser extent, for larger products.

The Need for Product Variation. There is an obvious need for product variation, and a great many strategies have been devised to accommodate this demand. The tendency to expect—and be able to obtain—an ever-larger variety of products has been a consistent trend throughout the past decades, and the speed with which new products enter the market is clearly accelerated as companies compete for market share and customers. The example of wood-based products illustrates the extent to which we have become used to variety. The simple plywood sheet used throughout the first half of the twentieth century has been supplemented by a large number of other wood-based products, ranging from particle, strand, and wafer sheet products to structural wood-based products reconstituted from long strands, thin veneers, as well as composite products that employ both lumber and glass-fiber/resin layers. Similar observations can be made in other areas.

There are many strategies to satisfy the demand for product variety, and these strategies impact the design and production processes that this book is primarily dealing with. Most of the broad characterizations in the following sections apply to product design as well as to architecture. There are, however, some significant differences that have to do with issues of scale and the fact that a product is usually prefabricated, while buildings typically consist of a mix of ready-made products, prefabricated, and partially customized components, as well as elements built on-site.

18.2 STANDARD PRODUCTS AND VARIATIONS: TRADITIONAL PROCESSES

A discussion of process principles inevitably has to begin by looking at standard products that are the result of highly deterministic mass production processes, because these processes are the origin of today's industrialized economies. Next, strategies of how to achieve a limited amount of product variety with standard products are reviewed. These include user configuration, modularity, and fabrication-side configuration.

Standard Consumer and Architectural Products

Standard products are normally associated with high-volume industrialized production on capital-intensive manufacturing and assembly facilities. Setup and tooling costs of the machines used in high-volume production are typically significant, and these mass production techniques can only operate cost-effectively for large production volumes of identical items. Mass-produced items are present everywhere in our daily lives, and little thought is usually given to the fact that thousands if not hundreds of thousands will be using exactly the same item. Typical assembled products are many consumer electronics products, most furniture, light fixtures, and clothes or shoes, to just name a few. Many buildings are at least partially assembled from mass-produced items such as standard doors and windows, suspended ceilings or raised floors, and others.

When designing products that will be produced at high volumes, designers obviously have to carefully consider the available manufacturing options: Manufacturing techniques with higher tooling and setup costs might be applicable here that would be impossible to justify for low-volume production. Plastic molding techniques, for example, are typically associated with a mass production mode.

CAD/CAM techniques have had a profound impact on the design and manufacturing of standard products. Many companies have embraced parametric design and analysis tools in order to reduce the time to market of their products and cut development costs. Integrated digital design environments as described in Chapter 12 are extensively used, often in combination with product data management (PDM) systems and related business software packages that help to control and manage complex interactions in companies. The improved efficiency of the design-to-manufacturing process has at least partially enabled today's tremendous product variety.

Standard products, such as standard doors and windows, the normalized light bulbs, are usually guided by a set of well-defined boundary conditions. Standards and other agreed-upon rules can be embedded into digital design environments, most typically as standard part libraries or predefined modeling macros. These are useful modeling aids that abbreviate what otherwise might be tedious and repetitive modeling tasks. Electronic marketplaces are increasingly used to purchase and distribute standard products, and connections between the designer's CAD drawing, the associated bill of quantities, specifications, and the databases of available products at online markets may only be a question of time.

Creating Variation with Standard Products

Despite a host of manufacturing strategies such as lean manufacturing or flexible manufacturing cells, mass production remains one of the most cost-effective ways of producing standard products in large volumes. It is less efficient, however, in producing the product variety that end users and designers expect, because this variety increases the complexity of production through additional setups, tools, training, and storage, to just name a few. All these factors ultimately increase cost (see Figure 18-1).

User-Side Configuration

One seemingly obvious way to achieve variation without leaving a mass production mode is to let the end user modify the standard product and customize it in the desired way. This approach exists both for consumer products and architectural products, but whereas the consumer product is typically assembled and configured by a layperson, the architectural product is assembled, configured, and installed by an expert (contractor). Design-for-assembly implications vary accordingly.

Configurations of this type can be as simple as finishing a product in the desired quality or choosing individual installing schemes for shelves or cabinets. In architecture, this type of customization is extremely common, since it allows the erection of unique buildings with cost-effective, mass-produced elements. Lumber and plywood products in lightweight timber construction, for example, are configured on-site, but the elements themselves are mass-produced on an industrial scale.

Digital Design Considerations

Some consumer product companies support online environments that allow users to visualize the possible configurations, but here the purpose is purely to provide visual assistance to the customer in choosing a configuration. Generally, companies do not track these visualization studies by the user, but registering more or less popular versions could surely impact the development of future products and is likely to become more common.

Since user-configured architectural products are often quite simple (sheets of plywood, tiles, etc.), sophisticated design development environments are more commonly used for the configuration process itself. Such configuration tools include the steel or timber design and detailing software discussed in Chapter 6, but the output would be traditional installation drawings instead of CNC instructions. Other design tools, such as those used for suspended ceiling systems or carpet design, enable the layout design and generate bills of quantities to facilitate the tedious specification and procurement process. Currently these tools are stand-alone environments that are disconnected from manufacturing and distribution processes. Future directions might include links to online market places or Web-based bidding and procurement environments.

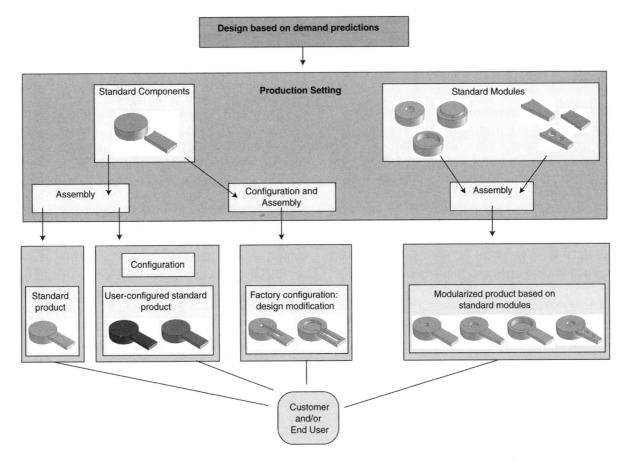

Figure 18-1 Creating variations with standard products and modularized products.

Modularity

A modular design approach is an additive design strategy that enables product variety by combining different standard modules that themselves may be mass-produced. In this discussion, the term "module" refers to a self-contained, distinct, and identifiable unit that serves as a building block for an overall structure. Modularity has functional and physical connotations to it. There are many examples in product design of modules that are primarily functionally defined, for instance, a power module. Although there usually are also some physical shaping and dimensional implications present, these considerations are not necessarily defining characteristics. The physical meaning of "module" refers to a standardized unit of size. In its more extreme form, a "modular" design thus generally refers to an overall design based on the use of a *prespecified dimensional array* (typically in the form of integral multiples of given dimensions) that serves to define the sizes and locations of all parts and subassemblies (locations of connection or interface points are often predefined as well). In building design, this concept is often associated with prefabricated building elements, whereas in electronics, it is used to structure the sizes and shapes of electronic devices to go on printed circuit boards with a highly

regularized hole spacing. This physically based notion of modular design is extremely important when it comes to manufacturing and assembly issues. Its general implication is that all modules are replaceable without completely disassembling the whole configuration. In most design circumstances, there are both functional and physical connotations to a modular design approach.

In architecture, modular design approaches are normally used in the spatial planning of any building to accommodate commonly available off-the-shelf building components such as standard bathroom or kitchen elements. One departs from these standard dimensions only at great cost. More specific constructs of "modular design" are used as well. For example, the term "modular housing" has long been associated with an approach wherein whole housing units are built according to standardized dimensions. Standardized units are then aggregated according to certain rules to form a larger development. The arrangement of the modules themselves is often used as the basis for architectural expression—for example, Moshe Safdie's original Habitat in Montreal that created a sensation at the 1967 World's Fair.

A notion inherently contained in modular design is the possibility of upgrading a modular system over time by exchanging selected modules. Alternatively, a modular system can be extended by adding new modules. In both scenarios, the interchangeability of parts and the standardization of connections need to be present in the system.

Digital Design Considerations

Parametric design environments are well suited to support modular design activities. The dimensionally driven nature of design features combines well with the regularity and systematic nature of modular design. Assembly models can be created that allow different modules (part file or subassemblies) to be displayed such that interferences and other design conflicts can be readily detected. Array features can efficiently support modular designs based on regularly spaced elements. The standards inherent in many modular design approaches (e.g., kitchen cabinet modules, masonry blocks) also make specialized design tools for certain systems feasible.

Preconfigured Standard Products

Leaving the customization of a standard product to either the end user (consumer products) or the contractor (architectural products) has the advantage of reducing the complexity of production by minimizing variety and allowing for the economy-of-scale effects of high-volume production systems. For architectural products, the disadvantage clearly is that on-site customization is generally less accurate and less productive than comparable off-site activities. These and other arguments have created great interest in the concept of preconfiguration and prefabrication in architecture, and preconfigured products today are widely used. On-site activities are usually limited to the assembly of these custom elements according to the installation drawings that are typically supplied. Timber and steel design and detailing software—discussed in more detail in Chapter 6—support design, computer-controlled production, and installation of preconfigured structural elements.

For consumer products, the concept of factory-configured standard products is equally common. Many standard products, for example, are produced in a range of factory-applied colors or finishes. Closely related is the notion of the *model,* a defined type of product that is produced in different variations of size, color, materials, or others. This approach is commonly encountered in the apparel or shoe industry, but it is also present in other products. It is a variation of the factory-configured standard product in that a single model—the basic type—is parametrically varied to suit individual needs. In the traditional setup, each variation is then fabricated as a standard product—in other words, in a production setting geared toward high-volume production.

Digital Design Considerations

Preconfigured standard products are products that truly benefit from digital design and manufacturing techniques, because fabrication processes need to provide for the variations that were traditionally produced on-site. There are many advantages to using a parametric modeling tool, since variations of a product are inherently simple to produce through parametric variations of part and assembly models. In product design, the digital tools employed are typically general-purpose, high-end parametric modelers (e.g., Pro/ENGINEER, SolidWorks), thus they are packages that combine with a variety of other tools to specifically support product data management and manufacturing activities.

In architecture this is the realm of many integrated solutions for building systems, as presented in Chapter 6. With few exceptions, they are not normally geared toward the designer, nor do they easily interface with digital models that are generated by the design team.

18.3 ARCHITECTURAL CONSTRUCTION AND ONE-OFF PRODUCTION

Erecting a building in an assembly mode of configured products clearly describes only one aspect of building. Most buildings also contain portions that are fabricated on-site through the direct processing of materials. Examples include on-site concrete and masonry construction, many cast floor finishes, wet-applied plaster, and others. CAD/CAM techniques currently affect this mode of construction relatively little, but a 3-D building model can clearly serve during the design process and also guide site-surveying techniques. Construction robots that operate either autonomously or are guided by the 3-D design model are still under development. Other processes such as the production of custom sets of masonry blocks or prefabricated concrete elements strive to render on-site activities more effective and improve productivity. These efforts are closely related to the concept of mass customization, as discussed in the next section.

In many ways parallel to on-site construction is the making of one-off, highly individualized products or construction elements by specialized fabricators. This mode of production remains largely craft-based, but it is increasingly supported by the advanced digital design and manufacturing techniques described throughout this book. The challenges of designing and making a unique object, for which little precedent may exist, has in fact been the focus of much of the current discussion on the use of CAD/CAM in architecture. Complexly shaped buildings are representative of this model. For unique elements that are mostly differentiated by their complex shapes, advanced parametric modeling tools have proven useful to represent shapes accurately and support fabrication through CNC techniques.

In extreme examples, design and fabrication may be contracted to companies outside the traditional building industry. The suspended technical library of the Yazaki Corporation Headquarters in Canton, Michigan, for example, was designed to take on the shape of a boat hull or ark—conveying the notion of safeguarding the collective knowledge of the company in a metaphorical vessel (see Figure 18-2). This regular but complexly curved shape was engineered by a naval engineer and manufactured by a boat builder, because even the most advanced architectural construction techniques were insufficient to generate the desired shape. The shape was ultimately hand-laminated as a wood-glass composite, over a mold built from CNC-cut profiles. The difficulties of such mixed teams go beyond problematic issues of file formats not being compatible among specialized digital environments from different industries. Approaches to collaboration and professional liability may vary as well.

18.4 MASS CUSTOMIZATION

The variations that can be created based on a mass-produced product are inherently limited. Modularity and configuration strategies inevitably lead to a smaller production volume for individual parts and subassemblies, and a lower production volume negatively affects the economy-of-scale effects that mass production is so dependent on. The relative inflexibility of mass production techniques not only limits product variety, but production relies on demand predictions that may or may not occur. Storage costs and the costs of discounts that may have to be granted in order to sell excess quantities can be substantial—if the demand for a product turns out to be below the production volume. Companies have been striving to reduce the risk of production without markets by reducing the time between demand prediction and bringing the product on the market (time to market). Lean manufacturing techniques, including just-in-time delivery and flexible manufacturing cells, were introduced mainly to improve flexibility and at the same time lower costs—thus breaking the traditional industrial dilemma whereby per-unit cost advantages were inevitably associated with large production volumes. These advances in manufacturing technology, when combined with the rapid introduction of information technology into the manufacturing world, brought about a different business model that claims to resolve the dilemma between variety and high production volumes: mass customization.

The fundamental premise of mass customization is to no longer manufacture products "blindly" according to a predicted demand, but instead allow production to be directly driven by actual orders. This reduces the cost for storage of unsold items and for costly discounts. Individual customers cannot only order individual quantities; the production processes are devised such that, within the typically modular design of a product, many individual variations can be accommodated. (See Figure 18-3.)

Generating individualized orders in significant quantities is only feasible if the corresponding manufacturing system is actually able to handle this individ-

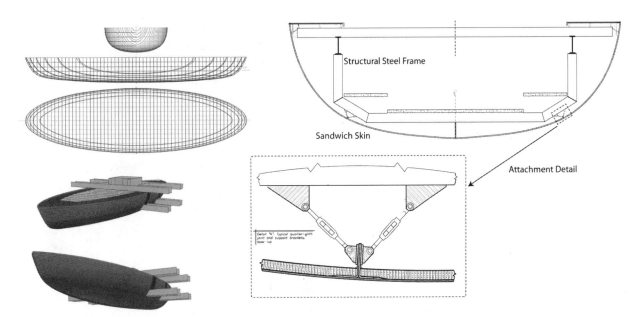

Figure 18-2 The Yazaki technical library: The line drawing (upper left) is typical of the 2-D representations for boat hulls employed in the marine industry. The detail (right) shows a sandwich skin suspended from a rigid steel frame. (Source: Yazaki Ark; lines by Steve Koopman; engineering by Dk1; built by Goetz Custom Boats)

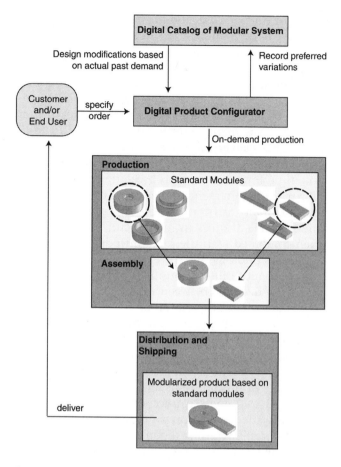

Figure 18-3 Schematic process diagram of mass customization.

can be delivered four to six weeks from the order. Similar techniques are employed to customize eyeglasses and other products where individualization may give the advantage of a better fit.

An important aspect of this direct interaction between the customer and the fabricator is referred to as the *learning relationship.* As the customer specifies the product variation that best suits his or her needs, this information is stored in the company's database and can be retrieved the next time the customer launches an order. The potential time savings for the customer create an incentive to keep purchasing from the same company. Companies can also use this information as a market analysis tool, allowing them to determine what modular variations to offer for future products. These types of customer bonds and learning relationships are more relevant for consumer products or services than for architectural construction products.

The competitive pricing of mass-customized products is what makes this business model so compelling and at the same time challenging to implement. How can a customized product be sold at a similar price compared to the equivalent mass-produced item? To streamline the ordering process, it is vital to automate the processing of large numbers of individualized orders. For this purpose, customers initially configure their product using a specific, system-integrated software or online environment. The choices available in these configuration tools are limited to the variation that a particular company can produce, thus guaranteeing that each individual order can be accommodated efficiently by the given process.

ualization efficiently—that is, without the downtimes, setup times, and high tooling costs normally associated with a change in product models or a model variation in high-volume production. Lean manufacturing and flexible manufacturing cells are key components of this process. Since these manufacturing systems are inevitably expensive to set up, it is important to point out that the success of mass customization hinges on large production volumes, but it can achieve an impressive variety of products.

Mass-customized products can be found on many levels of consumer products, as well as in services. Custom clothes and shoes are good examples of mass customization. Here, body-scanning techniques in specialized points of sale are usually employed to generate a 3-D model that is stored in the company's database (see Figure 18-4). For subsequent purchases of customized shirts, shoes, or suits, the customer can simply log on to a Web site or choose from a variety of models that can be produced in different material qualities and colors (modularity). Once an order is submitted, a cutting pattern is generated automatically and the selected material is cut accordingly. Assembly is often done manually, and custom-made apparel or shoes typically

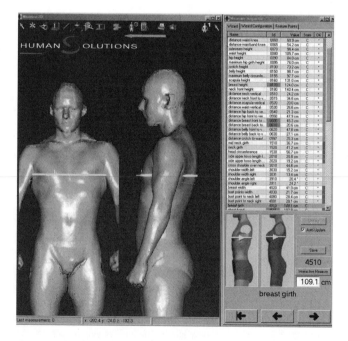

Figure 18-4 A body scanner generates digital data that can be used to configure custom-made clothes or shoes. (Source: Human Solutions)

Mass Customization in Architecture

Mass customization is beginning to make an impact on construction products. Many of the current approaches that integrate a system-specific design environment with its related manufacturing process bear resemblances of mass customization but in reality represent a distinctly different business approach. Compared to approaches of mass customization in consumer products or furniture, there are usually few if any direct connections between the product configuration software and the digitally driven manufacturing process. The traditional distribution of responsibilities between the design team and the contractors or fabricators makes any degree of automation between design and production presently a journey into legal no-man's-land.

Shop drawings exist for many good reasons and cannot easily be eliminated. The need to verify whether an architectural product or component is correctly designed and meets code clearly sets apart all attempts for mass customization with their counterparts in product design. Consumer products can be modularized in a way that restricts customization to the technically feasible. Verifying whether an architectural product and components meets code, represents the design intention, and can be manufactured is usually a much more complex undertaking involving a number of independent parties. There is usually no one party that is expert in all areas, and this specialization necessarily creates a need for design verification. Typically a given design environment has to be able to communicate with manufacturing facilities at many different companies. This makes any direct integration extremely difficult to achieve. A further problem in the building industry is its fragmentation: Fabricators are often small to mid-size companies, and the production volumes necessary to generate the economy-of-scale effects in a modularized production setting of mass customization are normally missing.

An approach that relates to mass customization is the custom manufacturing of large-format masonry blocks described in more detail in Chapter 6. This system combines a proprietary design interface that is directly tied into production. For the contractor, the slightly higher cost of customized masonry blocks compared to standard blocks is compensated for by the reduction in overall waste, the elimination of extensive storage areas on-site through just-in-time delivery, and most importantly, the improved construction productivity through prefabrication. These cost-saving factors are typical of mass customization. The configuration software used to generate customized masonry blocks, however, is only for use by the fabricator and not accessible to the architect or the builder. Design and production currently remain disconnected, strictly speaking not a case in mass customization.

A similar concept is Mero's system of steel space frames, an efficient, highly automated but proprietary design-to-manufacturing system for use only by the company itself (see Chapter 4). Within this modularized building system, customization of parts does not significantly affect cost, because all production is handled with the same CNC machining centers that are driven by NC files generated indirectly from Mero's proprietary software environment. Designers do not have direct access to the configuration software. Both custom masonry blocks and the Mero space frame system currently represent "islands of automation" with potential for mass customization.

The design and manufacturing of custom windows is a domain of successful mass customization. Since windows are both specified by architects or contractors, and purchased directly by homeowners, there are often two different design environments to configure the window. Laypeople typically specify the design together with a specialized dealer, using software with an interface particularly suited to individuals with little or no background in building construction and design. This configuration software limits the choices automatically to what can be manufactured by a given company. Choices include frame materials and finishes, different glazing systems, and others. The data is sent directly from the dealer to the manufacturer, where machine instructions can be generated automatically based on the design submittal. Some companies offer free downloadable software for use by architects, engineers, and builders that allows the design of a system-conform window without having to be present at a sales point or dealer.

Case Study: e-Skylight.com

This case study describes how a manufacturer of architectural skylights applied principles of mass customization in the production of small skylights, thus transitioning from a one-off custom production to a mass-customized production within a modular system. Architectural Skylight (ASC) of Waterboro, Maine, uses an object-oriented design approach to designing and manufacturing custom skylights. This system supplements AutoCAD with several plug-ins, including third-party software and programs developed by ASC. It allows technicians to import geometry generated by the architects, build upon this model, and generate a complete model of the skylight or curtain-wall parametrically in 3-D. The same model, after several post-processing steps, is used directly for CNC manufacturing of frame members and for the CNC cutting of custom glass sheets.

With this integrated approach to design and manufacturing well established and proven, ASC sought to expand its market by setting up a system capable of producing smaller skylights for small to medium-size commercial and residential construction. An online interface was set up, allowing customers to design custom skylights within the given manufacturing constraints. Within two and a half years of its implementation, over 65,000 skylights were designed online. The system is mostly used by glazing contractors, but also by architects and individual homeowners.

e-Skylight Process. The online design interface is structured into a series of simple steps that, at each level, enables a choice between either preselected options or the input of dimensions or desired performance values (see Figure 18-5). The design process starts with a selection among the four basic types. In the following steps all other parameters are defined, beginning with the basic dimensions, followed with a selection of frame and glass qualities and finishes. In case the user specifies dimensions that are beyond the range of the supported modularized product line, the system prompts an alert and points to the closest possible value. During the design process, an image displays a photorealistic rendering of the specific configuration. A quote for the custom skylight is instantly available online based on the 3-D model in the AutoCAD-based environment. This same model is eventually used to generate machine instructions for fabrication; it is also used to derive the bill of quantities, specifications, and all 2-D drawings (see Figure 18-6). Users can download the specifications, overview drawings, and construction details—all representing the specific version chosen during the online design session (see Figure 18-7).

Once the desired skylight is ordered, the glass dimensions are automatically generated from the 3-D model and electronically sent as text and drawing files to the glass fabricator. The desired glass type and coating are also included in this order, again derived from the bill of materials generated by the 3-D model.

Manufacturing. To minimize storage costs, e-Skylight does not store aluminum profiles in all available finishes. Once a skylight has been purchased, an affiliated metal finishing company automatically receives the

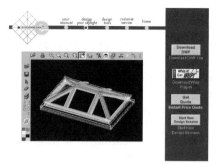

Figure 18-6 The 3-D model is evaluated in a CAD viewer online. (Source: E-Skylight.com)

order to finish a certain amount of a particular frame profile. This customized stock is then sent to e-Skylight just in time for the following machining processes.

Prior to any machining of metal profiles, the software system also creates a set of printed 2-D fabrication or shop drawings that are used for quality control, to guide the assembly of the unit in the shop, and to support the installation on-site (see Figure 18-8). The NC code is automatically generated from the 3-D model and sent to one of the machining centers (see Figure 18-9). The programming CAM software includes nesting routines that optimize material use of the customized frame stock. Technicians check the fabricated parts to the 2-D fabrication drawings.

A barcode system is employed throughout the manufacturing process to track each part during the various machining and finishing steps. Once all parts have been fabricated, units are assembled as far as possible to avoid any errors in the field and maintain a tight quality control (see Figure 18-10). Custom skylights are generally shipped within four weeks of the purchase.

Mass Customization—Business Paradigm of the Future?

In the 1990s, mass customization was praised as the business strategy of the future.[1] In the meantime, some promising attempts in the building industry have adapted this approach. Consumer product companies embraced mass customization much earlier, but some of the early attempts in mass customization have failed. Several large corporations no longer pursue markets of individualized products. Levi Jeans, for example, no longer produces individualized jeans, several custom-shoe companies went out of business, and Panasonic of Japan no longer offers customized bicycles through its subsidiary, NBIC. Many other companies have switched back to a mode of diversified mass production on flexible and lean manufacturing systems.

One of the main challenges of mass customization is the need to be cost-competitive with equivalent mass-produced items. This objective can only be achieved if

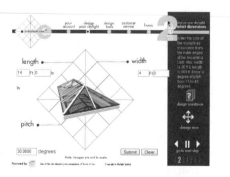

Figure 18-5 Online design interface of e-Skylight: selecting dimensions of a custom skylight. (Source: E-Skylight.com)

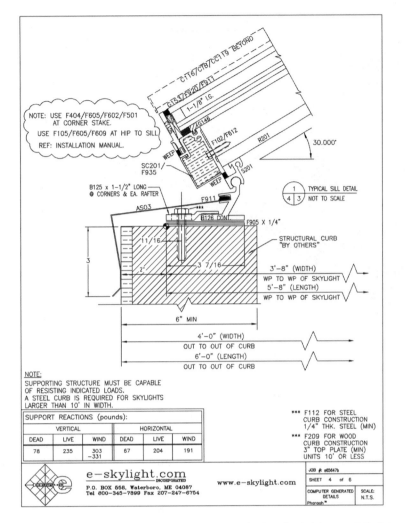

Figure 18-7 Edge details and other construction details are auto-generated and can be downloaded. (Source: E-Skylight.com)

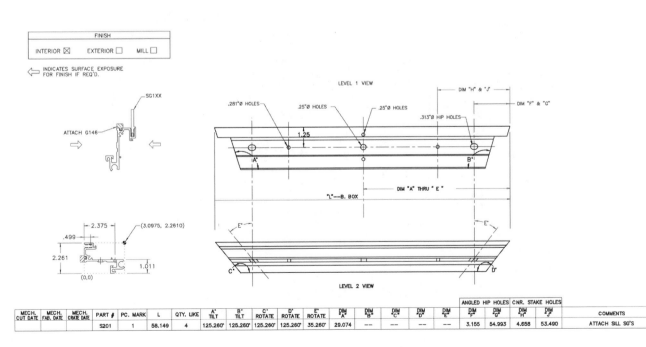

Figure 18-8 Fabrication drawing for assembly and quality control. (Source: E-Skylight.com)

Figure 18-9 CNC machining center for the fabrication of the skylight frames. (Source: E-Skylight.com)

the complete design-to-delivery process is highly stream-lined to eliminate any potential inefficiency. For customized architectural products or components, the industry-specific fragmentation is a major obstacle to mass customization. Only a few companies have successfully transitioned into mass customization, and with few exceptions those usually had a well-established market position in niche markets or were, such as the large win-dow manufacturers, among the market leaders in their field. Most of the successful mass customizers also pursue another business model at the same time—the manufacture of standard windows or, in the case of e-Skylight, designing and building high-end custom solutions for large projects. This diversification, and potential of transferring know-how between related production modes, is probably another reason for their success.

Figure 18-10 Assembly of a skylight before mounting of the glass. (Source: E-Skylight.com)

CHAPTER 19

Directions

19.1 EVOLVING CONTEXTS AND ROLES

A classic role of a concluding chapter is to summarize the salient issues, points, and findings of earlier chapters and to then look to the future. We have already seen examples of how the profession of architecture and the product design industry is continuously challenged to apply and exploit the development of digitally aided tools for design, engineering, and fabrication. What strategies can lead to the innovative application of the evolving digital design, engineering, and fabrication technology in design and architecture? How will the design, engineering, fabrication, and construction cooperation use newly developed tools to encourage creative works? Will the nature of collaboration change as the technology continues to be transformed? Will the nature of design itself change, and if so, how will this change impact the role of the designer?

Before we embark on future speculations, it may be helpful to examine the current relationship between the activities of planning and those of making and relate them to our inherited terminology of "design," "construction" (in architecture), and "manufacturing" (in industrial design). For it is this very terminology that created the most debate in our thoughts preceding the writing of this conclusion. What do we mean, for example, by "design"? And, in turn, how is that term affected by the impact of CAD/CAM?

The meaning of design varies greatly, depending on its subject and context. Design practice—or the context within which one practices design—is highly diverse: It may be a one-person effort, or a large-scale, geographically dispersed collaborative effort. So, clearly, an examination impacts not only our understanding (and thus definition) of design but also of the practice of design. As such, let's take a closer look at both terms and associated issues.

Design

Design, as a specialized activity of planning for making, is generally conceived of as an activity distinct from that of making. In a book of this nature the term becomes debatable; it seems less and less clear where the activity of design begins and ends, especially when much of the CAD/CAM-based processes inherently blur the boundary between representation and "direct" instruction for fabrication, or making. The first design mark may have already tied with it specific manufacturing or fabrication intentions or instructions in ways quite distinct from the designer's traditional first sketch. Perhaps one can argue that in this shared realm of direct data and instructions, the activities of design find themselves dispersed throughout the process in ways quite distinct from traditional processes of making. This blurring of the line where design occurs is a fundamental issue, as it is quite divergent from the way a design concept is traditionally created and developed. In the CAD/CAM realm, design activities exist in diverse scales and forms and run throughout the process from conception to implementation. They are no longer so clearly relegated to a single phase or phases.

So clearly, a traditional use of the term "design" in this context becomes tricky. In discussing the trajectory that an architectural idea takes toward its completion, we chose to use the terms "inception" and "implementation." Rather than suggest it as a process from design to construction, we wanted to frame it as a process between the start of an idea and the materialization of the idea in the built environment. As such, we will refer to it as a process of inception to implementation. Design and the activities of making (whether construction, fabrication, or manufacturing) are thus seen as activities that assist this transformation process and are dispersed, interlinked, and interdependent in disparate manners throughout this process.

Figure 19-1 illustrates these terms paired against relative complexity (is the task of inception simple or complex?) and the degree to which digital tools are used (is the fabrication highly dependent on CNC technology?). In this we can visualize a slightly different process landscape and use it to comparatively illustrate the process strategies that are emerging through the use of CAD/CAM tools in practice. There is probably at least a fourth if not fifth dimension to the variables. Certainly the practice context, for example, has an impact on design. In the spirit of simplicity, we have opted to treat the relationship between practice, project scale, and process in a separate discussion and diagram. However, it is clear that these issues are inextricably bound to each other and should be seen in light of this larger context.

Practice

Varying definitions of design are reflected in the varying scales, contexts, roles, relationships, and modus operandi of architectural practices. Certainly there is the familiar (and highly visible) model of the "signature" architect; this is a model deeply rooted in our tradition of architecture. In fact, the overwhelming majority of normative architecture in the world is less heroic and is produced anonymously outside of the traditional architectural practice context. Within this view, and particularly in view of the perspective ushered in by thinking about the product design world, the work of the signature architect ultimately addresses a niche market. The nature of design in the practice of a signature architect, a consultant, a small practice, and a corporate design department is certainly quite different. Affecting it are not only the nature of the practice, but its scale, the nature and scale of the project undertaken, and the process undertaken. It's not enough to think about the scale of practice, for example; one also has to consider the complexity of the projects undertaken. There can be a substantial difference in design complexity between designing a single-family house and a large institutional building. We recognize that there can be substantial differences in the complexity of the construction process itself and that this com-

plexity might be of a very different nature. The design and manufacturing of Gehry's EMP is certainly quite different in nature than the implementation of Boston's "Big Dig" infrastructure project. There is also a difference between what we will term (for lack of a better term) hand-based techniques and digitally driven techniques. Gaudi's Sagrada Familia is a highly complex and labor-intensive project, but it was completely dependent on handcrafted techniques for its original conception and implementation. Of late, its construction has been greatly aided by the introduction of CAD/CAM technology to complete this historic design. It exemplifies a process of traditional handcrafted conception being digitally assisted in its fabrication and construction (see Figure 19-2 A).

There are also differences in the ways in which practices are incorporating CAD/CAM processes and tools. There are practice models that use digital tools mostly in the inception process and rely primarily on traditional construction techniques for its implementation (see Figure 19-2 B). This is quite different from other practices that heavily depend on CAD/CAM tools throughout or for project implementation (see Figure 19-2 C). Comparing these practice models, it's impossible to draw definitive conclusions in recommending a model or method of digital practice, because these new technologies are inherently flexible (or continually being innovated) and are being employed as tools in innumerable ways under very different kinds of contexts and circumstances. What the interrelation of the various terminology suggests is that rather than coming to a single point of convergence, digital technologies are—in a contradictory manner—coming to multiple points of convergence whilst simultaneously coming to multiple areas of deconvergence.

19.2 TOPICAL DISCUSSION OF TECHNOLOGY, ARCHITECTURE, AND INDUSTRIAL DESIGN

Given the inception-to-implementation model, let's look at the question of future implications topically.

Issues in Technology
Information Technology and Digital Modeling
The recent explosion of developments in the broad arena of information technology has not only affected society at large but has had a profound impact on how buildings and products are represented, designed, analyzed, produced, and made available to users. The digitally based design and manufacturing techniques discussed in this book are a fundamentally important part of this larger information technology context.

The development of advanced digital modeling

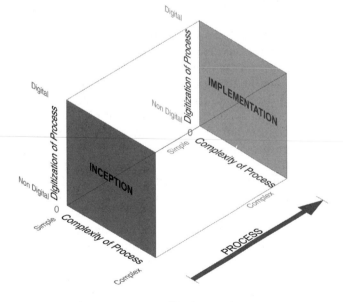

Figure 19-1 Charting inception and implementation processes.

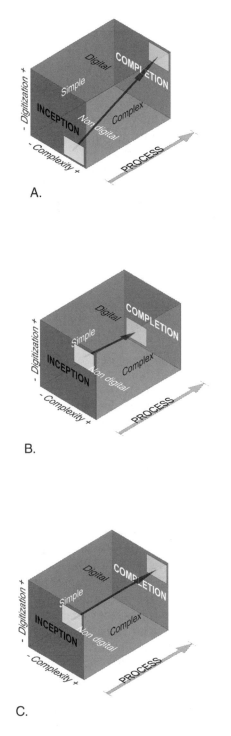

A.

B.

C.

Figure 19-2 Role of digital techniques in different project types.

ing assembly models, enables designers to explore ideas and develop design solutions in ways that were previously not possible. Rule-based procedures and the possibility for scripting unique design procedures allow for far more sophisticated models to be developed than those possible through simple dimensional variations. As experience with using parametric models grows, however, limits are invariably hit by designers. Many fundamental questions about how to best structure models for specific design uses remain.

These digital models also become not just representational but, in a sense, provide direct instructions to machines that subsequently actually make the models. The characteristics of these modeling environments, coupled with developments in numerically controlled production equipment (discussed below), are the fundamental enabling technologies for many high-profile developments in design thinking, including mass customization.

The development of knowledge-based approaches is allowing traditional manufacturing know-how to be built into design systems. Specific approaches, such as design for manufacturing or assembly, enable interactions between design and production to be more easily understood and exploited in a positive way. The ability to embed this kind of knowledge—as well as other kinds of knowledge—into a design system opens a wide door to future developments.

Other promising developments include "generative design" approaches (discussed more in the "Issues in Architecture" section coming up in the chapter) that are based on automated design algorithms. These algorithms both aid in form generation and take over the tedium of much of traditional detailed development.

When combined with other capabilities associated with the broader information technology context—including developments in remote communication and model sharing, Web-based interactions, and so forth—the digital environment right now provides more capabilities than the design professions have been able to implement or even absorb. Clearly, there are both challenges and opportunities here.

The Manufacturing and Production Environment

The development of computers and of control processes for machines have long gone hand in hand. The more recent evolution of computer-based numerical control processes has provided the once elusive link that allows digital modeling and the act of making something via both new and long-established manufacturing processes to be digitally connected. Their evolution has led to greater manufacturing productivity, more flexibility in the types of volumes of objects produced, greater precision and control in their execution, higher overall quality, and other benefits. Not only have existing man-

techniques that extend the use of 3-D models beyond schematic design visualization applications into design development, engineering, manufacturing, and other related domains is fundamental to digital design and manufacturing processes as they have developed into their mature forms. The ability to generate parametrically driven three-dimensional design models, includ-

ufacturing processes assumed new life and new capabilities, but new ones have been developed that are wholly a result of the exploitation of computer technologies. These range from precisely controllable cutting machines such as water jets to various casting methods based on the use of free-form solid fabrication ("rapid prototyping") models.

These new manufacturing processes have made possible increased flexibility in the production of parts and assemblies. Certainly it is possible to have unique parts designed and manufactured with quickness and ease. The ability to produce multiple part variations derived from a parametric digital model is a natural and fundamentally important capability in the CAD/CAM arena. While there are still economies of scale in producing any object, in carefully orchestrated production processes the principle of "repetition" is no longer the only governing principle for efficient and cost-effective production. In particular, it has become increasingly possible to achieve effectively the low-volume production levels that are relevant in many architectural settings, albeit it is in this domain that significant challenges yet remain.

These same manufacturing processes are not only linked to digital design models; they have also been connected with a whole series of other activities important in the production of a product. These activities span the spectrum of production concerns, including material resource planning and inventory control, various quality measurement and evaluation programs, distribution activities, and so forth. Many interesting approaches, such as "just-in-time" or "lean" manufacturing, relate to this larger sphere of activities and go far beyond the limited meaning of their popularized descriptors.

Many of the successes noted, however, have primarily been manifested in allied design and production professions and not in the building industry per se. At the moment, the building industry is still highly fragmented, consisting of diverse levels of technological sophistication. This ensures that the fabrication base for the building industry will remain for some time a mosaic of varying levels of more or less digitally integrated operations. With many operations and applications not currently CAD/CAM-integrated, obvious problems exist. Interchanges among even those currently digitally based remain problematic because of the diversity of approaches used and the different levels of development present. Still, the trend is a positive one of ever-increasing adoptions of digitally based manufacturing approaches. With time, it is clear that a more sophisticated building products industry will exist than is currently the case.

In summary, and as with information technology, there again appears to be already more available in the way of affordances that the manufacturing community can offer than there is an ability on the part of the design community to use or absorb them. Challenges and opportunities thus exist.

Issues in Architecture
New Architectural Forms

The emergence of new digital modeling techniques provided the impetus for developing architectural forms with complex geometries that were previously difficult at best to represent and subsequently build. Difficulties of representation have long been an inhibiting factor in visualizing and realizing complex shapes. New digitally based design environments have provided a powerful tool for designers in this regard.

Here we also see raised the whole question of generative design—as the term is used in relation to form finding in architecture—which has excited considerable interest and attention. As the term suggests, *generative design* broadly refers to the body of processes that, in one form or another, generate design. In the CAD/CAM arena, this usually has implications of automating the process of design, where design might be generally understood as a process of planning and organization. The term, however, is applied in a variety of frequently disparate contexts. For the most part, the term is used in two common ways: in relation to the process of overall form generation and in relation to automated system design. It is the first instance that is of direct concern at the moment. Here the term *generative shape design* is applied to the process of "form" generation, or the process that deals with the shaping of architecture. There is a large body of work and discussion that has experimented with the notion of form generation as represented in the work of architects such as Bernard Franken—in his work an architectural form is generated through the imposition of "forces" (such as water or traffic) onto an existing context or model. In his designs, a building is quite literally formed from the shaping of those forces. The role of the architect shifts from direct author to indirect author (shaping the forces that in turn shape the architecture). The shape is generated indirectly in an attempt to develop a formal architectural language. There are, of course, other ways in which the term is used in relation to form finding, such as seed algorithms or growth algorithms wherein designs evolve according to specific rules established by the designer. Again, the role of the architect shifts from being that of author to that of indirect author as shaper of rules or algorithmic structures that in turn shape the forms themselves.

The great majority of these explorations, however, have remained primarily within the digital realm. While attracting interest and speculation—even to the point of creating new design heroes seemingly overnight—disconnections to the world of materials and fabrication have remained disconcertingly evident.

Many of these highly speculative projects have remained unbuilt. Thoughtful observers have noted that remarkably little critical discourse has surrounded these same works.

While many of these explorations remained speculative, other projects have directly confronted the difficult question of how to transform digital design models into reality. In several cases, resulting buildings have generated wide interest within the profession and have often garnered wide public acclaim. Few members of the public at large, for example, have not seen images of the Guggenheim Museum in Bilboa, Spain, even if only as a backdrop or metaphor for other products displayed in TV ads. From more of a practice perspective, the works that have been realized have posed many complicated design development and implementation problems that in turn have led to many highly interesting technical and process innovations. Many of these innovations are potentially applicable to a wide range of building projects, free-form or not. Chapter 4 identified some of the more salient issues in relation to designing buildings with complex geometries.

In relation to the larger CAD/CAM arena, the use of specific manufacturing technologies within this design approach context is invariably directly related to implementing specific design intents, and less on developing more generically applicable strategies for manufacturing or construction efficiency. They are thus "design-pull" strategies that in turn affect how the overall design and implementation process is structured and implemented. As will be discussed more in the "Design Processes" section later in the chapter, the approach suggests the use of a master digital model that forms the basis for all related design and production activities that, ideally, would occur in a both seamless and coordinated way.

Elements and Components

In today's world, many of the most effective applications of CAD/CAM processes have not followed the master-model approach described previously. Rather, specialists have assumed more control over the design and fabrication of individual elements or components. This might be described as a technology-driven model, wherein many specific building elements and components are developed in light of an overall design but are not necessarily directly derived from it in an ostensibly seamless way.

These approaches are more clearly based on the limitations and affordances of specific materials and methods, and normally evolve from extensive professional engineering or fabrication expertise in specific domains. As such, the design and fabrication of individual elements and components can often be better optimized, and technological potentials and limits better explored, than is possible in the design-pull model

described previously. This whole process, in turn, has enabled designers to collectively produce buildings containing many highly sophisticated features, including many uniquely designed glass façades and roofs. As will be discussed more, this approach also has implications for how overall design and implementation processes are structured.

Building Systems

As seen in Chapter 6, fabricators of building systems have focused on transforming their services by integrating the CAD/CAM technology into vertically integrated design and manufacturing processes. To gain greater competitive advantage, some fabricators have developed proprietary software to facilitate rapid design, analysis, value engineering, and fabrication development. They have linked digital design and fabrication activities with database systems for product tracking, cost estimation, optimization, scheduling, and package sequencing. There have been successful developments in many different building system areas—including structural steel detailing, HVAC systems, windows and doors, curtain walls, and others.

Through the integrated approaches developed, component fabricators have expanded their services to afford unique designs within the limitations of their specialization. These technologies have also enabled expansions of product lines. In many cases, they allow their customers to specify the unique parameters of each building system, so that each system can be custom-configured to each building's engineering and construction. Economy is achieved through the parametric modification of basic typologies of each system's kit of parts. Thus, customization within limits can be offered within expanded product lines. Resulting configurations can each be evaluated with respect to design, performance, specification, and code compliance. Costs and schedules can be tracked. In some cases, direct linkages between the digitally based parametric model and actual CNC fabrication equipment for producing model variants have been successfully developed (in today's practice, this seemingly obviously desirable connection is often not fully realized in practical low-volume production situations).

Within the context of building system design, there has also been considerable interest in "generative design" techniques. It was noted previously that this phrase has two disparate meanings, one in relation to overall form finding, and the second in relation to system design. Applied to system design, the term refers to deep-rooted traditions and techniques of automated design in allied professions, such as shipbuilding and the aeronautical industry. Fundamentally, the term refers to digitally based environments that enable system designs (such as electrical or hydraulic) to be automatically generated by means of rule-based approaches.

This approach lends itself to those things (fundamentally, building systems) whose designs are primarily driven by quantitative criteria. The design of plumbing, electrical, HVAC, and other systems are being affected by these generative design approaches. Users (typically professional architects or engineers) input requirements into a generative design environment that in turn generates specific design characteristics for the building system (e.g., specific layouts and component features). In a typical application, connective points and parameters are defined, and the system generates its own design based on the prespecified rules and constraints. Upon its confirmation, the accompanying digital database can be subsequently used for fabrication. These generative approaches for common elements and systems will certainly not reduce design involvement, but they will allow designers to be freed from rote tedious tasks and to engage in the kinds of creative design explorations that they are best suited to do.

A highly interesting aspect of the use of "generative design" techniques in this regard is that professional knowledge has been captured and embedded in the design system. The term "knowledge-based systems" is thus often used in this general connection as well. In this application, the role of the professional becomes that of client advisor and facilitator.

All of these new processes inherently involve a change from the traditional shop drawing and submittal revision procedure so familiar to architects in traditional practice to one that is based on a digital model representation. There is also an implied or explicit accompanying fundamental change in the roles, relationships, and responsibilities of the designer, engineer, and fabricator. The realm of each practitioner's expertise and responsibility is expanded. There is more partnering in this collaboration. Will expert software of this type blur the boundary of professional specialization and/or promote further specialization?

Design Processes

The use and adoption of 3-D models have already impacted areas beyond direct digital design and manufacturing techniques. Basic approaches to developing representations and documents for project implementation processes are affected. Processes involving activities such as extracting needed 2-D representations from 3-D models, or using 3-D models as governing geometries or references, are significantly different from traditional implementation approaches based primarily on 2-D drawings.

For those designers who already use 3-D models as a basis for design collaboration and all phases of design development, it is clear that both design processes and the specific roles, responsibilities, and interactions of architects, consultants, and engineers have all been impacted. Traditional roles and relationships are challenged and cannot easily accommodate the kinds of processes suggested by adoption of these new technologies.

One series of questions arise at the very basic level of simply how a 3-D model is used by architects, engineers, and others involved in the design development process. What role does it serve? Who creates the model? Is it truly a shared model? Who has access to it for what purpose? Who can modify what? Who pays for it? How does use of a shared model affect legal responsibilities for things like errors or omissions? The list could go on.

There are also many basic questions about the appropriate level of the 3-D model detail that are largely unresolved (including levels of detail of assemblies, subassemblies, etc.). The level-of-detail issue also raises the question of strategy; including, for example, of what is usefully represented in 3-D and what is best represented in 2-D and how these representations relate to one another. The notion of a governing or master 3-D model arises again, but there is no clarity about how best to define a governing model, since the utility of how one is developed and structured is inextricably bound up with an office's broader approach to architecture and its collaborative relationships for each project. Conceptually, the question of what defines the nature of the master model thus becomes extremely interesting, including what is parametrically variable and what is not. The question goes to near the heart of how architecture is conceived.

A lot of these speculations still suggest that there is a seamlessness in not only technologies but in how design interactions are structured. For the most part, however, the current reality is that these process models are not as seamless as the scenarios suggest. Nonetheless, the seamless model remains interesting and suggestive of issues to consider. Long-established traditions and contractual models for assigning roles and responsibility models derived from older traditional building practices can be considered only marginally applicable. Many successes to date have been based on positive team building and nurtured relationships between participants. This welcome model may not, however, be feasible on an industry-wide basis. So where do we go here? New interaction modes and related contractual approaches may need to be developed.

In the fragmented building construction context, the varied levels of integrated digital practice may continue to offer opportunities for the fabricators to expand the digital application not only for its parametric product modeling and CNC fabrication. The value of fabricator dialogue during the design phase can be offered through an embedded expert database for building, in addition to its online advisory to users and designers. Just as the digital medium and the information technology environment can support geographically distant collaborations, it can further expand the consulting dialogue by "bringing the factory to the studio" from design inception to detail development; it can also "bring the studio to the factory and building site" during fabrication and construction.

Many of the innovative projects to date have benefited from partnered collaboration and negotiated bid projects, with unique forms built from one-off customized components. In contradistinction, most of the normative building projects work with an open-bid contract, incorporating numerous prefabricated components. Many of the market forces and technological factors favor an open-system framework for the building materials and products, in favor of highly specialized closed-system strategies. Could its flexible and accessible characteristics support an open-structured 3-D digital component model library? Can it be developed to be a complement of their physical reality? Perhaps the designers' generic building elements and components can be translated or substituted with fabricators' digital 3-D object-oriented models in the construction document and bid phases. These component digital models may have variable parameter definitions and customized performance specifications. These proprietary building element and component 3-D models, if readily substitutable with generic models, can translate a model of design intention into specific proprietary product and its fabrication instructions and associated database. It would be useful to consider the various factors that may be configured in a parametric model. Its parameters may be performance-driven, geometrically or algorithmically formatted, system- and assembly-linked, and process-delineated.

What is clearly evident in all of this is that the development and availability of 3-D models for design development and project implementation purposes has profoundly challenged conventional practices. New modes of design collaboration need to be explored and developed. It is an exciting area.

How can the creative dialogue between fabricator and designer be fostered in a normative project delivery process? Perhaps the 3-D models' embedded expert knowledge database can be augmented with manufacturers' online consultancy.

Project Management and Control

As we have seen, 3-D digital models can provide the basis for shared knowledge among all participants in the design process. While only briefly explored in Chapter 7, the use of 3-D models can also provide a sound basis for the many varied aspects of project management and control during the construction process, including communications among participants.

All of the basic issues noted in the previous section concerning how different participants in the design process relate to the 3-D model are also clearly relevant when it comes to an even more expanded group that addresses actual fabrication and construction issues. In the various case studies presented, we have seen several different models for how fabricators and constructors use 3-D models in the furtherance of their own obligations and objectives. New models of design collaboration are developing. Several approaches allow for more upfront involvement of fabricators and constructors in the design process.

Several fundamental tools have been developed to aid this kind of collaboration. Certainly, the possibility of shared models that can be remotely accessed is a key here. The extraction of information for purposes such as cost estimating and project scheduling—even at early design stages—is potentially far more possible or efficient via the use of 3-D models. Additionally, seemingly straightforward tools, such as joint fly-throughs by involved participants where the design model can be explored and annotated, can greatly facilitate an understanding of the design model and the construction challenges it poses. The use of 3-D models in construction planning also forms the basis for the exciting 4-D approaches under development that are based on successful network models showing task dependencies and time dimensions, but that render them highly understandable and more useful as communication and planning tools.

The use of various field devices for obtaining task information and instruction is not only possible but is being implemented. The linking of 3-D model geometries with actual 3-D site surveying has expedited the construction of complex building shapes. These same linkages also provide a new way of obtaining on-site field feedback for altering basic design modes in light of normal and/or unexpected changes that occur during construction. The accessibility of 3-D model geometrical and related information also opens the door for a number of potentially exciting construction innovations. Certainly, moves to "bring the factory to the site" via mobile CNC-based facilities can be further developed. The control of some construction equipment is already governed by digital data extracted from geometrical models. More innovations here can be anticipated—including the possible effective utilization of robotics.

Issues in Product Design and Architecture

The term "design" means a lot of different things to a lot of different people. This is no truer than when we examine the relationship between architecture and industrial design.

Within the context of this larger landscape, there are some generalizations that can be advanced about the nature of the construction industry. First, buildings are becoming more and more an assembly of products. These include "high-end" products such as windows, doors, ceiling systems, and lighting systems. They also include "low-end" products such as material products: plywood, drywall, and so on. Second, mass customization is beginning to cross the traditional divide between the industries of one-of-a-kind (architecture) versus mass production (industrial design). Third, interdependencies are developing between products and environments. Space impacts the kinds of products generated. The "invention" of the kitchen, as a specialized space in the house, for example, brought about the need for a whole series of specialized, task-oriented consumer products. Emerging issues, such as health care delivery to the home, are substantially impacting the conception of the household environment by tying together spaces, products, and services. We are seeing products (such as the Stala system discussed in Chapter 9) that are allowing for the customization of products for implementation within an architectural context. All in all, a different kind of relationship between architecture and product design is beginning to emerge.

Within this context, there are many areas of active interest to both the product design world and to the architectural world. Current models of mass customization are allowing companies—and their products—to diversify their offerings and address customer- or market-based differences. In the product design world, one critical question in the drive for new mass customization models is how to integrate the consumer's needs into the design and manufacturing process. Currently, in "personalization," one selects from a limited palate of options (as employed by the options-based personalization in the car industry), or the personalization of the simple products (such as Web-based features). The large challenge in terms of getting the consumer linked has been the haptic dimension. Many products rely on the tactile quality and ability to "try on" (as in the clothing industry) products. The current tools—or interfaces—between the customer and product manufacturer limit the kinds of products and strategies by which they are mass-customized.

These same general observations also have relevance to the architectural world, not only at the level of specific interfaces but more broadly as well. At the moment, for example, mass customization discussions take quite a different tone. The essential meanings underlying many of the same terms used in the product design world may be in danger of being lost. Is a building with uniquely designed elements, or even a series of buildings with sets of different part variations, really an example of "mass customization"? To the architect, perhaps the reference is meaningful. To the manufacturer that thinks in terms of tens of thousands, it is confusing and a misappropriation of the term. Clearly, there are many issues to be sorted out here.

Notes

CHAPTER 2

[1]Stan Davis, *Future Perfect,* and Joseph B. Pine, *Mass Customization: The New Frontier in Business Competition* (Boston: Harvard Business School Press, 1993).

CHAPTER 3

[1]Sydney Opera House credits: Jørn Utzon, architect, stage 1 and 2; Hall, Todd and Littlemore, architects, stage 3; Ove Arup & Partners, civil and structural engineers; Hornibrook, general contractors; Hoganas, ceramic tiles, prefabricated concrete; Boussois–Souchon–Neuvesel, glass suppliers; Quick-Steel Engineering Pty Ltd., sawing machinery and glass handling equipment; VASOB Glass Pty Ltd., glazing.

[2]Ove Arup and Jack Zunz, "Sydney Opera House," first published in *Structural Engineer* (March 1969). Reprinted in The *Arup Journal* (October 1973): 8.

[3]Vincent Smith, *The Sydney Opera House* (Sydney: Paul Hamlyn, 1974), 18.

[4]Arup and Zunz, "Sydney Opera House," *Structural Engineer,* "The contractor made use of the computer for the design of the erection arch, statistical control of concrete strengths and job costs." p. 19.

[5]Oswald L. Ziegler, ed., *Sydney Builds an Opera House* (Sydney: Oswald Ziegler Publications, 1973), 39.

[6]Arup and Zunz, "Sydney Opera House," *Structural Engineer,* 4–19.

[7]Ziegler, *Sydney Builds an Opera House,* 57.

[8]Harry Sowden, *Sydney Opera House Glass Walls* (Sydney: John Sands, 1972), 26–29.

[9]Piano + Fitzgerald is the architect for the Menil Collection.

[10]"Piano in Conversation," Interview with Roberto Fabbri. *A+U* E8903 Renzo Piano. p. 15. Piano on the use of the computer: "This potential lies not in its ability to facilitate whimsy, including biomorphic forms, because it can draw quickly and then control the manufacture of one-off components. Instead the computer's potential lies in its capacity to generate new forms, particularly ones related to those it is now revealing as underlying nature, which can serve as an encompassing discipline—especially useful if they result in an exceptional degree of integration between the building's various systems, as well as new levels of economy and efficiency in both performance and manufacture."

[11]Ibid. Renzo Piano's interview with Roberto Fabbri, p. 18.

[12]Notes from a conversation between Renzo Piano and author K. Kao on June 13, 1998.

[13]Peter Buchanan, *Renzo Piano Building Workshop, Complete Works,* volume 2 (London: Phaidon, 1995), 14.

[14]"Kansai International Airport, Passenger Terminal Building," *Process: Architecture* 122 (December 1994): 67.

[15]Ibid., 140.

[16]Ibid., 62.

[17]Buchanan, *Renzo Piano Building Workshop, Complete Works,* volume 3, 184.

[18]*Process: Architecture* 122, p. 62.

[19]Buchanan, *Renzo Piano Building Workshop, Complete Works,* volume 3, 154–155.

[20]Ibid., 200.

[21]Brian Forster's interview with author K. Kao. July, 1998. Emailed notes to author March 17, 2004.

[22]The Olympica development included a 45-story hotel, an office building designed by SOM, and 150,000 square feet of additional retail, commercial, and maritime elements designed by Gehry.

[23]Daniel Schodek, drawing upon his observations of the fish project at Harvard University Graduate School of Design, and from discussions with Frank O. Gehry and James Glymph.

[24]Bruce Lindsey, *Digital Gehry: Material Resistance Digital Construction* (Basel, Switzerland: Birkhauser, 2001) 38.

[25]Ibid., 32–38. Also reference discussions on Gehry's fish at Barcelona.

[26]The discussion on Fred and Ginger is indebted to Lamberti's research and documentation on the fabrication of the glazing and pre-cast concrete cladding. Andrea Lamberti, Unpublished Manuscript, Masters Research Paper "Fred and Ginger: Rasin Building Prague, Frank O. Gehry and Associates," Harvard University, Graduate School of Design, Fall Semester, 1995.

[27]Lamberti, p. 5.

[28]Ibid., Discussions with Masis Mesropian, Designer of Madusa, 1995.

[29]Annette LeCuyer, "Designs on the Computer," *Architectural Review* (January 1995): 4.

CHAPTER 4

[1]Mortenson, Michael E. *Geometric Modelling,* (New York: John Wiley & Sons, 1985) 18.

[2]Parts of this case study are based on S. Matsushima, "Collaboration in Architectural Design: An IT Perspective," thesis, Harvard University, 2003.

CHAPTER 5

[1]Christopher Mercier, GSD CADCAM conference, transcript. October, 2000,

[2]Ibid.

[3]Ibid.

[4]Ibid., "The process is repeated a number of times—the number being dependent on the complexity of a particular project. The physical model generated from digital models is an important check model for us."

[5]Ibid.

[6]Alberto De Gobbi, Permasteelisa, GSD CAD/CAM conference, transcript, October, 2000.

[7]Mercier.

[8]De Gobbi.

[9]Fred Adickes, C-Tek, GSD CAD/CAM conference, transcript, October, 2000.

[10]Mercier, op. cit.

[11]Ibid.

[12]Ibid.

[13]Tim Eliassen, TriPyramid, GSD CAD/CAM conference, transcript October, 2000.

[14]Mercier, op. cit. "Our office has learned over the years that it is important to not just propose these things in a computer or on a drawing or in a model and give it to somebody and say, look, this is what we want to make. In the construction industry there is a lot of 'No way.' "

[15]Ibid.

[16]Tim Eliassen.

[17]Ibid.

[18]Mercier, op. cit.

[19]Ibid.

[20]Blomberg.

[21]Damian Murphy, Dewhurst McFarlane, GSD CAD/CAM conference transcript, November, 2001.

[22]Blomberg.

[23]Ibid.

[24]Maguire, Architectural Skylights, GSD CAD/CAM conference transcript, November, 2001.

[25]Ibid.

[26]Ibid.

[27]Murphy, op. cit.

[28]Michael Samra, TriPyramid, GSD CAD/CAM conference transcript, November, 2001. "Here we started with something pretty good, allowing us to immediately translate this design into piece parts and to have a caster take a look at it to give us feedback on the weight of the part and its volume. The caster also analyzes it from a pure casting standpoint—depending on how the metal is going to chill they may suggest certain radii on corners."

[29]Ibid.

[30]Ibid.

[31]Charles Blomberg, GSD CAD/CAM conference transcript, November, 2001. "National Glass, the company that installed the glass, was only responsible for providing a watertight envelope. They had no responsibility for any movement or structural forces."

[32]Eliassen, op. cit.

[33]Ibid.

[34]Eliassen, "The foundry used our model to make a digital representation of the casting process in a program called Magma, actually showing the metal being poured and the metal cooling. This indicated that one part of our shape might cool too quickly, cutting off the supply of molten metal to the extremities. You can see the metal cooling, and after about 7 minutes and 21 seconds the piece is 50% solid. The program shows that the piece will develop porosity unless something is done to change the casting method. It is a porosity detector."

CHAPTER 6

[1]East Coast CAD/CAM, Littleton, Massachusetts; Shopdata, Garland, Texas; Metamation, United States, Japan.

[2]An example of products offered by Budde Sheet Metal.com. Budde Sheet Metal introduced CAD/CAM into its production. By 1996, all drawings were transferred to CAD/CAM production full-time. Using Solid Edge 1997, all components are created in 3-D solid models, and fabrication problems are worked out before the first component is produced. It uses CAD: Solid Edge V14, ACAD 2002, Inventor V8.0; and it uses CAM software: MetaMation–MetaCAM V4.

[3]David Derocher, president of East Coast CAD/CAM, in an interview with the author, November 25, 2003. The material cost savings through successful nesting is not significant if the metal sheet is 20-gauge or thinner.

[4]MetaCAM.

[5]Ibid.

[6]An example of fabrication offered by Budde Sheet Metal. Sheet-metal parts are cut using TRUMPF-TRUMAT IC L3030 3000-watt laser cutting machine, or punched using a flexible punch machine. Parts are taken through forming operation with a 150-ton press break with numeric gauging.

[7]David Derocher, East Coast CAD/CAM

[8]Ibid.

[9]The digital model was developed and is maintained by Puro, a Finland-based company specialized in modularized 3-D modeling.

CHAPTER 7

[1]The work of Martin Fisher and his team at Stanford University is of special interest here. Many articles have been published by this group, for example, Koo, Bonsang, and Fisher, Martin, "Feasibility Study of 4D CAD in Commercial Construction, *Journal of Construction Engineering and Management,* ASCE, 126(4), 251–260.

[2]Aspects of this approach have been pursued by different groups, but most notably Frank O. Gehry & Associates.

CHAPTER 8

[1]In 1878 George Eastman began to simplify the complex wet-plate process. In 1889 he developed the Kodak #2—the first camera with flexible film, and in 1900 his developments culminated in the coming to market of the $1 Kodak Brownie.

[2]Karl T. Ulrich and Steven D. Eppinger, *Product Design and Development* (New York: McGraw-Hill, 1995).

CHAPTER 9

[1]B. Joseph Pine, *Mass Customization: The New Frontier in Business Competition.* (Boston: Harvard Business School Press, 1993).

[2]Michael A. Cusumano and Kenaro Nobeoka, *Thinking Beyond Lean: How Multi-Project Management Is Transforming Product Development at Toyota and Other Companies.* (New York: Free Press, 1998).

CHAPTER 15

[1]There is no agreement on what the term "rapid tooling" actually means. In some instances, use of the term has been in connection with the act of making a tool as quickly as possible in order to reduce production time. This meaning is quite different than that used in this text.

[2]The Castings Development Centre in the United Kingdom has been a leader in the development of this process.

[3]In the seemingly similar lost-foam process described in Chapter 14, the molten metal consumes the largely carbon-based foam, and thus material characteristics are affected. The process is good for nonferrous alloys and irons, but not steel.

CHAPTER 16

[1]Geoffrey Boothroyd and Peter Dewhurst, "Product Design for Assembly", published by Boothroyd Dewhurst, Inc., 138 Main Street, Wakefield, Rhode Island, and also described in Boothroyd's *Assembly Automation and Product Design* (New York: Marcel Dekker, Inc., 1992.)

[2]Ibid.

CHAPTER 17

[1]J. A. Black, "The Design of Manufacturing Cells," American Society of Mechanical Engineers Publication (1988): 143.

[2] James P. Womack, Daniel T. Jones, and Daniel Roos, *The Machine That Changed the World* (New York: HarperCollins, 1991).

CHAPTER 18

[1]See B. Joseph Pine, *Mass Customization: The New Frontier in Business Competition* (Boston: Harvard Business Press, 1993) or F. T. Piller, *Kundenindividuelle Massenproduktion: Die Wettbewerbsstrategie der Zukunft* (München: Hanser Verlag, 1998).

Index